THE GREATEST MOVIES EVER

THE ULTIMATE RANKED LIST OF THE 101 BEST FILMS OF ALL TIME!

FULLY REVISED & UPDATED WITH NEW FILMS

THE GREATEST MOVIES EVER

THE ULTIMATE RANKED LIST OF THE 101 BEST FILMS OF ALL TIME!

Gail Kinn & Jim Piazza

Black Dog & Leventhal Publishers
New York

All photographs courtesy of Photofest, with the exception of the posters on the following pages, which are courtesy of Getty Archives: 93, 141, 150, 156, 237, 270; and the images on pages 16, 31 (top), 41 (bottom), 47 (bottom), 62, 85 (bottom), 86 (bottom), 125 (top), 147 (left), 149 (top), 159 (bottom), 165 (bottom), 191 (top), 197 (top), 204 (bottom), 206 (top), 240 (bottom), 252 (bottom), 253 (bottom), 263 (top), 273 (bottom), 275 (left), 296, and 299 (bottom), which are courtesy of Frank Vlastnik.

ISBN 13: 978-1-57912-890-6

The Library of Congress has cataloged the hardcopy edition as follows:

Kinn, Gail.
Four-star movies : the 101 greatest films of all time / Gail Kinn & Jim Piazza.
p. cm.
ISBN 1-57912-315-5
1. Motion pictures—United States—Plots, themes, etc. 2. Motion pictures—Plots, themes, etc. I. Title: 4 star movies. II. Piazza, Jim. III. Title.

PN1993.5.U6K49 2003
791.43'75—dc22
2003014848

Interior book design: Scott Citron and LuAnn Graffeo Blonkowski

Manufactured in China

Published by
Black Dog & Leventhal Publishes, Inc.
151 West 19th Street
New York, New York 10011

Distributed by
Workman Publishing Company
225 Varick Street
New York, New York 10014

g f e d c b a

To Alan, for standing by my side, and, as always, to Sarah.

Gail

To Frank and Adeline, Thelma Todd, and David, always.

Jim

Acknowledgments

THE AUTHORS, ONCE AGAIN, BOW DEEPLY TO EACH OTHER. Collaborating with friends sounds like fun but isn't always. We've been lucky twice. Our good fortune continues with editor Laura Ross, who cares as much as we do about the material and is reported to have killed on our behalf.

Thanks to J. P. Leventhal, who can almost always nail the most obscure photo in record time and took such an influential role in the process of movie selection; and to the designers Scott Citron and LuAnn Graffeo Blonkowski for putting together such a visually delightful and complicated design project. They were a constant joy to work with.

We are grateful to True Sims and Marie Mundaca, whose production skills are unsurpassed; to Katherine Furman, for keeping track of the photos; to Dara Lazar, for her assistance; and to hawk-eyed proofreaders Iris Bass and Kathy Brock, copyeditor Michael Driscoll, and indexer Ted Goodman. Special thanks to our original editor, Will Kiester, for his concept for the book.

To our friends at Photofest: We couldn't have done it without them and their wise and warm assistance. Deep thanks, also, to Frank Vlastnik and Manoah Bowman for their vast and obsessive knowledge of film stills (and everything else), and their invaluable contributions to the photographic aspect of this edition. Thanks also go to the Getty Archives. And finally, we wish to pay special tribute to all of the filmmakers whose work we honor here, who managed the miracle of making fiction as fascinating and thrilling as fact.

Special thanks from Gail: For all the shared nights at the movies, my family and friends, Mark, Hannah, Sarah, Linda, David, Ellen, Scott, Marianne, Paul, Judy, Tony, Ronni, Marty, Janis, Nathan, Elizabeth, Debra, and everyone out there in the dark. To my brilliant collaborator Jim. I couldn't have done it without you.

Special thanks from Jim: Among those who will always make my final cut are the inestimable David Ferguson, who had something vital to say about every selection and always keeps my "truth button" lit; devoted sisters Terry and Maryta; and of course, my wonderful collaborator, Gail Kinn, who chases down the stars with me.

CONTENTS

Introduction 9

1 Godfather I and II 10

2 Citizen Kane 17

3 Casablanca 20

4 Sunset Boulevard 23

5 Lawrence of Arabia 26

6 North by Northwest 29

7 The Wizard of Oz 32

8 Annie Hall 35

9 Chinatown 38

10 Singin' in the Rain 41

11 Nashville 44

12 Some Like It Hot 47

13 All About Eve 50

14 Psycho 53

15 Taxi Driver 56

16 Apocalypse Now 59

17 On the Waterfront 63

18 Gone with the Wind 66

19 To Kill a Mockingbird 69

20 The Searchers 72

21 La Dolce Vita 75

22 Double Indemnity 78

23 Pan's Labyrinth 81

24 Vertigo 84

25 Close Encounters of the Third Kind 87

26 GoodFellas 90

27 Jules and Jim 93

28 Funny Face 96

29 A Streetcar Named Desire 99

30 Saving Private Ryan 102

31 Strangers on a Train 105

32 It Happened One Night 108

33 The Graduate 111

34 It's a Wonderful Life 114

35 Raging Bull 117

36 The Best Years of Our Lives 120

37 The African Queen 123

38 Dr. Strangelove 126

39 Blade Runner 129

40 The Conformist 132

41 Schindler's List 135

42 The Lives of Others 138

43 Diner 141

44 City Lights 144

45 The Deer Hunter 147

46 8½ 150

47 Top Hat 153

48 Rules of the Game 156

49 2001: A Space Odyssey 159

50 Bonnie and Clyde 162

51 King Kong 165

52 Star Wars 168

53 The 400 Blows 171

In some of our favorite onscreen moments, actors share our enduring pleasure in getting lost at the movies (left to right): Salvatore Cascio and Philippe Noiret in *Cinema Paradiso*, Susan Sarandon and Robert Redford in *The Great Waldo Pepper*.

54 A Night at the Opera **174**
55 Slumdog Millionaire **177**
56 Night of the Hunter **180**
57 The Third Man **183**
58 Doctor Zhivago **186**
59 ET: The Extra-Terrestrial **189**
60 Invasion of the Body Snatchers **192**
61 Pinocchio **195**
62 Shadow of a Doubt **198**
63 Fargo **201**
64 Blue Velvet **204**
65 Jaws **207**
66 The Grapes of Wrath **210**
67 Do the Right Thing **213**
68 Wild Strawberries **216**
69 The Bicycle Thief **219**
70 Bringing up Baby **222**
71 Paths of Glory **225**
72 The Maltese Falcon **228**
73 Pather Panchali **231**
74 The Lady Eve **234**
75 The Last Picture Show **237**
76 One Flew Over the Cuckoo's Nest **240**
77 Rosemary's Baby **243**
78 Midnight Cowboy **246**
79 M*A*S*H **249**
80 American Graffiti **252**
81 The Producers **255**
82 Rashomon **258**
83 Cabaret **261**
84 Return of the King **264**
85 A Place in the Sun **267**
86 Red River **270**
87 The Conversation **273**
88 Grand Illusion **276**
89 L.A. Confidential **279**
90 Butch Cassidy **282**
91 Imitation of Life **285**
92 Raiders of the Lost Ark **288**
93 Spartacus **291**
94 The Manchurian Candidate **294**
95 The Seven Samurai **297**
96 A Hard Day's Night **300**
97 Atlantic City **303**
98 American Beauty **306**
99 Pulp Fiction **309**
100 The Shawshank Redemption **312**
101 Groundhog Day **315**
Chronology of the *Greatest Movies Ever* **318**
Index **318**

Introduction

TAKE TWO! Five years after its first edition—a millennia in movie time—it is time to reassess and re-evaluate our previous selection of the 101 films worthy of inclusion in *The Greatest Movies Ever*. There are seven new picks. We have eliminated some old favorites and returned them to the dusty back shelf. In their place are both reconsidered vintage gems and new films that have emerged as instant classics.

Compiling a definitive "Best List" is an audacious act—it's what separates mere movie lovers from downright cinemaniacs. It requires endurance, Machiavellian negotiating skills, and the willingness to lose your best friends. For those who truly care about ranking films, it's a blood sport (though the word sport may be a bit frivolous when referring to such vital matters as whether Ridley Scott's *Blade Runner* (#39) should appear higher on the list than Barry Levinson's *Diner* (#43), or whether they should be included at all. There were suspicious Hitchcockian red stains on the carpet following that particular decision).

Our personal narrowing-down of the universe of great films may seem arbitrary; but there is a reason behind every decision, whether or not you instantly agree. Are Steven Spielberg's *Close Encounters* (#25) and Bob Fosse's *Cabaret* (#83) among the best ever? Watch them again and judge them based on the arguments we present. We think you'll be surprised how well they hold up against very demanding standards. While it's impossible to lay down firm ground rules, there are certain significant attributes inherent in all these 101. Some are sterling prototypes that subsequent films would emulate. In *Blue Velvet* (#64), for example, David Lynch invents a surrealistic suburbia, a kind of fever dream from which would spring many other such alternative visions of "normal" American life, including those of Quentin Tarantino's *Pulp Fiction* (#99) and Sam Mendes' *American Beauty* (#98). The latter films in turn break cinematic ground in their own ways. Other films make the list because they are the most brilliant examples of their genre. John Huston's *The Maltese Falcon* (#72) could rightly be considered the seminal noir film; Howard Hawks' *Bringing Up Baby* (#70) and *The Lady Eve* (#74) are the Hope Diamonds of screwball comedy.

Many films were selected because of the particular excellence of the performances. Marlon Brando in Elia Kazan's *On the Waterfront* (#17) and *A Streetcar Named Desire* (#29) set a new standard in film acting, elevating those fine films to classic status. David Lean's *Lawrence of Arabia* (#5) and, yes, Billy Wilder's *Double Indemnity* (#22), are impossible to imagine without, respectively, Peter O'Toole's blazing intensity and Barbara Stanwyck's delectable malevolence.

While many of these films are considered "serious," some sing and dance, and often, it is the comedies that test the limits of the art form. If you'd like to argue that Mel Brooks's *The Producers* (#81) and Sam Woods's *A Night at the Opera* (#54)

(Left to right): Julia Roberts and Hugh Grant in *Notting Hill*; William Holden and Gloria Swanson in *Sunset Boulevard*.

can be described as genius collections of anarchic bits rather than traditional scenarios—we won't disagree. They include some of the most hysterically funny moments ever stamped on celluloid.

How, by the way, did we come up with the number 101? A certain symbolism was attached. That 101st slot should probably have remained empty, a kind of open parking spot for the reader. But, as you'll see, we couldn't resist filling it in ourselves. If you don't find your favorite movie on our list, perhaps you'll be inspired to come up with your own. In the final analysis, we suspect we won't be all that far apart. If you can do better than, say, #31, Alfred Hitchcock's just-about-perfect thriller *Strangers on a Train*, let us know.

The motion picture screen is a truly democratic terrain. If what we see up there can get us to think, feel, or go somewhere new, it really doesn't matter if it's Jean Renoir's *Grand Illusion* (#88) or Spike Lee's searing inner-city satire, *Do the Right Thing* (#67). *The Greatest Movies Ever* includes the full spectrum of what might be called art (*Pan's Labyrinth* [#23]) and what might just be considered popular (*Invasion of the Body Snatchers* [#60]). If, by some miracle of the creative process, a movie comes together and really delivers on its intention and promise, odds are good you'll find it here.

Should there be some noise made about the lack of silent movies (with one extraordinary exception, Charlie Chaplin's *City Lights* [#44], whose silence has always been a subject of loud debate), we did consider their inclusion early on. But we decided that that particular chapter of cinematic history is just too rich to sandwich in with a token choice or two, and requires a comprehensive list of its own. Another book, another time.

For those who haven't yet seen all of the films we've included, you're in for an enviable experience. While some of our entries have not yet been transferred to DVD, we're sure that will come in time. Greatness is never denied for long. Meanwhile, the vintage videos are well worth the search, as are screenings in the few remaining revival houses (the big screen still can't be beat!) and on cable networks devoted to classics.

As we suggested last time around, grab some popcorn and turn the page. Here come *The Greatest Movies Ever*—take two!

—Gail Kinn and Jim Piazza

1

THE GODFATHER 1972
THE GODFATHER, PART II 1974

FAMILY COMES FIRST

Unlike the mass-culture phenomenon of another era, Margaret Mitchell's *Gone with the Wind*, there was no great clamor for a film adaptation of Mario Puzo's labyrinthine crime-family epic. The novel's structure wasn't easily adaptable and, more importantly, the genre hadn't been surefire at the box office in years. The same could be said for the career of director Francis Ford Coppola, whose iffy assortment of early films hadn't exactly catapulted him to the top. But, by miraculous confluence—one of those celebrated but rare happy Hollywood accidents—director and project met by default, after Sergio Leone and Peter Bogdanovich passed on it. The result was a legendary romance between creator and material, the cinematic equivalent of Michelangelo's love-at-first-sight glimpse at that blank ceiling. The tremendous success of *The Godfather* gave Coppola the luxury of delving beneath the surface in *Part II*, taking a long look into the dark hour of Michael Corleone's soul. Both movies ask the question, What is true evil? The possible answer: a well-spoken, thoughtful young man forced to sacrifice his conscience and his family in order to become who—and what—he must be. The two movies culminate in a brooding Sicilian bonfire of greed, betrayal, and revenge, brilliantly played out by the greatest actors of their generation at their incendiary peak. There is almost nothing to be improved upon here. The films completely immerse us in a family and a universe like no other, one that, however briefly, becomes more earth-shatteringly important than our own.

Jim: A celluloid shrine to the acting gods. And, thanks to cinematographer Gordon Willis, *The Godfather* looks like a flip book of extraordinary paintings. Even the violence has the effect of gilt-framed art. *Part II* is such consummate storytelling, the beauty of it isn't the first thing you notice. De Niro's performance, among all these greats, is one for the ages.

Gail: In a country where there is no Great American Family Tragedy writ large, these films define us. They are Shakespeare's *Henry IV*, in which the prodigal son returns home to assume the role he must; Stendhal's *The Red and the Black*, a coming-of-age story in which a young man is seduced by power to become amoral and then immoral; and Eugene O'Neill's tragically predestined dysfunctional family. They are Italian opera and Greek tragedy...They are *us*.

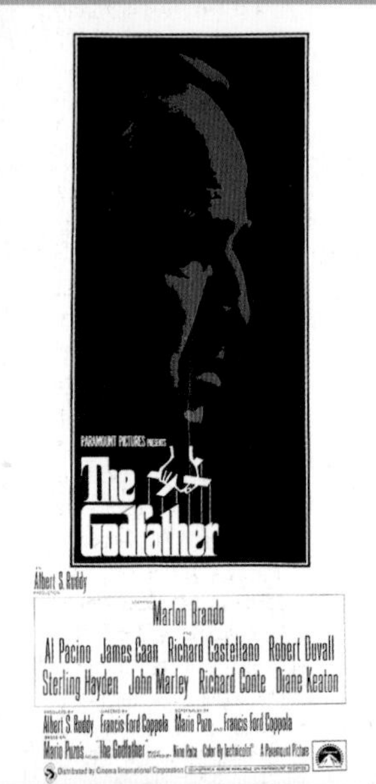

THE PLOT

The Godfather: Michael Corleone (Al Pacino), youngest son of a powerful capo di capi, comes home from World War II a decorated hero. An Ivy League education has fully Americanized him and he's broken with tradition by proposing to a non-Italian girl, Kay (Diane Keaton). They attend the wedding of his sister Connie (Talia Shire) during which his father, Don Vito (Marlon Brando), holds court in his study. Don Vito dispenses favors to be carried out by his attorney/surrogate son Tom Hagen (Robert Duvall) and Michael's older brothers, hot-tempered Sonny (James Caan) and Fredo (John Cazale). When a gang war is declared, Don Vito is targeted for death. As he clings to life in the hospital, Michael gets wind of another attempt to kill him. Michael outwits their foes and is now fully committed to retaliation. He prepares for his first taste of blood and, by so doing, forever gives up his dream of a normal life with Kay.

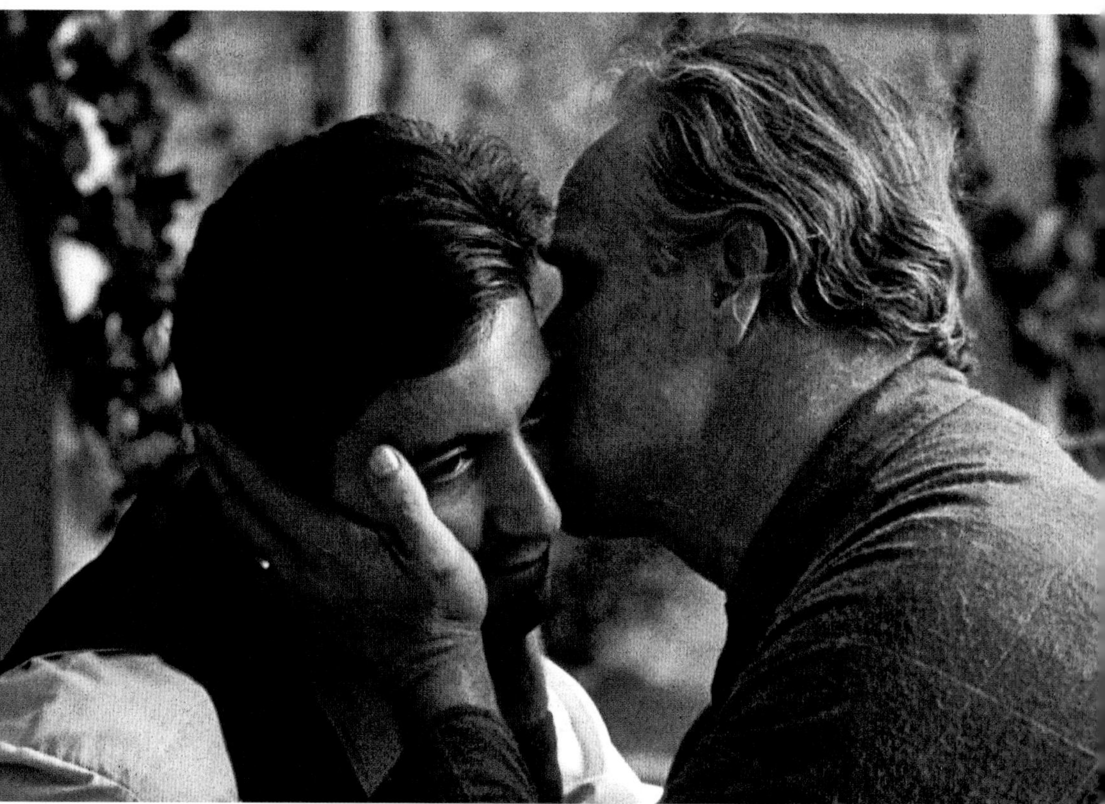

Vito passes the mantle to Michael with a kiss and, in so doing, effectively ends his youngest son's dream of a normal life.

THE PLOT

The Godfather, Part II: The crown rests heavily on the head of Michael Corleone (Al Pacino), don of America's most powerful "*mafiosa famiglia*." Betrayed at every turn by his unhappy wife Kay (Diane Keaton), his envious brother Fredo (John Cazale), his formidable business associate Hyman Roth (Lee Strasberg), and a valued underboss Frank Pentangeli (Michael Gazzo), he's forced to rule with an iron hand. No perceived enemy can be left standing. Even Fredo must suffer the consequences of his failed attempt to usurp Michael, who brilliantly outmaneuvers a Senate Hearing on Organized Crime and promises Kay their lives will return to normal. She knows it's a lie and naively threatens to take the children and leave him. He can't allow that. In counterpoint to Michael's tortured struggle, the early chronicles of his beloved father Don Vito's (Robert De Niro) rise to power in New York's Little Italy are vividly recalled.

"Don't ask me about my business, Kay." We are witness to the last moments of innocence before Michael is pulled into Corleone Incorporated. Diane Keaton more than held her own in this confluence of heavy-hitting actors. If Paramount execs had controlled casting, she would've been sitting here with Robert Redford as the Sicilian mob's heir apparent. Go figure.

THE ACTORS

Marlon Brando's Don Corleone, one of the most imitated performances ever, is by now as pervasive a film image as Chaplin's Little Tramp or Garland's Dorothy. The power of the portrayal is its focus on the physicality of the character. The old man's walk is by turns aggressive and suddenly agile, his demonic glare slowly melts into a mischievous grin. His death in the tomato garden at film's end was entirely improvised, as was his interplay with a kitten early on. (He was unconcerned that the loud purring created havoc with the sound.) Brando's infamous disregard for budgetary constraints led to his near loss of the role. Paramount was still steamed over his antics on the set of *Mutiny on the Bounty* (1962), which had led to financial disaster. He was the most iconoclastic screen actor of all time, an electric presence that overrode often mumbled performances and questionable self-discipline. His Stanley Kowalski in *A Streetcar Named Desire* (1951) changed the perception of film acting and created a new breed of male star. He topped it with *On the Waterfront* (1954), for which he earned his first Academy Award. His Oscar for *The Godfather* resulted in perhaps the most infamous moment in the Award's history, when he declined the statuette by proxy. His most memorable films include *Viva Zapata* (1952), *The Wild One* (1954) (in which he famously responded to the question "What are you rebelling against?" with "What have you got?"), his unlikely musical turn in *Guys and Dolls* (1955), *Reflections in a Golden Eye* (1967), *Last Tango in Paris* (1973), *Apocalypse Now* (1979), and his own wry imitation of Don Corleone in *The Freshman* (1990). (For more on Brando, see pages 60, 64, and 100.)

Al Pacino, who nearly didn't get the role the first time around (Paramount execs thought his early scenes were boring), is so thoroughly entrenched in the character you can easily imagine him living off-camera as Michael Corleone. "The pleasure of the film for me is looking back at the experience, that I survived it," he said. Coppola would probably never have made *The Godfather* without Pacino. "The first time I read the book I saw his face. He was always Michael." By the time *Part II* came along, a mere two years later, Pacino had already performed his second most iconic role, in *Serpico*. He was a full-fledged star now, with all the grace notes and burdens that implied. It perfectly suited the Michael in *Part II*, who'd come into his own during the same period. Previous to his *Godfather* breakthrough, there was *Me, Natalie* (1969) and *Panic in Needle Park* (1971). What followed was an avalanche of beautifully realized roles, in *Dog Day Afternoon* (1975), *...And Justice for All* (1979), *Cruising* (1980), *Scarface* (1983), *Sea of Love* (1989), *Dick Tracy* (1990), *The Godfather, Part III* (1990), *Frankie and Johnny* (1991), *Glengarry Glen Ross* (1992), and his Oscar-winning blind retired Army officer in *Scent of a Woman* (1992). That preceded his reteaming with De Niro in *Heat* (1995). Next came *Donnie Brasco* (1997), *The Devil's Advocate* (1997), *Any Given Sunday* (1999), *Insomnia* (2002), *The Recruit* (2003), and *Merchant of Venice* (2004).

Robert De Niro recalls the arduous debate about whether or not to wear a mustache as the young Don Vito. The discussion went on for weeks until it was finally resolved by the flip of a coin. (The 'stache stayed.) Though *Mean Streets* came out the same year, it was *Part II* and the accompanying Best Supporting Actor Oscar that made De Niro *the* De Niro. He can thank Coppola for his "lucky" timing. He'd tested for the roles of Sonny and Paulie in *The Godfather*, but Coppola thought he wasn't quite right for either. It allowed him the opportunity to take the role in *Bang the Drum Slowly* (1972) that Pacino had been forced to abandon to play Michael. De Niro was then freed up to play the young Vito Corleone in *Part II*, which was what Coppola had imagined for him all along. De Niro's credits are the essential graph of contemporary film, everything from his legendary *Taxi Driver* (1976) and *Raging Bull* (1980) to *Rocky and Bullwinkle* (2000), *The King of Comedy* (1983) to *Midnight Run* (1988) and *GoodFellas* (1990), with Pacino again in *Heat* (1995), and then as the comically conflicted mob boss of *Analyze This* (1999). He placed his stamp on *Cape Fear* (1991), *Casino* (1995), *Sleepers* (1996), *Cop Land* (1997), *Wag the Dog* (1997), *Meet the Parents* (2001), *The Good Shepherd* (2006), and ever onward. (For more on De Niro, see page 57, 91, and 118.)

Kay Corleone is the anti-Annie Hall, and it's to **Diane Keaton**'s credit that we're able to buy her in both roles. Kay's WASP rhythms are so completely at odds with Michael's Sicilian grand-opera mindset that a major clash is inevitable. The power of it comes equally from the two actors. Keaton matches Pacino's resilience, and when he finally slams the door in her face in their final scene, it's as if he's slamming it on whatever humanity he has left. Her follow-up to *The Godfather* series was *Looking for Mr. Goodbar* (1977), which introduced a young actor named Richard Gere. Then came her golden Woody Allen years, five films in all, crowned by her Oscar-winning *Annie Hall* (1977). She moved on to Hollywood royalty status as Warren Beatty's off- and on-screen partner in *Reds* (1981). She's had box-office successes with *Baby Boom* (1987) and *Father of the Bride* (1991), and has expanded her career to include writing and directing such well-received films as *Heaven*

(Continued on page 13)

Connie Corleone's wedding is a mob scene. "For better or worse," you bet.

THE GODFATHER CAST

Don Vito Corleone	Marlon Brando	Luca Brasi	Lenny Montana
Michael Corleone	Al Pacino	Paulie Gatto	John Martino
Kay Adams-Corleone	Diane Keaton	Bonasera the Undertaker	Salvatore Corsitto
Peter Clemenza	Richard S. Castellano	Albert "Al" Neri	Richard Bright
Tom Hagen	Robert Duvall	Moe Greene	Alex Rocco
"Sonny" Corleone	James Caan	Bruno Tattaglia	Tony Giorgio
Captain McCluskey	Sterling Hayden	Nazorine the Baker	Vito Scotti
"Connie" Corleone-Rizzi	Talia Shire	Theresa Hagen	Tere Livrano
Jack Woltz	John Marley	Phillip Tattaglia	Victor Rendina
Don Emilio Barzini	Richard Conte	Lucy Mancini	Jeannie Linero
Virgil "The Turk" Sollozzo	Al Lettieri	Sandra Corleone	Julie Gregg
Sal Tessio	Abe Vigoda	Mrs. Clemenza	Ardell Sheridan
Carlo Rizzi	Gianni Russo	Apollonia Vitelli-Corleone	Simonetta Stefanelli
Frederico "Fredo" Corleone	John Cazale	Fabrizio	Angelo Infanti
Ottilio Cuneo	Rudy Bond	Don Tommasino	Corrado Gaipa
Johnny Fontane	Al Martino	Calo, Bodyguard in Sicily	Franco Citti
Carmella "Mama" Corleone	Morgana King	Signor Vitelli	Saro Urzì

CREDITS

The Godfather Producer:
Alfred S. Ruddy/Paramount
The Godfather, Part II: Fred Roos, Gray Frederickson/Paramount
Director: Francis Ford Coppola
Screenplays: Mario Puzo, Francis Ford Coppola
Running time: *The Godfather*: 175 minutes; *The Godfather, Part II*: 187 minutes
Combined Budget: $19 million
Combined Box Office: $193 million

ACADEMY AWARDS

The Godfather
Best Picture
Best Actor: Marlon Brando
Best Adapted Screenplay: Francis Ford Coppola, Mario Puzo

ACADEMY AWARDS NOMINATIONS

The Godfather
Best Director: Francis Ford Coppola
Best Supporting Actor: Al Pacino, James Caan, Robert Duvall
Best Costume Design: Anna Hill Johnstone
Best Editing: William Reynolds, Peter Zinner
Best Music, Original Score: Nino Rota
Best Sound: Charles Grenzbach, Richard Portman, Christopher Newman

THE YEAR'S OTHER WINNERS

Best Director: Bob Fosse, *Cabaret*
Best Actress: Liza Minnelli, *Cabaret*
Best Supporting Actor: Joel Grey, *Cabaret*
Best Supporting Actress: Eileen Heckart, *Butterflies Are Free*

ACADEMY AWARDS

The Godfather, Part II
Best Picture
Best Director: Francis Ford Coppola
Best Adapted Screenplay: Francis Ford Coppola, Mario Puzo
Best Supporting Actor: Robert De Niro
Best Art Direction-Set Decoration: Dean Tavoularis, Angelo P. Graham, George R. Nelson
Best Music, Original Dramatic Score: Nino Rota/Carmine Coppola

ACADEMY AWARDS NOMINATIONS

The Godfather, Part II
Best Actor: Al Pacino
Best Supporting Actor: Michael V. Gazzo
Best Supporting Actor: Lee Strasberg
Best Supporting Actress: Talia Shire
Best Costume Design: Theadora van Runkle

THE YEAR'S OTHER WINNERS

Best Actor: Art Carney, *Harry and Tonto*
Best Actress: Ellen Burstyn, *Alice Doesn't Live Here Anymore*
Best Supporting Actress: Ingrid Bergman, *Murder on the Orient Express*

(Continued from page 11)
(1987) and *Unstrung Heroes* (1995). Her most recent best role: *Something's Gotta Give* (2003). (For more on Keaton, see page 36.)

James Caan, another veteran of Coppola's *The Rain People* (1969), was briefly considered for the role of Michael. His memorable death scene at a Jersey Turnpike tollbooth in *The Godfather* required nearly 200 "squibs" (fake blood pellets). Known for his wit and intelligence, Caan's career has bounced around wildly since his first appearance as a psycho in *Lady in a Cage* (1964). TV movie *Brian's Song* (1970) brought him a wide audience, and his *Rollerball* (1975) has become a cult classic. He appeared with Barbra Streisand in *Funny Lady* (1975) and made his directorial debut with *Hide in Plain Sight* (1980). He was detoured by drug addiction but caught a lucky comeback break with *Misery* (1990) after Warren Beatty dropped out of the project.

Robert Duvall had worked with Coppola previously on *The Rain People* (1969), and the director earmarked him for the role of loyal family outsider Tom Hagen. Considered the perfect team player and a strong supporting actor, Duvall had had few starring roles since his debut in *To Kill a Mockingbird* (1962). But when they came his way he took full advantage. One such opportunity, *Tender Mercies* (1982), led to a Best Actor Oscar. Coppola ingeniously cast him yet again, as the psychotically fearless Lt. Col. Kilgore in *Apocalypse Now* (1979). His ubiquitous presence in TV and films is marked by such highlights as *The Great Santini* (1979), *Lonesome Dove* (1989), *The Apostle* (1997), *A Civil Action* (1998), and as Robert E. Lee in *Gods and Generals* (2003). (For more on Duvall, see page 60.)

John Cazale, considered an "actor's actor" among his peers, was aced out of an Oscar nod for his deeply conflicted Fredo in *Part II*. "His work was so strong. We were sure he'd get the nomination," says Al Pacino. Cazale created yet another stir in *The Conversation* (1974), and as Pacino's hilariously anxious crime partner in *Dog Day Afternoon* (1975). "You knew you were in the presence of a great talent," adds director Sidney Lumet. Cazale met and fell in love with young Meryl Streep during a Shakespeare-in-the-Park production, but was diagnosed with terminal cancer before they could be married. His last film was *The Deer Hunter* (1978). (For more on Cazale, see page 274.)

Talia Shire, as the hopeful young bride turned world-weary Connie Corleone, bounded back as the plain, exuberant Aaaaa-drian! in the *Rocky* series. But what she really wanted to do was direct. She got her chance with *Before the Night/One Night Stand* (1994), as her acting career limped along with minor roles in TV miniseries and direct-to-video B films.

Lee Strasberg, revered and demonized capo of the Actor's Studio, counted Brando, Pacino, and De Niro among his prized students. The role of Hyman Roth was a very rare outing for Strasberg as an actor. He appeared once again with Pacino in *...And Justice for All* (1979).

Michael Gazzo, Oscar-nominated for his primitive, Old World (though often funny) Frank Pentangeli was previously a playwright; his *A Hatful of Rain* was a Broadway hit and a movie (1957). He was also credited with the screenplay for Elvis Presley's *King Creole* (1958).

BEHIND THE SCREEN

The production was plagued by bitter disputes between Coppola and Paramount Production Chief Robert Evans, who has since referred to him as "an evil person...a direct descendant of Machiavelli's prince. He's so seductive, so bril-

(Continued on page 15)

Young Vito Corleone begins his climb through the process of "elimination." Robert De Niro is the first and only American actor to win an Oscar for a performance in which no English is spoken. He passed up a few choice roles in *The Godfather* to land this one in *Part II*. A wise career move by all accounts.

“An actor’s a guy who, if you ain’t talking about him, he ain’t listening.”—Marlon Brando

Feigning a truce between the families, Michael agrees to meet with his father’s sworn enemy, Sollozzo, and his “bought cop,” Captain McCluskey. Sollozzo has chosen the spot, an out-of-the-way Italian restaurant in the Bronx. The Corleones have learned of its location in advance and a gun is planted in the men’s room. En route, Michael is briefly distressed when Sollozzo’s driver takes the bridge to New Jersey. But after a squealing U-turn, he realizes this was just to throw off any tails. It’s Michael’s first hit and his anxiety is palpable in the early stages of the meal. He’s already been searched by Sollozzo’s bodyguard, so when he goes to the bathroom there’s no suspicion at the table. He returns armed, and Sollozzo’s conversation comes across as just a muddle of words—Michael’s mind is elsewhere. This is his defining moment as a true son of the don and, finally, he takes it. A quick bullet is dispatched to Sollozzo’s head and another hits a stunned McCluskey in the throat. Then, according to plan, Michael drops the weapon and hurries out the door to a waiting car.

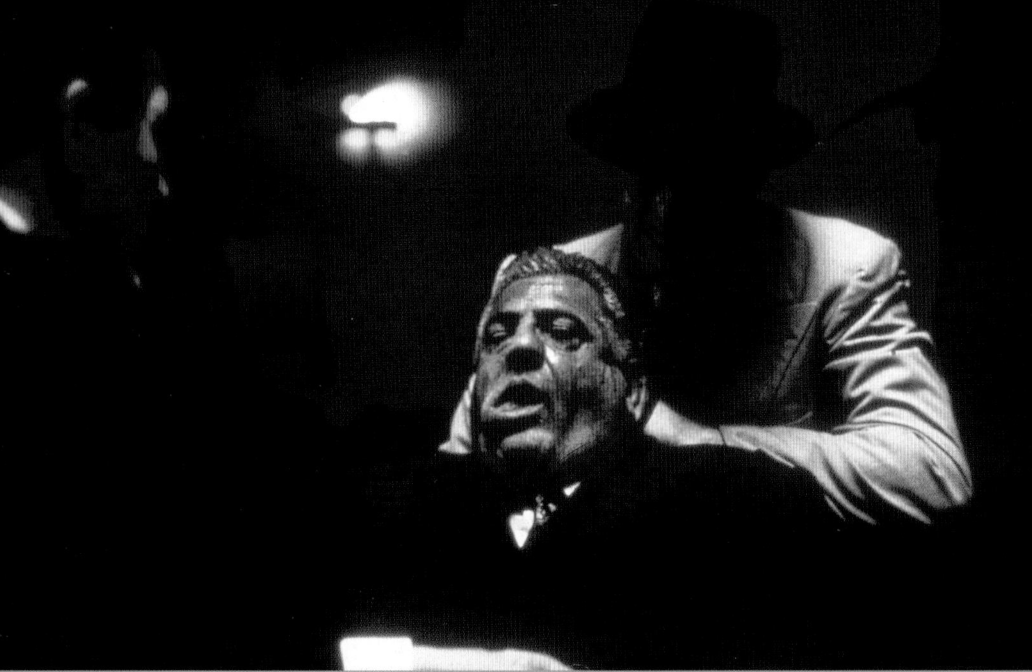

THE OTHER LISTS

- American Film Institute (Yes)
- Roger Ebert’s Top 100 (No)
- *Entertainment Weekly* (Yes)
- Internet Movie Database (Yes)
- Leonard Maltin (No)
- *Movieline* (Yes)
- National Society of Film Critics (No)
- *Premiere* Magazine (Yes)
- *Rolling Stone* Magazine (No)
- *Village Voice* (Yes)

“Luca Brasi sleeps with the fishes.” Unfortunate Brasi is part of a stunning, murderous montage of recrimination that is juxtaposed with Michael’s prayerful attendance at his son’s baptism. Rumors abounded that the film was unofficially sanctioned by the real Mafia and that many of its soldiers were cast as extras.

(Continued from page 13)

liant at bringing people into his web, he makes Elmer Gantry look like Don Knotts."

The word "Mafia" is never used in the screenplay.

Brando's Don Corleone mouth stuffing is on display at the American Museum of the Moving Image in Queens, New York.

Along with 23 murders, there are well over 50 scenes involving food and drink.

BEHIND THE SCREEN

Faded teen idol Troy Donahue played Merle Johnson, the man Connie wanted to marry. Merle Johnson was Donahue's real name.

The script called for a cameo return by Marlon Brando, a flashback to Don Vito's birthday. On the day of filming he was a no-show. Coppola thought fast, changed the scene to a surprise party, and we hear excited voices welcoming him in the next room. His unseen presence makes him the more formidable.

Inspired by crime legends from the first half of the twentieth century, De Niro wrapped a towel around his gun as a silencer as he went after Little Italy boss Don Finucci. When he fired off a round, the towel burst into flames. De Niro, on film, is clearly startled.

THE CRITICS

The Godfather:

"An enduring, undisputed masterpiece."
—Edward Guthmann, *San Francisco Chronicle*

"Overblown, pretentious, slow and ultimately tedious three-hour quasi-epic." —*Vogue*

The Godfather, Part II:

"It may be the most passionately felt epic ever made in this country." —Pauline Kael, *The New Yorker*

"Everything of any interest was thoroughly covered in the original film, but like many people who have nothing to say, *Part II* won't shut up."
—Vincent Canby, *New York Times*

NOTABLE QUOTES

"[Brando] gets to do a lot of takes. That's what I think stardom means."—Al Pacino

"I have the eyes of a dead pig."—Marlon Brando

"I don't know what people expect when they meet me. They seem to be afraid that I'm going to piss in the potted palm and slap them on the ass."—Marlon Brando

"Being a Hollywood star is death as far as I'm concerned. I don't want people to recognize me on the streets."—Robert De Niro

"My brother is the best director in the world—period."—Talia Shire

THE DIRECTOR

Francis Ford Coppola happily refers to the *Godfather* cycle as "the biggest home movie in history." His sister Talia Shire (as Connie), his daughter Sofia (as the christened baby), his father Carmine (as a shopkeeper)—they're all here. And, given his symbiotic relationship with Al Pacino and his deep affection for Diane Keaton and Robert De Niro, Coppola seems to direct in the manner of a paterfamilias at the head of the table. Prosciutto, cannoli, grappa, and scripts all around! The characters are as vividly real as the actors who portray them. With Pacino and De Niro, the set of *Part II*, in particular, was a firestorm of improvisation. "The script changed every day, like a newspaper," Coppola admits. Working at the piano bench alongside Fellini's legendary composer, Nino Rota, Coppola instinctively knew what the music would contribute. ("Those four bars there, repeat it again, slowly—that's Michael!") An early screening of *Part II* in San Francisco was a disaster. The audience was lost. Coppola knew at once he was cutting back and forth too much between the stories of Michael and Vito. He went from twenty cuts to twelve, allowing each segment to play itself out, letting the stories breathe. It was precisely what was required. While Coppola has been accused of playing the self-serving rebel with a camera, unconcerned by budgets or studio constraints, his heart's true appetite was for the story he was telling. Shaping and nurturing, Coppola functioned as the handmaiden as well as the architect of these two profoundly influential films. Previous to *The Godfather*, there was *You're A Big Boy Now* (1966), *Finian's Rainbow* (1968), and *The Rain People* (1969), though he was better known as a screenwriter on such seminal films as *Patton* (1970). On the heels of *Part II* came *The Conversation* (1974) and *Apocalypse Now* (1979). A sketchy period included *One from the Heart* (1982) and *The Cotton Club* (1984), before the success of the somewhat less ambitious *Peggy Sue Got Married* (1986). *The Godfather, Part III* (1990) was the critically toasted distant cousin of the trilogy—suffering, some felt, from the casting of daughter Sofia Coppola in a central role—and was followed by *Bram Stoker's Dracula* (1992), *Jack* (1996), and *The Rainmaker* (1997). (For more on Coppola, see pages 60 and 274.)

"I know it was you, Fredo." Michael gets his heart broken by his Judas brother. The payback will be a bit more painful for Fredo. Life tragically imitated art, as John Cazale died prematurely of cancer just two years after the film's release.

THE GODFATHER, PART II CAST

Michael Corleone	Al Pacino
Tom Hagen	Robert Duvall
Kay Adams-Corleone	Diane Keaton
Vito Corleone	Robert De Niro
Frederico "Fredo" Corleone	John Cazale
"Connie" Corleone-Johnson	Talia Shire
Hyman Roth	Lee Strasberg
Frankie Pentangeli	Michael V. Gazzo
Senator Pat Geary	G. D. Spradlin
Al Neri	Richard Bright
Don Fanucci	Gastone Moschin
Rocco Lampone	Tom Rosqui
Clemenza	Bruno Kirby
Genco	Frank Sivero
Young Carmella "Mama" Corleone	Francesca De Sapio
Older Carmella "Mama" Corleone	Morgana King
Deanna Dunn-Corleone	Marianna Hill
Johnny Ola	Leopoldo Trieste
Michael's Bodyguard	Amerigo Tot
Merle Johnson	Troy Donahue
Young Sal Tessio	John Aprea
Willi Cicci	Joe Spinnell
Sal Tessio	Abe Vigoda
Theresa Hagen	Tere Livrano
Carlo Rizzi	Gianni Russo
Vito's Mother	Maria Carta
Young Vito Corleone	Oreste Baldini
Don Francesco Ciccio	Giuseppe Sillato
Don Tommasino	Mario Cotone
Anthony Vito Corleone	James Gounaris
Mrs. Marcia Roth	Fay Spain
FBI Man #1	Harry Dean Stanton
FBI Man #2	David Baker
Carmine Rosato	Carmine Caridi
Tony Rosato	Danny Aiello
Policeman	Carmine Foresta
Bartender	Nick Discenza
Father Carmelo	Father Joseph Medeglia
Senate Committee Chairman	William Bowers
Michael's Buttonman #1	Joseph Della Sorte
Michael's Buttonman #2	Carmen Argenziano
Michael's Buttonman #3	Joe Lo Grippo
Impresario	Ezio Flagello
Tenor in "Senza Mamma"	Livio Giorgi
Girl in "Senza Mamma"	Kathleen Beller
Signora Colombo	Saveria Mazzola
Cuban President	Tito Alba

THE GREAT SCENE

"I didn't want your son, Michael. I wouldn't bring another one of your sons into this world!" Kay's sudden rage is no equal to the cold fury of her husband, who's become too well-practiced in the art of revenge. He'll make sure that she pays dearly.

THE GODFATHER, PART II

Kay has played the devoted wife for as long as she can, but her love and respect have evaporated. She gently informs Michael she's leaving with the children. He coldly reminds her that's not possible. Doesn't she know, after all this time, no one leaves him? He tells her she's just upset over her recent miscarriage, that's all: "We'll make another baby." She's aghast. "Are you blind, Michael? It wasn't a miscarriage, it was an abortion!" She's killed his son rather than subject any more children to this evil, this "Sicilian thing that's been going on for two thousand years!" Michael shakes with such rage he's in danger of imploding. He lunges, punching her so hard in the face she flies back onto the couch. Regaining control, he orders her out of his life. And, no, the children won't be leaving with her.

2

CITIZEN KANE 1941

IT'S LONELY AT THE TOP

The camera pulls up higher, higher, and still higher above the "costliest monument of a man to himself": Xanadu, the residence of the American newspaper magnate Charles Foster Kane (Orson Welles). As we look down, we see that the palace has become a warehouse for thousands of crated and uncrated works of art that Kane had been amassing for years. We feel a sense of vertigo not just from the height of the shot, but also from contemplating the immensity of the collection—a visual metaphor for the life of Kane. We reel at the sight of his bounty, as we've been reeling throughout the film, whose breakneck pace, its play with every conceivable camera angle, its inventive use of shadows, dissolves, deep focus, ceiling shots, overlapping dialogue, and a cacophony of offscreen sounds combine into a film masterpiece unlike any other. What's all this effort about? It's about how the story of a man's life gets told—if it ever can be told. *Citizen Kane* is seen by some as cold, and calculated only to puzzle and fool us. Others perceive a revelation with just the right measure of emotional impact. Whatever your conclusion, *Kane* is singularly responsible for changing our perceptions of the possibilities of film. And for that, we are indebted to the genius of Orson Welles and company.

Jim: Genuinely fascinating, brilliant and cold as a freezer. No wonder he needed that sled. Though very accessible, it's one of those movies that makes you feel smart for watching it. Probably responsible for more pseudo-intellectual conversations about the movies than any other.

Gail: In the end, watching *Citizen Kane* is like walking into your favorite room—you expect to find the furniture ingeniously and appealingly arranged, and, depending upon where you sit, you can always expect to see the pieces speak to each other from a new angle.

VERYBODY'S TALKING ABOUT IT!
It's Terrific!
ORSON
WELLES
CITIZEN
KANE
JOSEPH COTTEN
DOROTHY COMINGORE
EVERETT SLOANE
RAY COLLINS
GEORGE COULOURIS
AGNES MOOREHEAD
PAUL STEWART
RUTH WARRICK
ERSKINE SANFORD
WILLIAM ALLAND

'HE PLOT

oments after we approach a crumbling anadu through rusted gates, Kane is dead, ıispering his final word–"Rosebud"–as he ops a glass snow globe onto the floor. The eath of the newspaper magnate is big news, ıd his own bold, splashy, tabloid, *The New rk Inquirer*, is hungry to discover the meang of his elusive last word (though no one ctually heard him say it). Was it the nickname a lost love? A favorite pet? Kane's story is en told through a series of long flashbacks a overlapping, nonsequential accounts of e friends and acquaintances–none of whom e particularly reliable. We see Kane, with e help of his best friend, Jedediah Leland oseph Cotten), grow the *Inquirer* from a circution of 30,000 to the largest daily newspaper the country. He marries Emily Norton (Ruth arrick), the American President's niece. Kane ampaigns for governor, but the campaign is t short when his rival, Boss Jim Gettys (Ray ollins), reveals his affair with Susan Alexander orothy Comingore). Having alienated all ound him, Kane retreats to his unfinished alace with Susan. Lonely and in despair, ane grows more reclusive. Susan tires of their npty life and leaves him devastated.

The flight to power. "He happens to be the President, Charles, not you," says future wife Emily Monroe Norton Kane (Ruth Warrick) in an argument with Charles Foster Kane (Orson Welles) over the policies of her uncle, the President. "That's a mistake that will be corrected one of these days," replies Kane. Unfortunately, his prophecy will never come true. His first run for public office is ruined by a scandalous affair.

"Emily Monroe Norton Kane: Really Charles, people will think— Kane: —what I tell them to think!"

THE DIRECTOR

The 25-year-old trickster genius **Orson Welles**'s first film caused quite a stir upon its release, not the least of which was the fury—and the attempt to stop the film—of newspaper magnate William Randolph Hearst, upon whom the story was loosely based. In addition to the stink raised by Hearst, *Kane* caused critical wars that continue to this day over the meaning and structure of the film. Critic Pauline Kael nearly started a riot by accusing Welles of taking undeserved credit for the screenplay he coauthored with Herman J. Mankiewicz. Just what was Welles up to? Were all those fancy camera angles and that "Rosebud" business pieces of a puzzle designed to trick the audience, as Welles had done with his *War of the Worlds* radio broadcast? No matter. Orson Welles was the single most influential filmmaker in America, and though the movie did garner critical acclaim, it was a box-office disaster. The key fact of Kane's life, the loss of his mother, was actually Welles's story, not Hearst's. Welles's mother died when he was eight, and his father followed when he was twelve, at which time he became a ward of Chicago's Dr. Maurice Bernstein. After *Kane*, Welles told the more intimate story—hidden within *Kane*—of the importance of family life in *The Magnificent Ambersons* (1942), which was cut to shreds by the producers. Later, he made *The Stranger* (1946), *The Lady From Shanghai* (1948), a low-budget version of *Macbeth* (1948), then several projects that were never completed. He could have enjoyed the released of *Mr. Arkadin* (1955), but the film was taken away from him in the final stages of editing. He then directed *A Touch of Evil* (1958), *The Trial* (1963), *Chimes at Midnight* (1966), *F for Fake* (1974), and the never-completed *The Other Side of the Wind* (1970–76).

As a reporter assigned to get to the bottom of Rosebud and the Kane phenomenon, Jerry Thompson (William Alland) speaks to Kane's butler, the last man to have seen him alive, who claims to know about Rosebud. The bottom line is that nobody could have even known that Kane uttered "Rosebud," let alone what it meant to him, as no one actually heard Kane say it. Was this Welles' mistake or another one of his tricks? We'll never know.

THE CAST

Charles Foster Kane	Orson Welles
Jedediah Leland	Joseph Cotten
Susan Alexander Kane	Dorothy Comingore
Mrs. Mary Kane	Agnes Moorehead
Emily Monroe Norton Kane	Ruth Warrick
Boss James "Jim" W. Gettys	Ray Collins
Mr. Bernstein	Everett Sloane
Jerry Thompson/"News on the March" Narrator	William Alland
Raymond, Kane's Butler	Paul Stewart
Walter Parks Thatcher	George Coulouris
Signor Matiste, Susan's Opera Coach	Fortunio Bonanova
Mr. Rawlston	Philip Van Zandt
Kane's Father	Harry Shannon

THE ACTORS

Orson Welles's Kane is a fascinating character to watch; a larger-than-life figure, he is annoying, amusing, and bursting with energy and bravado throughout his young, ambitious manhood, then grows morose, tyrannical, and grotesque later in life. By the end of the film he has literally become a monster; his very walk is Frankensteinian. Though his many changing moods and the speed with which the story is told make him somewhat mysterious, you can at times feel his pain; you can see that his amassing of great wealth and innumerable material possessions was, in some measure, an unsuccessful attempt to fill the emptiness he experienced throughout his life, beginning with being taken from his mother. Welles acted throughout his troubled directing career, appearing in *Jane Eyre* (1944), the remarkable postwar drama *The Third Man* (1949), *A Man for All Seasons* (1966), *Is Paris Burning?* (1966), *Casino Royale* (1967), *Catch-22* (1970), and Henry Jaglom's *A Safe Place* (1971). In his last screen appearance he played himself in Jaglom's largely improvised *Someone to Love* (1987). Welles carried his directorial disappointments badly and became grotesquely obese. At his most desperate, he made the rounds of the talk-show circuit, appearing on Merv Griffin and other such venues. There he performed magic acts, then finally started hawking budget wine on TV commercials. His descent, ironically, came to mirror Kane's in far too many ways. (For more on Welles, see page 184.)

Though she appears only briefly in the beginning of the film to deliver her son as a ward to Walter Thatcher, **Agnes Moorehead**'s face bears a look of unforgettable motherly pain. It is the saddest of all moments in the film, save when Susan walks out on him decades later. Moorehead was a well-known character actress and a member of Welles's Mercury Players. She appeared in his *The Magnificent Ambersons*, for which she received an Oscar nomination (1942). During her career she would pick up four total nominations, for *Mrs. Parkington* (1944), *Johnny Belinda* (1948), and *Hush...Hush, Sweet Charlotte* (1965). To a younger generation she is best known as Samantha's conniving mother on the TV series *Bewitched* (1964–72).

Another Mercury Player, **Joseph Cotten**, performs the thankless role of the blindly loyal best friend to Kane, absorbing all the shocks of his friend's colossal ego without complaint. When Kane finally fires him for writing a bad review of Susan's opera, he takes it on the chin. It's a complex but unexamined relationship. Cotten rejoined Welles for *The Magnificent Ambersons* and *Journey Into Fear* (both 1942), the great Carol Reed thriller *The Third Man* (1949), and *Touch of Evil* (1958). Cotten was something of a Hollywood icon, appearing in Hitchcock's *Shadow of a Doubt* (1943) and other films, including *Gaslight* (1944), *Since You Went Away* (1944), *Duel in the Sun* (1946), *Under Capricorn* (1949), *Niagara* (1953), *Tora! Tora! Tora!* (1970), *Soylent Green* (1973), *Airport '77* (1977), and *Heaven's Gate* (1980). He died in 1994. (For more on Cotten, see page 184.)

Still another of Welles's Mercury Players, **Everett Sloane** as the excitable Mr. Bernstein, plays the eager right hand to the great newspaperman Kane. He also appeared with Welles in *Journey Into Fear* (1942), *The Lady*

CREDITS

Producer: Orson Welles/ RKO Pictures
Director: Orson Welles
Screenplay: Herman J. Mankiewicz, Orson Welles
Running Time: 119 minutes
Budget: $800,000

ACADEMY AWARD

Best Writing, Original Screenplay: Herman J. Mankiewicz, Orson Welles

NOMINATIONS

Best Picture
Best Actor: Orson Welles
Best Art Direction–Interior Decoration, Black-and-White: Perry Ferguson, Van Nest Polglase, A. Roland Fields, Darrell Silvera
Best Cinematography, Black-and-White: Gregg Toland
Best Director: Orson Welles
Best Film Editing: Robert Wise
Best Music, Scoring of a Dramatic Picture: Bernard Herrmann
Best Sound, Recording: John Aalberg

THE YEAR'S OTHER WINNERS

Best Picture: *How Green Was My Valley*
Best Director: John Ford, *How Green Was My Valley*
Best Actor: Gary Cooper, *Sergeant York*
Best Actress: Joan Fontaine, *Suspicion*
Best Supporting Actor: Donald Crisp, *How Green Was My Valley*
Best Supporting Actress: Mary Astor, *The Great Lie*

From Shanghai (1948), and *Prince of Foxes* (1949).

"Forty-nine acres of nothing but scenery and statues. I'm lonesome," complains Susan about their lives. **Dorothy Comingore** gives one of the more emotional performances in the film playing the shrill, angry Susan, for whom Kane builds an opera house (though she has little talent or interest in the art form), and who leaves the brooding, self-involved Kane despite having real feelings for him. Comingore appeared in small parts in *Mr. Smith Goes to Washington* (1939), *Five Little Peppers and How they Grew* (1939), and *The Hairy Ape* (1944), before being blacklisted during the House Un-American Activities Committee hearings.

THE CRITICS

"*Kane* was a picture that made you think anything was possible in film." —Martin Scorsese

"*Kane* is far and away the most surprising and cinematically exciting motion picture to be seen here in many a moon. As a matter of fact, it comes close to being the most sensational film ever made in Hollywood." —Bosley Crowther, *New York Times*

"A shallow masterpiece." —Pauline Kael, *The New Yorker*

BEHIND THE SCREEN

Welles bloodied his hands in the scene where Kane destroys Susan's room after she leaves him. "I really felt it," said the actor/director. He also broke his ankle when he ran down the stairs chasing Boss Gettys.

It wouldn't be an accident if watching *Kane* brought to mind the film *Stagecoach* (1939). Welles screened the film nearly 40 times while making *Kane*.

Welles's friends noticed that no one actually hears Kane say the word "Rosebud." When they asked him how anyone knew that he'd said it, Welles reportedly stared and said, "Don't you ever tell anyone of this."

Though the biographies of Hearst and Kane diverge, the real newspaperman tried to pull the film. Not only was he enraged by having his life smeared on the screen, he was distressed by the use of the word "Rosebud," which, according to Gore Vidal (a close friend of Hearst's), was Hearst's secret name for an intimate part of the anatomy of his longtime mistress, Marion Davies.

Joseph Cotten didn't sleep for 24 hours in order to appear drunk in the scene in which he decides he must write a bad review of Susan's premiere performance. Cotten slurred his words and mistakenly said "dramatic crimiticism," a goof that was left in the final film. In the scene Orson Welles looks surprised and then breaks into a smile.

THE GREAT SCENE

Kane and his wife's growing wealth—and their increasingly distant relationship—are reflected in the length of their breakfast table, which grows longer as the years go by.

Kane's marriage to the blue-blooded Emily is disintegrating. Crisply conveyed in a succession of shots of Kane and his wife at their breakfast table, we see their attitudes changing and the estrangement deepening over the span of years. In the last shot, they are icily silent—and Emily is reading the rival newspaper. Throughout these shots the table grows longer and longer, signifying both their increasing affluence and the growing distance between them. This is almost all we ever see of their relationship.

THE OTHER LISTS

- American Film Institute (Yes)
- Roger Ebert's Top 100 (Yes)
- *Entertainment Weekly* (Yes)
- Internet Movie Database (Yes)
- Leonard Maltin (No)
- *Movieline* (Yes)
- *Premiere* Magazine (Yes)
- *Rolling Stone* Magazine (Yes)
- *Village Voice* (Yes)

"Keep Ted Turner and his damn crayons away from *Citizen Kane*!"
—Orson Welles

"I think it would be fun to run a newspaper." Kane gets to play as he and his best friend, Jedediah Leland (Joseph Cotten), bedecked in pinstriped suits, and brandishing a pipe and a cigar, celebrate their retrenched newspaper and its new headquarters.

3

CASABLANCA 1942

"HERE'S LOOKING AT YOU, KID"

"The problems of three little people in this crazy world don't amount to a hill of beans," Rick (Humphrey Bogart) says to Ilsa (Ingrid Bergman). The movie begs to differ. And everything in this film matters, from lovers to criminals to a not-so-upstanding police chief. It all happens during World War II in Casablanca, which is either the crossroads to freedom or the place where you wait to die. Everything matters. Every word uttered in this film has wit. Every gesture, every turn of the head has import. *Casablanca* is that rare movie miracle, a film with not one inconsequential frame, not one insignificant line of dialogue. When we've wiped the tears from our eyes with a last chuckle over Rick's immortal closing line, "Louis, I think this is the beginning of a beautiful friendship," this hill of beans seems like the only thing in the world that *does* matter.

Jim: Its theme of sacrificed love for the sake of mankind is such an overwhelming myth. I mean, who does that except maybe Greek gods and Biblical heroes? Only actors of this caliber could make it believable, make us think we'd be capable of such behavior. Of course, they did have that song to back them up.

Gail: Don't even consider blinking during this film, in which every moment is inextricable from the whole.

THE PLOT

Expatriate Rick runs the café where everyone from refugees to escaped convicts goes when in Casablanca, the way station to freedom from the war in Europe. All the usual suspects can be found here, including the slippery police chief, Renault (Claude Rains), and the ivory-tickling Sam, who knows what not to play to remind Rick of his lost lover. That lover, Ilsa, suddenly shows up again and makes Sam play it. She's accompanied by her husband, the heroic resistance fighter Victor Laszlo (Paul Henreid). There's Ugarte (Peter Lorre), who has hidden murdered Nazis' transit papers with Rick, and a host of Nazis who intend to invade. Rick, the cynical hero, cannot put out the flames for Ilsa. In the end—though no one in the cast knew what the end would be—Rick puts political heroism above his own happiness. He pretends that Laszlo will escape on the plane alone, and that Ilsa will remain behind with him. In an intentional quick change he insists that she take flight and help the cause—and you can see the real shock on her face. "We'll always have Paris," he whispers.

Rick (Humphrey Bogart) can't hear the warnings of his devoted old friend Sam for all the turmoil in his mind over seeing his ex-lover Ilsa in Casablanca—their first meeting since she left him waiting at the train in Paris.

"Kiss me. Kiss me as if it were the last time."—Ilsa

THE DIRECTOR

Accepting his Oscar, the heavily accented director **Michael Curtiz** said, "So many times I have a speech ready but no dice. Always a bridesmaid, but never a mother." We knew what he meant, anyway. The director had a long and stunning career mostly determined by what producers offered him. Among his American films were *The Charge of the Light Brigade* (1936), *Angels with Dirty Faces* (1938), *Yankee Doodle Dandy* (1942), *Mildred Pierce* (1945), and *King Creole* (1958), with Elvis Presley.

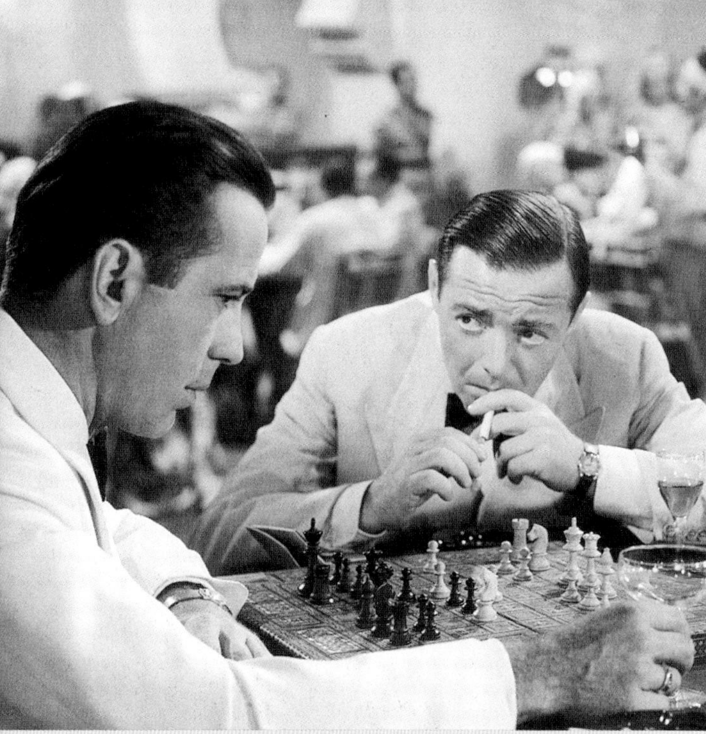

"Everybody comes to Rick's" to escape from the chaotic streets of Casablanca, World War II's melting pot of expatriates and criminals. Here Rick considers Ugarte's (Peter Lorre) request to hide his precious stolen Nazi transit visas.

THE CAST

Richard "Rick" Blaine	Humphrey Bogart
Ilsa Lund Laszlo	Ingrid Bergman
Victor Laszlo	Paul Henreid
Captain Louis Renault	Claude Rains
Major Heinrich Strasser	Conrad Veidt
Signor Ferrari	Sydney Greenstreet
Guillermo Ugarte	Peter Lorre
Carl, Rick's Café Manager	S. Z. Sakall
Yvonne, Rick's Girlfriend	Madeleine LeBeau
Sam	Dooley Wilson
Sascha, Bartender at Rick's Café	Leonid Kinskey

THE ACTORS

Humphrey Bogart's embittered expatriate barkeeper—"I stick my neck out for nobody"—tries to hide his loyalties and idealism. Bogart complained that he didn't even want to play the part. "This is the worst film we've ever come across," he said, and was shocked when the movie was a hit. The rest of his career is the stuff of Hollywood legend. He has George Raft's rejects to thank for making him into a proper star: *High Sierra* and *The Maltese Falcon* (both 1941). He continued playing the sympathetic tough guy in *To Have and Have Not* (1944), *The Big Sleep* (1946), *Key Largo* (1948), *The Treasure of the Sierra Madre* (1948), *In a Lonely Place* (1950), and *The Caine Mutiny* (1954), for which he received an Academy Award nomination. Bogart succeeded as well in such romantic comedies as *Sabrina* (1954), *We're No Angels* (1955), and *The African Queen* (1951), the latter earning him an Oscar. (For more on Bogart see pages 124 and 229.)

No other actress could shift her eyes downward in as heartbreaking and seductive a manner as **Ingrid Bergman**. Though the camera—and we—loved her, like Bogart, she didn't want the part, calling it "a fright." Indeed, the script changes every day and not knowing which man she would end up with affected Bergman. And it shows in her edgy performance. After this one, the hits kept coming. Her lyrical performances can be seen in *For Whom the Bell Tolls* (1943, Academy Award nomination), *Gaslight* (1944, Academy Award), *Spellbound* (1945), *Notorious* (1946), and *Joan of Arc* (1948). Touched by scandal when she left her husband and daughter for Italian director Roberto Rossellini, Bergman took her career to Italy, where she appeared in Rossellini's *Stromboli* (1949). She returned to the U.S. where she won an Oscar for *Anastasia* (1956). Among her later best films are *Cactus Flower* (1969) and *Murder on the Orient Express* (1974). She made her final appearance in Ingmar Bergman's *Autumn Sonata* (1978).

As freedom fighter Victor Laszlo, **Paul Henreid** had the distinct privilege of walking away with Ingrid Bergman. Often performing as the distinguished gentlemen, he appeared in *Goodbye, Mr. Chips* in England (1939), and returned to America for *Hollywood Canteen* (1944), *Four Horsemen of the Apocalypse* (1962), and *Exorcist II: The Heretic* (1977).

"We mustn't underestimate American blundering. I was with them when they blundered into Berlin in 1918," says the wry Captain Louis Renault, played with a crafty grin by **Claude Rains**. He was barely there for his great screen debut in *The Invisible Man* (1933). The studios tried to reprise the role but failed. Rains, however, succeeded in his film career in *Mr. Smith Goes to Washington* (1939), *Mr. Skeffington* (1944), *Notorious* (1946), in which he appeared again with Bergman, *Here Comes Mr. Jordan* (1941), *Now, Voyager* (1942), and *Lawrence of Arabia* (1962).

Peter Lorre's war profiteer hands a packet of illicit exit visas to Rick and says, "You know, Rick, I have many a friend in Casablanca, but somehow, just because you despise me, you are the only one I trust." The bug-eyed little man showed the filmgoing world that looks weren't everything in his powerful debut in the German-made *M* (1931). He escaped to Hollywood where he became one of the most caricatured of character actors in such films as *The Man Who Knew Too Much* (1934), *Secret Agent* (1936), *The Maltese Falcon* (1941), *The Mask of Dimitrios* (1944), *Arsenic and Old Lace* (1944), and *Beat the Devil* (1954). (For more on Lorre, see page 229.)

"As the leader of all illegal activities in Casablanca, I am an influential and respected

CREDITS

Producer: Hal B. Wallis/ Warner Bros.
Director: Michael Curtiz
Screenplay: Julius Epstein, Philip G. Epstein, Howard Koch
Running Time: 102 minutes
Budget: $957,000
Box Office: $4.1 million

ACADEMY AWARDS

Best Picture: Hal B. Wallis
Best Director: Michael Curtiz
Best Screenplay: Julius J. Epstein, Philip G. Epstein, Howard Koch, based on the play *Everyone Comes to Rick's* by Murray Burnett and Joan Alison

ACADEMY AWARD NOMINATIONS

Best Actor: Humphrey Bogart
Best Supporting Actor: Claude Rains
Best Cinematography, Black-and-White Arthur Edeson
Best Film Editing: Owen Marks
Best Score: Max Steiner

THE YEAR'S OTHER WINNERS

Best Actor: Paul Lukas, *Watch on the Rhine*
Best Actress: Jennifer Jones, *The Song of Bernadette*
Best Supporting Actor: Charles Coburn, *The More the Merrier*
Best Supporting Actress: Katina Paxinou, *For Whom the Bell Tolls*

man," says **Sydney Greenstreet**, proudly. The larger-than-an-armchair Greenstreet was a remarkable, versatile, and forceful presence on the screen. He appeared in a wide range of roles in such films as *The Maltese Falcon* (1941, Academy Award nomination), *The Mask of Dimitrios* (1944), *The Verdict* and *Three Strangers* (both 1946), *Flamingo Road* (1949), and *Malaya* (1950), among others. (For more on Greenstreet, see page 229.)

As the immortal pianist Sam of "play it again" fame, **Dooley Wilson** was actually a professional drummer who faked playing the piano. Dooley watched and copied pianist Elliott Carpenter's hand movements. Dooley appeared in other small roles in such films as *Night in New Orleans* (1942), *Stormy Weather* (1943), *Knock on Any Door* (1949), and the TV series *Beulah* (1952–53).

ROLE REVERSALS

Bogart was always considered the man for the job but studio publicity spread the word that Ronald Reagan and Ann Sheridan were to star.

George Raft tried to sweet-talk Jack L. Warner for the part.

Producer Hal B. Wallis considered Hedy Lamarr for the role of Ilsa.

Sam was originally conceived of as a woman, to be played by Hazel Scott, Lena Horne, or Ella Fitzgerald.

BEHIND THE SCREEN

Paul Henreid feared that playing a secondary lead, Victor Laszlo, would ruin his career as a leading man. Selznick loaned him out against his will.

Director Michael Curtiz's Hungarian accent confused everyone. When he asked a prop man for a "poodle" to appear in one scene, a dog was promptly produced. Curtiz screamed, "A poodle! A poodle of water!"

The last line of the film was producer Hal Wallis's idea, and it occurred to him three weeks after shooting ended. Bogart was called back in to dub it.

Max Steiner didn't want to use the song "As Time Goes By," and suggested composing an original song in order to qualify for royalties.

Rick never says, "Play it again, Sam." He says, "You played it for her, you can play it for me. Play it!" Ilsa says, "Play it, Sam. Play 'As Time Goes By.'"

That rage you sense through Bogart's smile may not always have been his character's. The actor disputed with his wife, Mayo Methot, who accused him of having an affair with Ingrid Bergman.

Many of the actors who played Nazis in the film were Jewish.

"Kiss me. Kiss me as if it were the last time," whispers Ilsa urgently. A moment before, Ilsa had confronted Rick at gunpoint to give her the transit papers. She weakens, drops the gun, and finally tells him the story of why she left him in Paris.

To maximize profits from foreign distribution of the film, the studio suggested that any unpleasant characters other than the Nazis should also be from an enemy country, namely Italy. This is why Ugarte, Ferrari, and the dark European pickpocket are Italian.

Everyone wanted Ilsa to remain with Rick, but too much was militating against it. After all, she was married to Victor, and adultery was *not* acceptable to the censors.

THE CRITICS

"*Casablanca* is one of the year's most exciting and trenchant films. It certainly won't make Vichy happy—but that's just another point for it." —Bosley Crowther, *New York Times*

"It's far from a great film, but it has a special appealingly schlocky romanticism, and you're never really pressed to take its melodramatic twists and turns seriously." —Pauline Kael, *The New Yorker*

THE GREAT LINE

"You know, Rick, I have many a friend in Casablanca, but somehow, just because you despise me, you are the only one I trust." —Ugarte

THE GREAT SCENE

In perhaps one of the most breathlessly romantic and heart-rending scenes on film, Ilsa tearfully threatens to shoot Rick if he doesn't give her the transit papers for Lazlo's escape. Rick refuses. Ilsa insists he put them on the table. Rick calls her bluff and tells her not only to shoot, but that she'll be doing him a favor. Seeing that Rick is ready to give up his life, she realizes the pain he has suffered because of her. She drops the gun and falls into his arms and cries, "Richard, I tried to stay away. I thought I would never see you again, that you were out of my life."

She tells him why she had to leave him in Paris and with that, kisses him passionately. Rick betrays his own pain, telling her, "The day you left Paris, if you knew what I went through. If you knew how much I loved you, how much I still love you."

THE OTHER LISTS

- American Film Institute (Yes)
- Roger Ebert's Top 100 (Yes)
- *Entertainment Weekly* (Yes)
- Internet Movie Database (Yes)
- Leonard Maltin (Yes)
- *Movieline* (Yes)
- *Premiere* Magazine (Yes)
- *Rolling Stone* Magazine (Yes)
- *Village Voice* (No)

4

SUNSET BOULEVARD 1950

HOLLYWOOD GOTHIC

Probably the most quoted screenplay outside of *All About Eve* (the same year, if you can believe it) and it's painfully clear what Hollywood has lost since—the power of the perfectly chosen word. This is trenchant, satirical *noir* with honest-to-God grownup characters. Sure, they're selfish users beyond redemption, but can they dress and talk! Unsentimental in the extreme and all the more fascinating for it, Billy Wilder may have wanted to show the dark underbelly of Hollywood in this one, but he also succeeded in making it more ineffably mythical. The irony here is delicious. Psycho ex-silent star Norma rails on about how "talk talk talk" ruined the movies. Not this one, baby.

Jim: A psychotic, over-the-hill movie star and her sulking rent-boy. It's like a night of eavesdropping at the Polo Lounge.

Gail: Wilder's savage powers of observation through script, lens, and direction make his depiction of Hollywood's thirst for immortality a true vampire story.

THE PLOT

ack screenwriter on the skids Joe Gillis William Holden) outraces the repo man and ides his car in the garage of a ghastly old everly Hills mansion. He's mistaken by the utler (Erich von Stroheim) for the undertaker e'd called to prepare the funeral for a be-)ved pet monkey. Joe is summoned to meet he lady of the house and recognizes her as he former silent-screen star Norma Desmond Gloria Swanson). When he comes clean bout who he is, she's intrigued. She's got a omeback script about Salome she's been vorking on and it might need some editing ere and there. Joe looks over the laughable ness and realizes this gig could put him ack in the chips. He thinks he's snared her ı his web but, too late, he realizes he's been aught in hers. Soon enough, she's seduced im and showered him with gifts. He grows oo spoiled to return to his old life despite he pleadings of a besotted young girlfriend ı the story department (Nancy Olson) who elieves in his talent. Joe's conscience is nally pricked and he plans to leave Norma. ut in her psychotic rage, she conceives a ifferent ending to his story. Joe's fate adds ew meaning to the term "typing pool."

"They had faces then!" Norma Desmond (Gloria Swanson) proclaims as she forces gigolo screenwriter Joe Gillis (William Holden) to watch one of her old silent epics. He's beginning to suspect Norma is off her rocker.

THE DIRECTOR

This was **Billy Wilder**'s favorite movie, though in the course of making it an argument with longtime cowriter/producer Charles Brackett ended their association. A feisty Jewish immigrant who'd escaped Nazi Germany, Wilder had a scathing, wry cynicism that served his *noir* scripts well. As a director, even better. In Norma's attempted suicide sequence, he called up to his overhead cameraman, "Johnny, it's the usual slashed-wrist shot...keep it out of focus. I want to win the foreign picture award." Wilder was deeply anxious and in tears after test audiences laughed at the opening scene in which Holden, as Joe Gillis, sits up on his morgue slab to tell the other corpses how he died. Wilder raced back to the studio to rewrite the now iconic opener in which Gillis narrates while floating facedown in Norma Desmond's pool. Underwater cameras weren't what they are now and for a clear image, Wilder came up with the idea of a mirror at the bottom of the pool to reflect the shot. He could be tyrannical with his actors but Swanson, for one, wound up adoring him. After her final shot, the mad scene on the staircase, she rushed childlike into his arms and wept. In defense of his opulent sets and cost overruns (Cecil B. DeMille charged him $20,000 for his brief scene and a quick retake), Wilder told reporters, "No man ever said to his wife, 'let's go see this picture, the director brought it in under budget'." Wilder launched his incomparable Hollywood career with the Ginger Rogers comedy vehicle *The Major and the Minor* (1942) but he was soon to show equal facility in any number of genres, including war drama with *Five Graves to Cairo* (1943), *noir* with *Double Indemnity* (1944) and "message pictures" with *The Lost Weekend* (1945). He easily pulled off romantic charmers like *Sabrina* (1954) and *Love in the Afternoon* (1957), both starring Audrey Hepburn. Among his later successes were *The Apartment* (1960), *The Fortune Cookie* (1966), and *The Front Page* (1974). (For more on Wilder, see page 48.)

"She was still sleepwalking along the giddy heights of a lost career—plain crazy when it came to that one subject: her celluloid self. The great Norma Desmond! How could she breathe in that house so crowded with Norma Desmonds? More Norma Desmonds and still more Norma Desmonds."

THE CAST	
Joe Gillis	William Holden
Norma Desmond	Gloria Swanson
Max Von Mayerling	Erich von Stroheim
Betty Schaefer	Nancy Olson
Sheldrake	Fred Clark
Morino	Lloyd Gough
Artie Green	Jack Webb
Cecil B. DeMille	Himself
Hedda Hopper	Herself
Buster Keaton	Himself
Anna Q. Nilsson	Herself
H. B. Warner	Himself

THE ACTORS

Gloria Swanson had been retired for almost twenty years when she got the call from Wilder and Brackett. "A screen test?" she steamed. "What the hell for, so you see if I'm still alive?" As a silent-screen diva, she'd calculated her stardom to the point where she once telegrammed her studio previous to her arrival at the Los Angeles train station: "Please arrange ovation." *Sunset Boulevard* put her back on the map, however briefly, but she lost her Oscar in a squeaker to newcomer Judy Holliday (*Born Yesterday*). She tried to turn *Sunset* into a Broadway musical in 1957, but couldn't wrangle the rights from Paramount.

Conversely, **William Holden**'s career exploded after *Sunset*, and he became the quintessential leading man in the 1950s with more successful Wilder collaborations including *Stalag 17* (1953 Oscar, Best Actor) and *Sabrina* (1954). A notorious ladies man and sex symbol, he will always be remembered by classic TV audiences as Lucy Ricardo's most embarrassing crush, the one that caused her to masquerade behind the fake nose that she ignited with a cigarette lighter. In true Hollywood Babylon fashion, Holden died after hitting his head on a table in a drunken fall.

This was **Erich von Stroheim**'s last film, and though he was nominated for Best Supporting Actor, he always referred to it patronizingly as "that butler role." He felt it was a step down after his superstar directorial career in the 1920s, which included *Queen Kelly* (1928) starring Swanson and produced by her then-lover, Joseph Kennedy. (For more on von Stroheim, see page 277.)

Talented but a little too dowdy-looking for stardom, **Nancy Olson** did better on the personal front with her marriage to *My Fair Lady* lyricist Alan J. Lerner.

BEHIND THE SCREEN

The name Norma Desmond is thought to have been a composite of murdered silent-film director William Desmond Taylor and the star who figured prominently in the investigation, Mabel Normand.

Von Stroheim, whose many skills didn't include driving, was forced to chauffeur Norma and Joe onto the Paramount lot. He managed to slam the vintage touring car into the famous entry gate.

THE CRITICS

"Casts a spell over an audience and holds it enthralled to a shattering climax. A powerful story of the ambitions and frustrations that combine to make life in the cardboard city so fascinating to the outside world." —Thomas Pryor, *New York Times*

"You bastard! You have disgraced the industry that made you and fed you!"—Louis B. Mayer to Billy Wilder, following a preview screening

CREDITS

Producer: Charles Brackett/ Paramount
Director: Billy Wilder
Screenplay: Charles Brackett, D. M. Marshman Jr., and Billy Wilder
Running time: 110 minutes
Box Office: $3.5 million

ACADEMY AWARDS

Best Screenplay: Charles Brackett, D. M. Marshman Jr., and Billy Wilder
Best Musical Score: Franz Waxman
Best Art Direction-Set Decoration: Hans Dreier, John Meehan, Sam Comer, and Ray Moyer

ACADEMY AWARD NOMINATIONS

Best Picture
Best Director: Billy Wilder
Best Actress: Gloria Swanson
Best Actor: William Holden
Best Supporting Actress: Nancy Olson
Best Supporting Actor, Erich von Stroheim

THE YEAR'S OTHER WINNERS

Best Picture: *All About Eve*
Best Director: Joseph L. Mankiewicz, *All About Eve*
Best Actor: Jose Ferrer, *Cyrano de Bergerac*
Best Actress: Judy Holliday, *Born Yesterday*
Best Supporting Actor: George Sanders, *All About Eve*
Best Supporting Actress: Josephine Hull, *Harvey*

ROLE REVERSALS

Montgomery Clift (first choice for Joe Gillis) would've been a perfect fit. But Mae West as Norma? Hard to imagine.

"All creative people should be required to leave California for three months every year."

—*Gloria Swanson*

"I am big. It's the pictures that got small."—Norma

The Paramount office summons Norma and she assumes her silent-movie mentor, Cecil B. DeMille, has decided to direct her triumphant return to the screen. With Joe and Max in tow, she arrives at the studio, where she's recognized by the old gatekeeper and waved in. DeMille learns of her arrival and escorts her onto the sound stage, where one of the lighting crew turns a blinding spot on her. Startled at first, she's quickly lost in the light, the only world she knows. Cast and crew give her a round of applause. She's in her glory, unaware that Paramount only called to borrow her vintage car for a Crosby/Hope road picture.

Norma and Joe head off to Paramount studios for an appointment with Cecil B. DeMille. Norma is under the impression he wants to direct her comeback. But ex-husband and current chauffeur Max (Erich von Stroheim) knows better; the studio just wants to borrow her vintage car for a period film.

"I just made pictures I would've liked to see."
—Billy Wilder

THE OTHER LISTS

- American Film Institute (Yes)
- Roger Ebert's Top 100 (Yes)
- *Entertainment Weekly* (Yes)
- Internet Movie Database (Yes)
- Leonard Maltin (Yes)
- *Movieline* (Yes)
- National Society of Film Critics (No)
- *Premiere* Magazine (Yes)
- *Rolling Stone* Magazine (No)
- *Village Voice* (Yes)

Police and media descend on Norma's mansion after Joe's body is found in the pool. She's completely lost her mind and has no idea what's going on. Max gently coerces her down the stairs after convincing her they're shooting a key scene from *Salome*.

5

LAWRENCE OF ARABIA 1962

ENIGMATIC SANDMAN

"Who are you?" a Suez Canal guard cries out to the blue-eyed Englishman swathed in native Bedouin robes. He's greeted with implacable silence. "Who are you?" he calls out again. T. E. Lawrence, as inhabited by Peter O'Toole, stands mute as if he, too, is trying to figure out the answer to that one. This human paradox of extreme self-deprecation and grandiose ambition, kindness, and sadomasochistic drive remains as mutable as the transcendent desert landscapes that swirl around him. He's Hamlet groping his tortured way through a Technicolor *National Geographic* layout. It's estimated that, if produced today without benefit of computer technology, the film would cost over $300 million. *Lawrence of Arabia* is a once-in-a-cinematic-lifetime phenomenon. Few stars or directors would ever agree to such a Herculean commitment. Aside from the factor of time, there were sandstorms and a sun so hot it couldn't be shot directly—Lean finally had to settle for a painting of it. He brilliantly co-opted the "abrupt cut" of New Wave French cinema. His favorite and the most famous in the film comes early, as Lawrence watches a match slowly burn down to his fingertips. At the last possible second he blows it out and—*voila!*—we're instantly transported to a startling tangerine dawn over the desert. The biographical filmmaker's deference to pace and structure takes precedence over hard, cold facts. While this may not be the definitive biography of T. E. Lawrence, and Robert Bolt's dialogue occasionally lapses into grandiose "historical epic-ese," Lean captures the essence. For all its sweeping adventure and stirring battles, a tinge of British prep-school homoeroticism emerges in the relationship between Lawrence and his inseparable companion, Sherif Ali, played by Omar Sharif. Lawrence is consumed by adolescent obsession, if not consciously for Ali, then for Arabia itself. It's a schoolboy crush played out on the world stage with guns, slaughter, and the inevitable heartbreak.

Jim: I'm always torn between where to look and what to feel. O'Toole's performance is so intricate and personal it could be played in a small room with a table and chair. I suspect if that's all Lean had to work with, he'd make it the most spectacularly constructed room, table, and chair in the history of film.

Gail: One of our most stunning screen spectacles. The vast and seductive desert landscape is so compelling it tends to obscure our vision of the subject at hand—but who's complaining?

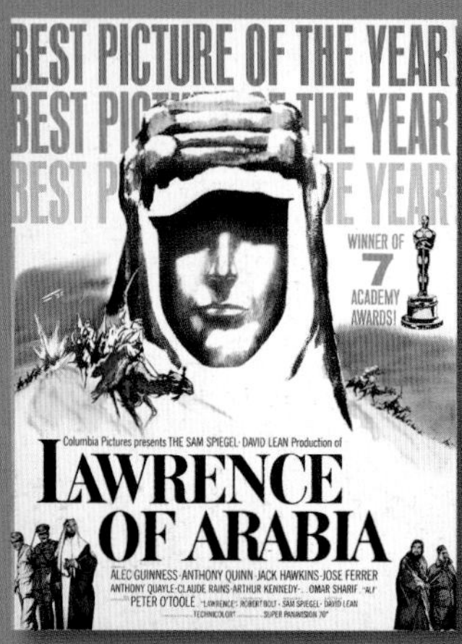

THE PLOT

A lowly British Army officer, T. E. Lawrence, has a rare knowledge of Mideast politics and culture, and is enlisted to see what he can do about organizing the disparate Arab tribes. The British need their assistance in fighting the Turks, allies of Germany in this vital stage of World War I. Lawrence is captivated by the exotic desert and its willful tribesmen, and quickly goes native after Prince Feisal pledges his support. Along with his new friend, Sherif Ali, Lawrence wins the key port of Aqaba and is proclaimed a hero. His now-bloated ego pushes him to the brink of daring. He's caught spying by the Turks, beaten, and raped. The experience transforms him into a vicious, often heedless warrior who kills for the pleasure of it. He miraculously manages to bring all the tribes together for the conquest of Damascus, but old blood feuds bring his dreams of unity to an end. Lawrence leaves Arabia despising himself for what he feels he's become—an abject failure in his mission and in his duty as a man of conscience. The world thinks otherwise.

Caught up in his own myth, Lawrence leads his adoring Bedouin forces to glory with the cry, "Take no prisoners!" Crews were on hand to rake the sand after each take.

"He was a poet, a scholar, and a mighty warrior. He was also the most shameless exhibitionist since Barnum and Bailey." —*Jackson Bentley, journalist*

THE DIRECTOR

David Lean imagined T. E. Lawrence as a man who "backed into the limelight," but once onstage, had a damnable time getting off. He'd dreamed of this project long before *The Bridge on the River Kwai*, whose success gave him the box-office clout to proceed. He had a brief flirtation with the idea of a Gandhi biopic but it was too soon after his death and "historical films force you to cut corners, always offensive to some." He had to make very firm decisions about Lawrence, his politics, and desert campaign, to say nothing of his dark personal nature. The scene in which Lawrence is savagely beaten by order of the Turkish Bey culminates in violent eroticism. Lean suggested sexual climax by focusing on José Ferrer as the Bey, standing in a doorway with an increasingly virulent cough. If this seems a bit prudish, consider Lean's background. Raised by devout Quaker parents, he was taught that films were sinful. That didn't keep him from embarking on a career that began as the action unit director for *In Which We Serve* (1942), and he moved forward with such classics as *Brief Encounter* (1945), *Great Expectations* (1946), and *Oliver Twist* (1948). After *Lawrence* came *Doctor Zhivago* (1964), *Ryan's Daughter* (1970), then a very long hiatus, which some attribute to the effect of critic Pauline Kael's withering comments on his work: "It's all so ploddingly intelligent and controlled, so distinguished." He should have relied on a comment he'd made years earlier: "I wouldn't take the advice of a lot of so-called critics on how to shoot a close-up of a teapot." Lean made a comeback with *A Passage to India* (1984). He'd begun work on Joseph Conrad's *Nostromo* at the time of his death. He could've easily eulogized himself with his own words: "I hope the moneymen don't find out that I'd pay them to let me do this." (For more on Lean, see page 187.)

Lawrence ponders the conquest of Damascus, as his blood brother, Ali, questions his sanity. (After two years on location, the cast was beginning to question Lean's.)

THE CAST	
T. E. Lawrence	Peter O'Toole
Prince Feisal	Alec Guinness
Auda abu Tayi	Anthony Quinn
Gen. Allenby	Jack Hawkins
Sherif Ali Ibn El Kharish	Omar Sharif
Turkish Bey	José Ferrer
Col. Harry Brighton	Anthony Quayle
Mr. Dryden	Claude Rains
Jackson Bentley	Arthur Kennedy
Gen. Murray	Donald Wolfit
Gasim	I. S. Johar
Majid	Gamil Ratib
Farraj	Michel Ray
Daud	John Dimech
Tafas	Zia Mohyeddin
Medical Officer	Howard Marion-Crawford

THE ACTORS

"I signed up for five months. I wound up staying for over two years." In the process **Peter O'Toole** also lost twenty pounds and his good health. "I find acting difficult. One hundred-thirty degrees in shade, sitting on a camel and covered in vermin doesn't make it easier." His was an extraordinary film debut, coming from practically nowhere (the Shakespearean stage, to be precise), in a role that was neither romantic nor fully heroic. Nonetheless, his deep intensity and startling good looks generated full-blast star power. Noel Coward famously cracked, "If he had been any prettier it would have been *Florence of Arabia*." O'Toole has since been drawn to extreme character roles in a succession of landmark films including *Becket* (1964), *The Lion in Winter* (1968), *Goodbye, Mr. Chips* (1969), *The Ruling Class* (1971), *Man of La Mancha* (1972), *The Stunt Man* and *Caligula* (both 1980), *My Favorite Year* (1982), *The Last Emperor* (1987), and *Venus* (2006). He has the dubious honor of tying with Richard Burton as the actor who's been nominated for the most Oscars (seven) without winning.

Omar Sharif was the only Arab actor to be cast in a leading role, perhaps partly due to his ability to speak English. Already an established star in the Mideast, he initially balked at the idea of a screen test but relented out of respect for David Lean. The film launched his international stardom and no actor has ever received a more spectacular introduction on film. Sharif's character, Sherif Ali, is first seen as a mere speck on the horizon, a figure on camelback, more mirage than real. (It was the first time a desert mirage had ever been captured on film.) No sound, not a stir as he slowly approaches. When he finally comes into focus in his darkly heroic black robes, he cuts a romantic figure reminiscent of Rudolph Valentino. Lean capitalized on that image in his follow-up epic, *Doctor Zhivago* (1965). *The Night of the Generals* (1967) was nearly lost in the uproar of his musical debut as sex-symbol Nicky Arnstein in *Funny Girl* (1968). It was to him that Barbra Streisand sang with the conviction of a woman in love on-screen and off: "To tell the truth it hurt my pride, the groom was prettier than the bride." His career never hit the same high, though he appeared in dozens of films including *The Tamarind Seed* (1974), *Crime and Passion* (1976), *Green Ice* (1981), and *Peter the Great* (1986). He's more comfortable touting his avocation as a world-class bridge player. (For more on Sharif, see page 187.)

Anthony Quinn was terrified to meet David Lean for the first time. "He looked more like a machine than a man, with those great eyes like a camera examining every inch of me." Lean wasn't sure he had the right stuff for the role of Auda abu Tayi, the fiercest tribal chief in Arabia. Quinn was determined to prove himself and the next day got in full costume and false nose. The extras, all locals, shouted, "It's Auda!" as he stepped out of his tent. Lean was convinced. Quinn's fear stayed with him during battle scenes in which the extras wielded swords and the pounding rush of camels could easily trample a man to death. Though Quinn wasn't nominated for an Oscar for his work here, he would be in 1964 for *Zorba the Greek*. He'd already won twice before, for *Viva Zapata* (1952) and *Lust for Life* (1956). That same year he appeared as the murderous strongman in Fellini's classic *La Strada* (1956). With more than 100 films to his credit, most of which feature him playing bigger-than-life characters, some of his career highlights include *Attila* (1959), *The Guns of Navarone* (1961), *The Shoes of the Fisherman* (1968), and *The Greek Tycoon* (1978).

Alec Guinness was a Lean veteran, with star turns in *Great Expectations* (1946), *Oliver Twist* (1948), and copping the Oscar for *The Bridge on the River Kwai* (1957). Having already played T. E. Lawrence on the stage, he found the role of Prince Feisal an equal challenge. He perfected just the right accent by listening intently to Omar Sharif, but the timing and delivery were pure Guinness. He got off some of the best-crafted lines in the film: "With Major Lawrence, mercy is a passion. With me, it is merely good manners. You may judge which motive is the most reliable." And, "No Arab loves the desert. We love water and green trees. There is nothing in the desert and no man needs nothing." In a career rich with unforgettable roles, along with the above mentioned, he's most closely associated with *Kind Hearts and Coronets* (1949), *The Lavender Hill Mob* (1951), *The Ladykillers* (1955), *The Horse's Mouth* (1958), *Our Man in Havana* (1959), and as a hero to a new generation of filmgoers in *Star Wars* (1977). (For more on Guinness, see pages 169 and 188.)

ROLE REVERSALS

Marlon Brando was the first choice for the role of Lawrence. When commitments interfered, Albert Finney was cast but lasted only four days. Spiegel and Lean tapped Peter O'Toole at Katharine Hepburn's insistence.

THE SET

The conquered city-on-the-sea, Aqabar, was actually reconstructed in Spain. Desert scenes were split among Spain, Jordan, and Morocco.

BEHIND THE SCREEN

The 1989 restoration, due in great part to the efforts of Steven Spielberg, was accomplished in the nick of time. The original negatives had nearly exhausted their usability.

Lawrence overcomes the desert and its inherent myths and mysteries.

CREDITS

Producer: Sam Spiegel/ Columbia Pictures
Director: David Lean
Screenplay: Robert Bolt and Michael Wilson
Based on the writings of T. E. Lawrence
Running time: 216 minutes
Budget: $12 million
Box Office: $20.3 million

ACADEMY AWARDS

Best Picture
Best Director: David Lean
Best Cinematography, Color: Freddie Young
Best Art Direction-Set Decoration, Color: John Box, John Stoll, Dario Simoni
Best Editing: Anne V. Coates
Best Score: Maurice Jarre
Best Sound: John Cox

ACADEMY AWARD NOMINATIONS

Best Actor: Peter O'Toole
Best Supporting Actor: Omar Sharif
Best Adapted Screenplay: Robert Bolt and Michael Wilson

THE YEAR'S OTHER WINNERS

Best Actor: Gregory Peck, *To Kill a Mockingbird*
Best Actress: Anne Bancroft, *The Miracle Worker*
Best Supporting Actor: Ed Begley, *Sweet Bird of Youth*
Best Supporting Actress: Patty Duke, *The Miracle Worker*

In its original release, 35 minutes were cut to satisfy theater operators who required more showings to make a profit.

THE CRITICS

"It's an astonishing, unrepeatable epic." –Michael Wilmington, *Chicago Tribune*

"Lawrence luxuriates in the tremendous." –Stanley Kauffmann, *New Republic*

"Lacks the personal magnetism, the haunting strain of mysticism and poetry that would be dominant in a film about Lawrence the mystic and the poet... it's just a huge, thundering camel-opera." –*New York Times*

Lawrence and Sherif Ali lead fifty men across the blazing stretch of desert known as the Sun's Anvil, en route to Aqaba. Near the end with half their men dead from exhaustion, they notice one of their loyal followers, Gasim, has fallen off his camel. Lawrence insists they turn around to look for him. Ali is horrified by the suggestion: "Gasim's time has come. It is written." Lawrence is adamant that "Nothing is written!" He will go back and he'll go alone if he must. Ali leads the others to water, where they rest before battle. Having assumed they've lost Lawrence to the desert, he's spotted in the distance with Gasim clinging to his saddle mount. Ali is overjoyed and the bedraggled but proud Lawrence is given a hero's welcome as he enters camp. Lawrence looks righteously at Ali: "You see? Nothing is written!" With that, he collapses.

NOTABLE QUOTES

"In Europe, an actor is an artist. In Hollywood, if he isn't working, he's a bum." –Anthony Quinn

"I can't stand light. I hate weather. My idea of heaven is moving from one smoke-filled room to another." –Peter O' Toole

"If you'd been any prettier, it would have been *Florence of Arabia*."–Noel Coward to Peter O'Toole

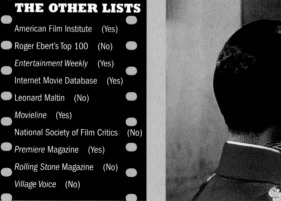

THE OTHER LISTS

- American Film Institute (Yes)
- Roger Ebert's Top 100 (No)
- *Entertainment Weekly* (Yes)
- Internet Movie Database (Yes)
- Leonard Maltin (No)
- *Movieline* (Yes)
- National Society of Film Critics (No)
- *Premiere* Magazine (Yes)
- *Rolling Stone* Magazine (No)
- *Village Voice* (No)

"You have a body, like other men." Lawrence is revealed as all-too-human while undergoing torture (and implied rape) at the hands of the Turkish Bey.

6

NORTH BY NORTHWEST 1959

PERFECT PITCH-HITCH

From the first eerie violin scratching in Bernard Herrmann's score, set against the glassy image of Manhattan's Lever House, you rightly suspect that this gem is Cartier. It's a glamorous, cross-country suspenser that gave Cary Grant, in the ripe sunset of his career, his lasting iconic image: the Wrong Man, in a very correct blue suit, outrunning a kamikaze crop duster. *North by Northwest* is among Alfred Hitchcock's least violent concoctions, opting more for comic release than nail-biting gasps. The anxiety in this case is of a more political nature, and the screenplay takes some daring (for the time) potshots at the cold war and CIA incompetence. Then there's the sex angle! There are enough steamy double entendres to melt the Hays Office. So much of the plot spins on what appears to be a one-night stand initiated by a cool blonde with an itch for anonymous encounters. Grant and Eva Marie Saint spend the second half of the movie attempting to legitimize their lust with conventional romance. And you really wish they wouldn't bother. Hitchcock seems to care little for the romance, either, and makes his feelings known in a corker of a final shot.

Jim: Luxurious talent in a postmodern dreamscape. If you ever get tired of this one, turn in your Blockbuster card and move to Pluto.

Gail: Who but Hitch would have his sexy duo on the run climbing up the large nostrils of a bunch of happy dead presidents? The master is having lots of classy, grown-up fun with this one, and thanks to him so are we!

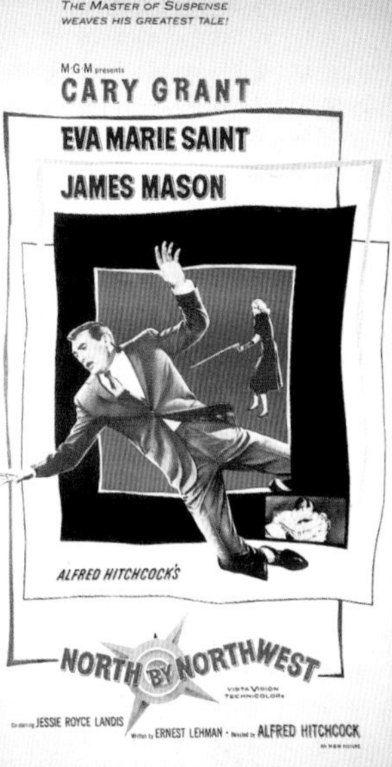

The Master of Suspense weaves his greatest tale!
M-G-M presents

HE PLOT

fateful coincidence leads Manhattan d exec Roger Thornhill (Cary Grant) to be istaken for an undercover Fed by a ring f foreign agents led by slippery Phillip Van-amm (James Mason). Roger is abducted nd marked for death. He miraculously es-apes but nobody will believe his story, not ven his own mother (Jessie Royce Landis). e agents have covered their tracks well. He ies to warn a UN official on their hit list, and inds up being framed for his murder. Roger, e most unlikely of fugitives, is on the run. e's abetted by femme fatale Eve Kendall va Marie Saint), who has her own dubious genda, and when the CIA takes notice, Roger in even more danger. He develops survival kills that surprise even him, as he desper-tely fights his way to the conclusion across e Presidential faces of Mount Rushmore.

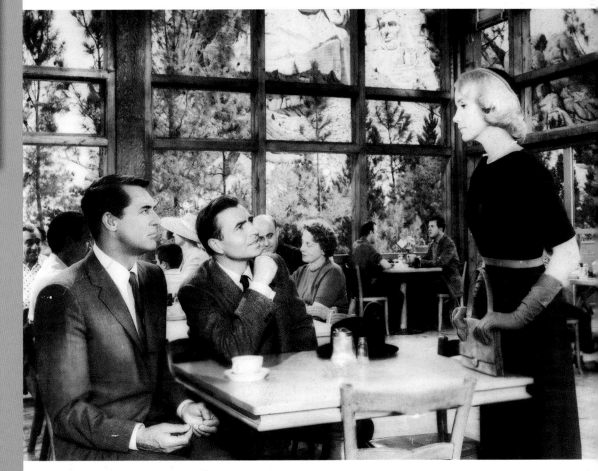

The Mount Rushmore cafeteria provides an unlikely stage for Roger (Cary Grant) and Eve (Eva Marie Saint) to dupe her lover and spymaster Vandamm (James Mason, center). Inside Eve's purse is a loaded gun that will shortly come into play.

"How does a girl like you get to be a girl like you?"—Roger Thornhill

THE DIRECTOR

"We're not making a movie, we're constructing an organ. We hit all the right chords and the audience responds accordingly. Someday, all we'll have to do is attach them to electrodes," Hitchcock confided in screenwriter Ernest Lehman. At the same time, **Alfred Hitchcock** was the master of exacting detail with his famous storyboarding technique. Beforehand he sketched every shot of the movie himself, leaving nothing to chance. The only moment of doubt in *North by Northwest* was a scene involving a bank of pay phones. The camera dollied from Martin Landau at one end to Eva Marie Saint on the other. It became clear that they were talking to each other. That was fine. But how did Landau get the number? Lehman was in Europe at the time and couldn't be reached. Hitchcock stopped shooting for the entire day until he'd figured out a reasonable rationalization for the scene. Hitchcock's first thriller, inspired by Jack the Ripper, was *The Lodger* (1926). Following *The 39 Steps* (1935) and *Sabotage* (1936), he answered the summons to Hollywood, where he struck gold the first time out with *Rebecca* (1940). *Suspicion* (1941) followed, along with the unsuccessful *Lifeboat* (1944)—remembered as a rare cinematic outing for stage legend, Tallulah Bankhead. After *Spellbound* (1945), a primitive early filmic treatment of psychoanalysis, came Hitchcock's Golden 1950s, which included *Rear Window* (1954), *To Catch a Thief* (1955), and his masterpiece, *Vertigo* (1958). (For more on Hitchcock, see pages 54, 85, and 106.)

Claiming his wives divorced him because he "led a dull life," Roger finds himself some deadly excitement when he gets mixed up with the desperately dangerous Eve.

THE CAST	
Roger O. Thornhill/George Kaplan	Cary Grant
Eve Kendall	Eva Marie Saint
Phillip Vandamm	James Mason
Clara Thornhill	Jessie Royce Landis
The Professor	Leo G. Carroll
Vandamm's Sister	Josephine Hutchinson
Lester Townsend	Philip Ober
Leonard	Martin Landau
Valerian	Adam Williams
Thornhill's Attorney	Edward Platt
Licht	Robert Ellenstein
Auctioneer	Les Tremayne
Dr. Cross	Philip Coolidge
Chicago Police Sergeant	Patrick McVey
Captain Junket	Ed Binns

THE ACTORS

This was **Cary Grant**'s fourth and final film with Hitchcock, and while there was great mutual respect, Grant could get touchy. At the time he was the biggest and highest-paid star in Hollywood, and he didn't like it when scenes didn't revolve around him. He was pleased, however, when the filming ran over schedule. His contract called for $10,000 per extra day. And this was 1958! Grant was notoriously tight with money and charged 15 cents for an autograph. While he suggested these funds were going to charity, those who knew him well weren't so sure. At least his film legacy is secure, with such classics to his credit as *She Done Him Wrong* (1933), *Holiday* and *Bringing Up Baby* (both 1938), *Gunga Din* and *His Gal Friday* (both 1939), *Notorious* (1946), *To Catch a Thief* (1955), *An Affair to Remember* (1957), and *Charade* (1963). (For more on Grant, see page 223.)

"You don't have to cry in this one, Eva," Hitch teased. "No more saintly parts for you." **Eva Marie Saint** was surprised by how easygoing the set was. Unlike Elia Kazan's direction during *On the Waterfront,* which included long, intimate, and involved notes, Hitchcock gave her only three instructions: (1) Lower your voice; (2) Don't use your hands; (3) Always look into Cary's eyes. *Northwest* would prove her career highlight, followed by lesser roles in lesser films like *The Sandpiper* (1965) and *The Russians Are Coming! The Russians Are Coming!* (1966). (For more on Saint, see page 64.)

BEHIND THE SCREEN

North by Northwest contains one of the most famous bloopers in film history. In the cafeteria scene in which Eve shoots George, a little boy sitting just behind her braces for the explosion by covering his ears.

Jessie Royce Landis, who plays Cary Grant's mother, was only one year older than he.

Hitchcock's signature cameo comes early. He rushes to catch a bus on a busy Manhattan street, only to have the driver slam the door in his face.

Alfred Hitchcock was nominated four times (*Rebecca, Lifeboat, Rear Window, Psycho*) but never won an Academy Award for Best Director. He received the Irving Thalberg Memorial Award in 1967.

THE MUSIC

Bernard Herrmann's elegant, twisting score is essential to the film's pace and sets up the opening credits with an eerie suspense. Ernest Lehman insists that without Herrmann, *North by Northwest* wouldn't have happened; he had introduced the screenwriter to Hitchcock.

THE SET

The Department of the Interior was horrified by the idea of actors shooting at each other on the Presidential faces of Mount Rushmore and banned Hitchcock from filming on the site. The scenes were shot in the studio on a mockup set with massive rear projections of the monument.

THE CRITICS

"*North by Northwest* is Alfred Hitchcock's ultimate wrong-man comedy. An empty Brooks Brothers suit (played with splendid insouciance by Cary Grant) is pushed further into the void when he inadvertently assumes the identity of a nonexistent secret agent. Thus cast in a role he cannot understand, the Grant character is a superb textual effect whose fantastic misadventures include the most bravura piece of editing in the Hitchcock oeuvre—the nearly silent rendezvous with himself in the horrifying vacuum of a Midwestern cornfield." —Jay Hoberman, *Village Voice*

"The director and Ernest Lehman, his scenarist, are not, to put a fine point on it, really serious about their mystery." —A. H. Weiler, *New York Times*

SEND IN THE CLONES

Silver Streak (1976)
Mission: Impossible II (2000)

NOTABLE QUOTES

"Film your murders like love scenes, and film your love scenes like murders." —Alfred Hitchcock

"I am a typed director. If I made 'Cinderella,' the audience would immediately be looking for a body in the coach."—Alfred Hitchcock

"The only really good thing about acting is that there's no heavy lifting."—Cary Grant

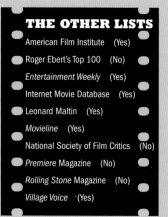

THE OTHER LISTS

- American Film Institute (Yes)
- Roger Ebert's Top 100 (No)
- *Entertainment Weekly* (Yes)
- Internet Movie Database (Yes)
- Leonard Maltin (Yes)
- *Movieline* (Yes)
- National Society of Film Critics (No)
- *Premiere* Magazine (No)
- *Rolling Stone* Magazine (No)
- *Village Voice* (Yes)

Roger is sent on a wild goose chase to middle-of-nowhere Iowa. The scene begins with a distraught but impossibly dapper Grant forced to ride on a Greyhound bus. He gets off, as ordered, on a dusty farm road where he waits for his mysterious "connection." And waits. And waits. Eight minutes of stillness, no background music, just the endless horizon of sun-baked flatlands. Then the distant buzz of a crop duster. Roger ignores it at first, then he suddenly realizes it's aiming for him! He's been set up! Where to hide? A lonely cornfield is his only hope and he dives for it. Deadly poison spews from the plane and Roger runs back to the road just as a full-throttle semi bears down on him. Needless to say, he'll miraculously survive. This is Cary Grant, after all. But Hitch has us going for a good, long, heart-pulsing stretch.

It's man versus machine as accidental double-agent Roger, hardly dressed for a hot day in the cornfields, runs for his life.

Roger takes an unofficial tour of the UN. Hitchcock was a master of the premise that an innocent man might get caught up in diabolical events beyond his control. The joke here is that Roger, a slick adman, is usually better at making up stories than relying on truth. No one believes his version of events, not even his dear mother.

CREDITS

Producer: Herbert Coleman
Director: Alfred Hitchcock
Screenplay: Ernest Lehman
Running Time: 136 Minutes
Budget: $4 Million

ACADEMY AWARD NOMINATIONS

Best Screenplay: Ernest Lehman
Best Editing: George Tomasini
Best Art Direction-Set Decoration: William Horning, Robert Boyle, Merrill Pye, Henry Grace, and Frank McKelvy

THE YEAR'S WINNERS

Best Picture: *Ben-Hur*
Best Director: William Wyler, *Ben-Hur*
Best Actor: Charlton Heston, *Ben-Hur*
Best Actress: Simone Signoret, *Room at the Top*
Best Supporting Actor: Hugh Griffith, *Ben-Hur*
Best Supporting Actress: Shelley Winters, *The Diary of Anne Frank*

7

THE WIZARD OF OZ 1939

THE PERFECT STORM

Less a movie than an American rite of passage, if you've never seen it, you could probably get a spot on the evening news. It's one of those perfectly realized inventions that almost seem like natural formations on the landscape—Mount Rushmore, Betty Crocker, the Golden Arches, *The Wizard of Oz.* A typical suburban Halloween, as if by official Munchkin decree, must have at least a dozen Dorothys, Scarecrows, and Wicked Witches. Proletariat pop aside, the movie is a magnet for the brainy elite (among them no less than Salman Rushdie), who've given it the "big, long words" treatment thanks to its symbolism and overripe Freudiana. (A winding yellow road to awareness, *whew!*) Add to that Judy Garland's ethereal, almost otherworldly performance, and you've got one of the most dreamed-about movies ever made.

Jim: After a million viewings, I'd love to reach that point where I could either take it or leave it. The Lollipop Guild? Come on! I'm almost up for an AARP renewal! But every damn time, even if I hear it from another room, I rush in, flop on the couch, and get happily lost all over again.

Gail: The most terrifyingly enchanting Hollywood spell ever to be cast on mesmerized, unwitting children. And there are enough messages hidden within for cultists to plumb for the rest of their lives.

THE PLOT

Lonely farmgirl Dorothy Gale (Judy Garland), ward of her dreary Auntie Em (Clara Blandick) and Uncle Henry (Charley Grapewin), dreams of a better place. She sadly sings "Somewhere Over the Rainbow" as she clutches her beloved dog Toto, whom she's managed to rescue from hateful spinster Elvira Gulch (Margaret Hamilton). Rather than give him up again, she runs away and encounters a "professor" (Frank Morgan) who convinces her to return home. She's caught in the grip of a furious tornado, gets clunked on the head, and "awakens" in a wonderful yet terrifying land beyond the rainbow, full of magical characters. Among them are several figures from her real life, transformed by imagination. Farmhands Hunk (Ray Bolger), Hickory (Jack Haley), and Zeke (Bert Lahr) become a Scarecrow, a Tin Man, and a Cowardly Lion. The four sing and dance their way down the Yellow Brick Road, bound for Oz and its all-powerful Wizard (Frank Morgan again), whom they hope will give them each what they most need. They're pursued by the Wicked Witch of the West (a transformed Elvira). Once before the Wizard, Dorothy and friends are rewarded with their hearts' desires. In Dorothy's case, with the help of Glinda, the Good Witch of the North, it's a return trip home to Kansas.

The four friends tremble before the door of the great and powerful Oz, hoping he'll grant their wishes. In the Frank Baum books, Oz is a very real place. In the final installment, Dorothy brings along her aunt and uncle and moves there for good. (Anything beats that ramshackle old black-and-white farm.)

"Toto, I've a feeling we're not in Kansas anymore." —Dorothy

THE DIRECTOR

"Man's man" director **Victor Fleming**, with his reputation for salvaging near-disasters, came aboard midway through, inheriting a project mired in overruns, mishaps, and rewrite nightmares. Key characters had come and gone and actors had been replaced. At his arrival, Garland was still playing Dorothy in a blonde wig. They hit it off at once, he affectionately calling her his little "Judelin," she idolizing him as a father figure. Garland had a nervous, uncontrollable laugh that often stopped the shooting cold. After one such outburst in a "duke out" with the Cowardly Lion, Fleming took her off to a quiet corner and slapped her hard across the face. It didn't faze her a bit (she was eager to kiss him on the nose in retaliation), but he was guilt-ridden. Not when it came to Frank Morgan, however. The two maintained a bitter feud throughout. Morgan, an old vaudevillian and an unfortunate alcoholic, railed against Fleming's demand that he play it straight, forgoing the easy slapstick laughs. By the time Fleming departed, three months later, to "rescue" *Gone with the Wind*, *Oz* was essentially on track and near completion. To his everlasting horror, no doubt, he refused a percentage of *GWTW* in lieu of salary after telling Selznick he had a great, big white elephant on his hands. (For more on Fleming, see page 68.)

"I'll get you, my pretty!" But it was the special effects that almost got poor Margaret Hamilton. She was dangerously burned in the "melting scene" and spent agonizing weeks recuperating. None of the fun of *Oz* came easy. Costumes were airless and hot, and there were several incidents of makeup poisoning.

THE CAST	
Dorothy Gale	Judy Garland
Toto	Terry
Professor Marvel/Wizard of Oz	Frank Morgan
Hunk/Scarecrow	Ray Bolger
Hickory/Tin Man	Jack Haley
Zeke/Cowardly Lion	Bert Lahr
Glinda the Good Witch	Billie Burke
Elvira Gulch/Wicked Witch	Margaret Hamilton
Uncle Henry Gale	Charley Grapewin
Auntie Em Gale	Clara Blandick
Nikko, Head Winged Monkey	Pat Walshe

THE ACTORS

Years later, the drug-addled but captivating **Judy Garland** entertained TV talk-show audiences with reminiscences of drunken Munchkins with inappropriately busy hands. She also squealed on her costars, claiming they were nasty old hams who kept trying to push her out of the shot. As it turned out, these tales were pure fabrication. While her ambitious stage mother and MGM chief Louis B. Mayer didn't do her any favors with the downers and diet pills, Garland's nature had an edge-of-destruction melodrama to it. It's what gave her performances their near-psychotic breathlessness. The laughs were always too quick and hysterical, the tears a sudden tsunami. To watch *The Wizard of Oz* and know what's going to happen to its beguiling young star is part of the experience. You begin to feel like a member of an early silent-movie audience that tries to warn the hapless heroine on-screen. Garland's personal doom shadows *Oz*, but what a legacy. Following her full-length feature debut in *Pigskin Parade* (1936), Garland was teamed with Mickey Rooney through most of her adolescence and teen years in such light fare as *Love Finds Andy Hardy* (1938), *Babes in Arms* (1939), and *Strike Up the Band* (1940). Maturity and marriage to director Vincente Minnelli resulted in sterling classics like *Meet Me in St. Louis* (1944) and *The Clock* (1945). Her teaming with Fred Astaire in *Easter Parade* (1948) was a sensation, but soon after *Summer Stock* (1950), personal woes set in and marked a long period of Hollywood banishment. She roared back with *A Star is Born* (1954), but was unable to top it. Her last film, *I Could Go On Singing* (1963), a melodrama about a singing legend in descent, was painfully autobiographical.

"After *The Wizard of Oz*, I was typecast as a lion." **Bert Lahr** added, "There aren't that many parts for lions." Like his fellow travelers on the Yellow Brick Road, **Ray Bolger** and **Jack Haley,** Lahr's career was launched in vaudeville and remained essentially stage-bound. Between these three accomplished song-and-dance men were dozens of hit Broadway shows and a sprinkling of earlier films. All pale in comparison to *The Wizard of Oz* which made each of them, along with **Margaret Hamilton**, icons—so long as they're remembered in costume.

BEHIND THE SCREEN

The real-life children of Dorothy and the Tin Man, Liza Minnelli and Jack Haley Jr., were briefly wed, 1974–78.

Two cast members, Margaret Hamilton and Terry (a.k.a. Toto), reunited on screen three years later in *Meet the Stewarts*.

The original pair of ruby slippers was auctioned off for $15,000 in 1971. Since then, six more pairs have emerged from the dusty MGM warehouse, each valued at more than $1.5 million.

CREDITS

Producer: Mervyn LeRoy/MGM
Director: Victor Fleming, Richard Thorpe (original scenes, uncredited), King Vidor (Kansas scenes, uncredited)
Screenplay: Noel Langley, Florence Ryerson, Edgar Allan Woolf
Running time: 101 minutes
Budget: $2.7 million
Box Office: $3 million (initial release)

ACADEMY AWARDS

Best Music, Original Score: Herbert Stothart
Best Song: "Over the Rainbow," Harold Arlen (music) and E. Y. Harburg (lyrics)
Special Junior Oscar: Judy Garland

ACADEMY AWARD NOMINATIONS

Best Picture
Best Art Direction: Cedric Gibbons, William A. Horning
Best Cinematography, Color: Harold Rosson
Special Effects: A. Arnold Gillespie (photographic), Douglas Shearer (sound)

THE YEAR'S OTHER WINNERS

Best Picture: *Gone with the Wind*
Best Director: Victor Fleming, *Gone with the Wind*
Best Actor: Robert Donat, *Goodbye, Mr. Chips*
Best Actress: Vivien Leigh, *Gone with the Wind*
Best Supporting Actor: Thomas Mitchell, *Stagecoach*
Best Supporting Actress: Hattie McDaniel, *Gone with the Wind*

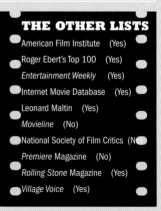

THE OTHER LISTS

American Film Institute (Yes)
Roger Ebert's Top 100 (Yes)
Entertainment Weekly (Yes)
Internet Movie Database (Yes)
Leonard Maltin (Yes)
Movieline (No)
National Society of Film Critics (No)
Premiere Magazine (No)
Rolling Stone Magazine (Yes)
Village Voice (Yes)

"Why, oh, why, can't I?" This is the closest Garland got to an Oscar—a Special Junior statuette. She was a shoo-in for Best Actress in 1954 for *A Star Is Born* and the cameras were all set to capture the big moment in the maternity ward, where she'd just given birth to son Joey Luft. But Judy lost to Grace Kelly in what Groucho Marx called "the biggest robbery since Brinks'!"

Lions and tigers and bears aside, the big moment comes early, simply, and in black and white. A dejected Dorothy, hugging Toto to her breast, yearns for escape in "Somewhere Over The Rainbow." She wants to fly like a happy bluebird, and in Garland's heartbreaking rendition, we want to migrate right along with her. She makes the incredible journey to Oz utterly believable, providing a bittersweet dimension to the story it doesn't have on its own. And in this moment we also see how unlikely Garland's stardom is: a little overweight, stuffed into a truly bad dress, a little weirdly old for the part, a definite hunch to her shoulders. (L. B. Mayer called her his "little hunchback.") Her very being, in this moment particularly, is a middle finger to the cookie-cutter studio system. Talent, by gum, overrides everything. Garland is the movie. This song makes it, and her, an instant legend. And yes, it's true—the studio suits wanted to cut it.

"HOW STRANGE WHEN AN ILLUSION DIES. IT'S AS THOUGH YOU'VE LOST A CHILD." —JUDY GARLAND

Look closely at the start of the "We're off to see the wizard" sequence and you'll spot a minor disturbance in one of the trees. For years, a Hollywood Babylon-like rumor spread that it was a member of the crew who'd been caught up in wires and fatally strangled. Not quite. It was an animal handler lunging for one of his escaped charges.

THE MUSIC

Composer Harold Arlen and lyricist E. Y. "Yip" Harburg were responsible for one of the most enduring original scores in film history. We seem to have been born knowing these songs. Happily, the lyrics aren't targeted for kids. Many are full of subtle and not-so-subtle political satire, and the Cowardly Lion, jumping the gun on Ellen DeGeneres by 55 years, pretty much outs himself in his soliloquy.

THE SET

The "tornado" was a 35-foot-long muslin stocking photographed against Kansas farmland in miniature.

THE CRITICS

"Remains the weirdest, scariest, kookiest, most haunting and indelible kid-flick-that's-really-for-adults ever made in Hollywood." —Owen Gleiberman, *Entertainment Weekly*

"It scared the hell out of me when I used to watch it between my fingers when I was a kid, and (though it might say too much about my own emotional development) I still get the heebie jeebies from a lot of it." —Paul Tatara, CNN

ROLE REVERSALS

Okay, here's the rundown: It was supposed to be Shirley Temple as guess who (Fox wouldn't lend her out); W. C. Fields as the Wizard (money jinxed the deal); Buddy Ebsen as the Tin Man (poisonous reaction to the makeup); and Gale Sondergaard as the Wicked Witch (just hated the makeup, period!).

"We're off to the see the Wizard!" But sadly, we won't enjoy "The Jitterbug" along the way. One of the most elaborate song-and-dance routines ever committed to film was cut from the final version. It was deemed too "contemporary" for the timeless, classic story.

8

ANNIE HALL 1977

THE PLEASURES OF ANHEDONIA

"A relationship, I think, is like a shark. You know? It has to constantly move forward or it dies. And I think what we got on our hands is a dead shark," says Alvy (Woody Allen) to Annie (Diane Keaton) as their impossibly complicated, affectionately incomprehensible, adorable, and endlessly challenging relationship looks like it's coming to its inevitable end. We recognized something about this dynamic, but we didn't know what it was called until Allen nailed the '70s boy-girl thing, which consisted of lots of freedom for ambivalence, pleasure, too much information, and all the words in the world with which to talk about it.

Jim: The anti-Barbie-and-Ken-doll love story. At long last, romantic leads too weird to envy.

Gail: Allen gave form and voice to the modern urban relationship with cinematic prowess unseen in American films up to that time. Often imitated, never duplicated.

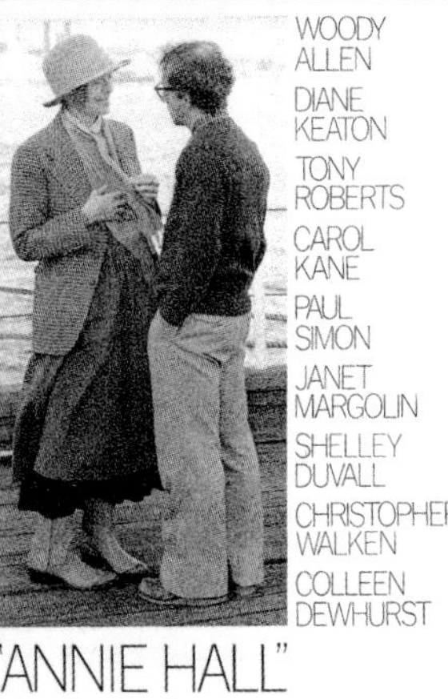

WOODY ALLEN
DIANE KEATON
TONY ROBERTS
CAROL KANE
PAUL SIMON
JANET MARGOLIN
SHELLEY DUVALL
CHRISTOPHER WALKEN
COLLEEN DEWHURST
'ANNIE HALL"
A new comedy.

'HE PLOT

arkly intellectual, chronically pessimistic wish comedian Alvy Singer falls in "loave" ith cat-lover and singer Annie, his complete pposite, a shy, nervous Midwestern WASP. What did you do? Grow up in a Norman ockwell painting?") He can't accept their fferences. He's always kvetching at Annie, ging her to change, plying her with books death, intimidating her into adult educa- on classes, and pestering her into bettering erself. He betters her right out of his life, ending her to California, where she becomes erself. Their affair is over, but the memory ngers on.

I don't want to chieve immortality hrough my work, I vant to achieve it by not dying."
—Woody Allen

Love in the big city isn't easy, but it can be oh-so-nice. Alvy and Annie start out nice. Alvy proclaims his feelings, saying, "Love is too weak a word for what I feel—I luuurve you, you know, I loave you, I luff you, two F's, yes I have to invent, of course I—I do, don't you think I do?" Sadly, the relationship can't sustain his incessant badgering for Annie to change.

"I thought of that old joke, you know. This guy goes to a psychiatrist and says, 'Doc, uh, my brother's crazy, he thinks he's a chicken,' and uh, the doctor says, 'Well why don't you turn him in?' And the guy says, 'I would, but I need the eggs.'"—Alvy

THE DIRECTOR AND ACTOR

On the set *Annie Hall*'s actors complained of **Woody Allen**'s cold and aloof demeanor. His mood improved, though, with his warm reception by the critics and at the box office. *Annie* was a smash, allowing the director carte blanche with future films. He continued to experiment with the newly minted seriousness of *Annie* in *Interiors* (1978), *Stardust Memories* (1980), *The Purple Rose of Cairo* (1985), and *Crimes and Misdemeanors* (1989). But nothing quite rose to the level of *Annie*, and some thought Allen's films had lost their spirit, having sacrificed humor to thoughtfulness. Claims of art imitating Allen's and Keaton's lives were disputed by Allen, who maintains that the film "...[is] so exaggerated that it's virtually meaningless to the people upon whom these little nuances are based. People got it into their heads that *Annie Hall* was autobiographical, and I couldn't convince them it wasn't." But we still haven't forgotten the pre-*Annie* Allen films that left us rolling in the aisles, including *Take the Money and Run* (1969), *Bananas* (1971), *Everything You Always Wanted to Know About Sex* (*But Were Afraid to Ask)* (1972), *Sleeper* (1973), and *Love and Death* (1975). Allen's recent movies continue in the more serious vein and include *Shadows and Fog* and *Husbands and Wives* (both 1992), *Manhattan Murder Mystery* (1993), *Bullets Over Broadway*, which earned him Oscar nominations for directing and cowriting (1994), *Mighty Aphrodite* (1995), *Deconstructing Harry* (1997), *Hollywood Ending* (2002), and *Matchpoint* (2005). Allen's personal life took a dramatic and morally troubling turn in the 1990s when he became involved with Mia Farrow's young stepdaughter, Soon-Yi Previn. Allen also found himself in court defending himself against accusations of sexually abusing his own biological child, Dylan. Most of his films star Allen as—what else?—a writer. What can we say about him that he hasn't already said?

There's hardly a moment when Alvy and Annie aren't arguing. Though the pink lights are Alvy's, he objects to Annie's smoking marijuana before they make love. In defense of her mood-enhancer, Annie says it relaxes her, so what's the problem? Alvy replies, "Well, I'll give you a shot of sodium pentathol. You can sleep through it."

THE CAST

Alvy Singer	Woody Allen
Annie Hall	Diane Keaton
Rob	Tony Roberts
Allison Portchnik	Carol Kane
Tony Lacey	Paul Simon
Pam	Shelley Duvall
Robin	Janet Margolin
Annie's Mom	Colleen Dewhurst
Duane Hall	Christopher Walken
Date	Sigourney Weaver

THE ACTORS

Diane Keaton, who had lived with Allen around the time of *Annie*, was born Diane Hall, and nicknamed Annie. About their real-life relationship, Keaton told Rex Reed, "Woody and I...we're beyond getting involved again with each other...He's my closest and dearest friend." *Annie Hall* began life as a murder mystery in which Annie was a secondary character. During the editing, however, her charm came to the fore and the film focused instead on Alvy and Annie's relationship. While the film focused on the lovers, the fashion world focused on Keaton's quirky costuming by Ralph Lauren. The androgynous tie, waistcoat, man's shirt and '30s-style pants became the fashion statement of '70s women. It also put Diane Keaton on the map as a style icon. Keaton made her own career without Woody in such films as *The Godfather* (1972), *Looking for Mr. Goodbar* (1977), *Reds* (1981, Academy Award nomination), and *The Little Drummer Girl* (1984). Keaton directed the documentary *Heaven* (1987), as well as *Unstrung Heroes* (1995), her first major feature as a director. She also directed an episode of *Twin Peaks* (1990). Later she appeared in *Father of the Bride* (1991) and *Father of the Bride, Part II* (1995), *Marvin's Room* and *The First Wives Club* (both 1996), *Sister Mary Explains It All* and *Town & Country* (both 2001). (For more on Keaton, see page 11.)

Shelley Duvall proved a perfect representative for the 1960s love affair with her typically spacey performance, telling Alvy, "Sex with you is really a Kafka-esque experience." Duvall would hardly have had a film career had it not been for director Robert Altman, who cast her first in *Brewster McCloud* (1970), and later in more prominent roles, among them *McCabe and Mrs. Miller* (1971), *Nashville* (1975), and her greatest role in *3 Women* (1977). She became a producer of prominent children's television, winning awards for such series as *Faerie Tale Theatre*, *Shelley Duvall's Tall Tales*, and *Shelley Duvall's Bedtime Stories*, and for the special *Mother Goose Rock 'n' Rhyme*.

Sigourney Weaver's screen debut was her nonspeaking part as Alvy's date near the end of the movie. Weaver's star shot into the stratosphere with the *Alien* movies, beginning in 1970, and she also appeared in *The Year of Living Dangerously* (1983), *Gorillas in the Mist* (1983) and *Ghostbusters* (1984).

Paul Simon showed up, too, though his performance proved that he was already in the right profession.

Tony Roberts played the first workaholic, modern urban careerist. We'll never be able to leave our telephone numbers with anyone without thinking of him.

THE CINEMATIC TECHNIQUES

It's Allen's most innovative film, one that borrows visual techniques from his European forefathers. To wit: Subtitles run across the bottom of the screen while people are talking that contradict what they actually say; the split-screen of the "world's apart" WASP and Jewish families; the grown-up Alvy hunched into his third-grade seat standing up to speak to the audience about his future; and Alvy alone on the screen simply talking to the audience about his dilemmas.

BEHIND THE SCREEN

When Alvy sneezed into the cocaine, it was no joke but a real-life, unscripted accident. Allen decided to leave it in the film when early audiences found it hysterically funny. It broke the audience up so much that Allen had to add more footage, allowing for a moment to recover so that the audience could hear the next joke.

Allen's speeches at the University of Wisconsin and on *The Dick Cavett Show* used actual material from his standup comedy performances. The original murder-mystery plot intended for *Annie* later found its way into Allen's *Manhattan Murder Mystery*.

CREDITS

Producer: Charles H. Joffe, Robert Greenhut/United Artists
Director: Woody Allen
Screenplay: Woody Allen, Marshall Brickman
Running Time: 94 minutes
Budget: $4 million
Box Office:$40 million

ACADEMY AWARDS

Best Picture
Best Director: Woody Allen
Best Actress: Diane Keaton
Best Screenplay: Woody Allen, Marshall Brickman

ACADEMY AWARD NOMINATIONS

Best Actor: Woody Allen

THE YEAR'S OTHER WINNERS

Best Actor: Richard Dreyfuss, *The Goodbye Girl*
Best Supporting Actor: Jason Robards, *Julia*
Best Supporting Actress: Vanessa Redgrave, *Julia*

Federico Fellini was Allen's first choice for the real-life artist/intellectual on the cinema line. When Fellini turned it down, the offer went to Luis Buñuel before falling to the awkward Marshall McLuhan.

The battle for a title for the film was pitched indeed, with Woody weighing in heavily for *Anhedonia* ("the inability to experience pleasure"). Marshall Brickman had a few ideas of his own, among them *It Had to Be Jew* and *Me and My Goy*.

In one of the many original endings, Alvy passes a billboard in Times Square lit up with the words, "What are you doing, Alvy? Go to California....It's OK. She loves you." Apparently this version disturbed Allen so much he was said to have thrown the reels into the Central Park reservoir.

THE CRITICS

"*Annie Hall* at last puts Allen in the league with the best directors we have." –Vincent Canby, *New York Times*

"[The film is] everything we never wanted to know about Woody Allen's sex life and were afraid he'd tell us anyway."–John Simon

Having been in therapy for fourteen years, Alvy tells Annie, "I'm gonna give him one more year, and then I'm going to Lourdes." The "Rashomon Effect" is at work when Annie and Alvy tell their therapists opposite stories about the same situation.

"If my film makes one more person miserable, I'll feel I've done my job." —Woody Allen

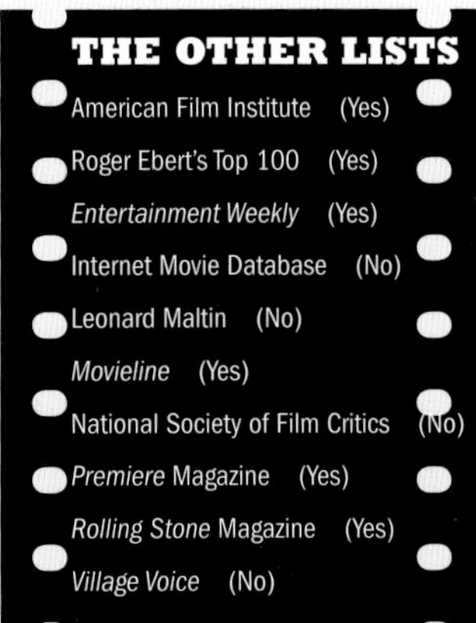

Alvy, seated in front of the traditional Easter ham at the Halls', envisions himself as a bearded and behatted Hasidic rabbi. The screen splits to show the incompatible worlds of the Halls and the Singers, Alvy's New York Jewish family, where food and arms fly across the table, and arguments, babbling about diabetes, heart disease, and unemployment provide the entertainment.

The families speak to each other across the screen: "How do you plan to spend the holidays, Mrs. Singer?" "We fast," he replies, explaining how in abstaining from food, Jews can atone for their sins. "What sins?" asks Mrs. Hall, "I don't understand." "To tell you the truth, neither do we."

Riding back together on a plane from Los Angeles where Annie has "discovered herself" and a new life, they know that the shark (their relationship) has finally expired.

9

CHINATOWN 1974

HIGH-WATER MARK

When screenwriter Robert Towne proposed *Chinatown* to producer Robert Evans, he described it as not so much a physical location but a metaphysical conundrum. Evans essentially responded with a less than metaphysical, "Huh?" But he also pushed the Go button. The result was one of the most creatively contentious, groundbreaking glories of the golden 1970s, a *noir*-oriented (pun intended) puzzler for a more cynical generation featuring a deviously kinetic poster boy for the era, Jack Nicholson. *Chinatown* is all mood, tone, and the faint rot of evil under the California sun. The movie does for 1930s Los Angeles what Fellini always did for Rome. It emerges not so much an actual location but…

Jim: Exotic as a dream. Nicholson, even with his nose wrapped in a bandage for half the movie, gives off so much star power LA is in danger of a blackout.

Gail: So visceral you can taste corruption like drinking water from a rusty pipe.

THE PLOT

Cocksure P.I. Jake Gittes (Jack Nicholson) is insulted when he's fed red herrings while trying to solve the murder of the LA Water Commissioner, Hollis Mulwray. He goes right to the source, the city's waterways, and deduces that someone is playing a highly profitable game of redirecting the flow. That someone could only be Mulwray's former business partner and father-in-law, the all-powerful Noah Cross (John Huston). Cross has reason to worry about Gittes getting too close. One of his goons (Roman Polanski) catches the detective in the wrong place at the wrong time and, with a flourish of his knife, warns Jake to keep his bloody nose to himself. As Jake continues to dig, all roads lead to Mulwray's mysterious widow, Evelyn (Faye Dunaway). She joins forces with Gittes, though fearful of her father, and in so doing falls in love with the detective. But there are more layers to the investigation, one involving the twisted relationship between Cross and his daughter. Though Gittes finally gets to the bottom of the fraudulent land grab, there's not much he can do about it. As witness to a final, awful bloodletting on the forbidding streets of Chinatown, Jake learns, to his tragic regret, that not all cases are open and shut.

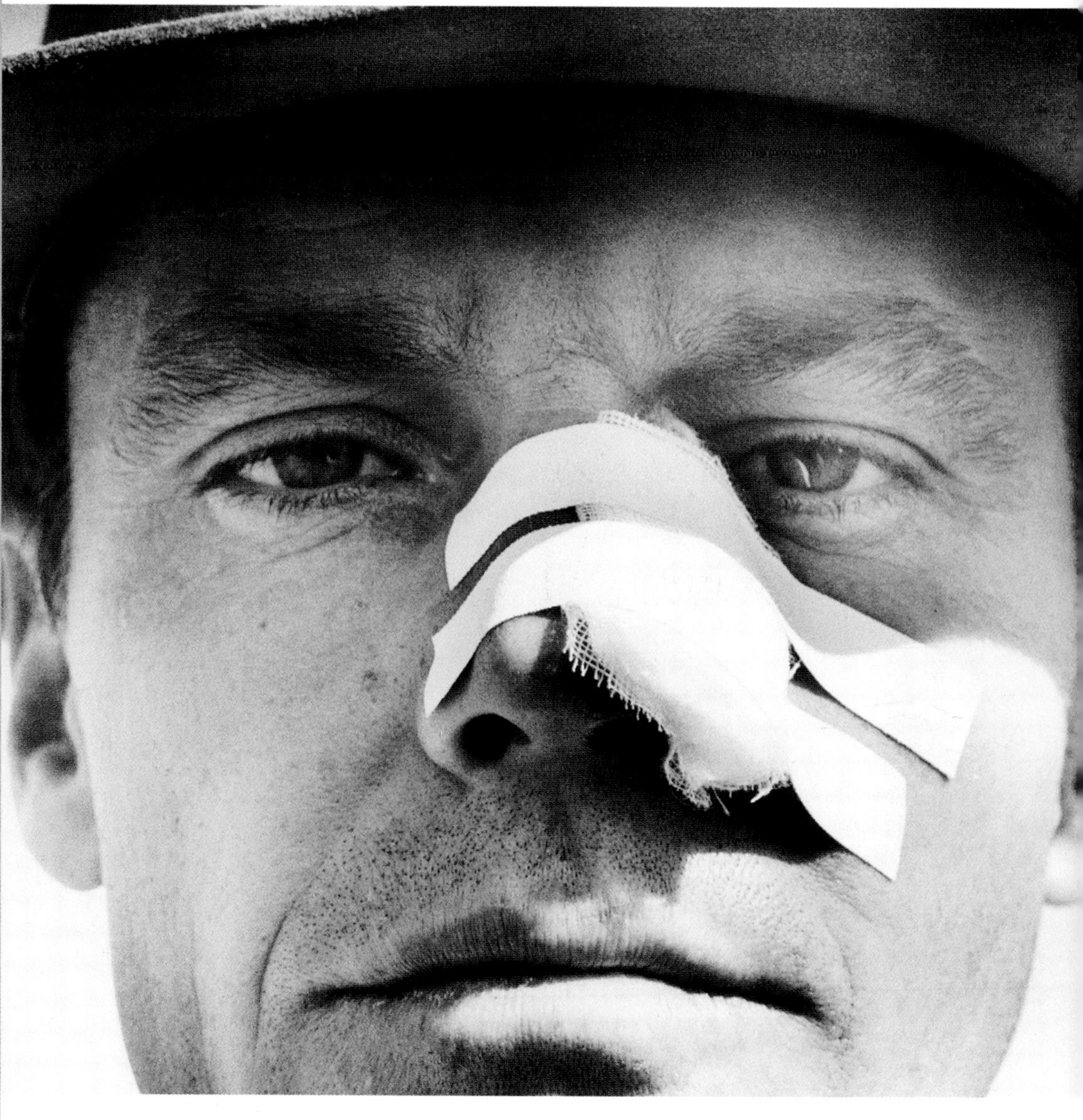

"You're a very nosy fellow, kitty-cat, huh? You know what happens to nosy fellows?" P.I. Jake Gittes (Jack Nicholson) painfully finds out from a knife-wielding thug (played by director Roman Polanski) while investigating suspicious doings at the reservoir.

"Forget it Jake. It's Chinatown."— Lt. Escobar

THE DIRECTOR

As a young Jewish fugitive in Holocaust Europe, **Roman Polanski** fashioned a fake foreskin out of wax in case he got caught by the SS. But the drama was just beginning for the diminutive Polish firebrand. The huge success of *Rosemary's Baby* (1963) was followed by the horrific slaying of his wife, Sharon Tate, by the Manson monsters. By the time *Chinatown* came along, Polanski wasn't much on optimistic endings. He fought bitterly with Robert Towne, whose original fadeout had Nicholson and Dunaway walking off into the sunset. Polanski was determined to show audiences that life is a chaotic nightmare without a sugar chaser. He showed little patience on the set and seemed to enjoy his sadistic approach to directing Dunaway. "Just say the words! Your salary is your motivation!" Producer Robert Evans admitted he was a Napoleon with the actors, but Nicholson soon warmed to his eccentricities and opened up his home to him. It was there, the following year, that he was caught by authorities with an underage girl in his bed. He returned to his roots as a fugitive in Europe, his tumultuous life having come full circle. His follow-up films include *Tess* (1979), *Frantic* (1988), and *The Pianist* (2002), for which he won an Oscar, and *Oliver Twist* (2005).

Evelyn Mulwray (Faye Dunaway) warns her demonic tycoon father, Noah Cross (John Huston, unseen), to keep away from "my daughter, my sister, my daughter, my sister..."

THE CAST	
J. J. "Jake" Gittes	Jack Nicholson
Evelyn Cross Mulwray	Faye Dunaway
Noah Cross	John Huston
Lt. Lou Escobar, LAPD	Perry Lopez
Russ Yelburton	John Hillerman
Hollis I. Mulwray	Darrell Zwerling
Ida Sessions	Diane Ladd
Claude Mulvihill	Roy Jenson
Man with Knife	Roman Polanski
Detective Loach, LAPD	Richard Bakalyan
Lawrence Walsh	Joe Mantell
Duffy	Bruce Glover
Sophie	Nandu Hinds
Lawyer	James O'Rear
Kahn, Evelyn's Butler	James Hong

THE ACTORS

Though **Jack Nicholson** was already a star (he'd done *Easy Rider* in 1969 and *The Last Detail* in 1973), this was the film that would make him a household name, and, specifically, a bedroom fantasy. Armed with that killer smile, a wardrobe Cary Grant might've arm wrestled him for, and some of the sharpest cynicism ever written for the movies, Nicholson embodies dapper worldliness. But his character is, at heart, a simple man who believes in certain home truths. When he's slowly but surely betrayed by them, the performance turns majestic. He's never been this good and once again it's proven true that the Oscar often goes to the right guy for the wrong role, i.e., *As Good As It Gets* (1997). Career highlights include *One Flew Over the Cuckoo's Nest* (1975), *The Shining* (1980), *Prizzi's Honor* and *Terms of Endearment* (1985), *A Few Good Men* (1992), *About Schmidt* (2002), and *The Departed* (2007). (For more on Nicholson, see page 241.)

Described by Robert Evans as "colder than Baskin-Robbins," **Faye Dunaway** seems, at first glance, oddly miscast. She's too stiff, an elegant mannequin that wouldn't fit Jake Gittes's idea of a hot romance. But Dunaway is never to be underestimated despite her obvious infatuation with her own stardom. Polanski would have none of her haughty airs and made her life on the set a daily misery. Berating her, yanking strands of her hair out by the roots, it's to her credit she didn't walk. But she must've known this was an iconic role and the surest route to Oscarville. As was the case with her costar, it was the Academy voters who took a head-scratching wrong turn. It took 20 years to honor Dunaway in the role by giving the Oscar to Kim Basinger for her pale imitation in *L.A. Confidential*. Dunaway could at least claim her own statuette for *Network* (1976) and a badge of courage for surviving the critical firestorm following the maligned *Mommie Dearest* (1981).

BEHIND THE SCREEN

Notorious iconoclast Polanski briefly suggested Anjelica Huston for the role of Evelyn. That would've made her real father, John, her on-screen incestuous father. Cooler heads prevailed. As it is, there's a weird moment when John Huston's Noah Cross asks Nicholson's Gittes if he's sleeping with his daughter. And of course, Nicholson was, on-screen and off.

In 1978, Polanski was charged with the statutory rape of a 13-year-old girl while at the home of his friend, Jack Nicholson. The director fled to Europe to avoid incarceration after a judge reneged on his offer of a plea bargain. He hasn't returned to America since, not even to accept his 2002 Oscar for direction of *The Pianist*.

THE CRITICS

"An art house movie in American mainstream drag. Seldom since Hitchcock's prime has a director displayed such a facility for making a commercial movie that is also a work of art."—James Verniere, *Boston Herald*

"Nicholson's performance is key in keeping *Chinatown* from becoming just a genre crime picture."—Roger Ebert, *Chicago Sun-Times*

SEND IN THE CLONES

Who Framed Roger Rabbit? (1988)
The Two Jakes (1990)
L.A. Confidential (1997)

NOTABLE QUOTE

"I don't really know what is shocking. When you tell the story of a man who is beheaded, you have to show how they cut off his head. If you don't, it's like telling a dirty joke and leaving out the punch line."—Roman Polanski

CREDITS

Producer: Robert Evans/ Paramount
Director: Roman Polanski
Screenplay: Robert Towne
Running time: 131 minutes
Box Office: $12.4 million

ACADEMY AWARDS

Best Original Screenplay: Robert Towne

NOMINATIONS

Best Picture
Best Director: Roman Polanski
Best Actor: Jack Nicholson
Best Actress: Faye Dunaway
Best Cinematography: John A. Alonzo
Best Art Direction: Richard Sylbert, W. Stewart Campbell, and Ruby R. Levitt
Best Costume Design: Anthea Sylbert
Best Music Score: Jerry Goldsmith
Best Editing: Sam O'Steen
Best Sound: Charles Grenzbach, Larry Jost

THE YEAR'S OTHER WINNERS

Best Picture: *The Godfather, Part II*
Best Director: Francis Ford Coppola, *The Godfather, Part II*
Best Actor: Art Carney, *Harry and Tonto*
Best Actress: Ellen Burstyn, *Alice Doesn't Live Here Anymore*
Best Supporting Actor: Robert De Niro, *The Godfather, Part II*
Best Supporting Actress: Ingrid Bergman, *Murder on the Orient Express*

THE GREAT SCENE

Gittes suspects Evelyn, the enigmatic femme fatale, may be a killer and confronts her in a rage. Who is that blonde she's got in the bedroom, her dead husband's girlfriend? Is she plotting to murder her as well? Evelyn comes apart as she admits the girl is her sister. Gittes isn't buying that and slaps her. "She's my daughter." Another slap. "She's my sister." Slap. "She's my sister and my daughter!" Gittes stops, overwhelmed by this confession of unimagined evil.

RIGHT: "I want the truth! I said, I want the truth!" After the shocking revelations of this most famous scene, there was no way screenwriter Robert Towne could provide Dunaway's Evelyn with a happy ending.

BELOW: Gittes is desperate to convince his nattily dressed pals on the LAPD that their fair city is under siege by "the big boys that control all the water."

> **"My mother never saw the irony in calling me a son-of-a-bitch."**
> **—JACK NICHOLSON**

THE OTHER LISTS

- American Film Institute (Yes)
- Roger Ebert's Top 100 (No)
- *Entertainment Weekly* (Yes)
- Internet Movie Database (Yes)
- Leonard Maltin (No)
- *Movieline* (Yes)
- National Society of Film Critics (No)
- *Premiere* Magazine (Yes)
- *Rolling Stone* Magazine (Yes)
- *Village Voice* (Yes)

10

SINGIN' IN THE RAIN 1952

SWINGIN' DOWN THE HALL OF MIRRORS

"Good Mornin', Good mo-o-o-or-ning." Ya know, last night I had the greatest dream. I dreamt we put on the best musical comedy ever. We could do it. We could take a whole bunch of songs already written by Arthur Freed and Nacio Herb Brown in the twenties, fill those in with some dancin' new tunes from Adolph Green and Betty Comden. We'll "Make 'em Laugh" with a knockout story that will snap the songs into place in a devilishly cynical and sardonic plot about Hollywood's panic during the transition to sound and its attendant resort to illusion (with which it is already well acquainted). We'll make it the wittiest musical of all time. Cyd Charisse will extend her endless legs in a "Broadway Ballet," and everybody's "Gotta Dance." We'll just slap together something great. We won't even care that we're all wet because we'll be so delighted just "Singin' in the Rain." It'll the best darn Hollywood musical of all time. We'll be on all the 100 all-time best movie lists...What? We won't get reviewed? We'll only get two Oscar nominations? And no wins, you say? And nobody will come? Hey—let's do it anyway.

Jim: Kelly, the proletarian Astaire, finally comes across as sexy in the way you always thought he should've but never quite did.

Gail: I'm smiling and I'm singin' and I'm dancin' in my living room with a broom. They just don't make 'em like this twice.

'HE PLOT

ı autobiography of Hollywood at the ıwn of the talkies wherein darlings of the ent screen—romantic silent-film star and vashbuckling matinee-idol Don Lockwood ›ene Kelly) and his glamorous, blonde ›-screen partner, diva Lina Lamont (Jean ıgen)—aren't in love but play the part at e behest of studio heads. Their next picture, *e Dueling Cavalier,* is to be their first sound n, and it's a musical, no less. Good God! na, who thinks very well of herself, can't lk, much less sing—but whines quite well, ank you. The diction coach is ditched for e dubbed voice of Don's talented aspiring- :tress girlfriend Kathy Selden (Debbie ›ynolds), whose voice is to be lip-synced by ıa. Don, however, must be true to himself ıd gives up the ruse of his screen-idol mance because he's fallen over the couch ' Kathy. He schemes his way into revealing ›r talents. Meanwhile everyone has a real ›od time givin' it to Hollywood.

It's 103 degrees inside Gene Kelly's body, but the rain seems to wash his fever down and our spirits up as he trips and splashes the puddles fantastic in his exhilarating dance to the title song. Maybe the fever helped him to fly? The dance certainly made film history.

"She can't act, she can't sing, she can't dance. A triple threat." —Don

THE DIRECTOR

Director **Stanley Donen** fed the creative forces at MGM for producer Arthur Freed, who produced more than 40 musicals at the studio. Kelly and Donen received codirector credits on this one, but it was Donen who infused it all with that witty edge. It was a "Let's put on a play!" kind of production to capitalize on the success of *An American in Paris*, for which Kelly won the Oscar. The grueling schedule on *Singin'* had everyone logging in nineteen-hour days. We have Donen (and Minnelli) to thank for most of the exhilarating musicals of the Golden Age: *On the Town* (1949), *Royal Wedding* (1951), and the remarkable *Funny Face* (1957). When the musical era went the way of the dinosaur, Donen turned to romantic comedies, including *Indiscreet* (1958), *Charade* (1963), *Bedazzled* and *Two for the Road* (both 1967), and a homosexual comedy, *Staircase* (1969). (For more on Donen, see page 97.)

Singin' in the Rain has a grand old time telling the story of the rabbits that had to be pulled out of a hat to make the first sound films. Life duplicated art when Debbie Reynolds herself—who couldn't dance—was tutored by Fred Astaire. The beloved star also required another voice behind some of her songs, even though she played the voice of a silent star in the film. She trained well, as shown in their song "Good Mornin'," where the tap-happy threesome—Gene, Debbie, and Donald O'Connor—danced their way over a couch with breathtaking finesse.

THE CAST

Don Lockwood	Gene Kelly
Cosmo Brown	Donald O'Connor
Kathy Selden	Debbie Reynolds
Lina Lamont	Jean Hagen
R. F. Simpson	Millard Mitchel
Dancer	Cyd Charisse
Roscoe Dexter	Douglas Fowley
Zelda Zanders	Rita Moreno

THE CRITICS

"Just about the best Hollywood musical of all time" —From Pauline Kael's program notes for the theater she was managing in Berkeley in 1958, which put the movie at the top of the charts.

THE ACTORS

Gene Kelly danced through his 103-degree fever to give us *Singin' in the Rain*, and we happily caught the bug. That rain he so enjoyed was one part water and the rest milk, which showed up better on film. (It also shrank his wool suit.) The terpsichorean tapper could also be a bit cruel in the interpersonal-communication department. He told poor teenaged Debbie, who'd never danced before, how badly she was doing. "I wasn't nice to Debbie," he said later. "It's a wonder she still speaks to me." Kelly's vigorous balletic and athletic dancing style was all his own. For his part, director Donen thought, "Gene was among the wonders of the twentieth century," and he was very glad Kelly never fulfilled his lifelong dream of playing shortstop for the Pittsburgh Pirates. After his first film, *For Me and My Gal* (1942), Kelly never let us forget him, appearing in such classics as *Anchors Aweigh* (1945), *The Pirate* (1948), *On the Town* (1949), and *An American in Paris* (1951). In the words of Paula Abdul, "Women love Gene Kelly. He's so handsome, so sexy and so self-assured." Thank you, Paula.

Nineteen-year-old **Debbie Reynolds** disappeared under a piano crying when Gene Kelly told her she couldn't dance. Fred Astaire came to her rescue, and it turned out she was a quick study. Still, Reynolds was quoted as saying that *Singin' in the Rain* and childbirth were the two hardest things she ever had to do. The mother of Carrie Fisher and ex-wife of Eddie Fisher had one of the more difficult Hollywood lives. She lost first hubbie Fisher to Elizabeth Taylor. Her second husband managed to squander both his fortune and hers. Reynolds won hearts throughout her career, which included roles in *The Catered Affair* (1956), *Tammy and the Bachelor* (1957), *How the West Was Won* (1962), and an Oscar-nominated performance in *The Unsinkable Molly Brown* (1964). When Hollywood stopped making musicals, Reynolds had to turn to the stage to earn a living. At one particularly low point, Reynolds confessed to living in her Cadillac. A serious Hollywoodophile, Reynolds has such an extensive collection of movie costumes and memorabilia that she now houses them in a hotel in Las Vegas. Daughter Carrie Fisher captured Reynolds best when she said, "My mother is so talented it's insane."

In a show-stealing performance, **Donald O'Connor**'s elastic face and rubber body twist around like a Gumby doll. He paid for it with three days of bed rest after performing "Make 'Em Laugh." We wondered if he might simply collapse. What's more, he had ideas, and suggested the title of the new sound film within the film be changed to *The Dueling Mammy*. A comment on *The Jazz Singer*, perhaps? He continued with costarring roles in *Call Me Madam* (1953), *There's No Business Like Show Business* (1954), and *Anything Goes* (1956). After his starring vehicle, *The Buster Keaton Story* (1957) flopped, his star began to fade. But he was good. Real good.

"**Jean Hagen** plays Judy Holliday with PMS," wrote critic Judy Gerstel of The National Society of Film Critics. For her trouble, which keeps us in stitches, she was deservedly nominated for Best Supporting Actress. Whenever her Lina Lamont can't seem to remember which flower arrangement holds the concealed microphone, her voice becomes a roar or a whisper as she turns her head back and forth. It's one of the great comic turns in film. Among Hagen's other films were *Adam's Rib* (1949) and *The Asphalt Jungle* (1950). She also played Danny Thomas's wife in the well-known television series *Make Room for Daddy* (1953–57).

That's **Rita Moreno**, yep, in the role of Zelda Zanders. It was her fourth picture in what was to become a spotty career that included *The King and I* (1956), *West Side Story* (1961), *Carnal Knowledge* (1971), and *The Ritz* (1976).

ROLE REVERSALS

Howard Keel was originally slated by studio heads to play the lead.

Can Oscar Levant really dance *that* well? Originally written for Levant, the role of Cosmo was played to perfection by Donald O'Connor.

CREDITS

Producer: Arthur Freed/MGM
Director: Stanley Donen and Gene Kelly
Screenplay: Betty Comden and Adolph Green
Running Time: 103 minutes
Budget: $2.5 million
Box Office: $7.7 (worldwide)

ACADEMY AWARD NOMINATIONS

Best Actress in a Supporting Role: Jean Hagen
Best Music, Scoring of a Musical Picture: Lennie Hayton

THE YEAR'S OTHER WINNERS

Best Picture: *The Greatest Show on Earth*
Best Director: John Ford, *The Quiet Man*
Best Actor: Gary Cooper, *High Noon*
Best Actress: Shirley Booth, *Come Back, Little Sheba*
Best Supporting Actor: Anthony Quinn, *Viva Zapata!*
Best Supporting Actress: Gloria Grahame, *The Bad and the Beautiful*

THE GREAT LINES

"Long people have short faces. Short people have long faces. Big people have little humor, and little people have no humor at all." –Cosmo

"Try to get this straight. There is nothing between us. There has never been anything between us. Just air." –Don

"Kathy Seldon as Juliet! As Lady Macbeth! As King Lear! You'll have to wear a beard for that one of course." –Don

BEHIND THE SCREEN

The film within the film within the film is enough to make you cry "Uncle." That's not always Reynolds' voice you hear dubbed over Lina Lamont's. Reynolds herself needed some help from friend Betty Noyes, who sang "Would You?" and "You Are My Lucky Star."

Once in a Lifetime (1932), a hilarious adaptation of the Moss Hart/George S. Kaufman play also set during the talkies panic, provided the original storyline.

Gene Kelly's two talented choreography assistants went uncredited: Carol Haney (*The Pajama Game*) and Gwen Verdon (*Can-Can*, *Damn Yankees*, *Sweet Charity*, and *Chicago*). And those were not always the sounds of the master's toes tapping in the "Singin' in the Rain" number. Some were added afterward by Gwen and Carol, who stood up to their tootsies in a container full of water to match the soggy on-screen action.

The film's original negative was destroyed in a fire.

The price of the fifteen-minute "Broadway" ballet number spiraled from $80,000 to $600,000 during production.

At Gene Kelly's request, the studio dug holes in the ground to create those puddles that he splashes in so deliriously.

THE OTHER LISTS

- American Film Institute (Yes)
- Roger Ebert's Top 100 (Yes)
- *Entertainment Weekly* (Yes)
- Internet Movie Database (Yes)
- Leonard Maltin (Yes)
- *Movieline* (Yes)
- National Society of Film Critics (No)
- *Premiere* Magazine (Yes)
- *Rolling Stone* Magazine (Yes)
- *Village Voice* (Yes)

Donald O'Connor in a positively, absolutely, indisputably exhilarating, intoxicating, and most certainly elevating, undeniably hysterical-making performance—not to mention rousing and carousing and utterly espousing of the greatness that a musical number can achieve. (*Whew.*) He's singin' and dancin'—or whatever you call what he does—to "Make 'Em Laugh."

RIGHT: Rubber-faced and triple-jointed Donald O'Connor stops the show with "Make 'Em Laugh." Worth the price of admission!

BELOW: Great Gams! Gun moll Cyd Charisse as just one of the dancers in the "Broadway" ballet shows how good—and self-consciously arty—dancing can get in this, her first duo, with Gene Kelly.

SONGS USED IN *SINGIN' IN THE RAIN*, AND THE PREVIOUS FILMS IN WHICH SOME APPEARED

"Singin' in the Rain," *The Hollywood Revue of 1929* (1929)

"Fit as a Fiddle" (original to film)

"All I Do Is Dream of You," *Sadie McKee* (1934)

"Make 'Em Laugh," similar to "Be a Clown" from *The Pirate* (1948)

"I've Got a Feelin' You're Foolin'," *Broadway Melody of 1936* (1935)

"The Wedding of the Painted Doll," *The Broadway Melody* (1929)

"Should I?" *Lord Byron of Broadway* (1930)

"Beautiful Girl," *Going Hollywood* (1933)

"You Were Meant for Me," *The Broadway Melody* (1929)

"Moses Supposes" (original to film)

"Good Morning," *Babes in Arms* (1939)

"Would You?" *San Francisco* (1936)

"Broadway Rhythm," *Broadway Melody of 1936* (1935), *Babes in Arms* (1939)

"You Are My Lucky Star," *Broadway Melody of 1936* (1935)

11

NASHVILLE 1975

GRAND OLD SOAP OPRY

Nashville is the jewel in Robert Altman's crown, no less than the high point of the 1970s anti-Hollywood revolution. With a camera as restless as a hitchhiker on amphetamines, the eccentric little bits and pieces finally come together in a rich tapestry of a plot. Altman uses the country-western music capital as a symbolic epicenter of every cheesy dream of fame, fortune, and immortality. The humor is improvisational and zany, and all the musical performers seem to be auditioning for our own personal pleasure. They're giving it all they've got, from the hysterically limited talents of a tone-deaf airport waitress to the glittery queens of America's jukeboxes.

Jim: Completely original and untouchable. Altman is so ahead of the curve, you begin to realize he *is* the curve.

Gail: An exhilarating mosaic of ambition, longing, and desperation in American lives and in the body politic, with knockout songs that capture all the high and low notes.

THE PLOT

Twenty-four disparate characters converge in a quite literal human traffic jam over a kaleidoscopic five-day period in Nashville. We meet the kings and queens of country-western music (played by Ronee Blakley, Henry Gibson, and Karen Black), a host of wannabes (Gwen Welles, Barbara Harris, Keith Carradine), hangers-on (Geraldine Chaplin, Shelley Duvall), smarmy frontmen (Ned Beatty, Michael Murphy) for a populist Presidential candidate, and an ominous drifter (David Hayward). Like a gathering storm, characters and events are swept toward a stunning climax that foreshadows one of the most celebrated tragedies of the late 1970s.

Haven Hamilton (Henry Gibson) and his pickled wife, Lady Pearl (Barbara Baxley), organize a "big old" Nashville welcome home for recuperating Barbara Jean (Ronee Blakley), the undisputed "Queen of Country."

"This is not Dallas. This is Nashville...They can't do this to us here in Nashville!"—Haven Hamilton

THE DIRECTOR

"I'm looking for surprises," **Robert Altman** commented at the start of the production. Disdainful of the Hollywood formula, the charismatic former bomber pilot opted for the family approach to moviemaking with himself as the paterfamilias. Even before shooting, *Nashville*'s 24 actors found themselves desperate to please "Big Daddy" and Altman played them accordingly for the best results. He would at once reward and admonish, coax and belittle. There were often passionate flare-ups on the set. Ronee Blakley proved difficult in her determination to find order in Altman's purposeful spontaneity. Barbara Harris was so appalled by the dailies, she pleaded for reshoots at her own expense. Altman, of course, refused. The final image he had in mind was far greater than the day-to-day concerns of actors who were asked to make it all up as they went along. (For more on Altman, see page 250.)

Runaway hillbilly wife "Albuquerque" (Barbara Harris) has come to Nashville in search of elusive fame. She'll do anything to advance her career, even sing one of her own ditties between laps at the Speed Way.

THE CAST

Norman	David Arkin
Lady Pearl	Barbara Baxley
Delbert Reese	Ned Beatty
Connie White	Karen Black
Barbara Jean	Ronee Blakley
Tom Frank	Keith Carradine
Mary	Cristina Raines
Opal	Geraldine Chaplin
L.A. Joan	Shelley Duvall
Barnett	Allen Garfield
Haven Hamilton	Henry Gibson
Private Kelly	Scott Glenn
Tricycle Man	Jeff Goldblum
Albuquerque	Barbara Harris
J. Triplette	Michael Murphy
Linnea Reese	Lily Tomlin
Sueleen Gay	Gwen Welles
Mr. Green	Keenan Wynn

THE ACTORS

Geraldine Chaplin, Keith Carradine, and **Barbara Harris** particularly disliked the roles they were assigned. Chaplin found her Opal to be pretentious in the extreme, and worried she wouldn't find the humor in her. Carradine, in real life unassuming and soft-spoken, couldn't find a core of goodness in his womanizing Tom Frank until **Lily Tomlin** reworked their key scene together. Harris, a Method actor, "became" Albuquerque, a free-spirited wanderer. She'd often vanish from the set and have to be tracked down. Altman threatened to fire her several times but was too smitten by her mesmerizing improvisational skills to do so.

Geraldine Chaplin, daughter of Charlie, appeared in Altman's *A Wedding* (1978), then significantly in *White Mischief* (1988), *The Age of Innocence* (1993), and *Talk to Her* (2002). **Keith Carradine**, another Hollywood off-spring, the son of John, earned important roles in *Pretty Baby* (1978), *The Moderns* (1987), and *The Ballad of the Sad Café* (1991). Lily Tomlin appeared in the ill-fated *Moment by Moment* (1978) with John Travolta, made a bigger splash in *Late Show* (1977), *Nine to Five* (1980), and Altman's *Short Cuts* (1993), and was particularly effective in *Flirting with Disaster* (1996).

BEHIND THE SCREEN

The original film was so long it was almost released as two parallel features: *Nashville Red* and *Nashville Blue*.

Altman was inspired to make *Nashville* after hearing Keith Carradine perform "I'm Easy" in his office.

Drugs and especially booze were prevalent during the production. Altman was battling his demons on the rocks, Barbara Baxley wept that she'd spent her entire salary on liquor, and Keenan Wynn often went on days-long benders during the shoot.

Carradine and on-screen lover Cristina Raines were involved in a tumultuous off-camera relationship as well.

Barbra Streisand attended a rough-cut screening of *Nashville* at Altman's home. When she didn't bother to compliment or comment on what she'd seen, he threw her out.

Nashville was unanimously despised by the country-western music elite. Loretta Lynn (the basis for Ronee Blakley's Barbara Jean) boycotted the premiere and cracked to a reporter, "I'd rather see *Bambi.*"

SEND IN THE CLONES

Magnolia (1999)
Boogie Nights (1997)

THE MUSIC

For authenticity, many members of the cast wrote and performed their own country-western songs: Henry Gibson: "200 Years, Keep A'Goin"; Lily Tomlin: "Yes I Do"; Ronee Blakley: "Down to the River," "Bluebird," "Tapedeck in His Tractor" (The Cowboy Song), "Dues," and "My Idaho Home"; Dave Peel: "The Heart of a Gentle Woman"; Keith Carradine: "Honey," "I'm Easy," and "It Don't Worry Me"; Allan Nicholls: "Rose's Cafe"; Karen Black: "Memphis," "Rolling Stone," and "I Don't Know If I Found It In You."

THE SOUND

Altman's innovation with sound (background voices given equal balance to central characters, e.g.) was perfected in *Nashville*. The loudspeaker oratory of Presidential candidate Hal Phillip Walker is heard in realistic concert with vital dialogue, background asides, and the ever-present twang of the plot-fueling music.

NOTABLE QUOTES

"I fiddle in the corner where they throw the coins. Where I can get my work done."—Robert Altman

ROLE REVERSALS

The character of Linnea Reese was created for and by Louise Fletcher, who was herself the daughter of two deaf parents and knew sign language. The role was eventually played by Lily Tomlin. Though Altman compensated Fletcher by recommending her for her Oscar-winning role in *One Flew Over the Cuckoo's Nest*, she never spoke to him again.

Gary Busey was originally slated for Keith Carradine's part.

THE CRITICS

"I've never before seen a movie I loved in quite this way: I sat there smiling at the screen in complete happiness. It's a pure emotional high, and you don't come down when the picture is over; you take it with you...The funniest epic vision of America ever to hit the screen." —Pauline Kael, *The New Yorker*

"*Nashville* is a vicious, malicious, occasionally witty look at grassroots America as it floats like navel lint into the vulgar Vegas of country-and-western music..." —Rex Reed, *New York Daily News*

Sexy but soulless womanizer Tom serenades shy Linnea in a nightclub with his killer ballad, "I'm Easy." Every other woman in the joint wants to believe he's singing for her. But tonight he's Linnea's. Trapped in a vacuous marriage, Linnea expresses the depth of her need to connect by gently tapping her hand on her breast. Her touching, embarrassed, desperate gaze meets his lying eyes as those take-me-to-bed-right-now lyrics pour out of him.

Emotionally fragile country-music queen Barbara Jean (Ronee Blakley) recuperates from yet another nervous collapse. Her manager/husband Barnett (Allen Garfield) has just about run out of patience with her. "Are you goin' nutsy on me again, Barbara Jean? 'Cause I won't stand for that!"

THE OTHER LISTS

- American Film Institute (Yes)
- Roger Ebert's Top 100 (Yes)
- *Entertainment Weekly* (Yes)
- Internet Movie Database (No)
- Leonard Maltin (Yes)
- *Movieline* (No)
- National Society of Film Critics (Yes)
- *Premiere* Magazine (Yes)
- *Rolling Stone* Magazine (Yes)
- *Village Voice* (No)

12

SOME LIKE IT HOT 1959

LEMMON TART

Comedy in the '50s was in serious transition. Lucy was allowed to be pregnant but Lenny Bruce wound up in jail for explaining how she got that way. Billy Wilder loved testing the business edge of the censor's scissors. *Some Like It Hot* is a risqué froth of raunchy jokes, sight-gags, and a stream of double entendres—starting with the title, which could either refer to sex, jazz, or Monroe's Orry-Kelly dresses, which accidentally-on-purpose make her look one bus stop short of naked. Conversely, her costars Lemmon and Curtis are the most overdressed men in the movies. Drag certainly wasn't new. (Milton Berle was in heels more often than not.) But what made the difference, and what keeps this one so remarkably fresh, is the degree of seriousness Lemmon and Curtis invest in their masquerade. They're cross-dressing for survival and, despite some of the "broad" strokes, they're passing for real, not winking at the audience. What's so especially tender is the sisterly bonding between them and Monroe's character. No bitchery, no conniving competition, these three over-the-top female creations ironically deliver an early blow for feminism, along with some of the biggest laugh lines in movie history. The last, famously, is the biggest of them all. If you've never heard it, well, "nobody's perfect."

Jim: Oscar voters should've been lined up against the wall, blindfolded, and given a last cigarette. A high crime in this case, especially for Lemmon, not to mention Marilyn, who, scratch your head, wasn't even nominated.

Gail: And we thought Hollywood never took on the subversive. Cross-dressing, impotence, and role-playing. We love you, Billy Wilder. You're one in a million.

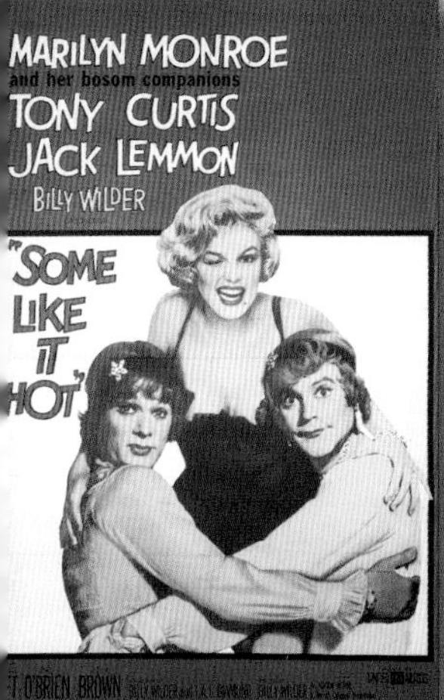

MARILYN MONROE
and her bosom companions
TONY CURTIS
JACK LEMMON
BILLY WILDER
"SOME LIKE IT HOT"

HE PLOT

ɔair of hapless Chicago musicians, Joe and ry (Tony Curtis, Jack Lemmon), are unlucky ough to witness the St. Valentine's Day ıssacre. Pursued by the mob, led by Spats lumbo (George Raft), they desperately flee wn disguised in drag as members of an all-l band bound for a two-week gig in Miami. th are smitten by its singer Sugar Kane arilyn Monroe), a curvaceous kitten in arch of a millionaire to love. As "older and ser gals," they eagerly take on the role of r mentors. Joe, in yet another disguise as a ry Grantish impotent millionaire, courts her, ile Jerry finds delusionary happiness with wealthy heir of his own, Osgood Fielding III e E. Brown). But when the mob shows up the hotel for a "convention," the boys are ce again on the run. After assorted chases d much mayhem, all ends happily for the ers—even, it seems, Jerry and Osgood. Well, body's perfect!

Jack Lemmon's Daphne spreads some joy around after being proposed to by millionaire Osgood. His delight almost lifts Monroe's spirits despite her deep well of off-screen depression. Billy Wilder reported that he was "glad he worked with her before her mind completely turned to Swiss cheese."

"Look at that! Look how she moves! That's just like Jell-O on springs. I tell you, it's a whole different sex!" —Jerry

THE DIRECTOR

Billy Wilder described the *Some Like It Hot* experience: "I knew we were in midflight, and there was a nut on the plane." He wasn't mentioning names but there was no question Monroe was at the top of the list. Magnanimous to a fault, Wilder had a genius for making actors do what he wanted without making it seem like his idea. A typical moment came when Monroe actually showed up to the set on time but refused to come out of her trailer. He quietly asked one of the girls in the band to get up onstage and sing one of Marilyn's songs in the film, "Runnin' Wild." When Monroe heard her, she immediately popped out her trailer and took the scene over, hitting every mark. She'd later comment to the press, "He's not a director, he's a dictator." He fired back: "I was lucky to get her before her mind completely turned to Swiss cheese." Near film's end, he was almost paralyzed with exhaustion but knew he'd captured something great. Would he have worked with Monroe again? Not on his life. But then again, if the results were this good, he might've happily risked it. Billy Wilder launched his incomparable Hollywood career with the Ginger Rogers comedy vehicle *The Major and the Minor* (1942), but he was soon to show equal facility in any number of genres, including war drama with *Five Graves to Cairo* (1943), *noir* with *Double Indemnity* (1944), and "message pictures" with *Lost Weekend* (1945). He socked it to the movie industry with *Sunset Boulevard* (1950), and pulled off romantic charmers like *Sabrina* (1954) and *Love in the Afternoon* (1957), both starring Audrey Hepburn. Among his later successes were *The Apartment* (1960), *The Fortune Cookie* (1966), and *The Front Page* (1974). (For more on Wilder, see pages 24 and 79.)

Still bath waters run deep as a contemplative Sugar (Marilyn Monroe) confesses her troubled romantic history to Joe/Josephine (Tony Curtis), in one of the film's most hilarious yet touching moments.

THE ACTORS

Jack Lemmon was relatively unknown to film audiences and was thrilled to be working at all. Wilder took him aside and said, "Look, when Marilyn finally gets something right, I'm going to print it. Keep your fingers out from where they don't belong." In other words, be a pro every waking minute and cover for her if she needs it. From Lemmon's first moment in a dress, he took to it with a flamboyant lack of restraint. His interpretation was classic music-hall mugging, double takes, and grand gestures. He and Curtis practiced their moves in ladies' rooms, hoping to pass. Lemmon was much better at it. *Some Like It Hot* made him an instant film legend and he was a virtual lock for the 1959 Oscar. Unfortunately, he was one of many victims of a runaway chariot race, *Ben-Hur*. Charlton Heston was caught in its tidal wave and surprised everyone with his win. When Lemmon finally got the Best Actor gold in 1972 for *Save the Tiger*, he admitted to the audience, "I had my speech all prepared in 1959." Among his signature films are *Mister Roberts* (1955), *The Apartment* (1960), *Days of Wine and Roses* (1962), *The Fortune Cookie* (1966), *The Odd Couple* (1968), *The China Syndrome* (1979), *Glengarry Glen Ross* (1992), and *Grumpy Old Men* (1993), made with his longtime comic sidekick, Walter Matthau.

Tony Curtis insisted he never made the infamous crack that "kissing Marilyn was like kissing Hitler." But if his patience was sorely tested by her endless delays and inability to remember lines, he only remembered the delight in working with her. She could be very "naughty" in their seduction scene on the yacht, grinding into his groin until he was aroused. It was Curtis who approached Wilder with the idea of Orry-Kelly making his and Lemmon's dresses. It was also his notion to do a Cary Grant voice in his alternating masquerade as the playboy millionaire. He had a less easy time maintaining his vocal pitch as Josephine and was intermittently dubbed. Curtis began his film career as a teen idol in such bare-chested roles as *Meet Danny Wilson* (1951) and *Son of Ali Baba* (1952). He stepped up in class with *Houdini* (1954) and *Trapeze* (1956), and in *Sweet Smell of Success* (1957) he proved himself an actor of dimension. But the roles weren't always an equal match, and aside from the few minor classics like *The Defiant Ones* (1958), and *The Boston Strangler* (1968), he was too often assigned less-than-sterling material such as *Taras Bulba* (1962). That role earned Curtis countless comic impersonations thanks to his Brooklyn-accented Middle Ages Cossack prince, to wit: "Yondah lies da castle of my fadduh." (For more on Curtis, see page 293.)

Wilder must've thought long and hard about the adage "be careful what you wish for" when he managed to get **Marilyn Monroe** for the role of Sugar. It was the most difficult period of her personal life; she was pregnant and her marriage to Arthur Miller was on the rocks. And while it was true that the simple line, "Where's that bourbon?" required 59 takes (even after the line had been taped in every drawer she opened), Monroe emerged perfectly on screen. As critic Roger Ebert notes, "What a work of art and nature is Marilyn Monroe. She hasn't aged into an icon, some citizen of the past, but still seems to be inventing herself as we watch her. She has the gift of appearing to hit on her lines of dialogue by happy inspiration." Her relatively brief life and career offered a reasonably solid legacy of films, including *All About Eve* (1950), *Niagara* (1953), *Gentlemen Prefer Blondes* (1953), *The Seven Year Itch* (1955), *Bus Stop* (1956), and *The Misfits* (1961). (For more on Monroe, see page 51.)

BEHIND THE SCREEN

Monroe's contract called for her to make only color films. Wilder talked her into doing black-and-white when he showed her how color film was translating Curtis and Lemmon's drag makeup as green.

Pregnant Monroe was considerably heavier than usual. She had a body stand-in for print publicity with her face superimposed on the photos.

Tony Curtis has never been shy about his own sexual ambiguity, using it to great advantage in his performance. "I was 22 when I arrived in Hollywood in 1948. I had more action than Mount Vesuvius; men, women, animals! I loved it, too. I participated where I wanted to and didn't where I didn't. I've always been open about it."

SEND IN THE CLONES

Tootsie (1982)
Victor/Victoria (1982)

THE CAST	
Sugar Kane	Marilyn Monroe
Joe (Josephine)/Junior	Tony Curtis
Jerry (Daphne)	Jack Lemmon
Spats Colombo	George Raft
Mulligan	Pat O'Brien
Osgood Fielding III	Joe E. Brown
Bonaparte	Nehemiah Persoff
Sweet Sue	Joan Shawlee
Sig Poliakoff	Billy Gray
Toothpick Charlie	George E. Stone
Beinstock	Dave Barry
Spats' Henchman	Mike Mazurki
Spats' Henchman	Harry Wilson
Dolores	Beverly Wills
Nellie	Barbara Drew

THE SET

The Florida scenes were shot at San Diego's historic Hotel Del Coronado, whose whimsical architecture inspired Frank Baum's Oz books.

THE CRITICS

"One of the enduring treasures of the movies, a film of inspiration and meticulous craft." —Roger Ebert, *Chicago Sun-Times*

"Let's face it. Two hours is too long a time to harp on one joke. The sight of Curtis and Lemmon teetering around on high heels wears awfully thin quickly, as does Curtis's imitation of a noted male movie star." —A. H. Weiler, *New York Times*

NOTABLE QUOTES

"I have discussed this with my doctor and my psychiatrist and they tell me I'm too old and too rich to [direct Marilyn Monroe] again."—Billy Wilder

"Making movies is a little like walking into a dark room. Some people stumble across furniture, others break their legs, but some of us see better in the dark than others. "
—Billy Wilder

"Sometimes I think it would be easier to avoid old age, to die young, but then you'd never complete your life, would you? You'd never wholly know yourself."—Marilyn Monroe

"They gave me away as a prize once—a Win Tony Curtis for a Weekend competition. The woman who won was disappointed. She'd hoped for second prize—a new stove."—Tony Curtis

"The worst part about being me is when people want me to make them laugh."—Jack Lemmon

Jerry bursts into the hotel room, still high from his night on the town with millionaire Osgood. Joe becomes increasingly concerned as Jerry flashes a huge diamond ring and announces their engagement. "We're planning a June wedding." Joe tries to impress upon him the fact that he can't possibly wed Osgood. Jerry is defensive, insisting Joe isn't too old for him and that, besides, he marries girls all the time. Joe is forced to remind him that he's not a girl. He's a guy. And why the hell would a guy want to marry another guy, anyway? Jerry looks at him like he's crazy, the answer is so obvious: "Security!"

ABOVE: "Just keep telling yourself you're a girl." Josephine and Daphne can barely keep their heads straight, never mind their seams, at bedtime on the train. Curtis couldn't maintain the upper register in his voice, and some of his dialogue had to be filled in by an actress. But the physical aspect of the performance was all his. (He borrowed gestures from his mother.)

BELOW: Cary Grant said of Marilyn Monroe, "She's half child, but not the half that shows." Ironically, here Tony Curtis does his own Grant imitation as Monroe tries to cure his "impotence" with her touching/hilarious busty, breathy nuance.

CREDITS

Producer: Billy Wilder/ United Artists
Director: Billy Wilder
Screenplay: Billy Wilder, I. A. L. Diamond
Running time: 120 minutes
Budget: $3.5 million
Box Office: $25 million

ACADEMY AWARDS

Best Costume Design, Black-and-White: Orry-Kelly

NOMINATIONS

Best Director: Billy Wilder
Best Actor: Jack Lemmon
Best Screenplay: Billy Wilder, I. A. L. Diamond
Best Art Direction-Set Decoration, Black-and-White: Ted Haworth, Edward G. Boyle
Best Cinematography, Black-and-White: Charles Lang

THE YEAR'S OTHER WINNERS

Best Picture: *Ben-Hur*
Best Director: William Wyler, *Ben-Hur*
Best Actor: Charlton Heston, *Ben-Hur*
Best Supporting Actor: Hugh Griffith, *Ben-Hur*
Best Supporting Actress: Shelley Winters, *The Diary of Anne Frank*

13

ALL ABOUT EVE 1950

BEST BETTE

"Eve. Eve the Golden Girl, the Cover Girl, the Girl Next Door, the Girl on the Moon. Time has been good to Eve. Life goes where she goes. She's the profiled, covered, revealed, reported. What can there be to know that you don't know?" Freeze-frame on the glamour girl in question. There's a triumphant smile on her flawless face and a treasured award for acting excellence in her manicured grip. Thus begins a timeless, unsentimental backstage epic that is more about the fear of aging and loss of power than the whizzbang life of the theater. Incredibly, Joseph Mankiewicz never slips into clichés or the easy artifice of camp. The two women at the center of the ego-collision, Margo Channing and Eve Harrington—by now hallowed archetypes of the genre—are as real and as Machiavellian as any contemporary corporate rivals. To dismiss *All About Eve* as merely a chick-flick or cult staple is to miss one of the great cinematic treasures. Mankiewicz's script dazzles and the white-hot cast burns holes through the screen.

Jim: It's as if Oscar Wilde had written for the movies—a hugely satisfying talkfest.

Gail: A savagely witty screenplay with an especially brave and knowing performance by Davis.

THE PLOT

As Broadway legend Margo Channing (Bette Davis) holds court in her dressing-room, the playwright's wife Karen (Celeste Holm) sweeps in with a dowdy little fan, Eve Harrington (Anne Baxter), who breaks their hearts with her little speech about a husband lost in the war and how Margo's performances have saved her from complete devastation. Margo takes her up at once and after seeing off her director/lover Bill Sampson (Gary Merrill) at the airport, she hires Eve as her Gal Friday. Margo's maid Birdie (Thelma Ritter) smells trouble. To her mind, Eve isn't quite the innocent she leads everyone to believe. Sure enough, at a party to welcome Bill back from LA, Eve wheedles Karen for an audition as Margo's understudy. Margo suspects Eve's duplicity and Bill accuses her of paranoia. The scene ends in their breakup. Karen plots to have Eve replace Margo onstage one night. Awestruck critic Addison DeWitt (George Sanders) is on hand and engineers her quick rise to stardom. Margo and Bill reunite in time to witness Eve win the theater's treasured Sarah Siddons Award. Eve is off to Hollywood but not before she encounters a little "Eve" of her own, the next in a long procession of them.

"Fasten your seatbelts, it's going to be a bumpy night," warns Broadway's reigning star, Margo Channing (Bette Davis, right). Her party guests are all ears as she rails at her conniving, covertly ambitious assistant, Eve Harrington (Anne Baxter, left).

THE DIRECTOR

As a writer/director in the age of the studio system, **Joseph L. Mankiewicz** was given unusually free rein despite a very close collaborative process with Zanuck. On the set, Mankiewicz demanded calm and quiet; he would not abide fits of temper from anyone, star or crew member. This conservatism was reflected in his technical style, straightforward camera work with only a few minor innovations, most notably the freeze-frame opening sequence. Long considered a women’s director (*The Barefoot Contessa* [1954], *Letter to Three Wives* [1949], *Cleopatra* [1963]), Mankiewicz happily asserted that women were innately more interesting characters. Asked how he knew so much about women, he shot back, “I’ve lived with them all my life!”

Margo arrives late for her understudy’s audition and learns that the duplicitous Eve has won the job. Margo jealously accuses her director/lover Bill Sampson (Gary Merrill) of falling in love with “Eve-Eve-Evil!”

THE CAST	
Margo Channing	Bette Davis
Eve Harrington	Anne Baxter
Addison DeWitt	George Sanders
Karen Richards	Celeste Holm
Bill Sampson	Gary Merrill
Lloyd Richards	Hugh Marlowe
Max Fabian	Gregory Ratoff
Phoebe	Barbara Bates
Claudia Casswell	Marilyn Monroe
Birdie Coonan	Thelma Ritter

THE ACTORS

Bette Davis’s career was drying up and her third marriage was on the rocks when the call came from Zanuck. She leapt at *All About Eve* as if it were a lifeline (“Joe Mankiewicz resurrected me from the dead!”), and after one look at her romantic lead, **Gary Merrill**, she was completely lost. Their affair shadowed the project, the sexual heat palpable on the set. They wed soon after wrapping and made a second film together, *Another Man’s Poison* (1951) that fell flat. By 1965, the marriage was well over and Merrill’s career had come to the point of *Run, Psycho, Run*. Davis was in the final horror-flick stage of her career, ignited by her surprise success in *What Ever Happened to Baby Jane* (1962). Her canon of iconic performances is almost unrivaled: *Of Human Bondage* (1934), *Jezebel* (1938), *Dark Victory* (1939), *The Little Foxes* (1941), *Now, Voyager* (1942), *Watch on the Rhine* (1943), *The Corn Is Green* (1945), *The Virgin Queen* (1955), *Pocketful of Miracles* (1961), and her last, *The Whales of August* (1987).

After hours, it was **Marilyn Monroe**’s bedroom conquests that captured attention. George Sanders and his wife, Zsa Zsa Gabor, would place bets as to how many callers knocked on Marilyn’s hotel room door in the course of a single evening. As an actress, she was dismissed as a “freaky dumb blonde” and it was to the astonishment of the cast and Zanuck (who once dismissed her as “unphotogenic”) that her star rose so swiftly after the film’s release. Though offered only walk-ons before *Eve*, she began to catch fire with *Clash by Night* and *Don’t Bother to Knock* (1952), and in 1953 came *Niagara* and *Gentlemen Prefer Blondes*, perhaps her most identifiable performance. She was a full-out phenomenon by *The Seven Year Itch* (1955), and with *Bus Stop* in 1956 and *Some Like It Hot* in 1959, she owned Hollywood. She had only one completed film left, *The Misfits* (1961), before her still-questionable demise from a drug overdose in 1962. (For more on Monroe, see page 48.)

George Sanders is unfortunately best known for the suicide note in 1972 in which he complained that he was bored and it was time to leave. None of his many films following *Eve* is memorable except for one, Disney’s animated *The Jungle Book* (1967), for which he provided the voice of the very nasty lion.

Anne Baxter would never have such a juicy role again and suffered through some awkward casting decisions, appearing as Mrs. Pharaoh in *The Ten Commandments* (1956) and as a Mexican roadhouse proprietor in *Walk on the Wild Side* (1962). She briefly starred in *Applause*, the Broadway musical version of *Eve*, in 1971. Despite their clashes over competing Oscar nominations for *Eve*, Baxter and Davis remained lifelong friends.

ROLE REVERSALS

Claudette Colbert lost the role of a lifetime thanks to a slipped disc. Bette Davis was grateful for the lucky break until her marriage to costar Gary Merrill soured.

BEHIND THE SCREEN

Bette Davis’s famous cocktail party dress was a last minute inspiration by the star. Designed by Edith Head, it was cut too large and wouldn’t stay up. Bette simply pushed the sleeves down off the shoulder, shoved her hands in its deep pockets, and stalked off to the shoot the scene.

All About Eve is sometimes referred to as the “three suicide movie” (George Sanders, Marilyn Monroe, and Barbara Bates).

CREDITS

Producer: Darryl F. Zanuck/ 20th Century Fox
Director: Joseph L. Mankiewicz
Screenplay: Joseph L. Mankiewicz, based on the short story “The Wisdom of Eve” by Mary Orr
Running time: 138 minutes
Budget: $1.4 million
Box Office: $4.2 million

ACADEMY AWARDS

Best Picture
Best Director: Joseph L. Mankiewicz
Best Screenplay: Joseph L. Mankiewicz
Best Supporting Actor: George Sanders
Best Costume Design, Black-and-White: Edith Head, Charles LeMaire
Best Sound Recording: 20th Century Fox sound department

NOMINATIONS

Best Actress: Bette Davis, Anne Baxter
Best Supporting Actress: Celeste Holm, Thelma Ritter
Art Direction: Lyle Wheeler, George Davis, Walter Scott, Thomas Little
Cinematography, Black-and-White: Milton Krasner
Editing: Barbara McLean
Musical Score: Alfred Newman

THE YEAR’S OTHER WINNERS

Best Actor: Jose Ferrer, *Cyrano de Bergerac*
Best Actress: Judy Holliday, *Born Yesterday*
Best Supporting Actress: Josephine Hull, *Harvey*

The Academy of Motion Picture Arts and Sciences named Bette Davis its first woman president in 1941. Her first order of business was to make that year's Oscar ceremony a charity event for the Red Cross. The Board refused to agree and she quit on the spot.

Bette Davis's headstone carries the inscription "She did it the hard way."

Celeste Holm got her start on Broadway as the original "Ado Annie" in *Oklahoma.*

Anne Baxter was the granddaughter of architect Frank Lloyd Wright. She'd been cast as Eve because of her resemblance to the original Margo, Claudette Colbert.

NOTABLE QUOTES

"Margo Channing was not a bitch. She was an actress who was getting older and was not too happy about it. And why should she be? Anyone who says that life begins at forty is full of it. As people get older their bodies begin to decay. They get sick. They forget things. What's good about that?"—Bette Davis

"I think it can be said fairly that I've been in on the beginning, rise, peak, collapse, and end of the talking picture."—Joseph L. Mankiewicz

"Acting is like rollerskating. Once you know how to do it, it is neither stimulating nor exciting." —George Sanders

SEND IN THE CLONES

A Face in the Crowd (1957)
The Fan (1981)
Bullets Over Broadway (1994)

THE CRITICS

"Mankiewicz would never again achieve such a pitch-perfect blend of wit and rueful wisdom." —Peter Travers, *Rolling Stone*

"*Sunset Boulevard* seems like the better film today, maybe because it fits our age of irony, maybe because Billy Wilder was a better director than Joseph Mankiewicz." —Roger Ebert, *Chicago Sun-Times*

THE OTHER LISTS

- American Film Institute (Yes)
- Roger Ebert's Top 100 (No)
- *Entertainment Weekly* (Yes)
- Internet Movie Database (Yes)
- Leonard Maltin (Yes)
- *Movieline* (Yes)
- National Society of Film Critics (No)
- *Premiere* Magazine (No)
- *Rolling Stone* Magazine (Yes)
- *Village Voice* (Yes)

The cocktail party in which Margo openly suspects Eve of undermining her is the banquet from *Macbeth* without the blood and ghosts. Margo's weapon of choice, aside from some of the best lines ever spewed, is a candy dish. As the hostess with a few too many martinis under her belt, she keeps checking to make sure the dish is filled. She wants a piece so badly, but she's always on a diet to stave off the likes of the younger, prettier Eve. Finally, as she lays it on the line for director/lover Bill, who defends Eve, Margo pops a piece of chocolate in her mouth and chomps down hard. You know she's thinking of Eve's lovely jugular.

Eve plays coy with critic Addison DeWitt (George Sanders) after standing in for Margo. He suggests she put a lid on her false modesty and allow him to hasten her stardom in his influential column. She pretends to be taken with him: "You take charge."

"There was more good acting at Hollywood parties than ever appeared on the screen." —Bette Davis

14

PSYCHO 1960

CUT-RATE MOTEL

"No one but no one will be allowed into the theater after the film has started. Not even the manager's brother, the President of the United States, or the Queen of England!" There was a further admonishment to audiences not to give away the secrets of the movie. In other words, don't tell your friends about the mother up in the creepy old house. Whether or not patrons were on their best behavior, and whether or not the movie scared them to death no matter how much of the plot was given away, the box office exploded. At one New Jersey drive-in, the waiting line was three miles long. Director Alfred Hitchcock sent his personal assistant to various theaters to gauge people's reactions upon exiting. She told him they were laughing with the same anxious relief that comes at the end of a roller-coaster ride. He was delighted. He had gambled on a low-budget "slasher flick," the first of the genre, and managed to change the way we see thrillers. The great trick in *Psycho* is Hitchcock's ability to make us care about a maniac. He introduced America to the vulnerable, boyishly charming monster next door.

Jim: The Oscars were at their cowardly worst with the snub of Perkins for the iconic performance that pretty much ended his career.

Gail: Why, that mean little dome of a man! Hitch obviously takes great pleasure in unleashing the most manipulative tricks in the book of cinematic frights, while delighting us in the utter cleverness of these contrivances. We hate to love him. But we do.

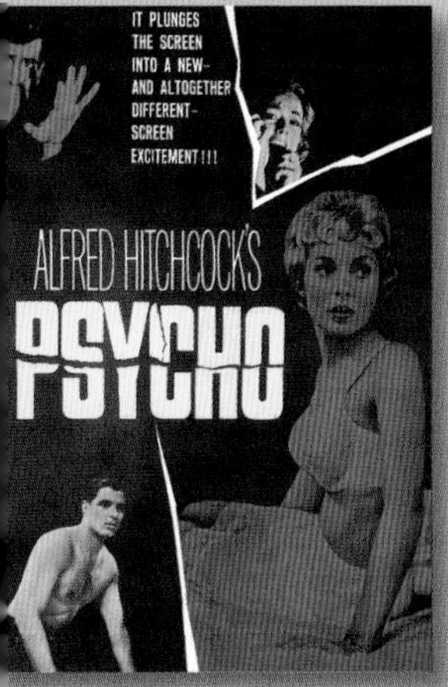

HE PLOT

arion (Janet Leigh), a Phoenix realtor's cretary, steals $40,000 from her boss finance her marriage to a cash-strapped ver (John Gavin). On the lam and exhausted m driving in the rain, she stops at an t-of-the-way motel run by a beleaguered ung man, Norman (Anthony Perkins), who es with his mentally disturbed mother. fore retiring, Marion decides to return the oney—and prepares for a soul-cleansing ower, unaware that Norman is spying on r through a hole in the wall. Moments er, she's brutally stabbed to death by his ranged mother. Or so we're led to believe. investigation into Marion's disappearance sults in another brutal murder and the ocking truth about Norman's unusual nd with Mama.

"Don't give away the ending. It's the only one we have." Undoubtedly, audiences snitched, but it didn't put a dent in the box-office numbers. *Psycho*'s structure was unique for the time, so it was hard to believe the story would end the way it did. Here, it looks as if we might be in for a bittersweet romance between a shy, lonely boy and a slightly older woman in need of rescue. Not quite.

THE DIRECTOR:

Alfred Hitchcock didn't care to work with young, new writers. But when his wife, Alma, admitted to loving the first scene that novice Joseph Stefano had written, Hitchcock was sold. It was said in Hollywood that "the Hitchcock touch has four hands and two of them are Alma's." From the beginning she was supportive of his notion of bringing big-name stars and quality direction to a low-budget, black-and-white film. Everything was done on the cheap, right down to the use of his TV-show camera crew. Well known for his "absolute camera," there would be no improvised action or dialogue. That sort of tight control led to Hitchcock's hatred of location shoots. He only shot one in *Psycho*, the used-car purchase while Marion is on the run. *Psycho* marked the end of his splashy, wide-screen Technicolor era. For all its scope, his follow-up film, *The Birds* (1963), is a smallish picture, as are *Torn Curtain* (1966), *Frenzy* (1972), and his last film, *Family Plot* (1976). (For more on Hitchcock, see pages 30, 85, and 106.)

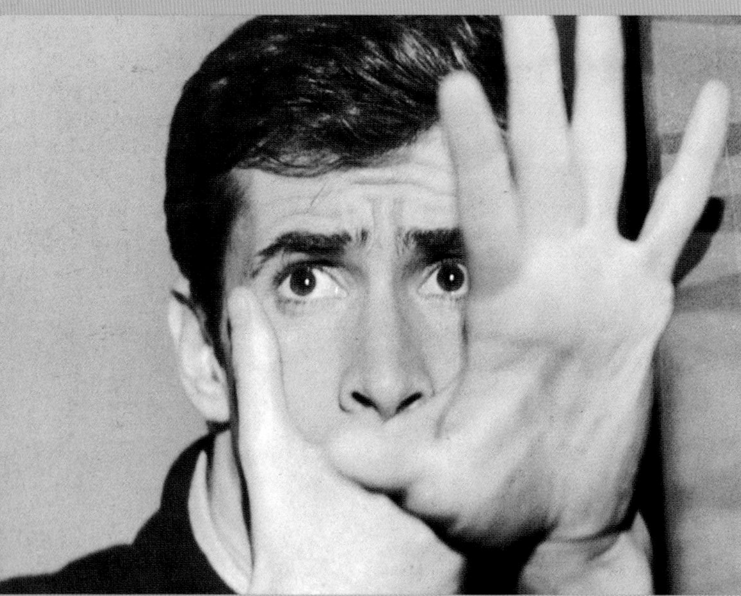

"You know what I think? I think that we're all in our private traps, clamped in them, and none of us can ever get out. We scratch and we claw, but only at the air, only at each other, and for all of it, we never budge an inch." Norman was speaking for himself but could easily be speaking for Perkins as well. After *Psycho*, he was confined to playing versions of the same role endlessly.

THE CAST

Norman Bates	Anthony Perkins
Marion Crane	Janet Leigh
Lila Crane	Vera Miles
Sam Loomis	John Gavin
Milton Arbogast	Martin Balsam
Sheriff Al Chambers	John McIntire
Dr. Richmond	Simon Oakland
George Lowery	Vaughn Taylor
Tom Cassidy	Frank Albertson
Eliza Chambers	Lurene Tuttle
Caroline	Patricia Hitchcock
Charlie	John Anderson
Highway Patrolman	Mort Mills

THE ACTORS

For **Anthony Perkins**, *Psycho* was a Faustian bargain: the role of a lifetime that he could never shake free of. He played the part with exacting detail, right down to the stutter at the mention of "Mother." Perkins made Norman Bates vulnerable and, for the first time, audiences saw a madman being controlled by his psychosis. His trauma was such that even after tossing poor Marion into the trunk and dumping her car in a swamp, audiences sweated it out, right along with Norman, when the car briefly stopped sinking. Perkins repeated the role three more times in sequels and died in 1990 of complications from AIDS. He left a statement to be released only after his passing. "I chose not to go public [with my illness] because, to misquote *Casablanca*, I'm not much at being noble, but it doesn't take much to see the problems of one old actor don't amount to a hill of beans in this crazy world." His A-list credits prior to *Psycho* include *Friendly Persuasion* (1956), *Fear Strikes Out* (1957), *Desire Under the Elms* (1958), and *On the Beach* (1959). His career's Act Two is memorable for *Pretty Poison* (1968), *Play It as It Lays* (1972) and *Mahogany* (1975).

Janet Leigh agreed to work with Hitchcock even before reading the script. It never occurred to her that it would be a problem to be killed off so quickly in the film. Challenged by Hitch's stricture that actors must adapt to his camera, she found her own motivations and claims to have enjoyed the challenge. When she saw the final cut of the shower scene, she screamed. She half-jokingly admits she hasn't taken a shower since. Leigh made her first major impact in *Little Women* (1949), but it was her marriage to screen-idol Tony Curtis that put her firmly on the Hollywood map. They costarred in *Houdini* (1953), after which she appeared in *Prince Valiant* (1954), *My Sister Eileen* (1955), *Touch of Evil* (1958), *The Manchurian Candidate* (1962), and *Bye Bye Birdie* (1963). Later on, Leigh took cameos in the horrors *The Fog* (1980) and *Halloween H20: 20 Years Later* (1998), the latter of which was filmed with her daughter, Jamie Lee Curtis. (For more on Leigh, see page 295.)

Vera Miles had been groomed for *Vertigo* (1958), and Hitchcock was irate when she became pregnant. She owed him one picture under her contract, and Marion's sister was the role she was forced to take, despite her marquee status at the time. Best known for her role in *The Searchers* (1956) and *Psycho*, she made one more classic, *The Man Who Shot Liberty Valance* (1962) before her career leveled off with B films and TV cameos.

John Gavin was a hot young actor under contract to Universal when *Psycho* was shot. Hitchcock found him acceptable, if a bit stiff, in the romantic scenes. (The director asked Janet Leigh if she could do something to spice things up between them.) Gavin's career was brief, and his most notable films include *Imitation of Life* (1959) and *Back Street* (1961). Rare for Hollywood, he was an outspoken conservative, and President Reagan appointed him ambassador to Mexico.

BEHIND THE SCREEN

Psycho is based on the true story of a Wisconsin schizophrenic, Ed Gein, who killed several neighbors. The woman he attacked in her shower was actually beheaded.

CREDITS

Producer: Alfred Hitchcock/ Paramount
Director: Alfred Hitchcock
Screenplay: Joseph Stefano, based on the novel by Robert Bloch
Running time: 109 minutes
Budget: $800,000
Box Office: $32 million

ACADEMY AWARD NOMINATIONS

Best Director: Alfred Hitchcock
Best Supporting Actress: Janet Leigh
Best Cinematography, Black-and-White: John L. Russell
Best Art Direction, Black-and-White: Joseph Hurley, Robert Clatworthy, George Milo

THE YEAR'S WINNERS

Best Picture: *The Apartment*
Best Director: Billy Wilder, *The Apartment*
Best Actor: Burt Lancaster, *Elmer Gantry*
Best Actress: Elizabeth Taylor, *Butterfield 8*
Best Supporting Actor: Peter Ustinov, *Spartacus*
Best Supporting Actress: Shirley Jones, *Elmer Gantry*

THE OTHER LISTS

- American Film Institute (Yes)
- Roger Ebert's Top 100 (Yes)
- *Entertainment Weekly* (Yes)
- Internet Movie Database (Yes)
- Leonard Maltin (Yes)
- *Movieline* (Yes)
- National Society of Film Critics (No)
- *Premiere* Magazine (No)
- *Rolling Stone* Magazine (No)
- *Village Voice* (Yes)

Hitchcock spread rumors about casting the role of the mother in order to keep the movie's big secret safe from industry snoops.

Hitch's cameo comes early. He can be spotted in a big cowboy hat outside Marion's office.

Psycho broke several taboos, not the least of which was that it marked the first time a toilet was seen and actually flushed in a movie.

"Thank you," was all Alfred Hitchcock said after being presented with the Irving Thalberg Memorial Award at the 1967 Oscars. No one before or since has delivered a briefer response.

THE MUSIC

Bernard Herrmann used an orchestra comprised entirely of strings, as if they were simply playing "guts." John Williams later used the three opening notes of the *Psycho* theme for his *Star Wars* score as an homage to Herrmann.

NOTABLE QUOTES

"*Psycho* gave me very wrinkled skin. I was in that shower for seven days—70 set-ups. At least [Hitchcock] made sure the water was warm." —Janet Leigh

SPECIAL EFFECTS

The shower scene required seven days of shooting and 70 camera setups for 45 seconds of footage. A nude body double was essential so that Hitchcock could determine the amount of water and steam required to cover up X-rated body parts. After exhaustive research, casaba melon was deemed best for the sound of a knife slashing into flesh. As for the most effective "movie blood," catsup was nixed in favor of chocolate syrup. The most difficult shot for Janet Leigh was the final one, in which the hand-focused camera slowly pulls back from her frozen, dead eye—while water is splashing on her. It took at least 20 takes, then a few more after Hitch's wife noted during a screening that Leigh had taken a breath. In a tribute to its unequaled montage editing, we don't even notice that Norman Bates isn't in the scene. In fact, Tony Perkins was away in New York the entire week. Several stand-ins, both male and female, played knife-wielding "Mother."

THE CRITICS

"What makes *Psycho* immortal, when so many films are already half-forgotten as we leave the theater, is that it connects directly with our fears: our fears that we might impulsively commit a crime, our fears of the police, our fears of becoming the victim of a madman, and of course our fears of disappointing our mothers." —Roger Ebert, *Chicago Sun-Times*

"There is not an abundance of subtlety or the lately familiar Hitchcock bent toward significant and colorful scenery in this obviously low-budget job . . . The consequence is his denouement falls quite flat for us. But the acting is fair." —Bosley Crowther, *New York Times*

Norman removes a painting from his office wall to reveal a peephole. Through it, he's aroused by the sight of Marion stripping down to her black brassiere and slip as she prepares to shower. She wraps herself in a towel and turns on the water. She steps into the tub and luxuriates in the rush of warmth. She doesn't notice the almost opaque outline of an older woman through the shower curtain. Suddenly, the curtain is torn open and, as Marion screams, our eyes go to the huge bread knife, Marion's naked stomach, her contorted, horrified face, the arm coming down, and the vain struggle. There is an unforgettable screech of discordant violins accompanying each deadly slash.

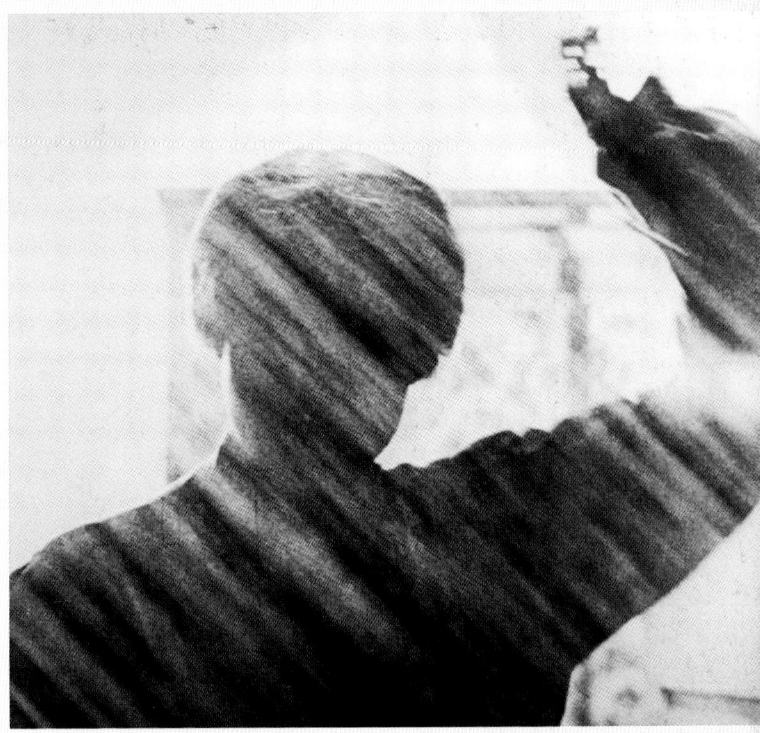

"Television has brought murder back into the home—where it belongs."—Alfred Hitchcock

"Bates Motel—twelve rooms, twelve vacancies." Hitchcock was later to comment, "Of course *Psycho* is a comedy. What else could it be?"

15

TAXI DRIVER 1976

MEAN STREETS

Gusts of steam rise up—as if from hell itself—over rain-slicked streets where hustlers and hangers-on roam the night. "Someday, a real rain will come and wash all this scum off the streets," says alienated, enraged Vietnam veteran Travis Bickle (Robert De Niro). It's part of his ongoing narration, spoken over a lamenting, saxophone score by Bernard Herrmann that clutches us in its embrace. We see Bickle's taxi from the ground up, a huge fortress where he avoids the sleeplessness that finds him day and night in his squalid room. We hate Bickle's violence, his twisted, off-kilter views of everything, but we cannot resist him either. He's handsome and he's got a kind of innocence: He's looking for something good, someone to connect with. We hear his thoughts through his diaries, which contradict what we see on the outside. Could he really have written those diaries? Is the ending a dream after death, or does he end up a hero? There are some things that don't quite add up, but Scorsese's dramatic, visual genius, the emotional resonance of the performances, and the power of the music combine like chemicals absorbed through the pores. The film leaves you staggering.

Jim: As much an historical document as gritty psychodrama, in *Taxi Driver* Scorsese captures the final moments of pre-Yuppie, pre-gentrified Manhattan. Once upon a time the city was actually dangerous and colorful enough to make this scenario plausible. Scorsese became intensely frustrated when thunderstorms ruined the continuity of the scenes in the Presidential volunteer office, forcing him to run over budget. The studios tried to force him to shoot against a wall instead of showing the city, but he considered New York to be a character in the film.

Gail: Bring your shields. This film has the power to hit you in the heart and the gut—and take you to places that you really don't want to go. It's contemporary urban American life at its creepiest.

THE PLOT

Vietnam veteran Travis Bickle (Robert De Niro) drives his taxicab as if it were an army tank rumbling through the dark, derelict-filled streets of New York. He'd like to mow down everyone he sees—except for Betsy (Cybill Shepherd), the blonde goddess he notices working in the office of a Presidential candidate. After he manages to take her on a misguided date to a porn movie, Betsy drops him, and Bickle slides deeper into his solitude, ever more desperate to take violent action against the world. He arms himself up to his Mohawk and sets out to assassinate the candidate. Meanwhile, he keeps running into a 12-year-old streetwalker, Iris (Jodie Foster), who once tried to get into his cab to escape her pimp, Sport (Harvey Keitel). Bickle spends one afternoon with her, not for her sexual services, but to "liberate" her. When secret service agents subvert his assassination attempt, he drives like a demonic force to Sport's place of business (a doorway), murders the pimp and everyone else, and is shot in the neck. Is he dead? It certainly looks that way, but in the next scene, newspaper accounts and letters from Iris's parents show that Travis is apparently a hero. We even see him at his old job talking to the guys, and, for one last ride, he picks up Betsy.

"God's lonely man" skulks around the city day and night in his taxi; he is incapable of sleep. The veritable tank is both Travis's (Robert De Niro) armor against and his access to the world, much preferable to the loneliness that awaits him in his dingy apartment.

"The days go on and on ... they don't end. All my life needed was a sense of someplace to go. I don't believe that one should devote his life to morbid self-attention, I believe that one should become a person like other people."—Travis Bickle

THE DIRECTOR

Martin Scorsese took Hollywood by storm, setting himself up as a director to watch with *Mean Streets* (1973) and, with *Taxi Driver*, cementing his place as an auteur of man's loneliness and entrapment within his nature. Scorsese's interest is always in studying character and psyche, and he has found some of the best actors to embody his obsessions. He found the perfect vehicle for his vision in De Niro. (For more on Scorsese, see pages 91 and 118.)

Travis runs into the 12-year-old prostitute Iris (Jodie Foster) over and over again on the streets of the city, and determines to "liberate" her from her tawdry life. He believes he's found a kindred lonely spirit. The only question is, Does she really want to be saved?

THE CAST	
Travis Bickle	Robert De Niro
Betsy	Cybill Shepherd
Wizard	Peter Boyle
Iris Steensma	Jodie Foster
"Sport" Matthew	Harvey Keitel
Charles Palantine	Leonard Harris
Tom	Albert Brooks
Concession Girl	Diahnne Abbott

THE CRITICS

"This ferociously powerful film is like a raw, tabloid version of *Notes from Underground*. Scorsese achieves the quality of trance in some scenes, and the whole movie has a sense of vertigo."
—Pauline Kael, *The New Yorker*

"*Taxi Driver* is in many ways a much more polished film than...*Mean Streets*, but its polish is what ultimately makes it seem less than the sum of its parts. At the end you feel cheated, as you do when the solution of a whodunit fails to match the grandeur of the crime."
—Vincent Canby, *New York Times*

THE ACTORS

Taxi Driver established **Robert De Niro** as a film icon. From the famous, improvised, "You talkin' to me?" target-practice-in-the-mirror sequence, to his locked-inside-himself inability to communicate with Betsy, Iris, or anyone but himself, De Niro is so good, so much the character he plays, that it seems we could never have known this man had De Niro not played him. One of the greatest American actors today, De Niro's performances in such films as *Raging Bull* (1980) and *The Godfather, Part II* (1974) are flawless, but in our collective unconscious we will always remember him as the lonely, angry, twisted Travis Bickle. "Now I see this clearly. My whole life is pointed in one direction. There never has been a choice for me." (For more on De Niro, see pages 11 and 148.)

Cybill Shepherd wasn't sure she understood or wanted the part of Betsy until she spent time with De Niro, who insisted that they meet each other in character. On their first encounter in the film, she almost falls for him, seeing him as poetic. Before *Taxi Driver*, Shepherd's film career was already on a roll with such movies as *The Last Picture Show* (1971), *The Heartbreak Kid* (1972), *Daisy Miller* (1974), and *At Long Last Love* (1975). After many feature failures, she returned to great success on television in the '80s and '90s with *Moonlighting* and the eponymous sitcom *Cybill*. (For more on Shepherd, see page 238.)

Harvey Keitel was originally slated to play a campaign worker for candidate Palantine. But he decided, instead, to play the small role of the pimp, Sport. It was a part intended for a black man, but Scorsese feared that the racist implications might cause a race riot. Keitel has appeared in many Scorsese films, including *Mean Streets* (1973), *Alice Doesn't Live Here Anymore* (1974), and *The Last Temptation of Christ* (1988), as well as *Thelma & Louise* (1991), *Bugsy* (1991, Academy Award nomination), *Reservoir Dogs* and *Bad Lieutenant* (both 1992), *The Piano* (1993), *Pulp Fiction* (1994), and *Clockers* (1995). Among his most recent films are *Holy Smoke* (1999), *The Grey Zone* (2002), and *Red Dragon* (2002).

Jodie Foster originally had problems with the role: "I spent four hours with a shrink trying to prove I was normal enough to play a hooker. Does that make sense?" Nothing made much sense—especially the fact that Jodie's character would so capture a real-life psycho's imagination that he would mimic the film and attempt to take the life of President Reagan to win Foster's love, as was the case with John Hinckley in 1981. Her appearance in the film launched Foster's fascinating career, in which she has moved from prostitute to feminist. She has appeared in such films as *Alice Doesn't Live Here Anymore* (1974), *Bugsy Malone* (1976), *The Hotel New Hampshire* (1984), *The Accused* (1988, Academy Award), and *The Silence of the Lambs* (1991). Among her later films are *Shadows and Fog* (1992), *Sommersby* (1993), *Nell* (1994), *Contact* (1997), *Anna and the King* (1999), and *Panic Room* (2002). Considered one of the more powerful women in Hollywood, Foster has also directed the movies *Little Man Tate* (1991) and *Home for the Holidays* (1995).

THE MUSIC

Bernard Herrmann died two hours after he conducted the *Taxi Driver* score, which is arguably his most magnificent. With its intoxicated, 1940s-style romantic sax, the score's lamenting character permeates the film and gives Travis Bickle a touching, seductive air. Everything in the film seems to move to its languorous rhythms, until it breaks into a dissonant and confusing composition that conveys the chaos of Bickle's psychosis; later, a percussive snare-drum theme takes over as, bent on mass destruction, Bickle goes into "training." Herrmann is best known for his work for Orson Welles (*Citizen Kane* and *The Magnificent Ambersons*), Alfred Hitchcock (eight films, among them, *The Wrong Man*, *Vertigo*, *North by Northwest*, and *Psycho*), François Truffaut (*Fahrenheit 451*), and Brian De Palma (*Sisters* and *Obsession*). Herrmann had great impact on content as well, as when he insisted that De Palma cut the third act from *Obsession*.

BEHIND THE SCREEN

After producers saw *Mean Streets* (1973), Scorsese was on the list to direct *Taxi Driver* —which had previously had Brian De Palma's name on it—but only if he could get De Niro to play the lead.

De Niro worked twelve-hour days for a month driving cabs as preparation for the role. He also studied mental illness.

De Niro's Mohawk was not real. Makeup artist Dick Smith created a bald cap that was glued to De Niro's head, and the Mohawk was made of thick horse hair.

Bernard Herrmann decided to write the score for the film after he watched Bickle pour Schnapps over his bread.

Harvey Keitel rehearsed with actual pimps to prepare for his role.

There are only two scenes in the film that don't focus on Bickle.

ROLE REVERSALS

Jeff Bridges was originally considered for the role of Travis Bickle.

President Rock Hudson? Sounds handsome enough. Hudson was originally considered for the role of candidate Charles Palantine but was committed to his TV series, *McMillan and Wife* (1971).

THE GREAT LINES

"The days go on and on...they don't end. All my life needed was a sense of someplace to go." —Travis

"You get a job. You become the job."—Wizard

"Loneliness has followed me my whole life, everywhere. In bars, in cars, sidewalks, stores, everywhere. There's no escape. I'm God's lonely man." —Travis

SCORSESE ON DIRECTING

"I became obsessed with the film and was really quite unpleasant to be around when I was making it, because I had to fight. Every day was a battle to get what I wanted."

"My attititude as a film director has always been...provocation. I want to provoke the audience."

"I know people are going to laugh...but you know, in a way both of them have this thread running through them of a love that's so strong, yet the two people involved can't get together. There's that same yearning, that same sense of want, and the frustration that comes from the demands of society and the way people are forced to live in it. In both stories, love comes to naught."—Comparing *Age of Innocence* to *Taxi Driver*

One of the more painful examples of Bickle's inability to communicate with or understand others occurs on his first date with Betsy, whom he takes to a porn movie. Offended and shocked by his odd choice of activity, she asks him if this is his usual date. His reply is painfully out of touch with the rest of the world—Betsy's world, that is. He didn't think it such a bad idea. Betsy responds, "Taking me to a place like this is about as exciting to me as saying: 'Let's f—k.'" (Behind Betsy is a blond prostitute, facing toward Travis in the same position).

He tries to apologize but by that time Betsy has hailed a taxi and dumps him.

The next scene is painful to watch. Travis is standing in a bare hallway, talking on a wall pay-phone to Betsy, apologizing for bringing her to the porn house: "Hello Betsy. Listen, uh, I'm sorry about the, the other night . . . Did you get my flowers in the . . .? You didn't get them? I sent some flowers, uh . . . Yeah, well, OK, OK. Can I call you again? Uh, tomorrow or the next day? OK. No, I'm gonna . . . OK. Yeah, sure, OK. So long.

CREDITS

Producer: Michael Phillips, Julia Phillips/Columbia Pictures
Director: Martin Scorsese
Screenplay: Paul Schrader
Running Time: 113 minutes
Budget: $1.3 million
Box Office: $21.1 million (U.S.)

ACADEMY AWARD NOMINATIONS

Best Picture
Best Actor: Robert De Niro
Best Supporting Actress: Jodie Foster
Best Music, Original Score: Bernard Herrmann

THE YEAR'S WINNERS

Best Picture: *Rocky*
Best Director: John Avildsen, *Rocky*
Best Actor: Peter Finch, *Network*
Best Actress: Faye Dunaway, *Network*
Best Supporting Actor: Jason Robards, *All the President's Men*
Best Supporting Actress: Beatrice Straight, *Network*

THE OTHER LISTS

- American Film Institute (Yes)
- Roger Ebert's Top 100 (Yes)
- *Entertainment Weekly* (No)
- Internet Movie Database (Yes)
- Leonard Maltin (No)
- *Movieline* (No)
- National Society of Film Critics (No)
- *Premiere* Magazine (Yes)
- *Rolling Stone* Magazine (No)
- *Village Voice* (Yes)

Bickle is shot after an attempt, first, to assassinate a political candidate, and then to kill a local pimp. He can be seen bleeding profusely from the neck in this impossibly high overhead shot—they had to cut a hole through the ceiling—characteristic of some of the more unusual and striking photography by Michael Chapman in the film.

16

APOCALYPSE NOW 1979

DARKNESS VISIBLE

We fly into Vietnam just above rows of treetops, the puck-puck rhythms of chopper blades beating to the mournfully trippy tune of the Doors' "The End." Dust swirls and a sudden cloud of colorful napalm fills the sky as the noise of the helicopter blades fades into the thrum of a ceiling fan and the upside-down head of Martin Sheen (as Captain Willard) comes into focus. He says the film's first line: "Saigon. Shit. I'm still only in Saigon." The ecstatic barrage of sound and light, of violence and drug-induced hyperactivity, the sensory overload of this stunning film evoke what we imagine to be the real, raw look and feel of the Vietnam War. This, in itself, is enough to make Coppola's expressionistic war film a masterpiece. Considered a muddled work by some for its failure to tell a cohesive story or to deepen its embryonic themes, it was also criticized by the director himself for not living up to the implied promise of an apocalyptic conclusion. Willard's mission to "terminate, with extreme prejudice, the most decorated soldier in the army, the AWOL and deranged Kurtz," who has become ineffective as a military man but effective as a savage warrior, failed to bring together all the film's ideas. Twenty-two years after its initial release, Coppola and company reworked the film from scratch, releasing *Apocalypse Now Redux* to fill in the missing pieces and clarify the basic themes, but it left viewers disagreeing once again about its achievements. Regardless of which version you view, this is a monumental film that succeeds on many levels. From the massive, genocidal, Wagnerian helicopter assault to the decadent *Playboy* pageant in the jungle, Coppola has imagined countless indelible moments and images on an awe-inspiring, epic scale. The film's surreal absurdities and its provocation of both horror at and identification with the cruelties of jungle war make this an experiential triumph. Triumphant as well is the way the group of soldiers responds to one another on their journey down a river into hell.

Jim: Tales of Coppola's megalomania, Sheen's heart attack, Brando's Brando-like behavior have inspired a great documentary and a hit play/indie comedy. As you watch the film, you can't help but recall the behind-the-scenes stuff as well. Rather than distract, I think it adds to the experience. The movie may be about Vietnam, but it also speak volumes about a particularly grandiose era in Hollywood and the excesses that can sometime result in art.

Gail: Martin Sheen's breakdown in his room in Saigon is one of the most terrifying pieces of acting on film. And it wasn't all acting.

'HE PLOT

aptain Willard (Martin Sheen), already eeply scarred by the war, is assigned the ission of locating and terminating Col. alter Kurtz (Marlon Brando), an AWOL 'een Beret hero. Drawn into the jungle by rces greater than his mission alone, Willard ets out by boat, along with "Chief" (Albert all), "Chef" (Frederic Forrest), the surfer ance (Sam Bottoms), and the ghetto-raised iller, played by a fourteen-year-old Laurence shburne. Their journey moves in an altered ate, to the beat of rock and roll, toward the nigmatic madman, the AWOL Captain Kurtz. s more than a trip up river; it's a terrifying urney into the heart of human darkness. In e end, Willard confronts the mad warrior his lair—where he is the self-appointed od—and he murders him as natives outside acrifice a cow. It is a blood frenzy reflective all that we now know about the savagery of purposeless jungle war with no end in sight.

"When I was here, I wanted to be there; when I was there, all I could think of was getting back into the jungle," says Capt. Benjamin L. Willard (Martin Sheen).

"You have to have men who are moral ... and at the same time who are able to utilize their primordial instincts to kill without feeling... without passion...without judgment...without judgment. Because it's judgment that defeats us." —Col. Kurtz

THE DIRECTOR

Francis Ford Coppola once declared that *Apocalypse Now* was not about Vietnam—it was Vietnam. Though his arrogant, perhaps drug-induced comments angered many, there is no question that the director made a transcendent, unforgettable, visually breathtaking film. Not a man to do anything small, Coppola had to mortgage everything he owned to finance the film. The emotional toll was even greater. Coppola threatened suicide several times during its making, and dealing with the unpredictable Brando was as difficult as braving the typhoons that threatened to shut down the whole picture—and, at times, did; the set had to be rebuilt after fierce tropical storms. The director lost 100 pounds in the process. The scale and grandiosity of Coppola's ambitions were even more than he could handle. "We had access to too much money and too much equipment," he said at a Cannes Film Festival news conference in 1979. "The making of this film was as epic and complex as the film itself, and the human drama inspired Eleanor Coppola (the director's wife) to chronicle it in her documentary, *Hearts of Darkness: A Filmmaker's Apocalypse* (1991). (For more on Coppola, see page 15 and 274.)

Kurtz (Marlon Brando), the "Green Beret gone insane," stands in the shadows waiting for Willard to finally confront him.

THE CAST

Col. Walter E. Kurtz	Marlon Brando
Lt. Col. William "Bill" Kilgore	Robert Duvall
Capt. Benjamin L. Willard	Martin Sheen
Engineman 2nd Class Jay "Chef" Hicks	Frederic Forrest
Chief Quartermaster Phillips	Albert Hall
Gunner's Mate 3rd Class Lance B. Johnson	Sam Bottoms
Gunner's Mate 3rd Class Tyrone Miller	Laurence Fishburne
Photojournalist	Dennis Hopper
Gen. R. Corman	G. D. Spradlin
Col. G. Lucas	Harrison Ford
Civilian (Jerry)	Jerry Ziesmer
Capt. Richard Colby	Scott Glenn
MP Sergeant #1	Bo Byers
Kilgore's Gunner	James Keane

THE ACTORS

Martin Sheen's is an intensely arresting and complex portrayal of an intelligence officer who travels into his own heart of darkness while being transported toward Colonel Kurtz's jungle compound. So seriously did Sheen prepare for the role that he suffered a heart attack as a result, but he managed to return after a brief rest to complete the film. Sheen's work is notable for its intensity, which can be seen early on in his role as a disaffected killer in *Badlands* (1973). After a long spell of distinguished television productions, including *The Execution of Private Slovik* (1974), as President John F. Kennedy in the miniseries *Kennedy* (1983), and as JFK's brother Robert in *The Missiles of October* (1974), he returned to film in *Gandhi* (1982), *The Dead Zone* (1983), *Wall Street* (1987), *Da* (1988), and *That Championship Season* (1982). His most recent roles have been in the comic caper *Catch Me If You Can* and *The Confidence Game* (both 2002), and *The Commission* (2003). He has become well known to TV viewers as the President of the United States in the popular series *The West Wing* (1999-2006).

You can't take your eyes off Oscar-nominee **Robert Duvall**, the wild-eyed, renegade warrior, who is both hilarious and terrifying as Colonel Kilgore. The napalm-sniffing surfer dominates the screen in his brief but powerful scenes. Duvall is unquestionably one of our greatest actors, playing in unforgettable roles such as that of the mafia family's consigliere in the first two *Godfather* movies (1972, 1974), the mad ex-fighter pilot father in *The Great Santini* (1979), the righteous detective brother of a fallen monsignor in *True Confessions* (1981), and a spent, alcoholic country-and-western singer in *Tender Mercies* (1983, Academy Award). (For more on Duvall, see page 13.)

Dennis Hopper plays the stoned photojournalist (based on the real life of Tim Page) with just the right balance of sanity and derangement. He is both Willard's unreliable guide and a crazed, desperate fool, who does and doesn't understand what is going on. He seems to have been around Kurtz's camp too long when he begins muttering that Kurtz is "a poet-warrior in the classic sense" and "we're all his children." The role was hardly a departure for Hopper, who has appeared as manic outsiders in such films as *Easy Rider* (1969), *Blue Velvet* (1986), and *Red Rock West* (1993). (For more on Hopper, see page 205.)

No one ever accused genius Method-actor **Marlon Brando** of delivering consistent performances. His *A Streetcar Named Desire* (1951) and *On the Waterfront* (1954) remain two of the greatest examples of his unique genius on film. Unfortunately, *Apocalypse Now* was one of the great disappointments. After hearing about the strange AWOL Green Beret, Kurtz, for three-quarters of the film, we finally meet him in the shadows, reciting poetry and making incoherent observations about man's fate. Brando makes this a climactic moment, regardless of his performance. The often-difficult actor gave Coppola a run for his $1 million advance, at times threatening to quit and keep the money. Coppola told his agent that he didn't care, and if they couldn't get Brando, they would try Jack Nicholson, Robert Redford, then Al Pacino. Brando eventually turned up—late, drunk, and 88 pounds overweight—and admitted he hadn't read the script or even *Heart of Darkness*, the book it was based on. When he finally read Coppola's script, he refused to do it. After days of arguments over single lines of dialogue, an ad-lib style of scripting was agreed upon, and it was shot according to Brando's stipulations

CREDITS

Producer: Francis Ford Coppola/ United Artists
Director: Francis Ford Coppola
Screenplay: John Milius, Francis Ford Coppola, Michael Herr (narration), based on the novella *Heart of Darkness* by Joseph Conrad
Running Time: 139 minutes
Budget: $31.5 million

ACADEMY AWARDS

Best Cinematography: Vittorio Storaro
Best Sound: Walter Murch, Mark Berger, Richard Beggs, Nathan Boxer

NOMINATIONS

Best Picture
Best Director: Francis Ford Coppola
Best Supporting Actor: Robert Duvall
Best Writing, Screenplay Based on Material from Another Medium: John Milius, Francis Ford Coppola
Best Film Editing: Richard Marks, Walter Murch, Gerald B. Greenberg, Lisa Fruchtman
Best Art Direction–Set Decoration: Dean Tavoularis, Angelo P. Graham, George R. Nelson

THE YEAR'S WINNERS

Best Picture: *Kramer vs. Kramer*
Best Director: Robert Benton, *Kramer vs. Kramer*
Best Actor: Dustin Hoffman, *Kramer vs. Kramer*
Best Actress: Sally Field, *Norma Rae*
Best Supporting Actress: Meryl Streep, *Kramer vs. Kramer*

"Disneyland. Fuck, man, this is better than Disneyland."— Gunner's Mate 3rd Class Lance B. Johnson

that he appear in shadows (because of his great girth). Improvising his lines, Brando chewed on a nut and said, "The human animal is the only one that has bloodlust. . . .Killing without purpose, killing for pleasure. . . .[Pause] I swallowed a bug." Unfortunately, he couldn't continue from there. (For more on Brando, see pages 11, 64, and 100.)

If Coppola had a repertory company of actors, **Frederic Forrest** would be right there in the middle. Many of his best roles have been in the director's films, including *The Conversation* (1974), *One from the Heart* (1982), and *Tucker: The Man and His Dream* (1988). He was nominated for a Best Supporting Actor Oscar for his performance as the army-deserter lover of a singer in the non-Coppola film *The Rose* (1979). Forrest's career has been erratic, including roles in such films as *The Two Jakes* (1990) and more recently *Shadow Hours* and *The Spreading Ground* (both 2000), and *To What Sweet End* (2002). But perhaps his best roles have been in large-scale made-for-TV movies, including *Lonesome Dove* (1989) and *Citizen Cohn* (1992).

As Chief Quartermaster Phillips, **Albert Hall** is the man who runs the boat. His despair over what he witnesses, though kept tightly under wraps, speaks volumes about the gravity of the situation, and stands in sharp contrast to his unstrung crewmembers. Hall has enjoyed a prolific career both in film—*The Fabulous Baker Boys* (1989), *Malcolm X* (1992), *Devil in a Blue Dress* (1995), *Courage Under Fire* (1996), and *Ali* (2001)—and in such television films as *Guyana Tragedy: The Story of Jim Jones* (1980), *Separate But Equal* (1991), *Get on the Bus* (1996), *The Tiger Woods Story* (1998), and *Getting Away with Murder: The JonBenet Ramsey Mystery* (2000).

Laurence Fishburne was only fourteen when he made *Apocalypse Now*, and it is said the experience had a profound effect on him. It shows in his vulnerable performance as Gunner's Third Mate Tyrone Miller. He also worked in Coppola's *Rumble Fish* (1983) and *The Cotton Club* (1984), Steven Spielberg's *The Color Purple* (1985), and Spike Lee's *School Daze* (1986), among others. But it wasn't until *King of New York* (1990), in which he played a former drug lord, that Fishburne made a real impact. That film was followed by *Class Action* and John Singleton's *Boyz N the Hood* (both 1991). Fishburne finally achieved leading-man status as an undercover narcotics agent in *Deep Cover* (1992), and his appearance as Ike Turner in *What's Love Got to Do With It?* (1993) scored him an Oscar nomination. Most recently he has appeared in *The Matrix* (1999), *Biker Boyz* (2003), *Mystic River* (2003), and *The Alchemist* (2004). And who can forget Fishburne as Cowboy Curtis in the children's TV series *Pee-wee's Playhouse*?

ROLE REVERSALS

Coppola had offered roles to Al Pacino, James Caan, Gene Hackman, Jack Nicholson, and—yes—Clint Eastwood, all of whom declined. Years later, Eastwood admitted he turned down the role that later went to Martin Sheen because he figured that, with him in the part, audiences would never doubt that the captain could and would kill Kurtz, and might even grow angrily impatient while waiting for Willard to deliver the coup de grace.

Brother of Ben Bottoms, Joseph Bottoms, and Timothy Bottoms, we best remember **Sam Bottoms** as the kid brother in *The Last Picture Show* (1971). In *Apocalypse Now,* he plays the professional surfer who gets more than he bargained for in the jungle. Bottoms has appeared in both film and television in *After School* (1989), *Sugar Hill* (1994), *Zooman* (1995, TV), *Thick and Thin* (1997, TV), *The Unsaid* (2001), and *Seabiscuit* (2003).

BEHIND THE SCREEN

Coppola kept shooting and shooting and shooting, accumulating miles and miles of exposed footage, without knowing precisely what story he wanted to tell or how he wanted to end it.

Back in the bad old days, Coppola claims in press notes for the new and improved *Apocalypse Now Redux*, "we were terrified that the film was too long, too strange, and didn't resolve itself in a kind of classical big battle at the end. . . .Twenty-two years ago, I was under more pressure to make this into what was then considered a 'normal' war film. Now I have the opportunity to widen the focus."

Coppola was required by the Philippine government to destroy the Kurtz compound after he was finished shooting. He photographed it being blown up and decided to use this footage over his closing 35mm credits. The destruction of the compound was later confused as an alternative ending to the film.

It is well known by now that the making of *Apocalypse Now* was fraught with trauma. (Sheen had a heart attack, the Philippine locations were politically and meteorologically unstable, and Coppola was reportedly in

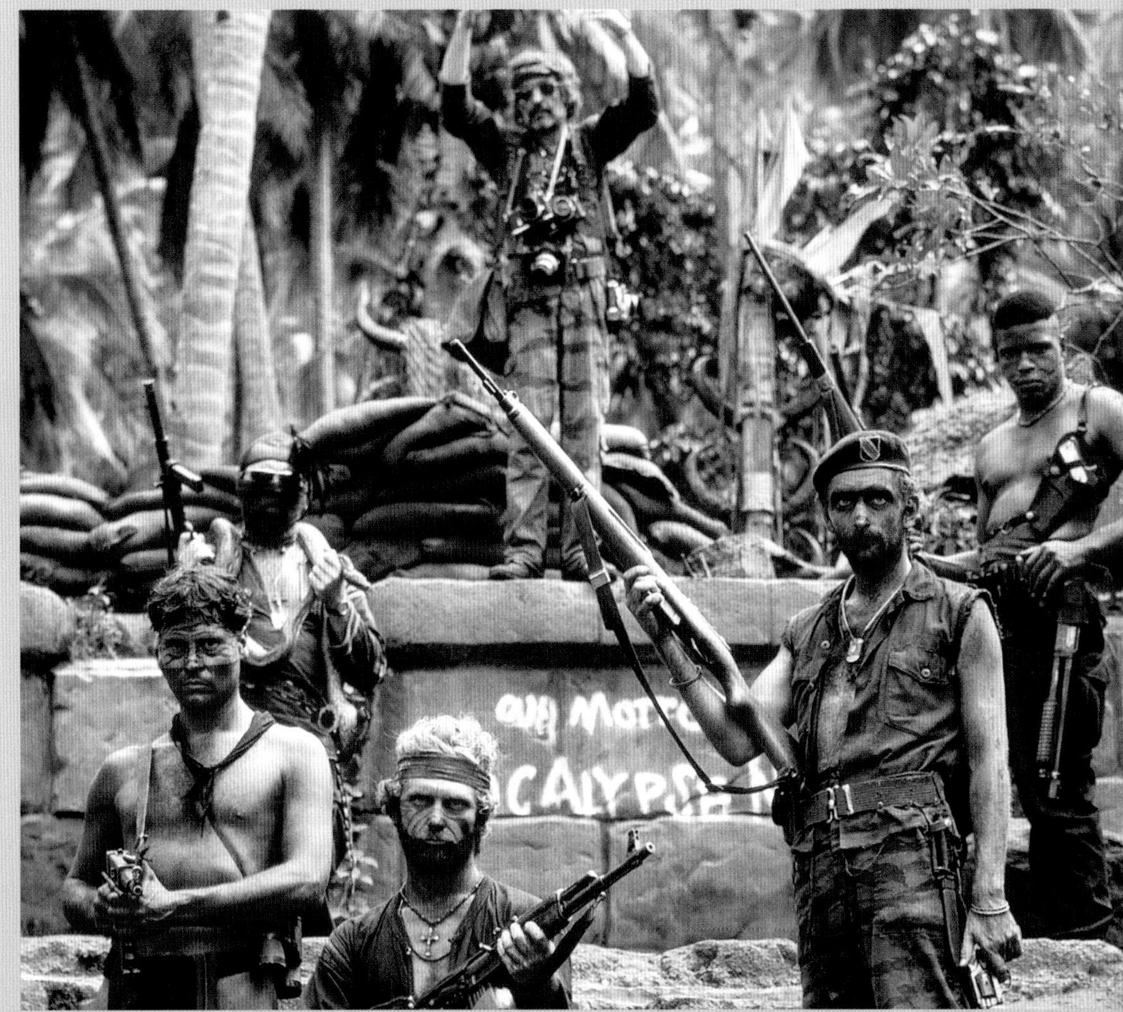

"I was going to the worst place in the world and I didn't even know it yet," says Willard during the journey to Kurtz's camp. Kurtz's undead cultists stand guard in front of his encampment. On top of the pyramid stands the photojournalist (Dennis Hopper) who shares Kurtz's visions with Willard.

a paranoid coke frenzy, to name a few.) Somehow, it only makes the grandiosity of the end result all the more impressive.

George Lucas was originally set to direct *Apocalypse Now* based on a screenplay by John Milius. Lucas's initial plan was to shoot the movie as a faux documentary on location in South Vietnam while the war was still in progress. Coppola, who was to be the executive producer, tried to get the film made as part of a production deal with Warner Bros. But the deal fell through, and Coppola went on to direct *The Godfather* (1972). By the time both men had enough clout to get the film made, Saigon had fallen and Lucas was making *Star Wars* (1977). Milius had no interest in directing the film, and Lucas gave Coppola his blessing to direct the film himself.

Originally scheduled to be shot over six weeks, the filming ended up taking sixteen months.

The cow slaughter in the climactic scene is real.

Ferdinand Marcos of the Philippines supplied the helicopters and pilots. Marcos's government also needed them for fighting the rebels, and sometimes withdrew them during filming, sending back different pilots unfamiliar with the filming.

When Sheen had a heart attack, Coppola was so worried that backing would be withdrawn by the studio and distributor that he kept it quiet, and explained Sheen's hospitalization as a result of "heat exhaustion."

Coppola had recklessly chosen to film on location in the Philippines during the rainy season, and was punished for his hubris when a typhoon destroyed his sets.

Sam Bottoms admits that he was on speed, LSD, and marijuana during the shooting of parts of the movie.

Coppola was unable to find a satisfactory way of ending the film until his wife, Eleanor Coppola, witnessed the Ifugao natives, who were being used as extras, performing an animal sacrifice.

According to editor Walter Murch, it took nearly two years to edit the movie, with an average of less than one cut per day.

THE CRITICS

"*Apocalypse Now* is a stunning work. It's as technically complex and masterful as any war film I can remember." –Vincent Canby, *New York Times*

"*Apocalypse Now* is a mixed bag, a product of excess and ambition, hatched in agony and redeemed by shards of brilliance." –Edward Guthmann, *San Francisco Chronicle*

Lt. Col. "I love the smell of napalm in the morning" Kilgore (Robert Duvall) announces his intentions to run a helicopter attack on a small village (in order to clear the way for good surfing).

Hepped-up renegade and surfing warrior Col. Kilgore (Robert Duvall), whose choppers feature loudspeakers playing Wagner's "Ride of the Valkyries" at top volume, sends his killer clippers off to attack a village so he can liberate the beach for surfing. The chopper swoops down on a yard full of children as Kilgore waxes rhapsodic, "You smell that? Do you smell that?. . .Napalm, son. Nothing else in the world smells like that. I love the smell of napalm in the morning. You know, one time we had a hill bombed, for twelve hours. When it was all over I walked up. We didn't find one of 'em, not one stinkin' dink body. The smell, you know that gasoline smell, the whole hill. Smelled like. . .victory. Someday this war's gonna end. . . ." The sequence is a mortifying display of senseless murder, and yet we thrill at the effectiveness of the technology. When a Vietnamese girl tosses a grenade into a helicopter, vengeance (reluctantly) fills our veins. We're both revolted by the spectacle and energized by its kinetic drive.

THE OTHER LISTS

- American Film Institute (Yes)
- Roger Ebert's Top 100 (Yes)
- *Entertainment Weekly* (No)
- Internet Movie Database (Yes)
- Leonard Maltin (Yes)
- *Movieline* (No)
- National Society of Film Critics (No)
- *Premiere* Magazine (Yes)
- *Rolling Stone* Magazine (No)
- *Village Voice* (No)

17

ON THE WATERFRONT 1954

MAKE MINE A BRANDO

"I was tasting vengeance that night and enjoying it. *On the Waterfront* is my own story; every day I worked on that film, I was telling the world where I stood and my critics to go and . . . themselves." While director Elia Kazan was attempting unsuccessfully to vindicate himself for naming the names of communists in Hollywood, he produced much more than a melodramatic, quasi-documentary about the evils of corrupt unions. Kazan unleashed a force of nature on the screen, a performance by an actor that was not a performance at all but an act of poetic truth revealed. Marlon Brando's Terry Malloy, the inarticulate lug whose simple and improvised gestures—like picking up a woman's glove, placing it on his thick dockworker's hand, and playing with it as if it spoke to him about the human heart—revealed something true about the experience of being alive. If Kazan failed to vindicate himself politically, and failed to make the perfect film, at least he had the judgment to say, "If there is a better performance by a man in the history of film in America, I don't know what it is." Neither do we.

Jim: The question that haunts me: Could Terry Malloy really have been a contender? If only he hadn't been stuck punching guys out on the dock, could he have made it punching them out in Madison Square Garden? The movie wants us to believe the latter would have meant salvation. Brando is far better at playing a loser, anyway. They always get the best dialogue.

Gail: It's tough to think of anything else when you've got Brando's greatest performance on the screen hitting you right between the eyes.

HE PLOT

wn-on-his-heels former boxer Terry Malloy arlon Brando) took a fall for the mob and s never stopped regretting it. He is con- ced by his brother Charley (Rod Steiger), vyer to the union, to take a non-job on the terfront for the same mob union boss who mpromised his future, Johnny Friendly (Lee Cobb). Not knowing he's being set up to ng another dockworker, Joey Doyle, who is ng to break the waterfront code of "d and (deaf and dumb) and testify against the on, Malloy unwittingly sets Joey up to be ırdered. Slow to pick up on what is going , he meets and falls badly for Edie Doyle a Marie Saint), the dead man's sister, who nfuses him by showing him what he has ne. Malloy has a weak sense of what his n powers are and what choices he has in now that he's owned by the mob. But his e for Edie makes him slowly realize what has done, and he grows tormented by his tions. Edie won't sit still for this one and ns forces with Father Barry (Karl Malden), o convinces her that Malloy didn't know out the setup. Meanwhile, sensing that lloy is getting skittish and considering tifying against the mob in court, Johnny nds Charley to kill his brother. He doesn't the job, the mob does it to him, and Terry ds him hanging on a wall. Terry testifies d the reign of the mob ends.

"Boy, what a fruitcake you are!" says Terry Malloy (Marlon Brando) to Edie Doyle (Eva Marie Saint) when she asks, "Shouldn't everybody care about everybody else?"

"Hey, you wanna hear my philosophy of life? Do it to him before he does it to you."— Terry Malloy

THE DIRECTOR

Just after naming names before the House Un-American Activities Committee, director **Elia Kazan** ran an ad in the *New York Times* to clear his name. It backfired. Then he made *Waterfront*. Kazan insisted that the story felt autobiographical, drawing a parallel with his being pilloried for naming names. No dice. Kazan's outstanding work with actors, which allowed for improvisation and was based on the Stanislavki Method, helped to usher in a new, more naturalistic style of acting. Kazan was interested in social issues as well as acting. Most of the cast members of *On the Waterfront* were good stage actors who had been part of the Group Theatre and the Actor's Studio. Kazan's care with actors also showed in such films as *Boomerang!* (1947), *Gentleman's Agreement* (1947, Academy Award-winner), about anti-Semitism, and *Pinky* (1949), about race relations. Kazan's breakthrough came with another Brando film, *A Streetcar Named Desire* (1951, Academy Award-winner). Kazan soon did for James Dean what he had done for Brando in *East of Eden* (1955, Academy Award nomination). He followed that film with *Baby Doll* (1956), *A Face in the Crowd* (1957), and *Splendor in the Grass* (1961), all of which looked like Kazan pictures but weren't as substantial as his earlier films. After years of inactivity, he made a comeback with *Reversal of Fortune* (1990). (For more on Kazan, see page 100.)

With brother Charley murdered by Johnny Friendly for not killing Terry after Terry testified against the mob union, which led to its downfall, Terry confronts Friendly, saying, "You think you're God Almighty, but you know what you are? You're a cheap, lousy, dirty, stinkin' mug! And I'm glad what I done to you, ya hear that? I'm glad what I done!"

THE CAST

Terry Malloy	Marlon Brando
Father Barry	Karl Malden
Johnny Friendly	Lee J. Cobb
Charley Malloy/Charley the Gent	Rod Steiger
Edie Doyle	Eva Marie Saint
Timothy J. "Kayo" Dugan	Pat Henning
Big Mac (Pier Boss)	James Westerfield
Truck (Goon)	Tony Galento
Tullio (Goon)	Tami Mauriello
Jimmy, kid with pigeons	Arthur Keegan
Goon	Abe Simon

THE ACTORS

"You had wires on your teeth and glasses and everything. You was really a mess," says **Marlon Brando**'s Terry Malloy to Edie, remembering her from grade school. Simple observations, but coming out of the mouth of an inarticulate, amoral, brutish ex-fighter, there's poetry in them. There's poetry and poignancy in his entire performance. Brando improvised not only his words but his odd physical gestures. Throughout the film, he seems to speak from an almost preconscious place, and we feel his presence like some force of nature. This performance opened up screen-acting to a naturalism heretofore unknown. He would reach that height only once again, in *The Godfather* (1972). (For more on Brando, see pages 11, 60, and 100.)

As Edie, sister of the slain worker, the blond, angelic New Jersey actress **Eva Marie Saint** awakens the conscience of Terry. Brando's depths of tenderness in turn awaken her love. She helps him to see and he helps her to feel. It was Saint's debut performance, and for her efforts she received the Best Supporting Actress Oscar. Though her star faded rather quickly, she had impact in *A Hatful of Rain* (1957), *North by Northwest* (1959), and *Exodus* (1960), among other films. She would much later appear on television as Cybill Shepherd's mother on *Moonlighting*. Her most recent film appearances include *Titanic* (1996) and *I Dreamed of Africa* (2000). (For more on Saint, see page 30.)

Rod Steiger, in his riveting, Oscar-nominated debut as Charley, plays him with the coiled, quiet desperation of a man who knows he is doing wrong but can see no other way to survive. He is caring when he should be cold-blooded. From his brilliant early performance in *Marty* (1955) to his studio mogul in *The Big Knife* (1955) and concentration camp survivor in *The Pawnbroker* (1965, Academy Award nomination), he went on to win an Oscar playing the redneck Southern sheriff in *In the Heat of the Night* (1967). More recently he has appeared in *Shiloh* (1997), *Body and Soul* (1998), and *Crazy in Alabama* (1999). Steiger died in 2002. (For more on Steiger, see page 187.)

"If you don't think Christ is down here on the waterfront, you got another think coming," says **Karl Malden**'s "takes it on the chin" Father Barry, referring to the mob-murdered waterfront worker. Though his performance is a little histrionic, it has moments of greatness. Malden was a regular in the Kazan repertory, winning himself an Oscar for his role in *A Streetcar Named Desire* (1951). He also appeared in *Boomerang!* (1947), *Baby Doll* (1956), *One-Eyed Jacks* (1961), *Birdman of Alcatraz* (1962), *Gypsy* (1962), *How the West Was Won* (1962), *Patton* (1970), *Nuts* (1987), and *Back to the Streets of San Francisco* (1992). He starred in the 1972–77 TV series *Streets of San Francisco* and was for many years the public face of the American Express card. ("Don't leave home without it!") (For more on Malden, see page 101.)

Lee J. Cobb's piercing eyes and pinched, angry mouth hit the right nerve as mob labor boss Johnny Friendly. A member of the famous Group Theatre, Cobb appeared on stage in Clifford Odets's *Waiting for Lefty* and *Golden Boy*. Though not a leading man, he played strong supporting roles in *The Song of Bernadette* (1943), *Boomerang!* (1947), *The Man in the Gray Flannel Suit* (1956), *12 Angry Men* (1957), *The Three Faces of Eve* (1957), and *The Exorcist* (1973), among others. He was a regular on the television series *The Virginian* (1962–66), and reprised his stage performance as Willy Loman, his greatest role, for a TV version of *Death of a Salesman* (1966).

CREDITS

Producer: Sam Spiegel/Columbia
Director: Elia Kazan
Screenplay: Budd Schulberg, based on "Crime on the Waterfront," a series of Pulitzer Prize-winning articles by Malcolm Johnson.
Running Time: 108 minutes
Budget: $910,000
Box Office: $9.6 million (U.S.)

ACADEMY AWARDS

Best Picture
Best Actor: Marlon Brando
Best Supporting Actress: Eva Marie Saint
Best Director: Elia Kazan
Best Writing, Story and Screenplay: Budd Schulberg
Best Film Editing: Gene Milford
Best Cinematography, Black-and-White: Boris Kaufman
Best Art Direction–Set Decoration, Black-and-White: Richard Day

NOMINATIONS

Best Supporting Actor: Lee J. Cobb
Best Supporting Actor: Karl Malden
Best Supporting Actor: Rod Steiger
Best Music, Scoring of a Dramatic or Comedy Picture: Leonard Bernstein

THE YEAR'S OTHER WINNERS

Best Actress: Grace Kelly, *The Country Girl*
Best Supporting Actor: Edmond O'Brien, *The Barefoot Contessa*

They were all contenders. **Tony Galento**, **Tami Mauriello**, and **Abe Simon**, Johnny Friendly's chief bodyguards, were all one-time heavyweight boxers and opponents of Joe Louis for the heavyweight world title.

THE CRITICS

"Moviemaking of a rare and high order." –A.H. Weiler, *New York Times*

"The director. . .and the writer start out to expose racketeering on the waterfront unions, and wind up trying to make a melodrama transcend itself. They fail but. . .it's a near-great film." –Pauline Kael, *The New Yorker*

NOTABLE QUOTES

"I put on an act sometimes, and people think I'm insensitive. Really, it's like a kind of armor because I'm too sensitive. If there are two hundred people in a room and one of them doesn't like me, I've got to get out." –Marlon Brando

"The only reason I'm here in Hollywood is because I don't have the moral courage to refuse the money." –Marlon Brando

"I'm a workaholic. I love every movie I've been in, even the bad ones, every TV series, every play, because I love to work. It's what keeps me going." –Karl Malden

ROLE REVERSALS

Kazan originally approached Frank Sinatra to play Terry Malloy (and it's a wonder he did, given Sinatra's purported connections to the real-life mob). Producer Sam Spiegel picked the right man: He favored Brando for his box-office power. Kazan said that he felt bad about the switch, but Sinatra "let me off easy."

Cool, blonde Grace Kelly was offered the role of Edie but turned it down to make *Rear Window* instead.

BEHIND THE SCREEN

According to Brando's biographer Carlo Fiore, something about the famous "contender" scene didn't ring true to the star. "The gun-pulling bit hits a bullshit note," said Brando.

Kazan claimed that the only improvising Brando did in the "contender" scene was to say, "Charley," over and over again.

Kazan approached playwright Arthur Miller for *Waterfront*, but when Miller learned of Kazan's naming of names, he turned him down.

Several scenes involving Brando had to be shot separately–the actor periodically had to leave the set early to see his therapist.

Many producers turned down the project, leaving Kazan with no other choice but producer Sam Spiegel, who was himself known as a tough, Johnny Friendly type.

Filmed on location in Hoboken, New Jersey, many of the extras used were real longshoremen from the Jersey docks.

Some of the real people behind the series of newspaper articles on the mob-controlled longshoreman's union became major characters in the film: Terry Malloy was really whistle-blower Anthony De Vincenzo; Father Barry was based on priest John M. Corridan; and Johnny Friendly was based on mobster Albert Anastasia.

Eva Marie Saint's agent made sure she was placed in the Best Supporting Actress race. Both Judy Garland and Grace Kelly were up for Best Actress.

"The only arithmetic he ever got was hearing the referee count up to ten." Caught between the debt he owes Johnny Friendly (Lee J. Cobb) for his mob job and his hatred of Friendly for forcing him to take a fall in a boxing match, Terry stands between Johnny and his brother Charley (Rod Steiger), unsure that there is anyone left he can trust.

"You was my brother, Charley, you shoulda' looked out for me a little bit. You shoulda' taken care of me just a little bit so I wouldn't have to take them dives for the short-end money." In the heartbreaking "I coulda' been a contender" scene, Terry bemoans that his brother let him take the fall in a boxing match he knows he could have won.

THE GREAT SCENE

Some say it was all improvised by Brando, while others say all the actor added was the repetition of his brother's name. No matter. The scene between two brothers, one of whom has been sent by his mob boss to compel his younger sibling not to testify, is as naked a portrayal of human frailty as has ever been put on screen. In the back seat of a cab, Charley points a gun at Terry, who almost lovingly pushes it away with the tip of his finger. In desperation, Charley enumerates his brother's failings as a boxer as if to justify his current troubles. "Look, kid. You coulda' been another Billy Conn. . ." His face a picture of unbearable loss, Terry replies, "It wasn't him, Charley, it was you. Remember that night in the Garden, you came down to my dressing room and you said, 'Kid, this ain't your night. We're going for the price on Wilson.'? You remember that? 'This ain't your night'! My night! I coulda' taken Wilson apart! So what happens? He gets the title shot outdoors on the ballpark and what do I get? A one-way ticket to Palooka-ville! You was my brother, Charley, you shoulda' looked out for me a little bit. You shoulda' taken care of me just a little bit so I wouldn't have to take them dives for the short-end money." Terry's final words are heartbreaking: "You don't understand. I coulda' had class. I coulda been a contender. I coulda' been someone, Charley, instead of a bum, which is what I am, let's face it. I'm a bum. It was you, Charley. "

THE OTHER LISTS

- American Film Institute (Yes)
- Roger Ebert's Top 100 (Yes)
- *Entertainment Weekly* (Yes)
- Internet Movie Database (Yes)
- Leonard Maltin (Yes)
- Movieline (No)
- *Premiere* Magazine (No)
- *Rolling Stone* Magazine (Yes)
- *Village Voice* (No)

18

GONE WITH THE WIND 1939

SCARLETT FEVER

David O. Selznick made Hollywood history by being the first studio chief to actually read an entire book. After doing so, he vowed to the American people that he would faithfully detail every page of Margaret Mitchell's epic on screen. Remarkably, he did just that, thanks in great part to his amphetamine-fueled micromanagement style. The final triumph is the result of three directors, over 20 uncredited writers (including F. Scott Fitzgerald), and the luminous Vivien Leigh, who provided one of the most complex performances in an era of stereotypic female images. She transforms Deep South soap opera into something resembling Greek myth. *Gone with the Wind* is designed big. It bowls you over, from that first, slow roll of the title, underscored by Max Steiner's haunting strains, to the final shot of indomitable Scarlett returning to Tara. Forget political correctness for a few hours and make popcorn.

Jim: A "must-see," at least once. I think it may even be a law in some states.

Gail: It's bigger than life, but we wouldn't have it any other way.

THE PLOT

Scarlett (Vivien Leigh), narcissistic young belle of the O'Hara cotton plantation Tara, is sick of war talk and only wants to marry the man of her dreams, Ashley Wilkes (Leslie Howard). But he's got designs on her sweet-natured cousin, Melanie (Olivia de Havilland). Scarlett isn't one for losing and spits fire, which delights her admirer, worldly Rhett Butler (Clark Gable), who vows to have her one day. The war wreaks havoc on the world they all knew. Scarlett, who'd married on the rebound, is suddenly widowed. Rhett's admiration for her is bolstered when she bravely helps Melanie deliver her baby as the city burns. Rhett helps them escape back to Tara where Scarlett's beloved father (Thomas Mitchell) has gone mad. She takes over the reins, fending off Union soldiers, carpetbaggers, and starvation itself. With war's end, Scarlett's second husband is killed in a raid to "protect her honor." Rhett finally weds her but is tormented by her apathy. When their daughter is killed in a riding mishap, the marriage hits the rocks. Scarlett realizes how much she loves him but it's too late. With a "frankly, my dear, I don't give a damn!" he's off. She determines she'll get him back but in the meantime, she'll find consolation at Tara.

Social butterfly Scarlett O'Hara (Vivien Leigh, far right) is the center of attention as usual, at a party at neighboring plantation Twelve Oaks. During the "Search for Scarlett," one of the greatest publicity coups in movie history, the public was invited to chime in with its favorites. Southerners rallied around one of their own, Tallulah Bankhead, daughter of an Alabama senator.

After escaping the burning of Atlanta, battling romantics Scarlett and Rhett Butler (Clark Gable) share a brief tender moment.

THE CAST

Rhett Butler	Clark Gable
Scarlett O'Hara	Vivien Leigh
Ashley Wilkes	Leslie Howard
Melanie Hamilton	Olivia de Havilland
Gerald O'Hara	Thomas Mitchell
Ellen O'Hara	Barbara O'Neil
Suellen O'Hara	Evelyn Keyes
Carreen O'Hara	Ann Rutherford
Stuart Tarleton	George Reeves
Brent Tarleton	Fred Crane
Mammy	Hattie McDaniel
Pork	Oscar Polk
Prissy	Butterfly McQueen
Jonas Wilkerson	Victor Jory
Big Sam	Everett Brown
John Wilkes	Howard C. Hickman
India Wilkes	Alicia Rhett
Charles Hamilton	Rand Brooks
Frank Kennedy	Carroll Nye
Aunt Pittypat	Laura Hope Crews
Uncle Peter	Eddie "Rochester" Anderson
Dr. Meade	Harry Davenport
Mrs. Meade	Leona Roberts
Dolly Merriwether	Jane Darwell
Belle Watling	Ona Munson

THE ACTORS

Up until *GWTW*, **Vivien Leigh** was most famous for her marriage-wrecking affair with Laurence Olivier. Settled into a Beverly Hills home for the duration, the unwed lovers could only meet covertly thanks to her ironclad morality clause. Leigh was obsessed with Olivier and torn between her own explosive stardom and his fear of being turned into Mr. Leigh. She was working 90 hours a week, risking her notoriously frail health. Her intense dislike of the brusque Victor Fleming didn't help, and she relied on Olivier's coaching in the role. When Olivier saw the completed film he was overwhelmed by her work and told friends, "I could never love someone who wasn't talented." The great romance finally ended and helped drive Leigh to a nervous breakdown. By the time of her second Oscar-winning performance, in *A Streetcar Named Desire* (1951), her world-famous beauty had faded. Her too-short career was significant for two other films, *The Roman Spring of Mrs. Stone* (1961), which featured a young Warren Beatty as an Italian gigolo, and *Ship of Fools* (1965), in which her mad scene hit uncomfortably close to home. (For more on Leigh, see page 100.)

Gary Cooper breathed a sigh of relief when he lost the role of Rhett Butler: "*Gone With The Wind* is going to be the biggest flop of all time and I'm glad it's going to be **Clark Gable** falling on his face and not me." Gable felt wrong for the part from the beginning and Selznick had to wait two years for him to commit. He'd been the public's first choice and that was that. Not much of an actor, Gable relied on his natural personality to shine through on screen. *GWTW* demanded a bit more than that, and the actor was in agony. It didn't help that Vivien Leigh was a consummate actress with considerable technique. Luckily, their mutual dislike came across as chemistry. (She complained that his breath was terrible.) Ironically, Gable's greatest performance came later, at the Academy Awards, where he was thought to be a shoo-in. But before the ceremonies began, he'd gotten a press leak that the Oscar would go to Robert Donat for *Goodbye, Mr. Chips*.Gable remained affable, even charming, betraying nothing of his profound disappointment. He would have to be content with the statuette he'd already won for *It Happened One Night* (1934). Following his service in World War II, he was a ubiquitous presence on-screen in such favorites as *Command Decision* (1948), *Across the Wide Missouri* (1951), *Mogambo* (1953), *Teacher's Pet* (1958), and his last, *The Misfits* (1961). (For more on Gable, see page 109.)

Leslie Howard enlisted as a pilot in the RAF and in 1943 was shot down over the Atlantic. Prior to *GWTW* he'd been England's most famous romantic hero, setting the girls to swoon in such classics as *Berkeley Square* (1933), *Of Human Bondage* and *The Scarlet Pimpernel* (both 1934), *Romeo and Juliet* (1936), and *Pygmalion* (1938).

Olivia de Havilland wept when she lost her Academy Award to history in the form of Hattie McDaniel, the first African-American recipient. Olivia's career thrived afterward with juicy roles in *To Each His Own* (1946), *The Snakepit* (1948), *The Heiress* (1949), *Lady in a Cage* (1964), and *Hush...Hush, Sweet Charlotte* (1964). But Hattie was stuck in the stereotypic roles of maids and suffered the outrage of the NAACP, which considered "Mammy" a giant step backwards.

BEHIND THE SCREEN

Selznick pulled a tremendous PR coup by turning the search for the actress who would play Scarlett into the biggest dragnet since the kidnapping of the Lindbergh baby. Screen tests of every available starlet who could manage a drawl became a national referendum.

CREDITS

Producer: David O. Selznick
Director: Victor Fleming
Screenplay: Sidney Howard
Running Time: 238 Minutes
Budget: $3.9 Million
Box Office: $200 Million

ACADEMY AWARDS

Best Picture
Best Director: Victor Fleming
Best Screenplay: Sidney Howard
Best Actress: Vivien Leigh
Best Supporting Actress: Hattie McDaniel
Best Art Direction: Lyle Wheeler
Best Cinematography, Color: Ernest Haller, Ray Rennahan
Irving Thalberg Memorial Award: David O. Selznick
Best Film Editing: Hal C. Kern, James E. Newcom

ACADEMY AWARD NOMINATIONS

Best Actor: Clark Gable
Best Supporting Actress: Olivia de Havilland
Best Effects, Special Effects: John Cosgrove, Fred Albin, Arthur Johns
Best Music, Original Score: Max Steiner
Best Sound Recording: Thomas T. Moulton

THE YEAR'S OTHER WINNERS

Best Actor: Robert Donat, *Goodbye, Mr. Chips*
Best Supporting Actor: Thomas Mitchell, *Stagecoach*

And then, of course, came that magic day of the filming of the burning of Atlanta. Selznick was interrupted by his brother Myron, an agent, who had a gorgeous, blue-eyed vamp on his arm. "David," he said, "I'd like you to meet Scarlett O'Hara." Vivien Leigh was suited up at once, and the rest is history. Terrific story but full of holes. Selznick knew all about Leigh, and she was high on his list from the start. He hadn't quite made up his mind, but she had. Leigh had determined the role was hers when she read the book in 1937 and was fully prepared when the time came.

Adolf Hitler was so determined to meet his idol, Clark Gable, that he offered a large sum to anyone who could briefly kidnap him and return him safely.

Vivien Leigh's smoking habit peaked during the filming of *Gone with the Wind* at four packs a day.

NOTABLE QUOTES

"Oh, Gable has enemies all right, but they all like him!" — David O. Selznick

"The only reason they come to see me is that I know that life is great–and they know I know it." –Clark Gable

"Some critics saw fit to say that I was a great actress. I thought that was a foolish, wicked thing to say because it put such an onus and such a responsibility onto me, which I simply wasn't able to carry."–Vivien Leigh

THE CRITICS

"The best and most durable piece of popular entertainment to have come off the Hollywood assembly lines. It's the stuff our movie dreams were made on–and mighty durable stuff it proves to be." –Judith Crist, *Atlantic Monthly*

"Is it the greatest motion picture ever made? Probably not, although it is the greatest motion mural."–Frank S. Nugent, *New York Times*

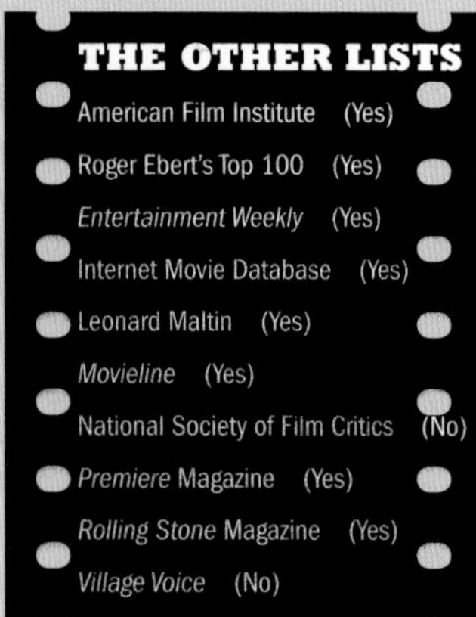

THE OTHER LISTS

American Film Institute (Yes)
Roger Ebert's Top 100 (Yes)
Entertainment Weekly (Yes)
Internet Movie Database (Yes)
Leonard Maltin (Yes)
Movieline (Yes)
National Society of Film Critics (No)
Premiere Magazine (Yes)
Rolling Stone Magazine (Yes)
Village Voice (No)

THE DIRECTORS

The saga behind the direction of *GWTW* could be a movie of its own. First up was **George Cukor**, the famed "woman's director," whose presence on the set delighted Vivian Leigh but made Clark Gable feel neglected. Gable eventually stormed off the set after shouting something to the effect that he wouldn't work with a "fag." (Some trace this to Cukor's having known Gable during the actor's youthful boy-for-hire days, and Gable hating the constant reminder.) Selznick placated Gable by luring away "man's man director" **Victor Fleming** from *The Wizard of Oz*. Fleming hit a wall with Leigh and tempers flared. At one point he rolled up his script, threw it at her, and told her to "shove it up her royal English ass!" Clearly, Fleming was under intense pressure, which Gable proceeded to add to. Gable thought it was unmanly to cry and refused to shoot the scene in which Rhett weeps in Melanie's lap. Fleming finally convinced him to do one take with crying, one without. Gable was forced to admit Fleming was right and agreed to his first on-screen tears. *GWTW* drained the juice out of Fleming, who was obsessed with "getting the damned thing finished." He would never attain such creative heights again. But for all that, his name will be forever linked to the incredible movie year of 1939. (For more on Cukor, see page 178; for more on Fleming, see page 33.)

THE GREAT SCENE

With Atlanta's ramparts about to be breached by Union troops, Scarlett rushes off to find a doctor to assist in the delivery of Melanie's baby. She makes her way to the railroad station that serves as an open-air hospital, and the horrified look on her face doesn't quite prepare us for what we're about to see. The camera pulls back and up, up, up, to show Scarlett in her billowy gown, standing amid a bloody, limb-torn sea of the dead and dying. The shot finally comes to rest on a torn Confederate flag waving listlessly in the wind.

19

TO KILL A MOCKINGBIRD 1962

CHILD'S PLAY

"You never know someone until you step inside their skin and walk around a little." For two young children, walking inside the skin of the victims of racism, poverty, and ignorance proved terrifying in 1932 Alabama, before the Civil Rights movement. *To Kill a Mockingbird* stands as Hollywood's first attempt to strike a knock-out blow to stubborn attitudes about race. More effectively, perhaps, it is a poetic tale about the innocence and maturation of two motherless children who learn responsibility and compassion during one blissful, mischievous, confusing, and dangerous summer in a small Southern town. In the film's meditative opening sequence, a child hums as she looks through a cigar box filled with the charms and talismans of childhood: a whistle, some marbles, an old pocket watch, and a pair of dolls. Everything that follows is filtered through young eyes: Is Boo, the mysterious young man next door, a crazy child killer who lives chained to his bed? We feel the vulnerability of the two young protagonists, as we see what they see. We understand their fear and the admiration they feel for their principled and loving father, as he turns the whole town upside down to defend an innocent black man accused of rape. Bucking the industry norm of the time, *Mockingbird* was filmed in luminous black-and-white, rendering quite literally the film's engagement with shades of gray. The film's quiet and steady lyricism keeps it from sinking into melodrama or sanctimony. *To Kill a Mockingbird* endures as one of the richest and most deft transcriptions of a great novel that we have, as well as one of our most indelible films.

Jim: Who's your daddy? Atticus Finch, we wish. If Hollywood had a Mount Rushmore, Peck's Atticus would be right up there with Jimmy Stewart's Mr. Smith and Sally Field's Norma Rae.

Gail: It's hard to believe we're watching Gregory Peck and not drooling over his striking good looks. It's undoubtedly because we're more captivated by the warmth of his connection to his children.

HE PLOT

summer, 1932, in a down-at-the-heels bama town. Widowed father and incor-tible lawyer Atticus Finch (Gregory Peck) oses his two young children, six-year-old ɔut (Mary Badham) and ten-year-old Jem ilip Alford), to the bitter realities of racism ən he takes on the defense of an innocent ck man, Tom (Brock Peters), charged with rape of a white woman. Though the fires ıatred burn all around them, the children nage to revel in the lazy days on cozy əets, making mischief by menacing Boo dley (Robert Duvall), the strange, elusive ng man in the creaky wooden house next ɔr. Despite threats and pressure from his ghbors, soft-spoken Atticus's devotion to tice prevails—but the outcome of the case, ch is being heard by an all-white jury, is a gone conclusion. Tom is found guilty and, spite of Atticus's brave attempt to safe-ard him, he is murdered by an angry mob. Soon, in a wooded grove, his children, too, the targets of this evil born of ignorance. t in time, they are swept up, into the com-ting arms of their longtime bogeyman—Boo dley. "Boo was our neighbor. He gave us soap dolls, a broken watch and chain, a fe, and our lives."

"There just didn't seem to be anyone or anything that Atticus couldn't explain," says the grown-up Scout in the voiceover that frames *To Kill a Mockingbird*. Gregory Peck's Atticus Finch has become synonymous with all that is noble, just, and gentle—and was his only Oscar-winning role.

"There's a lot of ugly things in this world, son." –Atticus to Jem

THE DIRECTOR

Bronx-born **Robert Mulligan**, although not a household name, comes close to New Wave status but loses it by consistently compromising his edge. He does, however, get high auteur marks for his child's-eye view of the world, his uncommon settings, and an unobtrusive camera style committed to intimate performances. "The trick [in working with children]," said Mulligan, "is to be sensitive to the fact that they're going to get bored." The performances of the three young actors in *Mockingbird* are a testament to Mulligan's ability to win large performances out of small people.

Mulligan won early regard for his TV dramas, which led him to Hollywood where, in addition to *Mockingbird*, he made six films with producer Alan J. Pakula, including his first feature, *Fear Strikes Out* (1957). Other career highlights include *Love with the Proper Stranger* (1963); *Baby, the Rain Must Fall* (1965); *Inside Daisy Clover* (1966); and *Up the Down Staircase* (1967). He came close to capturing an ineffable time but settled for nostalgic romance in *Summer of '42* (1971), which was followed by the memorable mediocrity *Same Time, Next Year* (1978). Some of the magic returned with *Clara's Heart* (1988) starring Whoopi Goldberg, and *The Man in the Moon* (1991), both of which revisit the lives of children.

"She was white and she tempted a Negro. She did something that in our society is unspeakable. She kissed a black man." Daring to speak the unspeakable in a Southern courtroom in 1932, Atticus (Gregory Peck) stands boldly beside the accused, Tom Robinson (Brock Peters)–but the verdict is a foregone conclusion.

THE CAST	
Atticus Finch	Gregory Peck
Scout	Mary Badham
Jem	Philip Alford
Dill	John Megna
Ewell	James Anderson
Mayella	Collin Wilcox
Tom Robinson	Brock Peters
Arthur "Boo" Radley	Robert Duvall
Sheriff Heck Tate	Frank Overton
Calpurnia	Estelle Evans
Miss Maudie	Rosemary Murphy
Mrs. Dubose	Ruth White

THE ACTORS

"The shot that got me the prize was the one where I walk out of the courtroom," said **Gregory Peck** to Robert Mulligan after winning the Academy Award. Peck's natural reticence and intelligence were keys to his performance as the earnest, noble, and moral Atticus Finch. "Greg allowed the kids to come to him. He didn't make a big fuss," said Mulligan. Peck's debut in *Days of Glory* (1944) led to his first Oscar nomination and his star-making role in *The Keys of the Kingdom* (1944). High-profile parts followed, in Hitchcock's *Spellbound* (1945), *The Yearling* (1946, Academy Award nomination), *Duel in the Sun* (1946), *Gentleman's Agreement* (1947, Academy Award nomination), *Twelve O'Clock High* (1949, Academy Award nomination), *Roman Holiday* (1953), *Moby Dick* (1956), and *The Man in the Gray Flannel Suit* (1956). Peck continued his long string of successes with *The Guns of Navarone* (1961), *Arabesque* (1966), *The Omen* (1977), and *The Boys from Brazil* (1978), in which he played Nazi doctor Joseph Mengele. In 1989, he received the American Film Institute's Lifetime Achievement Award.

Nine-year-old **Mary Badham**, at that time the youngest nominee ever for supporting actress, told director Robert Mulligan what it was like to play her part: "It's just like playing in the yard and somebody put a great glass globe around [me] and trapped [me] inside and now everyone's looking at [me]." Her expressive face and restless body showed courage, affection, and delight in her own mischievousness. According to the director, Badham wasn't very interested in acting but she was noticed by agent Betty Boatwright while the latter was down South casting the film. Badham's acting career after *Mockingbird* was minimal, with television roles in *Dr. Kildare* (1963) and *The Twilight Zone* (1964), and in films including *This Property Is Condemned* (1966) and *Let's Kill Uncle* (1966). Badham was pressed back into service in 2005 to appear in a cameo role opposite Keith Carradine in *Our Very Own*. She is currently an art restorer and college testing coordinator.

Mockingbird was thirteen-year-old **Philip Alford**'s film debut, but he had already begun his acting career on the stage, including a performance in *The King and I* under Robert Mulligan's direction. Like Badham, Alford was discovered down South during a talent search for the film. He initially refused the part but relented on condition that he would get to miss school. According to Mulligan, Alford had a hard time with Badham's high jinks, and the two were constantly at odds. Alford's brief acting career–almost exclusively on television–included roles in *Bristle Face* (1964), *Appalachian Autumn* (1969), *The Virginian* (1970), and *Fair Play* (1972). Alford is now a successful businessman.

CREDITS

Producer: Alan J. Pakula
Director: Robert Mulligan
Screenplay: Horton Foote (based on the novel by Harper Lee)
Running Time: 129 minutes
Budget: $2,000,000 estimate

ACADEMY AWARDS

Best Actor: Gregory Peck
Best Adapted Screenplay: Horton Foote
Best Art Direction: Alexander Golitzen and Henry Bumstead

ACADEMY AWARD NOMINATIONS

Best Picture
Best Director: Robert Mulligan
Best Supporting Actress: Mary Badham
Best Cinematography: Russell Harlan
Best Score: Elmer Bernstein

THE YEAR'S OTHER WINNERS

Best Picture: *Lawrence of Arabia*
Best Director: David Lean, *Lawrence of Arabia*
Best Actress: Anne Bancroft, *The Miracle Worker*
Best Supporting Actor: Ed Begley, *Sweet Bird of Youth*
Best Supporting Actress: Patty Duke, *The Miracle Worker*

When **Brock Peters** asked the director how he should play his tragic courtroom scene, Mulligan told him, "There's nothing I can tell you that you don't know about this man." Mulligan praised him most for not playing the victim. Born of African and West Indian parentage, Peters worked his way up from Harlem poverty. His powerful, noble face and heroic quality earned him his first stage role, Crown, in *Porgy and Bess* (1949). His film debut came in *Carmen Jones* (1954), which was followed by *The L-Shaped Room* (1962). He scored a Tony nomination for his starring role in the 1972 revival of *Lost in the Stars*. Peters read the eulogy for the funeral of Gregory Peck on June 16, 2003.

THE CRITICS

"The charming enactments of a father and his children in that close relationship that can occur at only one brief period are worth all the footage of the film." –Bosley Crowther, *New York Times*

NOTABLE QUOTES

"It was a sin to kill a mockingbird because mockingbirds don't do anything but make music for us to enjoy. . . . They don't do one

Tucked cozily into bed, Scout asks Atticus to let her see his watch. Her thin, gangly arms reach out to him as she pulls the watch from his pocket. She opens the cover with awkward fingers and reads aloud, "To Atticus, My Beloved Husband." She whines quietly about Jem's telling her that the watch would go to him someday. "Why?" she asks. Atticus replies, "It's customary for the boy to have his father's watch." Longing for her own treasure, Scout asks what she is to get. Atticus rewards her with the promise of her mother's pearl necklace and a ring. "I've put them away, and they're to be yours." Contented with his reply, she stretches her arms over her head and lowers them to rub her belly. Safe in her bed, with a small, reassured smile spreading across her face, she closes her eyes. She blinks awake and calls out quietly to Jem. "Was she pretty? Did you love her? Do you miss her?" The camera shifts to Atticus, sitting on the porch swing, listening, sad but accepting of his daughter's questions about the mother she would never know.

According to director Robert Mulligan, "Peck grew close to the kids. He taught Philip (Jem) how to play chess. The orphaned Mary (Scout), pictured here, spent time with Peck and his family. She would just fall into his lap between takes."

Jem (Philip Alford) and Scout (Mary Badham) examine another treasure mysteriously left in the hollow of a tree. They later discover that it was the mysterious and ultimately saintly Boo Radley who had been leaving them these talismans.

thing but just sing their hearts out for us." —Atticus to the children

"Some men in this world are born to do our unpleasant jobs for us... your father is one of them." —Maude to Jem

"No director can tell a kid how to act like a kid." —Robert Mulligan

"When Scout says 'Hey, Boo,' that was the reason to make this film. It was the smile from Scout to Boo." —Robert Mulligan

BEHIND THE SCREEN

The role of Dill is based on author Harper Lee's close childhood friend, Truman Capote.

Written on Peck's scripts were the words, "Fairness, courage, stubbornness, love."

"You have a pot belly just like my daddy," said Lee on the set. "Oh, Harper, that's great acting," replied Peck.

Speaking of the strained relationship between actors Anderson and Peters, Mulligan says, "I heard that there was some hostility going on between Brock and Jim. Was it Jim being a method actor? My hunch is that once he got into character he stayed in it. It was threatening to Brock. The only one he talked to was me."

Robert Duvall stayed out of the sun and dyed his hair to become the pale, oddly angelic Boo Radley.

"The studio didn't want to touch this property," explained Robert Mulligan, "until Gregory Peck said, 'I want to do it.'"

THE OTHER LISTS

- American Film Institute (Yes)
- *Entertainment Weekly* (Yes)
- Internet Movie Database (Yes)
- Leonard Maltin (No)
- *Movieline* (Yes)
- *Premiere* Magazine (No)
- Roger Ebert's Top 100 (No)
- *Rolling Stone* Magazine (No)
- *Village Voice* (No)

20

THE SEARCHERS 1956

DESTINY MADE MANIFEST

Director John Milius named his son after its main character, Buddy Holly wrote a song based on one of its most famous lines, and films by such directors as Martin Scorsese, Paul Schrader, George Lucas, and others have revisited its stark storyline, which follows Ethan Edwards's single-minded search for a niece who's been captured by natives. He is tormented by his need to find, but not necessarily save, her, as he now considers her one of "them." A cover story in *New York* magazine on *The Searchers* called it the most influential movie in American history. With its stunning vision of the literal and mythological landscape of the American West, its complex characterizations, and a simple story that speaks to the essence of the American character, *The Searchers* has become nothing less than a touchstone of American cultural history.

Jim: Here's a western even a Harvard graduate could love. It really is about something, and that something is the Eisenhower Era. It is more contemplative than we might've imagined for the period.

Gail: As breathtakingly composed as a Frederick Remington painting, with as many layers of meaning in both form and substance as a great myth. An indelible work of art. Get me to Monument Valley.

THE PLOT

Loner Ethan Edwards (John Wayne) returns home to a family counting on his protection. It's five years after the end of the Civil War and Ethan is still wearing his dusty Confederate uniform. Where has he been? Is the law after him? As his eyes find his sister-in-law Martha's, a secret love passes between them. Has the wanderer returned home to settle down and proclaim his illicit love? Learning that Comanches may be in their midst, Ethan leaves with Martin Pawley (Jeffrey Hunter), a part-Cherokee boy he saved as a child. "Hell, I could mistake you for a half-breed," says Ethan, revealing his fierce racism. Ethan and Martin return home to discover the ranch burned down and the family slaughtered by Comanches, except for one of his two nieces, Debbie, who has been abducted. He and Martin search for the girl, whom Ethan now considers a "squaw." In their travels they come to physical blows over Debbie's fate at Ethan's hands; in a comic moment, Martin accidentally marries a full-bodied squaw; and Ethan squares off with the Comanche leader, Scar. Up until the very last moments we don't know if Ethan will save Debbie or murder her.

It's considered one of the most influential movies in history. In mythological terms, it speaks of the struggle to wrench a civilized society out of the wilderness. It also speaks about the American character, about individuality, and about racism. Ethan Edwards (John Wayne) is the ultimate solitary man. He's eager to return home to his family, and yet he cannot remain.

"I love making pictures, but I don't like talking about them."—John Ford

THE DIRECTOR

"Take everything you've heard...everything you've ever heard...and multiply it about a hundred times...and you still won't have a picture of John Ford." —James Stewart

Having begun his career in silent films, **John "Pappy" Ford** was a master of expressive action without words. He had a unique gift for animating the screen with life and for capturing the poetry of the landscape and the lives of the American West. Already a four-time Best Director Oscar-winner (*The Informer* [1935], *The Grapes of Wrath* [1940], *How Green Was My Valley* [1941], and *The Quiet Man* [1952]), *The Searchers*, his 115th—and arguably his best—film, did not receive a single nomination. Often working with a stock company of beloved actors, Ford could bully them without fear; so great was their loyalty to him...with one exception. Henry Fonda never spoke to the director after a fistfight broke out on the set of *Mister Roberts* (1955). Ford is universally recognized as one of Hollywood's most brilliant directors, and one who mastered many genres, but his westerns ascended to the visionary. About his craft, Ford said, "Anybody can direct a picture once they know the fundamentals. Directing is not a mystery; it's not an art. The main thing about directing is: photograph the people's eyes." (For more on Ford, see page 211.)

Monument Valley is more than a place to director John Ford—who used the location in many of his films—it's a poetic state. It is the landscape from which the American character grew: fierce, solitary, and free.

THE CAST

Ethan Edwards	John Wayne
Martin Pawley	Jeffrey Hunter
Laurie Jorgensen	Vera Miles
Reverend Captain Samuel Johnson Clayton	Ward Bond
Debbie Edwards	Natalie Wood
Lars Jorgensen	John Qualen
Mrs. Jorgensen	Olive Carey
Chief Cicatrice (Scar)	Henry Brandon
Charlie McCorry	Ken Curtis
Brad Jorgensen	Harry Carey Jr.
Emilio Figueroa	Antonio Moreno
Mose Harper	Hank Worden
Wild Goose Flying in the Night Sky (Look)	Beulah Archuletta
Aaron Edwards	Walter Coy
Martha Edwards	Dorothy Jordan

THE ACTORS

Given that Wayne tended to play characters that were very much like himself—solitary, honest, and tough—it's likely that many viewers then and now regard **John Wayne** as the racist he played in *The Searchers.* Nothing could be further from the truth, but Wayne described his role as Ethan Edwards as one of his favorites. Wayne holds the record for the actor who played the most leading parts: 142. Among his other great westerns were *Stagecoach* (1939), *Red River* and *Fort Apache* (1948), *She Wore a Yellow Ribbon* (1949), *Rio Bravo* (1959), *El Dorado* (1967), *Rio Lobo* (1970), *The Man Who Shot Liberty Valance* and *How the West Was Won* (both 1962), *True Grit* (1969, Oscar), and *The Shootist* (1976). Wayne's performance as the tormented loner in *The Searchers* is universally recognized as one of his best...and we couldn't agree more. Of his work with the great director, Wayne lovingly said, "He kept calling me a clumsy bastard and a big oaf and kept telling me that I moved like an ox." Tough love between two tough guys. (For more on Wayne, see page 271.)

"I was told I had arrived when, during the shooting of *The Searchers*, they gave me almost as much ammunition as they gave John Wayne," said **Jeffrey Hunter**, whose youthful performance kept pace with the Duke's. He did so well that Ford cast him again in *The Last Hurrah* (1958) and *Sergeant Rutledge* (1960).

Natalie Wood suffered from a deep fear of drowning after having barely survived a drowning accident during the filming of *The Green Promise* (1949). So great was her fear that director Kazan had to lie—promising a stuntwoman—and trick her into doing the scenes at the water reservoir for *Splendor in The Grass* (1961). Unfortunately, her fear would prove a rational one. Wood died after falling off a yacht, ironically named *Splendor.* Wood won the heart of the American viewing public with such films as *West Side Story* (1961), *Gypsy* (1962), *Love with the Proper Stranger* (1963, Oscar nomination), *Bob & Carol & Ted & Alice* (1969), and *Diamonds are Forever* (1971). She also performed notably in several TV movies, among them *Cat on a Hot Tin Roof* and *From Here to Eternity*.

BEHIND THE SCREEN

Ethan's oft-quoted line from the film, "That'll be the day," inspired the famous song of the same name by Buddy Holly.

The Searchers was credited as a C. V. Whitney picture. The involvement of a Whitney, one of the wealthiest American industrial dynasties, added yet more weight to the film. Ironically, the producer was a descendant of Eli Whitney who produced guns and provided the weaponry for the conquest of the West.

The Production Code Office objected to the scene where Martin takes a bath as Laurie looks on.

The Searchers was one of the first movies to market itself with a "making of" documentary, which aired on TV and was hosted by Gig Young.

In a closing scene, Ethan stands in a wide stance within the frame of the doorway, grasping his right elbow with his left hand. The pose was not called for in the script but was struck by Wayne as a tribute to the memory of cowboy actor Harry Carey Sr., who employed the stance in silent westerns. Consistent with this tribute, director Ford cast Carey's widow (Olive) as Mrs. Jorgensen (the mother) and Carey's son Harry Carey Jr. as one of the sons (Brad).

CREDITS

Producer: Merian C. Cooper/ Warner Bros.
Director: John Ford
Screenplay: Frank S. Nugent, adapted from the novel *The Avenging Texans* by Alan Le May
Running Time: 119 minutes
Budget: $3.8 million

THE YEAR'S ACADEMY AWARD WINNERS

Best Picture: *Around the World in 80 Days*
Best Director: George Stevens, *Giant*
Best Actor: Yul Brynner, *The King and I*
Best Actress: Ingrid Bergman, *Anastasia*
Best Supporting Actor: Anthony Quinn *Lust for Life*
Best Supporting Actress: Dorothy Malone, *Written on the Wind*

THE OTHER LISTS

American Film Institute (Yes)
Roger Ebert's Top 100 (Yes)
Entertainment Weekly (Yes)
Internet Movie Database (No)
Leonard Maltin (Yes)
Movieline (Yes)
National Society of Film Critics (Yes)
Premiere Magazine (Yes)
Rolling Stone Magazine (Yes)
Village Voice (Yes)

When Ethan finally discovers Debbie he chases the terrified girl up a hill. He grabs her, and she looks at him in terror. Though he looks as though he is about to kill her, the moment their eyes meet he says, "Let's go home, Debbie," and we cry with relief.

"When I pass, I want to be remembered as 'John Ford—a guy that made Westerns.'"
—John Ford

Debbie Edwards (Natalie Wood) is protected by the loving arms of her half-brother, Martin Pawley (Jeffrey Hunter), against her uncle Ethan's conflicting desires to rescue or kill her. Debbie, kidnapped during a raid, has grown up Comanche. Ethan's hatred of Comanches obscures his judgment, which makes him see Debbie as "one of them."

In the famous confrontation scene between John Wayne and Natalie Wood, they run up the side of a hill in Monument Valley, Utah, and come down the other side of the hill in Bronson Park, Los Angeles (1,200 miles away!).

Natalie's eight-year-old sister, Lana Wood, played the young Debbie Edwards.

THE VISUALS

One-eyed director Ford (he wore a patch) had a singularly unerring sense of composition. Using dazzling, on-location VistaVision photography, he shot the landscape that shaped the American character in beautifully composed pastoral tableaux. Witness the many shots taken from dark interiors (houses and caves) that open up on the wilderness outside—establishing the distinction between civilization and the terrifying, untamed beauty of the land. The Jorgensens stand in a perfect triangle on the porch with Martha at the farthest point, looking out expectantly with the light illuminating their faces; framed against a monumental butte, the Jorgenson's Texas Gothic-style ranch house looks tiny, vulnerable, and proud; in the dark, silhouetted riders move gracefully across the top of a ridge. Veteran director Billy Wilder described Ford's filmmaking style: "John Ford rarely pans the camera. But when he does, the scene carries a tremendous wallop. Remember the shot of the stage in *Stagecoach* taken from a great height and coming toward you in a cloud of dust? Now the camera pans like fifteen degrees and you see the face of the Indian filling the screen and getting his gun ready. That film was made over 30 years ago. But the scene has never been improved on."

THE CRITICS

"*The Searchers* is arguably the best and most emotionally devastating western ever crafted. Ford came closest in *The Searchers* to edging the poetic majesty of his beloved Monument Valley with a despairing sense of shame."
—Peter Travers, *Rolling Stone*

"It's a peculiarly formal and stilted movie. You can read a lot into it, but it isn't very enjoyable. The lines are often awkward and the line readings worse, and the film is often static, despite economic, quick editing.
—Pauline Kael, *The New Yorker*

RIGHT: Laurie Jorgensen (Vera Miles) rushes to greet her intended, Martin, as he rides up with his rescued sister.

21

LA DOLCE VITA 1961

THE BITTER-"SWEET LIFE"

Federico Fellini shook up the buttoned-down Eisenhower era with this portrait of gasping decadence, Italian-style. Marcelo Mastroianni riding party girls like ponies at an orgy! Drag queens mixing it up with dwarves! American audiences may have feigned shock and disgust, but they stayed until the end. After all, this was art. In truth, it was satirical autobiography, Fellini having some fun with us and himself. In so doing, he also served as a visionary of the paparazzi culture to come. If, as some critics claim, *La Dolce Vita* is about the death of hope, bone-deep cynicism never looked so damned seductive. The actors are stunning and nightlife Rome looks spectacularly hip in plush velvet black-and-white. Warhol could have based his entire life-as-art movement on a single frame.

Jim: This is the one that gave us the jet set, vroom-vroom paparazzi, and sunglasses at night—*Ciao, bella*!

Gail: A visionary work. Its syncopated, frenetic design promises a dance of pleasure and leaves the viewer immobilized in the end.

HE PLOT

ndsome young gossip columnist Marcello bini (Marcello Mastroianni) covers the viable beat of swinging Rome's dusk-to-wn party scene. Along with his regular mpanion, nymphomaniac Maddalena nouk Aimée), Marcello travels in the clusive circles of the gorgeous, rich, and red even as he searches for some meaning his life. He hopes to find it in a vacuous nerican starlet, Sylvia (Anita Ekberg), then a phony made-for-TV religious miracle, and ally in his adulation of a gifted poet named einer (Alan Cuny). The latter proves his doing when he learns the tragic price of tistic integrity." Marcello gives up the ghost hope, tosses away his manuscript for a vel, and descends into the meaningless gy of pleasure for its own sake.

Marcello maintains a steady hand at the wheel. Mastroianni, the actor, approached his career in similar fashion. "I don't understand why these Americans have to suffer so much to identify with their characters. Me, I just get up there and act. It's great fun. There's no suffering in it."

"YOU ARE THE FIRST WOMAN ON THE FIRST DAY OF CREATION. YOU ARE MOTHER, SISTER, LOVER, FRIEND, ANGEL, DEVIL, EARTH, HOME." —MARCELLO

THE DIRECTOR

"Rome had become a big place in the 1950s, full of international types and lots of activity. It was a confusing carnival and I was being shoved along with it, not sure where I was going or what I wanted to do. And I wanted to get all that on film." And with that, **Federico Fellini** began work on *La Dolce Vita*, the film that finally slammed the lid on Italian neorealism. He'd done all that with *La Strada* and *Nights of Cabiria* and was ready to move on. Fellini envisioned *La Dolce Vita* as an episodic misadventure with seven chapters, though he denied the significance of the seven hills of Rome, the seven deadly sins, et al. But there was no denying his affection for symbolism. "Look, it's Jesus!" shout bikini-clad rooftop beauties as a massive religious icon is helicoptered overhead. That's the opening shot and precisely the message Fellini was after: the debasement of tradition with nothing to take its place. While *La Dolce Vita* is ripe for intellectualization, Fellini's approach was far more instinctive than cerebral. His wit could be crass, his images over the top (dwarves, bad drag queens, freaks, bust-clinging nun's habits) but he wasn't afraid to chart new territory. When critics complained that the climactic murder-suicide was left unexplained, Fellini responded, "People are so complicated, so confused and irrational in this age, that there are no simple explanations. The 'sweet life' with its happy endings and tidy resolutions, is absurd." Fellini's first solo directorial effort was *The White Sheik* (1952) followed by *I Vitelloni* (1953), which was the inspiration for George Lucas's *American Graffiti* and served as a particularly strong influence for Martin Scorsese's *GoodFellas*. Next came *La Strada* (1954) and *Nights of Cabiria* (1957), starring his wife, Giulietta Masina, who also led the cast of *Juliet of the Spirits* (1965). *8½* (1963) was the story of Fellini's own midlife crisis played out in grand style, and *Fellini Satyricon* (1970), his fantastical look at Ancient Rome, has since become a cult favorite. The autobiographical childhood memoir film, *Amarcord* (1973), is considered by many critics to be his best. (For more on Fellini, see page 151.)

Rome's premiere gossip columnist, Marcello Rubini (Marcello Mastroianni), begins his nightly rounds in the company of jet-set nymphomaniac Maddalena (Anouk Aimée). As they negotiate their glamorous way through the usual horde of paparazzi, Marcello pretends to be annoyed.

THE CAST

Marcello Rubini	Marcello Mastroianni
Sylvia	Anita Ekberg
Maddalena	Anouk Aimée
Emma	Yvonne Furneaux
Fanny	Magali Noël
Steiner	Alain Cuny
Marcello's father	Annibale Ninchi
Paparazzo	Walter Santesso
Robert	Lex Barker

THE ACTORS

Marcello Mastroianni served as the director's idealized image of himself, in *La Dolce Vita* as a younger, more impressionable Fellini, and later in *8½* (1963) as the more worldly filmmaker. Mastroianni despised his image as a "Latin lover." "I've played impotent, homosexuals, I don't always get the girl." But his numerous real-life romantic exploits with such celebrated beauties as Faye Dunaway and Catherine Deneuve (with whom he had a child) ran counter to the argument. Though his wife never left him, he played out the possible scenario in *Divorce, Italian Style* (1961), then bounced back with *Marriage, Italian Style* (1964), followed by *Casanova 70* (1965), and, perhaps his best late-career performance, *A Special Day* (1977), costarring Sophia Loren. (For more on Mastroianni, see page 151.)

Despite Mastroianni's supposed lack of attraction to costar **Anita Ekberg**, they remained great friends over the years and submitted themselves to a documentary late in life. By then the former Miss Sweden, once called "The Ice Maiden," had lost her battle with obesity. Following *La Dolce Vita*, she made her home in Italy, where she's still considered a national treasure.

Anouk Aimée, the restless nympho, Maddalena, went on to even greater fame and stellar reviews in *A Man and a Woman* (1966) before becoming the fourth Mrs. Albert Finney. **Lex Barker**, who played the faded musclebound star, Robert, unfortunately continued that role in real life.

ROLE REVERSAL

Dino de Laurentis suggested Paul Newman for the role of Marcello. Fellini was appalled, claiming Newman was a "goody-goody, a family man".

BEHIND THE SCREEN

During World War II, Marcello Mastroianni escaped a German POW camp and hid in Venice for the duration.

THE MUSIC

Composer Nino Rota was like the musical hum inside Fellini's brain. Theirs was one of the most intrinsic collaborations in movie history. Rota's haunting score for *La Dolce Vita* not only adds eccentric color and texture, it at times seems to advance the narrative. Very listenable on its own.

THE CRITICS

"Fellini has a deliciously sardonic wit, an uncanny eye for finding the offbeat and grotesque incident, the gross and bizarre occurrence that exposes a glaring irony."
—Bosley Crowther, *New York Times*

"Sacrilegious and obscene."
—The Vatican's *L'Osservatore Romano*

SEND IN THE CLONES

Darling (1965)
After Hours (1985)
Eyes Wide Shut (1999)

CREDITS

Producer: Giuseppe Amato, Franco Magli and Angelo Rizzoli
Director: Federico Fellini
Screenplay: Federico Fellini, Ennio Flaiano, Tullio Pinelli, and Brunello Rondi
Running time: 167 minutes
Box Office: $20 million

ACADEMY AWARDS

Best Costumes: Piero Gherardi

NOMINATIONS

Best Director: Federico Fellini

THE YEAR'S OTHER WINNERS

Best Picture: *The Apartment*
Best Director: Billy Wilder, *The Apartment*
Best Actor: Burt Lancaster, *Elmer Gantry*
Best Actress: Elizabeth Taylor, *Butterfield 8*
Best Supporting Actor: Peter Ustinov, *Spartacus*
Best Supporting Actress: Shirley Jones, *Elmer Gantry*

"I'm very much bigger than I was, so what? It's not really fatness, it's development."
—Anita Ekberg, today

One of the most iconic visuals of twentieth-century cinema is Anita Ekberg, barely contained by her strapless black dress, wading into Trevi Fountain. Fellini was awed by her impassive beauty, though Mastroianni claimed she reminded him of a storm trooper. The scene was shot on a frigid March night, but Ekberg seemed oblivious as she stood soaking wet in the cold. Mastroianni, on the other hand, fended off the elements with an entire bottle of vodka. By the time the cameras rolled, he was completely drunk. In an irony he might've loved, the fountain was turned off to memorialize his passing on December 19, 1996.

RIGHT: Desperate for a reason to care about anything at all, Marcello thinks he might find epiphany in the arms of the ultimate dream girl, Hollywood starlet Sylvia (Anita Ekberg). He'll follow her anywhere, even into the frigid waters of Trevi Fountain.

"IN THE MYTH OF THE CINEMA, OSCAR IS THE SUPREME PRIZE"

—FELLINI

THE OTHER LISTS

- American Film Institute (No)
- Roger Ebert's Top 100 (Yes)
- *Entertainment Weekly* (Yes)
- Internet Movie Database (No)
- Leonard Maltin (Yes)
- *Movieline* (Yes)
- National Society of Film Critics (No)
- *Premiere* Magazine (Yes)
- *Rolling Stone* Magazine (No)
- *Village Voice* (Yes)

LEFT: Following the suicide of his literary idol, Marcello loses all faith. Why pursue his dream of writing the great novel if it will all come to nothing? At a luxurious beach villa, he whips himself into an orgiastic frenzy hoping to dispel any last vestiges of hope.

22

DOUBLE INDEMNITY 1944

HER-FAULT INSURANCE

Walter: Suppose I bust out crying and put my head on your shoulder.

Phyllis: Suppose you try putting it on my husband's shoulder.

Courtship, Billy Wilder-style. It's a crackling battle of wits between two sexually charged burnouts with only an irritating husband and a gas chamber standing in the way of their happiness. Happiness is open to wide interpretation in this early LA *noir* wrought by genre masters at their peak. The book by James M. Cain, and the screenplay by Wilder and Raymond Chandler, offers an astonishingly well-conceived blueprint for murder. It helps that Barbara Stanwyck is the purring engine of this *Fatal Attraction* "psycho fatale" prototype. She doesn't bother making Phyllis sympathetic, instead she opts for calculating, silver anklet-jangling evil. You can't take your eyes off her for a second, it's like watching a predator tease her young before feasting on them. Unrepentant wickedness as refreshing and inventive as a powerful jazz riff.

Jim: The post-murder rendezvous in the grocery store, with Stanwyck in shades, is essential *noir*. The film is highly stylized, slightly absurd, and about the best way to kill two hours ever invented. A single viewing of *Double* isn't enough. Like a great song, you'll want to memorize every line and tough-talk along.

Gail : When it comes to *noir,* they don't get much darker or better than this. The dialogue crackles, Stanwyck sizzles, and MacMurray is the most vulnerable prey.

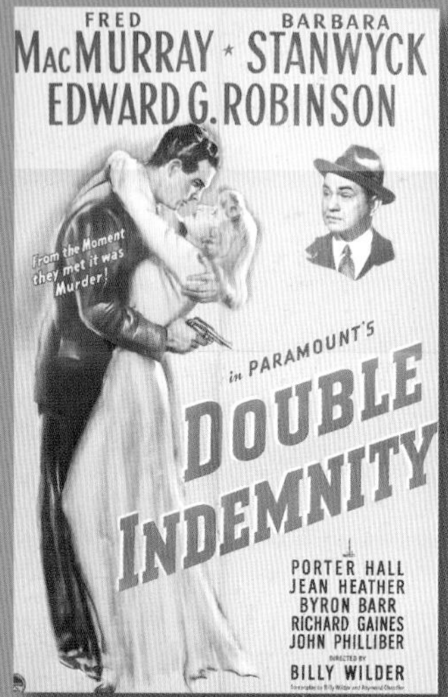

THE PLOT

Insurance salesman Walter Neff (Fred MacMurray) lives the solitary, booze-and-cigarette-fueled life of a confirmed bachelor. But he's anxious to change his ways when he comes upon blond siren Phyllis (Barbara Stanwyck) while making a house call. She plays hard-to-get as she slowly reels Walter in. She's got it in her head to do away with her older, tightfisted husband but she needs a plan. When Walter explains the idea behind his company's double-indemnity life insurance policy, which provides twice the amount if the insured dies accidentally, she's like a dog with a bone. Of course, she makes it seem like it is Walter's idea—and he's happy to kill anyone as long as Phyllis is the prize. Perfect motive for a perfect crime. Once her husband is dispatched as planned, Phyllis's true black-widow nature emerges, and Walter starts to sweat. He tries to back off, hoping to save himself, but that's not part of her game. When his claims adjuster boss (Edward G. Robinson) begins to suspect foul play, Walter knows the jig is up. His only possible hope is doing Phyllis in, but is it also possible she may be thinking along the same lines? Uh-huh.

"They've committed a murder and it's not like taking a trolley ride together where they can get off at different stops. They're stuck with each other and they've got to ride all the way to the end of the line and it's a one-way trip and the last stop is the cemetery."—Barton Keyes

"I killed him for money and for a woman. I didn't get the money. And I didn't get the woman."—Walter Neff

THE DIRECTOR

Billy Wilder was the only first-rank Hollywood director who'd lost his family in the Holocaust, so it's not surprising that his worldview would be something less than cheery. He felt it was his mission to share with American audiences the dark side of the human condition. It was especially ironic that Leo McCarey's relentlessly upbeat *Going My Way* would be *Double Indemnity*'s major rival for the 1944 Academy Awards. When McCarey's name was announced as Best Director, Wilder, either playfully or truly piqued, tripped him as he made his way up the aisle. "Working with Wilder was an agonizing experience and probably shortened my life," claimed cowriter Raymond Chandler, "but I learned as much about screenwriting as I am capable of." Wilder was a script man. The word, once written, was the Bible and took precedence over performance and technical aspects. *Double Indemnity*, along with his other masterpieces, *Sunset Boulevard* (1950) and *Some Like It Hot* (1959), are among the most quotable movies ever made. (For more on Wilder, see pages 24 and 48.)

"Do I laugh now, or wait 'til it gets funny?" Walter considers cutting his losses, but you don't walk away from a woman like Phyllis. Remarkably, Stanwyck had never played a bad-to-the-bone villainess. She would again, at least once more, in *A Walk on the Wild Side* (1962).

THE CAST

Walter Neff	Fred MacMurray
Phyllis Dietrichson	Barbara Stanwyck
Barton Keyes	Edward G. Robinson
Mr. Jackson	Porter Hall
Lola Dietrichson	Jean Heather
Mr. Dietrichson	Tom Powers
Nino Zachetti	Byron Barr
Edward S. Norton	Richard Gaines
Sam Garlopis	Fortunio Bonanova
Joe Peters	John Philliber

THE ACTORS

Wilder on **Barbara Stanwyck**: "An extraordinary woman. Never a fault, never a mistake—just a wonderful brain she had." But Stanwyck was initially wary of the role of Phyllis. "I had never played an out-and-out killer. And because it was an unsympathetic character, I was a little frightened of it." She appealed to Wilder, "I love the script and I love you, but I'm a little afraid," to which he responded, "Are you an actress or a mouse?" She was clearly the former, as her canon of classic films will attest. Among her greats are *Stella Dallas* (1937), *Golden Boy* (1939), *The Lady Eve* (1941), *Sorry, Wrong Number* (1948), *Titanic* (1953), *A Walk on the Wild Side* (1962), and just for fun, her Elvis movie, *Roustabout* (1964). She "retired" to '60s TV as the high-in-the-saddle matriarch of the hit series *The Big Valley*. (For more on Stanwyck, see page 235.)

Fred MacMurray stunned everyone with this performance. He was dubious about taking on the role, having been known primarily as an affable comedian with a quick but slightly insincere grin. In *Double Indemnity*, his solid all-American demeanor serves him and Wilder very well as we witness the dissolution of his already fading morality. He's the friendly door-to-door salesman who falls quickly from grace into the yawning pits of hell. It's a blow to the integrity of Oscar that MacMurray wasn't nominated. He was the object of Katharine Hepburn's desire in *Alice Adams* (1935), and after numerous Westerns and action war dramas, he reinvented his image for a series of Disney classics like *The Shaggy Dog* (1959) and *The Absent-Minded Professor* (1962). He paused for one last "bad guy" role in *The Apartment* (1960) before settling in as the befuddled, kindly dad in the long-running '60s TV series *My Three Sons*.

Edward G. Robinson, the intrepid claims adjuster who smells a rat, might've felt similarly about his own career. A consistently polished character actor with scores of classics to his credit, he was never nominated by the Academy and suffered the humiliation of a House Un-American Activities Committee subpoena. He shot to stardom in *Little Caesar* (1930) and never stopped working. His films include typical gangster fare like *I Am the Law* (1938), epics like *The Ten Commandments* (1956), classic *noir* like *Key Largo* (1948), Westerns like *Cheyenne Autumn* (1964), and cult sci-fi like *Soylent Green* (1973).

BEHIND THE SCREEN

Paramount production chief Buddy DeSylva was horrified by Barbara Stanwyck's blond wig: "We hired Barbara Stanwyck and here we get George Washington." The wig had been Wilder's idea but a month into shooting he realized his mistake.

Double Indemnity was based on a true-life murder in 1927. Ruth Snyder, a Queens, NY, housewife, and her girdle-salesman lover murdered her husband, who had taken out an insurance policy with a double-indemnity clause. The killers were quickly uncovered, and she was among the few women to get the electric chair. A harrowing tabloid photo (taken with a camera hidden in a reporter's pant leg) showed her body recoiling in mid-current.

Fred MacMurray's beefy good looks served as the original model for comic book superhero Captain Marvel.

In 1944, the IRS listed Barbara Stanwyck as the highest-paid woman in the United States, with a total annual income of $400,000

SEND IN THE CLONES

The Postman Always Rings Twice (1946, 1981)
Body Heat (1981)
The Last Seduction (1994)

ROLE REVERSAL

First-choice George Raft would only agree to play Walter if he were written as a "good guy."

Dick Powell lost the part due to contractual difficulties and never stopped kicking himself.

CREDITS

Producer: Buddy DeSylva/ Paramount
Director: Billy Wilder
Screenplay: Billy Wilder, Raymond Chandler, from the James M. Cain novel
Running time: 107 minutes

ACADEMY AWARD NOMINATIONS

Best Picture
Best Director: Billy Wilder
Best Screenplay: Billy Wilder, Raymond Chandler
Best Actress: Barbara Stanwyck
Best Cinematography, Black-and-White: John F. Seitz
Best Music: Miklos Rozsa
Best Sound, Recording: Loren L. Ryder

THE YEAR'S WINNERS

Best Picture: Leo McCarey, *Going My Way*
Best Actor: Bing Crosby, *Going My Way*
Best Actress: Ingrid Bergman, *Gaslight*
Best Supporting Actor: Barry Fitzgerald, *Going My Way*
Best Supporting Actress: Ethel Barrymore, *None but the Lonely Heart*

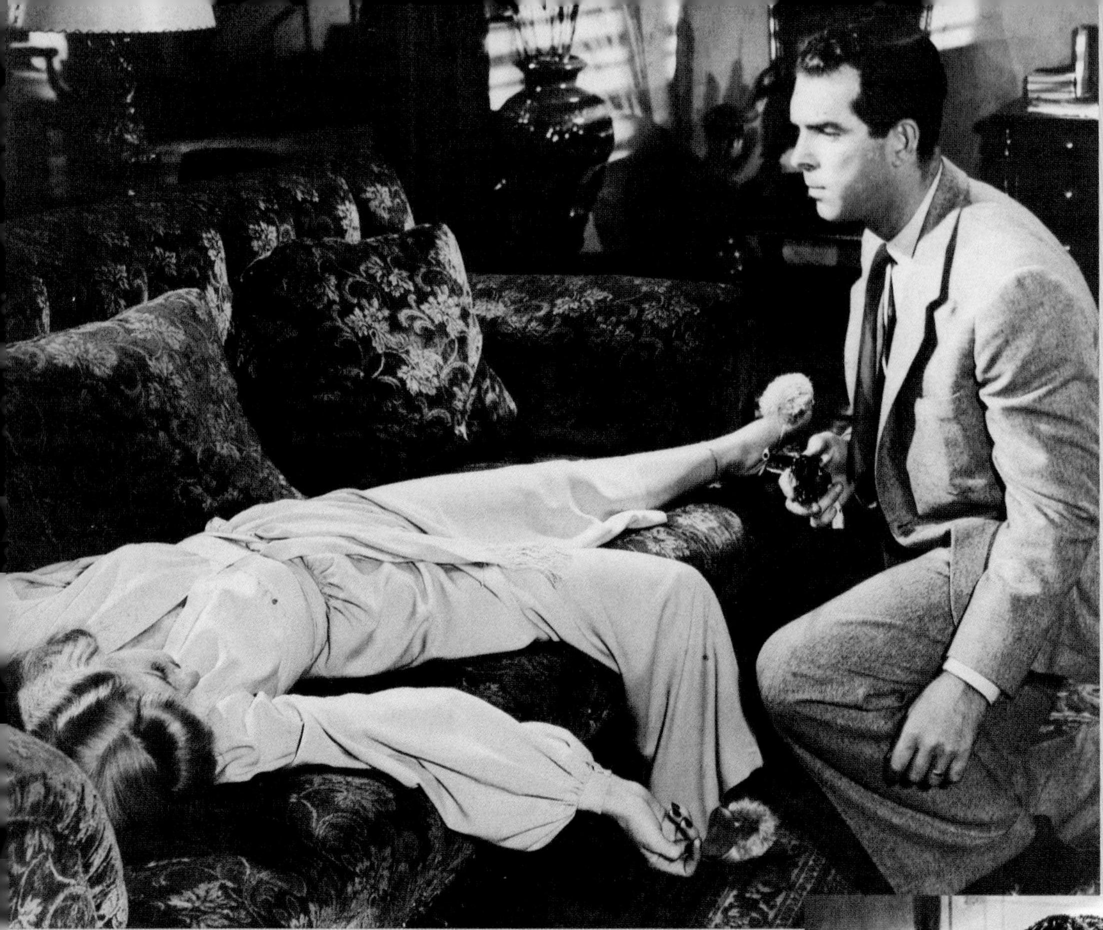

THE GREAT SCENE

"I'm in here, Walter," Phyllis calls out after quickly tucking a pistol beneath her sofa cushion. He enters the room with murder on his mind and closes the window on a neighbor's blaring radio. As he lowers the blinds, he tells her what he's thinking: how her death is the only option he has left. As he turns to her, he takes a bullet. He's somehow not surprised as he moves toward her, daring her to fire again at closer range. She lowers the gun, trembling. He's not buying her act and she understands.

"No, I never loved you, Walter, not you or anybody else. I'm rotten to the heart. I used you just as you said. That's all you ever meant to me. Until a minute ago, when I couldn't fire that second shot."

He easily wrests the gun from her, and her expression widens in surprise and fear as she feels the barrel against her chest. "Good-bye, baby."

"Bye, baby." Walter gives Phyllis the big kiss-off. *Noir* novelist James M. Cain's most famous stories (*Mildred Pierce, The Postman Always Rings Twice, Out of the Past*) invariably take romance on a deadly ride.

THE CRITICS

"With its shadowy monochrome photography and adultery-and-murder plotline, Wilder's film is arguably his sexiest, bleakest portrait of corruption. Nearly sixty years after its release, *Double Indemnity* is still a killer." —Matthew Seitz, *New York Press*

"The very toughness of the picture is also the weakness of its core. The principal characters lack the attractiveness to render their fate of emotional consequences. The ease of [Fred MacMurray's] fall is also questionable. One look at the lady's ankles and he's cooked." —Bosley Crowther, *New York Times*

"I once asked Barbara Stanwyck the secret of acting. She said: 'Just be truthful—and if you can fake that, you've got it made.'"

—Fred MacMurray

THE OTHER LISTS

- American Film Institute (Yes)
- Roger Ebert's Top 100 (Yes)
- *Entertainment Weekly* (Yes)
- Internet Movie Database (Yes)
- Leonard Maltin (Yes)
- *Movieline* (Yes)
- National Society of Film Critics (No)
- *Premiere* Magazine (Yes)
- *Rolling Stone* Magazine (No)
- *Village Voice* (No)

"You're not smarter, Walter . . . you're just a little taller." Barton begins to suspect his protégé, and from the look on Walter's face, already a dead man walking. "I couldn't hear my own footsteps." *Noir* dialogue doesn't get much wilder than Wilder: "I never re that murder could smell like honeysuckle."

23

PAN'S LABYRINTH 2006

OF FASCISTS AND FAIRY TALES

Goya meets Alice in Wonderland in this genre-obliterating tour de force. Guillermo del Toro performs magic as he juggles two improbable narratives: a political fable of brutal fascist Spain and an equally perilous fairy tale. Intermingling dark and shimmering special-effects imagery with an abiding respect for character, del Toro questions our notion of the polarity between reality and imagination. A young girl, Ofelia, confronted by the savagery of her sadistic stepfather finds refuge in the dank supernatural world beneath an ancient labyrinth. The child's fantasy world dazzles with spectacular creatures and terrifying games. It is, however, no easy escape from the horrors of its parallel reality. Del Toro pulls no punches. His film is graphically and unapologetically violent, rendering the audience exquisitely receptive to the seriousness of both cruelty and kindness. Visually seductive, it approaches the magical in its use of every element of filmmaking to give physical shape to the narrative's extreme shifts in emotion. As the film progresses, all schisms begin to merge. External and internal experience blend, defying viewers to determine where one ends and the other begins. After a time, we no longer care. In this labyrinth of a film, there is no end but what we make of it. Without imagination, del Toro is telling us, reality would be unbearable. Without a belief in the impossible, without the freedom to hope in the face of rigidity and terror, life would be senseless and without meaning. Ofelia's mother's warns her intrepid dreamer of a daughter, "Soon you'll see life isn't like fairy tales." Del Toro asks, "Are you sure?"

Jim: This four-star paella of pure evil and transcendent goodness is a rare "instant classic" that hits you in the gut, the heart, and the mind. *Cine delicioso.*

Gail: Del Toro's choreography of every element of filmmaking into an organic, seamless experience leaves you awed, exhilarated, and shaken to the core.

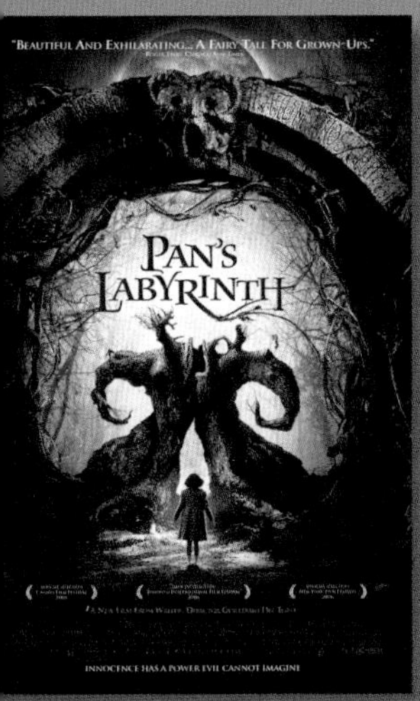

HE PLOT

opening titles read "Spain, 1944." The
' war has ended. Franco's Fascists exult
heir victory as they oppress the country.
ttered rebel insurgents hide out in the
ds and are hunted down by the victors.
ng Ofelia (Ivana Baquero), her arms full
airy-tale books, arrives at a forest outpost
her ailing, pregnant mother (Ariadna
. She meets her new stepfather, the Big
l Wolf captain (Sergi López), and despises
. That night, she follows an annoying drag-
y/fairy down to the center of an ancient
yrinth, where a hairy faun identifies Ofelia
the reincarnated princess Moanna. He
nises her eternal life upon the completion
hree tasks.

Desperate to flee her terrifying new life,
intrepid girl faces dire decisions at every
as she negotiates the twisted labyrinths
rutal politics, a dying mother, a coura-
us housekeeper (Maribel Verdú) who is
ng the rebels, and the denizens of her
lous fairy-tale world. In the end, she is left
nake the hardest choice of her life: sac-
e her baby brother or die. As reality and
gination merge, we are left to wonder, is
world truer than the other?

"My mother told me to be wary of fauns," says Ofelia (Ivana Baquero) to the ancient creature (Doug Jones), but Ofelia is not always a good listener. In her journey through the brutal and forbidding twin worlds of reality and fantasy, the girl finds that, in the end, she can only follow her own voice—for better or for worse.

"Don't you dare touch that girl. You won't be the first pig I've gutted." –Mercedes to the Captain

THE DIRECTOR

"It's the movie I've done that I like the most, that most resembles the things I thought I would do when I began directing." With *Pan's Labyrinth*, **Guillermo del Toro**, the self-proclaimed "Geek from Guadalajara," realizes a vision only hinted at in his previous work. Arguably the world's most accomplished fantasist, whose roots are in graphic design, del Toro has made six features since the age of twenty-nine, debuting with *Cronos* (1995). The artistic precursor to *Pan*, *The Devil's Backbone* (2001) was followed by *Blade II* (2002) and *Hellboy* (2004). Fans were disappointed when del Toro turned down the direction of *Harry Potter and the Prisoner of Azkaban* (2004). Del Toro's cinema is informed by all the arts: Goya, twentieth-century English storybook illustrator Arthur Rackham's gnarled creatures, the symbolist painters, and the more romantic Pre-Raphaelites. His own biography provides rich soil for a vivid imagist's menagerie. Raised by a strictly Catholic grandmother reminiscent of Piper Laurie in *Carrie*, del Toro says she made him mortify himself in self-punishment, placing metal bottle caps in his shoes so that the soles of his feet were bloodied while walking to school. She tried to exorcise from him his interest in fantasy and drawing monsters—but we're glad he remained possessed.

Ofelia (Ivana Banquero) risks reviving the terrifying "Pale Man" (Doug Jones) by ignoring the Faun's warning to avoid eating anything from the banquet table. The moment she samples a grape, the monster stirs to life and the chase is on.

THE CAST

Ofelia	Ivana Baquero
Capitán Vidal	Sergi López
Mercedes	Maribel Verdú
Fauno/Pale Man	Doug Jones
Carmen Vidal	Ariadna Gil
Dr. Ferreiro	Álex Angulo

"Politics is more fantasy that fairy tale. I don't believe in borders."
—Guillermo del Toro

THE ACTORS

"I believe in our duty to deal with children as if they were the ambassadors of a higher culture. To learn from them," said del Toro. Out of the one thousand girls he auditioned for the role of Ofelia, he could not have found a better teacher than the poised and darkly lovely **Ivana Baquero**. Del Toro sent her comics and fairy tales to help her "get more into the atmosphere of Ofelia and more into what she felt." Before her breakthrough performance at age twelve in *Pan* (the youngest Spanish actress to win the coveted Goya Award), Baquero appeared on Spanish TV and in a few small film roles. She will appear in del Toro's next film, *The Anarchist's Wife*, also set in Civil War Spain, due to be released in 2008. Speaking of the *Pan's Labyrinth*, Baquero commented, "At the same time it can bring you pain and sadness and scariness and happiness."

"Captain Vidal is the most evil character I've ever played in my career," said Catalan Spanish actor **Sergi López**. It's a shattering and terrifying performance in which a man's brutality is superceded only by his vanity and pride. Although known primarily as a Spanish actor, López's career took off in France, where he starred as a rootless Spanish immigrant. Perhaps Spain's most iconic villain, he is known to American audiences for his role in a British film directed by Stephen Frears, *Dirty Pretty Things* (2002). He has appeared in both Spanish and French productions alongside some of Spain's most famous actors, Javier Bardem, Victoria Abril, and Spanish legend Carmen Maura. Del Toro has said he is "in love" with López's work.

Maribel Verdú, to whom pinup Web sites are devoted, was cast against type as the earthy, subtle, and quietly powerful Mercedes. Del Toro chose her to play the compassionate revolutionary because he "saw a sadness in her . . . [he] thought would be perfect for the part." International audiences were seduced by her verdant sexuality as the "older woman" in *Y Tu Mama También* (2001). Verdú has appeared in almost fifty films since she started out on Spanish television at the tender age of thirteen. At fifteen, she began her film career in earnest, proving herself as one of Spain's most expressive actresses. In 2007, Verdú was invited to join the Academy of Motion Picture Arts & Sciences.

Doug Jones makes for a disturbing father figure as the gnarled faun who offers Ofelia the possibility of eternal life. (He also played the creepy Pale Man.) Del Toro was determined to cast Jones, with whom he had worked previously in *Mimic* (1997) and *Hellboy* (2004). He sent him an e-mail that insisted, "You must be in this film. No one else can play this part but you." Speaking of his work under prosthetics, Jones has said, "I have to make that a part of my being and my physicality and again, acting is a full body experience and that's a part of it when you're doing a costumed character." The only American on the set and the only non-Spanish speaker, Jones had to memorize his lines in Spanish, as well as Baquero's, so he would understand his cues. Perhaps not surprisingly, Jones started his performing

CREDITS

Production Companies: Tequila Gang, Esperanto Filmoj, Estudios Picasso, OMM, Sententia Entertainment Telecinco
Director: Guillermo del Toro
Screenplay: Guillermo del Toro
Budget: $19,869,000
Running Time: 119 minutes

ACADEMY AWARDS

Best Achievement in Art Direction–Set Decoration: Eugenio Caballero, Pilar Revuelta
Best Achievement in Cinematography: Guillermo Navarro
Best Achievement in Makeup: David Martí, Montse Ribé

NOMINATIONS

Best Writing, Original Screenplay: Guillermo del Toro
Best Foreign Language Film of the Year
Best Achievement in Music Written for Motion Pictures, Original Score: Javier Navarette

THE YEAR'S WINNERS

Best Picture: *The Departed*
Best Director: Martin Scorsese
Best Actor: Forest Whitaker, *The Last King of Scotland*
Best Actress: Helen Mirren, *The Queen*
Best Supporting Actor: Alan Arkin, *Little Miss Sunshine*
Best Supporting Actress: Jennifer Hudson, *Dreamgirls*

THE OTHER LISTS

American Film Institute (No)
Roger Ebert's Top 100 (Yes)
Entertainment Weekly (No)
Internet Movie Database (Yes)
Leonard Maltin (No)
Movieline (No)
National Society of Film Critics (No)
Premiere Magazine (No)
Rolling Stone Magazine (No)
Village Voice (No)

Captain Vidal (Sergi López) requires nothing more than a shot of whiskey before sewing up his own face. Nothing seems able to destroy or even deter this real-world monster.

The courageous rebel housekeeper, Mercedes, struggles with the Captain, fighting to free herself from imminent torture and death. With a kitchen knife she has concealed in her apron, she slashes at his face, catching him squarely in the mouth with the blade and opening a large gash in his face. Stunned and bleeding, the Captain stumbles back to his lair and, with preternatural composure, prepares himself for surgery. Exhibiting the same fastidiousness with which he polishes his boots and watch, he sets about sewing up his own mouth. He readies a small mirror and pulls thread through a needle. After throwing back a shot of whiskey, he begins to stitch with not much more than a wince. The dexterous self-surgery is shocking—but even more so is the fact that we are riveted to the scene. The audience, too, has learned not to flinch, even in the face of unendurable pain and evil.

career as a mime. Well known to television viewers for, among other things, his part on the award-winning *Buffy the Vampire Slayer*, he has made more than ninety commercials and music videos. Without prosthetics, he appeared in *Batman Returns* (1992), *Adaptation* (2002), and *Men in Black II* (2002), before his elegant performance in box-office smash *Hellboy* (2004) won him kudos.

THE CRITICS

"Magic realism leavened with moral seriousness, *Pan's Labyrinth* belongs with a handful of classic movie fantasies: Cocteau's *Orphée*, Charles Laughton's *The Night of the Hunter*, and Erice's *The Spirit of the Beehive*."
—J. Hoberman, *Village Voice*

"If this is magic realism, it is also the work of a real magician . . . *Pan's Labyrinth* is a swift and accessible entertainment, blunt in its power and exquisite in its effects."
—A. O. Scott, *New York Times*

BEHIND THE SCREEN

Cheat: A labyrinth would never have a dead-end, although this one does.

Del Toro sat next to Stephen King at a screening. Noticing the famous author squirming in his seat, del Toro was delighted. "That was the greatest moment of my life," he said.

The film was shot at the height of a drought, though the landscape of the film was intended to be lush and green.

Playing the Pale Man eating the fairies, Doug Jones had to bite into condoms filled with fake blood.

Del Toro, working at an inhuman pace, lost forty-five pounds while making the film.

OOPS!

When Ofelia bites her finger to drip blood into the mandrake, the tube of stage blood she is squeezing can be seen.

In the dramatic scene where Ofelia steals her brother from his crib, he is crying. When she turns around revealing the infant, we see that the baby is a motionless doll.

Upon entering the Pale Man's sanctuary, Ofelia picks up the basket containing the fairies given to her by the faun. When she turns, revealing the inside, the basket is empty.

Speaking of the scene where the doctor, along with the rebels, is coming through the forest, del Toro complained, "We had to substitute a digital head cloned from other frames because the goddamned guy [the doctor] looked at the camera."

Ofelia's despised stepfather (Sergi López) rules his fascist outpost with unparalleled cruelty matched only by his vanity and pride. There's not a speck of dirt on him as he investigates the bombing of a train by rebel insurgents.

24

VERTIGO 1958

FEAR OF FALLING

We are in a state of confusion. Nothing makes any logical sense. Threads of a mystery are picked up and dropped. There is a silent, beautiful woman, Madeleine Elster a.k.a. Judy Barton (Kim Novak), whose blonde hair is spun into a French twist a man could get lost in. Then there is the man, Scottie Ferguson (James Stewart), who suffers from acrophobia, which means that to fall is both his greatest fear and his deepest desire. He falls badly when he sees Madeleine, and pursues her through the streets of a mythic San Francisco. Scottie follows her to graveyards, to the ancient forest of sequoias, and he chases her up the winding, claustrophobic staircase of an old Spanish mission—fearing it is from there that she will take her plunge. Hitchcock is less interested in the mystery here than in the suspenseful struggle between love, identity, obsession, and death. He captured this enigma in cinematic terms that will haunt you for the rest of your life.

Jim: I guess maybe after about 120 viewings you might get a little sick of this one. It's one of those movies (really a filmed dream) you want to put on a permanent disc in your brainstem.

Gail: The visual poetry, the pull of the film's haunting landscape, and its portrait of the human longing for transcendence through love or art sends us down a new and intriguing pathway. Old Hitch is still playing with our heads, but this time he breaks through to our hearts.

THE PLOT

A dizzying rooftop chase that results in a fellow officer's death leaves San Francisco detective Scottie Ferguson (James Stewart) debilitated by acrophobia. Guilt-ridden, Scottie retires from the force and turns for comfort to would-be lover Midge (Barbara Bel Geddes), who tries to mother him back to his old self—but he is no longer sure who that is. Scottie is hired by an old college buddy to tail his suicidal wife, whom he actually plans to murder; the "wife" Scottie follows is actually the man's mistress, Madeleine (Kim Novak). Scottie becomes an unwitting pawn in his friend's murder plot and falls madly in love with Madeleine as the two descend into a macabre game of cat-and-mouse.

"There is no terror in the bang, only in the anticipation of it."
—Alfred Hitchcock

A part of detective Scottie goes down with him as his partner falls from a rooftop while chasing a suspect. In place of Scottie's former stability comes a debilitating case of acrophobia—both a fear of and a desire to fall—that leaves him unemployable. Hitchcock worked many years to capture the psychological state of vertigo on film, which he finally achieved by combining a forward zoom with a reverse tracking shot. Whatever it is . . . it works!

"If I let you change me, will you love me?"—Judy

THE DIRECTOR

Brilliant but notoriously difficult director **Alfred Hitchcock** was given to playing (often sadistic) practical jokes on his cast and crew. Some say the idea for the film was driven by the director's own obsession with Vera Miles (*The Wrong Man* [1957], *Psycho* [1960]), the actress he had wanted to cast but couldn't due to her pregnancy. So incensed at Miles's temerity in getting pregnant for the third time, Hitch told her "that two was sufficient, but that three was really obscene." He tried to replicate her with the many elegant blondes he cast in subsequent films. Novak paid for not being Miles when Hitchcock forced her to do endless retakes, reducing her to tears. *Vertigo*, his most personal film, reveals much about the director's own need for control and his obsession with the feminine "ideal," and about his determination to find in art the possibility to transcend daily life. Hitchcock's stunning output includes *The Man Who Knew Too Much* (1934), *The 39 Steps* (1935), *Sabotage* (1936), *The Lady Vanishes* (1938), *Rebecca* (1940, Best Picture), *Suspicion* (1941), *Shadow of a Doubt* (1943, the director's favorite), *Lifeboat* (1944), *Spellbound* (1945), *Notorious* (1946), *Strangers on a Train* (1951), *Dial M for Murder* and *Rear Window* (1954), *To Catch a Thief* and *The Trouble with Harry* (1955), the remake of his own *The Man Who Knew Too Much* (1956), *The Wrong Man* (1957), *North by Northwest* (1959), *Psycho* (1960), *The Birds* (1963), *Marnie* (1964), and *Torn Curtain* (1966). He returned to the pictures after a hiatus to make *Frenzy* (1972) and *Family Plot* (1976). (For more on Hitchcock, see pages 54 and 106.)

Scottie Ferguson's (Jimmy Stewart) fearful desire to fall in love with the mesmerizing Madeleine Elster (Kim Novak), a shop girl he has physically transformed to look and act like his memory of someone else, keeps him in a constant state of anxiety. Judy will do anything for his love, even if it's not her he actually desires.

THE CAST

John "Scottie" Ferguson	James Stewart
Madeleine Elster/Judy Barton	Kim Novak
Marjorie "Midge" Wood	Barbara Bel Geddes
Gavin Elster	Tom Helmore

THE ACTORS

When **Kim Novak** asked the maniacal director, "Mr. Hitchcock, what is my character feeling in relation to her surroundings?" there was silence on the set. Hitch replied, "It's only a movie, for God's sakes." When Novak complained about her dull wardrobe, Hitchcock retaliated with 24 takes of the attempted drowning sequence. (She couldn't swim and was afraid of the water.) Novak learned never to ask another question of the director. She was not particularly secure in herself to begin with, which proved a boon to her performance. She was so earnest and natural that she slipped through Hitchcock's tight grasp, which allowed her character to became deeply sympathetic. Novak's star shone brightest in the 1950s, when she appeared in a slew of classic American films, from *Picnic* (1955) to *Pal Joey* (1957).

Described today as the "Tom Hanks of his day," **James Stewart** was one of Hitchcock's favorite actors, an all-American Everyman. Hitch and Stewart shared the same agent and the production's profits, cementing their connection from the get-go. Yet, Hitchcock blamed the movie's failure on Stewart, claiming the actor was too old for the part. In *Vertigo*, Stewart played against type as a troubled romantic who loses all sense of the rational by falling desperately in love with an illusion. Stewart held onto superstardom for six decades, performing in such classics as *The Philadelphia Story* (1940), *It's a Wonderful Life* (1946), and Hitch's *The Man Who Knew Too Much* (1956). (For more on Stewart, see page 115.)

THE VISUALS

If you don't feel you're hallucinating the movie hasn't done its job, because that's what the director wanted. Hitchcock kept his camera focused on the older parts of San Francisco so that his audiences would hardly recognize it. He destabilizes us with such shots as the swirling staircase inside the mission, the pull toward the graveyard, and the chases across rooftops, all appearing under an inimitably eerie light. When Scottie first sees Madeleine in the restaurant, the light around her becomes unnaturally bright for a moment. In the bookshop, while Scottie hears the story of Madeleine's ancestor, it gets very dark; when he leaves, the store brightens again. As Judy emerges from the bathroom made up to look like Madeleine, she is backlit by a ghostly green light from a neon sign outside the window. (This color green appears throughout the film, even in the clothes that Madeleine wears.)

Ironically, composer Bernard Herrmann insisted that the San Francisco locale was a mistake (He also thought the idea of Stewart's obsession with a woman was ridiculous).

BEHIND THE SCREEN

The bell tower on the Mission Dolores isn't really there but was added through trick photography.

To get the lighting just right, Hitchcock reportedly spent a week filming a brief scene where Madeleine stares at a portrait in the palace of the Legion of Honor.

Hitchcock spent years trying to recreate the psychological state of dizziness or vertigo on film. He finally achieved it by combining a forward zoom with a reverse tracking shot. The effect is used several times in the film: in the opening sequence, when the officer falls from the roof of a building; and later, in the view down the mission stairwell (a shot that cost $19,000 for a mere few seconds).

The Brocklebank Apartments, where Kim Novak's character resides, still stand at 2000 Mason Street on the northern gable end of the Fairmont Hotel.

Vertigo, one of the famous "Five Lost Hitchcocks" (the others are *The Man Who Knew Too Much* [1956], *Rear Window* [1954], *Rope* [1948], and *The Trouble with Harry* [1955]), was unavailable for 30 years. It seems that Hitch bought back the rights to leave to his daughter. The films were re-released beginning in 1984.

Poorly received by U.S. critics upon its original release, this film is now hailed as Hitchcock's masterpiece.

The famous Hitchcock cameo appears about ten minutes into the film, when he walks past Gavin Elster's shipyard wearing a gray suit.

Due to a Guild strike, the famous score by Bernard Herrmann was the only one not conducted by the composer himself.

THE CRITICS

"There is something very darkly, very deviously funny in the spectacle of Stewart's meticulous effort to remake the shop girl into the femme fatale . . . *Vertigo*, like all Hitchcock films, is an elaborate balancing act, and he has found the means of pouring all the inherent ambiguities of the cinema into our collective unconscious." —Andrew Sarris, *New York Observer*

"You might say that *Vertigo* is all about how a dizzy fellow chases after a dizzy dame, the fellow being an ex-detective; and the dame being—well, you guess." —Bosley Crowther, *New York Times*

SEND IN THE CLONES

Obsession (1976)
Dead Again (1991)

"Somewhere in here I was born...and there I died," says the mysterious Madeleine as she and Scottie stand, overwhelmed, in a forest of Sequoias.

Scottie and Madeleine wander into the giant redwood forest at Big Basin. Scottie, bewildered and half-mad with love, asks Madeleine what she is thinking as she gazes trancelike into the huge sequoias. She answers gravely that she's thinking "of all the people who've been born and who died while the trees went on living . . . I don't like it, knowing I have to die." As they approach the stump of an ancient tree she continues, "Somewhere in here I was born . . . and there I died." Crazed with the bewildering effect of her words and mindful of her vision of suicide, Scottie prods her desperately: "Tell me. When were you born? Where? Tell me! Why did you jump?"

THE OTHER LISTS

- American Film Institute (Yes)
- Roger Ebert's Top 100 (Yes)
- *Entertainment Weekly* (Yes)
- Internet Movie Database (Yes)
- Leonard Maltin (Yes)
- *Movieline* (Yes)
- National Society of Film Critics (Yes)
- *Premiere* Magazine (Yes)
- *Rolling Stone* Magazine (Yes)
- *Village Voice* (Yes)

CREDITS

Producer: Alfred Hitchcock/ Paramount
Director: Alfred Hitchcock
Screenplay: Sam Taylor and Alex Coppel, based on the novel *D'entre les morts* by Pierre Boileau and Thomas Narcejac
Running Time: 127 minutes
Budget: $2.5 million
Box Office: $3.2 million

ACADEMY AWARDS

Best Sound: Hal Pereira, Henry Bumstead, Sam Comer, Frank R. McKelvy
Best Art Direction: George Dutton

THE YEAR'S OTHER WINNERS

Best Picture/Director: Vincente Minnelli, *Gigi*
Best Actor: David Niven, *Separate Tables*
Best Actress: Susan Hayward, *I Want to Live!*
Best Supporting Actor: Burl Ives, *The Big Country*
Best Supporting Actress: Wendy Hiller, *Separate Tables*

Scottie Ferguson (Jimmy Stewart) finds himself falling for a woman he's been hired to follow (Kim Novak)...but is it Judy Barton he's in love with–or the the mysterious Madeleine Elster? Lines blur as Scottie works to transform the needy Judy into his "Madeleine."

"The length of a film should be directly related to the endurance of the human bladder." –Alfred Hitchcock

25

CLOSE ENCOUNTERS OF THE THIRD KIND 1977

FAIRY TALES CAN COME TRUE

We're surrounded by sounds. A din of muffled voices, and behind it, a driving, foreboding orchestration. Together they conjure a force field driving everything in the universe toward some moment…by something outside this world. The enchanted, star-filled skies, dancing lights, and a monumental, volcano-like mountain to which the characters have been mysteriously drawn provide the backdrop for our greatest contemporary science-fiction film, one that recaptures the style of the otherworldly 1950s classics. Part *The Day The Earth Stood Still* (1951), part *North by Northwest* (1959), *Close Encounters* magically induces an awestruck bliss.

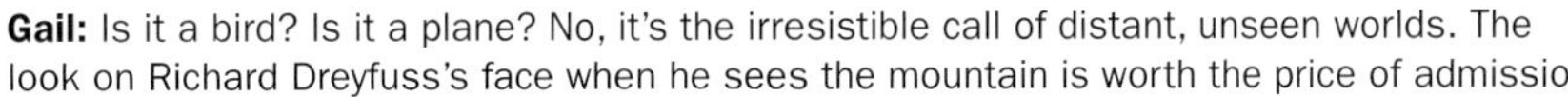

Jim: Call it *The X-Files* for the gentle of heart. The final third is transcendent, so completely beguiling that you can almost feel yourself levitating. It could only have been made in the late '70s, when big-budget Hollywood still allowed room for soulful ventures.

Gail: Is it a bird? Is it a plane? No, it's the irresistible call of distant, unseen worlds. The look on Richard Dreyfuss's face when he sees the mountain is worth the price of admission.

HE PLOT

hild (Cary Guffey) awakens to find his nbal-clanging toy monkey and other toys zing about his room. Drawn by something asing, he runs out into the yard as his ther shouts after him. Electrician Roy ary (Richard Dreyfuss) is called away by company to investigate a power outage d en route is burned by the blinding lights a UFO mothership. Half-mad to learn what foot, Neary terrifies his family when he s to give shape to a persistent internal on, first with shaving cream, then with his shed potatoes, and, finally, with dirt from backyard. "I have to know," he shouts. anwhile special agents are trying to pre- t the public from discovering the extrater- trial visitations by lying about unleashed ic gases. A French scientist decodes a set musical notes associated with the visita- ns, and using those tones, lures the friendly thership to land. Volunteers, joined by Roy, greeted by angelic extraterrestrials and ard the ship. They take off to the sounds of eavenly chorus of "When You Wish upon a r." Take me with you.

te: Spielberg, dissatisfied with the film's ddled midsection, reedited the picture and sued it in 1980 as "The Special Edition."

Little Barry Guiler (Carey Guffey) wakes to find—much to his delight—all his toys buzzing and clanging. He wanders downstairs and out the front door, lured by a beatific golden light. His mother, Gillian (Melinda Dillon), shouts after him but he's already gone, laughing with glee as he follows sounds—it's the extraterrestrials—only a child can hear.

"This means something. This is important." —Roy Neary

THE DIRECTOR

Though we have always loved the movie, **Steven Spielberg** has played Monday morning quarterback to his Academy Award nominee. Now a "grownup" with his own children, Spielberg says, "Twenty years later, I look at (*Close Encounters*) and I see a lot of naiveté, and I see my youth, and I see my blind optimism, and I see how I've changed. . . . I look at *Close Encounters* and I see a very sweet, very idealistic odyssey about a man who gives up everything in pursuit of his dreams—or his obsession. In 1997, I would never have made *Close Encounters* the way I made it in 1977 . . . I mean, that was just the privileges of youth. It's the one film I see that dates me." But the film's magic remains. Spielberg's compulsive attention to every detail was not lost on producer Julia Philips, who described her close encounter with the obsessive director: "It was either too easy or too hard to get Steven Spielberg's attention. That's why he was such a great director: For him it had to be perfect small moments between people, or Barnum & Bailey. Lots of directors were doing small moments but no one was doing the circus quite so well." Later, he would revisit the themes of *Close Encounters* with *E.T. The Extra-Terrestrial* (1982). (For more on Spielberg, see pages 103, 136, 190, 208, and 289.)

Having been blinded—and shaken—by the heavenly lights of a UFO, husband, father, and electrician Roy Neary (Richard Dreyfuss) drives his family to distraction by his sudden obsession with a mysterious volcanic formation, which he tries craft out of everything from backyard dirt to his dinner's mashed potatoes. What he's possessed by—though he hasn't a clue of it yet—is a mountain near a landing strip where a UFO will touch down.

THE CAST

Roy Neary	Richard Dreyfuss
Claude Lacombe	François Truffaut
Ronnie Neary	Teri Garr
Gillian Guiler	Melinda Dillon
David Laughlin	Bob Balaban
Project Leader	J. Patrick McNamara
Wild Bill	Warren J. Kemmerling
Jean Claude	Philip Dodds
Barry Guiler	Cary Guffey
Brad Neary	Shawn Bishop
Sylvia Neary	Adrienne Campbell
Toby Neary	Justin Dreyfuss

THE ACTORS

Richard Dreyfuss etched himself into our collective memories by playing with his mashed potatoes in *Close Encounters*. He'd impressed us before with his extraordinary performances in *American Graffiti* (1973), *The Apprenticeship of Duddy Kravitz* (1974), and *The Goodbye Girl* (1977), for which he won an Oscar, and he would continue to do so in *Tin Men* (1987). Later Dreyfuss spent time fighting off a well-publicized drug problem and making a comeback in *Down and Out in Beverly Hills* (1986). More recently, he starred as an avuncular professor in the short-lived TV series, *The Education of Max Bickford*. (For more on Dreyfuss, see pages 208 and 253.)

Spielberg's requisite child star was four-year-old **Cary Guffey**, whose performance in *Close Encounters* was so professional that only one take was usually required. On the set they dubbed him "One-Take Cary," and Spielberg had it printed on a T-shirt. Quite the realist, Guffey later said, "I don't want the greatest thing I do in life to be something I did when I was four years old." He never quite matched himself, but has had a respectable career in TV and other small movies, including the TV miniseries *North and South* (1985) and the movies *Night Shadows* and *The Bear* (both 1984).

French director **François Truffaut** made his American acting debut with *Close Encounters*. It was fitting casting, since the director's own films expressed his personal sense of wonder about the mysteries in people's lives. He is best known for his trilogy of films on the life of a romantic dreamer (and Truffaut surrogate) named Antoine Doinel (Jean-Pierre Léaud). Truffaut's appearance in *Encounters* lent the film a level of universality. (For more on Truffaut, see pages 94 and 172.)

Character-actress **Melinda Dillon** received an Oscar nomination for her performance in *Close Encounters* and another for her role in *Absence of Malice* (1981). Since making those films she's virtually disappeared from the screen.

Teri Garr, the exasperated wife in *Close Encounters*, has had a career to match. After strong and diverse supporting roles in *The Conversation* and *Young Frankenstein* (both 1974), and major parts in a number of others, she won an Oscar nomination for her performance in *Tootsie* (1982). Most of her subsequent work has been in TV movies.

THE CRITICS

"The final 30 to 40 minutes of the film . . . are what it's all about . . . This sequence, as beautiful as anything I've seen since *2001*, has been deliberately designed to suggest a religious experience of the first kind." —Vincent Canby, *New York Times*

ROLE REVERSAL

The role of Roy Neary was offered to Steve McQueen, Dustin Hoffman, and Gene Hackman.

CREDITS

Producer: Julia Phillips and Michael Phillips/ Columbia/Warner
Screenplay: Steven Spielberg, based on the book *The UFO Experience* (1972) by Dr. Allen J. Hynek
Running Time: 132 minutes
Budget: $20 million
Box Office: $171.7 million

ACADEMY AWARDS

Best Cinematography: Vilmos Zsigmond
Special Achievement Award for Sound Effects Editing: Frank Warner, Robert Knudson, Robert J. Glass, Don MacDougall, Gene S. Cantamessa

NOMINATIONS

Best Supporting Actress: Melinda Dillon
Best Director: Steven Spielberg
Best Film Editing: Michael Kahn
Best Original Score: John Williams
Best Art Direction/Set Decoration: Joe Alves, Daniel A. Lomino, Phil Abramson
Best Sound: Robert Knudson, Robert J. Glass, Don MacDougall, Gene S. Cantamessa
Best Visual Effects: Roy Arbogast, Douglas Trumball, Matthew Yuricich, Gregory Jein, Richard Yuricich
Best Cinematography

THE YEAR'S OTHER WINNERS

Best Picture: *Annie Hall*
Director: Woody Allen, *Annie Hall*
Best Actor: Richard Dreyfuss, *The Goodbye Girl*
Best Actress: Diane Keaton, *Annie Hall*
Best Supporting Actor: Jason Robards, *Julia*
Best Supporting Actress: Vanessa Redgrave, *Julia*

THE 100 RUNOFF

American Film Institute (No)
Roger Ebert's Top 100 (Yes)
Entertainment Weekly (No)
Internet Movie Database (Yes)
Leonard Maltin (No)
Movieline (No)
National Society of Film Critics (Yes)
Premiere Magazine (Yes)
Rolling Stone Magazine (No)
Village Voice (No)

Electrician Roy Neary gets lost on the road when he is sent out by his company to investigate a massive power outage. With his face buried in a map, he laughs to himself, "Help, I'm lost." Slowly, a cluster of bright lights float up behind him. Thinking they are the lights of an oncoming car, he waves them past, but instead they become more intense and rise up like a rocket over his truck. Startled, he jumps ten feet in the air. His flashlight suddenly catches sight of a row of mailboxes, rattling and moving back and forth as if in an earthquake. Suddenly he is bathed in blinding rays, colorful lights appear before him, and a deep musical tone vibrates within his truck. Then, just as suddenly as the commotion began, it stops, leaving in its wake a deafening silence split only by the barking of a lone dog. Just as he is about to get going, Roy looks up through his windshield to see a huge, flying object. A narrow beam of intense light shines down from it. Everything back to normal (?), his radio turns on, and he hears a flood of reports about other sightings.

"Help, I'm lost," cries Roy (Richard Dreyfuss) as he pores over a road map. Suddenly, a blast of light shoots into his truck, the radio starts jumping all over the dial, mail boxes begin swaying, and he realizes something very strange is going on.

The entire world—from India to Midwestern America—has heard the intoxicating five-note call of the mothership from outer space. Researchers from around the world (including UFO expert François Truffaut) finally find a way, through replicating those five notes (from Disney's "When You Wish upon a Star") to safely bring the mothership down to earth. They succeed and the magic moment arrives as extraterrestrials disembark from the ship and the earthbound stand entranced at their anxiously awaited—secret—meeting.

NOTABLE QUOTES

"I think that the Internet is going to effect the most profound change on the entertainment industries combined. And we're all gonna be tuning in to the most popular Internet show in the world, which will be coming from some place in Des Moines. We're all gonna lose our jobs. We're all gonna be on the Internet trying to find an audience." —Steven Spielberg

"Once a month the sky falls on my head, I come to, and I see another movie I want to make." —Steven Spielberg

"I don't think film acting is necessarily a triumph of technique. Film stardom is a friendship that happens between an audience and a performer. Its like you meet someone and you click with that person for whatever reason." —Richard Dreyfuss

BEHIND THE SCREEN

Spielberg claimed authorship of the script when he changed a good portion of the original one by Paul Schrader. Without a name to replace Schrader's, Spielberg took full credit.

Stars from other Spielberg films make appearances in *Encounters*, including an upside-down R2-D2 from *Star Wars* (1977) and the shark from *Jaws* (1975), which can be spotted when Jillian first sees the mothership up close in its hiding place in the rocks.

CBS refused Spielberg's request that Walter Cronkite play the broadcaster, so the director cast ABC's Howard K. Smith instead. The switch was made so late that Walter Cronkite's name is mentioned several times.

Talk about self-referential. When Ronnie Neary cuts out a newspaper article about the UFO sightings, two articles on *Star Wars* (1977) appear next to the UFO piece.

The look of the mothership was inspired by a giant oil refinery Spielberg saw while filming in India.

Cinematographer Vilmos Zsigmond overexposed the scenes with the extraterrestrials deliberately so they would appear fuzzy. When producer Julia Phillips saw the footage, she thought he'd made a mistake and ordered the film reprocessed. The next day, a furious Zsigmond told the lab to reprocess the film again the way he had originally wanted it. (Everything looked fine when they watched the revised dailies.)

Close Encounters holds the record for most cinematographers on a production—eleven, counting those on the special edition.

26

GOODFELLAS 1990

SCORSESE'S MOB HIT

"As far back as I can remember, I always wanted to be a gangster. To me, being a gangster was better than being President of the United States." And with mob informant Henry Hill's defiant introduction, underscored by Tony Bennett's full-throttle version of "From Rags to Riches," we're off. This in-your-face whiplash of a ride tears through New York City's underworld from the idealized 1950s to the druggy, frenetic 1970s. It's the violent flip-side of the American Dream, set to a driving pop beat and populated by low-lifes at the wheel. The movie is so packed with color, grisly humor, and the childish, spontaneous joy of mob life, there's an underlying message that crime, however briefly, pays. When Henry waxes nostalgic, we come oh-so-close to empathizing. The magic here is that even as the movie chronicles the bloody descent of its sleazeball characters, we're in the hands of an urban master of sheer entertainment. Despite its theme, it's a great big delicious movie-movie.

Jim: My favorite Scorsese. The music alone is enough to make you want to follow these wiseguys almost anywhere.

Gail: Scorsese is brilliant in his depiction of both the seductions and the utterly repellant subculture of the mob.

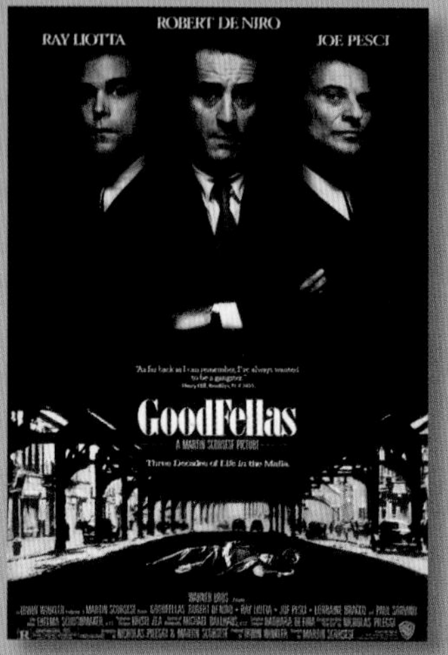

THE PLOT

Brooklyn Irish neighborhood kid Henry Hill (Ray Liotta) longs to be among the glamorous Caddy-driving gangsters he watches from his tenement window. He's soon "adopted" by don Cicero (Paul Sorvino), earns his stripes, and emerges a trusted insider. But as a non-Italian, he can never "make his button," a heartbreak shared by his longtime cohort Jimmy Conway (Robert De Niro). They're part of an inner circle that dances to the tune of psychotic but charismatic Tommy DeVito (Joe Pesci). With so much money out there and so many suckers begging to be taken, the good times roll for Henry and the boys. He's's the star of the show with the right clothes and the right girl on his arm, gorgeous Karen (Lorraine Bracco), whose innocence lasts only until the night he asks her to hide a gun for him. With marriage come responsibilities and a greater need for money. The "biggest heist of the century," an airport job, is in the works, but so is the inevitable greed among thieves. With so much cash on the table, longtime associates are getting bumped off at an alarming rate. Even the untouchable Tommy is gone. It's only a matter of time before Henry runs out of luck. Does he take his chances or turn State's evidence? Henry's life, like a dangerous dream, verges on collapse.

"When I was broke, I'd go out and rob some more. Everything was for the taking." Finally, it's Henry himself that gets taken—by the Feds. But not before one last desperate stop at the diner, his home away from home in good times and bad.

THE DIRECTOR

A child of the old New York neighborhoods himself, **Martin Scorsese** was drawn instantly to the story of Henry Hill, a star-struck outsider fascinated by the glamour of local mobsters. Scorsese knew all these amoral characters so well the set often had the feel of a perverse family reunion. Many of the old-timers, watching from the sidelines and putting in their two-cents worth, knew the real-life goodfellas in question. Scorsese's staccato energy and his ease with actors who speak his language made for a highly efficient, though often improvisational shoot. Pesci wrote and directed the "You think I'm funny?" scene at Scorsese's request. Chief among the familiar faces was, of course, De Niro, whose career has been a mirror to Scorsese's. A film scholar and lover of every form of cinema, high and low, Scorsese borrowed without apology from such diverse directors as Michael Powell, Hitchcock, and Truffaut. The ending shot of Pesci firing his weapon at the camera is a visual reference to *The Great Train Robbery* (1903), whose final frames have the villain, George Barnes, gunning at the camera. (For more on Scorsese, see pages 57 and 118.)

You don't want to push Tommy (Joe Pesci) around. He has a habit of getting even in ways you can't imagine.

THE CAST	
Jimmy Conway	Robert De Niro
Henry Hill	Ray Liotta
Tommy DeVito	Joe Pesci
Karen Hill	Lorraine Bracco
Paul Cicero	Paul Sorvino
Frankie Carbone	Frank Sivero
Sonny Bunz	Tony Darrow
Frenchy	Mike Starr
Billy Bets	Frank Vincent
Morrie Kessler	Chuck Low
Tutti Cicero	Frank DiLeo
Henny Youngman	Himself
Janice Rossi	Gina Mastrogiacomo
Tommy's Mother	Catherine Scorsese
Vinnie	Charles Scorsese
Karen's Mother	Suzanne Shepherd
Sandy	Debi Mazar

THE ACTORS

GoodFellas was a definitive high point for **Joe Pesci**, the only member of the cast to nab an Oscar. His speech was surprisingly brief ("This is an honor and a privilege, thank you."), explaining that he didn't prepare because he had no idea he'd win. He went on to play a slew of tough-guy cameos and a mild comic turn in his most famous other film, *My Cousin Vinnie* (1992). He reverted to slapstick criminality in *Home Alone* (1990) and *Home Alone 2* (1992), but was back to his old threatening mob ways in *Casino* (1995). (For more on Pesci, see page 118.)

A former soap star, **Ray Liotta** fought hard for the role of Henry Hill and finally convinced Scorsese he had the chops. Very particular about the direction of his career, he may have purposely eluded stardom with the forgettable *Unforgettable* (1996), *Cop Land* (1997), and a horrifying turn as the victim in *Hannibal* (2001) who watches his own brains being sautéed. "It would be nice to do a movie where I didn't have to choke the girl to get her."

A former model with a penchant for a tabloid-grabbing personal life (a very ugly breakup with actor Harvey Keitel and an equally fiery marriage to Edward James Olmos), **Lorraine Bracco** found her greatest celebrity as psychotherapist Dr. Melfi in *The Sopranos*, where she is joined by fellow *GoodFellas* alumnus **Michael Imperioli**.

"I don't like to watch my own movies—I fall asleep during my own movies." Luckily, audiences don't feel the same. **Robert De Niro** continues as the screen's most ubiquitous presence, lending his volcanic intensity to everything from *Casino* (1995) to *Rocky and Bullwinkle* (2000). (For more on De Niro, see pages 11, 57, and 118.)

BEHIND THE SCREEN

The F-word is used 246 times in the film (mostly by Joe Pesci's Tommy).

The real Henry Hill was relocated to Redmond, Washington, where he ran an Italian restaurant.

In the scene where Henry and Karen Hill are negotiating to enter the Witness Protection Program, former U.S. Attorney Edward McDonald played himself, reenacting what he did in real life.

Scorsese's mother plays Tommy's mother. She ad-libbed the dinner scene. Scorsese's father plays the prisoner who puts too many onions in the tomato sauce.

Scorsese has been divorced four times, most famously from actress Isabella Rossellini. Among his high-profile affairs are ones with Illeana Douglas and Liza Minnelli.

THE MUSIC

According to Scorsese, it's all about the jukeboxes. These mob hangouts would have the favorite records of the old-time bosses, and only when they died and new guys took over would the selections change. The soundtrack reflects this constant shuffle of power as we begin with Tony Bennett and Jerry Vale and ascend to Cream, the Rolling Stones, and the Who. Interestingly, Sinatra doesn't figure here. A snub or a request? His anthem at movie's end, "My Way," is sung by Sid Vicious.

THE CRITICS

"America's finest filmmaker at the peak of his form. No finer film has ever been made about organized crime—not even *The Godfather*."
—Roger Ebert, *Chicago Sun-Times*

"Is it a great movie? I don't think so. But it's a triumphant piece of filmmaking-journalism presented with a bio of drama. What's missing? We'll, there are no great voices. It has no arc, and doesn't climax; it just comes to a stop."
—Pauline Kael, *The New Yorker*

SEND IN THE CLONES

Reservoir Dogs (1992)
A Bronx Tale (1993)
Trainspotting (1996)
Donnie Brasco (1997)
The Sopranos (TV, 1999–2007)

CREDITS

Producer: Irwin Winkler/ Warner Bros.
Director: Martin Scorsese
Screenplay: Martin Scorsese, Nicholas Pileggi (from his novel *Wiseguy*, based on the real-life exploits of mob informant Henry Hill)
Running time: 148 minutes
Box Office : $48 million

ACADEMY AWARDS

Best Supporting Actor: Joe Pesci

ACADEMY AWARD NOMINATIONS

Best Picture
Best Director: Martin Scorsese
Best Screenplay: Martin Scorsese, Nicholas Pileggi
Best Editing: Thelma Schoonmaker
Best Supporting Actress: Lorraine Bracco

THE YEAR'S OTHER WINNERS

Best Picture: *Dances with Wolves*
Best Director: Kevin Costner, *Dances with Wolves*
Best Actor: Jeremy Irons, *Reversal of Fortune*
Best Actress: Kathy Bates, *Misery*
Best Supporting Actress: Whoopi Goldberg, *Ghost*

Scorsese holds us breathless with a one-take tracking shot during which mobster-in-training Henry sweeps his girl Karen into the hot, hot Copacabana. Henry ignores the waiting line in front of the famed 1950s nightclub and glides in through the back door, peeling off twenties as he goes. He swaggers like a movie star through hallways, kitchens, and finally into the main room, where a special table is rolled out, clothed, and plunked down ring-side just for them. Karen is awestruck ("You gave them each twenty dollars!") as headliner Henny Youngman fires off his first joke.

"One night, Bobby Vinton sent us champagne. There was nothing like it. I didn't think there was anything strange in any of this. You know, a twenty-one-year-old kid with such connections." Karen is clearly infatuated by Henry as they take in a ringside show at the Copacabana.

Knights of the goombah table in "happy" times. But once the big heist goes down and all the greed and double-crosses kick in, few will be left in a seated position. "When they found Carbone in the meat truck, it took two days to defrost him for the autopsy."

"For us to live any other way was nuts. Uh, to us, those goody-good people who worked shitty jobs for bum paychecks and took the subway to work every day and worried about their bills were dead. I mean they were suckers. They had no balls. If we wanted something we just took it. If anyone complained twice they got hit so bad, believe me, they never complained again."—Henry Hill

THE OTHER LISTS

- American Film Institute (Yes)
- Roger Ebert's Top 100 (Yes)
- *Entertainment Weekly* (No)
- Internet Movie Database (Yes)
- Leonard Maltin (Yes)
- *Movieline* (No)
- Nat'l Society of Film Critics (Yes)
- *Premiere* Magazine (No)
- *Rolling Stone* Magazine (No)
- *Village Voice* (No)

27

JULES AND JIM 1961

LA VIE BOHÈME

"I want a film I watch to express either the joy of making cinema or the anguish of making cinema," director François Truffaut once said. "I am not interested in all the films that don't vibrate." *Jules and Jim* stands as the embodiment of the director's manifesto of the Nouvelle Vague (new wave); it is arguably his greatest work. More an experience than an examination, this tragic story about two men in love with the same impossibly enigmatic woman (Jeanne Moreau) moves like a dance. It is in constant motion, always aware, however, of its inevitable end. But what does the femme fatale at the center of it all tell us? Does she speak of the joy or the sorrow of life as a free spirit living *la vie bohème*? Do her shifting moods—from charming and high-spirited to tyrannical and despairing—serve as a metaphor for the spirit of the period between World War I and World War II? Is there a conclusion to be drawn? Impossible. The film is a carousel, spinning with good talk and great friendship, with disappointed longings, reckless passion, and misguided notions. Only one thing is abundantly clear: this witty and sometimes cynically narrated fairy tale is entrancing for its visual and musical poetry, its technical inventiveness, and its loving, humanistic vision. It grabs hold of your heart and never lets it go.

Jim: If you want to say Truffaut pretty much invented the new wave and single-handedly changed the look and feel of film, you won't get much of an argument. It's easy to see the effect of *Jules et Jim* on such neo-American classics as *Bonnie and Clyde*. Even *The Graduate* has a tinge of Truffaut's legacy.

Gail: Scott and Zelda Fitzgerald would have liked this one, with its "pretty to think so" bohemian freedom that spirals into despair.

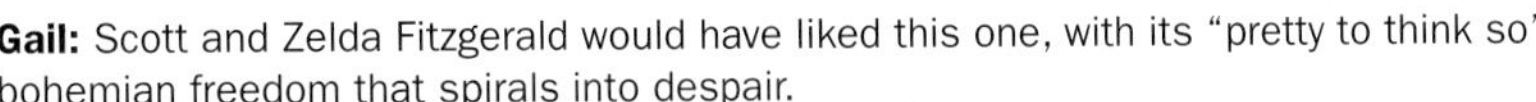

HE PLOT

Paris, 1912, and German-born Jules kar Werner) and French-born Jim (Henri re) are the greatest of artistic and llectual friends. They never tire of each er's company. Upon seeing an ancient ne carving of a woman's head, they fall ove with her lips and vow to find her. The parition appears—lips, flesh, and high rits—as Catherine. For a while the men are their love for this utterly seductive, fling Mona Lisa, a femme fatale of many ods (she jumps into the Seine when she not the center of attention), unsatisfiable sires, joyous energy, and an unreliable art. When Jim sees her favoring Jules, he nerously gives her over to his friend out ove. World War I breaks out just after ir wedding, and each man fears that his nd will appear on the other side of his e. After the war, Jim returns as a foreign respondent and visits Germany to see his nds, who now live in pastoral bliss with ir charming daughter. But Jim can sense mething unsettling under the surface; he s known all along that Catherine could ver be satisfied with one man, even though es is prepared to abide her indiscretions, luding her love for Jim. The men have wn to understand that their bohemian am has ended—but Catherine cannot.

Seemingly carefree and definitely careless, Catherine plays happily with her two lovers, seeing no reason why she should be restricted to one or the other. Jules (Oskar Werner) and Jim (Henri Serre, center) don't see it quite the same way, and try as they might to please her. Each man wants her for his own.

"She begs God to forgive her in advance...and believes he will."—Jules

THE DIRECTOR

Celebrated as much for his film theories as for the ebullient films themselves, **François Truffaut** began by making shorts and working as an assistant to Roberto Rossellini. But his artistic mentor was the poetic humanist Jean Renoir. Truffaut's first feature-length film, the semiautobiographical childhood story *The 400 Blows*, led to the great trilogy of *Stolen Kisses* (1968), *Bed and Board* (1970), and *Love on the Run* (1979), all films featuring the same actor, Jean-Pierre Leaud, as Antoine. One of the proponents of the French new wave school of cinema—characterized by a burst of new energy and spirit and the inspiration for the auteur theory of film celebrating the personal mark of a filmmaker on his work—Truffaut was an enormous influence to his generation. After *Jules and Jim* came a flood of films, including *The Wild Child* (1969), *Such a Gorgeous Kid Like Me* (1973), *Day For Night* (1973), *Small Change* (1976), *The Man Who Loved Women* (1977), and *Confidentially Yours* (1983). Another strain of Truffaut's filmmaking was darker, Hitchcockian works, including *The Bride Wore Black* (1968), *Two English Girls* (1972), *The Story of Adele H* (1975), *The Green Room* (1978), and *The Woman Next Door* (1981). His late films, including *The Last Metro* (1980), combined the two modes of his filmmaking. He died in 1984. (For more on Truffaut, see pages 88 and 172.)

Does Catherine (Jeanne Moreau) cease to exist if she is not the center of attention? So it seems. While the two friends are carrying on a conversation without her, she suddenly decides to throw herself into the Seine.

THE CAST	
Catherine	Jeanne Moreau
Jules	Oskar Werner
Jim	Henri Serre
Gilberte	Vanna Urbino
Albert	Boris Bassiak

THE ACTORS

Jeanne Moreau's greatest role was Catherine the Enigmatic in *Jules and Jim*. Appearing onstage in the *Comedie Francais* when she was in her 20s, she broke into film with Louis Malle's *Elevator to the Gallows* (1958), followed by *The Lovers* (1959). It was clear from the start that Moreau was as mercurial as her Catherine, capable of looking ugly one minute and becoming a great beauty the next. "Behind those eyes and that enigmatic smile is a woman with a mind," wrote critic Roger Ebert. Moreau embodied a new erotic freedom in films made during the 1960s, among them *La Notte* (1961), *Eva* (1962), *The Trial* (1963), *Diary of a Chambermaid* (1964), *Chimes at Midnight* (1966), and *The Bride Wore Black* (1968). During the 1970s Moreau took roles in a number of American films, including *Monte Walsh* (1970) and *The Last Tycoon* (1976), and later in *Going Places* (1974) and *La Femme Nikita* (1990). She stands out in world cinema as a singular feminine icon.

Oskar Werner plays the melancholy, worshipful Jules of the *ménage à trois*, the one to marry Catherine but not to keep her. Primarily a stage director, the soft-spoken Werner also turned his acting skills to a handful of important films, among them *Decision Before Dawn* (1951), *Lola Montes* (1955), *Ship of Fools* and *The Spy Who Came in from the Cold* (both 1965), *Fahrenheit 451* (1967), *The Shoes of the Fisherman* (1968), and, finally, *Voyage of the Damned* (1976). He died two days after Truffaut in 1984.

Henri Serre plays the more sophisticated and world-weary foreign correspondent who is also in love with Catherine, but with more or less open eyes. Little known to American audiences, Serre appeared in only two other films released in the U.S., *Street of the Crane's Foot* (1979) and *The Army Game* (1961).

THE CRITICS

"Elliptical, full of wit and radiance, this is the best movie ever made about what most of us think of as the Scott Fitzgerald period."
—Pauline Kael, *The New Yorker*

CREDITS

Producer: Marcel Berbert (uncredited)/Janus Films
Director: Francois Truffaut
Screenplay: Francois Truffaut, Jean Gruault, based on the novel by Henri-Pierre Roche
Running Time: 104 minutes

ACADEMY AWARD NOMINATIONS

Best Film Editing: Ferris Webster

THE YEAR'S WINNERS

Best Picture: *West Side Story*
Best Director: Robert Wise and Jerome Robbins, *West Side Story*
Best Actor: Maximilian Schell, *Judgment at Nuremberg*
Best Actress: Sophia Loren, *Two Women*
Best Supporting Actor: George Chakiris, *West Side Story*
Best Supporting Actress: Rita Moreno, *West Side Story*

Catherine grows increasingly despondent as the free-and-happy life continues to elude her. Though she is married to Jules and has a child with him, she continues to play musical beds, spending the night with Jim and professing her love for him.

Powerful scenes follow one after the other with a brevity that takes your breath away. In one scene Catherine sings a jaunty yet melancholy song she wrote. Sometimes she smiles, sometimes she closes her eyes breathing in the sadness, other times she smiles gaily and knowingly. Time, for once, seems to stop.

We met with a kiss
A hit, then a miss
It wasn't all bliss
Together we make our ways
In life's whirlpool of days
We go round and round
Together bound, together bound

TRUFFAUT ON DIRECTING

"I wanted the film to look like an album of old photographs."

"[Catherine] is totally fabulous. If you met such a woman in real life, you would see in her only faults—which the film ignores."

"You know what a French psychiatrist said: '*Jules and Jim* is about two children in love with their mother.'"

"One proceeds always by contrasts. If the situation is extraordinary, then one must force the actors to be naturalistic, and vice versa."

THE OTHER LISTS

- American Film Institute (No)
- Roger Ebert's Top 100 (No)
- *Entertainment Weekly* (Yes)
- Internet Movie Database (No)
- Leonard Maltin (No)
- *Movieline* (Yes)
- National Society of Film Critics (No)
- *Premiere* Magazine (Yes)
- *Rolling Stone* Magazine (No)
- *Village Voice* (Yes)

28

FUNNY FACE 1957

S'MARVELOUS

"Banish the black, burn the blue, and bury the beige—think pink!" And with that, we're off and dancing. From the inner sanctum of Manhattan's fashionista elite to the Champs Élysées and the top of the Eiffel Tower, this is undiluted Cinderella-time. The cliché is transformed by the magical presence of Audrey Hepburn, in the springtime of her career, and a still-formidable Fred Astaire in the late autumn of his. A teenager might find it hard to keep up as Fred hangs from a balcony rail and tangles with an imaginary bull with a sweep of a red satin-lined raincoat. Make that a very talented teenager. Writer Leonard Gershe was inspired by anecdotes of *Vogue*'s eccentric diva, editor in chief Diana Vreeland, and the legendary fashion photographer, Richard Avedon, whose wife, Doe, had been a model ambivalent about her career. It seemed like an unbeatable idea for a movie musical, and after putting the screenplay together, Gershe couldn't get himself arrested. It bounced around for years until falling into the lap of director Stanley Donen and producer Roger Edens, who knew just where to take it from there. With a major assist from one of the best scores George and Ira Gershwin ever wrote, and some very lucky casting (the singular Kay Thompson is more like a lucky weather front!), they were off. *Funny Face* is an ageless, delectable froth of a film, too substantive, to be a guilty pleasure. You can enjoy this one right out in the open. The kids may initially giggle at the '50s mannered gloss—but not for long. "*S'awful nice, s'paradise.*"

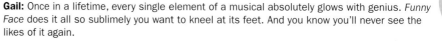

Jim: Just beneath the film's beautiful surface is that well of Hepburn wistfulness that makes you want to rush in and rescue her—from a big modeling career and true love! How empathetic is that? Bet you can't watch this one just once.

Gail: Once in a lifetime, every single element of a musical absolutely glows with genius. *Funny Face* does it all so sublimely you want to kneel at its feet. And you know you'll never see the likes of it again.

THE PLOT

Maggie Prescott (Kay Thompson), imperious editor in chief of *Quality* magazine, is bored, bored, bored by the latest issue. It needs oomph and "bizzazz!" At her command, the world is transformed into pink. Now, how about an issue devoted to the intelligent woman who hates to dress up. Along with ace photographer Dick Avery (Fred Astaire) and her creative team, Maggie invades one of those "dreary bookshops in Greenwich Village." They overwhelm the studious salesgirl, Jo Stockton (Audrey Hepburn). Dick is taken in by Jo's gamine charm and has a sudden urge to kiss her. Her world is abruptly transformed by love. Back at *Quality*, Dick convinces Maggie they've found their new golden girl in Jo. Maggie scoffs until he shows her a blowup shot from the bookstore. Jo is convinced to go along to Paris for a major fashion splash featuring the new collection of Paul Duval (Robert Flemyng). It will provide her with the chance to meet her philosophical hero, Flostre, in the Beatnik environs of Montmartre. She is devastated when Flostre's interest in her is revealed to be more physical than intellectual. She realizes that Dick is the only philosophy she needs. She rushes headlong into his arms to the lushly romantic strains of "S'Wonderful" and the glamorous fashion career that awaits her.

"Think pink!" Or red, if you happen to think Kay Thompson got robbed of a Best Supporting Oscar nomination. As the larger-than-life fashion editor Maggie Prescott, she makes *Funny Face* look like it's shot in 3-D when she's on-screen. Her talent and vitality are almost uncontainable.

"When I get through with you, you'll look like—what do you call beautiful ... a tree? You'll look like a tree."—Dick Avery

THE DIRECTOR

Stanley Donen's fearless camera, which at times seems to be tapping its tripod to the music, brought exterior shots to the big Hollywood musicals. *On The Town* (1948) was a benchmark—from the first second that its heroes debark at the Brooklyn Navy Yard, you know you're not on a tricked-out backlot. This is song and dance against the unmistakable palette of real life. In *Funny Face*, Donen's deep and abiding affection for Paris, Astaire, and Hepburn makes it impossible not to join in the love-fest. The weather helps capture the city's many moods, turning from sun to rain to fog and back again. Donen is most closely identified with Gene Kelly, having directed him in the hands-down classic *Singin' in the Rain* (1952). He'd worked with Astaire previously in *Royal Wedding* (1951), and would later direct Hepburn in two of her signature films, *Charade* (1963) and *Two for the Road* (1967). (For more on Stanley Donen, see page 42.)

Dig that crazy Empathicalism! Jo needs to free her inner-turmoil by escaping the fashion houses, dressing in black and dancing like a wild child to Stanley Donen's feline choreography. Hepburn's training as a ballerina is made gracefully apparent.

THE CAST

Jo Stockton	Audrey Hepburn
Dick Avery	Fred Astaire
Maggie Prescott	Kay Thompson
Professor Emile Flostre	Michel Auclair
Paul Duval	Robert Flemyng
Marion	Dovima
Specialty Dancer	Suzy Parker
Specialty Dancer	Sunny Hartnett
Hairdresser	Jean Del Val
Babs	Virginia Gibson
Laura	Sue England
Lettie	Ruta Lee
Dovitch	Alex Gerry
Armande	Iphigenie Castiglioni

THE ACTORS

"I was asked to act when I couldn't act. I was asked to sing "Funny Face" when I couldn't sing, and dance with Fred Astaire when I couldn't dance and do all kinds of things I wasn't prepared for. Then I tried like mad to cope with it." The daughter of a banker and Belgian countess, **Audrey Hepburn**'s much-envied thinness was the result of malnutrition suffered during World War II. She launched a dancing/modeling career in London in the late 1940s, and her steely ambition served her well. Discovered by the French author Colette, who chose her to star in the Broadway production of *Gigi* (1951), Hepburn was off and running, snagging an Oscar her first time out for *Roman Holiday* (1953). From there on it was magic time, at least on the screen, with *Sabrina* (1954), *War and Peace* (1956), *Love in the Afternoon* (1957), *Funny Face*, and *The Nun's Story* (1959) in quick succession. An iconic turn as Holly Golightly (a part that had been written for Marilyn Monroe) in *Breakfast at Tiffany's* (1961) fixed Hepburn's image forever as the wistful, ultra-stylish Bohemian with the dangling cigarette holder. She easily charmed Cary Grant in *Charade* (1963) but part two of her career came at the expense of two unhappy marriages and a minor scandal about her choice as Eliza in *My Fair Lady* (1964). It cost her an Oscar nomination and earned the wrath of the millions who had been pulling for Julie Andrews in the role she'd created. Hepburn responded with a top-drawer thriller in which she played a victimized blind woman, *Wait Until Dark* (1967), and a trenchant romantic comedy/drama, *Two for the Road* (1967), before a long retirement as Goodwill Ambassador for UNICEF. She made a comeback costarring with Sean Connery in *Robin and Marian* (1976) and a few forgettable TV miniseries before her untimely death on the eve of her 1993 Honorary Oscar. (For more on Hepburn, see page 178.)

After David O. Selznick viewed **Fred Astaire**'s screen test, he determined, "I am a little uncertain about the man, but I feel, in spite of his enormous ears and bad chin line, that his charm is so tremendous that it comes through even in this wretched test." Despite Astaire's vow that "I did not go into pictures to be part of a team," he will forever be remembered with a girl on his arm—most often, Ginger Rogers—in ten films beginning with *Flying Down to Rio* (1933). Along the way, he tapped, swooped, and spun with Joan Crawford in *Dancing Lady* (1933), Judy Garland and Ann Miller in *Easter Parade* (1948), and Cyd Charisse in *The Band Wagon* (1953). But there were also those mesmerizing solo turns in a ship's engine room to the contagious rhythm of "Slap That Bass," and dancing on the ceiling in *Royal Wedding* (1951). His singing seemed as offhanded and unaffected as his dancing, but he was a severe taskmaster who insisted, "choreography on screen is 80 percent brain work and 20 percent footwork." (For more on Astaire, see page 154.)

"I've discovered the secret of life. A lot of hard work, a lot of sense of humor, a lot of joy and a whole lot of *tra la la*." As a vocal coach at producer Arthur Freed's MGM Music Unit, **Kay Thompson** essentially taught Judy Garland how to steal a scene. Every nuance of a ballad, every tiny gesture that seemed "accidental" but managed to get audiences to their feet, belonged to Thompson. She had come up from the nightclub circuit with one of the most successful acts of all time, and made that great bent-crane of a body work to her advantage. As is apparent in "Clap Yo Hands," she effortlessly pulls off the impossible—she takes our eyes away from Astaire. A woman of diverse gifts, she's best known to millions of children for her classic *Eloise* books. Her longtime friend Roger Edens never considered anyone else for the role of Maggie Prescott.

THE MUSIC

Nearly the entire score of *Funny Face* was lifted from George and Ira Gershwin's 1927 Broadway hit of the same title, which also starred Fred Astaire. The addictive "Bonjour, Paree" is one of five specialty numbers penned by Roger Edens and Leonard Gershe.

ROLE REVERSALS

When Cyd Charisse passed on the role of Jo Stockton, Hepburn grabbed it, and, in so doing, passed up *Gigi*, which went to Leslie Caron.

CREDITS

Producer: Roger Edens/
Paramount Pictures
Director: Stanley Donen
Screenplay: Leonard Gershe
Music and Lyrics:
George and Ira Gershwin
Running Time: 103 minutes
Budget: $3 million

NOMINATIONS

Best Original Screenplay:
Leonard Gershe
Best Cinematography: Ray June
Best Costume Design:
Edith Head, Hubert de Givenchy
Best Art Direction-Set Decoration:
Hal Pereira,
George W. Davis, Sam Comer,
Ray Moyer

THE YEAR'S ACADEMY AWARD WINNERS

Best Picture/Best Director:
David Lean, *The Bridge On the River Kwai*
Best Actor: Alec Guinness,
The Bridge On the River Kwai
Best Actress: Joanne Woodward,
The Three Faces of Eve
Best Supporting Actor:
Red Buttons, *Sayonara*
Best Supporting Actress:
Miyoshi Umeki, *Sayonara*

THE CRITICS

"The musical that dares to rhyme Sartre with Montmartre—knocks most other musicals off the screen for its visual beauty, its witty panache, and its totally uncalculating charm."
—*Time Out*

"The songs of George and Ira Gershwin are the oldest thing in the picture, barring Mr. Astaire."
—Bosley Crowther, *New York Times*

BEHIND THE SCREEN

While Paris has never looked more romantic than in *Funny Face*, the production was bedeviled by violent political riots in the streets.

The irrepressible buoyancy of Kay Thompson may have grated on Astaire. She complained of his dark moods on the set and, in particular, his curtness to the young Hepburn.

Dovima was one of the most famous high-fashion models of the 1950s. She's forever immortalized by Richard Avedon in a black and white photograph wearing a ball gown and posed between two elephants.

The gauzily beautiful dance sequence at the abbey was a nightmare of mud and wet grass. Astaire and Hepburn could barely keep from slipping.

THE OTHER LISTS

- American Film Institute (No)
- Roger Ebert's Top 100 (No)
- *Entertainment Weekly* (Yes)
- Internet Movie Database (No)
- Leonard Maltin (No)
- *Movieline* (Yes)
- National Society of Film Critics (No)
- *Première* Magazine (No)
- *Rolling Stone* (No)
- *Village Voice* (No)

"No dancer can watch Fred Astaire and not know we should all have been in a different business."
—Mikhail Baryshnikov

RIGHT: Hepburn on herself: "My look is attainable. Women can look like Audrey Hepburn by flipping out their hair, buying the large sunglasses, and the little sleeveless dresses." Yeah, right.

BELOW: "Can't act. Can't sing. Balding. Can dance a little." That would be the consensus on the first screen test of the gentleman on the left. Astaire managed to overcome his critics quite nicely with 44 starring roles under his dapper belt, and, as lushly visualized here, some of the most spellbinding dancing ever filmed.

THE GREAT SCENE

Maggie sends Dick and Jo off on a fashion shoot, an exclusive layout of Paul Duval's new collection. She sharply reminds them the photos must be smart, different, and full of "bizzazz!" They begin on a rain-slicked avenue with only a bunch of balloons as props. Jo is clearly at a loss when Dick yells "Run!" She hesitates and he barks at her. "But which way do I run?" she cries. "That way!" She's off, and as the balloons escape her hands, he commands her to stop in her tracks. Click! Freeze-frame. Beautiful shot. Next is the train station and he wants her to think *Anna Karenina*. She's just lost her lover, she wants to die, and she's wearing a fabulous new traveling ensemble. He'd like tears in her eyes, and his assistant hurries to provide them from a bottle. She doesn't need them. Dick's brief kiss has made Jo think her love for him is hopeless. Click. Another perfect shot. Now to the opera house, where she runs down the magnificent stairway in a painterly emerald-green gown with billowing cape. "Your lover has just stood you up!" Dick directs her. "You're Isolde, a queen, you're furious!" Jo's got it by now. She's become her own storyteller. She turns imperiously with a flash of anger. Click! Wow! Then, on to the flower market, the fountains at L'Étoile by night, then the Louvre and the stairway leading up to "Winged Victory." Dick orders her into view. "No! Just tell me when you're ready." He yells "Go!" and she emerges from behind the statue in a dazzling red gown and veil. He's bowled over and barely gets the shot as she runs down the steps in giddy abandon. "Take the picture, take the picture!" she cries. Finally, the last shot—Duval's sumptuous wedding gown, and Dick and Jo are on location at an abbey alongside an idyllic lagoon. Jo is overwrought; this is such a lie for her. The happiness the picture is meant to evoke will elude her. She escapes to the water's edge. And it's there Dick finally realizes she's in love with him. Now it's his turn to be overwhelmed. As he sings "He Loves and She Loves," he takes her in his arms, and they waltz onto a raft, accompanied by swans, floating magically toward a flowery meadow. What a picture!

"I never thought I'd land in pictures with a face like mine."—Audrey Hepburn

29

A STREETCAR NAMED DESIRE 1951

METHOD TO THE MADNESS

Rape, nymphomania, and unbridled female lust collided with the Hays Motion Picture Code Office, which fought nearly to its death to protect fragile audiences from this "sordid, morally repugnant" Tennessee Williams masterwork. The Hays Office lost, and *Streetcar* is credited with shattering the censorship regulations—at least for a brief period of time. This flagrantly theatrical film, ironically, gave birth to Hollywood's age of neorealism, marking the demise of plot contrivance, musty acting technique, and faux back-lot atmosphere. It can't be stressed enough that Marlon Brando's performance here was a pioneering journey into the stratosphere. Moviegoers had never seen anything close to its raw power. As one critic remarked, "You can almost smell him."

Jim: This tale of an unhinged midlife Scarlett O'Hara versus a groin-thrusting brute, unfolding within a cramped, one-bedroom apartment, is among the most riveting dramas to be inspired by the New Orleans housing crunch.

Gail: We melt not only under the heat of Brando's animal appeal but under the oppressive humidity of decaying lives. Packs more artistic charge than a battery of strong melodramas.

HE PLOT

anche DuBois (Vivien Leigh), a fluttery inster with delusions of grandeur, arrives the tawdry French Quarter, broke and at e mercy of her younger sister Stella (Kim nter) and her brother-in-law Stanley arlon Brando). Stella, who is pregnant for e first time, is thrilled to have her. Stanley is mediately put off by her patrician façade d her obvious distaste for his brutish meanor. She tries to charm him but he ts right to it: what's become of the family tune? She laughs in his face. The DuBois's lle Rive plantation has been sold for back kes. She's got nothing but the costume welry and moth-eaten wardrobe she's come th. Blanche's influence on Stella begins to ate on Stanley. When she takes up with one his poker pals, Mitch (Karl Malden), Stanley ends to put a stop to it. He digs into her st to find plenty of skeletons. It seems that anche has been something less than a lady order to support herself. Stanley tips Mitch and he promptly reneges on his marriage oposal. Blanche is devastated. While Stella at the hospital delivering his child, a drunken anley confronts Blanche about her sordid st and rapes her. As a final defense against elty, she descends into the madness of mplete make-believe.

"Take a look at yourself here in a worn-out Mardi Gras outfit, rented for fifty cents from some rag-picker." A sadistically aroused Stanley Kowalski (Marlon Brando) shatters the delusions of grandeur harbored by his fragile sister-in-law, Blanche DuBois (Vivien Leigh).

"I have always depended upon the kindness of strangers." —Blanche DuBois

THE DIRECTOR

Elia Kazan had directed the Broadway production of *Streetcar*, and was initially unwilling to direct the movie. "It would be like marrying the same woman twice," he told Tennessee Williams. But Kazan finally consented when he thought about the challenge of opening the play up. He envisioned flashbacks to Blanche's life prior to New Orleans, but once written, he realized they diminished the story's intensity. He settled for harsh close-ups, and even had the apartment set constructed so that it could "shrink" as Blanche's suffocating paranoia closed in on her. Kazan, the ultimate Method director, was in perfect tandem with the Method prince, Brando—but Vivien Leigh was another story. He'd insisted on Jessica Tandy in the lead, but Warner Brothers wouldn't hear of it—they wanted star power. Leigh was slow to warm to Kazan and even slower to trust him. But once she did, they became fast friends. He admired her determination despite what he considered her "small talent." "She'd have crawled over broken glass if she thought it would help her performance," he recalled. "In the scenes that counted, she was excellent." Kazan's film career exploded after *Streetcar*, due in great part to his willingness to play along with the House Un-American Activities Committee. He "named names," fingering Communist sympathizers to ingratiate himself with the Hollywood studios. Those who suffered blacklisting as the result of Kazan's testimony never forgave him. Presented with an honorary Academy Award in 1998, he was greeted with tepid applause and more than a few scowls. He accepted his Oscar with an unapologetic nod and muttered to no one in particular, "I think I can just slip away now." His extraordinary if limited canon includes *Gentleman's Agreement* (1947), *Panic in the Streets* (1950), two more Brando vehicles, *Viva Zapata!* (1952) and *On the Waterfront* (1954), and James Dean's electrifying debut film, *East of Eden* (1955). (For more on Kazan, see page 64.)

"I don't want realism! I want magic." That being the case, poor Blanche may have come to stay at the wrong apartment. Stanley's primitive swagger is everything she claims to despise.

THE CAST

Blanche DuBois	Vivien Leigh
Stanley Kowalski	Marlon Brando
Stella Kowalski	Kim Hunter
Harold "Mitch" Mitchell	Karl Malden
Steve	Rudy Bond
Pablo Gonzales	Nick Dennis
Eunice	Peg Hillias
A Collector	Wright King
A Doctor	Richard Garrick
The Matron	Ann Dere
Mexican Woman	Edna Thomas
A Sailor	Mickey Kuhn

THE ACTORS

"Beautiful people make their own laws," **Vivien Leigh** was fond of saying. And to that end, she was fearless, promoting herself relentlessly to win the role of Scarlett O'Hara and then the real-life role of Mrs. Laurence Olivier. But the strain of competing with him was too much for her fragile mental health. By the time she began filming *Streetcar*, she was well on her way to a breakdown. Some insist the role hastened her demise. Though she won the Oscar and claimed that Brando's raw technique helped her immeasurably, it seems to have drained the juice out of her. Leigh made only three films after *Streetcar* and died at the age of 53. Her other indelible performances include *Gone with the Wind* (1939), *Waterloo Bridge* (1940), *Anna Karenina* (1948), and *Ship of Fools* (1965). (For more on Leigh, see page 67.)

Marlon Brando despised the character of Stanley Kowalski and was horrified that it elevated him to a sex-symbol status not seen since Rudolph Valentino. His muttering, stuttering, sweaty, ripped-T-shirt performance ushered in the era of Method acting on film, and the Oscar was his for the losing. But his bad-boy reputation, compounded by Humphrey Bogart's extravagant PR campaign on his own behalf for *African Queen*, left Brando the only major *Streetcar* cast member to go home empty-handed on Oscar night. Brando, of course, not only bounced back, he proceeded to transform the image of the contemporary American male hero. His acting choices, while not always praised, have almost always astonished: *The Wild One* (1954), *On the Waterfront* (1954), *One-Eyed Jacks* (1960), *Reflections in a Golden Eye* (1967), *The Godfather* (1972), *Last Tango in Paris* (1973), and *Apocalypse Now* (1979). (For more on Brando, see pages 11, 60 and 64.)

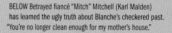

Streetcar was **Kim Hunter**'s movie high-water mark, thanks to the McCarthy blacklisting—which was abetted, ironically, by her own director, Kazan. After a long career on the stage, Hollywood made a monkey of her as "Zina" in the original 1968 *Planet of the Apes* series.

CREDITS

Producer: Charles Feldman/ Warner Bros.
Director: Elia Kazan
Screenplay: Tennessee Williams
Running time: 125 minutes
Budget: $1.8 million

ACADEMY AWARDS

Best Actress: Vivien Leigh
Best Supporting Actor: Karl Malden
Best Supporting Actress: Kim Hunter
Best Art Direction-Set Decoration, Black-and-White: Richard Day, George James Hopkins

NOMINATIONS

Best Picture
Best Director: Elia Kazan
Best Screenplay: Tennessee Williams
Best Actor: Marlon Brando
Best Cinematography, Black-and-White: Harry Stradling, Sr.
Best Costume Design, Black-and-White: Lucinda Ballard
Best Music: Alex North
Best Sound, Recording: Nathan Levinson

THE YEAR'S OTHER WINNERS

Best Picture: *An American in Paris*
Best Director: George Stevens, *A Place in the Sun*
Best Actor: Humphrey Bogart, *The African Queen*

BELOW Betrayed fiancé "Mitch" Mitchell (Karl Malden) has learned the ugly truth about Blanche's checkered past. "You're no longer clean enough for my mother's house."

Despite dozens of supporting roles, **Karl Malden**, with his signature nose, is best remembered as the guy in the Bogie hat reminding us not to leave home without our American Express cards, and for the 1972 *Streets of San Francisco* TV series. On the big screen he was featured in *Gypsy* (1962), *Cheyenne Autumn* (1964), *The Cincinnati Kid* (1965), and *Patton* (1969). (For more on Malden, see page 64.)

NOTABLE QUOTES

"A woman's charm is fifty percent illusion." —Vivien Leigh

"Kowalski was always right, and never afraid. He never wondered, he never doubted. His ego was very secure. And he had the kind of brutal aggressiveness that I hate. I'm afraid of it. I detest the character." —Marlon Brando

THE MUSIC

Alex North's brazen, ultra-sultry score makes you want to hop the next flight to the French Quarter, lean up against a wrought-iron balcony with a "lemon Coke and chipped ice," and give in to your secret "Della Robbia blue" desires.

THE CRITICS

". . . throbs with passion and poignancy . . . as fine if not finer than the play. Inner torments are seldom projected with such sensitivity and clarity on the screen." —Bosley Crowther, *New York Times*

"Kazan achieves a sort of theatrical intensity in which the sweaty realism sometimes clashes awkwardly with the stylization . . ." —*Time Out*

BEHIND THE SCREEN

Tennessee Williams clearly used elements from his own life. As a resident of the French Quarter, he incorporated specifics of the locale; there is indeed a "Desire" bus route. Stanley Kowalski was the name of one of his shoe factory coworkers back in St. Louis. Blanche DuBois was the name of a school librarian from his childhood.

THE OTHER LISTS
American Film Institute (Yes)
Roger Ebert's Top 100 (No)
Entertainment Weekly (No)
Internet Movie Database (No)
Leonard Maltin (No)
Movieline (No)
National Society of Film Critics (No)
Premiere Magazine (Yes)
Rolling Stone Magazine (No)
Village Voice (No)

Stanley's scream for "Stell-aaaahhh!" (Kim Hunter) brings her down the stairs, her anger at him diffused by sheer animal attraction.

THE GREAT SCENE

When Stanley physically lashes out at Stella, she and Blanche hightail it to the safety of an upstairs neighbor. Stanley, as sorrowful as a child who doesn't know his own strength, lets out a primal cry for his "Stell-aaaahhh!" She responds to the mating call, slowly descending the stairs with an expression of dopey lust. He buries his face in Stella's belly as she kneads his naked, brawny back. He picks her up and carries her inside like a caveman with his willing prize.

30

SAVING PRIVATE RYAN 1998

NO HEROES IN HELL

A GI slowly pushes a knife into an enemy soldier's heart, all the while whispering comforting, hushing sounds into the dying man's ear. This "war is hell" movie won't let up. The hellish first 30 minutes, Spielberg's documentary-style rendering of the D-Day invasion of Omaha Beach, is hardly bearable: Wounded, living bodies are pulled under the bloody surf like so many choking fish; a man, his arm blown off, picks up the limb as if to save it for some later use. Blinded by bombs and bullets, the soldiers can barely see ahead, let alone know in which direction they are supposed to stagger. Spielberg lays before us a visceral and devastatingly honest film experience that speaks more through action and emotion than words. But the brilliant director cannot seem to resist his urge to frame the story in sentimental conventions of the genre. When we find ourselves applauding at the Allies' victories, we know the movie is beginning to lie. It's difficult to ignore this transition into the predictable, but the harrowing vision of war that radiates from the screen is burned so deeply into your senses that, regardless of those Spielberg-ian niceties, you are ultimately left with the harrowing insight into the pain and tragedy of war.

Jim: For all the calamitous spectacle, what makes it for me is Hanks in a quiet moment telling his boys he's just a teacher back home.

Gail: Spielberg serves this film with an unprecedented rawness. An unusually nuanced ensemble performance, and a masterful treatment of the hell of combat.

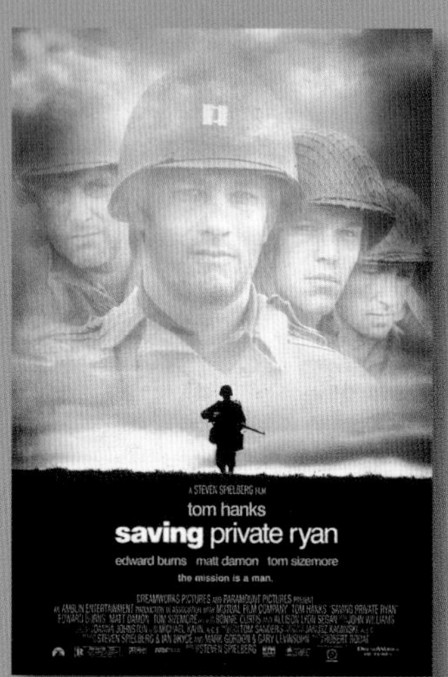

THE PLOT

Having endured the bloody invasion of Omaha Beach during World War II, a squadron of survivors under the leadership of Captain John Miller (Tom Hanks) is enraged by orders to go behind enemy lines in order to save one Private Ryan, whose three brothers have all been killed in combat. Though they're unaware of it, the orders have come from General Marshall (Harve Presnell). The soldiers see it as a PR ploy and are outraged that their lives will be risked to save one man. During the troops' journey through devastated villages strewn with bloody corpses, they encounter a Nazi sniper and later an enemy compound seen through the eyes of their awkward, bookish translator (Jeremy Davies). A medic is mortally wounded and the soldiers who try to save him cry out, "Tell us what to do. Tell us how to fix you." After going through a pile of dog tags taken from corpses, the men finally encounter Ryan, alive. Their resentment toward him is exacerbated by his refusal to leave. "These are my brothers now," he says. The men complete their mission, but there is more loss before they reach safety.

Captain John H. Miller (Tom Hanks) confronts the horror of the bloodbath he and his men must endure day after day.

"Ryan better be worth it. He better go home and cure some disease, or invent a longer-lasting light bulb."—Captain Miller

THE DIRECTOR

Though he described *Saving Private Ryan* as one of his least favorite films to make, director **Steven Spielberg** had to do it. His father, who had been a radio operator aboard a B-25 bomber in Burma, "intoxicated me with bedtime stories about the war." Indeed, among Spielberg's first stabs at filmmaking were war films that included *Battle Squad* and *Escape to Nowhere* (both 1961), featuring kids as World War II soldiers, including his sister, Anne Spielberg. Of the close to 20 films he has directed, four—*1941* (1979), *Empire of the Sun* (1987), *Always* (1989), and *Schindler's List* (1993)—are concerned with World War II. In a tour to promote the film, Spielberg said he had "a duty to warn people" about the extent of the violence on screen. "I just want people to know that this movie is extremely close to reality. This movie in effect may resensitize people who thought they were desensitized to violence." (For more on Spielberg, see pages 88, 136, 190, 208, and 289)

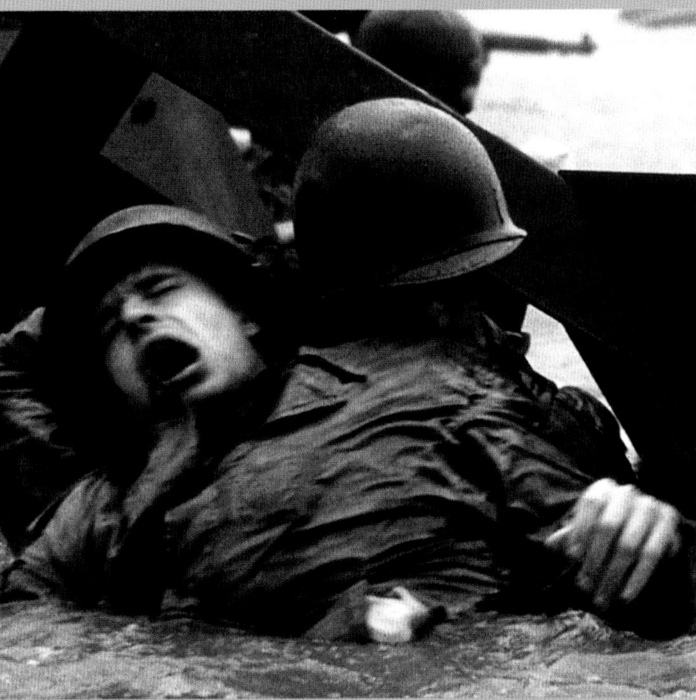

D-Day on Omaha Beach is so gut-wrenchingly horrifying we can barely watch it. Men drown as they try to drag themselves to shore; others lose limbs and begin to sink. This scene has to go on record as one of the most devastating depictions of the brutality and terror of war.

THE CAST

Capt. John H. Miller	Tom Hanks
Pvt. Richard Reiben	Edward Burns
Sgt. Michael Horvath	Tom Sizemore
Pvt. James Ryan	Matt Damon
Cpl. Timothy Upham	Jeremy Davies
Pvt. Stanley Mellish	Adam Goldberg
Pvt. Daniel Jackson	Barry Pepper
Pvt. Irwin Wade	Giovanni Ribisi
Pvt. Adrian Caparzo	Vin Diesel
Capt. Fred Hamill	Ted Danson

THE ACTORS

Tom Hanks, in one of his greatest but most understated roles, plays Capt. John H. Miller, an elusive and courageous soldier at war with his own terror. It hardly needs saying that Hanks is one of America's most celebrated and beloved actors. It took eight years after his debut in *He Knows You're Alone* (1980) before he won the career-making role of a reticent cross-dresser in the TV sitcom *Bosom Buddies* (1980–82). He went on to turn in winning performances in scores of films, including *Splash* (1984), *Big* (1988, Academy Award nomination), *Sleepless in Seattle* (1993), *Philadelphia* (1993, Academy Award), *Forrest Gump* (1994, Academy Award), *Apollo 13* (1995), *Cast Away* (2000), *Catch Me If You Can* (2002), and *Charlie Wilson's War* (2007).

Matt Damon's Pvt. James Ryan doesn't quite fit the bill of the working-class boy with integrity, but he carries it off with star quality. Damon is said to have spent his days following the director around so he could find out "what it was like to be Spielberg." The baby-faced Damon made his debut with a one-line role in *Mystic Pizza* (1988), followed by a star-making turn in *Courage Under Fire* (1996). He became a household name after collaborating with friend Ben Affleck on the screenplay for *Good Will Hunting* (1997), in which they co-star. Among his other films are *The Talented Mr. Ripley* (2000), *All the Pretty Horses* (2000), *Ocean's Eleven* (2001), and the Bourne films (2004, 2007).

Jeremy Davies playing Timothy Upham is one of the most terrifying and effective characters in the film. As the fragile, literary translator, it is clear that he does not belong there, and we tremble along with him during the climactic scene. After a stint doing TV movies and commercials, he was noticed by casting agents in a Subaru ad. Among Davies's films are *Twister* (1996), *Solaris* (2002), and *Dogville* (2003).

As Sgt. Michael Horvath, **Tom Sizemore** plays the gruff, John Wayne-ish soldier. Sizemore had a solid film career in the 1990s with his first break in a bit part in *Born on the Fourth of July* (1989), followed by bigger roles in *True Romance* (1993), *Natural Born Killers* (1994), *Devil in a Blue Dress* (1995), and *Heat* (1995). He won his first lead role in *The Relic* (1997), followed by *Bringing Out the Dead* (1999), and *Black Hawk Down* (2001). Sizemore, who suffered from substance abuse, turned his life around and now counsels teens. On *Ryan*, Spielberg threatened to reshoot the entire film if Sizemore failed a drug test even once. He credits the director with saving his life.

THE CRITICS

"*Saving Private Ryan* is a powerful experience. I'm sure a lot of people will weep during it. Spielberg knows how to make audiences weep better than any director since Chaplin in *City Lights*. But weeping is an incomplete response,

CREDITS

Producer: Steven Spielberg and Ian Bryce, Mark Gordon and Gary Levinsohn/Dreamworks
Director: Steven Spielberg
Screenplay: Robert Rodat
Running Time: 170 minutes
Budget: $70 million

ACADEMY AWARDS

Best Director: Steven Spielberg
Best Cinematography: Janusz Kaminski
Best Effects, Sound Effect Editing: Gary Rydstrom, Richard Hymns
Best Film Editing: Michael Kahn
Best Sound: Gary Rydstrom, Gary Summers, Andy Nelson, Ron Judkins

NOMINATIONS

Best Actor: Tom Hanks
Best Art Direction-Set Decoration: Thomas E. Sanders, Lisa Dean
Best Makeup: Lois Burwell, Conor O'Sullivan, Daniel C. Striepeke
Best Music, Original Dramatic Score: John Williams
Best Picture: Steven Spielberg, Ian Bryce, Mark Gordon, Gary Levinsohn
Best Original Screenplay: Robert Rodat

THE YEAR'S OTHER WINNERS

Best Picture: *Shakespeare in Love*
Best Actor: Roberto Benigni, *Life Is Beautiful*
Best Actress: Gwyneth Paltrow, *Shakespeare in Love*
Best Supporting Actor: James Coburn, *Affliction*
Best Supporting Actress: Judi Dench, *Shakespeare in Love*

THE OTHER LISTS

American Film Institute (Yes)
Roger Ebert's Top 100 (No)
Entertainment Weekly (No)
Internet Movie Database (Yes)
Leonard Maltin (No)
Movieline (No)
National Society of Film Critics (No)
Premiere Magazine (No)
Rolling Stone Magazine (No)
Village Voice (No)

letting the audience off the hook. This film embodies ideas. After the immediate experience begins to fade, the implications remain and grow." —Roger Ebert, *Chicago Sun-Times*

"What nags you about [the film] is the way Rodat's script, though solid and well-structured, has not broken through convention, has not elevated itself to a higher level (or even reached the best of the old level) the way the mind-bending scenes of combat have." —Kenneth Turan, *Los Angeles Times*

BEHIND THE SCREEN

Both Spielberg and Hanks waived their salaries in exchange for percentages, which took $30 million off the budget.

The film was based upon the true story of the Niland brothers.

Steven Spielberg thought Matt Damon too skinny for the role. When Robin Williams introduced Damon to Spielberg on the set of *Good Will Hunting* (1997), he must have gained some weight, because Spielberg decided that the actor was just right.

To get the actors in the mood to hate Private Ryan, all the principals underwent several days of grueling army training—except for Matt Damon.

Real amputees were used for the shots of people with limbs missing.

Among the many veterans of D-Day who applauded Spielberg for the film's authenticity, actor James Doohan (that's Scotty from *Star Trek*) commended the director for his honest portrait. Doohan lost the middle finger of his right hand and was wounded in the leg during the war.

Hanks plays it low-key. You know he's courageous, but he's also scared to death; something in his character makes him keep his own counsel, and he remains slightly aloof to his men. "I don't gripe to you. I don't gripe in front of you. You should know that."

A captured Nazi babbles, begs, and pleads with the GIs to spare his life. In desperation he regales the men with his love and knowledge of things American; he sings American anthems, praises Betty Grable's legs, even screams "Fuck Hitler!" But two of the men, Reiben and Mellish, still want his head, while the fragile translator Upham decries such action as a war crime and insists that the German must either be taken prisoner or freed. The prisoner is finally allowed to leave on condition that he find the nearest base and surrender to the Allies.

The most fragile member of the troop, and one of the film's most powerful characters, Timothy Upham (Jeremy Davies) comforts a crying child even as he himself is paralyzed with fear.

31

STRANGERS ON A TRAIN 1951

KILLER COMMUTE

Spectators at a tennis match swivel their heads back and forth, back and forth, following the ball. The camera finds one face in the center staring straight ahead, oblivious to the game. Deadly Bruno Antony might easily be mistaken for a daydreamer lost in reverie. And in keeping with the Hitchcock tradition of mundane evil, he couldn't look more affable. Like so many of the best thrillers of the era—*Double Indemnity* and *Leave Her to Heaven* come to mind—things really get cracking on a train, specifically in the bar car, a lost corner of glamour in the rush of time. We find ourselves grudgingly admiring Bruno for his snazzy skills with a cigarette lighter and the way he nonchalantly orders cocktails in mid-afternoon. (Perhaps the eerily well-mannered Hannibal Lecter was born right here in the heart of Hitchcock's darkness.) We can't help but find the bad guy more entertaining. So much more so than the sulky, banal hero who wins the equally good-looking but vacuous dame. In Hitchcock's world the good guy with the enviably untroubled existence always makes the ideal victim because, at heart, as much as we're supposed to identify with him, nothing gets our pulse racing, our imagination fired, like a dedicated villain.

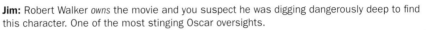

Jim: Robert Walker *owns* the movie and you suspect he was digging dangerously deep to find this character. One of the most stinging Oscar oversights.

Gail: And the hits just keep coming. Hitchcock never fails to amaze with his appetite for brilliant, malicious comedy. This one's got Robert Walker to define the mood; it also has the scene: the white knuckle-inducing reach for the cigarette lighter under a spinning carousel. Are you holding onto your arm?

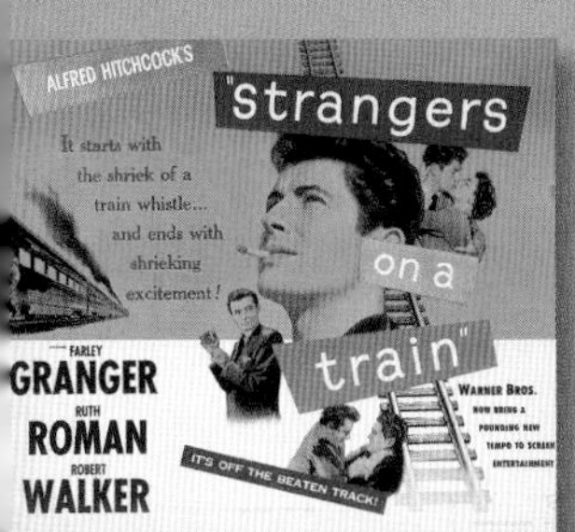

HE PLOT

arming sociopath Bruno Antony (Robert lker) encounters handsome tennis star y Haines (Farley Granger) on a train. He's d all the society columns and knows of y's plan to wed Senator Morton's beautiful ughter Anne (Ruth Roman). He also knows t Guy is still inconveniently married to his mer childhood sweetheart Miriam (Laura ot), a gold-digging tramp who won't give n up. Bruno suggests a wickedly inventive tch: he'll kill the wife if Guy will do him the or of knocking off his nasty old millionaire ner. The murders would appear entirely dom; the cops wouldn't have enough to ld a case. Guy thinks he's joking and gets at his station. But Bruno is convinced they ve an agreement and sets off to fulfill his d of the deal. He strangles Miriam after ateful ride through the Tunnel of Love. He ws increasingly impatient when Guy won't urn the favor. He begins to stalk him and in nal act of revenge, plants evidence at the ne of Miriam's murder. With cops closing Guy must somehow clear himself as the ck ticks down.

"I may be old-fashioned, but I thought murder was against the law." Tennis pro Guy Haines (Farley Granger) is put off by Bruno's (Robert Walker) suggestion of a killing exchange—his wife for Bruno's father—but he's nonetheless intrigued by the stranger. Walker's personality was thought to be dangerously close to the role, given his long history of violence and alcohol abuse.

THE DIRECTOR

Alfred Hitchcock was coming off a string of box-office flops (*Rope* [1948], *Under Capricorn* [1949], *Stage Fright* [1950]), and for the first time in his career felt he might be losing his touch. To hedge his bets he shot alternate endings for *Strangers*, one in which a passenger is dressed as a minister, another in which he's not. Hitchcock was concerned that there could be a backlash from religious conservatives. He was even more worried by Bruno's homosexuality and its effect on American audiences, so he considerably toned down the flirtation in the opening scene. The film's huge success inaugurated Hitchcock's golden age, a canon of classics including *Dial M For Murder, Rear Window* (both 1954), *North By Northwest* (1959), and his critical masterpiece, *Vertigo* (1958). (For more on Hitchcock, see pages 30, 54, and 85.)

"I still think it would be wonderful to have a man love you so much he'd kill for you." A party game gets a bit out of control as Bruno's twisted imagination makes him forget whose neck he's throttling. Walker's character is among Hitchcock's most affable maniacs, sharing dangerous company with Joseph Cotten in *Shadow of a Doubt* and Anthony Perkins in *Psycho*.

THE CAST

Guy Haines	Farley Granger
Anne Morton	Ruth Roman
Bruno Antony	Robert Walker
Senator Morton	Leo G. Carroll
Barbara Morton	Patricia Hitchcock
Miriam Joyce Haines	Laura Elliott
Mrs. Antony	Marion Lorne
Mr. Antony	Jonathan Hale
Police Capt. Turley	Howard St. John
Professor Collins	John Brown
Mrs. Cunningham	Norma Varden
Leslie Hennessy	Robert Gist

THE ACTORS

Robert Walker died less than two months after the film's release of complications resulting from acute alcoholism. Bruno Anthony is considered one of his most sensational performances, full of the actor's wry wit and mercurial intensity. Terrible eyesight, which kept him out of the war, caused him to squint, giving his characters an appealing vulnerability. His professional career started off well with marriage to an acting school sweetheart, Jennifer Jones. But after two children, she abandoned him for studio mogul David O. Selznick, who made her a star. "My personal life has been completely wrecked by David Selznick's obsession for my wife. What can you do to fight such a powerful man?" He married again, to the daughter of John Ford, the acclaimed director of westerns. When she filed for divorce claiming he beat her, John Wayne threatened to grind him to a pulp. Walker had his ardent supporters, among them Judy Garland, who costarred with him in his most engaging film, *The Clock* (1945). He followed that with *Till the Clouds Roll By* (1946), the biopic of composer Jerome Kern; and *One Touch of Venus* (1948).

One of the more famously handsome leading men of his generation, **Farley Granger** was a Hitchcock veteran (*Rope*, 1948). After a series of forgettable romantic dramas for MGM, Granger's boyish looks began to fade, and his talent wasn't enough to compensate. A stint in Italy ended with his return to the U.S. in a series of exploitation films, including *Rogue's Gallery* (1968), *Night Flight from Moscow* (1973), *The Slasher* (1981), *The Prowler* (1981), and *Deathmask* (1984).

The director's daughter **Patricia Hitchcock** was cast due to her striking similarity to **Laura Elliott**, who played Guy's trampy, doomed wife, Miriam. There's a moment in which Bruno sees her at a party, thinks she's the dead woman, and reacts accordingly. Patricia appeared in two other of her father's films: *Stage Fright* (1950) and *Psycho* (1960).

Ruth Roman, a striking Warner Brothers contract starlet, came with the production deal. She never completely took off as a star despite a long string of B movies including *Five Steps to Danger* (1957), *Look in Any Window* (1961), *Love Has Many Faces* (1965), *The Killing Kind* (1973), *Impulse* (1979), *Day of the Animals* (1977), and occasional appearances on TV's *Knot's Landing*. In 1956 she made headlines along with her young son as a survivor of the *Andrea Doria* ocean-liner disaster.

THE CRITICS

"A timeless treat, a marvelous display of Hitchcock's absolute mastery of his medium and a deliciously dark comedy as well." —Kevin Thomas, *Los Angeles Times*

"Mr. Hitchcock again is tossing a crazy murder story in the air and trying to con us into thinking that it will stand up without support." —Bosley Crowther, *New York Times*

BEHIND THE SCREEN

Alfred Hitchcock's cameo appearance is as a train passenger lugging a bass fiddle.

The breathless crawl under the carousel looked too dangerous, even to Hitchcock. He vowed never to direct such a stunt again.

Outtakes and close-ups of Robert Walker from *Strangers on a Train* can be seen in *My Son John* (1952). They filled in the gaps after his sudden death while filming.

Author Raymond Chandler was no fan of Hitchcock's. When the director pulled up at his house for a story meeting, Chandler yelled out the window, "Look at the fat bastard trying to get out of his car!" His wrath may have been warranted. Hitchcock pulled a fast one by optioning the rights to *Strangers on a Train* anonymously, thereby getting them dirt cheap —$7,500.

ROLE REVERSALS

William Holden was Hitchcock's first choice for tennis pro Guy Haines.

CREDITS

Producer: Warner Bros.
Director: Alfred Hitchcock
Screenplay: Raymond Chandler, from the novel by Patricia Highsmith
Running time: 101 minutes

ACADEMY AWARD NOMINATIONS

Best Black-and-White Cinematography: Robert Burks

THE YEAR'S WINNERS

Best Picture: *An American in Paris*
Best Director: George Stevens, *A Place in the Sun*
Best Actor: Humphrey Bogart, *The African Queen*
Best Actress: Vivien Leigh, *A Streetcar Named Desire*
Best Supporting Actor: Karl Malden, *A Streetcar Named Desire*
Best Supporting Actress: Kim Hunter, *A Streetcar Named Desire*

THE GREAT SCENE

Cops rush into an amusement park and fire a shot at Guy, the falsely accused killer. The bullet misses its target and hits the merry-go-round operator. He falls forward onto the controls, sending the ride into a berserk, racing spin. Children hang on for their lives, some of them thrilled by the excitement, as Guy and Bruno wrestle each other for control of the deadly evidence, a cigarette lighter. An old mechanic volunteers to crawl beneath the carousel to apply the brake. Bruno grabs a little boy and tries to fling him off. Guy saves the child but in so doing hangs dangerously over the edge. Bruno sadistically kicks at his hand, and it appears Guy will go careening into the void. The mechanic finally reaches the brake and hits it hard. The carousel screeches to a horrifying, bloody stop.

LEFT: Full-tilt-a-whirl! Guy and Bruno's carousel of death is one of Hitchcock's most nerve-jangling finales and went a long way to reestablishing his credibility at the box office.

THE OTHER LISTS

- American Film Institute (No)
- Roger Ebert's Top 100 (No)
- *Entertainment Weekly* (No)
- Internet Movie Database (No)
- Leonard Maltin (Yes)
- *Movieline* (Yes)
- National Society of Film Critics (No)
- *Premiere* Magazine (No)
- *Rolling Stone* Magazine (No)
- *Village Voice* (No)

"Man does not live by murder alone. He needs affection, approval, encouragement and, occasionally, a hearty meal."
—Alfred Hitchcock

"She was a tramp." Two escorts into the Tunnel of Love aren't enough for Guy's dispensable wife. She unwisely flirts with Bruno, who moments later will take her for a final moonlight stroll. Hitchcock was accused of ignoring his actors, forcing them to sink or swim according to their ability. He believed audiences came to see a story, not a particular performance.

32

IT HAPPENED ONE NIGHT 1934

LOVE AT FIRST FIGHT

Frank Capra broke the comedy mold when he added romance to the mix, creating a special brand of good-natured Depression escapism called screwball comedy, wherein an ill-matched man and woman go kicking and screaming into each other's arms—in overdrive. The exhilarating pacing of this film was largely practical, a function of Colbert's limited availability. Quick takes and multiple cameras were used to get the story moving (accounting for Gable's bare chest in the famous pajama scene). The result was pure "screwball": the most spirited and sexually provocative mini-genre of the day. *One Night* features the unforgettably macho Gable teaching the damsel-in-distress (or was she?) Colbert the ways of the world, including how to hitchhike (he fails, she succeeds), how to sleep on a haystack, and how to hang a curtain between their beds so they can sleep together out of wedlock. The film also benefited from having missed the Production Code's censorial scissors. Had the Code existed, the film surely wouldn't have. Call it cute, call it funny, it was love in the thirties—the *Annie Hall* of its day.

Jim: Colbert is an odd movie legend, with almost no memorable films to her credit. It doesn't help that she broke her back before she was to do *All About Eve*. This one is the best we've got of her, and it will do just fine. And Gable was never this natural or just plain likeable again.

Gail: The wit and the sophistication, the good-natured charm, and incandescent chemistry of this film make it a classic. They don't make 'em this way anymore, try as they might.

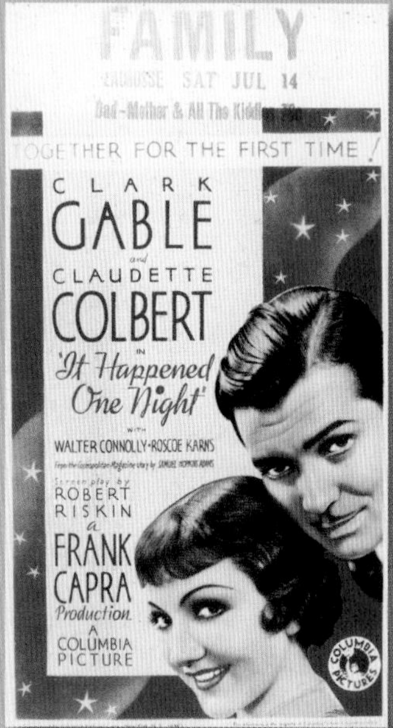

THE PLOT

A spoiled heiress, Ellie Andrews (Claudette Colbert) goes AWOL off the side of her father's yacht in search of freedom. She winds up on a rickety old bus populated by the usual proletarian suspects. She's headed for New York, where she will make her way to King Westley (Jameson Thomas), whom she plans to marry just to spite Dad. On the bus, she falls into the lap of Peter Warne (Clark Gable), a recently unemployed reporter who is immediately annoyed and fascinated by her . . . and who also sees a scoop. They exchange constant insults on the road while starving, sleep deprived, and occasionally living in sin (though a blanket hung between two beds keeps things kosher). Meanwhile, front-page headlines blare about the missing heiress who, finally too hungry to go on, makes it to the wedding with her father's assistance. Just before she ties the knot, though, Gable confesses his love and honorable intentions to Dad'ums. When the fateful moment arrives she says, "I don't," and the two are on the lam, again.

Sales of undershirts plummeted when Gable revealed nothing more than a bare chest beneath his shirt.

Alexander Andrews: "I asked you a simple question! Do you love her?"
Peter Warne: "YES!!! But don't hold that against me, I'm a little screwy myself!"

THE DIRECTOR

The film took all the awards at the Oscars, but it didn't make enough money to be held over for a second week at Radio City. Word of mouth did finally put it over the top. Critics praised the fast-paced farce that would usher in a whole new romantic genre: the screwball comedy. This was just the beginning of Sicilian-born director **Frank Capra**'s brilliant film career, which spanned nearly half a century. Starting out as a gag writer for silent-comedy kings Hal Roach and Mack Sennett, Capra directed films from weepies to adventures to comedies to whodunits, and took on issues in *The Younger Generation* (1929), *The Miracle Woman* (1931), and *The Bitter Tea of General Yen* and *American Madness* (both 1932). Capra's reputation was sealed as a director of sentimental films (though tarred with the sobriquet "Capra-corn"), and these were his true strength. Among them are *Mr. Deeds Goes to Town* (1936), *You Can't Take It With You* (1938, Oscar), *Lost Horizon* (1937), *Mr. Smith Goes to Washington* (1939), *Meet John Doe* (1941), and the black comedy *Arsenic and Old Lace* (released in 1944). After the war he formed Liberty Pictures, where he made the immortal *It's a Wonderful Life* (1946) and *State of the Union* (1948), both of which were box-office bombs. Later, Capra made a comeback with *A Hole in the Head* (1959) and *Pocketful of Miracles* (1961). (For more on Capra, see page 115.)

Runaway heiress Ellie (Claudette Colbert) is not so sure she likes the looks—or the profession—of her seatmate Peter Warner (Clark Gable), even though she does seem to need his protection.

THE CAST	
Peter Warne	Clark Gable
Ellie Andrews	Claudette Colbert
Walter Connolly	Alexander Andrews
Oscar Shapley	Roscoe Karns
King Westley	Jameson Thomas

THE ACTORS

"I feel as happy as a kid and a little foolish they picked me," said **Clark Gable** for his Best Actor Oscar as out-of-work journalist Peter Warne. He'd been loaned out to Columbia to make this film, which he had considered "punishment." Gable had sex appeal to spare, which is why he could get away with some of the more humiliating turns in the film. The studios cast him opposite their finest actresses in such films as *Mutiny on the Bounty* (1935, Academy Award nomination), *Wife vs. Secretary* (1936), *Idiot's Delight* (1939), and, of course, *Gone With the Wind* (1939). Gable's winning streak continued until, tragically, his new wife, Carole Lombard, was killed in a plane crash. He returned to Hollywood after enlisting in the Air Corps, but without his star quality. In *The Misfits* (1961), one of Gable's last films, director John Huston was able to draw on the actor's real-life pain. Gable's proposed epitaph? "He was lucky and he knew it." (For more on Gable, see page 67.)

Claudette Colbert was absolutely winning as the helplessly clever runaway heiress. And audiences continued loving her screwball style in *Bluebeard's Eighth Wife* (1938), *Midnight* (1939), and *The Palm Beach Story* (1942). Colbert proved herself as a dramatic actress as well, in *Drums Along the Mohawk* (1939), *Arise, My Love* (1940, her favorite film), and *Since You Went Away* (1944, Academy Award nomination). Time was not kind to the star, and her appeal had faded by the late 1940s and '50s. Her final appearances included *Parrish* (1961) and the television movie *The Two Mrs. Grenvilles*.

ROLE REVERSALS

Offers to play the role of Ellie went to no less than Miriam Hopkins, Margaret Sullivan, and Myrna Loy. Bette Davis was shooting *Of Human Bondage*. Colbert said no at first, but when Capra upped her salary, she became the heiress.

Gable's role was originally offered to Robert Montgomery, who said the script was the worst thing he'd ever read.

BEHIND THE SCREEN

Gable wasn't taking any chances when he accepted the role opposite Claudette Colbert. He told director Frank Capra that he would give the role a shot, but if things weren't going well after a few days, he would leave the production.

"All that French broad cares about is money," said Columbia's Harry Cohn. Claudette Colbert accepted *It Happened One Night* after an offer of $50,000 for four weeks' work.

Colbert hated the left side of her face and once painted it green to be sure that the cameraman wouldn't shoot it.

MGM lent out Gable to Capra as punishment for his money demands. He showed up drunk for his first meeting with the director. "Listen, he's no Clark Gable at home," said Carole Lombard.

It Happened One Night inspired a whole slew of screwball comedies, but apparently it inspired more. In Friz Freleng's unpublished memoirs, he cites several things from the film upon which Bugs Bunny and other cartoon characters were based: Oscar Shapely (Roscoe Karns) gave Bugs his personality; Peter Warne (Clark Gable) gave Bugs a way with a carrot; Alexander Andrews (Walter Connolly) and King Westley (Jameson Thomas) were inspirations for the characters of Yosemite Sam and Pepé LePew, respectively.

"They call me the King of Hollywood. I'm underendowed, I've got a mouthful of false teeth, and bad breath," said Clark Gable.

When Gable peeled off his shirt in *It Happened One Night* to reveal a bare chest, men's undershirt sales plummeted. Hard to believe, but true: Several shirt manufacturers tried to sue the studio.

At the Miami bus station, friends of Peter Warne (Clark Gable) refer to him as "the King" —Gable's nickname in real life.

CREDITS

Producer: Harry Cohn/ Columbia Pictures
Director: Frank Capra
Screenplay: Robert Riskin
Running Time: 105 minutes

ACADEMY AWARDS

Best Picture
Best Director: Frank Capra
Best Actor: Clark Gable
Best Actress: Claudette Colbert
Best Screenplay Adaptation: Robert Riskin, based on the story "Night Bus" by Samuel Hopkins Adams

THE OTHER LISTS

- American Film Institute (Yes)
- Roger Ebert's Top 100 (No)
- *Entertainment Weekly* (No)
- Internet Movie Database (Yes)
- Leonard Maltin (Yes)
- *Movieline* (No)
- National Society of Film Critics (No)
- *Premiere* Magazine (Yes)
- *Rolling Stone* Magazine (No)
- *Village Voice* (No)

Reclining on a fence at the side of the road, Ellie listens as Peter condescendingly explains to her how an expert hitchhikes. She's dubious. He's full of himself. "There's no end to your accomplishments, is there?" she sneers. "It's all in that ol' thumb, see? . . . that ol' thumb never fails," Peter says, and proceeds to demonstrate the many techniques for getting a car to stop on a dime. But no dice.

Ellie makes a wise crack about his thumbing technique. After watching twenty cars speed by, Ellie gets fed up with his display, she jumps off the fence, dusts herself off, and takes on the job herself. Peter snarls at the implication that she might know a better technique, to which Ellie replies, "Oh, you're such a smart alec. Nobody knows anything but you. I'll stop a car and I won't use my thumb."

She wiggles her way slowly to the road, raises her skirt seductively exposing a very shapely leg. A car immediately screeches to a halt.

THE GREAT SCENE

Defying the assumptions of journalist Peter Warne (Clark Gable) about spoiled heiresses, this one was game for just about anything—from sleeping in a haystack to sharing a room divided by a sheet. Here, Ellie is about to outwit Peter by succeeding where he has failed. She easily flags down a ride by using a little trick of her own.

At long last love emerges from its hiding place amidst the relentless hostility between the runaway heiress and the journalist who tries to scoop her story. As another screwball comedy so aptly observed, "All love begins in conflict."

NOTABLE QUOTES

"My advice to young filmmakers is this: Don't follow trends. Start them!" —Frank Capra

"I thought drama was when the actors cried. But drama is when the audience cries." —Frank Capra

"I worked like a son of a bitch to learn a few tricks and I fight like a steer to avoid getting stuck with parts I can't play." —Clark Gable

"Oh, Gable has enemies all right, but they all like him!" —David O. Selznick

"Why do you throw away five hundered dollars of our money on a test for that big ape? Didn't you see those big ears when you talked to him? And those big feet and hands, not to mention that ugly face of his?" —Jack Warner (to Mervyn LeRoy after LeRoy gave Clark Gable a screen test)

THE CRITICS

"No one has ever explained what gives this basically slight romantic comedy its particular—and enormous—charm." —Pauline Kael, *The New Yorker*

33

THE GRADUATE 1967

DEBUT CUM LAUDE

It's difficult to imagine a time when Dustin Hoffman didn't exist. *Midnight Cowboy*, *Rain Man*, and *Tootsie* are among the movies that make up our common frame of reference. But once upon a time he was a true beginner, an upstart who wasn't sure if his looks and personal style would translate onto the big screen. It's more than a matter of you-had-to-be-there, for if *The Graduate* were to open now as a comedic indie with an unknown, it might just cause the same earthquake it did way back when. Somehow the theme remains fresh, perhaps more so since the collapse of the get-rich-quick dot-com culture. Youth will always be stymied by the search for self. And if, as in Benjamin Braddock's case, he turns to cheap and easy sex as a bridge to responsibility, and if he then falls in love with his lover's daughter, hey, it's the 21st century. Be advised, though, that in 1967, such thoughts were positively incendiary. If any movie set off a revolutionary chain reaction, *The Graduate* did. It wasn't about the long-hair, hippie-dippie fringe. This was rebellion on the home front, amongst the solid middle class, and audiences went nuts. Hoffman's generation cheered, maybe over-related, but as with every generation, it was delighted to have found a hero of its own. Watch the film now and be transported—or simply look around and see that we haven't, in the end, come all that far.

Jim: The first half still makes me laugh harder than most movies in total. Hoffman is so hilarious in his rendezvous with Mrs. Robinson in the hotel bar, you can see why she just might fall for the boy. You find yourself cheering this odd couple on—and why not? I sometimes wish the story ended here.

Gail: Take one great soundtrack by Simon and Garfunkel and set the angst of the sixties generation to the tunes, and you have the movie that captured an era and embedded it in our collective unconscious for all time.

SEPH E LEVINE
E NICHOLS
VRENCE TURMAN
This is Benjamin. He's a little worried about his future.
HE GRADUATE
NE BANCROFT DUSTIN HOFFMAN · KATHARINE ROSS
DER WILLINGHAM BUCK HENRY PAUL SIMON
ON GARFUNKEL LAWRENCE TURMAN
E NICHOLS TECHNICOLOR PANAVISION

HE PLOT

League grad Benjamin Braddock (Dustin fman) comes home to upscale suburban without a clue as to what he wants to do his life. While hanging around over the mer, he's dragged, unwillingly at first, into overt affair with his father's law partner's , Mrs. Robinson (Anne Bancroft). Com-ations arise when his parents set him up a date with the Robinson daughter, Elaine tharine Ross). Her mother warns him end the relationship before it can begin. else. He tries hard to make Elaine hate but when she cries, he melts. He falls dlong in love. But how can he explain the ation with her mother? Before he gets chance, Mrs. Robinson beats him to the ch with her version of events, which are at all sympathetic to Benjamin. A devas-d Elaine backs away in disgust and hooks with her former fiancée Carl (Brian Avery). jamin rises to the occasion and takes eme measures in the hope of winning back.

"Benjamin, would this be easier for you in the dark?" The series of hotel room rendezvous are a high point of 1960s American film. Director Nichols's imaginative jump-cut montage covered the course of the affair in a matter of a few minutes. The most famous cut has Benjamin diving into a pool and landing in bed with Mrs. Robinson.

"Plastics."—Family friend offering career advice to Benjamin

THE DIRECTOR

"Maybe this movie is about a young man finding his way through madness," suggested **Mike Nichols** (born Michael Igor Peschkowsky in Berlin) as he mulled over a possible theme. It was the notion that unlocked the gold mine, the brilliant stroke that would become Nichols' trademark. He found fame very young with his groundbreaking comedy act with Elaine May. They brought a cerebral irony to the vaudevillian jokiness of 1950s comedy and changed the way America laughed. Before his Oscar-winning debut with *The Graduate*, he'd only been at the directorial helm once before (Broadway's *Barefoot In The Park*). Katharine Ross tells of how he rehearsed *The Graduate* cast relentlessly for three weeks until "we were ready to take it on the road." "He was doing what an artist does," says Dustin Hoffman. "He was painting. He was feeling his way as he went." Since his remarkable first outing with *Who's Afraid of Virginia Woolf* (1966), Nichols has directed such memorable films as *Catch-22* (1970), *Carnal Knowledge* (1971), *Silkwood* (1983), *Heartburn* (1986), *Working Girl* (1988), *Postcards from the Edge* (1990), *The Birdcage* (1996), *Primary Colors* (1998), *Wit* (2001), and the miniseries *Angels in America* (2003).

"I bet you're quite the ladies' man." The unsuspecting Mr. Robinson thinks it would be a terrific idea if Benjamin and his daughter Elaine got together. Comedy takes a backseat to emotional fireworks and an unforgettable moment as Anne Bancroft, soaked to the skin from the rain, is the target of a merciless camera. She appears to have aged twenty years from one moment to the next.

THE CAST

Mrs. Robinson	Anne Bancroft
Benjamin Braddock	Dustin Hoffman
Elaine Robinson	Katharine Ross
Mr. Braddock	William Daniels
Mr. Robinson	Murray Hamilton
Mrs. Braddock	Elizabeth Wilson
Hotel Desk Clerk	Buck Henry
Carl Smith	Brian Avery
Mr. McGuire	Walter Brooke
Mr. McCleery	Norman Fell
Mrs. Singleman	Alice Ghostley
Miss DeWitte	Marion Lorne
Woman on Bus	Eddra Gale

THE ACTORS

Dustin Hoffman spontaneously grabbed Bancroft's breast in the first hotel scene. Her numbed reaction cracked him up and he banged his head on the wall to keep from laughing into the camera. Nichols kept it in. Hoffman was still in shock over the fact that he'd actually won the role since the original story called for a blue-eyed, blond WASP of a guy. "I still believe today that Katharine (Ross) and I were the bottom of the barrel. I was convinced my screen test was just an excuse for Mike (Nichols) to score with Katharine." As with such icons as DeNiro and Pacino, Hoffman's filmography reads like a brief history of contemporary American cinema. Among his best are *Midnight Cowboy* (1969), *Little Big Man* (1970), *Papillon* (1973), *Lenny* (1974), *All the President's Men* and *Marathon Man* (both 1976), *Kramer vs. Kramer* (1979; Academy Award), *Tootsie* (1982), *Rain Man* (1988; Academy Award), *Dick Tracy* (1990), *Outbreak* (1995) and *Wag the Dog* (1997). (For more on Hoffman, see page 247.)

At 36, **Anne Bancroft** was only six years older than Dustin Hoffman. She was made up to look older, a burnt-out alcoholic and arch representative of the fuddy-duddy generation. But, at least according to *Chicago Sun-Times* critic Roger Ebert, she is the only character who transcends the film. "Mrs. Robinson is the only person who is not playing old tapes. She is bored by a drone of a husband, she drinks too much, she seduces Benjamin not out of lust but out of kindness or desperation. She is also sardonic, satirical, and articulate–the only person in the movie you would want to have a conversation with." Bancroft's most famous earlier role was Annie Sullivan, on-stage and in the Oscar-winning film version of *The Miracle Worker* (1962). Then came *The Pumpkin Eater* (1964). Following *The Graduate* were *The Prisoner of Second Avenue* (1975), *The Turning Point* (1977), and *The Elephant Man* (1980), the highlights of a career put on a back burner for her favorite role as Mrs. Mel Brooks.

Unless you count *Butch Cassidy and the Sundance Kid* (1969) and *The Stepford Wives* (1975), this was Mount Everest for **Katharine Ross**, who never really stopped working but couldn't seem to glom onto the right roles. She married actor Sam Elliott and is also a noted author of children's books.

BEHIND THE SCREEN

Fledgling producer Lawrence Turman borrowed $1,000 to option Charles Webb's 1962 novel.

In the scene in which Benjamin asks for a room from the desk clerk played by Buck Henry, Mike Nichols told Hoffman to play it as if he was asking for condoms from an elderly female pharmacist.

Dustin Hoffman's idea for a sequel has him still wed, though unhappily, to Elaine. They have a son with a girlfriend who catches Benjamin's eye. They begin an affair and essentially he becomes a second-generation Mrs. Robinson.

THE MUSIC

To remove the **Simon & Garfunkel** score would be the equivalent of decapitation. The songs function as landscapes of the characters' minds, and one in particular, "Mrs. Robinson," will probably remain a classic well into

CREDITS

Producer: Joseph E. Levine/ Lawrence Turman
Director: Mike Nichols
Screenplay: Buck Henry, Calder Willingham, from the novel by Charles Webb
Running time: 105 minutes
Box Office: $44 million

ACADEMY AWARDS

Best Director: Mike Nichols

NOMINATIONS

Best Picture
Best Actor: Dustin Hoffman
Best Actress: Anne Bancroft
Best Supporting Actress: Katharine Ross
Best Cinematography: Robert Surtees
Best Adapted Screenplay: Calder Willingham, Buck Henry

THE YEAR'S OTHER WINNERS

Best Picture: *In the Heat of the Night*
Best Actor: Rod Steiger, *In the Heat of the Night*
Best Actress: Katharine Hepburn, *Guess Who's Coming to Dinner*
Best Supporting Actor: George Kennedy, *Cool Hand Luke*
Best Supporting Actress: Estelle Parsons, *Bonnie and Clyde*

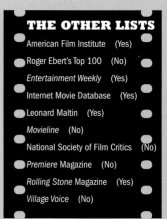

THE OTHER LISTS

American Film Institute (Yes)
Roger Ebert's Top 100 (No)
Entertainment Weekly (Yes)
Internet Movie Database (Yes)
Leonard Maltin (Yes)
Movieline (No)
National Society of Film Critics (No)
Premiere Magazine (No)
Rolling Stone Magazine (Yes)
Village Voice (No)

It's pouring but Benjamin and Elaine are too in love not to cancel the drive they'd planned. He pulls up in front of her house, but it's Mrs. Robinson who hops in. She demands he stop seeing her daughter. If not, she will make it very difficult. She'll tell Elaine about their affair. He doesn't believe she'd try that—not until he sees the determined look on her face. He must get to Elaine first, try to soften the blow. He dashes out of the car, up the stairs and into Elaine's bedroom. "Remember that married woman I told you about? She wasn't just anybody, she was… " The sight of Mrs. Robinson, soaked to the skin, standing outside the opened door, stops him. Elaine turns, realizes at once what he's been saying. Hysterical, she orders him out. As he departs he turns to see Mrs. Robinson up against the wall, stripped of her makeup and glamour. "Good-bye, Benjamin." She says it as if he's just passed away. And in a sense, the life he's known is quite suddenly over.

BELOW: Elaine, the prize, seems almost inconsequential in the tug-of-war between the ex-lovers. A moment later, Benjamin and Elaine will escape on a bus. Nichols wanted them to laugh throughout that final scene and kept the camera rolling until the laughter sputtered. The young romantics exchanged a confused look, as if to say "Now what?" A perfect ending.

"Are you having an affair with somebody, Benjamin?" The parsley-sage-rosemary-and-thyme are about to hit the fan. Listless college grad Benjamin Braddock's life takes a sudden and very traumatic turn.

the next millennium. When the Yankee legend Joe DiMaggio heard it for the first time he was deeply offended by the line: "Where have you gone, Joe DiMaggio?" It took some explaining to the notoriously humorless "Yankee Clipper" that the song was an homage to the American heroic ideal.

ROLE REVERSALS

If the original dream cast had been hired, we would've seen Robert Redford as Benjamin, Doris Day as Mrs. Robinson, Ronald Reagan as Dad, and Candice Bergen as Elaine. "A family of surfboards," Buck Henry called them. Redford was quickly nixed because Nichols felt he was too handsome and too self-assured.

THE CRITICS

"One of the best serio-comic social satires we've had from Hollywood since Preston Sturges was making them." —Bosley Crowther, *New York Times*

"*The Graduate* is a movie about a young man of limited interest, who gets a chance to sleep with the ranking babe in his neighborhood, and throws it away in order to marry her dorky daughter. " —Roger Ebert, *Chicago Sun-Times*

34

IT'S A WONDERFUL LIFE 1946

YOU CAN'T ALWAYS GET WHAT YOU WANT

"George Bailey, I'm going to love you 'til the day I die," whispers an adolescent Mary (Donna Reed) into George's (Jimmy Stewart) one deaf ear. Her words echo through time, imbuing the film with a sense of predestination. It's a good thing that George can't hear Mary, because he'd probably tell her to take a hike; he has other plans and none of them can be carried out in Bedford Falls. George wants to see the world: "I . . . I want to do something big, something important," he insists. Herein lies the conundrum of *It's a Wonderful Life*, which explains why the film wasn't popular when it was released. Though the luminous—and often sentimental—spiritual center of the film is the power of courage and friendship to surmount any obstacle, it is a dark film. What lingers even after George looks at how empty the life of his town, and his family, would have been had he never existed is the fact that George wanted more out of life, but fate always got in the way. Ironically, because of problems with the film's initial copyright, the movie fell into the public domain, and ultimately became extremely popular through repeated viewings. Having the film fall into the public domain almost seems like an act of grace performed by Clarence himself. Had we not had the opportunity to see it again and again, we would have missed experiencing the indelible power of this film. Every event in the movie—George's rescue of his brother from drowning, his discovery of the poisoned medicine, his terrible disappointments about not being able to leave Bedford Falls—and the depth of his love for Mary speak of something fundamental, something true about life. Like a great fable, it resonates with our feelings about living in the world.

Jim: Why wait until Christmas? When did this bittersweet tale of a man's contemplation of suicide become exclusively a holiday treat, anyway? It's a terrific film in July–or any time of the year you want to celebrate Stewart's underestimated gift as one of the screen's great dramatic actors.

Gail: On close inspection, this ultimately optimistic and charmingly sentimental film has darkness at its heart. But the movie shines through and reaches us at the most basic human level.

THE PLOT

From as early as the otherworldly opening, in which we hear people praying for George Bailey and angels discussing his case, we've got a lump in our throats that just won't go away. As George is poised on the brink of suicide, the angels review his early life. They recount how he saved his brother's life and became deaf in one ear; they speak of his rescuing a despondent pharmacist from accidentally delivering poison to a customer; and they talk of the early flowering of his love for young Mary. A quick cut to the future shows an eager George about to board a train for his first trip abroad–a trip he's been dreaming of since he was a boy. He reconnects with eighteen-year-old Mary, with whom he instantly falls in love, but not at the sacrifice of his big plans for the future. His plans change when his father is felled by a stroke. A disappointed George stays to run his father's loan office, eagerly awaiting his brother's return from the service, when he will once again try to board a train, this time for college. But once again, outside forces conspire to keep him home. He finally marries Mary, and they have a large family. Meanwhile, the building and loan company falters several times, and one final blow to the business pushes George to the brink of suicide. Clarence (Henry Travers), George's guardian angel, comes to his rescue by showing him how dismal the town would have been had he never lived. Ecstatic to have one more chance at life, George returns home to find that Mary has appealed to the townspeople, who empty their pockets to save George and the building and loan. Clarence earns his angel's wings, and it is a very merry Christmas for all.

Mary (Donna Reed) keeps her promise to love George (Jimmy Stewart) forever in this powerful fable of loss and love, and the things that make life worth living.

"One man's life touches so many others, when he's not there it leaves an awfully big hole."—Clarence

THE DIRECTOR

Frank Capra never intended *It's a Wonderful Life* to be pigeonholed as a Christmas picture; he had more on his mind. He wanted it to be special—a celebration of the lives and dreams of America's ordinary citizens, who try the best they can to do right by themselves and their neighbors. The public didn't love his movie in the beginning, but ultimately there was a happy ending...much delayed. Capra became Hollywood's poet of the common man in the 1930s with an extraordinary series of populist parables, including *Mr. Deeds Goes to Town* (1936), *Mr. Smith Goes to Washington* (1939), and *You Can't Take it With You* (1938), earning his films the sobriquet "Capra-corn." Capra also scored it big with *Lost Horizon* (1937) and *Arsenic and Old Lace* (1944). After World War II he made *It's a Wonderful Life* and *State of the Union* (1948), which were box-office failures. He later made a brief comeback with *A Hole in the Head* (1959) and *Pocketful of Miracles* (1961). (For more on Capra, see page 109.)

"No securities, no stocks, no bonds. Nothin' but a miserable little $500 equity in a life insurance policy. You're worth more dead than alive," says the soulless banker, Mr. Potter. But it's not his own money George feels so bereft about losing on this Christmas Eve, it is the money the town has entrusted to him. And the pain of it drives him to throw himself into the river.

THE CAST

George Bailey	James Stewart
Mary Hatch	Donna Reed
Mr. Potter	Lionel Barrymore
Uncle Billy	Thomas Mitchell
Clarence	Henry Travers
Mrs. Bailey	Beulah Bondi
Ernie	Frank Faylen
Bert	Ward Bond
Violet Bick	Gloria Grahame
Mr. Gower	H. B. Warner

THE ACTORS

"Sometimes I wonder if I'm doing a **Jimmy Stewart** imitation of myself," said the actor who became associated for all time as the earnest, kind, and wise small-town American male. Stewart was nominated for an Oscar for his wonderful performance as the tall, gawky boy with the shy downcast eyes and excitable personality. Stewart had previously nailed the Academy Award for *The Philadelphia Story* (1940), and was nominated for Oscars for *Mr. Smith Goes to Washington* (1939), *Harvey* (1950), and *Anatomy of a Murder* (1959). It was because of the darker story at the heart of *Wonderful Life* that Stewart was recognized for his dramatic gifts, which could be seen in such films as *Rear Window* (1954) and *Vertigo* (1958). Among his countless other films, Stewart starred in two John Ford westerns, *Two Rode Together* (1961) and *The Man Who Shot Liberty Valence* (1962).

Because of her performance as Mary, **Donna Reed**'s image is burned into our collective unconscious as the wholesome, good mother and all-American woman. Among her grittier roles, she was particularly outstanding as a prostitute in *From Here to Eternity* (1953). She also displayed her thespian gifts in John Ford's *They Were Expendable* (1945), *The Picture of Dorian Gray* (1945), and *The Benny Goodman Story* (1955). But Reed came home again to the role of dutiful wife and mother in the long-running TV sitcom *The Donna Reed Show* (1958–66).

The cruel Mr. Potter was not **Lionel Barrymore**'s most distinctive performance. The patriarch of the Barrymore acting clan was far better known for going very dramatic in unforgettable roles in *Grand Hotel* (1932), *Christopher Bean* (1933), *Dinner at Eight* (1933), *Treasure Island* (1934), *A Free Soul* (1931, Academy Award-winner), and *Key Largo* (1948). Barrymore appeared in the long-running *Dr. Kildare* series, from 1938 through 1947.

Thomas Mitchell's Uncle Billy is the lovable fool. Mitchell enjoyed a memorable career comprising roles in *Lost Horizon*, *Only Angels Have Wings*, *Mr. Smith Goes to Washington*, *Gone with the Wind*, and *The Hunchback of Notre Dame* (all 1939). He won an Oscar for *Stagecoach* (1939). He also performed in *Theodora Goes Wild* (1936), *Make Way for Tomorrow* (1937), *Our Town* (1940), *High Noon* (1952), *Destry* (1954), and *Pocketful of Miracles* (1961).

BEHIND THE SCREEN

Jimmy Stewart returned from service in World War II a burned-out case, but Lionel Barrymore convinced him to take the role of George.

Stewart was nervous about the phone scene kiss because it was his first screen kiss since his return to Hollywood after the war. Under Capra's watchful eye, Stewart filmed the scene in only one unrehearsed take, and it worked so well that part of the embrace was cut because it was too passionate to pass the censors.

The film originally ended with "Ode to Joy," not "Auld Lang Syne."

The final cut contained the drunken Uncle Billy yelling, "I'm all right, I'm all right," after he accidentally tripped over trash cans left on the sidewalk.

"Buffalo Gals," the film's theme song, was used as the name of the production company for

CREDITS

Producer: Frank Capra/ RKO Pictures
Director: Frank Capra
Screenplay: Frances Goodrich, Albert Hackett, Frank Capra, Jo Swerling, based on *The Greatest Gift*, by Philip Van Doren Stern
Running Time: 29 minutes
Budget: $3.18 million
Box Office: $3.3 million

THE YEAR'S ACADEMY AWARD WINNERS

Best Picture/Director: William Wyler, *The Best Years of Our Lives*
Best Actor: Fredric March, *The Best Years of Our Lives*
Best Actress: Olivia de Havilland, *To Each His Own*
Best Supporting Actor: Harold Russell, *The Best Years of Our Lives*
Best Supporting Actress: Anne Baxter, *The Razor's Edge*

THE OTHER LISTS

- American Film Institute (Yes)
- Roger Ebert's Top 100 (Yes)
- Entertainment Weekly (Yes)
- Internet Movie Database (Yes)
- Leonard Maltin (Yes)
- Movieline (Yes)
- Premiere Magazine (No)
- Rolling Stone Magazine (Yes)
- Village Voice (Yes)

the most representative television show of the baby boom generation, *thirtysomething*, a generation for which all the options in the world were, ironically, available.

The set for Bedford Falls was constructed in two months and was one of the longest sets ever made for an American movie. It covered four acres of the RKO's Encino Ranch. It included 75 stores and buildings, Main Street, a factory district, and a large residential and slum area. Main Street was 300 yards long, three whole city blocks!

Dalton Trumbo, Dorothy Parker, and Clifford Odets all did uncredited work on the script.

The film has been colorized because there is no copyright holder, but there has been an outrage in the film community over colorizing, so it is almost always broadcast in the original black-and-white.

While filming the scene where George prays in the bar, Jimmy Stewart has said that he was so overcome that he began to sob in earnest. Later, Capra reframed the shot so it looked like a tighter closeup, because he wanted to catch the genuinely anguished expression on Stewart's face.

THE CRITICS

"What is remarkable about *It's a Wonderful Life* is how well it holds up over the years; it's one of those ageless movies, like *Casablanca* or *The Third Man*, that improves with age." —Roger Ebert, *Chicago Sun-Times*

"Capra takes a serious tone here though there's no basis for the seriousness; this is doggerel trying to pass as art." —Pauline Kael, *The New Yorker*

"I'm gonna build things. I'm gonna build airfields, I'm gonna build skyscrapers a hundred stories high, I'm gonna build bridges a mile long . . ." George says to Mary. He is so smitten with his plans that he hardly notices he's falling in love.

THE GREAT SCENE

The last time George saw Mary she had bows in her hair. Now, at eighteen, on the night of the school dance, he is reintroduced to her, and he is breathless. He steals her away for a Charleston and they dance right into the pool, which has been opened up as a prank. Later, George, ridiculous in the tight football jersey that has replaced his wet clothes, escorts Mary, who is wearing a giant bathrobe, back home, singing an off-key duet of "Buffalo Gal" under the moonlight. It illuminates her face and her hair, and it's clear that George is falling for "the prettiest girl in town." Gawky and shy, he is about to place a courtly kiss on her lips when she playfully turns away and continues singing. It's clear that they are overcome with feelings for each other. Mary makes a wish that she might someday live in the old abandoned house they pass, and throws a rock into the window to seal their fate. George, growing rapturous, wishes a "whole hatful" of wishes for himself about conquering the world. "I'm shakin' the dust of this crummy little town off my feet and I'm gonna see the world! Italy, Greece, the Parthenon, the Coliseum. Then, I'm comin' back here to go to college and see what they know. And then I'm gonna build things. I'm gonna build airfields, I'm gonna build skyscrapers a hundred stories high, I'm gonna build bridges a mile long . . ." He then asks Mary what she wants, and before he knows it, he's practically proposed to her: "You—you want the moon? Just say the word and I'll throw a lasso around it and pull it down. Hey, that's a pretty good idea. I'll give you the moon . . . then you could swallow it. And it'll all dissolve, see? And the moonbeams that shoot out of your fingers and your toes and the ends of your hair . . . Am I talking too much?" A car rushes up to tell George that his father has suffered a mortal stroke. The evening they have shared, a harmonious moment out of time, has ended. And we sense instinctively that some of George's glorious dreams never will come to pass.

"Remember George, no man is a failure who has friends," says Clarence, George's guardian angel (Henry Travers). George is still having a hard time getting used to this guardian angel stuff—particularly since he has no wings.

35

RAGING BULL 1980

OTHELLO ON THE ROPES

Blood and sweat spew out of the boxing ring. A solitary hooded figure, monk-like, shadowboxes in slow motion as the camera circles the ring. Later, fat and swollen with defeat, the former boxer rehearses lines from Shakespeare in his seedy nightclub, then wails from a prison cell. The victory here is simply in watching this man: He is capable of unspeakable violence and of obsessive sexual jealousy, and has little sense of himself and his value in the world beyond what he can do with his fists—a man, in short, who is dragged under by his own nature. We cannot dismiss his failings; we ache for him not because he is sympathetic, but because we recognize him in ourselves.

Jim: When Method acting and the Atkins Diet collide. The sadomasochism of the boxing ring is even more shockingly embodied by what De Niro has done to his body for the sake of art. De Niro and his Method dieting program got a lot of the attention for this one, but Pesci and Moriarty pull their own considerable weight. The scene where Pesci is dragged from his house remains one of my most visceral moviegoing memories.

Gail: If you're open to it, there is grace in this foul, brutal, and artful vision of manhood at the lower depths.

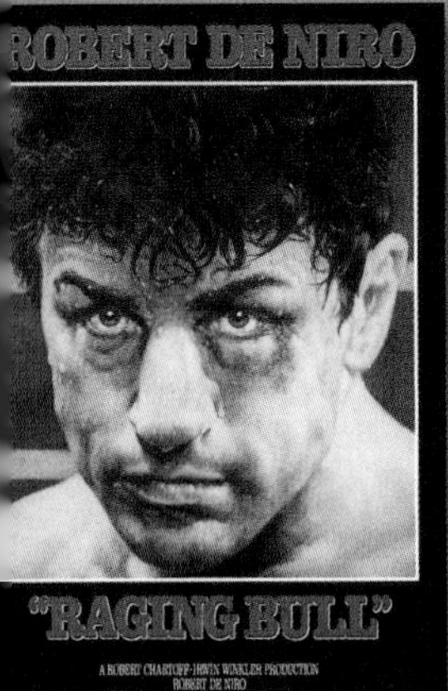

HE PLOT

is the story of the rise and self-ineered fall of middleweight boxer Jake Motta, a violent man trapped by his own ure. With the help of his ne'er-do-well ther, Joey, Jake earns a shot at the dleweight crown, but is made to take a It destroys him. He is further undone his irrational jealousy over Vickie, his utiful blond bride from the Bronx. La ta's inner demons and his inability to rcise rational thought or judgment isolate and magnify his brutal, animal instincts, ting him his wife, his title, his brother, his freedom.

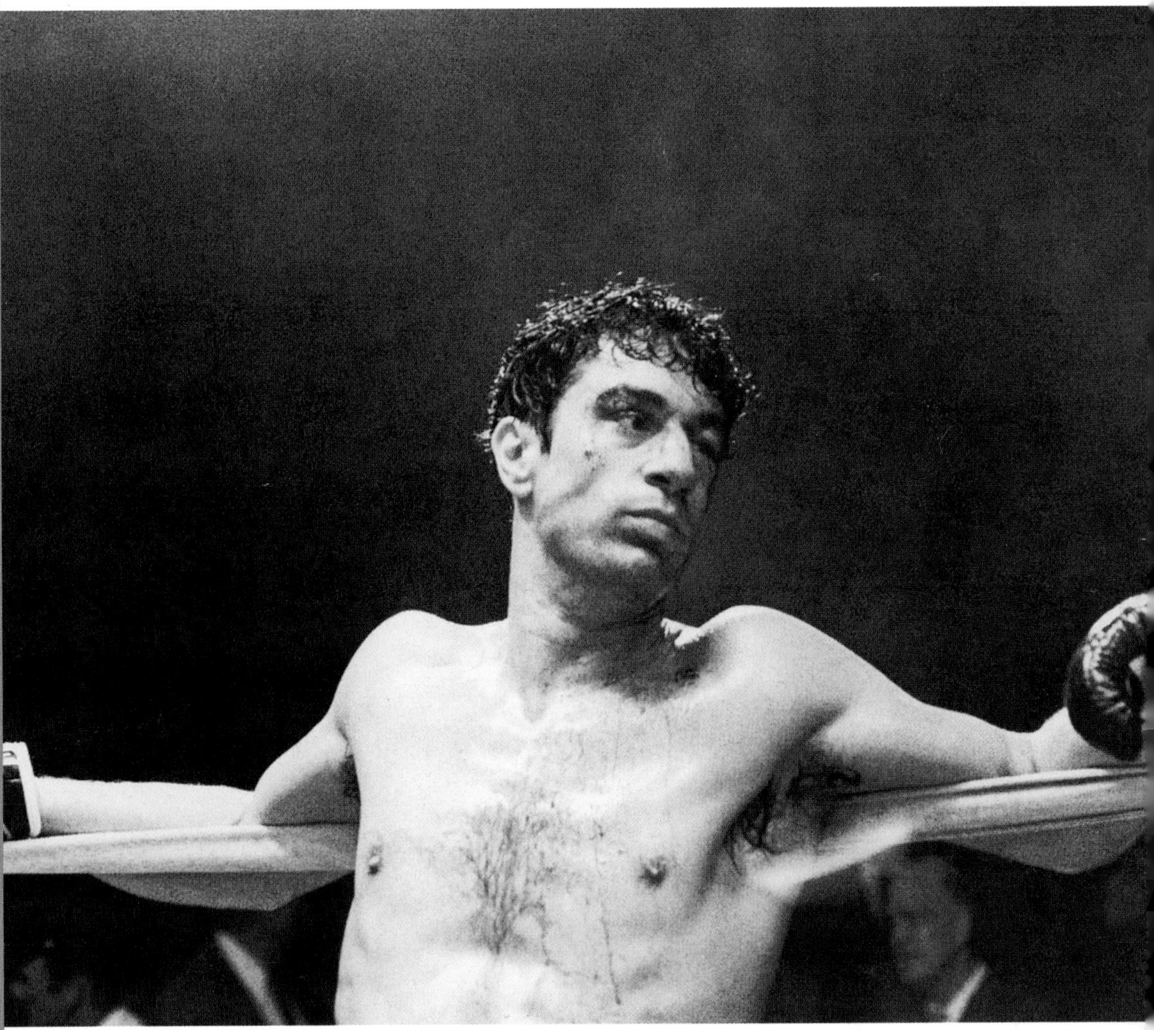

Jesus, according to Martin Scorsese. The tormented Jake (Robert DeNiro) is here and elsewhere filmed in a Christ-like pose as if taking hits for the sin of his very human, animal instinct for survival.

"You lose, you lose. You win, you still win." – Joey La Motta

THE DIRECTOR

De Niro, who brought La Motta's story to the attention of **Martin Scorsese**, had to force the director to take the story seriously and to stay with it after endless script revisions. When Scorsese was in the hospital after suffering an emotional and drug-related collapse, he reconsidered the life of La Motta and made a deep emotional connection, seeing Jake, like himself, as having overborrowed on his stores of goodwill. Scorsese's own despair seemed to be echoed by the boxer's inarticulate rage. As a result, the film became a deeply personal story. The director also found in the material the stuff of his most profound interest: the dynamic between human drives and the cultures that mold them, themes that resonate in others of his landmark films: *Mean Streets* (1973), *Taxi Driver* (1976), *GoodFellas* (1990), *The Aviator* (2004), and the Oscar-winning *The Departed* (2006). (For more on Scorsese, see pages 57 and 91.)

Jake turns his dreamgirl Vickie's (Cathy Moriarty) life into a living nightmare when he marries her and wastes their lives accusing her of sleeping with every man she sees.

THE CAST

Jake La Motta	Robert De Niro
Vickie La Motta	Cathy Moriarty
Joey La Motta	Joe Pesci
Salvy	Frank Vincent
Tommy Como	Nicholas Colasanto
Lenore La Motta	Theresa Saldana
Mario	Mario Gallo
Patsy	Frank Adonis
Guido	Joseph Bono
Toppy	Frank Topham
Charlie–Man with Como	Charles Scorsese

THE ACTORS

There are, and have been, few actors fiercer than **Robert De Niro**. In *Raging Bull* he reached the peak of his artistry and won the Academy Award. Method acting proved more a curse than a blessing when the actor accidentally broke Joe Pesci's rib in a sparring scene. De Niro's preparation to play Jake La Motta has become the stuff of legend. He sweat his way through relentless physical training, then entered three real-life Brooklyn boxing matches, winning two of them. He gained over 50 pounds to play the older La Motta, eating mountains of pasta in Italy. (Pesci lost weight for the same scene.) While preparing to play the fighter, De Niro met with La Motta himself to get a handle on him. The boxer was so impressed with De Niro that he insisted the actor could be a contender, and offered to manage and train him. (For more on De Niro, see pages 11, 57 and 91.)

Cathy Moriarty was only nineteen when she played the fifteen-year-old Vicki, but she played her with the sophistication of a married woman who has seen it all. Scorsese liked the fact that Moriarty had had no acting training. She rewarded his confidence when she received an Oscar nomination for her performance. Unfortunately, her subsequent career choices stalled a promising future, though she did manage two comebacks in *Soapdish* (1991) and *Matinee* (1993). She has appeared most recently in *Crazy in Alabama* (1999) and *Analyze That* (2002).

When De Niro saw **Joe Pesci**'s performance in a B movie, he asked the struggling actor to audition for him. At the time Pesci was working a musical act with fellow performer Frank Vincent I. De Niro struck gold when Pesci was cast as Jake's brother Joey. His intensity matched De Niro's scene for scene. Scorsese, however, felt that Pesci's response to Jake's imprecation, "Did you fuck my wife?" was too weak. The director told De Niro to ask him, "Did you fuck your mother?" That got him going and clinched the scene. Pesci continued to work brilliantly with Scorsese, particularly as a chilling wiseguy in *GoodFellas* (1990). (For more on Pesci, see page 91.)

Actor **John Turturro** made his film debut in *Bull* as the man at the table at Webster Hall. Since performing that role, Turturro has worked regularly with director Spike Lee, appearing in *Do the Right Thing* (1989), *Mo' Better Blues* (1990), and *Jungle Fever* (1991), and with producer/directors Joel and Ethan Cohen in *Miller's Crossing* (1990) and *Barton Fink* (1991). He's also appeared in *Desperately Seeking Susan* (1985), *The Color of Money* and *Hannah and Her Sisters* (both 1986), *The Sicilian* (1987), and *Five Corners* (1988). He appeared in Dennis Hopper's *Backtrack* (1989), and a pair of contemporary gangster films, *State of Grace* (1990) and *Men of Respect* (1991). His more recent credits include *Fearless* (1993), *Being Human* (1994), *Quiz Show* (1994), and *Search and Destroy* and *Clockers* (both 1995).

BEHIND THE SCREEN

In order to exaggerate Jake's increasing desperation and shrinking stature, Scorsese shot the later boxing scenes in a larger ring.

Chocolate was used for blood. It shows up better on black-and-white film.

The producer nixed the script after telling Scorsese and De Niro that La Motta was "a cockroach." The two did an uncredited rewrite to make La Motta more human.

The entire picture had only a few minutes of actual boxing, but those scenes took six weeks to film.

Scorsese's father, Charlie, is one of the mob wiseguys hanging around La Motta at a Copa nightclub table.

The original script included a scene of La Motta masturbating in his prison cell.

CREDITS

Producer: Robert Chartoff and Irwin Winkler/United Artists
Director: Martin Scorsese
Screenplay: Paul Schrader, Mardik Martin
Running Time: 129 minutes
Budget: $18 million
Box Office: $39 million

ACADEMY AWARDS

Best Actor: Robert De Niro
Best Editing: Thelma Schoonmaker

NOMINATIONS

Best Picture
Best Director: Martin Scorsese
Best Supporting Actor: Joe Pesci
Best Supporting Actress: Cathy Moriarty
Best Cinematography: Michael Chapman
Best Sound: Donald O. Mitchell, Bill Nicholson, David J. Kimball, Les Lazarowitz

THE YEAR'S OTHER WINNERS

Best Picture: *Ordinary People*
Best Director: Robert Redford, *Ordinary People*
Best Actress: Sissy Spacek, *Coal Miner's Daughter*
Best Supporting Actor: Timothy Hutton, *Ordinary People*
Best Supporting Actress: Mary Steenburgen, *Melvin and Howard*

THE BOXING SCENES

Scorsese's cinematic artistry is most evident in the boxing scenes, which have an almost elegiac, religious feel. In the ring, the tormented Jake seems to be taking punishment for the sin of not knowing quite how to be a man, and, more importantly, a human being. Impressionistically shot in slow motion from inside the ring, closeups show blood spurting, flying, and dripping from the ropes. Emotions are heightened by musical excerpts from Pietro Mascagni's *Cavalleria rusticana* and two other, lesser-known operas by the composer. Animal cries, bird shrieks, and the grating explosions of flashbulbs (actually, panes of glass being shattered) were used to create a sense of chaos. Melons and tomatoes were smashed to create the sound of landed punches. So special was this track that the original tapes were destroyed by the sound technicians to prevent them from being used again. We aren't consciously aware of all we're listening to, but we sense it.

The fights themselves were broken down into dozens of shots edited by Schoonmaker into duels consisting not of strategy but of punishing blows, with the camera only inches from the fists. Scorsese broke the rules of boxing pictures by staying inside the ring, and by changing its shape and size: Sometimes it's claustrophobically small, while other times it's long and narrow. The effect is dreamlike. In this nightmare, La Motta's inner demons do a dance of death. In the last fight with Sugar Ray Robinson the fighter looms over Jake, delivering endless, brutal blows, which end Jake's brief reign as champion.

"Why? Why? Why?...Why'd you do it? Why? You're so stupid...I'm not an animal. Why do you treat me like this? I'm not so bad," pleads Jake when he is alone in his prison cell where he has been thrown for soliciting prostitutes for his clients.

Bloated, bitter, and spent, La Motta, now a has-been boxer, runs a seedy night club, where he does standup and shouts obscenities. He is arrested on morals charges for soliciting prostitution clients. In one of the most emotionally eviscerating scenes on film, Jake, alone in his jail cell, slams head, fist, and shoulders into the wall, crying out, "Why? Why? Why? . . . Why'd you do it? Why? You're so stupid. . . . I'm not an animal. Why do you treat me like this? I'm not so bad."

THE CRITICS

"*Raging Bull* makes pain the measure of manhood. Not only pain inflicted, but pain endured. This is the big one, the title fight, and it's only art that's at stake. The sense of risk is palpable and the payoff is exhilarating. There's not a single pulled or wasted punch. The film is a perfect match of form and content."
—Amy Taubin, *Village Voice*

"It's about movies and about violence, it's about gritty visual rhythm, it's about Brando, it's about the two Godfather pictures—it's about Scorsese and De Niro's trying to top what they've done and what everybody else has done. Scorsese puts his unmediated obsessions on the screen, trying to turn raw, pulp power into art by removing it from the particulars of observation and narrative. He loses the lowlife entertainment values of prizefight films; he aestheticizes pulp and kills it."
—Pauline Kael, *The New Yorker*

RIGHT: Jake's brother Joey (Joe Pesci), though his steadfast manager and confidante, still gets gored by the raging bull whose paranoia destroys everything he loves.

THE OTHER LISTS

- American Film Institute (Yes)
- Roger Ebert's Top 100 (Yes)
- *Entertainment Weekly* (Yes)
- Internet Movie Database (Yes)
- Leonard Maltin (Yes)
- *Movieline* (Yes)
- National Society of Film Critics (No)
- *Premiere* Magazine (Yes)
- *Rolling Stone* Magazine (Yes)
- *Village Voice* (No)

36

THE BEST YEARS OF OUR LIVES 1946

PEACE IS HELL

"I don't care if it doesn't make a nickel. I just want every man, woman, and child in America to see it." And with that, Hollywood's master of the malapropism, producer Samuel Goldwyn, launched his project of love. He hired a veteran director of epic dramas, William Wyler, who in turn drafted cinematographer Gregg Toland of *Citizen Kane* fame to give the film his articulated "deep focus" treatment. The arch-realism combined with an unusually frank discourse on the plight of returning servicemen made this the biggest box-office bull's-eye since *Gone with the Wind.* The film's great discovery was Harold Russell, a real-life double amputee who'd lost his hands in an Army training accident. Audiences were mesmerized by the scene in which he showed his fiancée what she would have to deal with if she wed him. It's comparatively mild by today's standards (we don't actually see his stumps), but the scene's emotional power is timeless. The more subtly tragic figure is the otherwise handsome "flyboy" played by Dana Andrews. A great war hero, he comes home without much hope of anything more than his old job as a soda jerk. For him, the war years were truly the best of his life.

Jim: Dana Andrews's incredible performance is another major Oscar bypass. We don't buy that tacked-on happy ending for him, and from the look on his face before fadeout, neither did he.

Gail: If you have enough handkerchiefs around you might get through this groundbreaking portrait of the traumatic aftermath of war in the lives of the survivors and their families. Its wrenching honesty is matched by the nakedness of the performances.

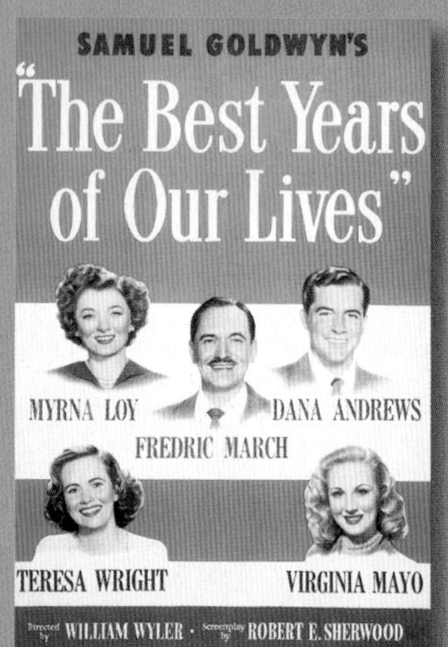

SAMUEL GOLDWYN'S
"The Best Years of Our Lives"
MYRNA LOY
DANA ANDREWS
FREDRIC MARCH
TERESA WRIGHT
VIRGINIA MAYO
WILLIAM WYLER · ROBERT E. SHERWOOD
MacKINLAY KANTOR · GREGG TOLAND

THE PLOT

Three veterans return to their idyllic hometown at the end of World War II to confront the overwhelming difficulties of fitting in. The oldest, Army sergeant Al Stephenson (Fredric March), has missed his children growing up and must deal with their discomfort. His wife Milly (Myrna Loy) remains loyally by his side despite his often embarrassing, ill-timed drunks. The handsome Air Force bombardier Fred Derry (Dana Andrews) realizes he's losing his party-girl wife Marie (Virginia Mayo) to a world he can neither afford nor understand. He turns to Al's daughter Peggy (Teresa Wright) for comfort only to fall impossibly in love. The sailor and former football hero Homer Parrish (Harold Russell) has lost his hands in a ship explosion. Though his fiancée Wilma (Cathy O'Donnell) still loves him, he must face the stark realities of his new way of life.

The first night home is a perfect excuse for a drunken night out. It helps if the guy who's playing your bar-owner uncle is none other than Hoagy Carmichael, who wrote, among some other pretty decent tunes, the classic "Stardust."

I've seen nothing, I should have stayed at home and found out what was really going on."—Al Stephenson

THE DIRECTOR

"This is not a story of plot, but a picture of some people, who were real people, facing real problems." **William Wyler** had served in the Air Force during the war, during which time he made the documentaries *The Fighting Lady* and *Memphis Belle*. *Best Years* was an extremely personal mission for him. "If anybody doubts my loyalty to my country, I'll punch him in the nose, and I don't care how old he is." He felt that returning servicemen were owed something, primarily an understanding of what they'd been through. Wyler brilliantly pointed up their sense of isolation in the early scene where Homer, Fred, and Al are flying back to Boone City together. They're looking down on their hometown to see "folks golfing as if nothing had ever happened." The three men are between two worlds, no longer a part of either. Wyler walked away with his third Best Director Oscar for this one, having won for *Mrs. Miniver* (1942) and for *Ben-Hur* (1959). For many years Bette Davis's lover off-screen, he's credited with three of her greatest performances: *Jezebel* (1938), *The Letter* (1940) and *The Little Foxes* (1941). Among his other highpoints are *The Heiress* (1949), *Detective Story* (1951), *Carrie* (1952), *Roman Holiday* (1953), *Friendly Persuasion* (1956), *The Children's Hour* (1961) and *Funny Girl* (1968). He was offered, but passed on, *The Sound of Music*, remarking, "I just can't bear to make a picture about all those nice Nazis."

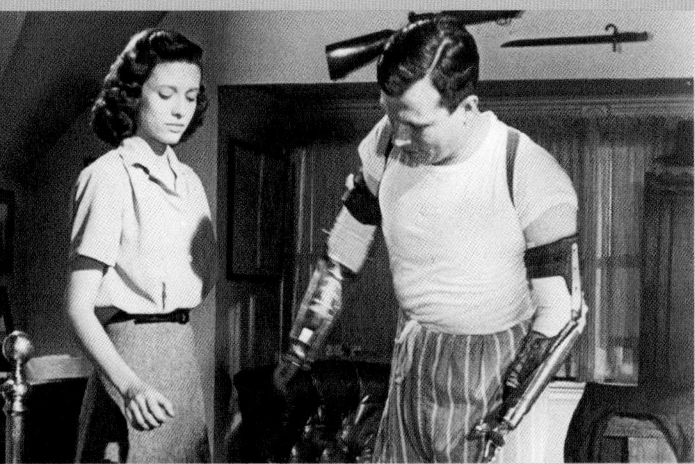

Wyler declared Harold Russell the most natural actor he'd ever worked with. This is the movie's killer scene, in which he lays out the hard truths about his handicap to his fiancée, Wilma. It was beyond mere performance; Russell was telling his real, very harrowing story to the world. His double Oscar win had the tearful audience on its feet.

THE CAST

Milly Stephenson	Myrna Loy
Al Stephenson	Fredric March
Fred Derry	Dana Andrews
Peggy Stephenson	Teresa Wright
Marie Derry	Virginia Mayo
Wilma Cameron	Cathy O'Donnell
Uncle Butch	Hoagy Carmichael
Homer Parrish	Harold Russell
Hortense Derry	Gladys George
Pat Derry	Roman Bohnen
Mr. Milton	Ray Collins
Mrs. Parrish	Minna Gombell
Mr. Parrish	Walter Baldwin
Cliff Scully	Steve Cochran
Mrs. Cameron	Dorothy Adams

THE ACTORS

Fredric March was among the canniest stars of his generation. His refusal to be typecast kept him open to a remarkable spectrum of roles, from the chilling *Dr. Jekyll and Mr. Hyde* (1932) to Garbo's romantic interest in *Anna Karenina* (1935) to a screwball comedic actor in *Nothing Sacred* (1937). He even had a turn as the Grim Reaper in *Death Takes A Holiday* (1934). Interestingly, in his two most famous roles, Al Stephenson in *Best Years* and Norman Maine in *A Star Is Born* (1937), he played alcoholics. And his big drunken scenes in each one found him speechifying in a tuxedo. He remained well dressed for *The Man in the Gray Flannel Suit* (1955) and as William Jennings Bryan in *Inherit the Wind* (1960).

"Because he has the best role, the most forthright and meaningful, **Dana Andrews** is privileged to give the best performance in the film," said Bosley Crowther in the *New York Times*. One of the most underrated male stars of his era, Andrews got his jumpstart late in *Laura* (1944) playing the lovesick detective to Gene Tierney's haunting mystery woman. Andrews made more than 80 films, most of which were undistinguished, as he battled acute alcoholism. *Best Years* was his watershed film, but *Where The Sidewalk Ends* (1950) and *Beyond a Reasonable Doubt* (1956) are worth a look.

Myrna Loy was pigeonholed "the perfect wife" by her studio and was stuck in the role for most of her career. She most famously appeared as the soused spouse of William Powell in *The Thin Man* series. She took a sabbatical from Hollywood for the duration of World War II, in which she served as a full-time volunteer on several fronts. She was one of the few stars who made the transition from silents, where she had often played Asian vamps. She was considered the beautiful ideal of the early 1930s, and with the oncoming popularity of cosmetic surgery, hers was the nose most women asked their doctors for. Following *Best Years of Our Lives*, she appeared in another box-office hit, *The Bachelor and the Bobby Soxer* (1947), followed by *Mr. Blandings Builds His Dreamhouse* (1948). Her final appearances on film were the unmemorable *Midnight Lace* (1960) and *Airport 1975* (1975).

Harold Russell had been spotted by Wyler in a military training film in which he displayed dexterity with his "hooks." The director was immediately taken by Russell's natural ease on camera and thought he had just the right look for Homer Parrish. The character's handicap was changed from spastic to double amputated hands. *Best Years* was his only film appearance until *Inside Moves* (1995) and *Dogtown* (1997).

An Oscar winner for Best Supporting Actress in *Mrs. Miniver* (1942), **Teresa Wright** did well by Wyler, who then cast her in *Little Foxes* with Bette Davis. She also made a smart impression on Alfred Hitchcock, who costarred her with Joseph Cotten in one of his most enduring classics, *Shadow of a Doubt* (1943). Her solid but plain appearance led to character roles very early on, and her film career suffered. By 1953 she was already playing the mother of Jean Simmons in *The Actress*, with just a six-year difference in their ages.

THE CRITICS

"Heart-wrenching, touching, and filled with emotional dynamite." —*Hollywood Reporter*

"No piece of entertainment, however intelligent and thrilling, or beautiful, can justify so Wagnerian a length." —*London Tribune*

SEND IN THE CLONES

Coming Home (1978)

NOTABLE QUOTES

"It's eighty percent script and twenty percent you get great actors. There's nothing else to it." —William Wyler

"Too caustic? To hell with the costs, we'll make the picture anyway." —Sam Goldwyn

CREDITS

Producer: Samuel Goldwyn
Director: William Wyler
Screenplay:
Robert E. Sherwood,
from the novel *Glory For Me*
by MacKinlay Kantor
Running time: 172 minutes
Box Office: $11.3 million

ACADEMY AWARDS

Best Picture
Best Director: William Wyler
Best Adapted Screenplay:
Robert Sherwood
Best Actor: Fredric March
Best Supporting Actor:
Harold Russell
Best Editing: Daniel Mandell
Best Musical Score:
Hugo Friedhofer

NOMINATIONS

Best Sound Recording:
Gordon Sawyer

THE YEAR'S OTHER WINNERS

Best Actress: Olivia de Havilland,
To Each His Own
Supporting Actress: Anne Baxter,
The Razor's Edge

THE GREAT SCENE

Fred Derry's brief glory days are as irrelevant now as the trashed bombers he once flew.

Fred Derry's life has hit bottom. He's being sued for divorce by his cheating wife, and he's lost the girl he truly loves as well as his job at the drugstore. He's decided to try his luck in another town despite his adoring father's protests. Dad begs Fred to stay on, but one look around their shack by the railroad tracks convinces him. He hits the road, leaving his many war citations behind. His dad begins to read the one he received with his Iron Cross. It recounts Fred's bravery as a bombardier over the German skies. His feats were nothing short of extraordinary. As his dad reads aloud to Fred's stepmother, his voice cracks almost imperceptibly. This is a man who never cries, but his tragic son's accomplishments, which he could never have imagined, have elevated the boy to the pantheon of heroes.

Fred Derry suffers the double horror of waking from a nightmare in a stranger's guest bedroom. He's not sure how he got there or, for that matter, where he's going. Dana Andrews gives the best performance of his alcohol-troubled career.

THE OTHER LISTS

- American Film Institute (Yes)
- Roger Ebert's Top 100 (No)
- *Entertainment Weekly* (Yes)
- Internet Movie Database (No)
- Leonard Maltin (Yes)
- *Movieline* (Yes)
- National Society of Film Critics (No)
- *Premiere* Magazine (Yes)
- *Rolling Stone* Magazine (No)
- *Village Voice* (No)

BEHIND THE SCREEN

Harold Russell was the only nominee in the history of the Academy Awards to win two for the same role: one for Best Supporting Actor and a second Honorary Oscar for his courage and patriotism.

Harold Russell was also the first Oscar-winner to sell his statuette at auction. He needed the money to pay for his ailing wife's surgery.

To ensure "reality," the actresses wore only street makeup and the actors wore none.

Director Wyler liked untrained Harold Russell's naturalness just fine. Wyler threw a fit when, behind his back, producer Goldwyn hired an acting coach for him.

A perfectionist behind the camera, his exhausted cast and crew dubbed the director "Once-more Wyler."

37

THE AFRICAN QUEEN 1951

LADY AND THE TRAMP STEAMER

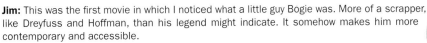

It isn't grit and a cranky steam engine that get the rickety *African Queen* down the Bora River—it's sheer star power. The German Navy, alligators, and leeches don't stand a chance against the likes of Humphrey Bogart and Katharine Hepburn at full-throttle. Both are a bit past their prime and it's a brilliant ploy to provide them with characters that aren't merely mature simulacra of their former images. Bogart, as an almost clownishly coarse, simpleminded lug with a taste for gin, completely submerges himself in the role of Charlie Allnut. You suspect this is the kind of character he would've loved to have been playing all along rather than those smoky, hard-boiled detectives. When he giddily imitates the animals on shore for Rose's pleasure, especially his routine as a very cute hippo, you can't quite believe this was Rick of *Casablanca*. Hepburn is more recognizable—it's almost impossible to hide her unique persona—but her Rose is a new creation, righteous fortitude underpinned with touching vulnerability, a combination more often evident later in her career. These two legends are fascinating to observe. That's good, because there's not much else to do—the plot is pure formula: Unlikely lovers meet, beat the odds, and live happily ever after at the Academy Awards.

Jim: This was the first movie in which I noticed what a little guy Bogie was. More of a scrapper, like Dreyfuss and Hoffman, than his legend might indicate. It somehow makes him more contemporary and accessible.

Gail: Like a chemical compound that explodes when the proper elements are combined, Bogie and Hep come together in a boat, and something absolutely charming and wonderful happens, the likes of which we'll never see again.

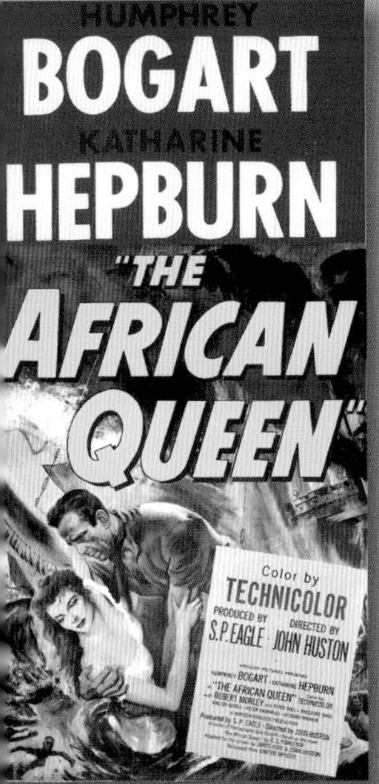

HE PLOT

:h the declaration of World War I, English ssionary siblings in German East Africa, se (Katharine Hepburn) and Samuel Sayer bert Morley), find themselves in the wrong ce at the wrong time. The advancing Huns :h their settlement and fragile Samuel s of shock. Shy but righteous Rose is to taken downriver by grizzled trader Charlie nut (Humphrey Bogart) on his steam-pow- d boat, the *African Queen*. Their natures lide from the very start. She will not simply out the war as he drunkenly suggests. e pushes him to navigate the full course the deadly river and attempt to blow up German tanker. Rose's grit is contagious d soon enough Charlie is in love, even er she dumps his gin overboard. They aculously survive the river, and a close counter with German sharpshooters, but ir hope of sinking the tanker is dashed by torm. They're taken prisoner and insist on ng wed before their execution. Fate spares m as the drifting wreckage of the *African een* completes their mission for them and lodes in the nick of time.

"You crazy, psalm-singing, skinny old maid!" Bogie's Charlie Allnut isn't one to mince words when he's full of gin. Given his round-the-clock drunken revels with director John Huston on and off the set, it's not easy to guess how a sober Bogie might've responded to Hepburn. But it sure looked like they were having the times of their lives.

"Nature, Mr. Allnut, is what we are put into this world to rise above."—Rose

THE DIRECTOR

Gleefully vice-ridden Renaissance man **John Huston** approached filmmaking with the fearlessness of one born to the business. The scion of a famed acting family, he made his directorial debut with *The Maltese Falcon* (1941), which resulted in a "beautiful friendship" with Bogart. They next collaborated on *The Treasure of the Sierra Madre* (1948), which costarred John's father, Walter, and *Beat The Devil* (1954). His drinking binges with Bogart during production were the stuff of legend and drove Hepburn to distraction. Huston was smart enough to bring on board the noted cinematographer Jack Cardiff, who captured the daunting beauty of the rugged river. Huston pursued large-themed projects and his signature manic energy resulted in such classics as *The Asphalt Jungle* (1950), *Moulin Rouge* (1952), *Moby Dick* (1956), and *The Misfits* (1961), which was the last film for Marilyn Monroe and Clark Gable. His direction of *Prizzi's Honor* (1985) led to his daughter Anjelica's Best Supporting Actress Oscar. As an actor he's most famous for his villainous role as Faye Dunaway's father in *Chinatown* (1974). (For more on Huston, see page 229.)

"A man alone, he gets to living like a hog." His character is far from anything Bogie had done before, and it makes you wonder what he might've been capable of had he not been so confined by his image. Those animal imitations are the stuff of Brando, his Oscar rival.

THE CAST	
Charlie Allnut	Humphrey Bogart
Rose Sayer	Katharine Hepburn
Reverend Samuel Sayer	Robert Morley
Captain of Louisa	Peter Bull
First Officer	Theodore Bikel
Second Officer	Walter Gotell
First Officer of Shona	Peter Swanwick
Second Officer of Shona	Richard Marner

THE ACTORS

"I'd like to be anything but an actor. It's such a foolish life." **Humphrey Bogart** hated wearing his hairpiece but the studio demanded it, claiming he had an image to maintain. Ironically, the role of childlike, big-hearted Charlie Allnut was a major departure from his usual tough-guy fare. It won him his first and only Academy Award and he campaigned hard for it. Luck was on his side; his major competition was the supposed shoo-in, Marlon Brando (for *A Streetcar Named Desire*), who lost votes as the result of his "bad boy" off-camera behavior. Bogart announced that if he won he was "not going to thank anybody. I'm just going to say I damn well deserve it." Despite several appearances in the early '30s, Bogart's career really began in earnest with *The Petrified Forest* (1936), followed by *Marked Woman* (1937), in which he shares the screen with Bette Davis. *Angels with Dirty Faces* (1938) led to another Davis vehicle, *Dark Victory* (1939), and *They Drive By Night* (1940). He entered his golden age with *Maltese Falcon* (1941), *Casablanca* (1942), *To Have and Have Not* (1944) in which he starred and fell in love with Lauren "You know how to whistle . . ." Bacall, *The Big Sleep* (1946), *The Treasure of the Sierra Madre* (1948), *Key Largo* (1948), and *In a Lonely Place* (1950). The post-*African Queen* period is highlighted by *The Caine Mutiny*, *Sabrina*, *The Barefoot Contessa* (all 1954), and *We're No Angels* (1955). (For more on Bogart, see pages 21 and 229.)

Katharine Hepburn was undaunted by the dangers of filming on location in Africa and maintained her sunny cynicism. In the scene in which she and Bogart have to drag the boat out of the marsh, the water teemed with alligators. Huston told her not to worry, he'd have the crew shoot at them. "They're afraid of the noise," he told her. Hepburn fired back, "But what about the deaf ones?" Thanks to Huston, her galvanic performance in *The African Queen* initiated a new and lasting image for her. Once dubbed "box-office poison," Hepburn went on to win a record four Oscars out of twelve nominations. A true Hollywood survivor, her enormous output includes *Morning Glory* (1933), *Little Women* (1933), *Bringing Up Baby* (1938, see page 222), *The Philadelphia Story* (1940), *Woman of the Year* (1942), *Adam's Rib* (1949), *Summertime* (1955), *Suddenly Last Summer* (1959), *Guess Who's Coming To Dinner* (1967), *The Lion in Winter* (1968), and *On Golden Pond* (1981). (For more on Hepburn, see page 223.)

THE SET

Huston, an avid wild-game hunter, loved Africa and was determined to shoot on location there. It would be only the third American film to do so. Setbacks and delays were routine, thanks to the constant challenge of alligators, soldier ants, and native extras who had a habit of looking directly into the camera during key scenes.

ROLE REVERSALS

The role of Rose had Bette Davis written all over it—it fact, it was written *for* her. She passed on the project for one reason or another over the years (once due to pregnancy). Proposed leading men included James Mason, David Niven, and John Mills.

BEHIND THE SCREEN

Katharine Hepburn, perfectly cast as the steely, righteous Rose, told all in a best-selling book, *The Making of the African Queen, or How I went to Africa with Bogart, Bacall and Huston and Almost Lost My Mind.*

Another book documenting the production, *White Hunter, Black Heart*, by Peter Viertel, was made into a 1990 movie by Clint Eastwood.

The infamous leeches, which made audiences' skin crawl as well as Charlie's, were made of rubber. Now that's acting!

Dysentery cost Hepburn 20 pounds by the time she'd finished shooting. Though a hearty survivor of location shoots, she developed a chronic eye infection after tumbling into Venice's Grand Canal during the filming of *Summertime* (1955).

As a sailor in World War I, Bogart suffered a partially paralyzed upper lip after a freak accident aboard a ship. The unusual effect on his face and voice served to create his screen image.

CREDITS

Producer: Sam Spiegel/ Paramount
Director: John Huston
Screenplay: John Huston, James Agee, based on the novel by C. S. Forester
Running time: 105 minutes
Box Office: $4.3 million

ACADEMY AWARDS

Best Actor: Humphrey Bogart

NOMINATIONS

Best Actress: Katharine Hepburn
Best Director: John Huston
Best Screenplay: James Agee, John Huston

THE YEAR'S OTHER WINNERS

Best Picture: *An American in Paris*
Best Director: George Stevens, *A Place in the Sun*
Best Actress: Vivien Leigh, *A Streetcar Named Desire*
Best Supporting Actor: Karl Malden, *A Streetcar Named Desire*
Best Supporting Actress: Kim Hunter, *A Streetcar Named Desire*

THE GREAT SCENE

Their boat stuck in the marshes, poor Charlie must drag it barefoot through the silt. He comes back on board and Rose screams at the sight of leeches stuck to his back. "If there's anything in the world I hate it's leeches!" he shudders with pure disgust and loathing. She starts to pull them off and he warns her ,"No! They'll just burrow their heads in. Salt, that's it, that'll make them fall off." She manages to get them all, even the ones clinging to his legs. He finally catches his breath and they try to push off with oars—no luck. Charlie and Rose exchange a look of dread. He has no choice but to get back in the infested water.

Rose (Katharine Hepburn) and Charlie (Humphrey Bogart) enjoy a rare moment of calm as they head down river to safety from the Germans. There will be no hiding from the mutual attraction that soon explodes between them, though. (No surprise that Bogie looks a bit hung over—he was reportedly reveling round the clock with director John Huston during filming.)

Katharine Hepburn was ordered by a studio exec, early in her career, never to smile. "It makes you look like a horse." She defied the edict, of course, but in repose there's something ineffably secretive and powerful about her, like a monarch withholding her personal suffering from her subjects.

THE CRITICS

"A film that has everything—adventure, humor, spectacular photography and superb performances." —*TV Guide's Movie Guide*

"*The African Queen* owes more to casting coups than to directorial acumen." —Andrew Sarris, *Village Voice*

"All Bogart has to do to dominate a scene is to enter it."
—Raymond Chandler

THE OTHER LISTS

- American Film Institute (Yes)
- Roger Ebert's Top 100 (No)
- *Entertainment Weekly* (No)
- Internet Movie Database (Yes)
- Leonard Maltin (No)
- *Movieline* (Yes)
- National Society of Film Critics (No)
- *Premiere* Magazine (No)
- *Rolling Stone* Magazine (No)
- *Village Voice* (No)

"The trouble with Bogart is he thinks he's Bogart."
—John Huston

38

DR. STRANGELOVE, OR: HOW I LEARNED TO STOP WORRYING AND LOVE THE BOMB 1964

BOMBS AWAY!

From its credits sequence showing the graceful midair refueling of a B-52 bomber set against a musical background of "Try a Little Tenderness," we know we're headed for a bumpy ride. The abuse of power has never been as maddeningly funny. Coming on the heels of the Bay of Pigs and the assassination of the American President, this savagely satiric film made plausible our worries about the bomb, the Russians, and doomsday. Kubrick's pantheon of eccentrics and grotesques with their fingers on the button is as absurd and riotously funny as it is paralyzing.

Jim: Cold War paranoia served up as Monty Python-esque satire. If you get the joke, you're in for a one-of-a-kind treat. If you don't, it could make for a very long night. The pacing is often glacial.

Gail: *Strangelove* broke hallowed ground with savage humor that reveled in the dark underside of technological progress and the American military character.

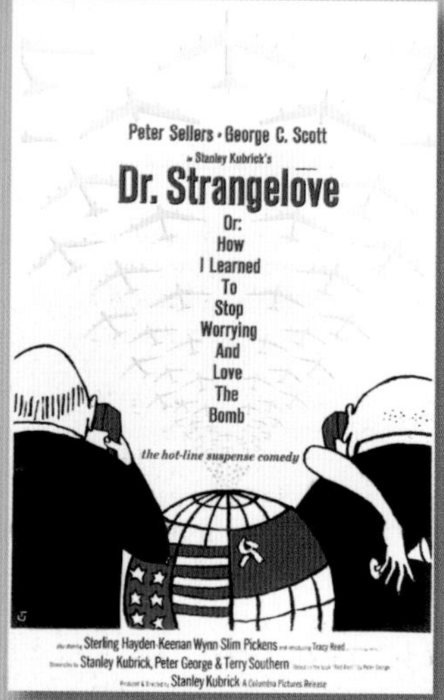

THE PLOT

At the height of the Cold War an accidental nuclear attack is launched by a psychotic bomb-group commander, Jack D. Ripper (Sterling Hayden). Cut to the cramped flight-deck interior of a B-52 sent on a preemptive strike against the Soviets. At the helm, the rabble-rousing flight commander, Major T. J. "King" Kong (Slim Pickens), dons a cowboy hat and is off to war—Whoopee! Cut to the cavernous underground war room where the bald, ridiculous President Merkin Muffley (Peter Sellers) alerts the Russians of the impending attack and instructs them to "shoot down the American bombers." After a series of disputes with the dead-on Khrushchev impersonator (Peter Bull) and explications of how the attack will play out by the Kissinger-esque Dr. Strangelove (also Sellers), the inevitable occurs and the world ends as mushroom clouds rise to the strains of "We'll Meet Again."

Can you be only a little psychotic? Brig. Gen. Jack D. Ripper (Sterling Hayden), who has blockaded himself inside his office, justifies his accidental release of a nuclear bomb over Russia to Capt. Lionel Mandrake (Peter Sellers): "I can no longer sit back and allow Communist infiltration, Communist indoctrination, Communist subversion, and the international Communist conspiracy to sap and impurify all of our precious bodily fluids." Mandrake, thank goodness, is still in possession of enough sanity to attempt to reach the President in order to prevent the inevitable outcome—nuclear annihilation.

THE DIRECTOR

They said it couldn't be done but **Stanley Kubrick** did it. He directed the first commercially successful political satire about nuclear war. The subject had been an obsession of the director's for years. Though originally written as a drama, the director transformed the novel on which the movie is based into a comedy because of its absurd premise: "How the hell could the President ever tell the Russian premier to shoot down American planes?" Though actors and crew were deeply affected by Kubrick's micromanagement on the set, they were eager to please. *Strangelove*'s success gave Kubrick the financial and artistic freedom to work on any project he chose, and he went on to direct *2001: A Space Odyssey* (1968), *A Clockwork Orange* (1971), *Barry Lyndon* (1975), *The Shining* (1980), *Full Metal Jacket* (1987), and *Eyes Wide Shut* (1999), before his premature death in 1999. (For more on Kubrick, see pages 160, 226, and 292.)

Taking his job very seriously: Upon receiving orders to institute code R (that's nuclear attack to you) Major T. J. "King" Kong (Slim Pickens) eventually rips off his flight gear and dons a cowboy hat with a yowl of "Yahoo!" By the end of the film he's straddling the bomb like a horse, riding it down to earth waving his hat into the sunset.

THE CAST	
Capt. Lionel Mandrake/President Merkin Muffley/Dr. Strangelove	Peter Sellers
Gen. "Buck" Turgidson	George C. Scott
Brig. Gen. Jack D. Ripper	Sterling Hayden
Col. "Bat" Guano	Keenan Wynn
Major T. J. "King" Kong	Slim Pickens
Russian Ambassador Alexi de Sadesky	Peter Bull
Lt. Lothar Zogg	James Earl Jones

NOTABLE QUOTES

"There used to be a me behind the mask, but I had it surgically removed." –Peter Sellers

"I writhe when I see myself on the screen. I'm such a dreadfully clumsy, hulking image. I say to myself, 'Why doesn't he get off? Why doesn't he get off?' I mean, I look like such an idiot. Some fat awkward thing dredged up from some third-rate drama company. I must stop thinking about it, otherwise I shan't be able to go on working." –Peter Sellers

THE ACTORS

Instead of the three roles he ultimately played, **Peter Sellers** was originally cast in four, but couldn't get the hang of the Texas accent for Major T. J. "King" Kong. In any case, Sellers broke his leg before he could do those scenes and Kubrick had to find another actor. Sellers was given free reign to improvise. "If you ask me to play myself, I will not know what to do. I do not know who or what I am," he once said. Sellers was brilliant in such films as, *Lolita* (1962), *What's New, Pussycat?* (1965), *I Love You, Alice B. Toklas* (1968), *The Magic Christian* (1969), *The Return of the Pink Panther* (1975), *Being There* (1979), and *Trail of the Pink Panther* (1982).

Infamous for, among other things, rejecting his Oscar for *Patton*, **George C. Scott** often said that his role in *Strangelove* was his favorite, and that he felt guilty getting paid for having so much fun. His fall in the war room when his character gets extremely agitated was in real life an accident. But it was so in character that Kubrick decided to keep it in. Scott also delivers one of the film's most devastatingly funny lines: "Mr. President, I'm not saying we wouldn't get our hair mussed, but I do say no more than ten to twenty million killed, tops, uh, depending on the breaks." Scott said of Kubrick, "He is most certainly in command, and he's so self-effacing and apologetic it's impossible to be offended by him." Scott has had a formidable career, including such films as *Anatomy of a Murder* (1959), *The Hustler* (1961, Oscar nomination), *The FlimFlam Man* (1967), *Petulia* (1968), *Patton* (1970, Oscar), *The Hospital* (1971), *The New Centurions* (1972), and *Hardcore* (1979). By the end of his career, he was reduced to starring in the TV sitcom, *Mr. President* (1987).

Kubrick never showed **Slim Pickens** ("Kong") the script nor told him the film was a black comedy. Instead, the director told him to play it straight. The results, are, well, pretty funny, intentionally or not. Kubrick cast Pickens's on the basis of his work in the western *One-Eyed Jacks* (1961). Pickens's major work was performed in TV movies, though he did appear in features, including *The Flim-Flam Man* (1967), *The Ballad of Cable Hogue* (1970), *Pat Garrett and Billy the Kid* (1973), *Blazing Saddles* (1974), and *1941* (1979).

You never saw **James Earl Jones** in a film before *Strangelove*. This was his debut.

BEHIND THE SCREEN

Originally, the ending had the Russians and Americans in the war throwing custard pies at each other. President Muffley took a pie in the face and fell down, prompting Gen. Turgidson to cry, "Gentlemen! Our gallant young President has just been struck down in his prime!" The gravity of the Kennedy assassination put an end to such hijinks; it all just cut too close to home.

The film's release was delayed from late 1963 to early 1964 in response to the Kennedy assassination on November 22, 1963.

The film included the following disclaimer: "It is the stated position of the United States Air Force that their safeguards would protect the occurrence of such events as are depicted in this film. Furthermore, it should be noted that none of the characters portrayed in this film are meant to represent any real persons living or dead."

Seller's strange German accent for *Dr. Strangelove* was adopted after hearing the 1950s crime photographer Weegee talking during an on-set visit.

Sellers had the cast in stitches when he portrayed Muffley speaking with a bad cold. It proved so disruptive that the director reshot the scenes with Sellers playing the role straight.

Major Kong's comment about the survival kit ("A fella could have a pretty good weekend in Vegas with all that stuff") originally referred to Dallas instead of Las Vegas, but was overdubbed after President Kennedy's assassination in Dallas.

"Alien hand syndrome," Strangelove's uncontrollable limb, is an actual affliction that can be caused by a stroke or other brain injury.

CREDITS

Producer: Stanley Kubrick/ Columbia Pictures
Director: Stanley Kubrick
Screenplay: Stanley Kubrick, Terry Southern, and Peter George, based on the novel by Mr. George
Running Time: 102 minutes
Budget: $1.8 million
Box Office: $9 million

NOMINATIONS

Best Picture: Stanley Kubrick
Best Director: Stanley Kubrick
Best Actor: Peter Sellers
Best Adapted Screenplay: Stanley Kubrick, Peter George, and Terry Southern

THE YEAR'S WINNERS

Best Picture: *My Fair Lady*
Best Director: George Cukor: *My Fair Lady*
Best Actor: Rex Harrison, *My Fair Lady*
Best Actress: Julie Andrews, *Mary Poppins*
Best Supporting Actor: Peter Ustinov, *Topkapi*
Best Supporting Actress: Lila Kedrova, *Zorba the Greek*

THE GREAT SCENE

The President phones the drunken Soviet premier Dmitri Kissof to warn him of the impending American air assault: "Well, I'll tell you what he did, he ordered his planes . . . to attack your country . . . I'm sorry, too, Dmitri. I'm very sorry . . . All right! You're sorrier than I am! But I am sorry as well. I am as sorry as you are Dmitri. Don't say that you are more sorry than I am, because I am capable of being just as sorry as you are. So we're both sorry, all right? All right."

"Well, I'll tell you what he did. He ordered his planes . . . to attack your country," President Muffley (Peter Sellers) tells Soviet President "Dmitri" in a friendly phone call, surrounded by his war room staff and Russian Ambassador Alexi de Sadesky (Peter Bull, far right).

Researchers at the University of Aberdeen who identified it named it "Dr. Strangelove Syndrome."

The dictionary definition of "merkin" (the President's first name) is "a pubic wig."

It was Sellers who brought Terry Southern in on a cowrite because he was a fan of Southern's novel *The Magic Christian*, the film version of which Sellers appeared in five years later.

When Sellers observed Kubrick wearing gloves to handle hot lights on the set, he thought them sinister. He decided it would be disturbing to wear one on his right hand (the one that was out of control) for the film.

The stock footage shown during the opening credits (a suggestive image of refueling military aircraft) had been used in *Santa Claus Conquers the Martians* (1964).

THE LOOK

Three sets are used in the film and the scenes shot on each one are characterized by a different camera style. Kubrick uses intense closeups inside the bomber; long, static shots show the eerily quiet war room; and shaky, documentary-style chaos during the attack on the Air Force base. Several standout shots include the tight closeup of the huge, cigar-puffing face of Ripper looming like something out of a nightmare; a contrasting shot of Turgidson ranting in the foreground while a dignified Mandrake looks on. Ironically, the most beautiful shots are those of the flyers speeding over ice, tundra, and evergreens. Finally, the most impressive shot of the film comes at the end: Major Kong rides the bomb into oblivion, whooping it up as he disappears toward the earth below.

THE CRITICS

"Dr. Strangelove . . . is beyond any question the most shattering sick joke I've ever come across. It is at the same time one of the cleverest and most incisive satiric thrusts at the awkwardness and folly of the military that has ever been on the screen." —Bosley Crowther, *New York Times*

THE OTHER LISTS

- American Film Institute (Yes)
- Roger Ebert's Top 100 (Yes)
- *Entertainment Weekly* (Yes)
- Internet Movie Database (Yes)
- Leonard Maltin (Yes)
- *Movieline* (Yes)
- National Society of Film Critics (No)
- *Premiere* Magazine (Yes)
- *Rolling Stone* Magazine (Yes)
- *Village Voice* (No)

Alarmed at reports that the bomb is on its way to Russia without the required Presidential release, President Merkin Muffley presses the highly volatile General "Buck" Turgidson (George C. Scott) for an explanation. More offended at the question than alarmed by its implications, Buck whines, "I don't think it's quite fair to condemn a whole program because of a single slip-up."

39

BLADE RUNNER 1982

FUTURE TENSE

There's a shivering lunatic, all bundled up from the cold, who talks into a pipe connected to his oversized fur coat as he manufactures lifelike eyes. Just outside his window, an open-air sushi bar provides scant refuge from the polluted drizzle. Up the street in a vast, smoke-lit, abandoned luxury apartment house, a lonely, dying genius puts the finishing touches on yet another of his sweetly humanistic toys. Just another day in "Apocalypse Soon" LA, as the questions "Why are we here?" and "How long have we got?" echo in the electronic smog. If you want to dig, there are plenty of messages beneath the surface. If you just want to sit back and immerse yourself in this visual feast, you won't need to understand a thing. In one of Harrison Ford's most enigmatic roles, he is bewildered, burned out, and desperate to feel something. As he commands hot-wired "replicant" Sean Young to tell him she loves him, it may break your heart in about 30 million pieces.

Jim: It's a gorgeous, bastard child of Stanley Kubrick and Steven Spielberg. Once you see *Blade Runner*, it really never goes away. Beautiful, sad—and all that incredible rental space just lying empty.

Gail: This is moviemaking of the pure experience kind. This visionary film of some future dystopia floods our senses with ingenious imagery that takes hold of us and won't let go.

HE PLOT

Angeles, 2019, and from the look of gs, the world has gone to hell in a hurry. city is a sprawling, rain-soaked slum ulated for the most part by beleaguered it-crawlers. Anyone with the proper creds to the upscale galactic colonies long . Ex-cop Dick Deckard (Harrison Ford) is trying to get through the sludge that's be- ie his life when he's approached for one detail. He's the best "blade runner" in the iness (a hunter of illegal humanoid rep- nts) and there are four particularly nasty s on the loose, on a murderous search a means to expand their shelf life of years. They're led by Roy (Rutger Hauer), ombat model," muscular dimwit Leon on Jones), gorgeous and dangerous Zhora nna Cassidy), and "pleasure model" Pris ryl Hannah). Deckard unwillingly takes the ignment and the weirdo tagalong cop who es with it, Gaff (Edward James Olmos). kard meets with the designer/manufac- r of replicants Dr. Tyrell (Joe Turkel) who oduces him to his lovely assistant Rachael an Young). Her tragedy is that she isn't yet re she's a replicant, having been given xtremely detailed memory chip. Deckard ins to fall in love with her despite himself, as he's caught in the deadly web of the se, he must also find a way to save Ra- el from her otherwise inevitable fate.

You never know who or what you'll run into while chasing replicants through the futuristic gloom of LA. Critics Gene Siskel and Roger Ebert did a double-"thumb"-take on the film, initially panning it, then reversing themselves shortly thereafter.

THE DIRECTOR

Taciturn former advertising wiz **Ridley Scott** felt boxed into a corner by studio suits. He was forced to tack on a happy ending after early preview audiences grumbled. "We had Harrison Ford and Sean Young heading off into the mountains. If you've got mountains like that, why the fuck are you living in that dark, rainy city? There's no logic to that ending." He was further induced to add a *noir* voiceover, Harrison Ford channeling Sam Spade, to make the storyline more accessible. "I was just really British, just grateful to be there. Now, I think back and think, 'Fuck them.' I should have said, 'No.'" Scott's track record of hits (*Alien* [1977], *Thelma & Louise* [1991], *Gladiator* [2000]) allowed him a director's cut re-release. All sins atoned for. It's the one to see. Previous to *Alien* was the sepia-toned period piece *The Duellists* (1977). The epic fairytale *Legend* (1985) starred a forest-wandering Tom Cruise, and Michael Douglas got a bloody taste of the Japanese mob in *Black Rain* (1989). Demi Moore added twenty pounds of muscle for *G.I. Jane* (1997), a forerunner to Russell Crowe's battered physique in *Gladiator*. Then came *Black Hawk Down* (2001), *Matchstick Men* (2003), and *American Gangster* (2007).

Scott directs sensational-looking deaths. Here, Zhora the Snake Charmer is put out of commission by Deckard when he discovers her reptile is as synthetic as she is—or was.

THE CAST	
Rick Deckard	Harrison Ford
Roy Batty	Rutger Hauer
Rachael	Sean Young
Gaff	Edward James Olmos
Bryant	M. Emmet Walsh
Pris	Daryl Hannah
J. F. Sebastian	William Sanderson
Leon	Brion James
Eldon Tyrell	Joe Turkel
Zhora	Joanna Cassidy
Hannibal Chew, Eyemaker	James Hong
Holden	Morgan Paull
Bear	Kevin Thompson
Kaiser	John Edward Allen
Taffey Lewis	Hy Pyke

THE ACTORS

With a nearly $6 billion total gross for his movies, **Harrison Ford** is the most successful and richest movie star ever. *Blade Runner* has the distinction of being one of his few financial flops, but the role of Deckard also elevated him to more than just a cartoon action hero. He's been quoted as saying that this is his least favorite role, which only reminds us that often actors, like betrayed lovers, are the last to know. Ford's greatest gift, the ability to express real fear in the critical scenes, serves him well here, especially in his climactic rooftop joust with replicant Roy. Ford's filmography is essentially a list of the biggest hits of the last twenty years, with a few clinkers to keep things interesting. Among his most iconic are *American Graffiti* (1973), *Star Wars* (1977), *Raiders of the Lost Ark* (1981), *Witness* (1985), *Presumed Innocent* (1990), *Patriot Games* (1992), *The Fugitive* (1993), *Clear and Present Danger* (1994), and *Air Force One* (1997). (For more on Ford, see pages 169 and 289.)

Former model and dancer **Sean Young** made her indelible mark in *Blade Runner* with those soulful eyes, a Joan Crawford hairdo, and a way with her cigarette under stress. Her career has been sketchy and unfocused since. Young is probably best known for her volatile offscreen antics. In 1989, former costar James Woods filed a harassment suit against her when she threatened bodily harm after he ended their affair. She steams up the screen in *No Way Out* (1987), *A Kiss Before Dying* (1991), *Ace Ventura: Pet Detective* (1994), and *Poor White Trash* (2001)

Edward James Olmos, as weirdly dapper cop Gaff, turns in one of the kinkiest screen performances since Joel Grey in *Cabaret*. It's hard to know what makes Gaff tick, but those tiny origami sculptures he litters the movie with are a continual fascination. Olmos, despite or because of his intense, pockmarked looks, has never stopped working and remains a major activist voice in the Latino community. His role in the era-defining series *Miami Vice* (1984) was followed up with the surprise hit, *Stand and Deliver* (1987). *Selena* (1997) interspersed years of TV miniseries, culminating in *An American Family* (2002).

Daryl Hannah, thanks to *Splash* (1984), forever America's dream mermaid, is almost unrecognizable here as Pris, the replicant party girl. She's touchingly punk, slutty, and vulnerable at all once, and manages to give Jane Fonda a run for her fitness money with that gleaming Nautilus thigh-hold around Deckard's neck.

Though Pauline Kael thought Dutch-born hunk **Rutger Hauer** should've taken the "Klaus Kinski Overacting Award" for *Blade Runner*, his dread-sexy Aryan replicant Roy is riveting to watch. This was the performance that launched years of villain roles for him in escapist B-movie fare such as *Blind Fury* (1990), *Buffy the Vampire Slayer* (1992), and *Omega Doom* (1996).

BEHIND THE SCREEN

Ridley Scott recently divulged that the character of Deckard is, in fact, a replicant. It throws an entirely new slant on the movie and managed to throw Harrison Ford for a loop. "We had agreed that he definitely was not a replicant." But if you watch some of Ford's reaction shots closely, especially when replicant-testing is mentioned, it makes perfect sense. *Blade* fanatics argue, however, that if he's a replicant, why is it he can't match them in a fight and, further, what accounts for his long law enforcement career—given their brief life spans?

Daryl Hannah's spellbinding karate moves were performed by a male stunt double in drag.

Ridley Scott optioned the book *The Bladerunners* by Alan Nourse, as well as its adapted screenplay by William Burroughs. All Scott wanted from the transaction were rights to the title.

MUSIC

Greek composer Vangelis's haunting score became an instant classic, the most successful aspect of *Blade Runner*'s initial release. It's nothing short of grand theft that it was overlooked by the Academy Awards nominating committee.

CREDITS

Producer: Michael Deeley/ Warner Bros.
Director: Ridley Scott
Screenplay: Hampton Fancher, David Peoples, from Philip K. Dick's novel *Do Androids Dream of Electric Sheep?*
Running time: 117 minutes
Budget: $28 million

NOMINATIONS

Best Art Direction-Set Direction: Lawrence G. Paull and David L. Snyder; Linda DeScenna
Best Visual Effects: Douglas Trumbull, Richard Yuricich, David Dryer

THE YEAR'S WINNERS

Best Picture: *Gandhi*
Best Director: Richard Attenborough, *Gandhi*
Best Actor: Ben Kingsley, *Gandhi*
Best Actress: Meryl Streep, *Sophie's Choice*
Best Supporting Actor: Louis Gossett Jr., *An Officer and a Gentleman*
Best Supporting Actress: Jessica Lange, *Tootsie*

The debate of *Blade Runner* cultists rages: Is he or isn't he? The argument that Deckard is a replicant can be made based on the fact that their eyes eventually cast a red glow—as his do when he brings Rachael (Sean Young) back to his place.

Lovely, sad-eyed Rachael refuses to believe she's a replicant and comes to Deckard with a photo of herself as a child in the arms of her late mother. Deckard is fresh out of compassion and cruelly destroys whatever dream of humanness she clings to. He tells her that her memories have been programmed. Remember the game of doctor and nurse she played with her brother? It never happened. The spider who hatched an egg outside her bedroom window when she was six? Pure fiction. Rachael, devastated and in tears, rushes out, and in so doing, pierces Deckard's heart. Her manufactured emotions have awakened his again.

SEND IN THE CLONES

Total Recall (1990)
Strange Days (1995)
Minority Report (2002)
A.I. (2002)

ROLE REVERSALS

Dustin Hoffman was the early choice to play Deckard.

CRITICS

"The world of *Blade Runner* has undeniably become one of the visual touchstones of modern movies."—Roger Ebert, *Chicago Sun-Times*

"Scott's creepy, oppressive vision requires some sort of overriding idea—something besides spoofy gimmicks . . . it hasn't been thought out in human terms. If anybody comes around with a test to detect humanoids, maybe Ridley Scott and his associates should hide."
—Pauline Kael, *The New Yorker*

THE OTHER LISTS

- American Film Institute (Yes)
- Roger Ebert's Top 100 (No)
- *Entertainment Weekly* (No)
- Internet Movie Database (Yes)
- Leonard Maltin (No)
- *Movieline* (Yes)
- National Society of Film Critics (No)
- *Premiere* Magazine (Yes)
- *Rolling Stone* Magazine (No)
- *Village Voice* (Yes)

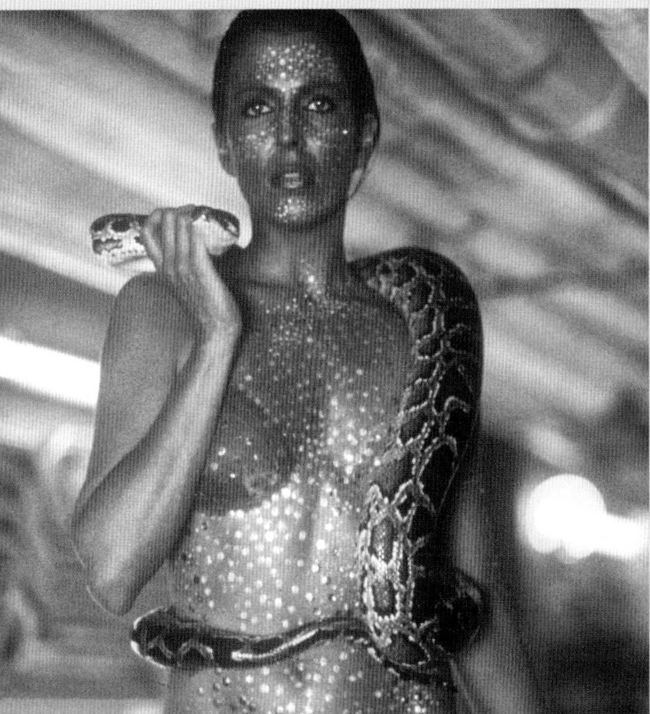

"Reality is that which, when you stop believing in it, doesn't go away," insists author Philip K. Dick, whose original title for the short story adapted here was "Do Androids Dream of Electric Sheep?" Maybe that should have been "electric boa constrictors"?

40

THE CONFORMIST 1970

HOW TO BECOME A FASCIST

Marcello moves deliberately, angularly, desperately, and guiltily through Fascist Italy, attacked by the shame of random memories of childhood homosexual abuse. All he wants is to be normal, to fit in. He'll do anything, including kill, to be one of the boys. Though beautifully and opulently stylized, utilizing unusual camera angles, the play of light and shadow, tints, textures, and patterns, Bertolucci succeeds in producing one of the most chilling and resoundingly truthful character studies of an individual, as well as a collective mentality, in this portrait of a weak man who succumbs to fascism for fear of being left out. The production design and the camerawork of Vittorio Storaro produce nothing less than the greatest images on film. The romantic yet taut stylization adds edge, never distance, from the reality with which we are faced: what a man is capable of doing to fit in.

Jim: You'll never forget that ending, with Dominque Sanda, incongruously glamorous in her heels and fur coat, running for her life in the woods. How can this be happening? The ease of betrayal, the "so what?" of murder in broad daylight. Will she outrun them? How can she? We're all her for a minute. You may forget to breathe.

Gail: Unquestionably one of the greatest works of film art, utilizing both style and content to achieve masterful ends. Trintignant's face and walk convey all we need to know of the genius at work both in front of and behind the camera.

THE PLOT

Marcello (Jean-Louis Trintignant), a spineless, upper-class intellectual painfully isolated from his peers, just wants to be a normal bourgeois man. But everything in his past, particularly his childhood homosexual abuse, works against it. He joins the Italian Fascist Party in 1938 and marries a trophy wife, Giulia (Stefania Sandrelli), to put his past behind him. The party officials ask him to murder his former professor in order to prove his loyalty. Burdened by ambivalence and fear, Marcello's situation is further complicated by his introduction to the professor's lusty, sexually audacious wife Anna (Dominique Sanda), with whom he becomes infatuated. Sex and violence are once again equated in his life—and in Bertolucci's notions about the nature of fascism. Marcello, the good, cowardly conformist, is confused, but nevertheless takes the easy way out. He abandons his morals, completes his mission, and is satisfied (?) that he has salvaged himself from his past.

A citizen of fascist Italy, Marcello (Jean-Louis Trintignant), having been abused as a child and feeling "different" because of it, wants nothing more than to fit in. He'll do anything to be considered normal. He joins the Fascists and agrees to murder an ex-professor . . . and more.

THE DIRECTOR

Easily one of the greatest contemporary international filmmakers, **Bernardo Bertolucci** began his life in film as assistant director to Pier Paolo Passolini, who became his mentor. Like Passolini, Bertolucci was passionate about both cinema and poetry. His first film, *The Grim Reaper* (1962) was a critical and commercial failure, but he returned brilliantly with *Before the Revolution* (1964). Before truly embarking on a full-time filmmaking career, the director made documentaries for Shell Oil. He then directed *The Conformist*, which put him on the map. Two years later he raised eyebrows—and other body parts—with his controversial, shocking, and erotically-charged *Last Tango in Paris* (1973), for which he received a Best Director Oscar nomination. There is hardly a Bertolucci film that does not have the director's mark. Among his later works are *1900* (1977), *Luna* (1979), and *The Last Emperor* (1987), which won Best Picture and Best Director Oscars. Upon accepting his award, Bertolucci made the now-famous observation of Hollywood as "the big nipple."

Marcello (Jean-Louis Trintignant) goes limp at the sight of his decadent, drug-addicted mother. Ashamed by her outrageous lifestyle and his entire childhood, he takes comfort in belonging to the Fascists, who are considered "normal."

THE CAST

Marcello	Jean-Louis Trintignant
Giulia	Stefania Sandrelli
Manganiello	Gastone Moschin
Professor Quadri	Enzo Tarascio
Il Colonnello	Fosco Giachetti
Italo	José Quaglio
Anna Quadri	Dominique Sanda
Lino	Pierre Clémenti
Madre di Giulia	Yvonne Sanson
Madre di Marcello	Milly
Padre di Marcello	Giuseppe Addobbati
Raoul	Christian Aligny

THE ACTORS

Like a weak Bogart, **Jean-Louis Trintignant**'s Marcello is capable of registering no emotion. His portrait of the ultimate sellout is stylized and at the same time deeply chilling. American audiences are quite familiar with Trintignant's appeal through such films as the classic *A Man and a Woman* (1966), and *My Night at Maud's* and *Z* (both 1969). The 1980s proved leaner for the actor, and he appeared in such relatively unknown films as *Confidentially Yours* (1982), *Under Fire* (1983), and *A Man and a Woman: 20 Years Later* (1986). He also had a terrific role in *Red* (1994). Trintignant was once married to actress Stephane Audran.

Stefania Sandrelli, Giulia, has appeared in over 100 international productions. Among those films, several are familiar to American viewers, including, *Divorce, Italian Style* (1961), *We All Loved Each Other So Much* (1974), and *Last Kiss* (2001). She worked for Bertolucci twice more, appearing in *1900* (1976) and *Stealing Beauty* (1996).

As Anna, the sultry wife of an antifascist, **Dominique Sanda** brings a voluptuous and dangerous sexuality to the film. Sanda began her career as a model and was discovered by director Robert Bresson, who cast her in his film *Une Femme Douce* (1969). She continued to impress audiences with her intense performances in *The Garden of the Finzi-Continis* (1971) and *The Mackintosh Man* (1973). Bertolucci worked with her again in *1900* (1977).

BEHIND THE SCREEN

The Conformist was cut by five crucial minutes known as the "Dance of the Blind" when first released in the U.S. The missing moments were restored in the 1994 reissue.

THE CRITICS

"It's a triumph of feeling and of style—lyrical, flowing, velvety style so operatic that you come away with sequences in your head like arias."
—Pauline Kael, *The New Yorker*

"Bertolucci will be faulted for his rather loving depiction of all of the very photogenic details of upper middle-class decadence. It does get to be a bit much when Marcello goes to call on his mother and finds her in bed, asleep, at noon, wearing a feathered bed jacket, a mask over her eyes, and waiting for a morphine fix . . . There are excesses in the film, but they are balanced by scenes of such unusual beauty and vitality that I couldn't care less."
—Vincent Canby, *New York Times*

THE OTHER LISTS

American Film Institute (No)
Roger Ebert's Top 100 (No)
Entertainment Weekly (Yes)
Internet Movie Database (No)
Leonard Maltin (No)
Movieline (No)
National Society of Film Critics (No)
Premiere Magazine (Yes)
Rolling Stone Magazine (Yes)
Village Voice (Yes)

CREDITS

Producer: Giovanni Bertolucci (executive producer), Maurizio Lodi-Fe (uncredited)/ Paramount
Director: Bernardo Bertolucci
Screenplay: Bernardo Bertolucci and Alberto Moravia (based on his novel)
Budget: $750,000
Running Time: 114 minutes

NOMINATIONS

Best Writing, Screenplay Based on Material from Another Medium: Bernardo Bertolucci

THE YEAR'S ACADEMY AWARD WINNERS

Best Picture: *The French Connection*
Best Director: William Friedkin, *The French Connection*
Best Actor: Gene Hackman, *The French Connection*
Best Actress: Jane Fonda, *Klute*
Best Supporting Actor: Ben Johnson, *The Last Picture Show*
Best Supporting Actress: Cloris Leachman, *The Last Picture Show*

Italo: *A normal man? For me, a normal man is one who turns his head to see a beautiful woman's bottom. The point is not just to turn our head. There are five or six reasons. And he is glad to find people who are like him, his equals. That's why he likes crowded beaches, football, the bar downtown. He likes people who are similar to himself. He does not trust those who are different. That's why a normal man is a true brother, a true citizen, a true patriot.*

Marcello: *A true fascist.*

Perhaps there is nothing more chilling than the scene that combines visuals of great beauty and acts of terrifying violence. Marcello, having decided to follow through on his directive to murder his former philosophy professor, now an antifascist, drives through the rapturously snowy forest to chase him down. He and a group of Fascist thugs surround the professor and stab him repeatedly, reminding one of a political assassination—the deliberate, hateful destruction of someone of a different mind.

Take no prisoners. Anna, left out in the forest to be shot by her husband's assassins, begs her lover Marcello to save her life. Alas, his bloodless heart is not moved. Though he loves her, Marcello wants desperately to remain in the good graces of the Fascists, so he leaves her to die.

"I think that when you go to see a movie—if we see it in the proper place, which is in the movie theater, and not the TV—we enter in a kind of a special light. There is this amniotic darkness, and we are going all together to dream the same dream. And this is the great thing of cinema; it is something that happens in a community, we are all together."
—Bernardo Bertolucci

The beautiful and sexually precocious Anna (Dominique Sanda) is the wife of the professor targeted for murder by the Fascists. Marcello is to be his assassin. When he falls in love with Giulia it raises uncomfortable feelings about his own disturbed childhood sexuality.

41

SCHINDLER'S LIST 1993

A RECORD OF HELL

A Jewish mother feeds diamonds wrapped in chunks of bread to her children in anticipation of their survival. An emptied street is filled with the contents of suitcases—shoes, toothbrushes, glasses—of Jews who just have been rounded up and taken away. A child escapes certain death by jumping off a truck filled with singing children headed for the gas chambers, and finds refuge in a cesspool along with other desperate children. These graphic scenes, and so many like them, filmed in documentary-style black-and-white, show us atrocity after atrocity with a frankness rarely seen in feature films. Other filmmakers had urged director Steven Spielberg not to take on this grave story, fearing that his facility for making entertainments might compromise the seriousness of the subject. He proved them wrong . . . up to a point. Spielberg is uncompromising for the most part, though some of the Jews fail to rise above stereotypes. Ben Kingsley's Stern is an eloquent exception. In several instances Spielberg resorts to histrionics, as in Oskar Schindler's fictional parting speech to "his" Jews, making for a tear-jerking, sentimental scene. Nevertheless, *Schindler's List* shows enormous restraint and provides rich insight into one of our darkest moments in history. The film does not use easy formulas but triumphs in its directness, in its power to terrify without numbing. Much of this is a result of the detailed images Spielberg has chosen to invoke a reality that is undeniable. In making a story, he has also created an historic record—and for that, we owe him our deepest gratitude.

Jim: Spielberg was out to prove he could make a film for adults and did so with resounding fervor—the images are indelible. The dirty little secret, of course, is, who bought all those tickets for his "kid" movies?

Gail: All his talent, experience, and good judgment served Spielberg well in this terribly close encounter with genocide.

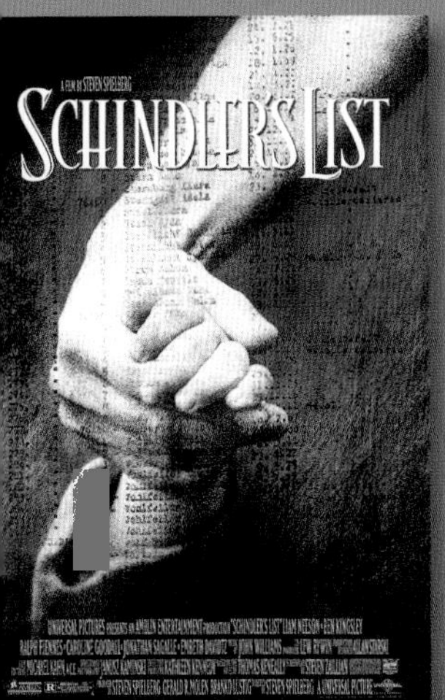

HE PLOT

s the dawn of World War II in Germany. kar Schindler, a greedy, womanizing, failed trepreneur and man-about-town, sees fit in the availability of cheap Jewish labor his new factory. He hires the reluctant hak Stern, who was an accountant before war, to run his business, and Stern does brilliantly. But soon the Jews are being nded up—the ghettos in which they were prisoned are being liquidated—and sent to ced labor/death camps. Schindler knows only hope of retaining his workers is to ort to politics. He ingratiates himself with highest-level Nazis, including the commandant of a forced labor camp, Amon Goeth alph Fiennes). It is soon clear, however, that eth is a sadist who kills Jews for sport, le Schindler is just trying to profit from m. With the Final Solution looming, Schinr must pull more and more strings to keep " Jews from being sent away. His greed is dually transformed into a desperate desire save the Jews from slaughter—possibly due his growing bond with Stern—and he transms his factory into a sham manufacturer bullet casings, though refusing to produce en one usable casing. As the pressure reases to release his workers to certain ath, he bribes Nazi officials until he is left stitute and a fugitive.

The greedy manufacturer Oskar Schindler (Liam Neeson) who, before the Jews were rounded up for slaughter, had been using them for cheap labor, now clutches onto a cattle car carrying "his" Jews. Schindler bankrupted himself to buy from the Nazis—and therefore save—1,100 Jews.

"They cast a spell on you, you know, the Jews. When you work closely with them, like I do, you see this. They have this power. It's like a virus."—Amon Goeth

THE DIRECTOR

"I've always been a victim of my own success," says **Steven Spielberg**. *Schindler's List* freed him of his label as the most reliably entertaining director in Hollywood. He proved the skeptics wrong. Restraining himself from exploiting the more dramatic aspects of the story, Spielberg relies on the power of facts. He explains his change of mission with the birth of his children, which "reawakened all my Judaism. The movie is the result of what I went through as a person." Somewhere in his motivation was the desire to "show the Nazis; I felt a lot of that in my heart." The tension was high while shooting in Krakow, Poland, and, according to the director, fights would break out in the hotels where Jewish-Israeli actors were living side by side with German businessmen of World War II vintage. Though *Schindler* was powerful not just for its subject matter but for the way in which it is represented, it shares the hallmarks of its director's lighter—but no less accomplished—fare. (For more on Spielberg, see pages 88, 103, 190, 208 and 289.)

"For six centuries there has been a Jewish Krakow. By this evening those six centuries will be a rumor. They never happened. Today is history," Amon Goeth (Ralph Fiennes) chillingly tells his friend Schindler. Goeth, who kills Jews for sport, takes target practice from his balcony overlooking the work camp.

THE CAST

Oskar Schindler	Liam Neeson
Itzhak Stern	Ben Kingsley
Amon Goeth	Ralph Fiennes
Emilie Schindler	Caroline Goodall
Helen Hirsch	Embeth Davidtz
Mila Pfefferberg	Adi Nitzan
Juda Dresner	Michael Schneider
Chaja Dresner	Miri Fabian
Danka Dresner	Anna Mucha

ROLE REVERSALS

Tim Roth was considered for the role of Amon Goeth.

Claire Danes was on Spielberg's list for a role, but she turned it down because he could not provide her with tutoring on the set.

THE ACTORS

Larger-than-life but undeniably human, **Liam Neeson**'s stirring portrayal of the exploiter-turned-rescuer Oskar Schindler presents an ambiguous and provocative character. What leads to his change of heart is not exactly stated. Neeson takes over the screen in most of his film appearances, which include *Excalibur* (1981), *The Good Mother* (1988), *Husbands and Wives* (1992), *Rob Roy* (1995), *Michael Collins* (1996), *Gangs of New York* (2002), *Love Actually* (2003), and *Kinsey* (2004).

British-born **Ben Kingsley** plays Stern, the accountant, with quiet dignity. Prodigiously gifted, Kingsley's performances have garnered nominations and Oscars, most notably for *Gandhi* (1982, Academy Award). He was also in *Betrayal* (1983), *Maurice* (1987), *Slipstream* (1989), *Bugsy* (1991, Academy Award nomination), *Death and the Maiden* (1994), and, in a fascinating departure from any role he'd played previously, *Sexy Beast* (2001).

With his bloated belly—the actor put on 20 pounds by drinking Guinness—as evidence of the slovenliness of his character, **Ralph Fiennes** was cast as Amon Goeth because, according to Spielberg, of his "evil sexuality." Goeth is a study not only in the sexuality but in the stupidity of evil. Appealed to through his vanity, when Schindler tells him he would be a bigger, more powerful man by pardoning the Jews instead of doing target practice on them, he rehearses a papal-like pardon in the mirror, and likes what he sees. It is a chilling scene and exceptionally revealing. Fiennes's work is varied but uniformly exceptional, and includes roles in such films as *Quiz Show* (1994), *The English Patient* (1996), *Oscar and Lucinda* (1997), and *Sunshine* (1999), and even in the slight romantic comedy *Maid in Manhattan* (2002).

BEHIND THE SCREEN

Several other directors were considered for the film, among them Billy Wilder, who contributed to the first draft of the screenplay. Martin Scorsese didn't feel he could do justice to the film as a Jew could. Spielberg himself offered director Roman Polanski the job, but he turned it down because the subject was too close to home (though he has now made his own Holocaust film, *The Pianist* [2003]). Polanski lived in the Krakow ghetto until the age of 8, and lost his mother to Auschwitz.

Based as it was on "living witness testimony," Spielberg turned one page of the Krakow ghetto liquidation scene into 20 minutes on screen.

Unable to get permission to film inside Auschwitz, Spielberg shot the death camp scenes outside the gates, on a set constructed as a mirror image of the real location on the other side.

The disembodied hand that places flowers on top of Schindler's grave in the last scene is Liam Neeson's and not Spielberg's, as was suspected by many viewers.

Spielberg refused to accept a salary for the film, calling such payment "blood money."

THE CRITICS

"Nothing in Spielberg's previous work prepares us for *Schindler's List* or for its mythical central figure, an unlikely angel dancing on the rim of hell. It's a stunning achievement. Its haunting, potent, jolting images turn it into another kinetic—and inextinguishable—Holocaust museum."
—Jay Carr, National Society of Film Critics

CREDITS

Producer: Steven Spielberg, Gerald R. Molen, Branko Lustig/ Universal
Director: Steven Spielberg
Screenplay: Steven Zaillian, based on the novel by Thomas Keneally
Running Time: 197 minutes
Budget: $25 million
Box Office: $317.1 million (worldwide)

ACADEMY AWARDS

Best Picture: Steven Spielberg, Gerald R. Molen, Branko Lustig
Best Director: Steven Spielberg
Best Art Direction-Set Decoration: Allan Starski, Ewa Braun
Best Cinematography: Janusz Kaminski
Best Film Editing: Michael Kahn
Best Music, Original Score: John Williams
Best Writing, Screenplay Based on Material from Another Medium: Steven Zaillian
Best Actor in a Leading Role: Liam Neeson
Best Actor in a Supporting Role: Ralph Fiennes
Best Costume Design: Anna B. Sheppard
Best Makeup: Christina Smith, Matthew W. Mungle, Judith A. Cory
Best Sound: Andy Nelson, Steve Pederson, Scott Millan, Ron Judkins

THE YEAR'S OTHER WINNERS

Best Actor: Tom Hanks, *Philadelphia*
Best Actress: Holly Hunter, *The Piano*
Best Supporting Actor: Tommy Lee Jones, *The Fugitive*
Best Supporting Actress: Anna Paquin, *The Piano*

"What isn't so harmless is the manipulating Spielberg does within the movie. In a much-criticized climactic scene, Spielberg distorts the facts to show Schindler breaking down in a speech to the Jewish factory workers. The episode never happened. Schindler was not a man to wear his emotions openly. Though the scene rings shockingly false, it fills what Spielberg discerns as the need for a big heroic moment." —Peter Travers, *Rolling Stone*

THE OTHER LISTS

- American Film Institute (Yes)
- Roger Ebert's Top 100 (Yes)
- *Entertainment Weekly* (Yes)
- Internet Movie Database (Yes)
- Leonard Maltin (Yes)
- *Movieline* (Yes)
- National Society of Film Critics (Yes)
- *Premiere* Magazine (No)
- *Rolling Stone* Magazine (No)
- *Village Voice* (No)

BELOW: Itzhak Stern (Ben Kingsley), Schindler's chief accountant, has a close call with certain extermination before Schindler "buys" him from the Nazis. Their adversarial relationship soon melds into a united force against the slaughter of innocents.

A horrifying mistake has been made. All of "Schindler's Jews" bound for safety are mistakenly sent to Auschwitz, where they are marked for death. A woman huddles in terror in the shower room, thinking that she is about to be gassed. In the nick of time Schindler manages, once again, to rescue "his" Jews.

A train carrying Schindler's women in cattle cars is mistakenly routed to Auschwitz, due to errors in paperwork. From the inside, a woman looks out to see a young Polish boy smile and draw a line across his throat. They arrive at the camp terrified. Their hair is shorn and they are sent into showers, where they huddle together, terrified that they are about to be gassed. When water comes out of the nozzles they cry in relief. The following morning the children are pulled from their parents. Schindler arrives just in time to stop them. "What are you doing? These are mine. These are my workers. They should be on my train. Their fingers polish the insides of metal shell casings. How else am I to polish the inside of a 45-millimeter shell casing? You tell me. You tell me!" he shouts to the commandant. The impact of this scene can hardly be felt on description. Suffice it to say that, even when you know the outcome, you still watch in horror. The rescue is barely a relief, too, knowing how many others have been left behind.

42

THE LIVES OF OTHERS 2006

STATE SECRETS OF THE HEART

The Lives of Others is the film the new Germany needed—but didn't particularly want to see. In a nation weary of its collective guilt complex, it seemed like a pile-on after countless ravaging tales of Nazi atrocities. But, as it turns out, cold war East Germany had its own methods of destroying lives, sometimes one damning audiotape at a time. With growing horror, as one perfectly structured scene follows another, we begin to learn that East Germany's stranglehold on its citizenry destroyed not just lives and careers but hope itself (the last thing that dies, we are reminded by a smirking, sadistic bureaucrat). It's more than ironic that from this desolate landscape, emptied of feeling, one of the most wrenching epiphanies in cinema rises from the ashes. Never before has the question of creative sacrifice been more devastatingly answered, amounting to a *Sophie's Choice* of art vs. survival. You get the sense that the film's sterling performances don't come simply from the actors digging deeply into their characters—but from their own memories of how it was just twenty years before. In its transcendent epilogue, *The Lives of Others* shows us the end of a nightmare and something more precious than any political movement—the opening of a lost man's soul.

Jim: This is one of the most perfectly imagined films I've ever seen. Every performance, every line of dialogue, every shot takes you one step deeper inside a quietly horrifying world that, up until twenty years ago, was completely real. And that final moment, *mein Gott!*

Gail: It is hard to think of any film in recent history that has given life to the implausible idea that a man can be so moved by his enemy that he will sacrifice his own cherished beliefs—the substance of his very existence—for something truer. In a word, redemptive (with a tad of a sentimentality at the end).

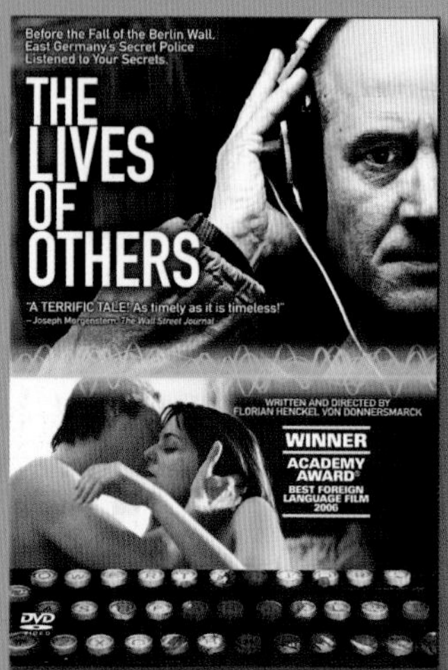

THE PLOT

East German theater director George Dreyman (Sebastian Koch) is the envy of a government minister, who orders him investigated by the Stasi, East Germany's secret police, so that he can snag Dreyman's beautiful actress-girlfriend, Christina-Maria (Martina Gedeck) for himself. Stasi operative Wiesler (Ulrich Mühe) is a party purist, unaware of the minister's true motives. He sets up his spy equipment in the attic of Dreyman's building and begins to listen in on the culturally rich, passionate lives of the lovers. At first, he maintains his objectivity but, when he deduces the real motive for the investigation, he makes the career-killing decision to save Dreyman from certain imprisonment for sneaking out an exposé of East Germany's soaring suicide rate. Wiesler is punished with a nowhere job, steaming open mail. With the fall of the Berlin Wall and the end to the cold war, an emotionally devastated Dreyman is free to examine his Stasi files and discovers Wiesler's sympathetic role and great sacrifice. He fashions a best-selling novel out of the story and dedicates it to Wiesler who, for the first time in his life, has been touched by another human heart.

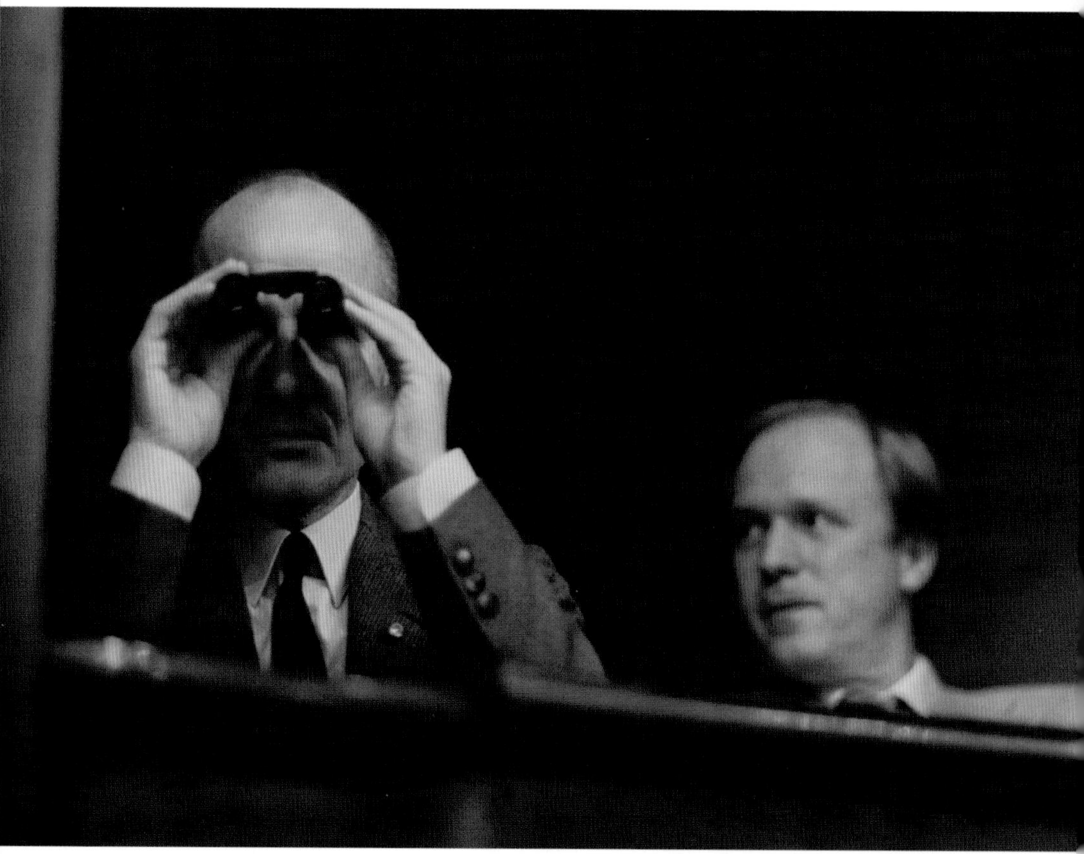

The unblinking eye of the beholder. Stasi operative Hauptmann Wiesler (Ulrich Muhe) thinks dashing playwright Georg Dreyman (Sebastian Koch) is just too good to be true, and insists on testing his loyalty to the party.

THE DIRECTOR

Florian Henckel von Donnersmarck, then thirty-three, was inspired by a comment made by Lenin that if he listened to the full "Passionata" by Beethoven, he'd never be able to finish his revolution. In effect, the tug of the heart can undermine the mechanisms of history. Donnersmarck was haunted by the image of a "company man" who is forced to listen to beautiful music as part of his duties and is somehow transformed by it. The director/screenwriter knew he'd struck gold with the premise of principle vs. feeling. He spent a year and a half researching the idea, and another year listening to the stories of both victims of the Stasi and former officers, some of whom remained proud of their work. The script took another year and a half to write and Donnersmarck participated in every detail. He was consumed by the notion of color palette, stripping the film of blue and red and replacing it with green and yellow to capture the essence of a particular time and place. He spent months hunting down analog equipment to perfect the image of predigital 1984.

Thirty-three-year-old director Florian Henkel von Donnersmarck remembers visiting relatives in East Berlin as a boy and wondering how a mere wall could separate two cultures so completely. The checkered reception of *The Lives of Others* in Germany made it clear that many still aren't ready to forgive or forget.

The Party's over. Georg is devastated to learn that his star and lover, Christa-Maria (Martina Gedeck), has been carrying on with the perversely uncouth Minister of Culture.

THE CAST

Georg Dreyman	Sebastian Koch
Hauptmann Gerd Wiesler	Ulrich Mühe
Christa-Maria Sieland	Martina Gedeck
Obersteulnant Anton Grubitz	Ulrich Tukur
Minister Bruno Hempt	Thomas Thieme
Paul Hauser	Hans-Uwe Bauer
Gregor Hessenstein	Herbert Knaup

THE ACTORS

The late **Ulrich Mühe** was the most important actor in Communist-controlled East Germany. In a case of art imitating life, there had been a Stasi secret police file on him since high school, where his early talent made it clear that he would rise high in his profession. His acting company, whose success was capped by his production of *Hamlet*, had within it three agents whose primary purpose was to report his every move. He was among the first to speak out against the oppressive regime in protests that would lead to its downfall in 1989. In preparing for *The Lives of Others*, he worried about how to play so much of his "listening" character in silence. Director Donnersmarck suggested he "not act, simply remember"—and that provided the key for him. His slow awakening from party apparatchik to an empathic heart was one of the most profound performances in modern cinema. How he managed to elude the Academy Awards nominating committee is one of its most perplexing mysteries.

Sebastian Koch, who bears a more than passing resemblance to the handsome young Peter Jennings, is one of Germany's most admired leading men, equally at ease onstage in Oscar Wilde's *An Ideal Husband*, in a long-running TV crime drama series, and on film in *The Lives of Others*. His role required that he play the complex piano composition "Sonata for a Good Man," so he spent months learning the piece by rote, understanding that the music lay at the heart of his character. The actor has since bought a grand piano and sometimes plays this sonata for guests, who remain unaware he can play nothing else.

"My audience doesn't want to know how many eggs I fry in the morning. I speak through my characters." **Martina Gedeck** might well be speaking on behalf of her own creation, in *The Lives of Others*, of a brilliant actress who betrays nothing of her tortured personal life on the stage. Previously, Gedeck's most famous role was the title character in *Bella Martha* (2001), remade in the United States in 2007 as *No Reservations*, starring Catherine Zeta-Jones. Gedeck's only English-language film was *The Good Shepherd* (2006), in which she played Hanna Schiller.

BEHIND THE SCREEN

The Lives of Others was refused by the Berlin Film Festival in 2005, the judges fearing it was just too painful a reminder of Germany's tortured past.

Ulrich Mühe's ex-wife filed a defamation suit after he and director Donnersmarck went on record with the allegation that she had spied on him for Stasi.

Trying to recreate Berlin of twenty-five years ago was almost impossible, given the graffiti that now covers many of its buildings. The crew would wash it off for a day's shoot only to find it rescrawled overnight.

Martina Gedeck wasn't invited by the director to attend the Oscar ceremonies. She was offered a ticket by the Academy but declined it.

SEND IN THE CLONES

A Hollywood remake is being considered by director Sydney Pollack.

For a preclone, consider Francis Ford Coppola's *The Conversation* (1974), page 273.

THE CRITICS

"Some of the movie's tensest moments take place with the most minimal of action—Weisler's simply listening through headphones, Dreyman's simply lying on his bed, a neighbor's simply looking through a door peephole, her whole life contingent on what she does about what she sees. In those nerve-racking pauses, von Donnersmarck conveys everything he wants us to know about choice, fear, doubt, cowardice, and heroism." —Lisa Shwarzbaum, *Entertainment Weekly*

CREDITS

Producer: Bayerischer Rundfunk (BR)/Sony Pictures Classics
Director: Florian Henckel von Donnersmarck
Screenplay: Florian Henckel von Donnersmarck
Running Time: 137 minutes
Budget: $2.5 million

ACADEMY AWARD

Best Foreign Film

THE YEAR'S OTHER WINNERS

Best Picture: *The Departed*
Best Director: Martin Scorsese, *The Departed*
Best Actor: Forest Whitaker, *The Last King of Scotland*
Best Actress: Helen Mirren, *The Queen*
Best Supporting Actor: Alan Arkin, *Little Miss Sunshine*
Best Supporting Actress: Jennifer Hudson, *Dreamgirls*

Overhearing is believing. In the essential and transformational moment of the film, a bloodless spy, Wiesler, is moved and forever changed by Georg's heart-wrenching piano tribute to a fallen mentor.

THE GREAT SCENE

Theater director Georg Dreyman has just received a call informing him that his beloved mentor has hanged himself. In a state of shock, he unwraps the man's birthday gift to him, the banned composition "Sonata for a Good Man." He sits down at the piano to play it. Upstairs in the attic with his spying headphones on, Wiesler is compelled by the music, having never heard anything of such indescribable beauty. It's art for the pure sake of itself. Aware of why Georg is playing it and feeling that he's somehow had a part in the man's suicide, Wiesler's otherwise inexpressive face is suddenly awash with tears. The State's firm grip on his heart has begun to come loose.

The Orwellian eeriness of Hauptman Wiesler's stiff-spine stroll down a totalitarian corridor is compounded by the fact that most of the action of the film takes place in 1984. It was within this very Hall of Records that detailed files of nearly every East German citizen were kept. In this pre-computerized bureaucracy, the amount of paperwork was staggering.

NOTABLE QUOTES

"You have no idea how many people are in prison here for senseless heroics." —Interrogator Grubitz to Christa-Maria

"Something doesn't feel right—there's something you're hiding." —Grubitz to Wiesler

"A filmmaker is the audience's therapist for two hours." —Florian Henckel von Donnersmarck

THE OTHER LISTS

Entertainment Weekly (No)
Internet Movie Database (No)
Movieline (No)
Premiere Magazine (No)
Roger Ebert's Top 100 (No)
Rolling Stone Magazine (No)

43

DINER 1982

THE LAST SUPPER

Growing up is hard to do in this extraordinarily sad, funny, and perfectly penned depiction of the lives of an aimless group of buddies at the end of an era. The guys are still hanging on and hanging out at their home at the edge of the universe—a Baltimore diner. At the end of the day, life at the greasy spoon holds the promise of vitality, of contact and connection, where there's a constant volley of jokes and jabs at best friends you know and like better than anyone, including wives or girlfriends. The sexual revolution and women's liberation haven't touched these guys yet—save one enlightened college chum—and all they can feel is loss; as far as they know there's nothing left to be found. Levinson's debut feature pushes the envelope of a very American genre and plumbs new depths of feeling. This multi-character study pulls such natural performances out of the promising cast that you're sure you've known every one of these guys your entire life. Each of them is infinitely more complex than he first appears to be; therein lies the genius.

Jim: Levinson is Baltimore's resident Woody Allen. He loves his hometown with a passion, and he doesn't require a formulaic plot to tell its story.

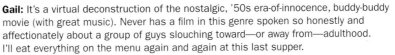

Gail: It's a virtual deconstruction of the nostalgic, '50s era-of-innocence, buddy-buddy movie (with great music). Never has a film in this genre spoken so honestly and affectionately about a group of guys slouching toward—or away from—adulthood. I'll eat everything on the menu again and again at this last supper.

HE PLOT

Christmas, late 1959, and Billy (Timothy y) returns home from college to be best n at the wedding of buddy Eddie (Steve tenberg). He meets up with his twenty-nething pals, who are still mostly hanging und the local diner. Everyone's identity well-being is under siege: Eddie is not so e marriage is the right move just yet and lives at home, preparing a make-or-break tball trivia test for his fiancée; Billy, the erficially clean-cut college boy, can't get old girlfriend out of his mind; Shrevie niel Stern), who marries unhappily cause that's the way you get sex) buckles der the weight of his own spiritlessness; d hairdresser Boogie (Mickey Rourke)—ross between James Dean and Warren atty's character in *Shampoo*—has the soul a poet and the problems of a confirmed nbler. Finishing off the quintet of disso-es who only come to life when they're at diner is Fenwick (Kevin Bacon), the ege dropout with a taste for alcohol d desperate pranks, the guy who gets all College Bowl questions right while tching it in his pajamas in the middle he afternoon.

(Clockwise) Clean-cut, studious Billy (Timothy Daly, far left) is already in college but is carrying a load of suppressed rage about an old flame; Shrevie (Daniel Stern) marries for the steady conjugal visits, but doesn't really care to embrace anything other than his record collection; a hair stylist with a poet's soul, Boogie (Mickey Rourke) can tell you all that's happening but can't do anything to stop his own solitary walk on the wild side of gambling; Fenwick (Kevin Bacon) can answer all the questions on "It's Academic," but can't finish school. Not seated at the table is Eddie (Steve Guttenberg), who is busy giving his fiancée a football quiz that will make or break the wedding.

"Do you ever get the feeling that there's something going on that we don't know about?" —Fenwick

THE DIRECTOR

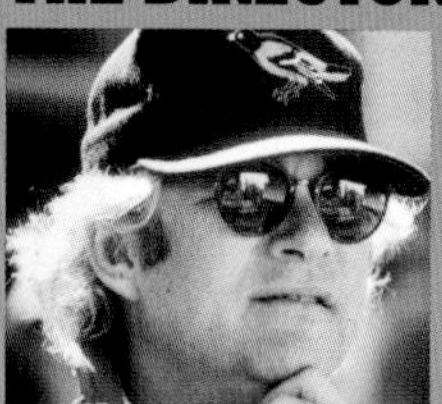

Director **Barry Levinson** shot all the diner scenes last so that the actors could warm to each other. It was the screenwriter's first time directing a feature and he proved himself a master of naturalism. The film was the first part of Levinson's "Baltimore Trilogy," followed by *Tin Men* (1987) and *Avalon* (1990). Among his many singular and much-lauded works are *The Natural* (1984), *Rain Man* (1988), *Good Morning, Vietnam* (1987), *Wag the Dog* (1997), *Possession* (2002), and *Envy* (2004). Levinson returned to his Baltimore childhood haunts in *Homicide*, his mid-1990s television series.

The Fells Point Diner in Baltimore is home to a group of five friends at the end of an era. It's the sure place to be to avoid facing the onrush of adulthood. They really don't want to be anywhere but here, forever. Pictured left to right, Timothy Daly, Mickey Rourke, Steve Guttenberg, and Daniel Stern.

THE CAST

Edward "Eddie" Simmons	Steve Guttenberg
Laurence "Shrevie" Schreiber	Daniel Stern
Robert "Boogie" Sheftell	Mickey Rourke
Timothy Fenwick Jr.	Kevin Bacon
William "Billy" Howard	Timothy Daly
Beth	Ellen Barkin
Modell	Paul Reiser
Barbara	Kathryn Dowling
Bagel	Michael Tucker
Carol	Colette Blonigan

THE ACTORS

Steve Guttenberg's subtly performed mama's boy was not to be revisited in any of his noisy performances in mainstream movies like *Can't Stop the Music* (1980), *Police Academy* (1984, and three of the five sequels), and *Cocoon* (1985).

Nice-boy graduate-student Billy, played by **Timothy Daly** (the grandson of the famous mayor of Chicago) isn't as squeaky clean as he appears. Struggling with his own demons, he hammers at the keys of a piano at a strip-joint as though he were pummeling a mugger. Daly's *Diner* debut would not lead to much of a career in features, but he's been kept busy on TV in the series *Wings*, the miniseries *Queen* (1993), the movie *Witness to the Execution* (1994), the Stephen King miniseries *Storm of the Century* (1999), and appeared in the feature film *Against the Ropes* (2003).

Ladies' man Boogie, played sensitively by **Mickey Rourke**, is the one character most clearly revealing an emotional life. Rourke was an actor worth watching in high-profile roles in *Body Heat* (1981), *The Pope of Greenwich Village* (1984), *Year of the Dragon* (1985), and *9 1/2 Weeks* (1986), and lesser-known films like *Barfly* (1987) and *Once Upon a Time in Mexico* (2003). His career, however, has tumbled, except in Europe, where he still has a large following. He's returned to boxing between infrequent films.

Kevin Bacon as Fenwick offers up an intense and moving breakout performance. He has also appeared in *Footloose* (1984), *Quicksilver* (1986), and *She's Having a Baby* (1988). Other films include *Criminal Law* (1989), *JFK* (1991), *A Few Good Men* (1992), *Apollo 13* (1995), *Mystic River* (2003), and *The Woodsman* (2004).

Ellen Barkin's Beth breaks your heart as the vulnerable, doesn't-have-a-clue wife. Her performance marked the debut of a great talent who continued to give her personal best in *Tender Mercies* (1983), *Daniel* and *The Big Easy* (both 1987), *Sea of Love* (1989), and *Into the West* (1993).

Paul Reiser takes nagging and self-denial to new depths in his hilarious portrait of the utterly marginal Modell. The stand-up comic took only a few turns in feature films, among them *Beverly Hills Cop* (1984 and the 1987 sequel), but achieved TV fame with his hit series *Mad About You* (1992–99). Reiser named his production company Nuance after an absurd exegesis his character gives in *Diner* on the word "nuance."

THE CRITICS

"It's rare to see a movie where the friendships seem as real, as lived-in as they do here . . . After the movie has ended, the closing credits come on, and we hear again on the soundtrack for several minutes the joyful, animated voices of the guys in the diner, ribbing and taunting each other. At the screening I attended no one got up to leave." —Peter Rainer, National Society of Film Critics

"Fresh, well-acted, and energetic American movies by new directors with the courage of their convictions are an endangered species. It isn't perfect, but even its unevenness is part of its appeal." —Janet Maslin, *New York Times*

SEND IN THE CLONES

The Low Down (2001)
Scotch and Milk (1998)
Dancer, Texas, Pop. 81 (1998)
Black & White & Red All Over (1997)
Mystic Pizza (1988)
Remembrance (1982)

CREDITS

Producer: Jerry Weintraub/ MGM/UA
Director: Barry Levinson
Screenplay: Barry Levinson
Running Time: 110 minutes
Budget: $5 million
Box Office: $14.1 million

ACADEMY AWARD NOMINATIONS

Best Screenplay: Barry Levinson

THE YEAR'S WINNERS

Best Picture: *Gandhi*
Best Director: Richard Attenborough, *Gandhi*
Best Actor: Ben Kingsley, *Gandhi*
Best Actress: Meryl Streep, *Sophie's Choice*
Best Supporting Actor: Louis Gossett, Jr., *An Officer and a Gentleman*
Best Supporting Actress: Jessica Lange, *Tootsie*

THE OTHER LISTS

American Film Institute (No)
Roger Ebert's Top 100 (No)
Entertainment Weekly (No)
Internet Movie Database (No)
Leonard Maltin (No)
National Society of Film Critics (Yes)
Premiere Magazine (No)
Rolling Stone Magazine (Yes)
Village Voice (No)

THE GREAT SCENE

Electronics salesman Shrevie, the lone married member of the tribe, loses his cool and reveals the emptiness at the heart of his marriage. Essentially, he lacks the depth to care about anything but his record collection. In this painful scene, he taunts wife Beth with her lack of knowledge of music: Shrevie asks Beth to test him on what's on the flipside of one record.

Beth: Why?

"Hey, Hey, Hey." 1958. Specialty Records. . . . See? You don't ask me things like that, do you? No! You never ask me what's on the flip side.

Beth: No! Because I don't give a shit. Shrevie, who cares about what's on the flip side of the record?

Shrevie goes into a rage about how important every aspect of a record is to him, from the label to the producer to the year it was made. He rants about the universe created around a song: who copied it; how it started a movement and a culture. Most importantly, he screams, "they take me back to certain points in my life, ok? Just don't touch my records, ever!" In a heartrending—yet empty as far as Beth is concerned—final note Shrevie remembers the music that was playing the night they met at the Modell sister's graduation party in 1955. "And "Aint That a Shame" was playing when I walked in the door!

BELOW: Boogie (Mickey Rourke) comforts Carol (Colette Blonigan). He's the only guy in the film who gets—understands—the women.

The only married couple in the group, Beth (Ellen Barkin) and Shrevie look like they're having a good time—but looks, as they say, can be deceiving. When Beth complains of loneliness, Shrevie launches a tirade, insisting that they have nothing in common.

NOTABLE QUOTES

"It gets harder and harder to make movies about human beings. These movies are like an endangered species. Everything is 'simplify, simplify' now. How many movies have sub-plots anymore?" —Barry Levinson

"We're talking about a very strange time [in Hollywood], to be honest. Writing by committee becomes much less about a vision. It is really about a piece of merchandise. We excuse movies like *Independence Day* (1996) that really lack logic and say, 'It doesn't make any sense, but it's a ride. I thought a movie was a movie and a ride was a ride." —Barry Levinson

"There are two types of actors: those who say they want to be famous and those who are liars." —Kevin Bacon

44

CITY LIGHTS 1931

QUIET RIOT

City Lights is one-stop shopping for both hardcore Chaplin fans and those who've never seen one of his films and wonder what the big deal was. It's a solo flight of comic invention that comes at you like some kind of clown miracle, and its elaborate slapstick sequences became templates for thousands of films that followed. It all looks spontaneous but, as they say, dying is easy, comedy is hard. It took Chaplin months to figure out how Virginia Cherrill's Blind Girl could plausibly mistake his Little Tramp for a rich man. Some 354 takes later, it came to him. Watch the scene and you won't see any sweat on that iconic brow. Is *City Lights* a silent movie? Well, it is and it isn't. It was made after the invention of sound, and sound there is—yet it features "dialogue cards" rather than spoken words. Chaplin was afraid that he'd lose his international fan base if they heard his voice but, in fact, they heard it here—disguised, of course. In the opening scene, dignitaries and politicians at the unveiling of a monument regale the crowd with the usual nonsense. Using his own voice through a filter, Chaplin provides them with officious noises in lieu of words. It works perfectly and the joke lands. As does just about every other one. Even in a small, throwaway moment, as the Tramp spins a bulky socialite across the dance floor, his footwork gets a laugh. And what is much, much more, *City Lights* has boundless heart. For those who think *The Great Dictator* is a bit broad or that the *King of New York* is slow, *City Lights* is just about perfect, a Swiss watch of comedy, every element lovingly crafted by a man who probably knew the power of film better than anyone.

Jim: Make no mistake, this is "intelligent" comedy. There's cunning behind those eyes and a fine art to the pratfalls. Oh, yeah, and by the way, it's hilarious. And heartbreaking.

Gail: A protest poem against the coming of sound and the loss of the ineffable—the gesture and the gaze—to the prosaic; it marked the end of film art as Chaplin knew it.

THE PLOT

A Tramp (Charlie Chaplin) encounters a beautiful Blind Girl (Virginia Cherrill) selling flowers, and she mistakes him for a man of means. Lovestruck, he buys a rosebud with his last coin. That night, he saves a drunken millionaire from suicide and is promised a generous reward—until the gin wears off and all of the gifts and promises are revoked. To save the girl from eviction, the Little Tramp submits to a prizefight and is creamed. The millionaire reappears with a hefty bankroll but, sober, he cries "thief." The Tramp manages to get the cash to the Blind Girl before he's nabbed. Much later, released from prison, he finds her in a shop of her own—no longer blind! The money he had given her paid for an operation. The pathetic little tramp watches her through a window, and she teases him with a flower and a coin—but as she takes his hand, she realizes he is her knight in shining armor.

"Can you see now?" the Little Tramp asks a blind girl who's been cured thanks to his love and sacrifice. Considered one of the defining moments in the history of cinema, Chaplin's great secret was that he wasn't acting.

THE INCOMPARABLE CHAPLIN

Born in 1889, the child of music hall performers, **Chaplin** was already a star in his native England by the time Mack Sennett hired him in 1913 and brought him to Hollywood. The film industry was in its infancy and eager for any new trick it could be taught. One desperate day on the set, Chaplin was called upon to quickly come up with something new. He borrowed a tight jacket from one actor, oversized shoes from another, a fake mustache the size of toothbrush, a bowler cap from another Sennett star, and added a cane from his own wardrobe. He penguin-walked in front of the camera and the Little Tramp was born. He would go on to become an iconic symbol of the silent era and well beyond.

By 1919, Chaplin had formed his own production company, United Artists, with great stars of the day Douglas Fairbanks and Mary Pickford. He could now make the films he wanted to make, using all of the time and money they required. It wasn't the money Chaplin was interested in—it was the freedom that money bought. His digs were always this side of ramshackle and, more often than not, he forgot to cash his checks from the studio. He never lived up to his means, although several of his wives managed to. He had four altogether, and the most famous was his last, Oona, daughter of playwright Eugene O'Neill. A daughter from that marriage, Geraldine, followed in her dad's footsteps in front of the camera. Chaplin lived long enough to experience every imaginable high and low resulting from a very public career. In the 1920s and '30s he was, hands down, the most famous and adored man in the world. He was the first actor to grace the cover of *Time* magazine. Adolf Hitler, hoping to steal a bit of his magic, modeled his mustache on the Little Tramp's. (He claimed to hate Chaplin, having been misinformed that he was Jewish, but is said to have watched *The Great Dictator*—Chaplin's great send-up of the Führer—no fewer than three times.)

Chaplin faced scandal in the form of a paternity suit (he was innocent but ended up paying a hefty settlement) and an investigation by Joseph McCarthy's red-baiting HUAC committee in the 1950s. He never became a U.S. citizen and rarely returned to England after being charged with cowardice for "hiding out" during the First World War. For most of his post-Hollywood life, Chaplin lived in Switzerland. At the height of his fame, he made hundreds of films, mostly comedy shorts—thirty-five in one year alone. That's a lot of jokes for a man who took himself very seriously. Possessing the body of an acrobat, the stamina of an Olympic athlete, the grace of a ballet dancer, and comic timing to match his closest though beloved rival, Buster Keaton, Chaplin also had a skill for pathos. The final scene in *City Lights* is a master class for anyone hoping to learn screen acting. On the surface of it, he does nothing but look into the face of the girl he loves . . . and smile. But oh, the volumes that smile speaks.

Highlights of Chaplin's many films include *A Woman of Paris* (1923), *The Gold Rush* (1925), *The Circus* (1928), *Modern Times* (1936), *The Great Dictator* (1940), *Monsieur Verdoux* (1947), and *Limelight* (1952).

THE CAST	
A Tramp	Charlie Chaplin
Blind Girl	Virginia Cherrill
Grandmother	Florence Lee
Eccentric Millionaire	Harry Myers
Butler	Allan Garcia
Prizefighter	Hank Mann

"All I need to make a comedy is a park, a policeman, and a pretty girl."
—Charlie Chaplin

The first meeting of the Tramp and the Blind Girl (Virginia Cherrill) required 354 takes. Marlon Brando, after being directed by uber-perfectionist Chaplin in *The Countess from Hong Kong*, claimed, "He was the most sadistic man I ever met."

BEHIND THE SCREEN

Chaplin and his leading lady, Virginia Cherrill, never had anything kind to say about each other. She was a spoiled, newly divorced socialite who, at one point, insisted on leaving the shoot early for a hairdresser's appointment. He tried to replace her with his *Gold Rush* costar, Georgia Hale, but by that time the film was too far along. Cherrill knew it, asked for double her salary, and got it.

The scene in which the Tramp and the Blind Girl meet was Chaplin's greatest challenge. Why would she mistake him for a rich man? He determined that the Tramp would avoid traffic by walking through an empty limousine's backseat. It was the slam of the expensive car door that provided the false clue.

Chaplin was an inveterate womanizer with a special affinity for underage girls. His affair and brief marriage to teen Nita Grey is said to have been the inspiration for Nabokov's *Lolita*.

Chaplin earned two honorary Academy Awards. The first came in 1928 (he supposedly used it as a doorstop) and the second in 1972. That ceremony was the occasion of Chaplin's first visit to the United States after many years of persecution by the FBI, who'd continually refused him a visa.

Chaplin's musical scores and compositions yielded two standards: "Smile" and "This Is My Song" (from the last film he directed, *The Countess of Hong Kong*, starring Sophia Loren and Marlon Brando).

CREDITS

Producer: Charlie Chaplin/ United Artists
Director: Charlie Chaplin
Screenplay: Charlie Chaplin
Running Time: 87 minutes
Budget: $1.5 million

THE YEAR'S ACADEMY AWARD WINNERS

Best Picture: *Cimmaron*
Best Director: Norman Taurog, *Skippy*
Best Actor: Lionel Barrymore, *A Free Soul*
Best Actress: Marie Dressler, *Min and Bill*

THE OTHER LISTS

American Film Institute (Yes)
Roger Ebert's Top 100 (Yes)
Entertainment Weekly (No)
Internet Movie Database (Yes)
Leonard Maltin (Yes)
Movieline (Yes)
Premiere Magazine (No)
Rolling Stone Magazine (Yes)
Village Voice (Yes)

Chaplin died on Christmas Day 1977 at his home in Switzerland. A year after his funeral, his body was stolen by a ring of extortionists who were caught weeks later. His second burial was beneath layers of cement to prevent further body-snatching attempts.

SEND IN THE CLONES

Woody Allen disguised as a robot in *Sleeper* and in the final shot of *Manhattan*, a tribute to the final shot in *City Lights*.

Steve Martin fighting with Lily Tomlin's soul—trapped inside his body in *All of Me*.

THE CRITICS

"If only one of Charles Chaplin's films could be preserved, *City Lights* would be the closest to representing all the different notes of his genius." —Roger Ebert, *Chicago Sun-Times*

NOTABLE QUOTES

The Tramp: Be careful how you're driving.
Drunken Millionaire: Am I driving?

Call him "Raging Huggy Bear." The Little Tramp is all over his opponent (Hank Mann) in a sublime boxing sequence that was the culmination of years of honing.

THE GREAT SCENE

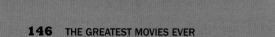

The Tramp steps into the prizefight ring with a killer of an opponent. He thinks he can stave off certain death by using politeness. He holds the rope for everyone to enter before him and, as the rivals approach for the customary handshake, he proceeds to hug his opponent like a long-lost love. Finally, the match begins in earnest. Charlie bobs and weaves, trying to survive by hiding behind the referee. It's an astonishingly choreographed pas de deux that leaves him untouched for the first round. Ultimately, he takes a punch and, as he falls back, the rope connected to the bell is tangled around his neck. Every time he moves, the bell rings to announce either the beginning or the end of a round. His tough-as-nails rival nearly collapses from confusion.

Hooked! The Tramp saves drunk millionaire (Harry Myers) from doing himself in. That cane Chaplin wields, along with the undersized bowler on his head, was auctioned off for over $150,000.

45

THE DEER HUNTER 1978

DEAD MEN WALKING

Released the same year as three other Vietnam films—*Coming Home, The Boys in Company C,* and *Go Tell the Spartans*—*The Deer Hunter* stands out from the rest for its epic ambitions. Its controversial portrayal of callous Vietnamese playing Russian roulette with the lives of POWs drew crowds of protesters. It is not an exaggeration to say that these scenes are nearly unwatchable in their graphic depiction of indifference to suffering. Apparently, the game was the director's fabrication and not an actual practice of the war. As viscerally hateful as they are, however, the scenes serve as a metaphor for the brutality of war. Anything less powerful might not have challenged the patriotic, buddy-buddy fervor with which the film's tight group of friends from a small steel-mill town enlist to prove their manhood and their deep love of country. But that country is no longer the same place for those who have returned, and they are no longer the same people they once were. What will survive of them remains to be seen, for everything has changed forever.

Jim: This one and *Godfather I* and *II* certainly, are the resulting magic of a certain place and time that allowed such a confluence of gifted actors to work together as an ensemble. They almost seem more content in their craft, somehow, than as solo super-novas.

Gail: Its brutal depiction of the inhumanity of war is matched by its devastating portrayal of the havoc the war has wrought on the lives that continue in its aftermath.

THE DEER HUNTER
ROBERT DE NIRO
THE DEER HUNTER
MICHAEL CIMINO

IE PLOT

ͣ close friends, Mike (Robert De Niro), (Christopher Walken), and Steve (John ge), steelworkers in a gray Pennsylvania , make arrangements for two important ous" rituals: the marriage of Steve, and deer-hunting trip. They play pool, drink, flirt, make love—and then they enlist. before going off the Vietnam, they take last hunting trip. Cool loner Mike speaks e hunt with reverence for its codes and s. He is not cruel. "A deer has to be n with one shot," he tells Nick. Cut to the mare of Vietnam where Mike and friends OWs brutally imprisoned. Prisoner after ner is fished out of his half-submerged to play Russian roulette with a loaded l. Mike can't bear it. He escapes with others. Time passes. Mike survives. Steve nt home a quadriplegic, but Nick is Mike comes home a troubled hero but ns to Saigon to find Nick, who is in a bling parlor, drugged and only half-alive, ng Russian roulette without any regard s life. Mike is shattered—he goes home, e is dead, too, in a way. He goes hunting an no longer shoot the buck that stands before him.

Of the three small-town buddies who enlist, one, Nick (Christopher Walken), is so dehumanized at the hands of his captors that he chooses to remain in Vietnam. Walken won a Best Supporting Actor Oscar for his staggering performance.

THE DIRECTOR

It was only his second feature—following *Thunderbolt and Lightfoot* (1974)—and **Michael Cimino** was the triple threat: producer, director, and screenwriter. *The Deer Hunter* won four Academy Awards, including Best Director, and five nominations altogether. Cimino's taste for things epic has rather informed his career and his approach to Hollywood. He rode on the coattails of *Deer Hunter* to direct the large and costly *Heaven's Gate*, which crashed and burned with epic proportions in 1980. The failure of this film virtually bankrupted the troubled United Artists. Cimino hoped to regain his stature with subsequent films like *Year of the Dragon* (1985), *The Sicilian* (1987), and *Desperate Hours* (1990), but all were box-office failures. His career is the stuff that movies are made of: a man of large talents whose taste for excess would prove his commercial undoing.

Submerged in rat-infested waters, contained within a bamboo cage, Mike (Robert De Niro, left) tries to calm the terrorized Steve (John Savage). Steve returns home a quadriplegic.

THE CAST	
Michael Vronsky	Robert De Niro
Stan	John Cazale
Steven	John Savage
Nick	Christopher Walken
Linda	Meryl Streep
John	George Dzundza
Axel	Chuck Aspegren
Steven's Mother	Shirley Stoler
Stan's Girl	Mary Ann Haenel
Linda's Father	Richard Kuss

THE ACTORS

As Mike, **Robert De Niro** is a leader among men, a man of few words who keeps his own counsel and upon whom life weighs heavily. De Niro's passion and intensity have informed his performances from the beginning. (For more on De Niro, see pages 11, 91, and 118.)

In order to get into—or out of shape—for his role, **Christopher Walken** ate only rice and bananas to attain that ravaged, hollow, and distant look he wears at the end of the film. As he says, "I don't need to be made to look evil. I can do that on my own." But as Nick, that evil look read more like inner turmoil, and it won him a Best Supporting Actor Oscar. Walken's early career on the stage (including a stint as a chorus boy) led to small but memorable performances in such films as *The Anderson Tapes* (1971) and *Annie Hall* (1977). In a surprise Astaire turn, Walken tapped brilliantly through *Pennies From Heaven* (1981). Since then he has played dramatic roles in such films as *The Dead Zone* (1983), *A View to a Kill* (1985), *At Close Range* (1986), *Biloxi Blues* (1988), and *King of New York* (1990). Walken has appeared in acclaimed TV dramas *Sarah, Plain and Tall* (1991) and its sequel, *Skylark* (1993). More recently he has taken on scene-stealing roles in *Batman Returns* (1992), *Wayne's World 2* (1993), and *Catch Me if You Can* (2002), and *Hairspray* (2007).

John Savage's Steve is the vulnerable, low-key buddy nearly destroyed mentally and physically by the war. Unlike De Niro's and Walken's, Savage's career did not take off after this performance but rather followed a more humble route with *Bad Company* (1972), and *The Killing Kind* and *Steelyard Blues* (both 1973). He played another emotionally devastated man, a cop, in *The Onion Field* (1979), and a suicidal crippled man in *Inside Moves* (1980). His varied career also includes *Hair* (1979), *Salvador* (1986), *Do the Right Thing* (1989), and *The Godfather, Part III* (1990).

The Deer Hunter was actress **Meryl Streep**'s second film performance. In it she plays the shy young woman who becomes Nick's girl by tacit agreement. But her heart belongs to Mike, and when Nick doesn't return, she briefly becomes Mike's lover. Arguably the best actress working in American films today, Streep seems to transform herself into whatever character she portrays—garnering praise from some and judgments of "coldness" from others. She has matched—and will soon outdo—Katharine Hepburn's record for the most nominations. Her screen debut in *Julia* (1977) led to her meteoric rise in such films as *The Seduction of Joe Tynan* (1979), *Manhattan* (1979), *Kramer vs. Kramer* (1979, first Oscar for Best Supporting Actress), *The French Lieutenant's Woman* (1981, Academy Award nomination), *Sophie's Choice* (1982), *Silkwood* (1983, Academy Award nomination), *Out of Africa* (1985, Academy Award nomination) *Ironweed* (1987, Academy Award nomination), *A Cry in the Dark* (1988, Academy Award nomination) and *Postcards From the Edge* (1990, Academy Award nomination). Streep later warmed up in such comedies as *Defending Your Life* (1991) and *Death Becomes Her* (1992). Her more recent films include *The River Wild* (1994) and *The Bridges of Madison County* (1995), the remarkable *The Hours* (2002, Academy Award nomination), and *The Devil Wears Prada* (2006).

John Cazale plays the lowlife Stan, a nervous alcoholic who might at any moment lose his cool. Engaged to Meryl Streep in real life, Cazale was ill with cancer while filming *Hunter*, and died shortly thereafter. He appeared in only five films in his career, and all of them were nominated for Best Picture. He debuted in *The Godfather* (1972), then made *The Godfather, Part II* (1974), *The Conversation* (1974), and *Dog Day Afternoon* (1975). (For more on Cazale, see pages 13 and 274.)

The womanizing Axel was **Chuck Aspegren**'s only role in a film.

THE CRITICS

"A big, awkwardly, crazily ambitious, sometimes breathtaking motion picture that comes as close to being a popular epic as any movies about this country since *The Godfather*. [Cimino] tried to create a film that is nothing

CREDITS

Producer: Michael Cimino, Michael Deeley, John Peverall, Barry Spikings/ Universal Pictures
Director: Michael Cimino
Screenplay: Michael Cimino, Louis Garfinkle, Quinn K. Redeker, Deric Washburn
Running Time: 183 minutes
Budget: $15 million
Box Office: $49 million

ACADEMY AWARDS

Best Picture
Best Supporting Actor: Christopher Walken
Best Director: Michael Cimino
Best Film Editing: Peter Zinner

NOMINATIONS

Best Sound: Richard Portman, William L. McCaughey, Aaron Rochin, C. Darin Knight

THE YEAR'S OTHER WINNERS

Best Actor: Jon Voight, *Coming Home*
Best Actress: Jane Fonda, *Coming Home*
Best Supporting Actress: Maggie Smith, *California Suite*

less than an appraisal of American life in the second half of the twentieth century." —Vincent Canby, *New York Times*

"The meandering, sometimes shrill, raw film has been extremely controversial on many accounts—political and emotional. The flawed, extravagantly expensive film is often pretentious, ambiguous, overwrought, and excessive, and loosely edited, with under-developed character portrayals and unsophisticated, careless film techniques." —Tom Dirks, *100 Best Movies, International Movie Database*

BEHIND THE SCREEN

Cazale was so sick that the filmmakers were often forced to work around him.

The scene where John Savage and Robert De Niro are being rescued by a helicopter from a river in the Vietnamese jungle turned into a real-life near-miss caught on camera. As the helicopter rose they anxiously signaled to the crew that they were in jeopardy. And that's exactly what we witness.

A live round was put into the gun during some of the Russian roulette scenes to raise the level of tension. (The gun was checked to ensure that the bullet was never in the chamber.)

Cimino's original rough cut was four hours long, prompting the studio to furtively hire an editor to cut it down to two hours. When test audiences responded positively to the director's original four hours, they rehired him to do a new cut down to three hours.

It was a hot summer when the film was shot, though the film was to take place in autumn. The art directors had to brown the grass and pull all the leaves off the trees, and the actors had to feign chills while mopping their brows between takes.

THE GREAT SCENE

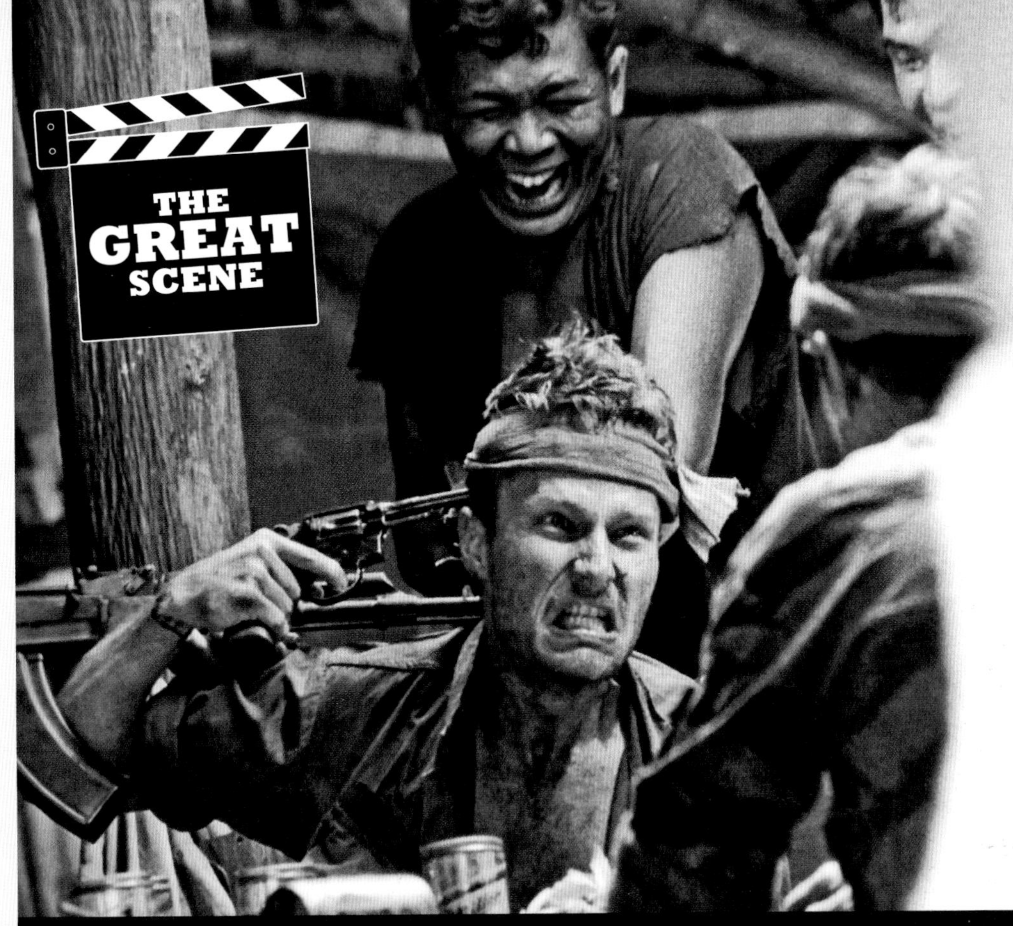

Steve (John Savage), a prisoner of war along with his friends Mike and Nick, is forced to play Russian Roulette in a Vietnamese gambling den. Though he survives the game, he emerges from the war traumatized and broken, physically and emotionally. All three friends will be irrevocably ravaged by the war.

Kept inside bamboo cages in rat-infested waters, POWs are pulled out one at a time to play Russian roulette with their captors—and their lives. Seated across from them at the table, the Vietnamese captors place a gun in each man's hand and force him to raise it to his temple. One chamber holds a live bullet. Bets are placed on whether or not the shot fired will be the fatal one. The excited players scream over and over again in Vietnamese for each of the men to *shoot, shoot!* A soldier's sweaty face turns ashen and twisted in terror. The gun is fired. Another man is pulled from the water.

THE OTHER LISTS

- American Film Institute (Yes)
- Roger Ebert's Top 100 (No)
- *Entertainment Weekly* (No)
- Internet Movie Database (No)
- Leonard Maltin (Yes)
- *Movieline* (No)
- National Society of Film Critics (No)
- *Premiere* Magazine (No)
- *Rolling Stone* Magazine (No)
- *Village Voice* (No)

The soldier returns home a different man. Kate (Meryl Streep) opens the door to find Mike, the man she secretly loves—though she is Nick's girl—alive. Her joy is immense. Though he looks the victorious soldier, the war has changed him in ways that he is only beginning to understand.

46

8½ 1963

MIDLIFE CIRCUS

At 40, Federico Fellini was suffering near-suicidal anxiety. Luckily for the history of cinema, he transformed his camera into a relentless mirror in hope of a cure. The original title of this film, *A Beautiful Confusion*, is remarkably apt. We float through a mosaic of exotic images Fellini hoped would shake him loose and inspire his artistic rebirth. Never a slave to the script, here he tosses it aside almost completely and flies by the seat of his pants. Where are we going next? A Dante-esque steam room, a farm of nurturing but ultimately rebellious women, a rocket ship launching pad guarded by a tap-dancing old sailor? Who cares? The man may have been deeply troubled, but his confidence at the wheel of this runaway vehicle is exhilarating. A gush of visual astonishments await as we journey through the mind of a genius who's essentially psychoanalyzing himself. More than a little like dreaming with your eyes open.

Jim: Anxiety and introspection, Fellini-style. Grotesque and unnervingly beautiful. The gravity-defying opening gives way to another rarefied phenomenon, Sandra Milo. *Mamma mia!*

Gail: When's the last time you saw a Hollywood movie that took on the internal life of the artist? It's so wonderfully European in its engagement of the subject of creativity. With its striking visual imagery and arresting contrasts in black and white, this one is bewitching.

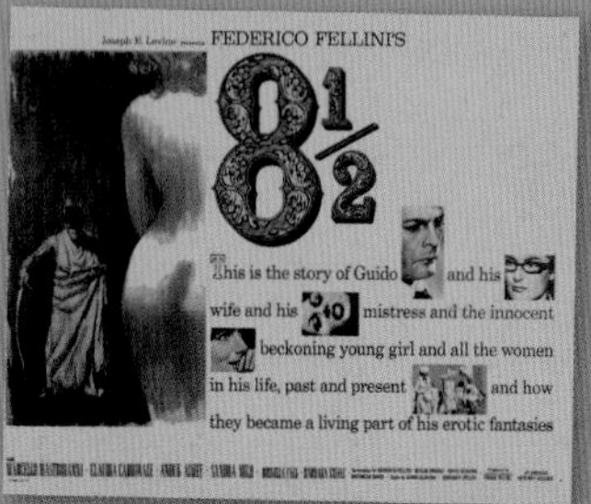

THE PLOT

Famed film director Guido Anselmi (Marcello Mastroianni) has gone dry. With a new project set to go before the cameras and no script, Guido plumbs his memories of childhood and his hidden desires for inspiration. He plays out such fantasies as the meeting of his wife (Anouk Aimée) and his mistress (Sandra Milo), even as he waxes nostalgic for the gargoyle of a whore he'd encountered as a schoolboy. Still far from ready to tell a commercial story, Guido is dragged kicking and screaming to a press conference on the massive, unfinished set of a film he has not yet envisioned. As he's barraged with questions, he ducks under a table and pulls a gun. But his suicidal desperation finally leads him to the understanding that life is only a show, a gala circus, and his spirit is renewed.

"My work is my only relationship to everything."

—Federico Fellini

Artistically exhausted, Guido suspects the joke is on him. Even as he dons a comic nose for effect, he wonders if there's any point in going on with his charade of a career. Never, before Fellini, had a filmmaker exposed his internal dilemma with such naked honesty.

"I have nothing to say but I want to say it."—Guido

THE DIRECTOR

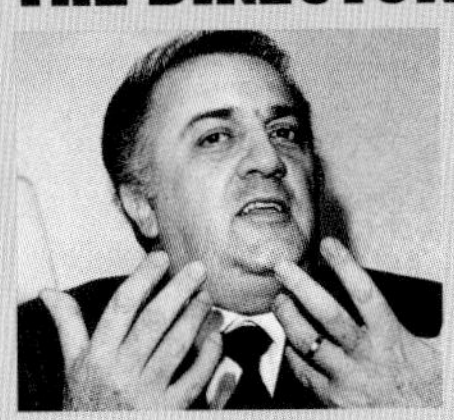

Federico Fellini was ready to chuck the entire project until he was inspired to transform his doppelgänger hero, Guido, from a writer to a film director. Still unclear as to the shape of the film, he dispensed with traditional trappings and dared to show the process of creation as it was happening. Though treated like a god by most Italians, Fellini maintained his self-deprecating nature. He appeared affable, but that was a mask for his limited interest in others. Once he had learned an actor's or writer's secrets, explored their potential fully, he let him or her go without a thought. Still, there was a long line of hopefuls eager to be used by him. They guessed rightly that they were in the presence of celluloid's Michelangelo, a peerless artist whose work remains timeless thanks to its highly personal content and his ability to capture perfectly the essence of contemporary culture. While filming *8½*, he asked a producer friend if it would find an audience in America. The man responded, No, Americans weren't ready for such an array of visual metaphors. It went on to win the Oscar for Best Foreign Film. (For more on Fellini, see page 76.)

Guido's voracious mistress Carla is content to simply be his creation. Once again, the film mirrors Fellini's life. He and Sandra Milo were extramarital lovers for years, and he simply let the scandal play out on screen. Milo, like Carla, trusted her director completely.

THE CAST

Guido Anselmi	Marcello Mastroianni
Claudia	Claudia Cardinale
Luisa Anselmi	Anouk Aimée
Carla	Sandra Milo
Rossella	Rossella Falk
Gloria Morin	Barbara Steele
French Actress	Madeleine LeBeau
Fashionable Woman	Caterina Boratto
La Saraghina	Eddra Gale
Producer	Guido Alberti
Director	Mario Conocchia
Production Secretary	Bruno Agostini
Production Inspector	Cesarino Miceli Picardi
Writer	Jean Rougeul

THE ACTORS

Marcello Mastroianni attended acting school with Fellini as a young man and they remained joined at the hip for the rest of their lives. Mastroianni was his on-screen persona and was the elegant exception to Fellini's rule never to use an actor in more than two films. Until he turned the character into a director, Fellini worried, "How am I going to ask Marcello to play a writer again? He'll end up believing he's one and he'll write a novel!" The director and his star enjoyed strikingly similar personal lives with wives who remained loyal despite their endless strings of affairs. In the film, the details of Guido's philandering are an uncomfortable but necessary detail. The irony is that Mastroianni was cheating on his wife with Anouk Aimée, his fictional missus. Life never really came close to imitating art in *Divorce, Italian Style* (1961), which was followed by *Marriage, Italian Style* (1964). He was a fascinating gigolo at midlife in *Casanova '70* (1965) and was particularly moving as a shy gay man under the murderous reign of Mussolini in *A Special Day* (1977), costarring Sophia Loren. (For more on Mastroianni, see page 76.)

Anouk Aimée had played the glamorous nymphomaniac in *La Dolce Vita*, but here Fellini cast her as the long-suffering wife, Luisa. The actress was quite vain about her appearance, and wasn't keen on smoking on screen because it made her squint. As it was, her eyesight was very weak; off screen, she wore thick glasses. Fellini forced her into them for Luisa, ordered her to chain-smoke, and even trimmed her unusually long eyelashes to complete the dowdy portrait. (For more on Aimée, see page 76.)

Sandra Milo, the zaftig, insatiable mistress, Carla, had quit the business and refused Fellini's request for an interview. But he knew she was perfect for the role and he showed up at her home unannounced, bringing along a cameraman to shoot a screen test. While filming, the two fell madly in love and maintained a seventeen-year extramarital relationship. Her film career was almost entirely confined to Europe but she appeared once again, famously, in Fellini's *Juliet of the Spirits* (1965).

La Saraghina, the indelible, fleshy whore whose very image in *8½* has become an Italian icon, was played by **Eddra Gale**, an opera singer from Milwaukee.

BEHIND THE SCREEN

Sandra Milo admitted that in all their years together, she and Fellini never made love in a bed.

Fellini's preproduction began with an ad in the newspaper asking that "any woman who thinks she's possessed of a rare, classical beauty" come for an interview. A mob scene resulted, and from that, Fellini selected his gallery of grotesqueries.

The title *8½* has no meaning. It has been thought to be the number of Fellini's completed projects, but it doesn't add up.

The luscious starlet **Claudia Cardinale** Fellini cast as the director's innocent Italian muse, was, in fact, from Tunisia.

THE CRITICS

"A movie like this is like a splash of cold water in the face, a reminder that the movies really can shake us up, if they want to. Ironic that Fellini's film is about artistic bankruptcy but seems richer in invention than almost anything else around." —Roger Ebert, *Chicago Sun-Times*

"*8½* may be the worst movie ever made by a major Italian director. A disgusting piece of self-exhibitionism." —Joseph Bennett, *The Kenyon Review*

BEHIND THE SCREEN

Fellini was a big fan of action/adventure comic books. An early writing assignment was the Italian translation of *Flash Gordon*.

Fellini's muse and famously patient wife, Giulietta Masina, died just five months after he did in 1996. She was his frequent star and made her indelible mark in *La Strada* (1954), *Nights of Cabiria* (1957), *Juliet of the Spirits* (1965), and *Ginger and Fred* (1986) .

CREDITS

Producer: Angelo Rizzoli/ Embassy Pictures
Director: Federico Fellini
Screenplay: Federico Fellini, Ennio Flaiano, Tullio Pinelli, Brunello Rondi
Running time: 135 minutes

ACADEMY AWARDS

Best Foreign Language Film
Best Costume Design, Black-and-White: Piero Ghirardi

NOMINATIONS

Best Director: Federico Fellini
Best Original Screenplay: Federico Fellini, Ennio Flaiano, Tullio Pinelli, Brunello Rondi

THE YEAR'S OTHER WINNERS

Best Picture: *Tom Jones*
Best Director: Tony Richardson, *Tom Jones*
Best Actor: Sidney Poitier, *Lilies of the Field*
Best Actress: Patricia Neal, *Hud*
Best Supporting Actor: Melvyn Douglas, *Hud*
Best Supporting Actress: Margaret Rutherford, *The V.I.P.s*

Guido is at last inspired to portray his life as the circus he imagined as a child. At film's end all the people who've shaped his identity come out for a curtain call. Orson Welles once remarked that Fellini's films "are a small-town boy's dream of the big city. His sophistication works because it's the creation of someone who doesn't have it."

The opening shot immerses us in a massive traffic jam in Rome. Hundreds of vehicles are stopped dead in their tracks with very little emotional reaction from drivers. Most stare straight ahead into the void. The camera seems genuinely confused by the tie-up as it searches everywhere for the cause. It finally comes to rest in the backseat of Guido Anselmi's car. Suddenly, the car begins to fill up with smoke. Guido struggles to free himself from the deadly fumes, kicking and clawing desperately at the windows. He's ignored by the drivers on either side of him. Finally he emerges from the roof of the car, like an embryo struggling out of the birth canal. As a wind rustles ominously, Guido floats up above the traffic and out over a beach, where he discovers that his leg is tied to a kite string. He's the kite! Down below, a man cuts the string and Guido plummets into the sea.

THE OTHER LISTS

- American Film Institute (No)
- Roger Ebert's Top 100 (No)
- *Entertainment Weekly* (Yes)
- Internet Movie Database (No)
- Leonard Maltin (Yes)
- *Movieline* (Yes)
- National Society of Film Critics (No)
- *Premiere* Magazine (No)
- *Rolling Stone* Magazine (No)
- *Village Voice* (No)

Evocative childhood memories emerge of sweetly deranged La Saraghina, the village whore who danced for a few coins and did far more for a loaf of bread. The priests called her "the devil incarnate." Little Guido couldn't have disagreed more.

"They come for you in the morning in a limousine; they take you to the studio; they stick a pretty girl in your arms . . . They call that a profession? Come on!"—Marcello Mastroianni

47

TOP HAT 1935

DEPRESSION BLUES CHASER

Fred Astaire and Ginger Rogers shimmer across the dance floor in a timeless, spaceless whirl called romance. This is the stuff that dreams are made of. Hollywood in its Golden Age may have fashioned a dream factory, churning out illusions hundreds of films at a time, but the pleasure we get from watching Astaire-Rogers is real. They were a force of nature. Astaire was grace made corpus. The Berlin score keeps our toes tapping and our hearts beating with, among others numbers, "Fancy Free," "No Strings," "Isn't it a Lovely Day to be Caught in the Rain," and "Top Hat, White Tie, and Tails" (in which Astaire uses his cane to shoot down the chorus of dancers). It was a time—the Depression—that needed a dream. The dream, however, lasts forever.

Jim: In a perfect world, this one would be nineteen hours long and they wouldn't even stop dancing for a cup of coffee.

Gail: Ginger Rogers's body arched over Fred Astaire, who holds her up with a finger. All this and heaven, too. Kismet!

EY'RE DANCING CHEEK-TO-CHEEK AGAIN!
FRED
ASTAIRE
GINGER
ROGERS

TOP
HAT
MUSIC AND LYRICS BY
IRVING
BERLIN
EDWARD EVERETT HORTON
HELEN BRODERICK
ERIK RHODES · ERIC BLORE
Directed by MARK SANDRICH

HE PLOT

? Who said anything about a plot? rybody just gets everybody else's identity ng, resulting in an array of silly behavior ong the ridiculously wealthy at the height ne Depression. Fred and Ginger make r way through a splendidly ornate and eal backdrop of art deco Venice, complete floating nightclubs. Formerly free-spirited) strings, no connections") hoofer Jerry ers (Astaire) and model Dale Tremont gers), who believes Jerry is married to her friend, dance around and around before ng into each other's arms. But Dale's best id doesn't seem to care that her putative band is spending all his time dancing Dale. Finally, Dale realizes that he *isn't* and he realizes that she *is* her—and ybody's happy, in a saucy kind of way. e sense?

"Hollywood is like an empty wastebasket."—Ginger Rogers

THE DIRECTOR

Though it seems as though everything happens by grace alone, there is, in fact, a human director behind the Astaire-Rogers films. Silent-film director **Mark Sandrich** tried his hand at sound, but he turned out to have a tin ear. He was given one more go at it and nailed his future with the Oscar-winning *So This Is Harris* (1932), allowing him to dance with the gods. Sandrich was blessed to direct seven of the dance team's films: *Roberta* and *Top Hat* (both 1935), *Follow the Fleet* (1936), *Swing Time* (1936), *Shall We Dance* (1937), *Carefree* (1938), and *The Story of Vernon and Irene Castle* (1939). *Top Hat* was the fourth of nine films that Fred Astaire and Ginger Rogers appeared in for RKO (between 1933 and 1939), and it became the studio's greatest box-office hit of the '30s.

With top hat, white tie, and tails twirling, Astaire is poetry in motion. Whether defying gravity by dancing on the ceiling or taking a broomstick as his partner, he casts a spell on the audience through the sheer glory of his movement. No one has ever done it better, before or since. It's as if he is in love with the space itself and wants to do everything in it that's possible.

THE CAST

Jerry Travers	Fred Astaire
Dale Tremont	Ginger Rogers
Horace Hardwick	Edward Everett Horton
Alberto Beddini	Erik Rhodes
Bates	Eric Blore
Madge Hardwick	Helen Broderick
Flower Clerk	Lucille Ball (uncredited)

THE ACTORS

The evaluation of **Fred Astaire**'s first screen test is infamous by now: "Can't act. Can't sing. Balding. Can dance a little." Doing everything with Olympian perfection, Astaire, alas, had a human frailty. Big Hands. To mask this unseemly attribute Astaire would curl his middle two fingers while tripping the light fantastic. In addition to the Sandrich-directed movies, Astaire graced many other films, among them *Funny Face* and *Silk Stockings* (both 1957), which featured music by such other immortals as Cole Porter and Jerome Kern. He also played a number of non-hoofing roles, including *On the Beach* (1959). The effect of Astaire on our nervous systems is nothing less than overstimulating. Astaire said it best: "Of course, Ginger was able to accomplish sex through dance. We told more through our movements instead of the big clinch. We did it all in the dance." And for the astonishing choreography we must also thank Hermes Pan.

The actress who won an Oscar for her role in *Kitty Foyle* (1940) was never given due credit for her serious acting work. A child performer with an aggressive stage mother, **Ginger Rogers** danced her way through childhood, and when she grew up she helped Fred light up the dance floor beginning with *Flying Down to Rio* (1933) and continuing through *Roberta* (1935), *Swing Time* and *Follow the Fleet* (both 1936), *Shall We Dance?* (1937), *Carefree* (1938), and the more serious *The Story of Vernon and Irene Castle* (1939). When asked why the team wasn't called Ginger and Fred, Rogers replied, "Because it's a man's world."

Erik Rhodes's suave, Continental gigolo Beddini, who utters the musical words, "Beddini, you are so pretty. I'm so glad you're not skeeny," appeared once before with Astaire-Rogers, in *The Gay Divorcee* (1934).

Edward Everett Horton, Horace Hardwick to you, has the singular distinction of appearing in nearly every Hollywood comedy of the thirties. Playing a high-strung fussbudget, Horton made a great foil for the charming men with whom he appeared, most notably Astaire.

Bates, the eccentric among eccentrics, is performed with caustic wit by **Eric Blore**. He had a prolific career throughout the thirties and the fifties, which included roles in such other Astaire-Rogers films as *Flying Down to Rio* (1933), *The Gay Divorcee* (1934), *Swing Time* (1936), and *Shall We Dance* (1937).

BEHIND THE SCREEN

Songs that were written for this film but made it into other ones include "Wild About You," "Get Thee Behind Me, Satan," and "You're the Cause."

All of Irving Berlin's songs from the film reached the top of the popular music charts at the time.

"For the men the sword, for the women the whip," observes Beddini in his infinite wisdom. The Hays censors didn't agree and changed his dictum to, "For the women the kiss, for the men the sword."

During "Cheek to Cheek," Rogers' gown shed so many feathers that Astaire became exasperated and insisted something be done. The feathers were sewn down, causing delays, but you can still see them flying. The big to-do earned Astaire the nickname "Feathers."

The two-minute production number "Piccolino" was filmed in one take.

ROLE REVERSALS

Impossible!

THE CRITICS

"The fourth pairing of Fred Astaire and Ginger Rogers and the first with a screenplay written specifically for them, *Top Hat* is the quintessential Astaire-Rogers musical, complete with a silly plot, romance, dapper outfits, art deco sets, and plenty of wonderful songs and dance numbers. " —*TV Guide*

CREDITS

Producer: Pandro S. Berman/ RKO Radio Pictures
Director: Mark Sandrich
Screenplay : Dwight Taylor and Allan Scott, based on the play *The Girl Who Dared*, by Alexander Farago and Aladar Laszlo
Running Time: 99 minutes
Budget: $609,000
Box Office: $3.2 million (worldwide)

ACADEMY AWARD NOMINATIONS

Best Picture
Best Art Direction: Carroll Clark, Van Nest Polglase
Best Dance Direction: Hermes Pan
Best Music/Song: "Cheek to Cheek," Irving Berlin

THE YEAR'S WINNERS

Best Picture: *Mutiny on the Bounty*
Best Director: John Ford, *The Informer*
Best Actor: Victor McLaglen, *The Informer*
Best Actress: Bette Davis, *Dangerous*

It's "Cheek to Cheek" time . . . and oh what a touch. The dance begins with Rogers carefully avoiding Astaire, dancing only by his side. Astaire suddenly spins her close to him and away again, close and away. It is arguably their most romantic dance. Dale is grace itself in an ice-blue satin gown covered with ostrich feathers. They whirl, solitary, around the dance floor. Fred twirls her deep into his arms, and finally she melts in surrender. The orchestra rises to a climax and the dancers come to rest against the terrace wall as if having made love. (Which they have, after all.)

BELOW: "Beddini, you are so pretty. I'm so glad you're not skeeny," sings Alberto Beddini (Erik Rhodes), fashion designer and love interest (or so he thinks) of model Dale Tremont (Ginger Rogers). When he discovers Jerry Travers's (Fred Astaire) designs on his "beloved," Beddini challenges him to a duel.

NOTABLE QUOTES

"They tend to overdo the vulgarity [in contemporary films]. I'm not embarrassed by the language itself, but it's embarrassing to be listening to it, sitting next to perfect strangers." –Fred Astaire

"After all, it's not as if we were Abbott and Costello. We did have careers apart from each other." –Ginger Rogers, on her partnership with Astaire

"People think I was born in top hat and tails." –Fred Astaire

"Of course, Ginger was able to accomplish sex through dance. We told more through our movements instead of the big clinch. We did it all in the dance." –Fred Astaire

THE OTHER LISTS

American Film Institute (No)

Roger Ebert's Top 100 (No)

Entertainment Weekly (No)

Internet Movie Database (No)

Leonard Maltin (No)

National Society of Film Critics (Yes)

Premiere Magazine (No)

Rolling Stone Magazine (No)

Village Voice (No)

48

RULES OF THE GAME 1939

L'AMOUR FOU

The passing of an age when heroism and great romance were still possible is already afoot when André Jurieux returns from his first solo transatlantic flight to discover that the woman for whom he had made the heroic flight did not come to greet him. And from this point on, Renoir watches through long, undisturbed takes the collapse of an era when heroism was possible and class privilege prevailed with all of its trappings, including the suppression of truth and humanity. There is something inexplicably right, beautiful, and simply complex about this film, a tragic and witty comedy of manners set in the grand weekend country chateau of the Jewish Marquis de Cheyniest. Seductions, murderous chases, and the drawing-room sexual triangulations of the French aristocrats (as well as those of the downstairs help) are recorded by the filmmaker with equal parts amusement and seriousness. Games, universal betrayals, and lies are renewed with every sip of a cocktail, by formidable people who "should know better." They are presented without judgment, though, as is the brutal hunting party which follows its own heartless tradition. It was certainly no accident that such a film, an allegory for World War II, would be made by the great director just as the Germans occupied France. Parisians felt so demoralized by Renoir's subtle indictment of the social order that they rioted at the film's opening. As a result, thirty-three minutes were cut. *Rules* was banned as morally perilous during the German occupation, and the original negative was ultimately destroyed during World War II. Universally considered one of the greatest films ever made, the movie's relative lack of structure, its sense of surprise and improvisation, its ability to slip so seamlessly from farce to tragedy, make it a film like no other.

Jim: It's vital to remember that, once upon a time, films could be so powerful as to cause audiences to riot, pummel the ushers, and threaten the director with something akin to a guillotine. And this was a comedy!

Gail: Formless yet formidable; sad and beautiful in its depiction of a cruel society on its last legs, no one but Renoir could make a film of such enormous human contradictions and ironies so compassionate and still so rigorous.

THE PLOT

When aviator André Jurieux (Roland Toutain), upon his return from a heroic transatlantic flight, discovers that his lover is not among the crowd, he breaks the first rule of society and declares his pain over national radio. Meanwhile, at the palatial Paris home of his married beloved, Christine de la Cheyniest (Nora Gregor), preparations are being made for a weekend shooting party at their country estate. Both wife and husband Robert (Marcel Dalio) have heard the broadcast. Christine, fearing that Robert will get the wrong idea, clarifies that she is not having an affair with Jurieux but that he is simply a friend. All of this prompts him to fly off to his mistress to break up the affair that he is having. Octave (Jean Renoir), a friend to both André and to the Marquis suggests that all of the confirmed and putative lovers be invited for the weekend to clear the air and establish that nothing untoward has been happening. The local aristocracy arrive at the house and the air fills with gossip of the latest infidelities. Christine is applauded for her handling of the André situation when she publicly explains that she and he are only dear friends. Meanwhile the maidservant to Christine, Lisette, has been flirting wildly with Octave and carrying on with another servant, infuriating her husband, the gamekeeper. Soon, everyone goes off to the very civilized shooting party where many rabbits run unsuccessfully for their lives. They all return for an all-night party. They flirt and chase one another through the house, raising the ire of cuckolded husbands and jealous lovers. Fights break out and, in the end a gun is shot, signaling, perhaps, the true end of this society and an era.

The very married Christine de la Cheyniest (Nora Gregor) confides her confusions about whom to love to one of her would-be lovers—really a great old friend—Octave (Jean Renoir).

THE DIRECTOR

Jean Renoir was the son of the Impressionist painter Auguste Renoir, and his films show the same pure delight in life and light as his father's paintings. *Rules of the Game* is his most pessimistic work, but it has the warmth and humanity that are a hallmark of all his films. Renoir is among the greatest European filmmakers, and *Rules* is the most highly considered—appearing on the top of the best of the best international film lists—even greater than his better-known work *The Grand Illusion* (1937). Having grown disturbed by France's complacency over the German occupation, Renoir made *Rules of the Game* to help his countrymen to look at themselves. "The rules of the game," said Renoir, "are those which must be observed in society if one wishes to avoid being crushed." He chose the drawing room comedy to make his thoughts known in a form close to the hearts of the French. Renoir worked extensively with improvisation and used anything that would help elucidate character. *Rules*, with its free-form construction was, the director said, "probably the most improvised of all my movies." Because of his primary interest in character, everything, including the use of the camera, was restrained in order to allow the drama to unfold naturally. His use of deep focus photography furthered that goal in that it allowed many players to share equal emphasis in a scene. In this case, deep focus literally brought the fates of the upper and lower classes together, one of his most important themes. Renoir began directing in the 1920s, financing his films by selling some of his late father's paintings. Among the greatest of his French films are the thriller *La Chienne* (1931), a mystery *La Nuit du Carrefour* (1932) and the tragic *Boudu Saved from Drowning* (1932), which Paul Mazursky remade as *Down and Out in Beverly Hills* (1986). He turned to politics with *The Crime of Monsieur Lange* (1936) and *Grand Illusion* (1937). Renoir came to the United States and made such films as the thriller *Swamp Water* (1941) followed by some marginal movies and then the beautiful story of sharecroppers, *The Southerner* (1945), which earned a Best Director nomination. Renoir went to India to make *The River* (1951), an adaptation of Rumer Godden's novel, *The Golden Coach* (1953), and finally returned to France to film *Only the French Can/French Can-Can* (1955). The *slight The Little Theatre of Jean Renoir* (1971) was his last film. (For more on Renoir, see page 277.)

Christine welcomes home national hero André Jurieux (Roland Toutain, center) upon his return from a celebrated solo transatlantic flight which he announced on radio he had done for her. Octave, a good friend to both, looks on.

THE CAST

Christine de la Cheyniest	Nora Gregor
Lisette, her servant	Paulette Dubost
Mme. de la Plante	Odette Talazac
Geneviève de Marras	Mila Parély
Mme. de la Bruyère	Claire Gérard
Jackie, Christine's niece	Anne Mayen
Radio-Reporter	Lise Elina
Robert de la Cheyniest	Marcel Dalio
Marceau	Julien Carette
André Jurieux	Roland Toutain
Schumacher	Gaston Modot
Octave	Jean Renoir

THE ACTORS

Octave is played by **Jean Renoir** himself and, like a director, the character is the chief maker of arrangements in the film; as the weekend unfolds, he attempts to keep the uncontrollable under control. He is the emotional center of the film, and the man who vainly tries to make sense of this doomed society only to find, in the end, that he is as confused as everyone else. His acting is comic, slapstick, and wonderful.

Nora Gregor plays Christine with an innocence that comes to her naturally. An operetta star and a real-life aristocrat and sometime actress who would commit suicide in the late 1940s, her weaknesses as an actress were used by Renoir to advantage rendering her performance a very moving one. The Austrian actress's flawed French and slightly remote quality were perfect for the role of an outsider. As the Marquis's troubled wife, Gregor is realistically hesitant and confused and easily believable as the focus of so much love. Compared to her selfish maid, vibrantly played by Paulette Dubost, Gregor's Christine is thoroughly innocent, the victim of a mistaken belief that she understands "the game." The actress's first talking picture was *Olympia* (1930), and she made a number of films in France and Germany until 1945.

As Lisette, **Paulette Dubost** manages to be both very appealing and appropriately vague as the blithe and careless maid. Dubost is a prolific actress, having made more than 150 movies for French film and television.

Robert de la Cheyniest, the self-indulgent host with many sides to his personality, is played brilliantly by **Marcel Dalio** (whose original name was Israel Moshe Blauschild). He is the ultimate deceiver, his eager, anxious facial expressions more theatrical than real, making him the perfect master of ceremonies for the events at hand. Yet, his face also betrays a gentleness, and, as he says, a need to avoid causing pain. His childish eagerness when showing off his mechanical toys is almost heartbreaking. Dalio, a Jew, fled Paris in 1940 just ahead of the German invasion, eventually reaching Lisbon with his wife, where they obtained visas to Chile, but on reaching Mexico they learned that these were forgeries. They eventually obtained temporary Canadian passports and ended up in the U.S. With his wife, he fled France ahead of the invading Germans who used his portrait on posters as representative of "a typical Jew." Dalio also appeared in Renoir's *Grand Illusion* (1937), and is memorable to American audiences for his roles in *Casablanca* (1942), *The Song of Bernadette* (1943), *To Have and Have Not* (1944), *Gentlemen Prefer Blondes* (1953), *Sabrina* (1954), *The List of Adrian Messenger* (1963), and *Catch-22* (1970) in addition to his numerous European films. (For more on Dalio, see page 277.)

André Jurieux is played by **Roland Toutain** with just the right sense of being an outsider in society. Though he is a hero, there is really no place within polite society for anyone who stands out. Toutain has appeared in more than forty French films.

THE CRITICS

"Perhaps the most influential of all French films, and one of the most richly entertaining." —Pauline Kael, *The New Yorker*

"Exactly what Jean Renoir has in mind when he wrote, performed in, and directed *The Rules of the Game*, is anybody's guess. Here we have a baffling mix of stale sophistication, coy symbolism, and galloping slapstick that

CREDITS

Producer: Claude Renoir/ Janus Films
Director: Jean Renoir
Screenplay: Carl Koch and Jean Renoir
Running Time: 110 minutes

THE YEAR'S ACADEMY AWARD WINNERS

Best Picture: *Gone with the Wind*
Best Director: Victor Fleming, *Gone with the Wind*
Best Actor: Robert Donat, *Goodbye, Mr. Chips*
Best Actress: Vivien Leigh, *Gone with the Wind*
Best Supporting Actor: Thomas Mitchell, *Stagecoach*
Best Supporting Actress: Hattie McDaniel, *Gone with the Wind*
Honorary Award for Outstanding Juvenile Performance: Judy Garland, *The Wizard of Oz*

THE OTHER LISTS

American Film Institute (No)
Entertainment Weekly (Yes)
Internet Movie Database (No)
Leonard Maltin (No)
Movieline (Yes)
Premiere Magazine (Yes)
Roger Ebert's Top 100 (No)
Rolling Stone Magazine (Yes)
The Village Voice (Yes)

almost defies analysis."—*New York Times*, 1950 (before release of restored version)

"A deeply personal statement of unusual richness and complexity. Renoir set out to make a masterpiece, closely following the literary tradition of Beaumarchais—who also foreshadowed the fall of a decadent aristocracy on the eve of the French Revolution." —Eugene Archer, *New York Times*, 1961

SEND IN THE CLONES

Smiles of a Summer Night (1955)
The Shooting Party (1984)
Scenes from the Class Struggle in Beverly Hills (1989)
Gosford Park (2001)

BEHIND THE SCREEN

After the film was destroyed a batch of outtakes was discovered—though the glimmer of Renoir's genius was visible in what had been left, nonetheless. Much work over two years time, with the help of the director, was done to patch the film back together to its original state.

A restored version of *Rules of the Game*, with only one or two variations from the original, was released in 1959. It was instantly hailed as a classic and is generally ranked as one of the top ten films of all time. It's said that when one of the original crew members saw it, he wept at the sight of it restored. The Venice Film Festival premiere of the restored version quickly put the film onto nearly every list of greatest films ever made, a position it has justly retained.

Alain Resnais considered this film the most overwhelming experience he had ever had at the cinema.

Marquis Robert de la Cheyniest (Marcel Dalio),Christine's husband and master of the country house in which all the rules of the game of society have been broken—workers seducing the aristocrac aristocracy flitting in and out of each other's wives's and husbands's beds—is being tidied up from his own chase after his lover, Mme de la Bruyere, by his servant Marceau (Julien Carette).

Perhaps the most troubling, galvanizing, and symbolic scene in the film is the brutal shooting expedition. Renoir extracts great power from the slaughter of the rabbits, an act done with the utmost cool by the aristocrats partying in the country. The shooters, dressed in traditional hunting garb, all stand behind blinders and observe their prey like players in a drama made for their amusement. What makes the scene all the more wrenching is the beautiful pale light in which the massacre that is played by the rules of that particular game takes place. The players return to the chateau to then carry out their own hunting expedition after one another. In the end, one of them is caught at the end of a barrel, too. He is shot dead by accident.

The aristocracy does one last tango, as all assembled look judgmentally upon some of the unsightly behavior of the rambunctious staff.

49

2001: A SPACE ODYSSEY 1968

BONE OF CONTENTION

With the five heraldic notes of "Thus Spake Zarathustra," an ape discovers the first weapon. Soon, a computer is taking on a life of its own. Kubrick's aim was always high, but this time he shot his arrow past the stars and into the heavens to explore his ideas about man's place in the universe, extraterrestrial life, and the lives and deaths of intelligence and the imagination. Some of us are left baffled and others utterly engaged. Regardless of where you stand, one thing is certain: Kubrick showed how far the frontiers of film could be pushed. Before *2001* there was no *Star Wars*, no *Close Encounters*, no *E.T.*—but to call this a "space film" would be like calling Cezanne's *Apples* fruit. The film is a profound work of the imagination and should be heard like music, read like poetry, and seen like a painting in motion.

Jim: Kubrick invented the visual dictionary of cinematic high-tech imagery. Before *2001*, all we had was Flash Gordon. Taking this one for granted would be like shrugging off the Declaration of Independence.

Gail: It's nothing less than a pioneering artist's hallucinatory portrait of man's existence through time.

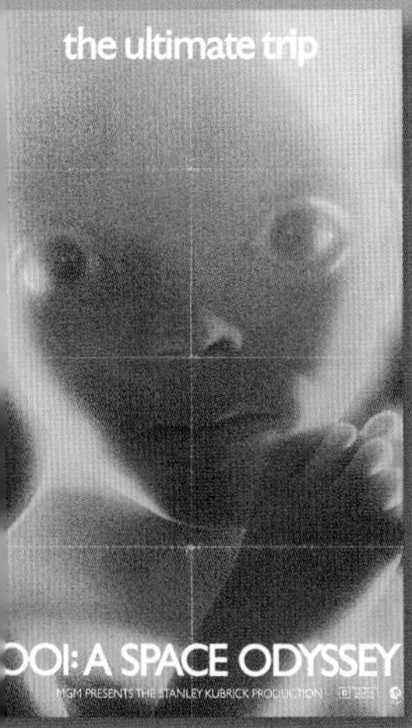

IE PLOT

ded into movements like a symphony, 1: *A Space Odyssey* explores man's tact with an extraterrestrial intelligence takes the form of a big black slab, erwise known as the Monolith. First tact: four million years ago. Prehistoric s encounter the stone slab and learn se bones as weapons and tools. An tosses a bone into the air and it is sformed into a docking spaceship. The ond Monolith is revealed when man ches the moon, enduring the endless y routines on the trip—including zero-ity toilets. The third Monolith, found near ter, draws astronaut Dave Bowman (Keir ea) into a star gate, and he is cast off a journey through inner and outer space. nwhile HAL, the ship's artificial—and chotic—intelligence plays mind games the ship's mechanisms and loses his mind after an electronic lobotomy. In the act, the enfeebled Bowman finds himself risoned in a human zoo drawn from his imagination. He dies with the Monolith is bedside and is reborn a "Star Child," dy for the next leap forward.

Rock of ages. An ape sees an enormous shiny black shape that looks like nothing else in his landscape, and he is inspired to throw a bone into space which travels millions of years. Who knows whence the process of evolution came? Could be that big, black Monolith.

THE DIRECTOR

"I tried to create a visual experience, one that bypasses verbalized pigeonholing and directly penetrates the subconscious with an emotional and philosophical content . . . I intended the film to be an intensely subjective experience that reaches the viewer at an inner level of consciousness, just as music does . . . You're free to speculate as you wish about the philosophical allegorical meaning of the film," said the director, **Stanley Kubrick**, whose fear of flying was—judging from the above statement—limited to airplanes and did not affect his flights of fancy. (Kubrick was so afraid of flying that he did most of his editing on the *Queen Elizabeth 2* and while traveling across the United States by train.) The director was obsessed with the possibilities of extraterrestrial life, and his conviction that it was inevitable compelled the making of this film. As always, he supervised every detail of production, and his staff accepted this, enthralled by the director's passion. If the auteur theory survives it is for the purpose of understanding careers such as Kubrick's, whose films, among them *The Killing* (1956), *Paths of Glory* (1957), *Lolita* (1962), *A Clockwork Orange* (1971), and *The Shining* (1980), manifest his idea that "writers or painters or filmmakers function not because they have something they particularly want to say. They have something that they feel." (For more on Kubrick, see page 127, 226, and 292.)

In the last stages of evolution, according to Stanley Kubrick, a new "Star Child" will be born, one who will bring a universal knowledge of existence instead of the limited human understanding.

THE CAST

Dr. David "Dave" Bowman	Keir Dullea
Dr. Frank Poole	Gary Lockwood
Dr. Heywood R. Floyd	William Sylvester
Moonwatcher	Daniel Richter
Dr. Andre Smyslov	Leonard Rossiter
Elena	Margaret Tyzack
Dr. Halvorsen	Robert Beatty
Dr. Roy Michaels	Sean Sullivan
HAL 9000	Douglas Rain (voice)
Mission Controller (voice)	Frank Miller
Ape	Bill Weston
Aries 1B Lunar shuttle captain	Ed Bishop

THE ACTORS

"I know I've never completely freed myself of the suspicion that there are some extremely odd things about this mission," said the computer HAL 9000 (voiced by **Douglas Rain**), who was always right, terrifyingly so. With his menacing, probing, glassy red eye and his emotionally overwrought performance, HAL remains the most memorable character in the film . . . aside from the apes, of course.

Kubrick liked **Keir Dullea**'s blank good looks for the role of Bowman, and he was right on the money. Apparently, though, Dullea was too blank for Hollywood, and scored only a few other starring roles—all great performances—in *The Hoodlum Priest* (1961), *David and Lisa* (1962), and *Bunny Lake Is Missing* (1965). After *2001*, Dullea mostly appeared in Canadian productions and B thrillers until he reprised the Bowman role in the sequel, *2010* (1984), of which Kubrick had no part.

ROLE REVERSALS

Nigel Davenport and Martin Balsam were considered for the voice of HAL before Douglas Rain landed the job.

BEHIND THE SCREEN

According to Roger Ebert, who was there, "To describe that first screening as a disaster would be wrong, for many of those who remained until the end knew they had seen one of the greatest films ever made. But not everyone remained. Rock Hudson stalked down the aisle, complaining, 'Will someone tell me what the hell this is about?'"

Kubrick's "designer" monkey suits were so authentic that many people, including Academy voters, never knew the apes weren't real.

Stranger than fiction: According to Isaac Asimov, Stanley Kubrick wanted to protect himself against any losses in case extraterrestrial intelligence was discovered before the film's release. When he approached Lloyd's of London for insurance they turned him down. Imagine that!

Though the screenplay was written primarily by Kubrick and the novel primarily by Clarke, Kubrick was to have been credited as second author on the front of the novel, but didn't like the idea. He deliberately withheld his approval to avoid compromising the release of the film, which, according to his wishes, was released first.

We might be humming North instead of Richard Strauss had Kubrick followed through on his original plan to have Alex North, his collaborator on *Spartacus* (1960), score the film. But Kubrick was so pleased with the effect his playing of classical music had on the set, he decided to use it in the film.

One of the first drafts of the script had narration. Generally panned by critics when previewed, Kubrick cut 20 minutes for its public release, but still failed to win over the film critics.

Take one step past each letter of "HAL" and where do you land? "IBM." Co-screenwriter Arthur C. Clarke wouldn't take credit for the sly joke, though, insisting that HAL stands for Heuristic Algorithmic Computer. Had he realized this little etymological trick, he would have changed the name, or so he says.

CREDITS

Producer: Stanley Kubrick/MGM
Director: Stanley Kubrick
Screenplay: Stanley Kubrick, Arthur C. Clarke
Running Time: 141 minutes
Budget: $10.5 million
Box Office: $190.7 million (worldwide)

ACADEMY AWARDS

Best Effects, Special Visual Effects: Stanley Kubrick
Best Art-Set Decoration: Anthony Masters, Harry Lange, Ernest Archer

NOMINATIONS

Best Director: Stanley Kubrick
Best Original Screenplay: Stanley Kubrick and Arthur C. Clarke

THE YEAR'S OTHER WINNERS

Best Picture: *Oliver!*
Best Director: Carol Reed, *Oliver!*
Best Actor: Cliff Robertson, *Charly*
Best Actress: Katharine Hepburn, *The Subject Was Roses*
Best Supporting Actor: Jack Albertson, *The Subject Was Roses*
Best Supporting Actress: Ruth Gordon, *Rosemary's Baby*

THE OTHER LISTS

American Film Institute (Yes)
Roger Ebert's Top 100 (Yes)
Entertainment Weekly (Yes)
Internet Movie Database (Yes)
Leonard Maltin (Yes)
Movieline (Yes)
National Society of Film Critics (No)
Premiere Magazine (Yes)
Rolling Stone Magazine (Yes)
Village Voice (Yes)

HAL, the ship's supercomputer, refuses to accept that he is failing and spies on the astronauts as they plot his demise. Bowman asks him to open the pod doors. HAL refuses and intimates that he knows that Bowman thinks he's blown his fuse. But he won't cede control of the ship. "This mission is too important for me to allow you to jeopardize it," threatens HAL in his deceptively mild voice. Bowman feigns innocence, but the computer is still a little too smart, despite its failing circuitry. HAL insists that he cannot allow Bowman to take any action. Bowman can't imagine how the computer has figured this all out when HAL makes it ominously clear that he has become a kind of Big Brother. "Dave, although you took thorough precautions in the pod against my hearing you, I could see your lips move."

THE GREAT SCENE

If you can't trust a super-intelligent computer, who can you trust? HAL, the ship's artificial intelligence, seems to have lost his mind and begins toying with the ship's mechanisms. His most violent act is to direct an external pod to kill one of the astronauts by cutting off his air.

THE CRITICS

"The world's most extraordinary film . . . as exciting as the discovery of a new dimension in life." —*Boston Globe*

"The movie is so completely absorbed in its own problems, its use of color and space, its fanatical devotion to science-fiction detail, that it is somewhere between hypnotic and immensely boring . . ." —Renata Adler, *New York Times*

KUBRICK ON FILM

"[Extraterrestrial intelligence] may have progressed from biological species . . . which are fragile shells for the mind at best, into immortal machine entities . . . and then transformed into beings of pure energy and spirit. Their potentialities would be limitless and their intelligence ungraspable by humans . . . they would ultimately possess the twin attributes of all deities—omniscience and omnipotence." —Stanley Kubrick

"A director is a kind of idea and taste machine; a movie is a series of creative and technical decisions, and it's the director's job to make the right decisions as frequently as possible." —Stanley Kubrick

Though fascinating to the imagination, daily living in the spaceship is as much of a grind as life on earth in the 21st century. There's jogging and there's sleeping (in tomb-like cells). And eating doesn't seem to be as much fun when most food looks like paint chips.

50

BONNIE AND CLYDE 1967

FRESH BLOOD

Hellbent banjos set the pace as a stolen jalopy tears across a dull yawn of Texas plain. For the thrill-struck, radiant young couple on the run, the Great Depression is over. They're racing into the sunrise of an anti-Hollywood revolution. A vast new youth audience suspicious of war and the politicians who make it are hungry for antiheroes. Glamorous killers—high school handsome Warren Beatty in spats and an unknown Faye Dunaway in a beret and heels—rob banks armed with guns and grins, idealized models of restless discontent. Just a few years later Patty Hearst will be caught by a bank's security camera, semiautomatic in hand, with a smile not dissimilar to Dunaway's Bonnie. The story behind the movie couldn't have been more Cinderella: It featured two young journalists who'd never written a screenplay, a director with a limited track record, a brazen young sex symbol desperate to earn his stripes as a producer, and a cast that, for the most part, no one had ever heard of. *Bonnie and Clyde* ushered in a new attitude on Saturday nights at the Bijou. You could no longer rely on a happy ending, love didn't conquer all, and comedy didn't come without a harsh kick in the backside. And the faces you fell in love with on the screen might not be the faces you'd want to meet up with in a dark alley.

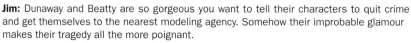

Jim: Dunaway and Beatty are so gorgeous you want to tell their characters to quit crime and get themselves to the nearest modeling agency. Somehow their improbable glamour makes their tragedy all the more poignant.

Gail: It's the Depression, after all. How ya' gonna keep 'em down on the farm after an exhilarating shooting spree? Poetically speaking, this movie makes it all make sense.

THE PLOT

Bored East Houston diner waitress Bonnie Parker (Faye Dunaway) catches ex-con Clyde Barrow (Warren Beatty) trying to hotwire her mama's car. He gives her a dimpled smirk and she's lost. He could very well be her ticket out of dull anonymity. He guarantees it when he accepts her dare to rob a grocery store and drives off with her in a stolen car. He convinces her that together they could make history—as long as she puts her romantic notions aside. Her sexual attraction is stymied by his impotence, but both compensate with escalating danger. They meet up with a bored gas station attendant C. W. Moss (Michael J. Pollard), who's delighted to be their getaway driver. They begin to hit banks, often comically at first, but Clyde is forced to kill for the first time when a bank manager clings to their car. Texas Ranger Frank Hamer (Denver Pyle) grows obsessed with their capture even as they taunt him. Clyde inducts his adored older brother Buck (Gene Hackman) into the gang despite Bonnie's clash with his hysterical wife Blanche (Estelle Parsons). As their fame grows, the gang's exploits become more daring. Buck is the first of them to die, slowly and painfully, after a shootout with cops. Blanche is captured, blind as the result of a stray bullet, and helps Hamer devise Bonnie and Clyde's inevitable, bloody moment of reckoning.

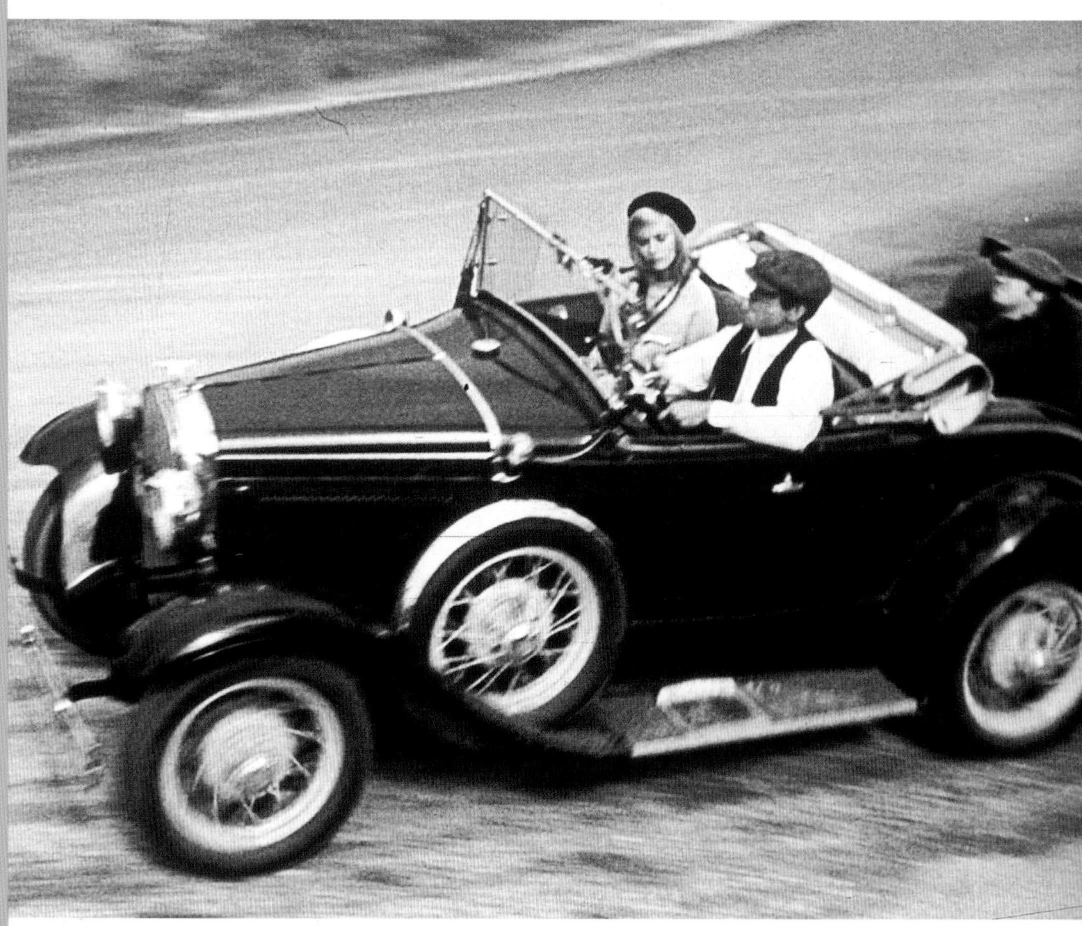

"I'm Clyde Barrow and this is Miss Bonnie Parker. We rob banks!" And with that, these glamorous criminal lovers are off and running into movie history. Few studios wanted to touch the project, but producer/star Warren Beatty was relentless. Many critics came down hard but later recanted in highly publicized re-reviews.

"You know what, when we started out, I thought we was really goin' somewhere. This is it. We're just goin', huh?" —Bonnie

THE DIRECTOR

Arthur Penn had pretty much given up on movie directing after an unhappy experience on *The Train* (1964), starring Burt Lancaster. "But Warren can be the most persuasive, relentless person I know," according to Penn, and he soon capitulated. He brought with him a great deal of theatrical experience (he had a Broadway hit at the time, *Wait Until Dark*) and as a result of his stagecraft, relied heavily on the script's structure. "At my invitation, screenwriters are always welcome on the set. I want them there, and I like them there." He also had reverence for his cast. "You learn again and again what fantastic things an actor can do and bring into a situation." Penn began his Hollywood career with *The Miracle Worker* (1962) and followed up *Bonnie and Clyde* with *Alice's Restaurant* (1969) and *Little Big Man* (1970). *Night Moves* (1975) and *The Missouri Breaks* (1976), with Marlon Brando, marked his gradual exit from the pantheon of hot new American directors. He all but disappeared until *Four Friends* (1981) and *Penn and Teller Get Killed* (1989).

"At least I ain't a liar. I told you I wasn't no lover boy." But in this version of the Bonnie and Clyde saga, their romance is consummated. Beatty's image as a sex god had to be maintained for the sake of the box-office.

THE CAST

Clyde Barrow	Warren Beatty
Bonnie Parker	Faye Dunaway
C. W. Moss	Michael J. Pollard
Buck Barrow	Gene Hackman
Blanche	Estelle Parsons
Frank Hamer	Denver Pyle
Ivan Moss	Dub Taylor
Velma Davis	Evans Evans
Eugene Grizzard	Gene Wilder

THE ACTORS

Warren Beatty was sick of being simply a heartthrob; he'd never really taken to the job description. In his very first film, *Splendor in the Grass* (1961), he showed an unusual lack of respect for the Hollywood star-making machine. He'd been mentioned as a possible nominee for Best Supporting Actor and irately demanded that he either be entered in the Best Actor category or nothing at all. He got his wish, and he won. Beatty was out to make the kind of movies that inspired him; Truffaut turned him on to the *Bonnie and Clyde* script, which he loved and optioned at once. Even after the completed film was buried by a vindictive Jack Warner, Beatty used the glowing reviews and cover of *Newsweek* to battle for a re-release, unheard of at the time. It went on to become a classic, thanks exclusively to Beatty's efforts. It also made him immensely rich. He'd taken a minuscule salary to star ($200,000) in exchange for 40 percent of the future gross. Following *McCabe and Mrs. Miller* (1971), and *The Parallax View* (1974), he primarily starred in films he produced and had an extraordinary run with *Shampoo* (1975), *Heaven Can Wait* (1978), and the critically acclaimed *Reds* (1981), which he produced and directed, before an infamous stumble with box-office dud *Ishtar* (1987). He recouped somewhat with *Dick Tracy* (1990), and fared far better with *Bugsy* (1991) and his raffish political satire *Bulworth* (1998).

Faye Dunaway's outfits in the film set off a fashion explosion, and for a time it seemed every other woman on the street was wearing a Bonnie beret. Dunaway's highly stylized acting, evident in so many of her follow-up roles (*Chinatown* [1974], *Network* [1976], and *Mommie Dearest*, [1981]), was muted here. While it's not fair to say this was her best work, the childlike vulnerability on display rarely revealed itself again. (For more on Dunaway, see page 39.)

Pauline Kael found **Gene Hackman**'s Buck Barrow the most consistent performance in the film. His nomination for Best Supporting Actor propelled him into his next major role in *The French Connection* (1971). From then on, he was golden. His career highlights include playing the villainous Lex Luthor in *Superman* (1978), roles in *Reds* (1981), *Mississippi Burning* (1988), *Class Action* (1991), *Unforgiven* (1992), *Crimson Tide* and *Get Shorty* (both 1995), and his riotous full-drag performance in *The Birdcage* (1996). (For more on Hackman, see page 274.)

Estelle Parsons's sometimes over-the-top but compellingly eccentric performance (she escapes a police raid on her home hysterically waving a spatula) won her the only Oscar in the cast. While a prime character actress who worked consistently, she is perhaps best remembered as Roseanne's dotty mother in the long-running eponymous TV hit.

Michael J. Pollard has had one strange career, essentially playing himself in nearly fifty movies, none of which matched the quality of this one, for which he earned a Best Supporting Actor nomination. Coincidentally, he and Beatty had both appeared in the early TV series *The Many Loves of Dobie Gillis*.

ROLE REVERSAL

Producer Beatty envisioned Bob Dylan as Clyde until he realized that his own presence on screen was vital at the box office.

Jane Fonda took a pass on the role of Bonnie.

SEND IN THE CLONES

Badlands (1973)
Kalifornia (1993)
Natural Born Killers (1994)

CREDITS

Producer:
Warren Beatty/Warner Bros.
Director: Arthur Penn
Screenplay: David Newman, Robert Benton
Running time: 111 minutes
Budget: $2.5 million
Box Office: $23 million

ACADEMY AWARDS

Best Supporting Actress:
Estelle Parsons
Best Cinematography:
Burnett Guffey

NOMINATIONS

Best Picture
Best Director: Arthur Penn
Best Actor: Warren Beatty
Best Actress: Faye Dunaway
Best Supporting Actor:
Michael J. Pollard
Best Supporting Actor:
Gene Hackman
Best Original Screenplay:
David Newman, Robert Benton
Best Costume Design:
Theadora Van Runkle

THE YEAR'S OTHER WINNERS

Best Picture:
In the Heat of the Night
Best Director: Mike Nichols,
The Graduate
Best Actor: Rod Steiger,
In the Heat of the Night
Best Actress:
Katharine Hepburn, *Guess Who's Coming to Dinner*
Best Supporting Actor:
George Kennedy,
Cool Hand Luke

THE WRITERS

Robert Benton, born and raised in Waxahachie, Texas: "I'd grown up hearing all the stories about Bonnie and Clyde. My father went to their funeral in 1934. Everyone knew someone who'd been robbed or kidnapped by them. Any farmer that had an old car that didn't work, they'd take it out, shoot it full of holes, pour some animal blood on it and show it off as the car Bonnie and Clyde were killed in." **David Newman** agreed to cut the sexual threesome of Bonnie, Clyde, and C. W. "We risked alienating audiences from what we so badly wanted—that they would love and identify with Bonnie and Clyde from the outset, so that by the time they start doing violent things, it was too late for the audience to back away from [them]."

THE CRITICS

New Yorker critic Pauline Kael's enthusiastic defense of *Bonnie and Clyde* essentially launched her career and ended that of Bosley Crowther. Crowther had made it his personal crusade to bury the film. When it backfired, the venerable but stodgy *New York Times* critic was unceremoniously replaced.

"The audience is alive to it. They are not given a simple, secure basis for identification; they are made to feel but are not told how to feel . . . The laughs keep sticking in our throats because what's funny isn't only funny . . . I think that Bonnie and Clyde, though flawed, is a work of art . . . By making us care about the robber lovers, [it] has put the sting back into death." —Pauline Kael, *The New Yorker*

"It is a cheap piece of bald-faced slapstick comedy that treats the hideous depredations of that sleazy, moronic pair as though they were as full of fun and frolic as the jazz-age cutups in *Thoroughly Modern Millie*." —Bosley Crowther, *New York Times*

BEHIND THE SCREEN

Studio chief Jack Warner was horrified when Warren Beatty got down on his knees with a vow to kiss his feet if he gave him the money to make the film.

First-time screenwriters Newman and Benton were desperate to get either Jean-Luc Godard or François Truffaut to direct.

At the studio screening, Jack Warner informed Beatty and director Penn, "If I have to get up and pee during this you'll know the movie stinks." He went off to the bathroom so often Penn agonized that "the longest and most diuretic film in human memory finally came to an end."

"That *Bonnie and Clyde* movie made it all look sort of glamorous, but like I told them teenaged boys sitting near me at the drive-in showing: Take it from an old man who was there. It was hell."—W. D. Jones, former Barrow gang member

THE GREAT SCENE

They know it's got to happen. They've been robbing banks, killing people, and they have no intention of being taken alive. It's just a matter of time—but not today, of all days. The Texas sun is shining down on them. Bonnie is happy again, munching her green apple. Clyde is just happy she's happy as he drives them down a dappled country road. The left lens of his sunglasses is knocked out, making him look like a careless schoolboy. They spot DJ's dad, and he waves them over to help change his tire. Suddenly he ducks under his truck, birds fly away in fright, and Clyde looks confused. He looks at Bonnie, still in the car. And then it happens: the barrage of bullets, 187 of them finding their mark. The camera slows as Bonnie and Clyde's bodies do their involuntary dance of death, writhing, seeming almost to rise back up. He finally rolls onto his back and she topples across the seat, her arm dangling at an unnatural angle.

> "The difference between directing yourself and being directed is the difference between masturbating and making love."
> —Warren Beatty

THE OTHER LISTS

- American Film Institute (Yes)
- Roger Ebert's Top 100 (Yes)
- *Entertainment Weekly* (Yes)
- Internet Movie Database (No)
- Leonard Maltin (Yes)
- *Movieline* (No)
- National Society of Film Critics (No)
- *Premiere* Magazine (Yes)
- *Rolling Stone* Magazine (Yes)
- *Village Voice* (No)

"Some day, they'll go down together/ They'll bury them side by side/ To a few, it'll be grief/ To the law, a relief/ But it's death for Bonnie and Clyde." The final stanza of a poem written, in real life, by the multitalented Bonnie Parker.

51

KING KONG 1933

APE OVER NEW YORK

Released at the height of the Great Depression, *King Kong* broke all previous box-office records, opening simultaneously at New York's two largest theaters, the Roxy and Radio City Music Hall. It was that rarest of monster movies, appealing to both young and old, the well-educated and the less so. Scholars have long attempted to reason out its curious appeal. There's something to the idea that Kong symbolizes the last great stand of primitive man against the onslaught of modern technology. There's also something more psychologically provoking and amusing about the frustrated sexuality of this unusually tall, dark hero and what he might hope to accomplish with the pint-sized blonde in his clenched fist. Remarkably, it still manages to fascinate and terrify.

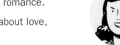

Jim: The first and best unrequited (we hope, for her sake!) inter-species romance.

Gail: A magical, larger-than-life horror story that cuts to primal feelings about love, abandonment, and greed.

¡Panico
EN LA CIUDAD DESPAVORIDA!
KONG
FAY WRAY
ROBT. ARMSTRONG
BRUCE CABOT

HE PLOT

gle filmmaker Carl Denham (Robert Arm- ng) hears rumors of exotic Skull Island, re prehistoric creatures supposedly still n. He hires a starving young actress, Ann row (Fay Wray), off the street and they off into the sunset with more than a hint omance. The island natives go wild for nde Ann, abduct her, and ready her for rifice to the behemoth killer gorilla, Kong. her than devour her, Kong loses his gi- tic heart—and his freedom. Captured and ught to "Jazz Age" New York City as the ul- ate freak show, he's presented as a behe- th in chains on a great stage. The black-tie wd gasps at the sheer size of him. When g sees Ann standing beside Armstrong at podium, he goes insane with jealousy. He aks free of his bonds and the audience omes an hysterical stampeding mob. Kong apes in pursuit of Ann. He crushes every- g in his path until he gets hold of her. The htmare culminates on top of the Empire e Building as Kong futilely battles a fleet pitfire biplanes. As he finally loses hold plummets to the pavement, we are left to der who is "civilized" and who is wild.

Kong takes a direct approach to dating, and she'll soon prove to be a handful. Nothing less than the U.S. Air Force will be called out to save Ann from Kong's big night on the town.

THE DIRECTORS

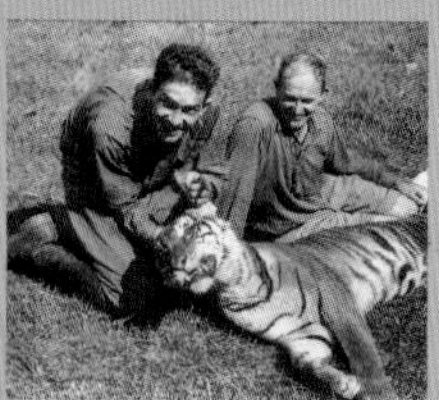

Like his fictional hero Carl Denham, **Ernest Schoedsack** was a nature-film documentarian and something of a showman, himself, in his signature pith helmet and dapper adventurer pose. His longtime collaborator, **Merian Cooper**, was an ace pilot in World War I and a fellow lover of the wild. Interestingly, they opted to shoot the entire film within the confines of the studio, entrusting its success to the ingenious technical innovations of Willis O'Brien. Cooper briefly took over as RKO studio chief before teaming up with John Ford in a production company that oversaw some of Ford's finest efforts, among them *She Wore a Yellow Ribbon* (1949) and *The Searchers* (1956). Ironically, Cooper died within hours of *King Kong*'s leading man, Robert Armstrong.

Kong drops by the village for a sacrificial human lunch and, as usual, is greeted with much excitement by the tribe.

THE CAST	
Ann Darrow	Fay Wray
Carl Denham	Robert Armstrong
Jack Driscoll	Bruce Cabot
Captain Englehorn	Frank Reicher
Charles Weston	Sam Hardy
Native Chief	Noble Johnson
Witch King	Steve Clemente

THE ACTORS

Nicknamed "The Queen of Scream," Canadian-born **Fay Wray** (her real name) rose from the ranks of silent-movie extras to costarring roles in early talkie Westerns, then a slew of horror flicks culminating in *King Kong*. When told she'd be working with one of Hollywood's biggest leading men, she thought it was to be Cary Grant. Given the technical process involved, she of course never met the mighty ape (whose working model was merely 18 inches high). Wray thought she screamed too much in *Kong* and many critics at the time agreed with her. But considering she was being filmed in those extended, lung-bursting scenes by herself, reacting to nothing more than thin air, the lady must be given her due. Kong was to be her lasting claim to fame, and her career peaked and dipped shortly afterward. Given her most famous image, squirming in Kong's giant paw, Wray wryly titled her autobiography *On the Other Hand*. Like her, **Robert Armstrong** (Carl Denham) made dozens of movies before and after, but he'll only be remembered for this one.

BEHIND THE SCREEN

Willis O'Brien, a pioneer in the use of stop-motion photography, used an 18-inch model of King Kong covered in rabbit fur. The miniature was shot frame by frame, repositioned each time, then edited together as animation. O'Brien then perfected rear-projection techniques that used animation and actual footage of Fay Wray to make them appear to be in the same shot.

Censors took scissors to several scenes, including one in which Kong removes some of Wray's clothes, tickles her, then sniffs his finger.

THE MUSIC

The inimitable Max Steiner (*Gone with the Wind, Theme from a Summer Place, Casablanca*) was a major contributor to *King Kong*'s success. The score is haunting, wildly romantic and, at times, goose bump-inducing. He's credited with providing the monster with a sympathetic, tragically heroic aura.

THE SET

King Kong was a backlot production whose most "realistic" set was the high-walled tribal village on Skull Island. It stood for another six years (and can be seen in countless jungle adventures) before being used as fodder in *Gone with the Wind*'s burning of Atlanta sequence. The village design remains a head-scratcher to *King Kong* trivia buffs. Why would the natives have constructed a huge doorway for Kong to enter if they were so deathly afraid of him?

THE CRITICS

"In this age of technical perfection, [*King Kong*] uses its very naiveté to generate a kind of creepy awe." —Roger Ebert, *Chicago Sun-Times*

"It's a film-long screaming session for [Wray], too much for any actress and any audience." —*Variety*

SEND IN THE CLONES

The Son of Kong (1933)
Mighty Joe Young (1949)
The 7th Voyage of Sinbad (1958)
King Kong (remake, 1976)
Jurassic Park (1993)

NOTABLE QUOTES

"The scene with the monster spider stopped the picture cold, so the next day back at the studio, I took it out myself." —Merian C. Cooper

CREDITS

Producer: David O. Selznik/ RKO
Directors: Merian C. Cooper, Ernest B. Schoedsack
Screenplay: Merian C. Cooper (story) and Edgar Wallace
Running time: 100 minutes
Budget: $600,000
Box Office: $5 million

THE YEAR'S ACADEMY AWARD WINNERS

Best Picture: *Cavalcade*
Best Director: Frank Lloyd, *Cavalcade*
Best Actor: Charles Laughton, *The Private Life of Henry VIII*
Best Actress: Katharine Hepburn, *Morning Glory*

"At the premiere of *King Kong* I wasn't too impressed. I thought there was too much screaming . . . I didn't realize then that King Kong and I were going to be together for the rest of our lives, and longer."

—Fay Wray

THE GREAT SCENE

Kong's last stand atop the Empire State Building, then the tallest building in the world, is as indelible a movie image as we have. In a tragic irony, the 1976 remake placed the ape atop one of the towers of the World Trade Center.

Kong stomps through the skyscrapers, tossing subway cars around like toys, until he eyes his beloved Ann through her apartment window. He takes her in hand and, in search of safe harbor, climbs the concrete jungle's highest tree, the Empire State Building. In a breathtaking distance shot, biplanes buzz around him like bullet-spewing bees. Kong gently lays Ann down on a vertiginous ledge before lashing out, grabbing one of the planes and sending it crashing to the street below. Then comes his own tumultuous topple down the side.

THE OTHER LISTS

- American Film Institute (Yes)
- Roger Ebert's Top 100 (No)
- *Entertainment Weekly* (Yes)
- Internet Movie Database (No)
- Leonard Maltin (Yes)
- *Movieline* (Yes)
- National Society of Film Critics (No)
- *Premiere* Magazine (Yes)
- *Rolling Stone* Magazine (Yes)
- *Village Voice* (Yes)

Peeping Kong stands on his tiptoes to glimpse into the boudoir of his beloved Ann Darrow (Fay Wray) as she's consoled by her fiancé, explorer Carl Denham (Robert Armstrong).

52

STAR WARS 1977

OUT OF THIS WORLD

Clear away the mega-conglomerate merchandising of toys, video games, and McDonald's novelty glasses, and you'll find a terrific little movie full of naive hope and endless charm. Created by ageless wunderkind George Lucas, *Star Wars* is a stewpot of every idea that ever appealed to his boyish wonder. He credits as an influence Kurasawa's *The Hidden Fortress* (1958) in particular, which tells the story of two sixteenth-century peasants who rescue a kidnapped princess and escort her through enemy territory. From there, toss in a few bits from Arthurian Legend (the Evil Empire vs. a Camelot-like galaxy), *The Wizard of Oz* (Obi-Wan Kenobi doesn't die so much as disappear beneath his flowing robe), the classic Hollywood Westerns (the intergalactic saloon full of gunslingers and seriously ugly mugs), and a generous helping of the *Flash Gordon* Saturday matinees of yore. Lucas freely admits his borrowing, but it's all in how he puts it together, like a cinematic four-star chef with a gift for spice and magic. Every aspect of *Star Wars* has a warm and fuzzy familiarity, yet feels entirely original. *Star Wars* is one of those rare phenomena that invite "think-pieces" by major writers, big books, and elaborate Web sites full of details right down to Luke Skywalker's shoe width. You can choose to become pleasantly lost in its surrounding universe or simply smile and occasionally grip your armrest. Any experience more fun than this one is probably illegal in some states.

Jim: I love the conceit of titling this series debut "Episode IV." The impact of that—you think, "Where have I been, what have I missed?" It gives an instant impression that the story has always been around, a simple fact of American life. There's a brilliant sense of humor behind that, and it cradles you throughout the whole movie.

Gail: What makes a sci-fi story stay with you forever is the emotional reality from which it springs, and *Star Wars* is brilliant in disguising but evoking those details of our everyday lives. How many times have you been in a restaurant or bar since seeing the film when you've said, "This is just like the bar scene in *Star Wars*?"

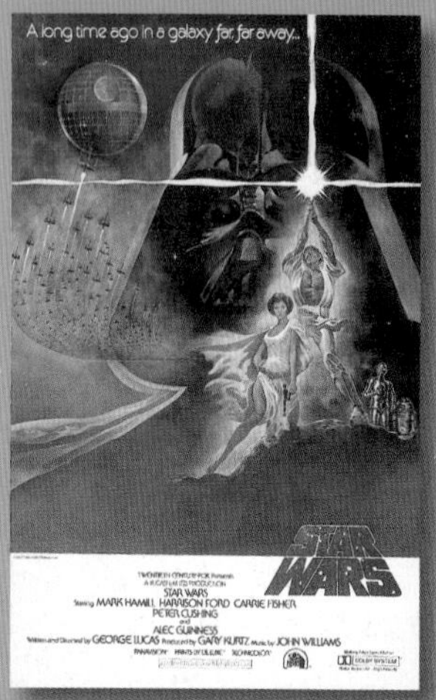

THE PLOT

An evil empire overseen by Darth Vader (David Prowse/James Earl Jones) vows to crush the last pocket of resistance. Its ambassador of hope, Princess Leia (Carrie Fisher), is kidnapped but she's already programmed battle plans into robot R2-D2 who, along with his 'droid sidekick C-3PO, escapes to Tatooine. After falling into the hands of farm boy Luke Skywalker (Mark Hamill) C-3PO mentions the name of Obi-Wan Kenobi (Alec Guinness), the great arbiter of the Force, an ancient religion of Zen mind control and magic. Luke brings them to the old hermit who fought alongside his father in the Clone Wars. Luke fears Empire goons are on his tail, and sure enough, his aunt and uncle are murdered in his absence. He and Obi-Wan arrange for a voyage to the rebel station during a visit to a wild inter-species bar. They hire arrogant mercenary pilot Han Solo (Harrison Ford) and his Wookie partner, Chewbacca (Peter Mayhew). They're targeted by Vader and their ship is pulled into the Death Star by magnetic force. Once inside, they rescue Leia, whose ego clashes with Solo's almost at once. Moments later, they lose Obi-Wan in a final duel with Vader. Obi-Wan is happy to sacrifice his life, as his spirit now inspires Luke. Luke joins a squadron of fighter pilots that hope to target the Death Star's one miniscule flaw. Self-serving Solo comes to his aid at the last moment. Their victory marks the ultimate triumph of good over evil and the birth of a New Hope.

"An elegant weapon for a more civilized age." Obi-Wan Kenobi explains the laser light saber ritual of the Jedi Knights to Luke, whose father had been the greatest Jedi of them all.

THE DIRECTOR

George Lucas fought the movie studio wars, unable to get any big guns behind his "weird little sci-fi project." Finally, 20th Century-Fox kicked in, trusting Lucas to come up with something to equal the success of his *American Graffiti* (1974). The production was riddled with challenges and near-disasters. There had never been a call for the technical wizardry required here, and Lucas relied on a very young crew of inventive engineers ("the average age was probably about 24") and Madison Avenue animation specialists. If they could breathe life into the Pillsbury Doughboy, they could certainly create this chessboard of colorful creatures. Finally, Lucas had something to show. He invited his upstart director pals to a rough-cut screening, and most thought it was a full-out disaster. Only Spielberg was optimistic. Lucas wasn't deterred, as he fought for and finally won the rights to the *Star Wars* sequels from the studio. This was at a time when it wasn't certain he could even finish the first episode. Sick with asthma, Lucas couldn't bear the strain of directing and told friend and screenwriter John Milius he thought he'd make more money from the sci-fi toys based on the film than *The Godfather* made. He often wished he could just make porn movies. "Low overhead, no problems with locations. If you didn't like the room, you could just rent another one." After *Star Wars* broke all box-office records, Lucas retired from directing—but 22 years later he made his comeback with *Star Wars: Episode I, The Phantom Menace*, and other films in the series. His Skywalker Ranch in Modesto, California, the site of Industrial Light and Magic, took five years to construct, and provides all the creative and technical challenges inherent in a Lucas film. Spielberg fondly admits, "We love to play at George's house—he has the best toys." (For more on Lucas, see page 253.)

THE CAST

Luke Skywalker	Mark Hamill
Han Solo	Harrison Ford
Princess Leia Organa	Carrie Fisher
Grand Moff Tarkin	Peter Cushing
Ben (Obi-Wan) Kenobi	Alec Guinness
See Threepio (C-3PO)	Anthony Daniels
Artoo-Detoo (R2-D2)	Kenny Baker
Chewbacca	Peter Mayhew
Darth Vader	David Prowse
Voice of Darth Vader	James Earl Jones
Uncle Owen	Phil Brown
Aunt Beru	Shelagh Fraser
Chief Jawa	Jack Purvis
General Dodonna	Alex McCrindle
General Willard	Eddie Byrne
Red Leader	Drewe Henley
Red Two (Wedge)	Dennis Lawson
Red Three (Biggs)	Garrick Hagon
Red Four (John "D")	Jack Klaff
Red Six (Porkins)	William Hootkins
Gold Leader	Angus MacInnes
Gold Two	Jeremy Sinden
Gold Five	Graham Ashley
General Taggi	Don Henderson
General Motti	Richard LeParmentier
Commander #1	Leslie Schofield

RIGHT: "That malfunctioning little twerp." C-3PO is quick to lose patience with his squat sidekick R2-D2, but their endearing comic relationship has been compared to that of Laurel and Hardy.

THE ACTORS

Mark Hamill got his start on TV in soap operas and the hit series *Eight Is Enough*. He rightly suspected *Star Wars* would be a huge success, but just before its release he was involved in a serious car accident. Resulting plastic surgery dramatically altered his appearance, as is evident in the sequels. While on the set, he didn't get off accident-free either. In the garbage disposal scene, he held his breath underwater so long he broke blood vessels in one side of his face, and had to be shot thereafter in profile. After appearing in the war epic *The Big Red One* (1980), Hamill starred in the two *Star Wars* sequels, *The Empire Strikes Back* (1980) and *The Return of the Jedi* (1983). He now confines himself primarily to cartoon voiceovers.

Star Wars was essentially the dawning of the **Harrison Ford** screen legend. His low-key charisma, devil-may-care sex appeal, and lopsided grin are balanced by a talent for expressing real fear in tense scenes. Note, in particular, his rooftop fight to the death in *Blade Runner* (1982). In his spectacularly successful *Raiders of the Lost Ark* (1981), he once again manages to bring a brooding, yet wry dimension to a comic-strip character. The highest grossing star in movie history, he's received only a single Oscar nomination (*Witness*, 1985). Ford appears to best advantage in such action thrillers as *Patriot Games* (1992), *The Fugitive* (1993), and *Air Force One* (1998). He tried his hand at romantic comedy in *Working Girl* (1988) and *Sabrina* (1995), but fans much prefer to see him running for his life. (For more on Ford, see pages 130, 254, and 289.)

Carrie Fisher was born famous, the first child of America's sweetheart couple of the 1950s, Eddie Fisher and Debbie Reynolds. While she caused a sensation as a nymphet in her screen debut, *Shampoo* (1975), and will always be remembered as the helmet-braided Princess Leia, Fisher has long since turned to writing. Her thinly veiled autobiography, *Postcards from the Edge*, became a Meryl Streep vehicle (1990) directed by Mike Nichols, and she continues to write screenplays. Her occasional film cameos include appearances in *When Harry Met Sally* (1989) and *Austin Powers* (1997). A talk-show host and regular guest, she wittily deconstructs her single working mom status, her past battles with drugs, and her unusually brief marriage to Paul Simon ("We were both very short").

Alec Guinness was considered among the top British actors of his generation, an elite list that includes Laurence Olivier and John Gielgud. He is a ubiquitous presence in this book, for his roles in *Lawrence of Arabia* (1962), *Dr. Zhivago* (1965), and for his elegantly conceived, Oscar-nominated Obi-Wan Kenobi in *Star Wars*. (For more on Guinness, see pages 27 and 187.)

ROLE REVERSALS

George Lucas would've been happy with Sissy Spacek as Princess Leia, thereby allowing

CREDITS

Producer: LucasFilm/
20th Century Fox
Director: George Lucas
Screenplay: George Lucas
Running time: 121 minutes
Budget: $11 million
Box Office: $780 million

ACADEMY AWARDS

Best Editing: Paul Hirsch, Marcia Lucas, Richard Chew
Best Art Direction–Set Decoration: John Barry, Norman Reynolds, Leslie Dilley, Roger Christian
Best Effects, Visual Effects: John Stears, John Dykstra, Richard Edlund, Grant McCune, Robert Black
Best Costume Design: John Mollo
Best Music, Original Score: John Williams
Best Sound: Don MacDougall, Ray West, Bob Minkler, Derek Ball
Special Achievement Award: Ben Burtt (for sound effects, voices)

NOMINATIONS

Best Picture
Best Director: George Lucas
Best Supporting Actor: Alec Guinness
Best Original Screenplay: George Lucas

fellow director Brian de Palma to have Carrie Fisher for *Carrie (1976)*. But Fisher was wary of nude scenes and opted instead for *Star Wars*. Had she not worked out, Lucas had Jodie Foster waiting in the wings.

Peter Mayhew was offered the role of Darth Vader but asked to play a good guy, Chewbacca, instead.

THE SAGA CONTINUES

Star Wars: Episode V–The Empire Strikes Back (1980)
Star Wars: Episode VI –The Return of the Jedi (1983)
Star Wars: Episode I–The Phantom Menace (1999)
Star Wars: Episode II–Attack of the Clones (2002)
Star Wars: Episode III–Revenge of the Sith (2005)

BEHIND THE SCREEN

Lucas claims that Harrison Ford was "the most serendipitous" casting coup. Ford had been working as a carpenter in the production office, and when an extra body was needed for the reading of the screenplay, he was asked to pitch in. According to Lucas, Ford read the lines for Han Solo better than any other contender. There may be more to the story, considering Ford had had a minor role in Lucas's previous hit, *American Graffiti* (1974).

Chewbacca was inspired by Lucas's dog, "Indiana." His voice was the result of overlays of various animals, including badgers, elephants, and camels.

R2-D2 got his name from a basic cinematic filing system: "Reel Two, Dialogue Two."

James Earl Jones didn't feel his participation as the voice of Darth Vader deserved screen credit in the film's original release.

The ingenious sound designers were inspired by everyday sources. Engine blaster-ignitions were the rotating click of parking meters, and the swoosh of the space ships consisted of the rattle of air-conditioning units.

Lucas asked for merchandising rights, and the studio, which didn't think that would amount to anything, gave them up without pause.

THE CRITICS

"A new classic in a rousing movie tradition: a space swashbuckler." –Gary Arnold, *Washington Post*

"George Lucas's breakaway sci-fi hit never quite feels soulful or emotionally engaging." –Peter Stack, *San Francisco Chronicle*

THE SET

The scenes on Luke's desert home planet, Tatooine, were shot in Tunisia and Death Valley, California. The rest of *Star Wars* was filmed on location inside the brains of George Lucas and his Oscar-winning Production Designer John Barry. The final sequence, a ceremony for the rewarding of heroic medals, is reminiscent of *The Wizard of Oz* and *Triumph of the Will*, and includes regiments of cardboard soldiers.

THE MUSIC

The *Star Wars* theme, as memorable and stirringly American as anything by John Phillip Sousa, was composed by the ubiquitous John Williams. The score went on to become the best-selling original music-only soundtrack of all time. Williams's credits could fill a phone book, and include most of the epic smash hits of the last three decades, from *Jaws* (1975) to *Jurassic Park* (1993), *Schindler's List* (1993), *The Patriot* (2000), and *Harry Potter and the Sorcerer's Stone* (2001).

NOTABLE QUOTES

"Acting in *Star Wars* I felt like a raisin in a giant fruit salad, and I didn't even know who the cantaloupes were."–Mark Hamill

"I don't really know who I am. Quite possibly, I don't exist at all."–Alec Guinness

"I do movies to stimulate me. I have got more money than I can handle."–Harrison Ford

"George, you can type this shit, but you sure can't say it."–Harrison Ford commenting on Lucas's *Star Wars* screenplay

"I'm a product of Hollywood. Fantasy is not unnatural to me–it's my reality."–Carrie Fisher

"I think we took a wrong turn." Not according to adoring audiences, they didn't. Princess Leia, Luke, and Han are an intergalactic variation on the classic screwball romantic comedy threesome. They banter, flirt, and compete with the zesty charm of Katharine Hepburn, Cary Grant, and James Stewart.

THE GREAT SCENE

"This is Red Five. I'm going in." A courageous Luke takes his chances against Darth Vader in the grand finale dogfight, but he's got the Force on his side, along with a surprise backup.

A brave squadron of rebel pilots suits up for battle after viewing the blueprint of the Death Star. They have only "one shot in a million" to target a microscopic flaw. But if one of them can get to it, Darth Vader's floating empire of evil will explode. Luke and Leia are disgusted by Solo's refusal to risk his neck to help–he's got his reward money, that's all he cares about. He clearly likes Luke and calls after him, "May the Force be with you." Luke says nothing as he and R2-D2 board. And they're off, with Vader's goon squad on their tails. One after another, the rebel pilots are blown to smithereens. With only a few left and the clock ticking down on Vader's destruction of the rebel planet with his Death Ray, Luke swoops into Dogfight Alley, a sub-level concourse leading to that pocket of vulnerability. In the shootout, R2-D2 is knocked out of commission. But just as Luke prepares to launch his weapons, Vader zeroes in. Solo vindicates himself by showing up at the last possible minute to protect Luke's back. Luke relies on the Force to guide him and there's nothing Vader can do to stop him now. "One shot in a million"–coming up!

THE OTHER LISTS

- American Film Institute (Yes)
- Roger Ebert's Top 100 (No)
- *Entertainment Weekly* (No)
- Internet Movie Database (Yes)
- Leonard Maltin (Yes)
- *Movieline* (No)
- National Society of Film Critics (No)
- *Premiere* Magazine (No)
- *Rolling Stone* Magazine (No)
- *Village Voice* (Yes)

53

THE 400 BLOWS 1959

CAUSE FOR A REBEL

There are so many beautiful and extraordinary choices made by director François Truffaut in telling this intimate story of adolescent delinquency that it is difficult to know how to parse them. The grace and perfection of *The 400 Blows* has become the standard against which all films on the subject are judged, and Jean-Pierre Léaud's portrayal of Antoine Doinel is the one to which all young performers are compared. Though thirteen-year-old Antoine's existence seems a life sentence of bad luck with parents and teachers, his truant days and nights on the streets of Paris—and in its movie theaters—offer him a sense of freedom and possibility. He does nothing truly wrong, yet he is caught up in endless punishments. The one time he does do something wrong—he steals a typewriter from his father's office—he is caught as he tries to return the machine. Antoine's face is a portrait of sadness and detachment, having suffered at such an early age. During a Punch-and-Judy show in the park, the young faces in the audience twist and turn with delight, in contrast to Doinel's, which registers worry, reminding us that he is still only a child. Truffaut captures the simple honesty of this boy most beautifully in one of the most moving scenes of the film as Antoine is interviewed by a therapist at a reform school. All we see during the interview is Antoine's face as he fidgets and talks about his life and how he has gotten into this predicament. His reactions are among the most honest we have seen on the screen. When, at the end of the film, Antoine escapes the detention center, he runs and runs until he reaches the seashore, the first time in his life he has seen the sea. The moment takes your breath away. The camera zooms into a freeze frame, showing Antoine looking directly into the camera, caught between land and sea, between prison and freedom, and between present and future. And we wonder, what will be his fate?

Jim: Considering most of the pablum being doled out by Hollywood at the time, visionaries like Truffaut hit a veritable mother lode simply by trading in honest human emotion. The closest Hollywood ever came to portraying the terrors of childhood this realistically was Margaret O'Brien smashing her snowman in *Meet Me in St. Louis*.

Gail: If the only new wave to ever wash up on our shores was *The 400 Blows*, it would have made a splash heard 'round the world. So intimate and poetic is this autobiographical portrait of growing up tough that you cannot take your eyes off the screen when young Doinel is present.

[T]E PLOT

[T]e-year-old Antoine Doinel (Jean-Pierre [Léau]d) lives in a tiny apartment with his [moth]er and stepfather, who are poor and [gen]erally inattentive. Antoine is tormented [by h]is teacher (Guy Decombie), who pegs [him] as a troublemaker, though most of the [time] Antoine's problems are just due to bad [luck]. At home, he cannot finish his homework [and] rather than return to school without it, [he s]kips school, saying he was sick. The next [time] he misses class, he makes the excuse [that] his mother has died. When his mother [show]s up at school, he is in deep trouble. The [moth]er (Claire Maurier) is a loose blond who [is ca]ught having an affair by her truant son. [His s]tepfather (Albert Rémy) is sometimes [frien]dly and companionable, but can be [shor]t-tempered and grumpy. Neither parent [seem]s to care much about what happens to [Anto]ine. His only escape from the oppression [of ev]eryday life is to avoid school with his [best] friend, go to the fairground, or visit the [cine]ma. Eventually, he deduces that it would [be b]etter to run away. By the end of *The 400 [Blow]s*, Antoine is a juvenile delinquent. He is [sent] to prison by his parents after stealing [a typ]ewriter. He is transferred to a juvenile [dete]ntion center from which he escapes . . . [to wh]at end, we don't know, but we root for [his lib]eration.

Getting deeper into hot water, Antoine steals a typewriter from his father's office, only to be caught when he tries to return it. His parents allow him to be sent to jail as punishment.

"He aggravates me."—Antoine's father

THE DIRECTOR

"I demand that a film express either the joy of making cinema or the agony of making cinema. I am not at all interested in anything in between," wrote director **François Truffaut**. There are a few moments of joy but much agony for young Antoine Doinel in *The 400 Blows*, which is all the more painful for being an autobiographical film; Truffaut grew up under very similar circumstances. The movies saved Truffaut's life, he said again and again. Cinema transformed a delinquent student, gave him something to love, and with the encouragement of film critic André Bazin, Truffaut became a critic and then made this, his first film, all before his 27th birthday. It was one of the founding films of the French new wave, which is characterized by a simple love of moviemaking and espouses an intimate, honest style. Truffaut also laid the groundwork for the "auteur" theory—the critical assumption that the director is the primary creator of a film—in a 1954 article that inspired a generation of European filmmakers. After *The 400 Blows*, director and star continued to collaborate, following Antoine through all the stages of his life, from young love to marriage, from parenthood to adultery, through jobs, divorces, and the various pains of life. The "Antoine Doinel Stories" include *Love at Twenty* (1962, part of a multi-episode film), and the features *Stolen Kisses* (1968), *Bed and Board* (1970), and *Love on the Run* (1979). As Truffaut said of Léaud, "Jean-Pierre interests me precisely because of his anachronism and his romanticism: he is a nineteenth-century man." Truffaut followed the Doinel series with *Shoot the Piano Player* (1960), *Jules and Jim* (1961, arguably his best film), *The Soft Skin* (1964), his science-fiction entry *Fahrenheit 451* (1966), his Hitchcock tribute *The Bride Wore Black* (1968), *Mississippi Mermaid* (1969), *Day for Night* (1973, Oscar), *Small Change* (1976), *The Last Metro* (1980), and *Confidentially Yours* (1982). Truffaut also tried his hand at period dramas, including *The Wild Child* (1970), *The Story of Adele H* (1975), and *The Green Room* (1978). He ended his career with the comedy *The Man Who Loved Women* (1977) and the drama *The Woman Next Door* (1981). Some critics complained that Truffaut's later films did not match the explosive quality of his early work, but Joseph McBride noted in them "an even more profound richness of emotion." (For more on Truffaut, see pages 88 and 94.)

Always the one to be caught, Antoine gets upbraided by his teacher—who is predisposed to disapproving of the boy—once again.

THE CAST

Antoine Doinel	Jean-Pierre Léaud
Gilberte Doinel	Claire Maurier
Julien Doinel	Albert Rémy
"Petite Feuille," the French teacher	Guy Decomble
Mr. Bigey	Georges Flamant
Rene	Patrick Auffray

THE ACTORS

He was Truffaut's perfect alter ego, therefore it must have seemed like magic both to Truffaut and the thirteen-year-old **Jean-Pierre Léaud** when they found each other. Léaud, like Truffaut, had been a juvenile delinquent and was expelled from several schools by the time he was thirteen. Léaud read in a newspaper that Truffaut was looking for a young actor and immediately won the part. His sad, distant face, a face that shows the wounds he has suffered, is deeply resonant in every frame of the film. There is a heartbreaking honesty in his eyes, and never the look of a "bad seed." After appearing in the Antoine Doinel films, Léaud played roles for Truffaut in *Two English Girls* (1971) and *Day for Night* (1973), and Truffaut even dedicated *The Wild Child* (1970) to him. Léaud also made films with Jean-Luc Godard, including *Pierrot le fou* (1965), *Made in USA* and *Masculine-Feminine* (both 1966), and *La Chinoise* and *Weekend* (both 1967). Léaud was unforgettable in Jean Eustache's *The Mother and the Whore* (1973) and in Bertolucci's *Last Tango in Paris* (1973). He has continued to act in such films as Godard's *Detective* (1985), *With All Hands* (1986), *36 Fillette* (1988), and *I Hired a Contract Killer* (1990). Among his most recent films are *Irma Vep* (1996), *A Matter of Taste* (2001), *Le Pornographe* (2001), and *Folle embellie* (2003).

THE CRITICS

"Let it be noted without contention that the crest of the flow of recent films from the 'new wave' of young French directors hit these shores with the arrival of *The 400 Blows*. M. Truffaut has here turned out a picture that might be termed a small masterpiece."—Bosley Crowther, *New York Times*

"Francois Truffaut's *The 400 Blows* is one of the most intensely touching stories ever made about a young adolescent."
—Roger Ebert, *Chicago Sun-Times*

TRUFFAUT ON DIRECTING

"I didn't think of the reaction the public was going to have. I simply wanted to show a child in a situation that was new to him and because I wanted to avoid clichés—say, showing him on a roller coaster—I chose the centrifuge."
—François Truffaut (on the scene where Antoine rides the centrifuge)

"The final freeze was an accident. I told Léaud to look into the camera. He did, but quickly turned his eyes away. Since I wanted that brief look he gave me the moment before he turned, I had no choice but to hold on it: hence the freeze." —François Truffaut

BEHIND THE SCREEN

When Antoine and a friend are suspended from school, they go gallivanting around town. At one point they pass a wall of posters and flyers, and they pull off a picture of Harriet Andersson in a shot from Ingmar Bergman's *Sommaren med Monika* (1953), also about two young lovers who run away from home to "live their own life."

The title of the film comes from the French idiom "*faire les quatre cents coups*," which means "to raise hell."

A widely circulated, possibly apocryphal story says that the Weinstein brothers attended this movie expecting a sex flick. They were so astounded by what they saw that their entire perspective on movies changed, eventually leading them to found Miramax.

CREDITS

Producer: François Truffaut
Director: François Truffaut
Screenplay: François Truffaut, Marcel Moussy
Running Time: 94 minutes

ACADEMY AWARD NOMINATIONS

Best Writing, Story and Screenplay Written Directly for the Screen: François Truffaut, Marcel Moussy

THE YEAR'S WINNERS

Best Picture: *Ben-Hur*
Best Director: William Wyler, *Ben-Hur*
Best Actor: Charlton Heston, *Ben-Hur*
Best Actress: Simone Signoret, *Room at the Top*
Best Supporting Actor: Hugh Griffith, *Ben-Hur*
Best Supporting Actress: Shelley Winters, *The Diary of Anne Frank*

THE OTHER LISTS

American Film Institute (No)
Roger Ebert's Top 100 (Yes)
Entertainment Weekly (No)
Internet Movie Database (No)
Leonard Maltin (Yes)
Movieline (Yes)
Premiere Magazine (No)
Rolling Stone Magazine (Yes)
Village Voice (Yes)

nly happy night of his life, or so it seems, Antoine's mother decides that the whole family should go to the movies. It's the first and last time we see them all smiling.

THE GREAT SCENE

Antoine Doinel's relentless bad luck seems to break for a a moment when his mother—after telling his teacher, "We can no longer cope"—comes to fetch him from school after he has gone missing for the night. She embraces him as never before, calling him "poor sweetie." She proceeds to shower him with affection, giving him a bath, and after toweling him, putting him to bed. As he lies there she speaks to him about her own youthful rebellion, and she makes a deal with Antoine. If he promises to do well on his English composition, she will reward him with money. Inspired by this, Antoine reads Balzac, becoming so passionate about the writer that he lights a candle for him. At dinner, the shrine catches fire and the father shrieks, "Stupid idiot, what were you doing?" Antoine cries, "It was an homage to Balzac for my French composition." Once again unable to deal with the boy, the father threatens to send him away to military school. Suddenly his mother decides to "change the mood" and suggests they all go to the movies. It becomes a rapturous night, filled with music and laughter and ice cream; the three hold hands, a real family for the first time. The following morning the teacher screams at Antoine once again, accusing him of plagiarizing in his beloved composition, "Search for the Absolute," about his grandfather's death. "I didn't copy," the boy swears plaintively. The teacher reads the composition, which lovingly paraphrases the master whose words have become Antoine's own. He is sent to the principal's office once again.

"My Dear Parents, I understand the gravity of my lie. After this we can't live together anymore, so I'll try my luck elsewhere...And when I've made good I'll come back and explain everything."

—Antoine

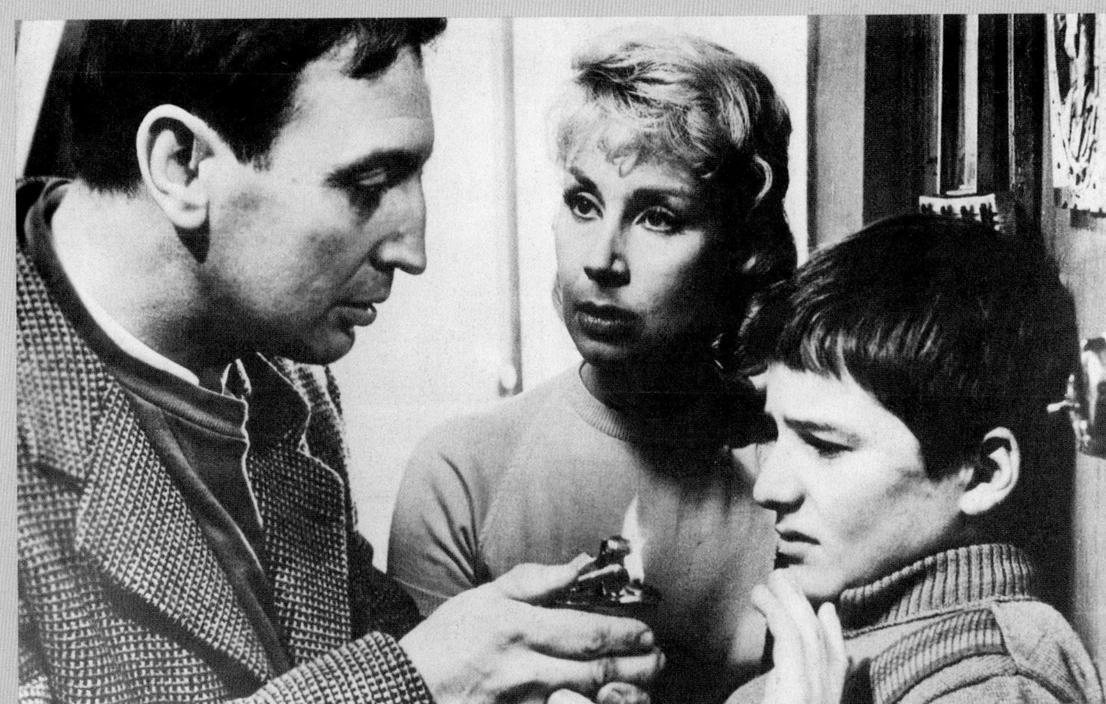

"He aggravates me," says Antoine Doinel's father Julien (Albert Rémy) when a candle in a shrine Antoine (Jean-Pierre Léaud) has made to honor Balzac sets fire to a curtain. Antoine had promised his mother (Claire Maurier), who tries to protect him against his father's anger, that he would write a wonderful composition on Balzac for school.

54

A NIGHT AT THE OPERA 1935

MAKE THAT THREE HARD-BOILED EGGS

The Marx Brothers did nothing less than break the sound barrier. Imagine going from silent films to Groucho's relentless, aggressively nonsensical witticisms. Try this scene: As Mr. Driftwood, Groucho is trying to convince a wealthy opera lover, Margaret Dumont (Mrs. Claypool), that he is in love with her after she has spied on him dining with another woman. "It's rather difficult to believe that when I find you dining with another woman," challenges Mrs. Claypool. "That woman?" replies Driftwood, "Do you know why I sat with her?" "No," she answers. "Because she reminded me of you," says the slippery Driftwood. "Really?" asks Claypool. "Of course," he insists. "That's why I'm sitting here with *you*. Because you remind me of you. Your eyes, your throat, your lips! Everything about you reminds me of you. Except you." Does it make any sense? Would you want it to? The Marx Brothers gave the world a handful of the most sacred cow-bashing satires of Hollywood history. They just had no respect. Groucho had the devastatingly destructive words, Chico had the dumbfounded charm, and Harpo, oh Harpo, he had the poetry. Their style of surrealistic, anarchic humor, which came from their naked contempt for authority and their habit of upending codes of social behavior, was as eternal as Chaplin's Little Tramp, though it couldn't have been more different. And the public embraced their scam wholeheartedly.

Jim: Its wild comic success is in part a tribute to the supporting players, who were happy to be made fools of by the Brothers Anti-Grimm. The zinger lines come at you like a spray of bullets. A dozen viewings later, you may have caught half of them.

Gail: "Make that three hard-boiled eggs!" That's a meal you won't get to eat because you'll be choking with laughter.

THE PLOT

There is no plot to speak of and everything happens in a helter-skelter manner with little logic or explanation—but here goes: Otis B. Driftwood (Groucho Marx) tries to interest Mrs. Claypool (Margaret Dumont) in a nebulous opera he promises to produce. Enter Harpo, stage left, who is the brutally banished valet of an opera tenor, Rodolfo Lassparri (Walter Woolf King). Chico is the manager of struggling young tenor Ricardo Baroni (Allan Jones). Groucho and Chico attempt to negotiate a contract for Jones, which results in scraps of paper that they throw away. Soon everyone boards a ship bound for New York. Groucho sneaks on by carrying Mrs. Claypool's trunk, in which Chico and Harpo are stowed away. The trunk is placed in a stateroom and Groucho opens it to find his friends curled up into balls. The steward comes to the room to take a food order and the fun begins: "Have you got any stewed prunes?" asks Groucho. "Sure," the waiter replies. "Well, give them some hot coffee," says Groucho. "That'll sober them up." And on it goes with more and more people filling up the stateroom until somebody opens the door and they all come tumbling out. Eventually everyone gets to the opera and wreaks havoc. The boys slip the sheet music for "Take Me out to the Ballgame" into the score for *Il Trovatore*. As the orchestra begins playing it, Chico starts hawking peanuts and popcorn. Chico and Harpo, dressed as peasants, riot onstage and are hauled off to jail. Enough said?

"Is my aunt Minnie here?" asks one of the thousands of people who seem to find their way into Groucho's stateroom. When room service arrives, Groucho and company order everything on the menu and Harpo honks his horn repeatedly to add two, no three, hard-boiled eggs to every order.

I saw Mrs. Claypool first. Of course, her mother really saw her first, but there's no point in bringing the Civil War into this." –Otis B. Driftwood

THE DIRECTOR

Former real estate broker and pipeline worker **Sam Wood** became a distinguished and prolific filmmaker known not for comedy but for drama, with such films to his credit as *Goodbye, Mr. Chips* (1939), *Our Town*, *Kitty Foyle* and *The Natural History of a Woman* (all 1940), *The Devil and Miss Jones* (1941), *The Pride of the Yankees* and *Kings Row* (both 1942), *For Whom the Bell Tolls* (1943), and *Saratoga Trunk* (1945). Wood was also one of the uncredited directors of *Gone with the Wind* (1939). He later served as the president of the Motion Picture Alliance for the Preservation of American Ideals, and in 1947 provided key testimony before the House Un-American Activities Committee.

Otis B. Driftwood (Groucho Marx) is all set for sailing. Though he has no ticket for the ride, he nevertheless avails himself of kingly service by allowing the porters to carry him into his stateroom while lying on top of his trunk. Nothing's too good for this pauper.

THE CAST	
Otis B. Driftwood	Groucho Marx
Fiorello	Chico Marx
Tomasso	Harpo Marx
Rosa Castaldi	Kitty Carlisle
Ricardo Baroni	Allan Jones
Rodolfo Lassparri	Walter Woolf King
Herman Gottlieb	Sig Ruman
Mrs. Claypool	Margaret Dumont

THE ACTORS

Groucho Marx, with his monstrous eyebrows, his boot-black mustache, and the ubiquitous cigar in a mouth that spoke nonstop, conniving chatter, was the spearhead of one of the funniest comedy teams of all time. And he couldn't have done it without the singular comedic help of **Chico**, the Italian ripoff artist, and **Harpo**, the silent skirt-chaser. Anarchy, absurdity, scam-artistry, and slapstick clowning only begin to define what makes their funny so funny. Encouraged early on by their mother Minnie, they broke into Broadway in 1925 with *The Cocoanuts*, which was reprised in a film in 1929. With that the brothers left for Hollywood and made films like *Monkey Business* (1931), *Horse Feathers* (1932), *Duck Soup* (1933), *A Night at the Opera* (1935), and *A Day at the Races* (1937). After producer Irving Thalberg's death, the boys just weren't the same. The best of the rest were *Room Service* (1938), *At the Circus* (1939), *Go West* (1940), and *The Big Store* (1941). After splitting up for a time, they were reunited in *A Night in Casablanca* (1946) and *Love Happy* (1949). Groucho went solo for *Copacabana* (1947), *Double Dynamite* (1951), and *Skidoo* (1968). He also had a big career in radio, particularly on the famous *You Bet Your Life* in 1947, which moved to TV in 1950, where he reigned for 11 years.

"I've been sitting right here since seven o'clock," complains **Margaret Dumont** to Groucho, who replies, "Yes, with your back to me. When I invite a woman to dinner I expect her to look at my face. That's the price she has to pay." Margaret Dumont's aristocratic dowager is the perfect foil for Groucho's irreverent swindler. Known best for her roles in seven Marx Brothers films—*The Cocoanuts* (1929), *Animal Crackers* (1930), *Duck Soup* (1933), *A Night at the Opera*, *A Day at the Races* (1937), *At the Circus* (1939), and *The Big Store* (1941)—Dumont appeared in over 30 films during her career. Groucho wasn't the only comic for whom she played the straight woman; she appeared in W. C. Fields' *Never Give a Sucker an Even Break* (1941), Laurel and Hardy's *The Dancing Masters* (1943), Jack Benny's *The Horn Blows at Midnight* (1945), Danny Kaye's *Up in Arms* (1944), and Abbott and Costello's *Little Giant* (1946). She was still at it in 1962 when she took a cake in the face in *Zotz!*

BEHIND THE SCREEN

Was Mel Brooks' *The Producers* based on a scrapped plot for *A Night at the Opera*? Some say so. The original storyline had Groucho as the producer of an opera.

Director Sam Wood's first directorial effort with the Marx brothers made Harpo bleed. Wood was such a perfectionist that he made Harpo retake a scene where he is hanging from ropes over and over until his hands were cut and swollen.

Interestingly, some of the material for the film was pretested before live audiences. The revised script was made more cohesive as a result.

THE CRITICS

"Corking comedy with the brothers at par and biz chances excellent." *—Variety*

"A very funny movie slowed down by MGM's expensive production values and idiotic song. "—Jeffrey M. Anderson, *San Francisco Examiner*

CREDITS

Producer: Irving Thalberg/MGM
Director: Sam Wood
Screenplay:
James Kevin McGuinness (story),
George S. Kaufman,
Morrie Ryskind; Al Boasberg
(dialogue, uncredited);
Buster Keaton (uncredited)
Running Time: 92 minutes

THE YEAR'S ACADEMY AWARD WINNERS

Best Picture:
Mutiny on the Bounty
Best Director:
John Ford, *The Informer*
Best Actor:
Victor McLaglen, *The Informer*
Best Actress:
Bette Davis, *Dangerous*

THE OTHER LISTS
American Film Institute (Yes)
Roger Ebert's Top 100 (No)
Entertainment Weekly (No)
Internet Movie Database (No)
Leonard Maltin (No)
Movieline (No)
Premiere Magazine (No)
Rolling Stone Magazine (No)
Village Voice (No)

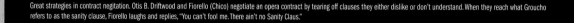

Great strategies in contract negitation. Otis B. Driftwood and Fiorello (Chico) negotiate an opera contract by tearing off clauses they either dislike or don't understand. When they reach what Groucho refers to as the sanity clause, Fiorello laughs and replies, "You can't fool me. There ain't no Sanity Claus."

THE GREAT SCENE

Groucho and Chico negotiate a contract for Chico's opera tenor by tearing off sections of the contract that they believe are unimportant or don't understand. Groucho holds his copy at a distance as if he can't read it. "If my hands were a little longer I could read it," he says. Then he casually asks, "You haven't got a baboon in your pocket, have you?" They continue tearing off whole sections. "Now what have you got? " Chico asks. "I've got about a foot and a half," says Groucho. "How much have you got?" Chico is upset, "How come your contract is longer than mine?" Groucho answers logically, "You must have been out on a tear last night." They finally come to the last item. Groucho says, "That's what they call the sanity clause." Chico looks at him and laughs smartly, "You can't fool me. There ain't no Sanity Claus." And with that they throw away the contracts and shake hands on the deal.

In the finest Marx tradition, the boys scam their way into the halls of great wealth and pomposity. Here they drive the great tenor Lassparri (Walter Woolf King) into a state of hysteria, while happily imbibing his bounteous liquor reserves.

55

SLUMDOG MILLIONAIRE 2008

MUMBAI MAMBA

Mumbai, India's chaotic, burgeoning city where massive wealth has erupted on a base of extraordinary poverty is the star of *Slumdog Millionaire.* Visually dazzling, kinetic, much of it shot with hand-held camera and backed-up with driving music and breathless editing, *Slumdog* tells the spirited and cruel story of Jamal, an orphan from the slums who becomes a contestant on the Indian game show phenomenon, "Who Wants to Be a Millionaire?" Suspected of cheating, Jamal is arrested and interrogated and, against all odds, he wins a staggering 20 million rupees—and is reunited with the love of his life—finding the answers to all of the questions in his own harrowing life story. *Slumdog* defies simple summation as a rag-to-riches story. Danny Boyle constructs something wholly original out of the standard tragic romance that has defined Bollywood from 1950s through to the 1980s when India worked to lift itself from hunger and poverty. He has crafted a distinctly cinematic experience of life in this impossibly modern and ancient city that doesn't quit, and permeated it with horror and hope. Here barefoot, parentless children scuttle across winding rumpled rooftops, splash in fetid laundry pools thick with brightly colored fabrics, play tag in sweaty traffic-clogged streets beneath chrome and glass behemoths rising up everywhere around them. As dark as it is buoyant, and verging on stereotype—but always a shivering hair-breath away—*Slumdog* transcends categorization with its fresh view of Indian culture, its great heart and sensitivity to its young (often untutored) performers and, most of all its irresistible storytelling.

Jim: The stench of Mumbai's gutter brutality keeps this romantic fable from floating off on a magic carpet. That said, poverty and sub-human conditions have never looked so gorgeously colorful.

Gail: *Slumdog* succeeds, beyond its fresh use of cinematic narrative, by Boyle's unique filtering of classic Bollywood themes through a Western lens.

E PLOT

l Malik, 18, sits across from his interrogator dia's television sensation, "Who Wants to Millionaire." He is one question away from nillion dollars when he's arrested on sus- of cheating. Without any education how this boy have come this far? That's the tion that drives Mumbai police, particularly uspicious inspector ("even doctors and rs cannot come close to the 20m rupee "), to arrest and brutally interrogate Jamal atedly with beatings and electrocutions. lm moves backward and forward in time g us from Jamal's impoverished childhood e of the self-proclaimed, Three Musketeers, with older brother Salim, and Jamal's ed Latika. Left homeless and parentless attack in which Jamal's mother is killed, hildren learn how to beg, swindle tourists, freight trains, survive savage clashes with , and bear up with life on the streets. The escape torture in an orphanage via freight But Jamal and Latika are heartbreakingly rated when she is unable to catch his out- hed hand from the moving train. Jamal's h for her becomes his greatest motiva- life. It is also, we come to realize, what les him to answer each question in the asingly tense game show.

"[Mumbai] a great place to tell a melodramatic story. You can use melodrama in a way that has gone out of fashion for us. It has gone into fantasy movies; our extremes of storytelling have been pushed into superheroes, or Narnia-type things. Those films are very, very popular, because we still want to see that kind of storytelling, but our more regular, more realistic films are more subtle affairs. This setting allows you to be outrageous." —Danny Boyle

"A few hours ago, you were giving chai for the phone walahs. And now you're richer than they will ever be. What a player!"

THE DIRECTOR

Danny Boyle English director of disparate film genres, from zombies to sci-fi oddities including *Shallow Grave* (1994), *Trainspotting* (1996), *28 Days Later* (2002), *Millions* (2004) and 2010 Best Picture nominee, *127 Hours*, broke into a world of new possibilities when he dared to make *Slumdog*. Though his oeuvre is diverse, several elements always inform a Boyle film: they are raw, shocking, exhuberant and stylistically over-the-top. Boyle's fans report *Slumdog* seemed to "come out of nowhere." Said Boyle, "India is very seductive to cinematography. It's a place that makes you want to go 'Wow!' I didn't want to make that kind of film. I wanted to make something more subjective, because I was a visitor, and I didn't want it to feel like a visitor's film. I wanted it to feel like the characters' film, and they were all from Mumbai, and mostly from the slums."

Boyle had never been to India before making *Slumdog*. In the brief eight months he filmed in Mumbai, Boyle unearthed a Dickensian city–complete with his own Oliver Twist. "The style in this film felt dictated by what it felt like to move to Mumbai and live there for eight months," said Boyle. "We tend to separate the extremes. The poor–and there are a lot of them there–they're included in the society. That is why it is such an exciting place to go as a storyteller." It's that vision and Boyle's triumph at using Indian themes filtered through a Western lens, that made *Slumdog* Boyle's own film.

Jamal looks out over the Mumbai.

THE CAST

Dev Patel	Jamal K. Malik
Saurabh Shukla	Sergeant Srinivas
Anil Kapoor	Prem Kapur
Freida Pinto	Latika
Irrfan Khan	Police Inspector
Azharuddin Mohammed Ismail	Youngest Salim
Ayush Mahesh Khedekar	Youngest Jamal
Rubina Ali	Youngest Latika
Chirag Parmar	Young Arvind
Tanay Chheda	Middle Jamal
Ashutosh Lobo Gajiwala	Middle Salim
Siddish Patil	Older Arvind
Tanvi Ganesh Lonkar	Older Salim

THE ACTORS

Dev Patel English actor Patel was first noticed by Boyle's daughter for his performance in the British Television teen drama *Skins* (2007), one of his first roles. He'd had no previous acting experience when his mother found the casting ad in a newspaper. Said Patel, "the first day of shooting I didn't really know what to do." *Slumdog* was his first feature. He also found love on the set with Freida Pinto.

Freida Pinto was an Indian model for two years and did some amateur theatre before getting her big break when director Boyle picked her in an audition. Between 2006-2007, she anchored "Full Circle," an international travel show. She later auditioned for the part of Bond Girl Camille in the James Bond, *Quantum of Solace* (2008) but lost out the role to Olga Kurylenko.

Anil Kapoor starred as a guest on the original "Who Wants to Be a Millionaire" and won 5,000,000 rupees. Kappor was raised in a Chawl–an Indian tenement–in Tilak Nagar; Punjabi was his native language. A loner, and an ardent fan of Bollywood, Kapoor devoted his life to making it as a film star against all odds. His first lead role was in *Woh 7 Din* (1983) followed by roles in almost 100 films. He won the National Film Awards, India for his performance in *Pukar* (2000).

Irrfan Khan appeared in a small role in *Salaam Bombay* (1988) and conducted acting-workshops for the children of the film. He appeared in various soap operas, tele-historicals series, and several unsuccessful Indian features until his breakthrough as the lead in *The Warrior* (2001) getting him notice in international film festivals. His first Bollywood main lead role came in the movie *Rog* (2005). He can also be seen in 2010 in the notable U.S. television series *In Treatment*

THE CRITICS

"[We are] witnessing a phenomenon: a dramatic proof that a movie is about how it tells itself. It is one of those miraculous entertainments that achieves its immediate goals and keeps climbing toward a higher summit."

–Roger Ebert, *Chicago Sun Times*

"Slumdog Millionaire, an almost ridiculously ebullient Bollywood-meets-Holywood concoction–and one of the rare "feel-good" movies that actually makes you feel good, as opposed to merely jerked around."

–Scott Foundas, *The Village Voice*

"There is a mismatch here. Boyle and his team, headed by the director of photography, Anthony Dod Mantle, clearly believe that a city like Mumbai, with its shifting skyline and a population of more than fifteen million, is as ripe for storytelling as Dickens's London [...] At the same time, the story they chose is sheer fantasy, not in its glancing details but in its emotional momentum. How else could Boyle get away with assembling his cast for a Bollywood dance number, at a railroad station, over the closing credits? You can either chide the film, at this point, for relinquishing any claim to realism or you can go with the flow–surely the wiser choice."

–Anthony Lane, *New Yorker*

CREDITS

Producer: Christian Colson
Production Companies: Celado Films; Film4; Pathé Pictures International
Director: Danny Boyle
Co-Director, India: Loveleen Tandan
Screenplay: Simon Beaufoy (based on novel *Q&A* by Vikas Swarup)
Cinematography: Anthony Dod Mantle
Running Time: 120 minutes
Budget: $15,000,000
Box Office: $377,000,000 worldwide as of 2011

ACADEMY AWARDS

Best Picture
Best Director: Danny Boyle
Best Cinematography: Anthony Dod Mantle
Best Editing: Chris Dickens
Best Original Score: A.R. Rahman
Best Original Song ("Jai Ho"): A.R. Rahman (music), Gulzar (lyrics)
Best Sound: Ian Tapp, Richard Pryke, Resul Pookutty
Best Adapted Screenplay: Simon Beaufoy

NOMINATIONS

Best Original Song ("O Saya"): A.R. Rahman, Maya Arulpragasam
Best Sound Editing: Tom Sayers, Glen Freemantle

THE YEAR'S OTHER WINNERS

Best Actor: Sean Penn, *Milk*
Best Actress: Kate Winslet, *The Reader*
Best Supporting Actor: Heath Ledger, *Dark Knight*
Best Supporting Actress: Penelope Cruz, *Vicky Cristina Barcelona*

THE GREAT SCENE

Slumdog is a perpetual motion machine of great scenes. Arguably one scene could stand out as "unforgettable." Young Jamal, clutching a crumpled picture of his Bollywood hero runs to get an autograph when the star makes an appearance, seemingly in the middle of a human waste-dump. Bad luck for Jamal when nature erupts in his intestines. A row of primitive "port-a-potties" stand lined up on a ridge; queues of waiting men move slowly to their destiny. Earthy, farty sounds and—one assumes—smells emerge. Jamal's gotta go; he can barely contain himself. With his turn comes visible relief. But when he gets up to leave, he cannot. His laughing friends have locked the door. Panicked but undaunted Jamal jumps down feet first into the excrement. He emerges smiling, racing headlong, covered in dung like a fudge covered ice cream cone (it's actually peanut butter and chocolate). Clutching his crumpled picture, he reaches straight into the crowd (who are only too glad to make way for this brown, oozing malodorous figure) to score an autograph. Victorious, he raises his signed picture high up in the air, his white teeth smiling through s....It is a moment of sheer exuberance

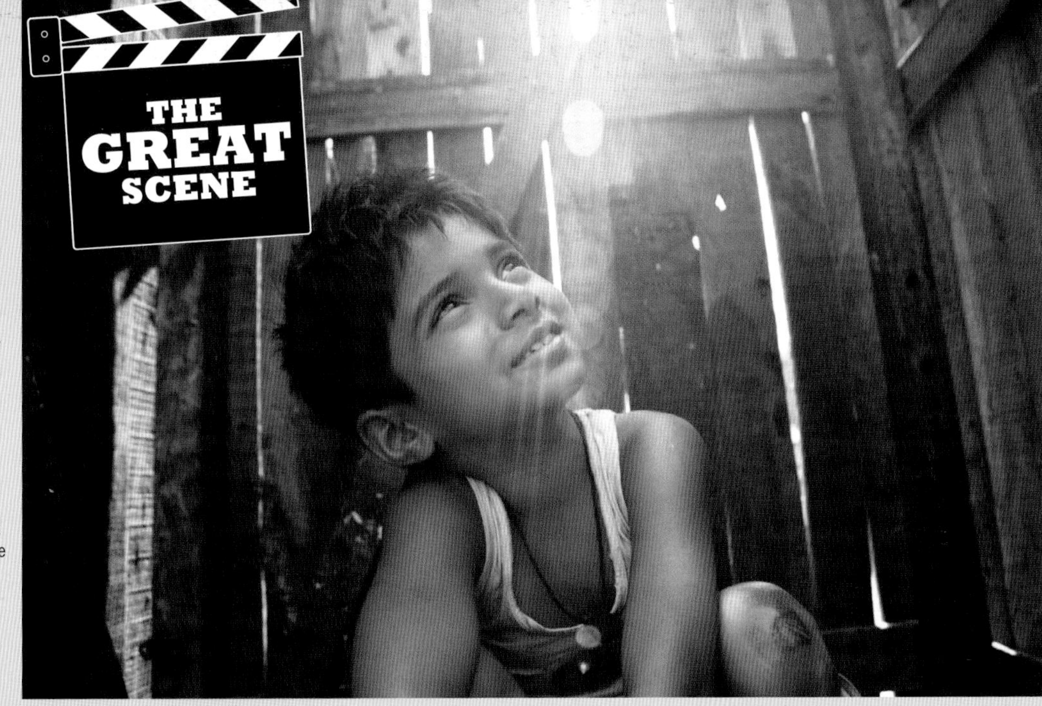

Relieved to be relieving himself, young Jamal smiles in anticipation of getting his Bollywood idol's autograph not yet aware of what he will have to "get through" to win the prized signature.

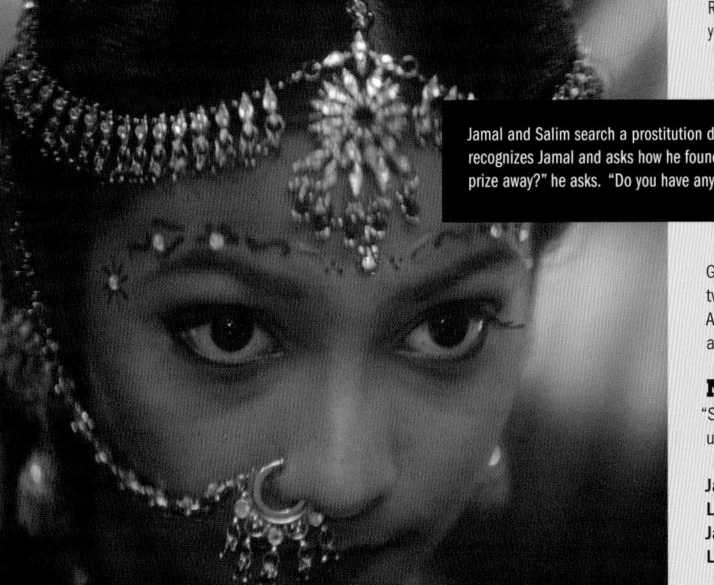

Jamal and Salim search a prostitution district and eventually find Latika, who is practicing her dancing, and dressed in a bejeweled sari. Latika instantly recognizes Jamal and asks how he found her. Before he can answer, Maman appears with his thugs. "You really thought you could walk in here and take my prize away?" he asks. "Do you have any idea how much a virgin girl is worth?" Salim takes his money and shoots him dead.

ACADEMY GOLD

Slumdog Millionaire was nominated for 10 Academy Awards in 2009 and won eight, the most for any film of 2008, including Best Picture, Best Director, and Best Adapted Screenplay. It also won seven BAFTA Awards (including Best Film), five Critics' Choice Awards, and four Golden Globes. The film was dubbed in Hindi for Indian release as *Slumdog Crorepati*.

THE MUSIC

The *Slumdog Millionaire* soundtrack was composed by A. R. Rahman, who planned the score for over two months and completed it in two weeks. Danny Boyle has said that he chose Rahman because "not only does he draw on Indian classical music, but he's got R&B and hip hop coming in from America, house music coming in from Europe and this incredible fusion is created." Rahman won the 2009 Golden Globe Award for Best Original Score and won two out of three nominations for the Academy Awards, including one for Best Original Score and one for Best Original Song for "Jai Ho."

NOTABLE QUOTES

"Shut up! The man with the Colt 45 says shut up" —Salim

Jamal: I knew you'd be watching.
Latika: I thought we would meet only in death.
Jamal: This is our destiny.
Latika: Kiss me.

Jamal:[seeing the Taj Mahal] Is this heaven?
Salim: You're not dead Jamal.
Jamal: What is it? Some hotel?

BEHIND THE SCREEN

Rubina Ali, who played the role of the youngest Latika, published a memoir, *Slumgirl Dreaming* (2009), including her experience in filming *Slumdog*.

Claims were made that the real slum children cast in the film were underpaid. Producers have disputed this and report that a trust fund held by their parents had been set up to be released when they turned 18, provided they continue their education until that time. Recently, when it was reported that the parents spent the money and that one of the fathers tried to sell Ali, Boyle created a new fund out of the parents' reach.

The Mercedes Benz that could be seen driving through the slums appears logo-less. Benz asked that the identification be removed out of concern that the car's status may be seen in the wrong light.

Slumdog almost didn't make it to the silver screen as it was originally slated for DVD release only.

THE OTHER LISTS

American Film Institute (No)
Roger Ebert's Top 100 (Yes)
Entertainment Weekly (Yes)
Internet Movie Database (Yes)
Leonard Maltin (No)
Movieline (No)
National Society of Film Critics (Yes)
Premiere Magazine (No)
Rolling Stone Magazine (No)
Village Voice (No)

56

NIGHT OF THE HUNTER 1955

HOLY TERROR

This is the quintessential Depression Gothic that alchemizes horror, religion, and sex into an iconic fable about the power of children. The broad-stroke performances, especially by Robert Mitchum at his most erotically evil and Lillian Gish as the mother figure of all mother figures, are the anchors for a film that is unusually free of the era's smoothed-over production standards. The same camera that zooms in on the playground discovery of a gruesome murder can also unleash magic in an extended boat ride through nature at its most improbably serene. The serenity doesn't last, of course, not with the terrifying Reverend Harry Powell (Robert Mitchum) blighting the landscape. "Doesn't he ever sleep?" bemoans the little boy who's being chased by Powell for his daddy's hidden money. The pulsing subtext (sometimes not so sub) is sex. The want of it, the fear of it. Mitchum's erect switchblade tearing through a trouser pocket elicits not only dread but the kind of gallows wit that only a Hitchcock crony such as director Charles Laughton might go for. And while he's at it, he's more than happy to skewer red-white-and-blue religious hysteria and, of course, that most durable of double-edged American precepts: that money may be the root of all evil but it's also the quick-claim cure. Rich black and luminescent white cinematography by Stanley Cortez, the master behind *The Magnificent Ambersons*, frames stylized sets that might've been traced from Grant Wood paintings.

Jim: Mitchum's role is as fine a Christmas present as any movie star ever got. He's like a weather front in this one, scary as hell and hilarious.

Gail: Move over, Hannibal Lecter. Mitchum's predatory widow killer and would-be child killer is one of the spookiest psychopaths to hum down an expressionist landscape.

THE PLOT

Evangelical psychopath Harry Powell (Robert Mitchum) weds young widow Willa (Shelley Winters), whose bank robber husband had been his cellmate. He beats her on their honeymoon in lieu of "sinful" sex, and harps on her two children, John and Pearl, for the whereabouts of Daddy's hidden stash. It's in Pearl's ragdoll, but they're not telling. When Willa becomes wise to his true intent, he murders her and the children run for their lives, into the warm and cozy arms of an eccentric spinster, Rachel Cooper (Lillian Gish). In the final showdown, it is the intrepid Rachel, shotgun at the ready, who is the last one standing.

"Would you like me to tell you the little story of right-hand/left-hand? The story of good and evil?" Preacher creature Harry Powell (Robert Mitchum) is possessed of a villainy so relentless that the performance takes on a satirical edge. It propels a film that could've been merely a cracking good horror story into the realm of the classics.

"It's a hard world for little things." —Rachel Cooper

THE DIRECTOR

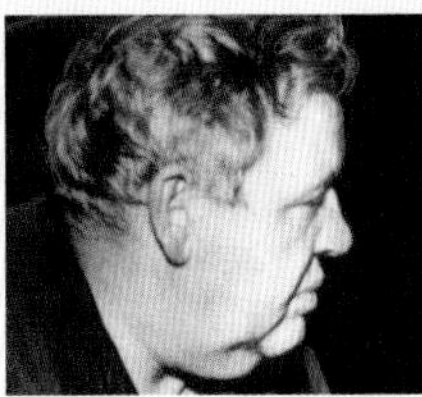

British-born **Charles Laughton** was the consummate character actor despite several iconic leading roles, most famously the titular king in *The Private Life of Henry VIII* (1933). Self-admittedly ugly ("I have a face that would stop a sundial") but not so forthcoming about his homosexuality, he remained wed to his best friend, Elsa Lanchester (*Bride of Frankenstein*) for the duration of his astonishing Hollywood run. The look of the film makes his admiration for D. W. Griffith apparent. He even procured his idol's greatest star, Lillian Gish. While he left the direction of the kids to Mitchum, Laughton rewarded his macho star with the most affecting performance of his career. The timing wasn't right for a voluptuous expressionist voyage and the studio couldn't begin to know what to do with it. It wound up in Saturday matinee release, where it suffered a quick unnatural death. Enraged by the poor reception of *The Night of the Hunter*, both critically and financially, Laughton vowed never to direct another film and kept his promise.

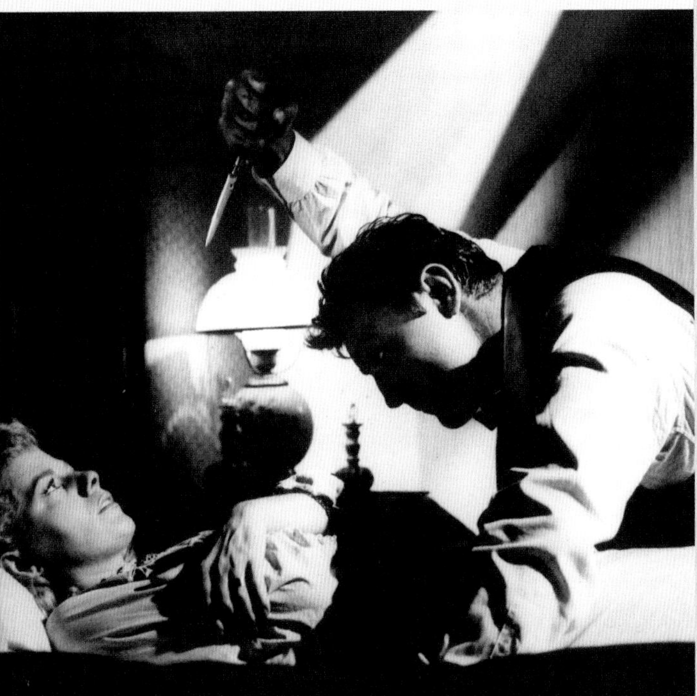

Every married couple has a bad night but this looks like the last one for ill-fated Willa Harper (Shelley Winters). For Winters, death was a great career move. In her first major film, *A Double Life*, she died at the end of Ronald Colman's dagger; in *A Place In The Sun*, Montgomery Clift drowned her; in *Lolita*, she ran into the path of a speeding car; and in *The Poseidon Adventure* she suffered a fatal, waterlogged heart attack.

THE CAST

Harry Powell	Robert Mitchum
Willa Harper	Shelley Winters
Rachel Cooper	Lillian Gish
John Harper	Billy Chapin
Pearl Harper	Sally Jane Bruce
Ben Harper	Peter Graves
Icey Spoon	Evelyn Varden
Walt Spoon	Don Beddoe
Birdie Steptoe	James Gleason
Ruby	Gloria Castillo

THE ACTORS

The *noir* genre of the 1940s and '50s was the perfect match for "bad boy" **Robert Mitchum**. His lethargic sexuality and shifty gaze provided the ideal antidote to postwar mom-and-apple-pie America. Laughton considered Mitchum the only Hollywood actor who could play Macbeth. As for Mitchum, he liked to pretend he was just strolling through his career. He claimed he only made movies to score women, pot, and easy money, commenting, "Movies bore me, especially my own." In fact, there was tremendous skill behind the casual exterior. He was a poet, a musician, a singer (none of his singing roles were dubbed), and one of the most durable stars in the business. He played indelible roles in such films as *From Out of the Past* (1947), *Cape Fear* (1962), and *Ryan's Daughter* (1970). His buoyant career managed to survive his brief imprisonment for drug possession in 1949. About life behind bars, he commented, "It's like Palm Springs without the riff-raff."

"They abide and they endure," says **Lillian Gish**'s Rachel of her brood of adoptive children as the movie comes to an end. The words might also apply to her resume of extraordinary films. She and her sister Dorothy were discovered by D. W. Griffith in 1912 and Lillian, whose face radiated an ethereal innocence, became his most famous star in such films as *Birth of a Nation* (1915), *Intolerance* (1916), and *Orphans of the Storm* (1922). By the 1930s, her Hollywood status faded and she returned to the stage, where she both starred and directed. Her movie comeback was rewarded with a Best Supporting Oscar nomination for *Duel in the Sun* (1946). She more than held her own alongside Bette Davis in *The Whales of August* (1987), although *The Night of the Hunter* is considered her most memorable role.

"You gotta play mothers, otherwise you won't have a long career in Hollywood," advised the shoot-from-the-hip **Shelley Winters**. She won her two Oscars doing just that, in *The Diary of Anne Frank* (1959) and *Patch of Blue* (1965). Having studied acting with Laughton, she made her first big impression as the nymphet waitress who gets strangled by Ronald Colman in *A Double Life* (1947). But her big break came as the pregnant and disposable girlfriend of Montgomery Clift in *A Place in the Sun* (1951). She aired her private life in a series of autobios in which she kissed and told on nearly every male star in Hollywood. Despite her former sex-bomb image (she taught Marilyn Monroe how to pose), she's probably best remembered as the plump, waterlogged Belle Rosen in *The Poseidon Adventure* (1972). (For more on Shelley Winters, see page 268.)

ROLE REVERSAL

The role of Preacher Powell was originally offered to Gary Cooper who flat-out refused it, thinking it would be a career killer.

Jane Darwell was set to play Rachel until Laughton decided to hold out for the legendary Gish.

BEHIND THE SCREEN

Rumors abound that Laughton was so appalled by Agee's deadweight script that he tossed it out and wrote one himself. Not completely true. He had Agee cut it by half and served as editor in chief.

Laughton despised children and had Mitchum step in to direct the kids.

Mitchum, in turn, despised Shelley Winters and not so jokingly suggested she should've done only the scene in which her dead body is found floating under water.

CREDITS

Producer: Paul Gregory/ United Artists
Director: Charles Laughton
Screenplay: James Agee
Running Time: 93 minutes
Budget: $800,000

THE YEAR'S ACADEMY AWARD WINNERS

Best Picture: *Marty*
Best Director: Delbert Mann, *Marty*
Best Actor: Ernest Borgnine, *Marty*
Best Actress: Anna Magnani, *The Rose Tattoo*
Best Supporting Actor: Jack Lemmon, *Mr. Roberts*
Best Supporting Actress: Jo Van Fleet, *East of Eden*

THE OTHER LISTS

- American Film Institute (No)
- *Entertainment Weekly* (No)
- Internet Movie Database (No)
- Leonard Maltin (No)
- *Movieline* (Yes)
- *Premiere* Magazine (Yes)
- Roger Ebert's Top 100 (Yes)
- *Rolling Stone* Magazine (Yes)
- *Village Voice* (Yes)

Although Mitchum chided John Wayne for wearing lifts in his shoes, he himself fudged the stats on his height, exaggerating by an inch or two.

Laughton cheats on the perspective in the scene when John spies Powell on horseback on the horizon; Mitchum's stand-in for the scene was a midget.

LOVE/HATE RELATIONSHIP

Mitchum's L-O-V-E and H-A-T-E knuckle tattoos have been mimicked in dozens of films, most famously in his later hit, *Cape Fear*, and comically in *The Rocky Horror Picture Show*.

THE CRITICS

"What a compelling, frightening and beautiful film it is! And how well it has survived its period. Many films from the mid-1950s, even the good ones, seem somewhat dated now, but by setting his story in an invented movie world outside conventional realism, Laughton gave it a timelessness." –Roger Ebert, *Chicago Sun-Times*

NOTABLE QUOTES

"Salvation is a last-minute business, boy." —Harry Powell

"Don't he never sleep?" —John Harper

"Get your state troopers out here. I got something trapped in my barn." —Rachel, after wounding Powell with buckshot

There's no walking on water for Reverend Powell, but he'll sink to any level to get his hands on that stash of money. John Harper (a very effective Billy Chapin) rows as if his life and that of his sister Pearl (Sally Jane Bruce) depended on it. It does!

Rachel sits anxiously in her kitchen chair, shotgun in her lap, awaiting Powell's return for the children. Outside the window, we see Powell leaning against the fence, happy to simply wear her down until he can make his move. He begins to sing a favorite hymn. "Leaning, leaning, leaning on the everlasting arm…" he croons, and pious Rachel can't help joining in. For a brief moment the hunter and the hunted come together in harmony.

Mother Goose got her gun! The feisty, pure-hearted guardian, Miss Cooper (Lillian Gish), waits out the skulking Powell, even as she briefly harmonizes with him.

57

THE THIRD MAN 1949

ONLY THE SHADOW KNOWS

The theater falls into darkness. From the strings of a zither comes a mockingly jaunty, utterly irresistible rag commenting on the moral and physical decay of postwar divided Vienna. On screen, dreamlike, documentary-style images of ruins and rubble, and a dead body floats by in a dry riverbed. These sights lead into the expressionist nightmare city, always in darkness, where cobblestone streets cast a mysterious metallic glow, and where huge baroque gargoyles and vaulting staircases linger but no longer elevate. Today the city belongs to no one save thieves, black marketeers, and foreign powers vying for control. Into this corrupt world steps the witless American Holly Martins (Joseph Cotten), who hadn't planned on spending his trip chasing a corpse—or his girl. If at times the tilted camera angles of this masterpiece seem a bit too stylish, overheated, and theatrical, we'll suffer it gladly. The artfulness at work is staggering, summoning the experience of living out of joint in a world without bearings. And the zither, like the deceit and corruption, jangles our nerves long after the movie has ended.

Jim: Terrifically entertaining and easy to grasp, yet somehow makes you feel terribly clever and sophisticated for watching it. A neat trick. And that music—dangerously addictive.

Gail: Hold onto your seats, this pretty little picture will take you on a ride through the fever dream of postwar Europe, down eerie cobblestone streets and through muck-slick sewers. If that's not enough, try to follow the sudden appearances and disappearances of one Harry Lime—Orson Welles, a very bad guy, depending, of course, upon what you know about him.

IE PLOT

n't get it," says Holly Martins, but the erican pulp Western author doesn't know half of what he doesn't know about this upt, post-World War II European city ulated by crooks, spies, and refugees. He arks the train and almost immediately ns that Harry Lime (Orson Welles), the hood friend at whose urging he has come, e most infamously dead person in town. e searching for the truth behind Harry's th, he falls—all over himself—in love with y's girl, Anna Schmidt (Alida Valli), who ms herself to remain in rotten Vienna . . . in love with Lime. Holly is shocked to n from a police inspector of his once h-admired friend's moral decay. It seems made a bundle black-marketing diluted cillin, resulting in the illness and death any children. Despondent over what he knows of Harry, Holly leaves Vienna, and girl, still uncertain of the truth about his d.

Is Harry Lime (Orson Welles) about to kill his friend Holly Martins (Joseph Cotten) by throwing him out of the swinging car atop a Ferris wheel? Is he trying to justify his black-marketing? Whatever he's up to, he certainly delivers a chilling speech on the relative productivity of warring cultures over peaceful ones in the now famous "cuckoo clock" lecture (see page 185).

THE DIRECTOR

It was artful director **Carol Reed**'s second picture based on a Graham Greene thriller, after *The Fallen Idol* (1948), but this time he did it his way. Reed reconstructed the script into a political allegory centering on the corruption of Harry Lime. He changed Greene's happy ending, closing instead on a cemetery, the same one at which the film began. He also adjusted characterizations so that Anna is a much more powerful character, no longer the daughter of Hungarian Nazis but a refugee of communist Czechoslovakia. Holly Martins is reduced to an American wimp. Before making *The Third Man*, Reed proved himself with *Odd Man Out* (1947) and *The Fallen Idol* (1948). He later made another Greene-based picture, *Our Man in Havana* (1960), to great acclaim. *The Third Man*, however, remains his most unforgettable film.

The film ends as it began with Anna Schmidt (Alida Valli) walking out of the cemetery where Harry Lime has just been buried . . . twice. This time, it's for keeps. In between, Holly Martins (Joseph Cotten) has fallen badly for the Czech refugee who still loves Harry, for better or for worse, for the charmer or for the murderer. She loves Harry for whatever it is he may be.

THE CAST	
Holly Martins	Joseph Cotten
Anna Schmidt	Alida Valli
Major Calloway	Trevor Howard
Harry Lime	Orson Welles
Porter	Paul Hoerbiger
"Baron" Kurtz	Ernst Deutsch
Dr. Winkel	Erich Ponto
Popescu	Siegfried Breuer
Old Woman	Hedwig Bleibtreu
Sergeant Paine	Bernard Lee
Crabbin	Wilfrid Hyde-White

THE ACTORS

Orson Welles makes one of his—in fact, *the*—most dramatic entrances in screen history. Though he makes only lightning-bolt appearances (literally) in and out of dark corners in *The Third Man*—and on that Ferris wheel, of course—his cherubic, cunning, and smirking face looms over the entire film. Like his unknowable character in *Citizen Kane* (1941), Lime remains one of the most enigmatic figures in all of film. Though the movie's attention to composition, long shots, disorienting close-ups and tilted camera angles was pure Welles, he had little to do with the making of the movie save for the rewrite of his dialogue and the penning of one of the film's greatest speeches—on the advent of the "cuckoo clock." (For more on Welles, see page 18.)

It took some daring to play one of the most befuddled, awkward, drunken, and, yes, cynical men in a world of toughs, but **Joseph Cotten** took on the role of Holly Martins and got the message across: America didn't have a clue about what post-World War II Europe was all about. Cotten plays acolyte to Welles's big man. He would reprise this role in a different form in Welles's *Citizen Kane* (1941). (For more on Cotten, see pages 18 and 199.)

The tough-minded yet tender Anna Schmidt, lover of Harry Lime—no matter who he really is—was played with dignity at just the right pitch by **Alida Valli**. She makes the role stand as a testament to womanly resolve. From 1934 to 2002, Valli appeared in more than 100 films, mostly European, but she made several appearances on American television—in *Dr. Kildare* and *Combat*. From the sublime to the ridiculous, some might say. She lives in Croatia.

ROLE REVERSALS

Harry Lime could only have one face, and it was that of the two-faced imp, the ornery Orson Welles. But producer David O. Selznick thought Noel Coward had what it took. Well, maybe he had half the face. We're grateful that Carol Reed insisted on Welles.

Director Carol Reed originally wanted James Stewart for the role of Holly Martins; producer David O. Selznick signed on Joseph Cotten, who was under contract to his production company at the time.

BEHIND THE SCREEN

Carol Reed put his own fingers through the sewer grate for the shot of those crawling digits reaching out for escape. Welles had had his fill of the slimy lower depths and left before the scene was shot.

Welles starred in a radio series *The Lives of Harry Lime* (1951-52), based on the early adventures of his character in *The Third Man*.

True-life British double agent Kim Philby—Greene's superior in the British Secret Intelligence Service—was Graham Greene's role model for the character of Harry Lime.

Theme composer Anton Karas had never played outside beer and wine gardens in Vienna (where Carol Reed discovered him). His score became the number one hit for eleven weeks in 1950. The instrumental version by Guy Lombardo also reached number one in 1950, and four other versions also charted that year. The music even made an appearance on the flip side of one of Herb Alpert's bigger hits. Karas had based the piece on an étude he found in a book of zither compositions.

CREDITS

Producer: Alexander Korda, Carol Reed and David O. Selznick
Director: Carol Reed
Screenplay: Graham Greene
Running time: 104 minutes

ACADEMY AWARDS

Best Cinematography, Black-and-White: Robert Krasker

NOMINATIONS

Best Director: Carol Reed
Best Editing: Oswald Hafenrichter

THE YEAR'S OTHER WINNERS

Best Picture: *All the King's Men*
Best Director: Joseph L. Mankiewicz, *A Letter to Three Wives*
Best Actor: Broderick Crawford, *All the King's Men*
Best Actress: Olivia de Havilland, *The Heiress*
Best Supporting Actor: Dean Jagger, *Twelve O'Clock High*
Best Supporting Actress: Mercedes McCambridge, *All the King's Men*
Honorary Award: Fred Astaire

THE OTHER LISTS

- American Film Institute (No)
- Roger Ebert's Top 100 (Yes)
- *Entertainment Weekly* (Yes)
- Internet Movie Database (No)
- Leonard Maltin (No)
- *Movieline* (Yes)
- National Society of Film Critics (Yes)
- *Premiere* Magazine (Yes)
- *Rolling Stone* Magazine (Yes)
- *Village Voice* (Yes)

THE CRITICS

"The creation of a sensibility terribly old and wise, and most of all very European; it was the very essence of world-weary sophistication." —Laura Miller, Salon.com

"The feeling here . . . is that Reed is deserting intelligence for a lyrical-romantic kick, the precocious use of space, perspective, types of acting (stylized, distorted, understated, emotionalized) and random, seemingly irrelevant subject matter . . . It uses such tiresome symbol-images as a door that swings with an irritating rhythm as though it had a will of its own. . ." —Manny Farber, *The Nation*

THE GREAT SPEECH

Lime holds Holly hostage in a high, swinging Ferris wheel car. Will he push his friend? Well . . . what he does instead is deliver one of the most perverse short speeches on character in history: "In Italy for 30 years under the Borgias they had warfare, terror, murder, and bloodshed, but they produced Michelangelo, Leonardo da Vinci, and the Renaissance. In Switzerland they had brotherly love—they had 500 years of democracy and peace, and what did that produce? The cuckoo clock."

NOTABLE QUOTES

"I'm not very fond of movies. I don't go to them much." —Orson Welles

"I started at the top and worked down." —Orson Welles

"I'm not bitter about Hollywood's treatment of me, but over its treatment of Griffith, Von Sternberg, Von Stroheim, Buster Keaton, and a hundred others." —Orson Welles

THE GREAT SCENE

The "dead" Harry Lime (Orson Welles) is very much alive in the sewers beneath Vienna's ruined streets. Detectives pursue him through the rank, labyrinthine channels.

Anna has just told Holly that the only person her cat purred for was Harry. As she speaks, the camera crawls through the plants on the windowsill and then outside to the darkened street below, where we find the cat running across the metallic cobblestones and landing in a doorway, where it nestles against a pair of shiny black men's shoes. We can't see the man inside those shoes, but if our synapses are firing we gasp when we realize what is afoot (so to speak). It's the most amazing entrance in film history. What follows is a closeup of a mocking choirboy face looking up toward the window. Holly gives chase to the figure, which disappears down into the sewers.

Everything has come to a standstill in post-World War II Vienna, except for all the corruption and black-marketeering. Of all places to stage a meeting, pulp-fiction writer Holly Martins (Joseph Cotten) waits for his once greatly admired friend Harry Lime (Orson Welles)—who is supposed to be dead—in an empty amusement park. Harry had better explain why he isn't dead—or, rather, why he shouldn't be considering what Holly has heard about his friend's activities during the war.

58

DR. ZHIVAGO 1965

FALLING HARD ON THE STEPPES

It seems as though almost every music box made since 1965 plays the evocatively sentimental "Lara's Theme," and countless women born around the time of the film's release bear the name of Julie Christie's love-haunted blonde. At the height of the film's popularity, few young men didn't at least consider the possibility of a Cossack shirt and a mustache. The reverberations were all the more remarkable given that *Dr. Zhivago* was almost universally dismissed by critics and initially fizzled at the box office. Director David Lean, his own severest critic, realized he'd cut the movie all wrong in haste. He went back to the editing room and nearly blinded himself from overwork as he redid the entire film, afterward shipping new prints to theaters across the country. The numbers turned around almost immediately, and the film went on to become one of the most successful romantic epics of all time. It was Lean's obsession that his adaptation of Pasternak's autobiographical novel be immaculately realized. No detail eluded his scrutiny. Period underwear was de rigueur for everyone in the cast. The rats scurrying on the stairs leading to Lara's flat had to be auditioned. And Communist revolutionaries, at least in Lean's version, had to know their place—the background. "It's fundamentally a story about human beings, not politics," Lean insisted. The bittersweet triangle of a handsome poet and the two women he loves struck a chord everywhere but at the Kremlin; *Dr. Zhivago* was banned in Russia until 1994.

Jim: Even the snow banks look like they just came out of makeup, and given Lean's exacting standards, they may have. Watch for the lighting of Christie's eyes—the same shade of blue as O'Toole's in *Lawrence of Arabia*. And the same love interest—Sharif. It makes you wonder if Lean was making the same epic over and over.

Gail: You just want to climb into this exquisite movie and find a poet in a Cossack shirt who will take you into his arms against the background of snow-filled Moscow streets.

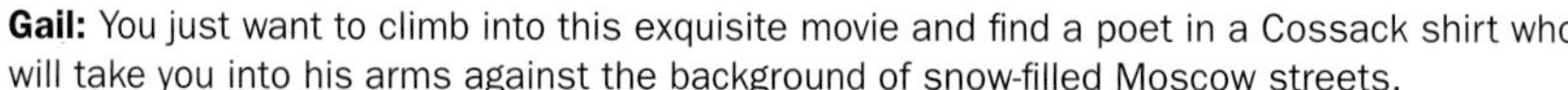

THE PLOT

Physician/poet Yuri Zhivago (Omar Sharif) is engaged to Tonya (Geraldine Chaplin), a young Moscow socialite. At a Christmas ball, they witness the shooting of tycoon Komarovsky (Rod Steiger) by his teen lover, Lara (Julie Christie). One look at her and Zhivago is obsessed. They encounter each other again on the Russian front during WW I, where she's volunteered as a nurse while searching for her political firebrand husband, Pasha (Tom Courtenay). Zhivago and Lara fall in love but don't act upon it. He returns to Moscow to find the Revolution has erased his past life. His home is now a commune and his half-brother Yevgraf, a highly placed officer (Alec Guinness), advises him to escape while he can; his poetry has been deemed subversive. The family flees to Tonya's family estate where they settle into a simple cottage. Yuri rediscovers Lara in the nearby town, deserted by her husband, now a powerful party leader. He's torn between her and pregnant Tonya. Before he can make a decision, he's kidnapped by the army. He escapes to reunite with Lara. With his own family in Paris, he, Lara, and her daughter take refuge at the estate until Komarovsky comes to them with the promise of safe passage. Yuri tricks her into going without him. He can't leave his beloved Russia, his muse. He watches Lara disappear into the distance, never to see her again.

"Good marriages are made in heaven...or some such place." Zhivago (Omar Sharif) and Lara (Julie Christie) must content themselves with idyllic, if illicit, rolls in the Russian hay. Lara, the devoted mistress, doesn't ask for more. After all, this is a David Lean film, and in his male-dominated universe, women either serve as décor or as prizes to be fought over.

"There are two kinds of women, and you, as we well know, are not the first kind. You, my dear, are a slut."—Komarovsky to Lara

THE DIRECTOR

Like a commander in the field of battle, **David Lean** oversaw a production staff of thousands and loved the power. Omar Sharif recalls that he almost never complimented anyone. But when he did, it was like a blessing from the Pope. His films took years to complete and he only gave up when the money ran out. Sam Spiegel, the producer of *Lawrence of Arabia*, remarked, "I had to get him out of the desert or he'd still be shooting the movie today." Lean lived for film; it was his only real passion. His view of the final product was intractable. When famed cinematographer Nicholas Roeg protested Lean's insistence on "Hollywood-style lighting," he was summarily fired. This was the same man who so valued one of his low-level technicians that he gifted him with his beloved Mercedes at the end of the production. Lean's output was, well, lean, but each film was intricately devised and unforgettable. He began with *Great Expectations* (1946), to be followed up by *Oliver Twist* (1948). His later career included *Hobson's Choice* (1954), *The Bridge on the River Kwai* (1957), his most acclaimed film, *Lawrence of Arabia* (1962), *Ryan's Daughter* (1970), and, finally, *A Passage to India* (1984). (For more on David Lean, see page 27.)

THE CAST

Yuri Zhivago	Omar Sharif
Lara Antipova	Julie Christie
Tonya	Geraldine Chaplin
Komarovsky	Rod Steiger
Gen. Yevgraf Zhivago	Alec Guinness
Pasha/Strelnikov	Tom Courtenay
Anna	Siobhan McKenna
Alexander Gromeko	Ralph Richardson
Sasha	Jeffrey Rockland
Yuri, younger	Tarek Sharif
Bolshevik	Bernard Kay
Kostoyed	Klaus Kinski
Liberius	Gérard Tichy
Razin	Noel Willman
Professor Kurt	Geoffrey Keen
Amelia	Adrienne Corri
Petya	Jack MacGowran
Engineer at Dam	Mark Eden
Old Soldier	Erik Chitty
Beef-Faced Colonel	Roger Maxwell
Delegate	Wolf Frees
Female Janitor	Gwen Nelson
Katya	Lucy Westmore
Train Jumper	Lili Muráti
Political Officer	Peter Madden

"I don't really know who I am. Quite possibly, I do not exist at all."—Gen. Yevgraf Zhivago

THE ACTORS

Omar Sharif was coached by his director to "do nothing." His character, Yuri Zhivago, is a poet, and Lean wanted the entire film to be seen through his eyes, the point of view of the artful observer. Sharif began to panic when he saw the early dailies and the abundance of closeups of his moist gaze looking off into the horizon. Lean told him not to worry, insisting that it would all pay off by the end of the film. Sharif knew better than to argue. He had served him well enough in *Lawrence of Arabia* (1962) to earn him an Oscar nod. Following *Zhivago*, *The Night of the Generals* (1967) was nearly forgotten in the excitement of Sharif's musical debut, *Funny Girl* (1968). Among his other memorable films are *The Tamarind Seed* (1974), *Crime and Passion* (1976), *Green Ice* (1981), and *Peter The Great* (1986). (For more on Sharif, see page 27.)

Considered one of the sexiest stars of all time, **Julie Christie** found fame very early after her brief debut in *Billy Liar* opposite Tom Courtenay (1964). *Doctor Zhivago* came directly on the heels of *Darling* (1969), the film that would earn her a Best Actress Oscar. Following *Petulia* (1968) and *The Go-Between* (1970), her famous liaison with Warren Beatty provided her with some of her best roles, including ones in *McCabe and Mrs. Miller* (1971), *Shampoo* (1975) and *Heaven Can Wait* (1978). The thriller *Don't Look Now* (1973) preceded a brief appearance as herself in *Nashville* (1975). The sci-fi screamer *Demon Seed* (1977) marked the decline of her Hollywood years, but she recouped with an Oscar nomination for the appropriately titled *Afterglow* (1997).

Geraldine Chaplin, at 20, had created a sensation in Paris in a new ballet. She was the girl of the moment on every magazine cover, and that's how Lean noticed her. "I'm sure he was thinking, oh, Charlie Chaplin's daughter, good PR. And she looks Russian!" Chaplin recalled. She recounted a great to-do over what color dress she'd wear in her first scene, where she disembarks a train from Paris. The designer insisted on gray. Lean said no. When they tried white, Lean eyed her up and down, then said loudly, "It makes her teeth look yellow." Chaplin was humiliated. After more fuss, Lean finally decided on pink. A childhood debut in her father's *Limelight* (1952) led to a supporting role in his last film, *A Countess from Hong Kong* (1966). Robert Altman cast her perfectly in *Nashville* (1975), and she appeared next in *Welcome to L.A.* (1977). Decades of French and Spanish films led to the international release *White Mischief* (1988) and Martin Scorsese's *The Age of Innocence* (1993). (For more on Chaplin, see page 45.)

Rod Steiger, the only American actor in the film, was convinced that Lean hated him. "He expected us to treat the script like the Bible. Anyone who didn't . . . " Steiger, a past-master of the emotionally instinctive Method, relied on improvisation to create solid moments. In a scene on the sleigh after his first dinner with the young Lara, he asked the director to hold the camera a bit longer. He wanted to try something. "I felt Julie was anticipating that first kiss," Steiger recalled. He kissed her on cue, paused for a second, then jumped her and stuck his tongue down her throat. Christie was startled and fought him, triggering the hateful reaction she'd need to show toward him later in the film. The scene stayed, though Lean wasn't happy that it was Steiger's idea. In only his second film, *On the Waterfront* (1954), Steiger's intensity matched Brando's and guaranteed him a long career of remarkable performances like those in *The Pawnbroker* (1965), *In the Heat of the Night* (1967), *Lucky Luciano* (1974), and *The Player* (1994). (For more on Steiger, see page 64.)

Outspoken **Tom Courtenay** was never afraid to bite the hand that fed him: "The film business is absurd. Stars don't last very long. It's much more interesting to be a proper actor." Nonetheless, he was the only actor in *Dr. Zhivago* to receive an Oscar nomination, garnered for his portrayal as Pasha, the schizophrenic young idealist turned political tyrant. His film career was off like a shot with

Producer:
David Lean-Carlo Ponti/MGM
Director: David Lean
Screenplay: Robert Bolt, based on the novel by Boris Pasternak
Running time: 197 minutes
Budget: $11 million
Box Office: $186 million

ACADEMY AWARDS

Best Adapted Screenplay: Robert Bolt
Best Cinematography, Color: Freddie Young
Best Costume Design, Color: Phyllis Dalton
Best Art Direction-Set Decoration, Color: John Box, Terence Marsh, Dario Simoni
Best Music, Score: Maurice Jarre

NOMINATIONS

Best Picture
Best Director: David Lean
Best Supporting Actor: Tom Courtenay
Best Editing: Norman Savage
Best Sound: A. W. Watkins, Franklin Milton

THE YEAR'S OTHER WINNERS

Picture: *The Sound of Music*
Director: Robert Wise, *The Sound of Music*
Actor: Lee Marvin, *Cat Ballou*
Actress: Julie Christie, *Darling*
Supporting Actor: Martin Balsam, *A Thousand Clowns*
Supporting Actress: Shelley Winters, *A Patch of Blue*

The Loneliness of the Long Distance Runner (1962), which he followed up with *Billy Liar* (1964). Following *King Rat* (1965), *The Night of the Generals* (1967), and *A Dandy in Aspic* (1968), he essentially vanished from the screen until his triumphant Oscar-nominated return in *The Dresser* (1983). He went on to make *Let Him Have It* (1991) and *Nicholas Nickleby* (2002).

David Lean considered **Alec Guinness** his talisman after their charmed collaborations on *Bridge on the River Kwai* (1957), and *Lawrence of Arabia* (1962). While he appears in only four scenes in *Dr. Zhivago*, he seems to play a major role thanks to the energizing force of his on-screen persona. Guinness's career is an essential map of outstanding mid-twentieth-century films, including appearances in *Great Expectations* (1946), *Oliver Twist* (1948), *The Lavender Hill Mob* (1951), *Our Man in Havana* (1960), *The Quiller Memorandum* (1966), *Star Wars* (1977), *A Passage to India* (1984), and *A Handful of Dust* (1988). (For more on Guinness, see pages 27 and 169.)

"I don't like my face at all. It's always been a great drawback to me." And in truth, the famously eccentric **Ralph Richardson**'s merely average looks kept him from many of the great screen roles won by his peer Laurence Olivier. Olivier, along with John Gielgud, considered him the greatest English actor of his generation. Unlike many of his stage-bound counterparts, he loved making movies, and could be seen in such classics as *Anna Karenina* (1948) and *The Heiress* (1949), which got him an Oscar nomination. *Exodus* (1960) was followed by *Long Day's Journey Into Night* (1962). His final film, *Greystoke* (1984), earned him a posthumous Oscar nod.

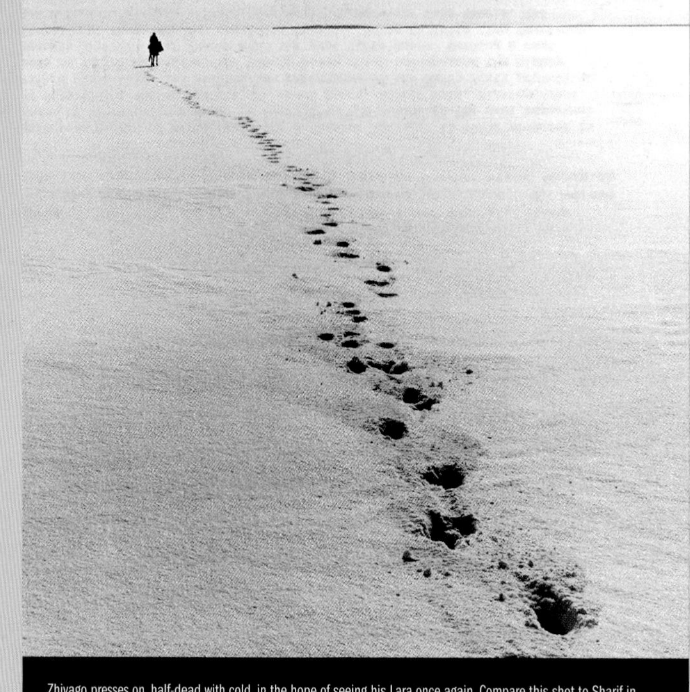

Zhivago presses on, half-dead with cold, in the hope of seeing his Lara once again. Compare this shot to Sharif in *Lawrence of Arabia* as a mirage-like figure approaching across the desert, increasingly fearsome. Here, he's receding toward the horizon, a pathetic soul, as if love has somehow used him up.

Two years after his abduction by the revolutionary army, Zhivago manages to escape in the midst of a blizzard. He slogs through weeks of bitter cold and starvation until he's more dead than alive. He senses movement from behind and his half-frozen face registers shock as he realizes he's standing on a railroad track. He heaves himself to the side just in time to avoid being struck by a speeding locomotive. After learning his family has evacuated to Moscow, he makes his way to Lara's flat. He finds the key in the old hiding place, behind a loose brick, with a note attached. She's heard of his arrival; she'll be back soon. He makes his way up the stairs, looks into the mirror at his ravaged face, and, before he can attempt to clean himself, collapses.

ROLE REVERSALS

Carlo Ponti optioned the property as a vehicle for his wife, Sophia Loren. But when it came down to it, Lean had the final word: "She's too tall for Lara."

BEHIND THE SCREEN

Boris Pasternak regretfully declined the Nobel Prize for his novel, fearing that if he traveled to Stockholm he wouldn't be let back into his beloved homeland.

Pasternak's real-life mistress, Olga, the model for Lara, was sent to a work camp following his death. Moscow wanted her to pay the price for his dissidence.

In the scene in which a peasant woman chases after the train to give Zhivago her baby, Sharif lost his grip on the actress Lili Muráti and she actually fell under the wheels. She survived, but nearly lost her legs. To the angry astonishment of the cast, Lean decided to keep the shot in. After Muráti was taken off in an ambulance, he called for her double to be dressed to finish the scene. "What am I supposed to do? I'm making a movie!" he insisted.

Sharif's own son plays the very young Yuri Zhivago.

Costume designer Phyllis Dalton sadly regrets the pouffed-up hairdos that forever mark Zhivago as a '60s film.

Sharif waxed his hairline and sported a wig to effect Pasternak's own dramatic image. He also wore elastic facial "pulls" to give his cheekbones a higher Slavic angle.

A night shoot required thousands of Spanish extras to sing the "Internationale," the universal Communist anthem. Local villagers woke thinking their despised leader, Generalissimo Franco, was dead, and they ran out into the streets to celebrate. Franco's police broke up the party quickly.

THE MUSIC

Composer Maurice Jarre argued bitterly with Lean about "Lara's Theme." He felt it wasn't his best effort, too cloyingly sweet. But Lean insisted it stay in. "When you win your Academy Award, you'll say thank you, Mr. Lean, you were right." He did.

THE SET

The Soviet Union at the time was of course off limits, and most of the film was shot in Spain. A recreation of Moscow was constructed in Madrid's outskirts. It took 800 workers eighteen months to complete. Geraldine Chaplin recalls that the homes weren't typical movie-set façades, but had fully constructed interiors. The famous "ice palace" was created by applying a coating of beeswax followed by sprays of ice-cold water. All four seasons were represented in the script; fall would turn to spring overnight, thanks to a tireless crew painting the leaves and laying out white sheeting to look like snow on the horizon.

THE CRITICS

"The movie is something that should be experienced by everyone at least once in a lifetime." —Marjorie Baumgarten, *Austin Chronicle*

"(Screenwriter) Bolt has reduced the vast upheaval of the Russian Revolution to the banalities of a doomed romance." —Vincent Canby, *New York Times*

THE OTHER LISTS
American Film Institute (No)
Roger Ebert's Top 100 (No)
Entertainment Weekly (No)
Internet Movie Database (No)
Leonard Maltin (No)
Movieline (No)
National Society of Film Critics (No)
Premiere Magazine (No)
Rolling Stone Magazine (No)
Village Voice (No)

59

E.T. THE EXTRA-TERRESTRIAL 1982

MY ALIEN, MYSELF

"You could be happy here, I could take care of you. I wouldn't let anybody hurt you. We could grow up together, E.T." The other famous homeless soul in filmdom, Dorothy, never got as good an offer. Alas, like Dorothy in *The Wizard of Oz*, all E.T. wanted to do was go home . . . or at the very least, phone. With its elevating religious allusions—a heavenly finger reaching out to touch another as in Michelangelo's painting on the Sistine Chapel ceiling—its parable-like story of a lonely boy from a broken home finding comfort in an equally lost extraterrestrial, Spielberg's masterful control of the medium in this warm and exhilarating classic of childhood innocence, loneliness, courage, love, and transcendence takes the camera down to E.T./child-level so that we see, like children, how threatening and overwhelming the adult world can be. And we get it . . . somewhere between the eyes, in the lump in our throats, and at the center of our hearts.

Jim: I'd love to have little Drew's screaming reaction shot on a loop. Makes me laugh every time.

Gail: As always the master Spielberg knows where all the spigots are, and he turns them on quite deftly here. Pass the tissues; I'm having too good a time.

IE PLOT

aceship lands on Earth and leaves out one of its passengers, E.T. When a ıg boy, Elliott (Henry Thomas) discovers little alien (no bigger than he), he whisks away and slips him into his room. But e's no keeping this baby in the closet. E.T. only gets out and into plenty of mischief, lso finds his way into the boy's heart—a t that, with the separation of his parents the everyday perils of childhood, badly ds a friend. So touched by his alien, tt begins to share E.T.'s emotions: When becomes deathly ill, so too does Elliott. two learn from each other, and protect another from all the bad grownups, icularly Keys, the desperate scientist king E.T. E.T. finally gets to phone home, his call is answered.

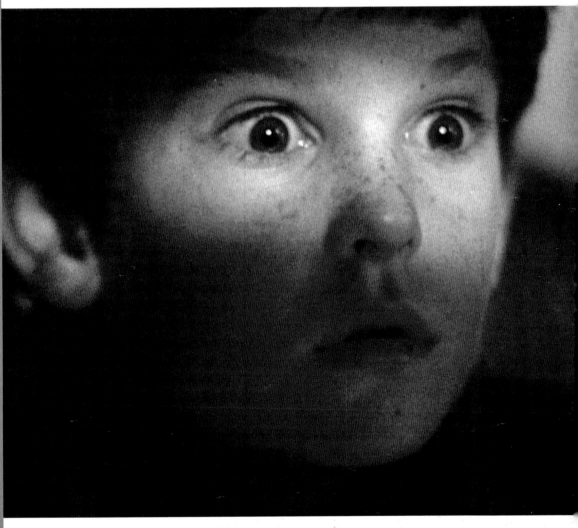

Elliott (Henry Thomas) is blinded by a heavenly light that at once thrills and terrifies him. The light speaks to him—and out of it steps E.T. "I'm keeping him," says the boy.

"E.T. phone home." —E.T.

THE DIRECTOR

He often shows shooting stars, features children in danger, makes references to Disney, and uses powerful flashlights in dark scenes . . . he's also one of the richest and most successful producer/directors in Hollywood. With all the "best of" awards going to *Gandhi* that year, director **Steven Spielberg** probably wanted to go home and forget the phone. His most personal work, *E.T.* explores both the child's sense of wonder at life and his loneliness upon the breakup of his family. But rather than sink into the mire, the director uses his own experience to make an on-target, timeless film. He is, in short, the most commercially influential director in all of Hollywood history. At 21 this college dropout signed a multi-film deal with Universal. When he directed her in his first effort, a segment on TV's *Night Gallery* (1969), Joan Crawford told a reporter during an interview, "Go interview that kid, because he's going to be the biggest director of all time!" A few more early successes, including the TV movie *Duel* (1971) and his first feature, *The Sugarland Express* (1974), and Spielberg took his place in the pantheon. *E.T.* remains one of the director's classics, and was his largest grosser up to that time. Among the films in his treasure chest are *Jaws* (1975), *Raiders of the Lost Ark* (1981), *Poltergeist* (1982), *The Color Purple* (1985), *Schindler's List* (1993), and *Saving Private Ryan* (1998). His more recent films include *A.I. Artificial Intelligence* (2001), *Minority Report* (2002), and *Catch Me If You Can* (2002). In 1995 Spielberg also gave birth to a multimedia empire, along with David Geffen and Jeffrey Katzenberg, called Dreamworks SKG. (For more on Spielberg, see pages 88, 103, 136, 208 and 289.)

Far from his world and unable to "phone home," E.T. becomes gravely ill. Elliot, whose own home seems to be unraveling in the wake of divorce, tries to care for his best friend, but becomes ill himself.

THE CAST	
Elliott	Henry Thomas
Mary	Dee Wallace-Stone
Michael	Robert MacNaughton
Gertie	Drew Barrymore
Keys	Peter Coyote
Greg	K. C. Martel
Steve	Sean Frye
Tyler	C. Thomas Howell

THE ACTORS

That lovable cross between Albert Einstein, Carl Sandburg, and a pug, **E.T.** won our hearts like a newborn baby. He's particularly moving when, at the end of the film, the mothership arrives to retrieve him. E.T. sees a figure that looks much like him standing in the light. Could it be his mother?

Henry Thomas plays Elliott, the boy who wails, "He came to me," as if he was born to the part. Look closer and you'll better appreciate the artlessly affecting emotional honesty of Thomas's performance as Elliott, the suburban youngster who bonds so closely with E.T. that they come to share feelings of fear, exhilaration, and, in one of the movie's most amusingly inspired scenes, inebriation. Thomas has also appeared in *Legends of the Fall* (1995) and *Curse of the Starving Class* (1994), and more recently in *All the Pretty Horses* (2000) and *Gangs of New York* (2002).

The descendent of a legendary acting family and goddaughter to Steven Spielberg, **Drew Barrymore** was five when she played Gertie, the Energizer bunny younger sister of Elliott. In early adolescence her thriving career sank under the weight of alcohol and drugs (and a resulting suicide attempt), sounding a disturbing note from her family's past. In 1990 she coauthored a book about her drug dependence and rehabilitation. After this she stole headlines again—sensationally—by posing nude for a national magazine. It took a few tries in small roles in TV movies, a costarring role in the well-received independent feature *Guncrazy* (1992), and a sexy walk-on in *Wayne's World 2* (1993), until she finally got back to the limelight with *Boys on the Side, Mad Love*, and *Batman Forever* (all 1995), and more recent films like *The Wedding Singer* (1998), *Charlie's Angels* (2000), and *Riding in Cars with Boys* (2001).

Peter Coyote, as the villainous scientist who can't wait to get under the skin of E.T., plays his part with unusual subtlety. Like his director, Coyote convinces us that he's been waiting for contact with extraterrestrials all of his life. Among Coyote's prolific output are *Tell Me a Riddle* (1980), *Cross Creek* (1983), *Jagged Edge* (1985), *Bitter Moon* (1992), *Execution of Justice* (1999), *A Time for Dancing* (2000), *Midwives* (2001), *Femme Fatale* (2002), and *A Walk to Remember* (2002).

THE CRITICS

"*E.T.* . . . may become a children's classic of the space age . . . it's full of the timeless longings expressed in children's literature." —Vincent Canby, *New York Times*

"It is arguably the most overrated motion picture to arrive in theaters during the 1980s." —James Berardinelli, *Reelviews*

CREDITS

Producer: Kathleen Kennedy and Steve Spielberg/ Amblin Entertainment/ Universal Pictures
Director: Steven Spielberg
Screenplay: Melissa Mathison
Running Time: 115 minutes
Budget: $10.5 million
Box Office: $701.4 million (worldwide)

ACADEMY AWARDS

Best Sound Effects Editing: Charles L. Campbell, Ben Burtt
Best Effects, Visual Effects: Carlo Rambaldi, Dennis Muren, Kenneth Smith
Best Music, Original Score: John Williams
Best Sound: Robert Knudson, Robert J. Glass, Don Digirolamo, Gene S. Cantamessa

NOMINATIONS

Best Picture
Best Cinematography: Allen Daviau
Best Director: Steven Spielberg
Best Film Editing: Carol Littleton
Best Screenplay Written for the Screen: Melissa Mathison

THE YEAR'S OTHER WINNERS

Best Picture: *Gandhi*
Best Director: Richard Attenborough, *Gandhi*
Best Actor: Ben Kingsley, *Gandhi*
Best Actress: Meryl Streep, *Sophie's Choice*
Best Supporting Actor: Louis Gossett, Jr., *An Officer and a Gentleman*
Best Supporting Actress: Jessica Lange, *Tootsie*

THE OTHER LISTS

American Film Institute (Yes)
Roger Ebert's Top 100 (Yes)
Entertainment Weekly (Yes)
Internet Movie Database (No)
Leonard Maltin (Yes)
Movieline (Yes)
National Society of Film Critics (No)
Premiere Magazine (No)
Rolling Stone Magazine (No)
Village Voice (No)

NOTABLE QUOTES

"Before I go off and direct a movie I always look at four films. They tend to be: *The Seven Samurai*, *Lawrence of Arabia*, *It's A Wonderful Life*, and *The Searchers*." –Steven Spielberg

BEHIND THE SCREEN

In order to express pain, Henry Thomas called upon the Method and remembered the day his dog died. He was cast immediately.

Can you spot Harrison Ford in the movie? No? That's because his scene was cut. Spielberg thought the actor's presence would simply be too distracting.

In the Halloween scene, a child dressed as Yoda from *The Empire Strikes Back* (1980) enters the picture, catching E.T.'s eye just as a piece of John Williams' Yoda theme is played.

Rumor had it that M&M's lost the product placement award to Reese's Pieces, which became the most famous candy in the world as a result of its appearance in the film. M&M apparently backed out after anticipating the film would melt at the box office.

Ronald and Nancy Reagan enjoyed their own private screening with Spielberg manning the White House projector.

All guns were pulled from the 20th anniversary re-release edition in 2002, costing Spielberg $100,000 for digitally removing a scene that featured the weapon prominently. He had regretted using the scene and said he would remove it if he ever reissued the film.

Spielberg intentionally worked on *E.T.* and *Poltergeist* simultaneously in 1982 as a matched set. *E.T.* represented suburban dreams, and *Poltergeist*, suburban nightmares.

Look around Elliot's room and you'll find a menagerie of *Star Wars* toys. George Lucas paid back the compliment by featuring *E.T.*'s possessions in *Star Wars: Episode I* (1999).

The original story idea belonged to director John Sayles, but when he left the project the script was taken over by Melissa Mathison (Harrison Ford's ex-wife), who made it her own.

Though Michael Jackson recorded the theme song "Someone In The Dark," it was never used.

"Once a month the sky falls on my head, I come to, and I see another movie I want to make."
–Steven Spielberg

THE GREAT SCENE

Can love make you fly? Absolutely. All you need is a bicycle, an extraterrestrial to whom you're utterly devoted, and a bunch of insensitive scientists who are hunting him down. Up and away you go!

How to choose? Is it the scene where Elliot's mother looks into his closet filled with toys and among them we see a motionless E.T., blending perfectly with his stuffed-animal surroundings? Or is it the Halloween scene that features E.T. dressed as a ghost, allowing us to see the world through his eyes as he peeks through the holes in the sheet? Perhaps you cannot tear the image of those soaring, flying bicycles from memory? Any one you choose will do. They're all classics.

Gertie (Drew Barrymore) opens the closet door to discover E.T. among her stuffed animals. Unlike her mother, Gertie notices that he's not just another furry plaything.

60

INVASION OF THE BODY SNATCHERS 1956

SLEEPLESS IN SANTA MIRA

"Santa Mira was like any other town. People with nothing but problems," intones an unearthly calm shrink. "Love. Desire. Ambition. Faith. Without them, life's so simple, believe me." No, this is not a commercial for Prozac. The good doctor is trying to induce his friend Miles to just close his eyes so that an alien pod can take over his mind. It's a quietly chilling moment from one of the most effective paranoid thrillers of all time, a stripped-down cheapie that manages to get everything right. *Body Snatchers* is clearly a vehicle for quintessential '50s propaganda, a Red-baiting "doze at your own peril" Cold War alarm. But it manages to rise above the message and, like the aforementioned pods, take on a complete life of its own. With almost no special effects, director Don Siegel swiftly transforms a world of suburban normalcy into a realm of unimaginable horror, precisely because it's all done in the clear light of day, in a context as familiar (for the time) as Wheaties, Chevy coupes, and chain-smoking housewives.

Jim: That haunting image of a frenzied Kevin McCarthy standing in the middle of freeway traffic screaming "You're next! You're next!"–I don't think I would've given him a lift either.

Gail: No special effects were needed to make this paranoid vision of a world in which people are stripped of real feelings and, like lemmings, follow every convention. Totally terrifying.

THE PLOT

Small-town doctor Miles Bennell (Kevin McCarthy) is confronted by several patients who complain that their loved ones "don't seem right"; it's as if their emotions have been drained. While dining with his old flame, Becky (Dana Wynter), he gets a call from friends, Jack (King Donovan) and wife Teddy (Carolyn Jones), who've found a bizarre "pod clone" in the house. It's not quite alive and has no fingerprints. That night, on a hunch, he breaks into Becky's basement to find her pod clone. He carries Becky off, reunites with his friends, and concludes that they have some kind of alien menace on their hands. They must get word to the world outside Santa Mira. But it's too late for Jack and Teddy, who fall asleep and allow their minds to be absorbed by the pods. Miles and Becky make a run for it but the whole town is after them now. They take refuge in the hills and Miles can only pray that Becky will stay awake long enough to be rescued.

Running away from home takes on a terrifying slant when your hometown is running after you.

THE DIRECTOR

"I think so many people have no feeling about cultural things, no feeling of pain, of sorrow. I wanted to get it over and I didn't know of a better way to get it over than in this particular film." **Don Siegel** was most at home with straightforward stories, an embattled, isolated hero facing the despair of contemporary American life. His films aren't frilly with excess and he manages to establish characters quickly. A fine example is when Miles and Becky rush to the home of his writer friend Jack, who's found a dead-ringer clone lying on his pool table. The moment is bizarre, over the top, but with just a few lines of dialogue, all the relationships are immediately clear and very real. Siegel even manages to sneak in some wit while he's at it. His lean, stripped-down-to-essentials style is what drew the young Clint Eastwood to him and together, they made several films including *Coogan's Bluff* (1968), *Two Mules for Sister Sara* (1970), *The Beguiled* (1971), *Dirty Harry* (1972), and *Escape from Alcatraz* (1979). Eastwood said of his director mentor, "If there's one thing I learned from Don Siegel, it's to know what you want to shoot and to know what you're seeing when you see it." Siegel worked well with other Hollywood macho icons, too, including Steve McQueen in *Hell Is for Heroes* (1962), Lee Marvin in *The Killers* (1964), Charles Bronson in *Telefon* (1977), and John Wayne in his cinematic farewell, *The Shootist* (1976). Add to this list Bette Midler in *Jinxed!* (1982), a misstep that ended his career on a sour note, but didn't dim his reputation for hard-hitting, economic storytelling and throat-grabbing action.

THE CAST

Dr. Miles Bennell	Kevin McCarthy
Becky Driscoll	Dana Wynter
Dr. Dan Kauffman	Larry Gates
Jack Belicec	King Donovan
Teddy Belicec	Carolyn Jones
Nurse Sally Withers	Jean Willes
Police Chief Nick Grivett	Ralph Dumke
Wilma Lentz	Virginia Christine
Uncle Ira Lentz	Tom Fadden
Stanley Driscoll	Kenneth Patterson
Officer Sam Janzek	Guy Way
Anne Grimaldi	Eileen Stevens
Grandma Driscoll	Beatrice Maude
Eleda Lentz	Jean Andren
Jimmy Grimaldi	Bobby Clark
Dr. Ed Pursey	Everett Glass
Mac Lomax	Dabbs Greer
Baggage Man	Pat O'Malley
Restaurant Owner	Guy Rennie
Martha Lomax	Marie Selland
Charlie, the Meter Reader	Sam Peckinpah
Pod Carrier	Harry J. Vejar

BEHIND THE SCREEN

Sam Peckinpah served as dialogue director for the film, as well as playing a small role.

Producer Walter Wanger had just been released from prison, where he'd been serving a term for shooting the lover of his movie-star wife, Joan Bennett.

THE ACTORS

Kevin McCarthy's relatively brief career as a leading man led to character roles and cameos in nearly 100 films. (He was particularly memorable in a witty piece of casting—the 1978 remake of *Invasion of the Body Snatchers*.) Brother of the author Mary (*The Group*) and cousin of Presidential candidate Eugene, McCarthy received an Oscar nomination for *Death of a Salesman* (1951). Most of his films fall within the sci-fi/horror genres and are not particularly distinguished, but for the most part they have enjoyed popular success: highlights include *Piranha* (1978), *The Howling* (1981), and *Twilight Zone: The Movie* (1983).

Dana Wynter's cool British glamour makes her an odd choice as the love interest of a small-town doctor—which adds to the intriguing strangeness of the film. In the midst of their breathless escape on foot, she resembles nothing more than a royal princess clutching her cashmere sweater, and the strapless dress she wears in her first scene is worth the price of admission. Wynter enjoyed a B-movie career as a Hollywood contract-player, working in only a handful of films that are still familiar today, including *The List of Adrian Messenger* (1963) and *Airport* (1969).

The supporting cast is a veritable Who's Who of 1950s TV. You may recognize **Carolyn Jones** from *The Addams Family*; **Virginia Christine**, also known as "Mrs. Olsen" of Folgers Coffee commercial fame; and **Richard Deacon** from *The Dick Van Dyke Show*. And, in case you missed him, that's director **Sam Peckinpah** in the role of the meter reader.

THE REMAKE

The remake of *Invasion of the Body Snatchers* (1978) was directed by Phillip Kaufman, written by W. D. Richter, and was promoted with the tagline, "You'll never close your eyes again." It starred Donald Sutherland and Brooke Adams with honorary cameos by the original *Body Snatchers* director, Don Siegel, as a cab-driver, and Kevin McCarthy as "a running man" on the freeway. Rounding out the cameo cast are Leonard Nimoy as the all too suspiciously logical Dr. Kibner, and an uncredited Robert Duvall as "the priest on a swing." The location has been changed from little Santa Mira to cosmopolitan San Francisco, which, famous for its New Age movements and idiosyncratic cults, suits the theme perfectly. Richter's script gets plenty of solid laughs out of the fact that "being podded" is an elevation of the human spirit. One of its glassy-eyed adherents remarks, "Don't be trapped by old concepts." Formidable *New Yorker* critic, Pauline Kael, was one of its most ardent cheerleaders: "*Invasion of the Body Snatchers* (the remake) is more sheer fun than any movie I've seen since *Carrie* and *Jaws*."

CREDITS

Producer: Walter Wanger/ Allied Artists
Director: Don Siegel
Screenplay: Donald Mainwaring, from the novel by Jack Finney
Running time: 80 minutes
Budget: $300,000

THE YEAR'S ACADEMY AWARD WINNERS

Best Picture: *Around the World in 80 Days*
Best Director: George Stevens, *Giant*
Best Actor: Yul Brynner, *The King and I*
Best Actress: Ingrid Bergman, *Anastasia*
Best Supporting Actor: Anthony Quinn, *Lust for Life*

Nothing perks up a quiet evening at home more than finding a doppelgänger pod stretched out on your pool table. Miles and his friends are understandably curious.

Miles and Becky hide out in a mountain tunnel after having eluded the entire town of "pod people." They struggle to stay awake and therefore human, desperate for a bit of hope. They hear a beautiful aria in the air. Could real people be nearby? An exhausted Becky stays behind while Mile investigates. He finds only a pod farm with a blasting radio. He returns to find Becky slumped over. He picks her up, runs, then falls in the mud. He leans down for what will probably be their last kiss. He suddenly pulls away in horror. "I fell asleep, Miles." She's been transformed into one of them. In a mindless, droning voice, she entreats him to join her in her trouble-free new world. He won't—so she screams for the others. He's forced to run for his life—still hellbent on somehow saving the world.

LEFT: "I'm so tired." Miles makes the fateful decision to leave Becky for "just a minute." A lot of bad things can happen in a Santa Mira minute.

BELOW: "You're next!" This is one of the great iconic images of 1950s sci-fi. Kevin McCarthy reprised the scene in the 1978 remake to hilarious effect.

THE CRITICS

"One of the few authentic science fiction classics." —Andrew Sarris, *Village Voice*

"Tense, off-beat piece of science-fiction." —*Variety*

SEND IN THE CLONES

Village of the Damned (1960)

THE OTHER LISTS

- American Film Institute (No)
- Roger Ebert's Top 100 (No)
- *Entertainment Weekly* (Yes)
- Internet Movie Database (No)
- Leonard Maltin (No)
- *Movieline* (No)
- National Society of Film Critics (No)
- *Premiere* Magazine (No)
- *Rolling Stone* Magazine (Yes)
- *Village Voice* (No)

61

PINOCCHIO 1940

DON'T KNOCK WOOD

"A boy who won't be good, might just as well be made of wood." Pretty and soft-spoken as the Blue Fairy may be, she doesn't suffer fools. Though Pinocchio has only been alive for a moment and has no idea who, where, or what he is exactly, he's given the full drill on flesh-and-blood alchemy. If he doesn't prove himself to be courageous and true of heart, he'll remain nothing more than an adorable bit of "naughty" pine. After a quick song and dance with a cat, a fish, and his maker, Geppetto, he's trundled off to school in the company of an insect. And this is no private school with a fancy curriculum for the "specially challenged." In 1940, childhood was a sink-or-swim proposition. It's remarkable, then, how extraordinarily well *Pinocchio* has held up in the era of the pampered tot. How do concerned parents explain an old bachelor's burning desire for a little boy? Or the haphazard babysitting technique of a dandified cricket who oversleeps and allows his charge to be kidnapped by drunken "talent scouts"? While Pinocchio's days are fraught with danger, young viewers remain glued. They may have caught the film's subliminal message: Life without risk is a plastic imitation.

Jim: A classic from the days when animations were painstakingly conceived dreams rather than computer downloads. Story and characters aside, it's just so beautiful to look at.

Gail: The sheer visual delight of the animations themselves, the camera panning, zooming and dollying to give this film its sense of freedom and invention, holds up incredibly well—better, in many cases, than some of the best modern animation. And the characters, Jiminy Cricket most of all, earn their rightful place in our memories.

E PLOT

y old wood-carver Geppetto showers his tions on a kitten and a goldfish, all the dreaming of a son. He wishes upon a hat his latest creation, an adorable pup- could be human. Sure enough, Pinocchio his first breath of life, but the Blue Fairy s he must prove himself brave and true e full boyhood can be bestowed. To lead n the straight and narrow, she dubs our tor, Jiminy Cricket, his official conscience. tation awaits Pinocchio as he wends his o school. He's taken up by a sly fox and to a sideshow. The Blue Fairy appears asks him why he didn't do as he was told. os and his nose grows a bit. He proceeds another white lie and this time his nose hes out so far that a leafy branch with t of birds pops up. Pinocchio is horrified she warns him never to lie again. With his nose recedes and she rescues him ne time, but no more. Poor Pinocchio is again kidnapped and brought to Plea- sland, where bad boys are transformed onkeys. Thanks to Jiminy, he escapes in to save Geppetto, who's been swallowed whale. The Blue Fairy awards his efforts real" boyhood—but we know he's been ving like a real boy all along.

"When you wish upon a star" you just might wind up with a dynamic little cricket as a permanent houseguest. Jiminy narrates the tale of Pinocchio with all the panache of a "kid friendly" Noel Coward.

"WHAT?! You mean you take your orders from a grasshopper?"—Lampwick

THE CREATOR

A Missouri farmer's son and a true American original, **Walt Disney** turned a rodent into a king, a pumpkin into a coach, and a duck into a dear. He oversaw 81 features in his lifetime and, during the Depression, the Disney Studios were the only ones in Hollywood running in the black. His first major full-length animation, *Snow White and the Seven Dwarves*, caused a sensation in 1938 and earned him a specially designed Academy Award with seven little Oscars resting on a single base. A relentless perfectionist, he learned lessons from *Snow White* and applied them to *Pinocchio*, which was three years in the making. It required the efforts of 750 artists, 80 musicians, 1,500 shades of color, and one million drawings. *Pinocchio* was the first full-feature use of Disney's exclusive "multi-plane" camera, which tracked animation in the way other cameras track live action, providing a unique sense of depth and prospective. The exceptional success of these first two features led Disney to create *Fantasia* (1940), which he hoped would elevate American audiences with its mix of classical music and cartoon characters. It was his first flop and he stopped just short of disowning it. He apologized to the public and promised to do better next time. If not better, he certainly did it bigger. Among other things, there were two theme parks to come, one carved out of the walnut orchards of Anaheim, California, the other from stretches of Orlando palms. Among some of his most enduring features are *Dumbo* (1941), *Bambi* (1942), *Wind in the Willows* (1949) *The Legend of Sleepy Hollow* (1949), *Cinderella* (1950), *Davy Crockett* (TV series, 1954), *20,000 Leagues Under the Sea* (1954), *Zorro* (TV series, 1957), *Old Yeller* (1957), *The Swiss-Family Robinson* (1960), *The Absent-Minded Professor* (1961), and *Mary Poppins* (1964). Contrary to tabloid myth, Disney wasn't fast-frozen upon his death in 1966. He was cremated and interred in Los Angeles' cemetery to the stars, Forest Lawn.

"Heigh, diddle-de-dee," it's an actor's life for me!" J. Worthington Foulfellow tempts naive Pinocchio with the oldest come-on of all: overnight stardom. All singing, all dancing, no school!

THE CAST/VOICES

Pinocchio	Dickie Jones
Barker	Don Brodie
J. Worthington Foulfellow	Walter Catlett
Lampwick	Frankie Darro
Jiminy Cricket	Cliff Edwards
Stromboli/The Coachman	Charles Judels
Geppetto	Christian Rub
The Blue Fairy	Evelyn Venable

BEHIND THE SCREEN

There's a Web site exclusively devoted to reports of hidden Mickey Mouse images throughout *Pinocchio*.

After a brief stint as a child actor, mostly in Westerns, Dickie Jones, the voice of Pinocchio, became a banker and realtor.

Upon accepting his customized gold statuette for *Snow White* in 1938, Walt Disney was the first to refer officially to the Academy Award as "Oscar."

Disney's most revered creation, Mickey Mouse, first saw the light of day in 1928 in the animated "talkie," *Steamboat Willie*.

In 2002, Miramax released a live-action remake of *Pinocchio*, starring the Italian "Jerry Lewis," Roberto Benigni, as the (rather long-in-the-tooth) wooden boy. After it was completed, Benigni's voice had to be overdubbed as his Italian accent was too thick to understand. The film took a critical beating, and quickly made its way to video stores.

PARTICULAR PLEASURES

Keep one eye on the clock, or in this case, clocks. Geppetto's cozy little chalet is chockful of them, each a brilliant invention that comes with its own little story.

The underwater sequence allowed Disney's animation team to explore fantastical aquatic movement. Mildly terrifying demons and lush-tailed cuties of the deep are beautifully choreographed.

Arguably the most charming moment, and certainly the best song in *Pinocchio* is "I've Got No Strings," performed by the little-boy puppet shortly after he's sold to a traveling gypsy show. If you'd like to hear an alternative version, check out Barbra Streisand's fifth album, "*My Name Is Barbra*."

THE OTHER LISTS

- American Film Institute (No)
- Roger Ebert's Top 100 (Yes)
- *Entertainment Weekly* (No)
- Internet Movie Database (No)
- Leonard Maltin (No)
- *Movieline* (No)
- National Society of Film Critics (No)
- *Premiere* Magazine (No)
- *Rolling Stone* Magazine (No)
- *Village Voice* (No)

THE CRITICS

"A marvel and a joy to behold, it's the real thing. It's the stuff that dreams—and nightmares—are made of." —*TV Guide*

"*Pinocchio* is without a doubt the most passive and simple-minded of the Disney cartoon heroes." —Roger Ebert, *Chicago Sun-Times*

CREDITS

Producer: Walt Disney
Directors: Hamilton Luske, Ben Sharpsteen
Screenplay: Aurelius Battaglia, William Cottrell, Otto Englander, Erdman Penner, Joseph Sabo, Ted Sears, Webb Smith, from the book by Carlo Collodi
Running time: 88 minutes
Budget: $2.4 million
Box Office: $40.4 million

ACADEMY AWARDS

Best Music, Original Score: Leigh Harline, Paul J. Smith, Ned Washington
Best Song: "When You Wish upon a Star" Leigh Harline (music), Ned Washington (lyrics)

THE YEAR'S OTHER WINNERS

Best Picture: *Rebecca*
Best Director: John Ford, *The Grapes of Wrath*
Best Actor: James Stewart, *The Philadelphia Story*
Best Actress: Ginger Rogers, *Kitty Foyle*
Best Supporting Actor: Walter Brennan, *The Westerner*
Best Supporting Actress: Jane Darwell, *The Grapes of Wrath*

"A lie keeps growing and growing until it's as clear as the nose on your face."
—The Blue Fairy

A blooming proboscis is just one of poor Pinocchio's anatomical problems. On the not-very-pleasureable Pleasure Island, his mischievous behavior results in a pair of donkey ears. Luckily, his conscientious little friend Jiminy is on hand to help guide him toward "real boyhood."

Pinocchio is abducted and taken by speeding coach to Pleasure Island. He falls under the sway of the delinquent Lampwick, who instructs him in the singular joys of cigars, beer, and fistfights. The Island is a wonder of childish delights: rides, candy, even a model home ready for happy destruction. By night's end, all the other boys have vanished and Lampwick and Pinocchio must entertain themselves at the abandoned pool hall. Jiminy sneaks onto the Island to discover its terrible secret—all the naughty boys are turned into jackasses for work in the salt mines. He finds Pinocchio just as the horrified puppet-boy sprouts long ears, a tail, and a hee-haw.

Pinocchio manages to trick Monstro "the Great Whale" into exhaling Gepetto and crew from his belly. Monstro isn't happy about missing a meal and pursues our little hero with a vengeance.

62

SHADOW OF A DOUBT 1943

BLOOD RELATIONS

Hitchcock's personal favorite is an extraordinary war film that never once mentions the war. The story is a metaphor for evil coming home to roost among the unwary, a clarion call to those who believe that if they just cover their ears and eyes to the most repugnant aspects of human nature, they will be spared. Of course it is a murder story as well—and the real victim is homespun, red-white-and-blue innocence. It's a perverse and perfect touch that the master of psychological terror would choose Thornton Wilder as his storyteller, the author of that quintessential American portrait, *Our Town*. But, on close inspection, Wilder's work has a bittersweet edge, a sadness that life isn't quite how we want it to go. What better way to get things rolling than with a restless but naive young girl-next-door longing for something a bit dangerous to spark up her safe little life. A visit from her namesake Uncle Charlie, the debonair gentleman with tailored pockets jammed with cash, a taste for fine champagne, and a scandalous wit is just the ticket. If only he had a conscience to go with it all. His familial visit is nothing more than a last hideout before the authorities close in. His lovely young niece, longing for excitement, will get far more than she bargained for. Like her country, on the precipice of the worst years of the war to come, she finally sees the truth. She awakens from her dream to see a living nightmare and is, ironically, empowered at last. Unlike most of Hitchcock's beleaguered heroines, she learns just in time how to fight back. After that, whatever happiness she can find, she has earned.

Jim: There's always something else going on with Hitchcock besides the plot. An uneasiness about the world, as if it might betray us at any minute. Even his rare happy endings make you wonder if they're even possible.

Gail: Hitchcock tramples our dreams of idyllic small-town life and then goes after our longing for glamorous escape from its doldrums. It's the mischievous director at his most psychologically adept.

THE PLOT

Dapper serial widow killer Charlie Oakley (Joseph Cotten) escapes an East Coast dragnet and hightails it to his sister's home in sleepy Santa Rosa, California. He charms the unwary locals but something boils beneath the surface. His namesake niece, Young Charlie (Teresa Wright), is suspicious when he blows a fuse while discoursing on the world's inherent evil. A detective (Macdonald Carey) tracks Charlie down but needs proof to arrest him. He asks Young Charlie for help and she grudgingly agrees, hoping he's wrong. Uncle Charlie is on to her and plots to kill her. She bravely suggests he leave town instead. She'll give him time to get a jump on the law. He hops on a departing train and pulls her up with him. As he attempts to toss her off at high speed, he slips and is killed instead. Santa Rosa gives him a hero's funeral, unaware of his true identity.

"He didn't trust people. Seemed to hate them. He hated the whole world." But adoring older sister Emma (Patricia Collinge) refuses to see the murderous truth in the face of her visiting brother Charlie (Joseph Cotten).

"Hitchcock considered this to be his finest American movie and he may have been right." –Pauline Kael

THE DIRECTOR

"The camera lies, you know, and when it does, you have to accommodate it." **Alfred Hitchcock** was one of the first directors to understand how vital the camera is to storytelling. He had no interest in simply filming a rehearsed scene with prosaic reaction shots. In the library scene in which Young Charlie discovers her uncle's murderous past while perusing the newspaper, Hitchcock's written direction calls for the camera to react like "a sharp intake of breath." He even penned some of the dialogue. In Uncle Charlie's blistering, psychotic ramble about the rich widows who "eat and drink their money," the director added his own colorful description of them as "horrible, faded, fat greedy women." Considered Hitchcock's first true American film, he loved *Shadow of a Doubt* best because of the familial atmosphere generated by cast, crew, and townsfolk. It didn't hurt that the location was the epicenter of California wine country and Hitchcock, at 300 pounds, was a connoisseur of all fine things edible and potable. (For more on Hitchcock, see pages 30, 54, 85, and 106.)

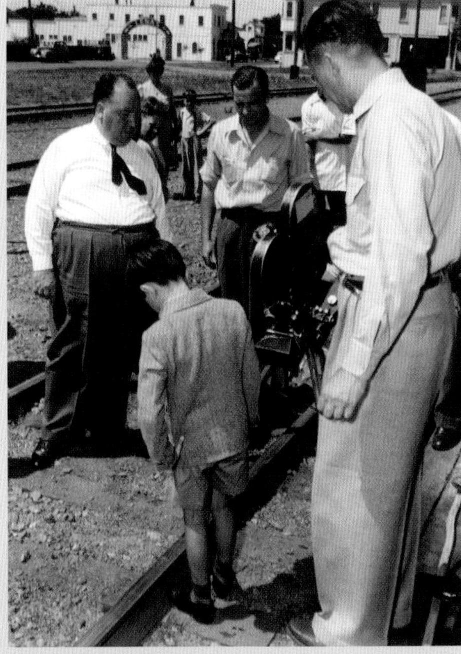

"Man does not live by murder alone. He needs affection, approval, encouragement, and, occasionally, a hearty meal," quipped the mighty Hitchcock. He had ballooned to 300 pounds by the time he wrapped *Shadow of a Doubt*. He was delighted by the shooting location, the heart of California's wine country.

THE CAST	
Charles "Uncle Charlie" Oakley	Joseph Cotten
Charlotte "Charlie" Newton	Teresa Wright
Emma Newton	Patricia Collinge
Joseph Newton	Henry Travers
Ann Newton	Edna May Wonacott
Detective Jack Graham	Macdonald Carey
Herbie Hawkins	Hume Cronyn

"Well, if I was gonna kill you, I wouldn't do a dumb thing like hitting you on the head. First of all, I don't like the fingerprint angle."
–Herbie Hawkins

THE ACTORS

With disarming modesty **Joseph Cotten** claimed, "I didn't care about the movies, really. I was tall. I could talk. It was easy to do." One of our best, if underappreciated character actors, he delivers handsomely in this rare leading role. It was his only outing as a villain and he clearly relished the opportunity. Hitchcock was a great admirer and enjoyed Cotten's off-camera personality that could, by turns, be erudite and hilariously caustic. There's an extraordinary moment in this film when the camera slowly zooms in on his face as he gives his "greedy widows" speech. The wholesome facial planes grow more severe, the affable eyes take on a hooded-cobra glint. It's as if he's allowing the camera to enter the dark side of his soul. The 1940s were remarkable for Cotten, who appeared in seminal films including *Citizen Kane* (1941), *The Magnificent Ambersons* (1942), *Gaslight* (1944), *Duel in the Sun* (1946) and *The Third Man* (1949). What followed was a busy but less than stellar career, primarily in B westerns and TV guest spots.

"I only ever wanted to be an actress, not a star." **Teresa Wright** made sure of that by refusing to pose for cheesecake studio shots. Her career took off with an unprecedented roar, and she scored Academy Award nominations for her first three movies: *The Little Foxes* (1941), *Mrs. Miniver* (1941), and *The Pride of the Yankees* (1941). She took home the Supporting gold for *Miniver* and, after a bit of a lull, came back in 1946 with *The Best Years of Our Lives*. She remembered meeting Hitchcock in his office and having him lay out the entire story of *Shadow of a Doubt* for her. "I was mesmerized. The final film, almost shot by shot, was exactly the way he told it to me that day." Wright wasn't content with playing the role of Young Charlie as written, fearing that her character's relationship with Macdonald Carey's detective was just too "boy meets girl." Along with Patricia Collinge, who played her mother, she rewrote the romantic scene in the garage, during which the two never touch.

BEHIND THE SCREEN

The inspiration for *Shadow of a Doubt* was Earle Leonard Nelson, the real-life "Merry Widow Murderer" of the 1920s.

The movie includes a twin motif. There are two Charlies, two detectives, a bar named "Til Two" and two scenes apiece that take place at the dinner table, in the garage, at the railroad station, and at church. There are even two wine toasts.

Hume Cronyn's turn as Herbie Hawkins, the nerdy murder-obsessed neighbor, marked his film debut.

The owners of the house Hitchcock selected for the film were so thrilled, they had it gussied up and painted. Just what the director didn't want. His crew had to return it to the slightly dilapidated quality he'd been drawn to.

Hitchcock was quick to take advantage of a lucky break from nature. As Uncle Charlie's train pulls into Santa Rosa station, the lighthearted scene with skipping children and dappled sun is briefly overshadowed by a dark cloud.

ROLE REVERSALS

Hitchcock's first choice for Uncle Charlie was the dapper William Powell and, for Young Charlie, his *Rebecca* star, Joan Fontaine.

SEND IN THE CLONES

Charade (1963)
Blue Velvet (1986)
Sleeping with the Enemy (1991)
The Last Seduction (1994)

NOTABLE QUOTES

"Do you know the world is a foul sty? Do you know if you rip the fronts off houses you'd find swine? The world's a hell. What does it matter what happens in it?" –Uncle Charlie

"Go away, I'm warning you. Go away or I'll kill you myself. See . . . that's the way I feel about you." –Young Charlie

CREDITS

Producer: Universal
Director: Alfred Hitchcock
Screenplay: Gordon McDonell, Thornton Wilder
Running Time: 108 minutes

ACADEMY AWARD NOMINATIONS

Original Screenplay: Gordon McDonell, Thornton Wilder

THE YEAR'S OTHER WINNERS

Best Picture: *Casablanca*
Best Director: Michael Curtiz, *Casablanca*
Best Actor: Paul Lukas, *Watch on the Rhine*
Best Actress: Jennifer Jones, *The Song of Bernadette*
Best Supporting Actor: Charles Coburn, *The More the Merrier*
Best Supporting Actress: Katina Paxinou, *For Whom the Bell Tolls*

The clock is always set at 2:00 at the 'Til Two bar, where young Charlie experiences the shocking realization that her uncle has a horrible secret life.

THE OTHER LISTS

- American Film Institute (No)
- *Entertainment Weekly* (No)
- Internet Movie Database (No)
- Leonard Maltin (No)
- *Movieline* (Yes)
- *Premiere* Magazine (No)
- Roger Ebert's Top 100 (No)
- *Rolling Stone* Magazine (No)
- *Village Voice* (No)

THE GREAT SCENE

Young Charlie runs out of the house, unable to control her secret knowledge of her Uncle Charlie's homicidal madness any longer. He chases after her, pulls her into a sleazy bar to lay out the macabre facts of life. "You live in a dream and I've brought you nightmares," he tells her as he grips her wrists. Her face is a map of terrified awakening. She's in the company of a monster. Pure evil has entered her safe little universe and, for the first time, she knows what real fear feels like.

WHERE'S THE HITCH?

When he made *Shadow of a Doubt*, Hitchcock had not yet become known for his cameo appearances. He shows up about fifteen minutes into the film, playing cards in the train's bar car. In his next feature, *Lifeboat*, he appears 80 pounds lighter, as a "before and after" photo in a newspaper ad. From that point on, he made sure that his cameos came early in his films, so as not to distract audiences from the suspense. By then they'd caught on and made a game out of looking for him.

Some of Hitchcock's more creative appearances include being pushed through an airport in a wheelchair in *Topaz* and winding a clock in *Rear Window*. He had a special fondness for musical instruments as props: *In Strangers on a Train*, he struggles to get a double bass on board; he ambles along with a violin case in *Spellbound*; and he lugs a cello in *The Paradine Case*. While he appears early on in *North By Northwest* as a harried New Yorker who's just missed his bus, there are those who swear he pops up later on—in drag—onboard a train.

Teresa Wright was a rare brunette in the pantheon of Hitchcock blondes. The only actress to be nominated for an Academy Award for each of her first three films, Wright got top billing over the veteran star, Joseph Cotten. Her last appearance before her death in 2005 was in John Grisham's *The Rainmaker*.

63

FARGO 1996

NORTHERN EXPOSURE

Like the blinding snow into which every shot seems to disappear, *Fargo* keeps you wondering where it's going. Just when you think this is a mundane but bloody crime thriller the camera turns its lens on the private life of the pregnant chief of police, Marge (Frances McDormand), and it turns into a celebration of quotidian married life. What you'll see when the windshield wipers clean off the snow is that the substance of this film can be viewed in the details—comic, savage, and, dare we say it, loving. Yes, more attention is paid to the color of the sock on a human leg that is slowly being eaten by a wood chipper than to any plot twist, but what really makes you stop and say, "Yah, this is some special film," is that, beneath it's jaundiced take on small-town life, there's a lot of heart. Like when Marge encourages her teddy-bear husband that his bird painting on a three-cent stamp is more important than a regular stamp because "whenever they raise the postage, people need the little stamps."—Yah, that's love.

Jim: The Coens' *"film blanc"* masterwork tells us what greed and too much snow can do to people. Aside from committing murder, it can make them hysterically funny.

Gail: This movie tricks you into falling in love—a little—even as you're repulsed by degenerate killers and doubled over with laughter at the "Thanks a bunch, and yah sure, you betcha" Minnesotans.

a film by
Joel & Ethan Coen
Fargo
a
homespun
murder
story

[TH]E PLOT

[A]round incompetent car salesman Jerry [Lund]egaard (William H. Macy) is in serious [deb]t. He hatches an ill-fated plan to have [his w]ife kidnapped in order to extort ransom [mon]ey from her wealthy, tightwad businessman [fath]er, Wade (Harve Presnell). Before long, [inno]cent people are killed by the bumbling, [Frida]y *the 13th*-style, hired killers (Steve Bus[cem]i and Peter Stormare). Enter the cheerful, [una]ssuming, very pregnant, and very smart [Mar]ge Gunderson (Frances McDormand), the [local] police chief. She handles everything [with] understated aplomb, gently criticizing her [not]-too-bright partner: "I'm not sure I agree [with] you 100 percent on your police work [ther]e, Lou." In between sharing meals with her [hus]band and picking up some night crawlers [for h]is fishing trip, she takes time out to hunt [dow]n the killer, trekking knee deep in snow, [takin]g weather reports from the "How ya doin'" [neigh]bors, and interrogating a very rude Lun[dega]ard—"Sir, you have no call to get snippy [with] me." When he goes missing during an in[tervi]ew, she follows his tracks to the killers just [as o]ne of them is being consumed by a wood [chip]per and the other tries, unsuccessfully, to [esca]pe across a vast wasteland of ice. At the [end] of the day, Marge and Norm settle down in [bed i]n front of the TV and exchange pleasant[ries] just as cozy as a pair of fluffy slippers.

Straight-shooting and very pregnant policewoman Marge Gunderson (Frances McDormand) pursues clues to the whereabouts of two murderers the way one might wonder where one put his or her car keys.

"And I guess that was your accomplice in the woodchipper." –Marge Gunderson

THE DIRECTOR

Though **Joel** usually gets the credit for directing all of the **Coen Brothers** films, it is common knowledge that both he and **Ethan** direct, write, produce, and edit all of their films together, winning them the sobriquet "The Two Headed." And the "Roderick Jaynes" always credited with editing doesn't even exist. In *Fargo*, the brothers went back to their home state of Minnesota to capture the climate (cold) and the people (ordinary and nonplussed), but also to infuse *Fargo* with something their other films lack: warmth and heart. It all began with *Blood Simple* (1984), whose genre-bending sounded a wake-up call for all cinephiles. Many films followed: *Miller's Crossing* (1990), *Barton Fink* (1991), *The Hudsucker Proxy* (1994), *The Big Lebowski* (1998), *O Brother, Where Art Thou?* (2000), *The Man Who Wasn't There* (2001), and the Oscar-winning *No Country for Old Men*.

As dumb as his blue hood, Jerry Lundegaard (William H. Macy) does everything he can to mess up his own nefarious plans. His hired kidnappers turn out to be psycho killers; his father-in-law hates him and gets killed as the scheme unfolds; and all Lundegaard can do by way of comforting his young son is to send him up to his room. When one of the killers questions him about their arrangement, he stutters, "Well, that's, that's, I'm not gonna go inta, inta–See, I just need money."

THE CAST	
Marge Gunderson	Frances McDormand
Jerry Lundegaard	William H. Macy
Carl Showalter	Steve Buscemi
Wade Gustafson	Harve Presnell
Gaear Grimsrud	Peter Stormare
Jean Lundegaard	Kristin Rudrüd
Scotty Lundegaard	Tony Denman
Norm Gunderson	John Carroll Lynch

THE ACTORS

When **Frances McDormand** explained her casting in Coen Brothers' films by saying, "The fact that I'm sleeping with the director may have something to do with it," she was only telling half of the tale. The other part of the story is that she's a gifted actress able to knit herself seamlessly into each role. McDormand made her debut in *Blood Simple* (1984), and followed up with *Raising Arizona* (1987), and *Miller's Crossing* (1990). She wandered out on her own and earned herself an Oscar nomination for *Mississippi Burning* (1988), which led to roles in *The Butcher's Wife* (1991), *Lone Star* (1996), *Paradise Road* (1997), *Almost Famous* and *Wonder Boys* (both 2000), *The Man Who Wasn't There* (2001), *Laurel Canyon* (2002), and *Miss Pettigrew Lives for a Day* (2008).

William H. Macy should have nailed an Oscar for the performance of a lifetime as Jerry, the hapless husband and father . . . and procurer of murderers. It's therefore unthinkable that he had to beg the directors for the role. When the Coens didn't get back to him after two readings, the actor with the Howdy Doody face flew to New York and said, "I'm very, very worried that you are going to screw up this movie by giving this role to somebody else. It's my role, and I'll shoot your dogs if you don't give it to me." Macy had appeared on stage regularly in David Mamet's plays. In *Fargo*, he takes a totally spineless, colorless, dull, almost invisible character and makes his desperation into a force field as palpable as that of the outrageous killers he hires. Macy has appeared in such films as *The Client* (1994), *Mr. Holland's Opus* (1995), *Ghosts of Mississippi* (1996), *Boogie Nights* and *Wag the Dog* (both 1997), *A Civil Action* (1998), *Magnolia (1999)*, *Door to Door* (2002), *The Cooler* (2003), and *Thank You for Smoking* (2005).

Before finding his way to the screen, **Steve Buscemi** was trying to start fires on stage as an actor and a stand-up comedian, and put them out as a real-life firefighter. Fortunately, he put down his hose and his microphone and made his way to *Fargo* to play the role of a demented criminal who lacks the ability to shut up and spends most of the film bleeding from a hole in his cheek. Buscemi has appeared in the Coens' *Miller's Crossing* (1990), *Barton Fink* (1991), *The Hudsucker Proxy* (1994), and *The Big Lebowski* (1998). His face and performances have stood out from the rest in many films, including *Billy Bathgate* (1991), *Reservoir Dogs* (1992), *Things to Do in Denver When You're Dead* and *Somebody to Love* (both 1995), *The Wedding Singer* (1998), *Big Daddy* (1999), *Ghost World* (2001), and *The Island* (2006).

Discovered by Ingmar Bergman and borrowed from one Swedish winter-hinterland for another, **Peter Stormare** plays the silent but evil "desperado" to chilling effect. Stormare began his acting career at the Royal National Theatre of Sweden and acted in many Shakespeare plays as well as serving as the Associate Artistic Director at the Tokyo Globe Theatre. Since his role in *Fargo* he has appeared in *The Lost World: Jurassic Park* (1997), *The Big Lebowski* (1998), *8mm* (1999), *Chocolat* (2000), *Dancer in the Dark* (2000), and *Minority Report* and *Windtalkers* (both 2002).

CREDITS

Producer: Ethan Coen/ Gramercy Pictures
Director: Joel Coen, Ethan Coen (uncredited)
Screenplay: Joel Coen, Ethan Coen
Running Time: 95 minutes
Budget: $7 million

ACADEMY AWARDS

Best Actress: Frances McDormand
Best Screenplay: Ethan Coen, Joel Coen

NOMINATIONS

Best Picture
Best Supporting Actor: William H. Macy
Best Cinematography: Roger Deakins
Best Director: Joel Coen
Best Film Editing: Ethan Coen, Joel Coen

THE YEAR'S OTHER WINNERS

Best Picture: *The English Patient*
Best Director: Anthony Minghella, *The English Patient*
Best Actor: Geoffrey Rush, *Shine*
Best Supporting Actor: Cuba Gooding Jr., *Jerry Maguire*
Best Supporting Actress: Juliette Binoche, *The English Patient*

THE OTHER LISTS

American Film Institute (No)
Entertainment Weekly (No)
Internet Movie Database (No)
Leonard Maltin (Yes)
Movieline (No)
National Society of Film Critics (Yes)
Premiere Magazine (No)
Roger Ebert's Top 100 (Yes)
Rolling Stone Magazine (Yes)
Village Voice (No)

THE CRITICS

"*Fargo* begins with an absolutely dead-on familiarity with small town life in the frigid winter landscape of Minnesota and North Dakota. Then it rotates its story through satire, comedy, suspense, and violence, until it emerges as one of the best films I've ever seen. To watch it is to experience steadily mounting delight, as you realize the filmmakers have taken enormous risks, gotten away with them, and made a movie that is completely original, and as familiar as an old shoe." –Roger Ebert, *Chicago Sun-Times*

"All the main players are perfect, but *Fargo* isn't." –Kim Williamson, *Box Office Magazine*

"Nobody became an actor because he had a good childhood."
–William H. Macy

BEHIND THE SCREEN

Because spring was approaching and the snow kept melting, filming of outdoor scenes had to be constantly moved across Minnesota, North Dakota, and Canada.

In the kidnappers' cabin, Bruce Campbell, who appeared in *The Hudsucker Proxy*, can be seen on the fuzzy TV screen.

Though the credits indicate that the film is "based on a true story," it is not.

When working on her Minnesota accent for the film, Frances McDormand worked with Larissa Kokernot, who played Hooker #1. McDormand referred to her accent and mannerisms as "Minnesota Nice."

With the exception of *The Hudsucker Proxy* (1994), Steve Buscemi ends up dead in every Coen Brothers' film, and with each death his remains get smaller. Only part of his leg is left intact after being "wood-chipped."

Though it's called *Fargo*, none of the movie was shot there.

Norm's competition for the duck stamps—the Hautmans—are three real brothers who frequently win federal and state wildlife stamp competitions.

NOTABLE QUOTES

"Most women's pictures are as boring and as formulaic as men's pictures. In place of a car chase or a battle scene, what you get is an extreme closeup of a woman breaking down. I cry too, maybe three times a week, but it's not in closeup. It's a wide shot. It's in the context of a very large and very mean world." –Frances McDormand

Carl Showalter (Steve Buscemi) walks around most of the film with half of his cheek blown off—and he was "kinda funny-looking" before. But it isn't the quality of life that matters to Carl, it's the money. His relationship with his increasingly psychotic partner, Gaear Grimsrud (Peter Stormare) begins to disintegrate as plans go awry.

Police chief Marge questions two strippers who had apparently been hired to service the killers. Her deadpan questioning and the hooker's equally deadpan but stupid answers are classic examples of the film's humor. Marge asks the hooker what the men looked like. "Well, the little guy, he was kinda funny-looking," one of them replies. How so, asks Marge trying to get her to be a little more specific. All she can come up with is, "I couldn't really say. He wasn't circumcised." Pressing on, Marge asks if the woman can tell her more. In that same, sleepy deadpan she replies, "No. Like I say, he was funny lookin'. More n' most people even." Marge responds to the useless information: "Oh you betcha, yah."

Isn't it romantic? Marge congratulates her husband Norm (John Carroll Lynch) when his bird painting is selected for the three-cent stamp. When he complains that it's such an unimportant stamp, Marge encourages him saying, "Whenever they raise the postage, people need the little stamps."

64

BLUE VELVET 1986

LISTENING WITH YOUR INNER EAR

A bright red fire truck sails in slow motion down the street as a fireman waves it on. Children float across, led by loving crossing guards. The whole town is saturated in hyperrealistic light and color. Clean-cut Jeffrey (Kyle MacLachlan) finds a crack in its facade when he discovers a severed ear on a back road. The temptation to determine its source leads him to the dark side of town, where attraction and repulsion, perversion and love live side by side. David Lynch's fever dream, though it pushes the limits of the palatable, is deeply affecting in its honesty, and, yes, its innocence. How strange and terrifying is the adult world to the child who is seeing it for the first time? Lynch explores this using his own kind of visual poetry. Thank-yous ought to go to Lynch from Quentin Tarantino and the Coen brothers for freeing them to go where no mainstream filmmakers had ever gone before.

Jim: Those who find this too weird forget what country they're living in. But if certain scenes get too intense for you, just shut your eyes and hide under Kyle MacLachlan's chin.

Gail: The Hardy Boys meet the Marquis de Sade in this visually and aurally overheated, overripe, and overreal journey into the nexus between the normal and the profane.

THE PLOT

It's a typical day in sunny Lumberton when Jeffrey Beaumont (Kyle MacLachlan) returns home to visit his sick father. He encounters a severed ear on his path and he follows it to the wilder side of the white picket fence. Along with his new girlfriend, Sandy Williams (Laura Dern), the prettiest girl in town and the daughter of the police detective on the case, Jeffrey finds that beneath the daytime facade lurks a world of fetishism and violence. Initiated into the dark side, as a voyeur to the rape of nightclub singer Dorothy Vallens (Isabella Rossellini) by the menacing, nitrous oxide-sniffing Frank Booth (Dennis Hopper), who is holding her child and her earless husband hostage in the apartment of a transvestite pimp, Jeffrey ultimately makes everything right. And with that, Sandy's vision of the "Blinding Light of Love" shines once again over the neighborhood. But still something's not exactly right with the scene.

Nice guy Jeffrey Beaumont (Kyle MacLachlan) trips over a severed ear on a back road and takes a walk on the wilder side of sexuality. While attempting to protect the fragile Dorothy Vallens (Isabella Rossellini), who is threatened by a psycho killer holding her family hostage—and who has her own ideas about lovemaking—Jeffrey finds himself a little thrilled by the knife.

"It's a strange world. Isn't it?" —Sandy Williams

THE DIRECTOR

Growing up in Montana, in a town not unlike Lumberton, **David Lynch** spent a lot of time wandering in the woods, observing—and enjoying—his surroundings. "It was a dream world, with a blue sky, planes droning overhead. There were fences, green grass, cherry trees . . . But on the cherry tree, there's this pitch oozing out—some black, some yellow. Meals seemed to last five hours and naptime seemed endless." Lynch's world was not too far a cry from Lumberton. It's the "ooze," this sense of violated innocence, that possesses his film. This is the primal stuff from which Lynch's art springs. A painter, Lynch became interested in film while in art school. His first feature, *Eraserhead* (1978), established him as a brilliant young stylist. He later made *The Elephant Man* (1980) and the disappointing *Dune* (1984), then went on to win the prize at the Cannes Film Festival for *Wild at Heart* (1990). With the surreal TV series *Twin Peaks* (1990), he achieved cult status and inspired many HBO shows to come. His comedy series *On the Air* (1992) was less successful.

Girl-next-door Sandy Williams (Laura Dern), whose detective father is now looking for the source of the severed ear, falls for Jeffrey. Though she devoutly believes in a bright and beautiful world, she can't deny—or resist—her curiosity about the dark, mysterious world below.

THE CAST	
Dorothy Vallens	Isabella Rossellini
Jeffrey Beaumont	Kyle MacLachlan
Frank Booth	Dennis Hopper
Sandy Williams	Laura Dern
Mrs. Williams	Hope Lange
Ben	Dean Stockwell

THE ACTORS

"I've got to play Frank. Because I am Frank!" insisted **Dennis Hopper** when other actors found the character too loathsome. Hopper's c.v. reads like something off the police blotter. From the start Hopper, once a child actor, was banned from the MGM lot when he responded aggressively to Louis B. Mayer, who didn't cotton to him playing Shakespearean roles. A natural rebel, Hopper appeared in *Rebel Without a Cause* (1955) and *Giant* (1956), both of which starred James Dean, whom he considered a mentor. Throughout the 1970s Hopper was a notorious drinker and drug user. He was arrested once when he was found ranting and naked in the street. Many of his roles at that time, including those in *The Trip* (1967) and *Apocalypse Now* (1979), fit the psycho part. But Hopper also turned in fine performances in *The American Friend* (1977), *Hoosiers* (1986), and *Flashback* (1990). He was nominated for an Oscar for the latter two films. In the real world Hopper was a player in the pop art scene as a collector and a published photographer. (For more on Hopper, see page 60.)

Isabella Rossellini is the subject of the film's most humiliating moments. The glamorous, beautiful daughter of Ingrid Bergman (whom she closely resembles) and director Roberto Rossellini had the remarkable courage to wander—unglamorously—naked over a suburban front lawn. She became an actress after a successful modeling career, and made her debut performance in *A Matter of Time* (1976), followed by *White Nights* (1985). She and director Lynch were lovers for several years and appeared together in *Zelly and Me* (1988). After making *Blue Velvet*, Rossellini continued to choose offbeat, unflattering roles in independent pictures, with the exception of *Cousins* (1989), a misguided remake of the French comedy *Cousin, Cousine* (1975). Her other films include *Siesta* and *Tough Guys Don't Dance* (both 1987), and she teamed up with Lynch again in his harrowing *Wild at Heart* (1990). Among her later works are *Death Becomes Her* (1992) and *Fearless* (1993). She was briefly married to director Martin Scorsese.

One could consider **Kyle MacLachlan** an alter ego for the young Lynch. There's a kindred feeling between actor and director as witnessed by MacLachlan's starring roles in most of Lynch's work, including *Dune* (1984), *Twin Peaks: Fire Walk with Me* (1992), and the television series, *Twin Peaks*, originated by Lynch and Mark Frost. He also appeared in *Rich in Love* (1993), *The Flintstones* (1994), and *Showgirls* (1995), and appeared in HBO's hit series *Sex and the City*. He dated Laura Dern after their romantic turn in *Blue Velvet*.

"It's really fun to act like a bimbo. But it's fun to act like a bimbo only when people know that you really aren't one," says **Laura Dern**, who was a natural for the soft-focus part of the innocent, pretty, blond next door with a subtle taste for the lower depths. The daughter of Bruce Dern and Diane Ladd, Dern has a gift for showing the greater dimensionality behind her virginal looks. Dern went over to the wild side in Lynch's *Wild at Heart* (1990), in which she played a much looser cannon. Among her always-quality performances are such films as *Alice Doesn't Live Here Anymore* (1974), *Foxes* (1980), *Mask* and *Smooth Talk* (both 1985), *Rambling Rose* (1991), and *Jurassic Park* and *A Perfect World* (both 1993).

BEHIND THE SCREEN

"No one wanted to touch it with a ten-foot barge pole," said Paul D. Sammon, group vice president, De Laurentiis Entertainment, referring to the distributors. "The film was looked at as a freak, and I don't think David ever knew."

Woody Allen called it the best movie of 1986. It was the same year his own *Hannah and Her Sisters* won three Academy Awards.

CREDITS

Producer: Fred C. Caruso/
Dino De Laurentiis
Director: David Lynch
Screenplay: David Lynch
Budget: $6 million
Box Office: $8.6 million

ACADEMY AWARD NOMINATIONS

Best Director

THE YEAR'S WINNERS

Best Picture: *Platoon*
Best Director: Oliver Stone, *Platoon*
Best Actor: Paul Newman, *The Color of Money*
Best Actress: Marlee Matlin, *Children of a Lesser God*
Best Supporting Actor: Michael Caine, *Hannah and Her Sisters*
Best Supporting Actress: Dianne Wiest, *Hannah and Her Sisters*

THE OTHER LISTS

American Film Institute (No)
Roger Ebert's Top 100 (No)
Entertainment Weekly (Yes)
Internet Movie Database (No)
Leonard Maltin (No)
Movieline (Yes)
National Society of Film Critics (No)
Premiere Magazine (Yes)
Rolling Stone Magazine (Yes)
Village Voice (No)

Primal bliss with Dorothy (Isabella Rossellini) is just a few inhalations away—or so Frank (Dennis Hopper) hopes. Dorothy better hope so, too—since Frank is holding her family prisoner in the next room.

THE GREAT SCENE

In perhaps the most unnerving scene in the movie, Jeffrey and Dorothy find themselves in an apartment where her family is being held hostage. In the filthy, overlit drug den, a hyped-up pimp, Ben (Dean Stockwell), a friend of Frank's, is dressed up like some kind of clown/game-show-host-in-heat, complete with mascara, lipstick, and an unlit cigarette in an elegant holder. His ghoulish presence engages the terrible tension between desire and repulsion to which the whole film has been alluding. As he leans seductively against a wall he lip-syncs Roy Orbison's "In Dreams," his face freakishly lit by the eerie, surreal light from the mechanic's lamp he uses as a microphone. Several feet away, Frank stands listening with a kind of childish desperation for . . . comfort? Pleasure? We don't know what he's looking for, but he's clearly not finding it. As a result he becomes increasingly agitated; though he tries in every twisted way he can, Frank cannot be gratified.

The original, four-hour version contains a scene in which Jeffrey watches a date rape at a college dance. He does nothing until he is heard by the rapist and then, to protect himself, yells, "Hey shithead. Leave her alone."

THE CRITICS

"This is American darkness—darkness in color, darkness with a happy ending. Lynch might turn out to be the first populist surrealist—a Frank Capra of dream logic." —Pauline Kael, *The New Yorker*

"Plotless, pretentious, and putrid."
—Michael Medved, *Previews*

ROLE REVERSALS

Val Kilmer turned down the role of Jeffrey, calling the film "pornography." According to the actor, once he saw the screen version, he wished he'd taken the part.

Molly Ringwald, who was originally offered the role of Sandy, had to turn it down after her mother objected to the movie's graphic content.

"I'm not a real film buff. Unfortunately, I don't have time. I just don't go. And I become very nervous when I go to a film because I worry so much about the director and it is hard for me to digest my popcorn."
—David Lynch

"You're a neat girl," says Jeffrey to Sandy (Laura Dern), who represents the bright world where all is simple and pure. But it is the dark and scary underworld that both Jeffrey and Sandy are inexorably drawn to. They do manage to make it back to the sun . . . for a while, anyway.

65

JAWS 1975

RATTLING THE FOOD CHAIN

When it comes down to it, this one really isn't about a shark. Except for the occasional flash of a tail fin, we don't even see the beast until the last third of the movie. What *Jaws* deals with, what imbues the narrative with such relentless suspense, is the primordial fear we bring to it. Those phantom terrors that lurk beneath the surface, that are too elusive to control. Steven Spielberg gets as much bang for the buck, perhaps more, in the scenes that don't involve the shark. There's a moment on the beach when Police Chief Brody is scanning the water for any sign of the monster. The sight of an old man's gray cap jolts us as much as anything. *Jaws* was the first summer blockbuster, a season previously confined to the release of schlock B movies. It transformed the way Hollywood did business, to say nothing of the way it transformed beach-going. Coastal resorts and concessions lost a fortune even as Universal raked it in.

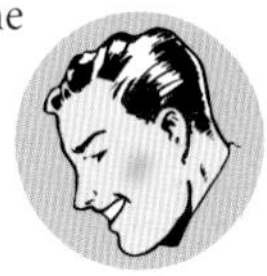

Jim: Note the prim morality of the opening scene: casual sex on the beach, a drunken swim and chomp, chomp, gulp. This one may have set the moral standard for teen-slasher films to come. "Bad girls" are the first to die and they always die painfully.

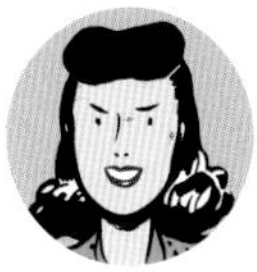

Gail: Spielberg knows how to build a story and, once again, he doesn't disappoint. By the time we get to the best scenes (on the boat), we're prepped and hungry for the worst. And we get it good.

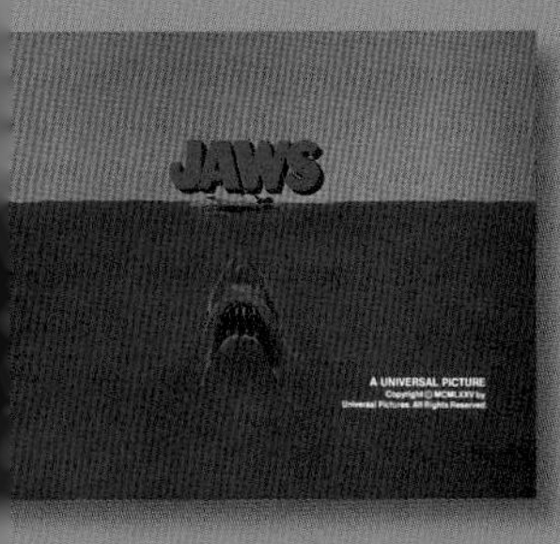

IE PLOT

.yville Island, Massachusetts, relies almost ely on summer beach tourism. When e Chief Brody (Roy Scheider) suspects al girl has been killed by a shark, sleazy or Vaughn (Murray Hamilton) orders a r-up. But another attack on the crowded h ignites a media frenzy and Vaughn is d to offer a bounty. Grizzled old shark er Quint (Robert Shaw) comes forward, bes young marine biologist Matt Hooper hard Dreyfuss). Despite Brody's fear of r, he and Matt head out to sea with Quint nt down the man-eating Great White. t entertains them with the skin-crawling of a World War II carrier that sank in in- d waters, and how his many shipmates me lunch to dozens of circling sharks. morning, Brody is the first to get a look at monster, and he realizes that they may not early well enough equipped. But Matt has sed a special underwater blind to draw his in safely. The shark seems infuriated by 's disrespect and makes quick work of the aption, nearly killing him in the process. oard, Quint taunts the beast who quite lly takes the bait until there's nothing f the grisly old hunter but a screaming ory. With the boat sinking and the shark hungry, Brody had better think fast. He es up with a plan that allows for only one ect shot." If he can pull it off, he and Matt aved. If not . . .

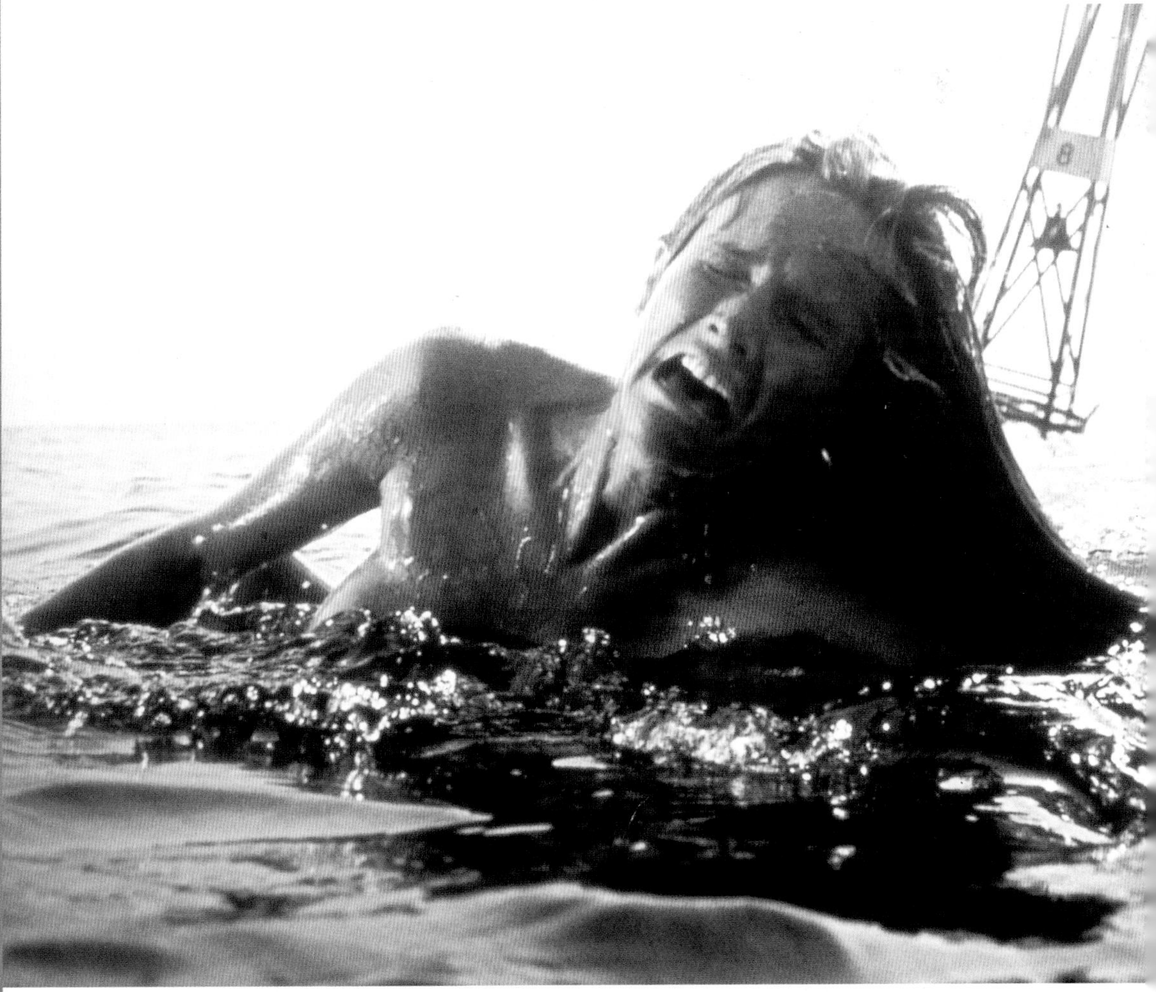

"God help me!" In what is probably the most terrifying "woman in jeopardy" moment on film since *Psycho*, a lascivious midnight swim will be the last for blonde man-bait Chrissie (Susan Backlinie). She desperately rings the buoy bell for help—then it all goes deathly quiet.

"We're going to need a bigger boat."—Brody, after getting his first look at the behemoth

THE DIRECTOR

"When I think of *Jaws*, I think of a period when I was younger than I am now. I think because I was younger I was more courageous or more stupid—I'm not sure which. So when I think of *Jaws*, I think of courage and stupidity, with both things existing underwater." When he first read the book, **Steven Spielberg** was reminded of his early film *Duel* (1971), in which a beleaguered motorist on a lonely road is pursued by a sadistic, faceless trucker. He agreed to direct *Jaws* on the condition that the shark wouldn't appear for at least the first hour. "I really wanted this movie to be shot at water level, the way we are when we're treading water." Some of the inventive shots he used here to ratchet up our anxiety level (the unique lighting of fog, for example) reappeared in many of his later films, whose box-office successes elevated him to Hollywood royalty. Among his remarkable hits are *Close Encounters of the Third Kind* (1977), *Raiders of the Lost Ark* (1981), *E.T.* (1982) Oscar-winner *Schindler's List* (1993), *Jurassic Park* (1993), *Saving Private Ryan* (1998), and *Minority Report* (2002). (For more on Spielberg, see pages 88, 103, 136, 190 and 289.)

A day at the beach with some bite to it, thanks to a mechanical Great White shark dubbed "Bruce."

THE CAST	
Chief Martin Brody	Roy Scheider
Quint	Robert Shaw
Matt Hooper	Richard Dreyfuss
Ellen Brody	Lorraine Gary
Mayor Larry Vaughn	Murray Hamilton
Ben Meadows	Carl Gottlieb
Deputy Lenny Hendricks	Jeffrey Kramer
Chrissie Watkins	Susan Backlinie
Cassidy	Jonathan Filley
Estuary Victim	Ted Grossman
Mike Brody	Chris Rebello
Sean Brody	Jay Mello
Mrs. Kintner	Lee Fierro
Alex M. Kintner	Jeffrey Voorhees
Ben Gardner	Craig Kingsbury

THE ACTORS

Roy Scheider, Oscar nominee for *The French Connection* (1971), ran into Spielberg at a party, expressed his fascination for the story of *Jaws*, and suggested himself for the role of Chief Brody. The director agreed that he'd be perfect. He was the only star of the original to appear in the less-than-comparable sequel. He made far more of an impression in *Marathon Man* (1976) and in his signature role as the choreographer Bob Fosse in *All That Jazz* (1979). Another law enforcement role came with *Blue Thunder* (1983), followed by *The Men's Club* (1986), *The Russia House* (1990), the exquisitely bizarre adaptation of William Burroughs' *Naked Lunch* (1991), John Grisham's *The Rainmaker* (1997), the TV series *Third Watch* (1999), and *Citizen Verdict* (2003).

Two walk-on appearances in 1967, in *The Graduate* and *Valley of the Dolls*, couldn't have prepared audiences for the stardom that was to come for **Richard Dreyfuss**. He made his first real impression in *American Graffiti* (1973), then revealed his flair for obnoxious charismatics in *The Apprenticeship of Duddy Kravitz* (1974). At 29 he was one of the youngest Best Actor Oscar winners for *The Goodbye Girl* (1977), and followed up in another Spielberg sensation, *Close Encounters of the Third Kind* (1978). Despite the occasional personal scandal involving drugs and car wrecks, he's rarely been far from camera range. His last, most popular role was the title character in *Mr. Holland's Opus* (1995). (For more on Dreyfuss, see pages 88 and 253.)

The classical British actor/playwright **Robert Shaw**, star of Oscar-winner *A Man for All Seasons* (1966), will forever be remembered as Quint, the over-the-top, blustering con man of the sea. Shaw, who died in 1978, wasn't particularly proud of that fact. "*Jaws* was a story written by a committee. A piece of s**t!" he insisted. Just before his death, he appeared in *Black Sunday* and *The Deep* (both 1977).

BEHIND THE SCREEN

Jaws nearly derailed Spielberg's career, thanks to budget overruns. It took three mechanical sharks, each dubbed Bruce (the name of Spielberg's lawyer), before the techies got it right. The first one sank and the mouth of the second wouldn't open.

Susan Backlinie, who plays the ill-fated Chrissie, suffered more than a few aches and pains after being pulled from side to side by 300-pound weights to simulate the tugging and chomping of the "shark."

The palpable tension between Robert Shaw and Richard Dreyfuss in their scenes together was easy for them to muster. Shaw had taken an instant dislike to the feisty young actor and made his feelings quite well known.

Serious overruns and mishaps had the grumbling film crew ready to jump ship. Spielberg was so exhausted after completing the final shot, he hopped into a departing speedboat and shouted "I shall not return!"

THE MUSIC

John Williams composed the most successful seven notes in the history of film. The five belonging to the "alien call" from *Close Encounters* and the two-note "shark theme" cello-and-bass scrapes from *Jaws*. His opening notes for *Star Wars* were affectionately borrowed from *Psycho*.

THE CRITICS

"One of the most effective thrillers ever made." —Roger Ebert, *Chicago Sun-Times*

"It doesn't help that this particular facsimile (the shark) looks like a foam-rubber pillow with the zipper open."—*Village Voice*

CREDITS

Producer: Richard D. Zanuck, David Brown/Universal
Director: Steven Spielberg
Screenplay: Peter Benchley, Carl Gottlieb, based on Benchley's novel
Running time: 124 minutes
Budget: $8.5 million
Box Office: $260 million

ACADEMY AWARDS

Best Music, Original Score: John Williams
Best Film Editing: Verna Fields
Best Sound: Robert L. Hoyt, Roger Heman Jr., Earl Mabery, John R. Carter

NOMINATION

Best Picture

THE YEAR'S OTHER WINNERS

Best Picture: *One Flew Over the Cuckoo's Nest*
Best Director: Milos Forman, *One Flew Over the Cuckoo's Nest*
Best Actor: Jack Nicholson, *One Flew Over the Cuckoo's Nest*
Best Actress: Louise Fletcher, *One Flew Over the Cuckoo's Nest*
Best Supporting Actor: George Burns, *The Sunshine Boys*
Best Supporting Actress: Lee Grant, *Shampoo*

Brody, Quint, and Matt set their traps for the shark, bracing themselves for the vindictive monster that lies in wait. They settle in for the night, sharing a bottle of brandy below deck as Quint recounts his horrifying tale of war. He was aboard the ill-fated *Indianapolis* that delivered the A-bomb to Japan. En route home, it was sunk and more than 1,100 men were cast into the water: "Didn't see the first shark for about half an hour, a tiger, thirteen-footer. So we formed ourselves into tight groups . . . the idea was, the shark comes to the nearest man and he starts poundin' and hollerin' and screamin'. Sometimes the shark goes away. Sometimes he wouldn't go away. Sometimes that shark, he looks right into ya, right into your eyes. Y'know, the thing about a shark, he's got lifeless eyes, black eyes, like a *doll's* eyes. When he comes after ya, he doesn't seem to be livin' until he bites ya, and those black eyes roll over white, and then—aww, then you hear that terrible high-pitched screamin', the ocean turns red, and in spite of all the poundin' and the hollerin', they all come in and rip ya to pieces . . . in that first dawn, we lost a hundred men."

THE OTHER LISTS

- American Film Institute (Yes)
- Roger Ebert's Top 100 (No)
- *Entertainment Weekly* (Yes)
- Internet Movie Database (Yes)
- Leonard Maltin (Yes)
- *Movieline* (No)
- National Society of Film Critics (No)
- *Premiere* Magazine (Yes)
- *Rolling Stone* Magazine (Yes)
- *Village Voice* (No)

THE GREAT SCENE

Quint (Robert Shaw) shows off a few physical mementos of his past tangles with sharks. His harrowing tale of the SS *Indianapolis* is based on fact. The inspiration for *Jaws* was a real-life incident on the New Jersey Shore in the summer of 1916.

"You open the beaches on the 4th of July, it's like ringing the dinner bell for Chrissakes." Brody and Matt try to shout some sense into the corrupt little mind of sleazeball Mayor Vaughn. The local graffiti artists seem to have found a way to "edify" the tourists.

ROLE REVERSALS

Jaws author Peter Benchley wanted the most obvious blockbuster box-office casting, including Robert Redford, Paul Newman, and Steve McQueen. Spielberg had his heart set on Lee Marvin for "Quint." When he passed, it was offered to Sterling Hayden but Hayden was already in hot water with the IRS, which would've taken a serious bite out of his acting income. He wanted Spielberg to pay him as a writer in order to avoid the mess but that sounded much too risky. Shaw was in.

NOTABLE QUOTES

"I drink too much. Will you tell me one great actor who doesn't drink?" —Robert Shaw

"I don't think film acting is necessarily a triumph of technique. Film stardom is a friendship that happens between an audience and a performer. It's like you meet someone and you click with that person for whatever reason."—Richard Dreyfuss

SEND IN THE CLONES

Mako: The Jaws of Death (1976)
Tintorera . . . Bloody Waters (1977)
Tentacles (1977)
Piranha (1978)
Jaws 2 (1978)
Killer Fish (1979)
Crocodile (1981)
Jaws 3-D (1983)
Jaws: The Revenge (1987)

66

THE GRAPES OF WRATH 1940

HOME OF THE BRAVE

"I been thinking about our people living like pigs and good, rich land layin' fallow. Or maybe one guy with a million acres and a hundred thousand farmers starvin'. And I been wonderin' if all our folks got together and yelled . . ." says a hungry and angry Tom Joad (Henry Fonda), whose tenant-farming family—along with thousands of others, both in the film and in reality—was chased from its home by banks and land agents during the Depression and the Dust Bowl drought. Though *The Grapes of Wrath* was based on the Pulitzer Prize-winning novel by John Steinbeck—and Hollywood never saw an important, best-selling book it couldn't love—it's still difficult to imagine how a film that is in spirit socialist (albeit directed by a Republican) was produced by an industry that was terrified by the union movement. Nevertheless, those hungry egos starved for significance brought us one of the most important and poetic documentary-style renderings of a terrible chapter in American history. *Wrath* is one of the most beautiful films ever made. Every frame is masterfully composed, though each one depicts unimaginable poverty and abuse. Its evocative use of black-and-white (though color was available) is reminiscent of the work of the period's great still photographer of migrant laborers, Dorothea Lange. Many scenes are set in darkness, with faces outlined by the light of a flickering candle; its stirring performances and its straightforward portrait of the injustices committed against broken yet courageous people put this one into the time capsule.

Jim: A high-minded treatment of utter desolation. While it leaves out some of the most shocking scenes in the novel, it could serve as a mission statement for the radical left. If you can get past Jane Darwell's terribly proper elocution (about as Okie as Greer Garson), you'll find her heart and emotions in the right place.

Gail: There are many movies here, each imbued with a powerful pathos for the lives it recounts: one, a straightforward, cruel Depression story; two, a sentimental story of the working American's basic goodness and triumphant spirit; three, an epic drama about the death of the American agrarian class and its transition to a new frontier.

THE PLOT

The laconic Tom Joad (Henry Fonda), just released from jail for committing "HOME-i-cide," hitches a ride home to find nothing but darkness and a wailing wind, everyone gone save the half-crazed ex-preacher Casy (John Carradine), and Muley (John Qualen), a neighbor deranged from the trauma of surrendering his land. Seems the Depression and the Dust Bowl have left all the tenant farmers in Oklahoma penniless, and the banks and land trusts have bulldozed everything in sight. Tom finds his way to his family and together they pile all their possessions onto a huge jalopy of a truck. Half keeled over with people and mattresses, the improbable vessel heads out for California. Flyers sent to thousands of hungry migrant laborers have promised work. Their journey is a tale of life in Hoovervilles littered with humans, trash, and barking dogs, of discrimination, starvation, and corrupt cops, and of exploitation by wealthy farmers who employ workers in exchange for a pittance. Some renegades without families strike and attempt to organize for better wages, and lose their lives in the process. Maintaining hope against all reason, the Joads travel down Route 66 in this fallen Eden of California and unwittingly land in a government-sponsored agricultural colony run by a benign, FDR-like caretaker who gently points them to showers, bathrooms, clean cabins, and the Saturday night dance. At the point when they seem most stable, Tom, who has already broken his parole, is tracked down by the police and must leave the bosom of his family and escape to places unknown.

Just released from prison, Tom Joad (Henry Fonda) finds ex-preacher Casy (John Carradine) at the side of the road near his family's abandoned home. Casy tells him of the poverty and hunger resulting from the Depression and the Dust Bowl drought, and how the bankers and land agents have appropriated everyone's home and chased them off the land, including the Joads. Tom determines to find them.

THE DIRECTOR

It is supremely ironic, but not inexplicable, that **John Ford**, a confirmed Republican, would make a film with socialist leanings (though his Ma Joad does question the welfare system, wondering whether it would do more harm than good to feed the hungry children in the Hooverville in which the Joads are camped). But there are many messages in Ford's epic. His directorial maxim that "the main thing about directing is photographing the people's eyes" was preeminent in this film. Best known for his magisterial Westerns, Ford won Best Director Oscars for *The Informer* (1935), *How Green Was My Valley* (1941), and *The Quiet Man* (1952). He snubbed the Academy on this one and told reporters, "I love making pictures, but I don't like talking about them, for as long as the fish are biting." (For more on Ford, see page 73.)

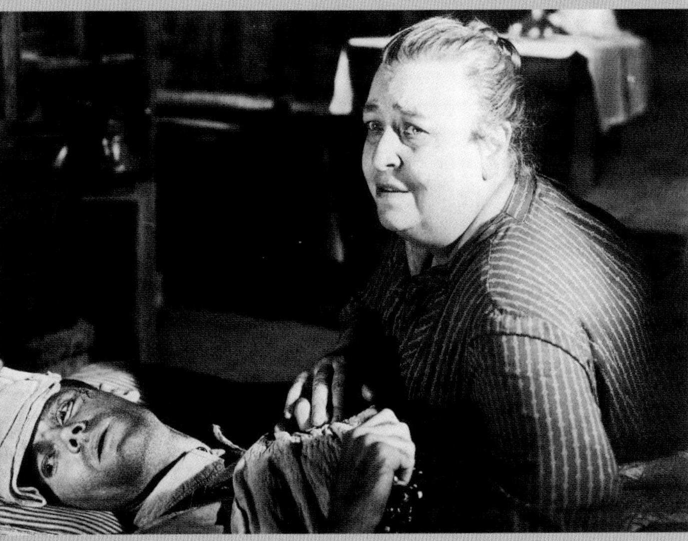

Earning a Best Supporting Actress Award for her earthy, heartfelt performance as Ma Joad, Jane Darwell plays an archetypal Mother Courage, concerned about the fortunes of her family while at the same time inspiring them with her integrity and grit. Here she comforts Tom who, wounded, has escaped after a group of migrant workers attempting to organize for a living wage were attacked by henchmen for the landlords.

THE CAST

Tom Joad	Henry Fonda
Ma Joad	Jane Darwell
Casy	John Carradine
Grandpa	Charley Grapewin
Rose of Sharon	Dorris Bowdon
Pa Joad	Russell Simpson
Al	O. Z. Whitehead
Muley	John Qualen
Connie	Eddie Quillan
Grandma	Zeffie Tilbury
Noah	Frank Sully
Uncle John	Frank Darien
Winfield	Darryl Hickman
Ruthie	Shirley Mills
Bert	Ward Bond
Bill	William Pawley

THE ACTORS

In one of his richest and most defining performances, **Henry Fonda**'s is a portrait of a spirit in transition. With his pent-up anger as an unmercifully harassed Okie, he begins to learn about fighting back, only this time without his fists. His face registers great depths of emotion and a mind at war with injustice. His slow, almost motionless gait is unmistakable; and his arms seem to dangle from his sides as if he hasn't yet figured out how to use them. The greatest injustice here—and it would take decades to right it—was that he didn't grab the Oscar for this one. His was a brilliant career in which his characters—and he—were always identified with a level of integrity that Fonda himself questioned, including classic westerns and dramas such as *Drums Along the Mohawk* and *Young Mr. Lincoln* (both 1939), *The Ox-Bow Incident* (1943), *My Darling Clementine* (1946), *Fort Apache* (1948), and, later, *Mister Roberts* (1955), *12 Angry Men* and *The Wrong Man* (both 1957), and *Fail-Safe* (1964). Not as celebrated but equally gifted in comedic roles, particularly in *The Lady Eve* (1941), Fonda could play deadpan comedy and execute pratfalls with the best of them. His later years brought disappointing roles but he went out victorious, finally winning his outrageously delayed Oscar for the crotchety gramps in *On Golden Pond* (1981). (For more on Fonda, see page 235.)

Jane Darwell was so identified with her role that she said, "I've played Henry Fonda's mother so often that, whenever we run into each other, I call him 'son' and he calls me 'Ma', just to save time." Darwell's Ma Joad is one of the great populist Mother Earth heroines of film, and she played her with a heart as big and bounteous as her body, winning herself an Academy Award for her effort. It was the crowning achievement of a 50-year screen career, during which she appeared in more than 200 movies. Darwell made her Hollywood debut in *Huckleberry Finn* (1931), and continued in feature roles in *The Scarlet Empress* (1934), *All That Money Can Buy* (1941), *My Darling Clementine* (1946), and *There's Always Tomorrow* (1956).

"I got nothin' to preach about no more, that's all. I ain't so sure of things," says the haunted ex-preacher Casy, played with Shakespearean intensity by **John Carradine**. In organizing workers, Casy finds the spirituality he's lost, and is murdered for it. Carradine worked virtually nonstop in scores of films, including many of John Ford's classics, among them, *Stagecoach* and *Drums Along the Mohawk* (both 1939), and *Captains Courageous* (1937). With his gaunt face and glaring eyes, he was built for such horror films as *Dracula in the House of Frankenstein* (1944), and *House of Dracula* (1945). His later, more distinguished films, include *The Last Hurrah* (1958), *Cheyenne Autumn* (1964), *The Last Tycoon* and *The Shootist* (both 1976), *The Howling* (1981), and *Peggy Sue Got Married* (1986). David, Keith, and Robert, three of his sons, have also become familiar faces on the big screen.

ROLE REVERSALS

The original cast called for Beulah Bondi as Ma Joad, James Stewart as Al, and Walter Brennan as Pa Joad.

BEHIND THE SCREEN

Had there been another chapter to the novel, it would tell the story of how the children of the landless migrant workers would become among the richest Americans. These fortunate sons and daughters were on the scene just

CREDITS

Producer: Darryl F. Zanuck
Director: John Ford
Screenplay: Nunnally Johnson
Running Time: 128 minutes

ACADEMY AWARDS

Best Actor: Henry Fonda
Best Supporting Actress: Jane Darwell
Best Director: John Ford

NOMINATIONS

Best Picture
Best Film Editing: Robert L. Simpson
Best Sound, Recording: Edmund H. Hansen
Best Writing, Screenplay: Nunnally Johnson

THE YEAR'S OTHER WINNERS

Best Picture: *Rebecca*
Best Actor: James Stewart, *The Philadelphia Story*
Best Actress: Ginger Rogers, *Kitty Foyle*
Best Supporting Actor: Walter Brennan, *The Westerner*

THE OTHER LISTS

American Film Institute (Yes)
Roger Ebert's Top 100 (Yes)
Entertainment Weekly (Yes)
Internet Movie Database (Yes)
Leonard Maltin (Yes)
Movieline (No)
Premiere Magazine (No)
Rolling Stone Magazine (No)
Village Voice (No)

as California began to reap the riches of the war industry.

Because there was strong resentment of Steinbeck's book among people who didn't want their stories told, the filmmakers had to disguise the nature of the film they were making. Since much of the film was made on location—particularly the drive down Route 66—locals were told the film was an innocuous romance called *Highway 66*.

THE CRITICS

"*The Grapes of Wrath* is just about as good as any picture has a right to be; if it were any better, we just wouldn't believe our eyes."
—Frank S. Nugent, *New York Times*

"The movie version is full of 'They can't keep us down, we're the people,' sort of thing, and a viewer's outrage at the terrible social injustices the film deals with is blurred by its gross sentimentality. This famous film, high on most lists of the great films of all time, seems all wrong—phony when it should ring true . . ."
—Pauline Kael, *The New Yorker*

NOTABLE QUOTES

"I am not a very interesting person. I haven't ever done anything except be other people. I ain't really Henry Fonda! Nobody could be. Nobody could have that much integrity."
—Henry Fonda

"I've made some of the greatest films ever made—and a lot of crap, too."
—John Carradine

"I'm not that pristine pure, I guess I've broken as many rules as the next feller. But I reckon my face looks honest enough and if people buy it, Hallelujah." —Henry Fonda

"Wherever there's a fight so hungry people can eat, I'll be there," says Tom to his mother in a moving and oft-quoted farewell speech. In violation of his parole, Tom must flee into the night—he sees that police have already been sniffing around his cabin. Mother and son have no idea where or whether they will ever see each other again. The scene may be a bit stagey, but thanks to to the penetrating performances it still hits very real notes of pain and courage under brutal circumstances.

Tom is forced to leave once the police track him down for his parole violation. The farewell scene between Tom and Ma is famously powerful. Having been radicalized by the inhumanity he has witnessed, particularly the murder of Casy for organizing the workers, Tom's final words to her speak of the unity. Unfortunately, his speech rings hollow. Nevertheless, the entire scene, like several others between Tom and his mother, is stirring. This ending is far more optimistic than that of the novel. Tom:

"Well, maybe it's like Casy says: A fella ain't got a soul of his own, just a little piece of a big soul—the one big soul that belongs to ever'body. Then . . . then, it don't matter. I'll be all around in the dark. I'll be ever'where—wherever you can look. Wherever there's a fight so hungry people can eat, I'll be there. Wherever there's a cop beatin' up a guy, I'll be there. I'll be in the way guys yell when they're mad—I'll be in the way kids laugh when they're hungry an' they know supper's ready. An' when the people are eatin' the stuff they raise, and livin' in the houses they build—I'll be there, too."

"It's a good picture. It's meaty and down-to-earth. But I think it needs a happier ending."
—Darryl F. Zanuck

Ma Joad (Jane Darwell) throws the last remnants of her home into the fire before the family sets off to try their luck in California. The sharp-edged lighting is a hallmark of this visually breathtaking film.

67

DO THE RIGHT THING 1989

WAKE UP!

Why doesn't the movie theater just blow up into a race riot? All of the tension is there in Sal's Pizzeria in Bedford-Stuyvesant, where everyone who comes in for a slice is black and every photo on the wall is white (and where the boss is cheap with the cheese). Director Spike Lee conducts this politically explosive film as if it were a symphony, with each character playing his part. It is by turns angry, funny, and touching—a latter-day fable of life among the disenfranchised. The soundtrack—which is a character in itself—is, by turns, an original, gentle folk opera (à la Aaron Copland), a loud rant from a boom box, and a series of pop and jazz riffs. The cinematography is beautifully theatrical, bathed in bright, warm hues and full of inventive, abrupt cuts and in-your-face close-ups. Did middle-class Lee have the right to explore the 'hood even though he didn't come from it? Is his ultimate message a violent or a peaceful one? There are questions raised here as never before: smartly, originally, and provocatively.

Jim: With his unique spin and fearless theatricality, Lee is about as close as it comes to an inner-city Orson Welles on a budget.

Gail: Good-natured, disturbing, provocative, and full of rage, this is a beautifully scored, ingeniously shot, and intelligently directed film that started a new African-American cinema.

E PLOT

emperature's rising on the streets of ord-Stuyvesant on the hottest day of the and the locals escape to the corner pizze-uggin' Out (Giancarlo Esposito) demands Sal (Danny Aiello) replace the white faces e wall of his shop with black ones. The cuts away to take us on a tour through the , introducing us to the members of the ly peaceful community, including Mookie e Lee), Sal's delivery boy who, though mannered, knows he's in a dead-end job; layor (Ossie Davis), an old drunk who's ryin' to make it through the day and do e good; Radio Raheem (Bill Nunn), who ts himself with the help of his blasting n box; Mister Señor Love Daddy (Samuel ckson), the local deejay who watches the ts from his window while spinning records commenting on the scene; Smiley (Roger veur Smith), a retarded boy who wanders treets selling the only photograph ever of Martin Luther King Jr. and Malcolm X her; and three middle-aged men who, like Greek chorus, spend their days sitting r an umbrella observing the comings and s of the neighborhood. Buggin' Out chal-s Sal with a boycott one sweltering night everyone in town is looking for comfort in izzeria. The tension builds and Mookie fi-throws a garbage can through the window. lace is looted and set ablaze.

With the temperature on the thermometer and in the community nearing the danger zone, Da Mayor (Ossie Davis, left), the street's conscience, argues with Mookie (Spike Lee), the pizza delivery boy, about the growing tensions in the neighborhood.

THE DIRECTOR

"I've been blessed with the opportunity to express the views of black people who otherwise don't have access to power and the media. I have to take advantage of that while I'm still bankable." Politically outspoken filmmaker **Spike Lee** took the film world by storm and gave birth a new African-American cinema. After making an acclaimed student short, *Joe's Bed-Study Barbershop: We Cut Heads*, Lee was able to amass enough money to finance his first feature, *She's Gotta Have It* (1986). With his second film, *School Daze* (1988), Lee was already receiving major studio backing. *Do the Right Thing*, which followed, was controversial not only for its subject matter but because Lee, a graduate of Morehouse College, was not sufficiently "street" (he made no mention of drugs in the film), but rather a middle-class black man talking about a life he didn't lead. He went apolitical for his next film about jazz, *Mo' Better Blues* (1990), and followed it with an interracial love story, *Jungle Fever* (1991); a biography, *Malcolm X* (1992); a family portrait, *Crooklyn* (1994); a crime drama, *Clockers* (1995); and an ambitious statement about crime and punishment, *The 25th Hour* (2003). Lee has also served as producer on *Drop Squad* (1994), and *New Jersey Drive* and *Tales from the Hood* (both 1995).

Sal's Pizzeria seemed a peaceable kingdom until somebody complained about the absence of any black faces on the walls. Before the tensions, Vito (Richard Edson, far left) was a friend to delivery-boy Mookie; and Sal (Danny Aiello, center) saw himself as the nice guy who had fed everyone since they were babies. But Pino (John Turturro, far right) was a racist from the start: "I detest this place like a sickness," he says in one of his many rants.

THE CAST

Sal	Danny Aiello
Da Mayor	Ossie Davis
Mother Sister	Ruby Dee
Vito	Richard Edson
Buggin' Out	Giancarlo Esposito
Mookie	Spike Lee
Radio Raheem	Bill Nunn
Pino	John Turturro
ML	Paul Benjamin
Coconut Sid	Frankie Faison
Jade	Joie Lee
Officer Ponte	Miguel Sandoval
Officer Long	Rick Aiello
Clifton	John Savage
Mister Señor Love Daddy	Samuel L. Jackson
Tina	Rosie Perez
Smiley	Roger Guenveur Smith
Ahmad	Steve White
Cee	Martin Lawrence

THE ACTORS

Danny Aiello, who wrote much of his own dialogue for the film, performs with an admirable subtlety; we feel both his love and his anger toward his clientele. Aiello's has become a familiar face as a cop, gangster, and working-class Italian. He made his screen debut in *Bang the Drum Slowly* (1973), and went on to make such prominent films as *The Godfather, Part II* (1974), *The Front* (1976), *Bloodbrothers* (1978), *Fort Apache, The Bronx* (1981), *Once Upon a Time in America* (1984), *The Purple Rose of Cairo* (1985), *Radio Days* (1987), and *Moonstruck* (1987). His more recent films have been less notable, among them, *Mistress* (1991), *Sicilian Code* (2000), and *Dinner Rush* (2001).

A legend in his own time, **Ossie Davis** earned the right to play Da Mayor, the voice of peace and goodwill on the streets of the 'hood, having been a leader in the civil rights movement. He joined Martin Luther King Jr.'s crusades and later eulogized Dr. King and Malcolm X at their funerals. As a playwright, Davis wrote and directed *Escape to Freedom: The Story of Young Frederick Douglass*, *Langston*, and the acclaimed *Purlie Victorious*. He later wrote the screenplay for and directed the film *Cotton Comes to Harlem* (1970), and appeared in Lee's *School Daze* (1988), *Jungle Fever* (1991), and *Malcolm X* (1992), as well in *Grumpy Old Men* (1993) and many other films and TV miniseries. Davis was married to actress Ruby Dee, with whom he made the TV series *Ossie and Ruby!* in 1980.

Ruby Dee's Mother Sister sits in her window complaining about the scene and giving Ossie Davis a hard time. Before making her big Broadway debut in *Anna Lucasta*, Dee performed with the American Negro Theatre in the 1940s. With few roles for black women in film, Dee managed to debut in *No Way Out* (1950), and continued on to play roles in *The Jackie Robinson Story* (1950), *Edge of the City* (1957) and *Jungle Fever* (1991). She was Oscar-nominated for *American Gangster* (2007).

This film marked the debut of **Rosie Perez** as Tina, the in-your-face, screechy-voiced girlfriend of Mookie. (She also dances under the film's opening credits.) She went on to appear in *Night on Earth* (1991), *White Men Can't Jump* (1992), *Fearless* (1993, Academy Award nomination), *It Could Happen to You* (1994), *Riding in Cars with Boys* (2001), and *Human Nature* (2002).

John Turturro as Pino is the high-tempered racist who serves as the nerve center of the film. Schooled in the theater, Turturro has carved an eccentric place for himself in such films as *Raging Bull* (1980), *Desperately Seeking Susan* (1985), *The Color of Money* (1986), *Mo' Better Blues* (1990), *Barton Fink* (1991), *Jungle Fever* (1991), *Quiz Show* (1994), *O Brother, Where Art Thou?* (2000), and *Collateral Damage* (2002).

Samuel L. Jackson is deejay and observer Mister Señor Love Daddy, perhaps the cooooolest character in Lee's film. Like Lee, Jackson graduated from Morehouse College, but was briefly suspended after taking several members of the board of trustees hostage. Jackson paid his Hollywood dues appearing in small roles in *Coming to America* (1988), *Sea of Love* (1989), and *GoodFellas* (1990). He worked with Lee in *School Daze* (1988), *Mo' Better Blues* (1990), and *Jungle Fever* (1991). He has played major roles in *Amos & Andrew* and *National Lampoon's Loaded Weapon 1* (both 1993), *Pulp Fiction* (1994), *Freedom Land* and *Snakes On a Plane* (both 2006). (For more on Jackson, see page 310.)

CREDITS

Producer: Spike Lee/Universal
Director: Spike Lee
Screenplay: Spike Lee
Running Time: 126 minutes
Budget: $6.5 million
Box Office: $27.5 million

ACADEMY AWARD NOMINATIONS

Best Supporting Actor: Danny Aiello
Best Original Screenplay: Spike Lee

THE YEAR'S WINNERS

Picture: *Driving Miss Daisy*
Director: Oliver Stone, *Born on the Fourth of July*
Actor: Daniel Day-Lewis, *My Left Foot*
Actress: Jessica Tandy, *Driving Miss Daisy*
Supporting Actor: Denzel Washington, *Glory*
Supporting Actress: Brenda Fricker, *My Left Foot*

THE OTHER LISTS

- American Film Institute (Yes)
- Roger Ebert's Top 100 (Yes)
- *Entertainment Weekly* (Yes)
- Internet Movie Database (No)
- Leonard Maltin (No)
- *Movieline* (No)
- National Society of Film Critics (Yes)
- *Premiere* Magazine (Yes)
- *Rolling Stone* Magazine (Yes)
- *Village Voice* (No)

Martin Lawrence's career began with an appearance doing stand-up on the TV talent show *Star Search*. His big break came with *Do the Right Thing*, and he went on to emcee HBO's *Def Comedy Jam*, eventually landing his own, aptly-named and risqué hit TV series *Martin* (1992-97). He later released *You So Crazy!* (1999), a vulgarity-laced stand-up film that became one of the highest-grossing concert movies of its time. Lawrence starred in big box-office films *Bad Boys* (1995), *Nothing to Lose* (1997), and *Life* (1999). He'd become so big that his salary broke the ten-million-dollar mark for *Big Momma's House* (2000). Most recently he has made *What's the Worst that Could Happen* (2001) and *Martin Lawrence Live: Runteldat* (2002).

ROLE REVERSALS

Spike Lee originally wanted Robert De Niro for the role of Sal.

NOTABLE QUOTES

"What's the difference between Hollywood characters and my characters? Mine are real." –Spike Lee

"Making films has got to be one of the hardest endeavors known to humankind. Straight up and down, film work is hard shit." –Spike Lee

THE CRITICS

"With *Do the Right Thing,* which he wrote, produced, directed, and stars in, Mr. Lee emerges as the most distinctive American multi-threat man since Woody Allen." –Vincent Canby, *New York Times*

"As with his previous films, Lee's *Thing* develops twice too many major characters. . . . The result, inevitably, is a meandering affair that eschews linear storytelling in favor of vignettes tied together in only the loosest way. While the film is seldom boring, its general lack of focus does seem to blunt much of the drama that its final explosive sequence might have engendered." –*Box Office* Magazine

BEHIND THE SCREEN

Rosie Perez appeared nude from the neck down, fearing that showing her face would feel exploitative. She kind of liked it, though, and has appeared—nude and with her face showing—in other movies.

Radio Raheem's description of his four-finger rings (which read "Love" and "Hate") is an homage to the character Robert Mitchum played in *The Night of the Hunter* (1955).

Spike Lee wrote the *Do the Right Thing* script in only two weeks.

"Stay black," chants Buggin' Out (Giancarlo Esposito) who is mad as hell about the white pizzeria and just can't take it anymore. His complaint that the wall of the 'hood's favorite hangout is covered with pictures of white people when all of its customers are people of color, eventually escalates into a race riot on the hottest night of the summer.

THE GREAT SCENE

In a terrifying scene that goes for the jugular, a chorus of the ugliest racial epithets is tossed like a bastketball by members of every race in the neighborhood. No one escapes the cut: Mookie: "Pino, fuck you. Fuck your fucking pizza and fuck Frank Sinatra." Pino curses him—along with Michael Jackson—back. Then it's Mookie's turn to get the racist stuff out: "Dago-wop-guinea-garlic-breath-pizza-slinging, spaghetti-bending-Vic Damone-Perry Como-Luciano Pavarotti . . . motha' fucker." And Pino comes back with: "You gold-chain-wearing-fried-chicken-eating-monkey-ape-babboon-big-time-fast-runnin'-high-jumpin'-spear-chucking-and-360-degree-basketball-dunkin'-spade-molignan. Take your fuckin' pizza and go the fuck back to Africa." Finally, Mister Señor Love Daddy, tries to calm things down: "Whoa! Hold up. Time out. Time out! Ya'all take a chill. Ya need to cool that shit out and dat's da double truth, Ruth!"

BELOW: The mercury finally blows—and all of the anger and the wear and tear of life on the mean but homey streets of Bed-Stuy are taken out on Sal's Pizzeria, which is looted and set ablaze.

68

WILD STRAWBERRIES 1957

STRANGE FRUIT

"His face shone with secretive light, as if reflected from another reality . . . It was like a miracle," wrote director Ingmar Bergman of his star's performance as a man who travels across an emotional universe from encrusted feelings to openness and love. Victor Sjöström's Isak Borg, a withdrawn, cantankerous, stubborn, and elitist scientist, gives one of cinema's great performances dealing with aging and self-transformation. In *Wild Strawberries*, Bergman reveals a humor and warmth toward his subject matter unequalled in any film he made before or after. When people speak of Bergman's great films they usually refer to *The Seventh Seal* (1958), *Persona* (1966), or *Cries and Whispers* (1972). But *Wild Strawberries*, though it is "Bergman-esque" in its interest in dreams, the surreal, alienation, and the questions of the existence of God, is unlike any Bergman film at its heart. There is optimism, clarity, directness, and structural integrity here, while his other films tend to leave viewers in the dark, at a loss. Bergman takes Borg (whose full name means Ice Palace) on a journey between present and past, dream and reality, during which he subtly and unconsciously learns to see the origins of his indifference to people, and the disappointments of his emotionally calcified existence. By the end of his journey he is changed, renewed by his reluctant though growing understanding of the opportunities for human contact that newly surround him. The Swedish title, *Smultronstallet*, actually translates as "strawberry field patch," which is regarded in Swedish culture as a place of rebirth. This film stands as a triumph of the redemptive powers of human connection, a notion the director explored, usually with pessimism, throughout his life and career.

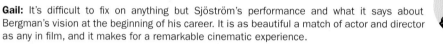

Jim: If this is your first shot at Bergman, don't hesitate to invite your therapist over to watch with you. This director-cum-Swedish institution uses intense symbolism the way Woody Allen relies on punchlines. And don't forget, this is Woody's idol, so make that a Freudian therapist.

Gail: It's difficult to fix on anything but Sjöström's performance and what it says about Bergman's vision at the beginning of his career. It is as beautiful a match of actor and director as any in film, and it makes for a remarkable cinematic experience.

THE PLOT

Grouchy, stubborn, and egotistical Professor Isak Borg (Victor Sjöström), a 78-year-old widower, sets out on a long car ride to receive an honorary degree from his old university. He is accompanied by his pregnant daughter-in-law, Marianne (Ingrid Thulin), who doesn't much like her cool father-in-law and is planning to separate from her husband. Their journey is punctuated by a series of hitchhikers, each of whom sets off either dreams or reveries into Borg's troubled past. The first group consists of two men and a woman—adored by both men—named Sara, who is a double for the lover of Isak's past (and who is played by the same actress, Bibi Andersson). They remain with him throughout his journey. Next, they pick up an embittered middle-aged couple who have just been in an auto accident. The pair exchange such terrible vitriol and venom that Marianne stops the car and asks them to leave. Borg finally arrives at his destination and picks up his prize, which proves an empty ritual. That night, he bids a loving good-bye to his young friends, to whom the once bitter old man whispers, "Remember me." As he goes to bed in his son's home, he is overcome by a sense of peace and dreams of a family picnic by a lake. Closure and affirmation of life have finally come, and Borg's face radiates joy.

"You have been accused of guilt. . . . I'll make a note that you haven't understood the charge," says Isak's (Victor Sjöström) teacher, during one of the many paranoid dreams he has before receiving a disinguished honor for his career as a scientist.

"A doctor's first duty is to ask for forgiveness."—Teacher to Isak Borg, in a dream

THE DIRECTOR

"There has always been a problem I have tried to tackle. Who am I and where do I come from, and why have I become what I am? I know less about myself now than I did ten years ago," said **Ingmar Bergman** when speaking about the themes in *Wild Strawberries*. It's an interesting statement by a man who directed a film in which the main character comes to know himself. It's clear that *Wild Strawberries* was a very personal film for Bergman, and he said so himself when describing the movie as an attempt to explore his own anguish over his relationship with his distant father. The dream sequences are based on Bergman's own dreams. One could say that all of Bergman's films are personal in that they explore the dilemmas the director struggled with throughout his career, of alienation, guilt, and family relationships. Bergman's work is known for its often-obscure symbolism, use of dreams, intimacy, and surrealism. His oeuvre includes a romantic comedy of manners, *Smiles of a Summer Night* (1955); *The Seventh Seal* (1957), which revolves around a chess game with death; *The Silence* (1963), which explores loneliness and loss of faith; *Persona* (1966), about an actress who suffers a breakdown and her relationship with her nurse; *Cries and Whispers* (1972), in which a family awaits death, and for which Bergman received a Best Director Oscar nomination; and *Fanny and Alexander* (1983), a deeply affecting re-imagining of Bergman's own childhood that earned the Academy Award for Best Foreign Language Film.

In one of Isak's dreams, he delights in the company of his cousin Sara (Bibi Andersson). He loves her, but was destined to lose her to his brother.

THE CAST	
Professor Isak Borg	Victor Sjöström
Sara	Bibi Andersson
Marianne Borg	Ingrid Thulin
Evald Borg	Gunnar Björnstrand
Agda	Jullan Kindahl
Anders	Folke Sundquist
Viktor Sjöström	Björn Bjelfvenstam
Isak's Mother	Naima Wifstrand
Mrs. Alman	Gunnel Broström
Karin, Isak's wife	Gertrud Fridh
Aunt Olga	Sif Ruud
Sten Alman	Gunnar Sjöberg
Henrik Åkerman	Max von Sydow

THE ACTORS

Victor Sjöström was coaxed out of retirement by Bergman to give one of his greatest performances in *Wild Strawberries*. Sjöström's character's losses accumulate until he has nothing left but the satisfaction of his own self-involvement. Like Shakespeare's King Lear, he is left hollow and empty, until he finally finds his bare and open self. There is indeed something miraculous about an actor who slowly and imperceptibly transforms himself from an utterly convincing stingy old man to someone who has realized the redemptive power of connection and generosity. Sjöström, himself a celebrated director, is best known for his silent work in the 1920s. He traveled to Hollywood, where he made his most celebrated film, *The Phantom Chariot* (1920), notable for its own bold narrative construction, in which one flashback sequence leads to the next. Sjöström continued to make major films like *The Scarlet Letter* (1926) and *The Wind* (1928), both starring Lillian Gish, and *He Who Gets Slapped* (1924). The director returned to Sweden in the 1930s and abandoned directing to become an actor.

As Sara, **Bibi Andersson** plays both Borg's childhood sweetheart who left him to marry his brother and a charming, energetic young woman who reminds him of that lost love. Andersson was one of the liveliest performers in Bergman's famed "repertory company." He gave her a small part in his film *Smiles of a Summer Night* (1955), and more prominent roles in *The Seventh Seal* (1957) and *Brink of Life* (1958), for which she won the Best Actress Award at Cannes. Her later films for Bergman included *The Touch* (1971), *Scenes From a Marriage* (1973), and two of his most complex works, *Persona* (1966) and *The Passion of Anna* (1969). Andersson has also worked in the U.S. in such films as *Duel at Diablo* (1966) and *I Never Promised You*

CREDITS

Producer: Alan Ekelund/ Janus Films
Director: Ingmar Bergman
Screenplay: Ingmar Bergman
Running Time: 90 minutes

THE YEAR'S ACADEMY AWARD WINNERS

Picture: *The Bridge on the River Kwai*
Director: David Lean, *The Bridge on the River Kwai*
Actor: Alec Guinness, *The Bridge on the River Kwai*
Actress: Joanne Woodward, *The Three Faces of Eve*
Supporting Actor: Red Buttons, *Sayonara*
Supporting Actress: Miyoshi Umeki, *Sayonara*

Isak (Victor Sjöström) picks up a bubbly, charming young hitchiker (Bibi Andersson), along with her two beaus. Her vibrancy remind him of his young love, Sara, and her adoration of him renews his spirit.

a Rose Garden (1977), as well as in films beneath her talents including *The Kremlin Letter* (1970), *The Concorde: Airport '79* (1979), and *Exposed* (1983).

Ingrid Thulin plays the sad, gentle, and warm daughter-in-law of Borg with an expressiveness that begs for close-ups—and she gets them. Thulin is a classic Bergman actress for those qualities, which David Thompson describes as her "tragic face, the unforgettable image of the anxiety that surrounds Bergman's world." In addition to other Swedish films, she has appeared in Bergman's *The Face/The Magician* (1958), as the mistress in *Winter Light* (1963), as the lesbian nymphomaniac in *Hour of the Wolf* (1968), and as one of the three sisters in *Cries and Whispers* (1972). She made her way to America, where she appeared in Vincente Minnelli's *The Four Horsemen of the Apocalypse* (1962); to France, where she performed in Alain Resnais's *La Guerre est Finie* (1966); and to Italy for Visconti's *The Damned* (1969). She made her last film, *La Casa del Sorriso*, in 1990.

THE OTHER LISTS
American Film Institute (No)
Roger Ebert's Top 100 (No)
Entertainment Weekly (No)
Internet Movie Database (No)
Leonard Maltin (No)
Movieline (No)
Premiere Magazine (Yes)
Rolling Stone Magazine (No)
Village Voice (No)

At journey's end, Isak's cool and disinterested relationship with his daughter-in-law Marianne (Ingrid Thulin) has been transformed into a generous and loving one. They embrace for the first time before he falls into a rapturous dream of childhood.

"No form of art goes beyond ordinary consciousness as film does, straight to our emotions, deep into the twilight room of the soul."

—Ingmar Bergman

At the end of his long journey, after having received his award, Borg lies in bed and says good-night to his daughter-in-law. For the first time, this grouchy old man tells her how highly he thinks of her. It is the first time we see a light, a spark of loving life in his eyes. He falls asleep and into a dream in which his sees his beautiful young cousin and asks where his parents are. It is the first dream in which the old man can communicate with the dream figures of his childhood. His cousin runs with him through the tall grass to the edge of a cliff, across which he can see his mother and father gently resting near a lake in the summer sun. They wave at him and we see the same light in his eyes that he has just shown his daughter-in-law. Rather than the sentimental or clichéd moment this could be, the scene says everything that need be said, truly and honestly, about the possibility and glory of an almost miraculous personal transformation.

69

THE BICYCLE THIEF 1948

WHEEL OF FORTUNE

The destruction and poverty left in the wake of World War II, persuaded many Italian film directors that they could no longer make the typical melodrama—based as that was on what they believed to be Fascist principles. Out of this realization was born a new, loosely defined style of filmmaking called neorealist, which emphasized naturalistic settings and straightforward stories about real people. *The Bicycle Thief's* story is that of a desperately poor father who finally lands a job as a poster hanger, only to have all hope of work and security stolen from him when a street thug runs off with his only ticket to the job: his bicycle. His anxious, helpless, and futile search for the bicycle through the streets of Rome accompanied by his young son one long Sunday, has the poignancy and irony of a Charlie Chaplin film in which a little man is buffeted by an indifferent society. What gives De Sica's film it's unforgettable quality is not only our identification with the father and son, but with the wealth of secondary characters, often comic, who follow along on the tragic adventure of seeking a bicycle which they never find. Though the film was made without any professional actors, it was written with the camera exclusively in mind. It is the faces, more than anything, that propel us into the story.

Jim: Without a single battle scene, this is truly the story about what war can do to the human spirit. This is not the pretty Italy of package tours, but a crumbling culture amid the ruins. Prepare to have your heart completely broken. But in a good way!

Gail: The futile search for the bicycle that would save Antonio's life and family would be unbearable to watch if it did not have embedded within it flashes of the comic in everyday life. It is hard to let go of this father and son as they disappear, in despair, into the crowd.

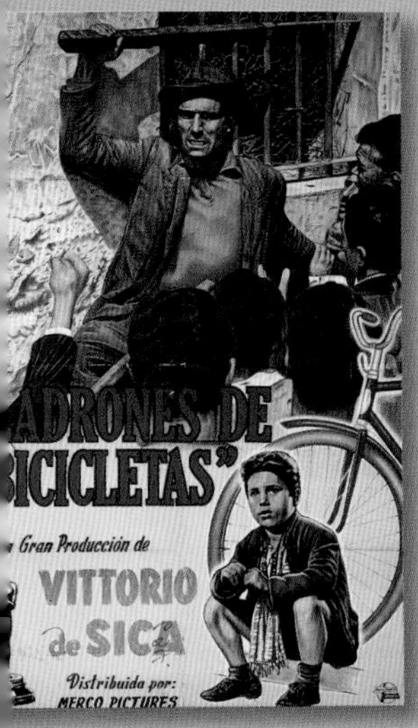

E PLOT

Sunday after Antonio's (Lamberto Maggiora- velihood is stolen from him, he sets out with oung son (Enzo Staiola) and an assortment ends on a tragi-comic hunt for a stolen bi- . They search through a secondhand bicycle ket, crowded with sullen people and tough e, without luck. On their own, father and son a quick burst of hopeful excitement when ather sees a suspicious-looking fellow. They he old man into a mission and then a church, a succession of funny and grim encounters priests and poor congregants, again without . Growing tired and hopeless, Antonio takes his despair on Bruno. He slaps him across ace. They spot the thief once again. This time nio chases him into a brothel where, comi- , he pushes Bruno outside. He drags the thief, has had an epileptic seizure, into the street neighbors crowding around him in support. n Bruno finally brings a policeman to search hief's apartment, there is no bicycle. Forlorn utterly without hope, Antonio attempts to l a single bicycle out of a doorway. He is ght immediately. Bruno sees the calamity runs to the aid of his father. No charges are sed. Father and son are speechless with ne and exhaustion as they take each other's d and walk away together, weeping softly, disappearing into an anonymous crowd.

Having grown weary walking the city streets all day in search of his stolen bicycle—the only barrier between his family and starvation—Antonio (Lamberto Maggiorani) and son Bruno (Enzo Staiola)—two nonprofessional actors—fall into despair of ever finding the precious vehicle.

THE DIRECTOR

Vittorio De Sica grew up in Naples, Italy, and started out as an office clerk in order to raise money to support his family. He was increasingly drawn towards acting, and made his screen debut while still in his teens. Best known for his light, earthy acting roles opposite Italy's most famous sex goddesses at the time, Gina Lollobrigida and Sophia Loren, De Sica continued to act in films in order to finance his own projects. He turned to directing in 1940, making comedies, but with his fifth film, *The Children Are Watching Us* (1942), his depth and sensitivity were made more than apparent, and his particular gift at working with actors, particularly children, illuminated his work. Credited with being one of the founders of the postwar Italian neorealist school of filmmaking, De Sica is world-renowned. He worked with writer Cezare Zavattini on both *Shoeshine* (1946) and *The Bicycle Thief*, which won special Oscars before the foreign film category was officially established. When his films started failing at the box office, he returned to work more regularly as an actor, becoming an international star of great repute. However, he returned to directing making *Two Women* (1961) for which Sophia Loren won a Best Actress Oscar. He continued making such memorable films as *Marriage, Italian Style* and *Yesterday, Today, and Tomorrow* (both 1964), winning another Oscar for the latter, *The Garden of the Finzi-Continis* (1971) a powerful study of anti-Semitism which brought him a fourth Oscar, and his final film, *A Brief Vacation* (1973).

Antonio catches up with the bicycle thief (Vittorio Antonucci) who is staunchly protected by neighbors against his criminal accusations. Overwhelmed by the scene, the thief falls into—or fakes—an epileptic seizure.

THE CAST

Antonio Ricci	Lamberto Maggiorani
Bruno	Enzo Staiola
Maria	Lianella Carell
Baiocco	Gino Saltamerenda
The Thief	Vittorio Antonucci
The Beggar	Guilio Chiari
Fausto Guerzoni	Amateur Actor
The Rest of the Cast	Amateur Actors and Actresses

THE ACTORS

The actors do their jobs well, possibly because they're not entirely acting. De Sica chose to use amateurs rather than professional actors in order to stay close to reality. He discovered **Lamberto Maggiorani** in Rome working as an electrician. He is superb as the anguished workman, performing with subtlety, expressing his changing moods with perfect pitch and power. His force was recognized and the unknown electrician went on to have a real acting career in Italian films.

Enzo Staiola plays his young son Bruno with a firmness that fully reveals the rugged determination and yet the latent sensitivity of the boy. Watching him, we feel that this is a face we will see again, and we do in Italian films.

The only professional actor was the thief, **Vittorio Antonucci**. For the few moments we see him, Antonucci strikes the right note of the rough-hewn, shabby thief. Ironically, *The Bicycle Thief*, was the only film he made while the amateur actors went on to have full careers.

ROLE REVERSALS

Producer David O. Selznick wanted Cary Grant to star as the Roman bill-poster. De Sica suggested Henry Fonda instead, an idea which Selznick rejected on the grounds that he was not "box-office" enough.

BEHIND THE SCREEN

Financing for the film was difficult to get, and, for a moment, De Sica was enticed by David O. Selznick's offer to back the film.

On his own, De Sica raised approximately $100,000 from friends and other Italian financial sources.

THE CRITICS

"De Sica has artfully wrapped [*The Bicycle Thief*] into a film that will tear your heart, but which should fill you with warmth and compassion. People should see it—and they should care." —Bosley Crowther, *New York Times*

"If Visconti and Rossellini invented neorealism in *Osession* and *Open City* and then invested it with the ultimate profundity of *La Terra Trema* and *Paisan*, De Sica milked it dry with *Shoeshine* and *The Bicycle Thief*. Lacking an insight into the real world, De Sica relied instead on tricks of pathos that he had learned too well as an actor. It is unlikely that any of the Big Four would have made *The Bicycle Thief* in the De Sica-Zavattini manner." —Andrew Sarris, *Village Voice*

"Fellini comes closer to creating a viable symbol of humanity than does De Sica with his whining protagonist in *The Bicycle Thief*." —Andrew Sarris, *Village Voice*

CREDITS

Producer: Alessandro Cicognini and Vittorio De Sica (uncredited)
Director: Vittorio De Sica
Screenplay: Vittorio De Sica and Cesare Zavattini
Running Time: 93 minutes
Box Office: $332,930

HONORARY ACADEMY AWARD

Most Outstanding Foreign Film released in U.S. (1949)

ACADEMY AWARD NOMINATIONS

Best Screenplay: Vittorio De Sica and Cesare Zavattini

THE YEAR'S OTHER WINNERS

Best Picture: *All the King's Men*
Best Director: Joseph L. Mankiewicz, *A Letter to Three Wives*
Best Actor: Broderick Crawford, *All the King's Men*
Best Actress: Olivia de Havilland, *The Heiress*
Best Supporting Actor: Dean Jagger, *Twelve O'Clock High*
Best Supporting Actress: Mercedes McCambridge, *All the King's Men*

THE OTHER LISTS

- American Film Institute (No)
- *Entertainment Weekly* (No)
- Internet Movie Database (No)
- Leonard Maltin (No)
- *Movieline* (No)
- National Society of Film Critics (Yes)
- *Premiere* Magazine (Yes)
- Roger Ebert's Top 100 (Yes)
- *Rolling Stone* Magazine (No)
- *The Village Voice* (No)

Having spent more than half the day walking the cobblestone streets, Antonio sees his son grow weary and depressed, and decides to raise their spirits by treating them both. "To hell with it! You want a pizza?" says the father to the now smiling Bruno. As they are seated the camera pans to another table where a preciously dressed boy and his affluent family are dining on platters of pasta. "To eat like that, you need a million lire a month at least," Antonio tells his son. Realizing that they can't even afford the pizza, they order up some bread and mozzarella, which the boy gobbles up happily while the father despairs.

Antonio proudly carries his new bicycle for his job as poster hanger, which was paid for by his wife's pawning of the sheets from their beds.

Glad that he will be working, wife Maria (Lianella Carell) prepares Antonio, dressed in his new work uniform, for his first day on the job.

70

BRINGING UP BABY 1938

INTO THE WOODS

"Now it isn't that I don't like you, Susan, because, after all, in moments of quiet, I'm strangely drawn toward you, but—well, there haven't been any quiet moments!" rants David (Cary Grant), the boring paleontologist who is helpless in the face of the ruthless force of nature called the opposite sex. In this case, the opponent is Susan (Katharine Hepburn), and she draws him kicking and screaming into madness, a.k.a. love (and sexual liberation). You can't watch this, the best screwball comedy ever made, without letting go of all rationality as you descend into its absurd parallel universe—and it's a very Shakespearean *As You Like It* universe at that. But, like David, who whines, "I know we ought to go now, but somehow I can't move," we wouldn't leave it for the world.

Jim: Some of the biggest laughs don't come from the punch lines—they're inspired by Hepburn's outfits. Speaking of which, the torn gown in the nightclub sequence is comic delirium. I don't want to watch this movie; I want to live in it.

Gail: The confounding and exhilarating perils of romance have never seemed as crazy—or as charmed.

THE PLOT

A daft (but terribly delightful) heiress (Katharine Hepburn) with a dog named George, a pet leopard named Baby, and a rich aunt who has a million dollars, goes gaga for a nervous, uptight, bespectacled paleontologist (Cary Grant) who has just acquired the bone (intercostals clavicle) he needs to complete his precious dinosaur skeleton. He's also counting on getting a million dollars from the heiress's aunt for his work, and is engaged to be married the following day. Everything goes wrong (or right, depending on your point of view). The paleontologist can't shake off the heiress, who's a train wreck. Hungry for a bone, George (the dog) steals the intercostals clavicle; the befuddled paleontologist and the besotted heiress disappear into the Connecticut woods in search of the dog in order to find the bone; and Baby (the leopard) is on the loose. The paleontologist emerges with the bone and Susan and finds himself helplessly, hopelessly in love and liberation.

David's (Cary Grant) bookish paleontologist is no match for wacky heiress Susan (Katharine Hepburn), who's falling in love with him whether he likes it or not. Despite his best efforts to avoid her, they always seem to end up in a fix together. Soon, he is going to have to take her home, having stepped on her iridescent dress, tearing off the entire back.

"The love impulse in men frequently reveals itself in conflict."—Dr. Lehman

THE DIRECTOR

If it's a **Howard Hawks** film, regardless of genre, it's tough-minded, not a little cynical, and smart (smarter than your average Hollywood film). Hawks had a particular fascination with sex roles, which is why many of his male characters end up wearing women's clothing. Not only did Grant don a boa-collared robe in *Baby* but he also wore tight army skirts in *I Was a Male War Bride* (1949). In an interview, Peter Bogdanovich asked Hawks if the lighting for *Baby* wasn't inordinately dark for a comedy. The director grinned, "Well, it was a complete tragedy for Cary, wasn't it?" There's definitely a dark side to the film. Perhaps Hawks was thinking of the real-life tragedy that became his inspiration for the film: During the making of *Mary of Scotland* (1936), by the (also) bespectacled director John Ford, he and Hepburn fell in love. Her strong-mindedness and her unique playfulness with the very serious director made for quite a (mis)match. Ford nearly left his family for her. Hawks made brilliant films in a number of genres, including the mother of all mafia films, *Scarface* (1932), the screwball comedy, *Twentieth Century* (1934), which made Carole Lombard a star, *Only Angels Have Wings* (1939), his remake on overdrive of *The Front Page* with a female lead, *His Girl Friday* (1940), Lauren Bacall's debut, *To Have and Have Not* (1944), *The Big Sleep* (1946), *Red River* (1948), *Monkey Business* (1952), *Gentlemen Prefer Blondes* (1953), *Rio Bravo* (1959), and his only Oscar nomination, *Sergeant York* (1941). In 1974 Hawks received an Honorary Oscar. (For more on Hawks, see page 271.)

It's no wonder that David is on the floor. If he could find a chair to sit in, he'd probably fall out of it. It's all the work of Susan, who has unleashed her destabilizing feminine force upon this impervious, buttoned-up scientist. Somehow, he can't stop her. It all goes to show that love can be hazardous to your health.

THE CAST

Susan	Katharine Hepburn
David	Cary Grant
Major Applegate	Charles Ruggles
Slocum	Walter Catlett
Aunt Elizabeth	May Robson
Dr. Lehman	Fritz Feld
Alice Swallow	Virginia Walker
George	Asta

THE ACTORS

In jail—never mind how they got there—Susan tries to make things better by telling David that once the authorities know who they are, they'll release them. To that David replies, "When they find out who *you* are they'll pad the cell." Despite her brilliant comic performance in *Baby*, **Katharine Hepburn** was branded box-office poison, and was forced to buy out her RKO contract. She showed them. Hep went on to become one of the most honored screen actresses, earning four Oscars and eight more nominations. She led all actresses on the American Film Institute's (AFI) list of top 100 U.S. love stories. Briefly wed to Ludlon Smith, her affair with Spencer Tracy was one of Hollywood's great romances. Few actresses have had as legendary a career as Hepburn's. (For more on Hepburn, see page 124.)

"How can all these things happen to just one person?" asks the bumbling and befuddled paleontologist, David. And we're hysterical. Laughing at the very debonair **Cary Grant**? Impossible. Yet there he is playing the master of the pratfall and the goofy double take. Kate's Susan is as daft as he, only crafty. What a match. They'd come out fighting again in the classy romantic comedy *The Philadelphia Story* (1940). Grant led AFI's list for top male love objects. He was the light that brightened some of the greatest screwball comedies. (For more on Grant, see page 30.)

BEHIND THE SCREEN

While pretending that she and David are gangsters, Susan calls David "Jerry the Nipper," which was Grant's nickname in *The Awful Truth* (1937). David protests to the police, "Officer, she's making it up from motion pictures she's seen!"

Baby did so badly at the box office that Howard Hawks was fired from his next production at RKO.

Silent-film comedian Harold Lloyd was Hawks's model for Grant's performance in *Baby*.

THE CRITICS

"It may be the American movies' closest equivalent to Restoration comedy." —Pauline Kael, *The New Yorker*

"A farce you can barely hear above the precisely enunciated patter of Miss Katharine Hepburn and the ominous tread of deliberative gags. In *Bringing up Baby* Miss Hepburn has a role that calls for her to be breathless, senseless, and terribly, terribly fatiguing. She succeeds and we can be callous enough to hint it is not entirely a matter of performance." —Frank S. Nugent, *New York Times*

HAWKS ON DIRECTING:

"There's action only if there is danger."

"A good movie is three good scenes and no bad scenes."

"When you find out a thing that goes pretty well, you might as well do it again."

NOTABLE QUOTES

"Acting is a nice childish profession—pretending you're someone else and at the same time selling yourself." —Katharine Hepburn

"Once a crowd chased me for an autograph. 'Beat it, ' I said, 'go sit on a tack!' 'We made you, ' they said. 'Like hell you did, ' I told them." —Katharine Hepburn

"Everybody wants to be Cary Grant. Even I want to be Cary Grant." —Cary Grant

CREDITS

Producer: Howard Hawks/RKO
Director: Howard Hawks
Screenplay: Dudley Nichols, Hagar Wilde
Running Time: 102 minutes

THE YEAR'S ACADEMY AWARD WINNERS

Best Picture: *You Can't Take It with You*
Best Director: Frank Capra, *You Can't Take It with You*
Best Actor: Spencer Tracy, *Boys Town*
Best Actress: Bette Davis, *Jezebel*
Best Supporting Actor: Walter Brennan, *Kentucky*
Best Supporting Actress: Fay Bainter, *Jezebel*

THE OTHER LISTS

American Film Institute (Yes)
Roger Ebert's Top 100 (Yes)
Entertainment Weekly (Yes)
Internet Movie Database (No)
Leonard Maltin (No)
Movieline (Yes)
National Society of Film Critics (No)
Premiere Magazine (Yes)
Rolling Stone Magazine (Yes)
Village Voice (No)

Susan is so in love with David that she feels compelled to steal his clothes. He emerges from her bedroom draped in a boa-collared satin robe, much to the mortification of Susan's wealthy aunt (from whom he was to receive his million-dollar endowment) who says, "Well, you look perfectly idiotic in those clothes." At the end of his rope, David insists that he isn't wearing his own clothes—that somehow they've gone missing. "But why are you wearing *these* clothes?" To which David, half-insane with frustration replies, "Because I just went GAY all of a sudden!" (The audience could not have failed to get the double meaning in this: it was widely rumored that Grant himself was gay.)

THE GREAT SCENE

"I went gay all of a sudden," shouts David (Cary Grant) by way of explaining his cross-dressing. See, Susan's so in love with David that she has to steal his clothes so he won't leave her. Then he ends up in her clothes and . . . well . . . that makes sense. Doesn't it?

"The only really good thing abou acting is that there's no heavy lifting."

–Cary Grant

"When they find out who you are they'll pad the cell," shouts David to Susan. Try as he might, the baffled bone collector (Cary Grant) just can't get a fix on who this female creature (Katharine Hepburn) is, or what she could possibly want from him.

71

PATHS OF GLORY 1957

FRENCH FRONT ROW

"You are an *idealist*!" a venomous old general spits out like a curse. He might have been dressing down Stanley Kubrick himself, a director committed to the notion that a well-aimed film could change hearts and minds. *Paths of Glory* brought early fame to Kubrick and became the first of his antiwar trilogy, which also included *Dr. Strangelove* (1964) and *Full Metal Jacket* (1987). *Paths of Glory* is the only one based on fact, but its story is so grotesquely evil that it could pass for darkly satiric fiction. When Kirk Douglas was asked to come on board, he responded, "Stanley, I don't think this picture will ever make a nickel, but we have to make it." He was right about it not making much noise at the box office, but it created international shock waves just the same. France was so incensed by the damning portrait of its military that it banned the film for eighteen years. The Academy Awards seems to have taken its marching orders from Paris. Despite the extraordinary script and what was probably the best performance ever by Douglas, the film failed to pick up a single nomination. This may have been a result of co-screenwriter Jim Thompson's blacklisting as a former member of the Communist Party. Kubrick certainly couldn't be accused of rattling his sword at windmills. The hypocritical targets of his wrath were lining up on his front step.

Jim: A powerful story and a great script overcome the thudding American accents. The French Front by way of Des Moines.

Gail: It took twenty-two years to get this one made, but when he finally did it, Kubrick succeeded in making one of the most brutal, beautiful, and horrifying antiwar war movies ever.

E PLOT

he winter of 1916 and the Germans are d just outside of Paris by an entrenched h Army. While few are dying, no ground is made. Pressured by politicians to make ess at any cost, two ego-bloated French als, Broulard (Adolphe Menjou) and u (George Macready) devise an attack ed to failure. Colonel Dax (Kirk Douglas) sts the order, but he knows it's hopeless ue. On the eve of battle, he sends Lieu- t Roget (Wayne Morris) on surveillance Corporal Paris (Ralph Meeker) and Private ne (Ken Dibbs); Roget panics and tosses nade, killing Lejeune. Paris vows to report Next day is a charnel house of slaughter; men are machine-gunned as soon as limb out of the trenches. When the last angs back in confusion, Mireau catches of them and demands they be fired upon. ders are refused. In a pique, he then s them all to be executed for cowardice. horrified, but the old man must be pla- . Three men, one from each division, will bitrarily chosen for court-martial. Paris ong them, thanks to Roget's efforts. Dax ds them before a kangaroo court led by ictive prosecutor (Richard Anderson). The verdict is a travesty. As the clock ticks on the march to the firing squad for the Dax's threatens to blackmail Broulard e hope of changing his mind.

"Medals are no defense." The past heroics of Corporal Paris (Ralph Meeker) and Colonel Dax (Kirk Douglas), don't count when the vanity of egocentric generals is at stake. Kubrick's first major film was inspired by a real-life incident during the horrific WWI Battle of Verdun in which thousands of French soldiers perished in a pointless, suicidal mission.

"These executions will be a perfect tonic for the entire division. There are few things more fundamentally encouraging and stimulating than seeing someone else die."—General Broulard

THE DIRECTOR

Even this early in his career, **Stanley Kubrick** was making himself known for his exacting attention to technical detail. Special lenses were designed for each of his films and lighting always played a key role in his storytelling. In this film, the brighter the light, the more horrifying the scene. The glaringly sunny morning of the execution, for example, casts no shadow on the inhuman cruelty being played out. Kubrick, known for his sometimes exasperatingly extended shooting schedules, was not intimidated by budgetary constraints. The "last meal" sequence inside the military lockup took 68 takes to please him. Jack Nicholson, star of Kubrick's later horror epic *The Shining* (1980), said of him, "He gives new meaning to the word 'meticulous.'" Kirk Douglas clearly had no reservations about his ability when he teamed up with him again for the explosive hit *Spartacus* (1960). Kubrick's output was lean, but each of his films created a sensation—sometimes negative, but never ignored. His canon includes *Spartacus* (1960), *Lolita* (1962), *Dr. Strangelove* (1964), *2001: A Space Odyssey* (1968), *A Clockwork Orange* (1971), *Barry Lyndon* (1975), *The Shining* (1980), *Full Metal Jacket* (1987), and *Eyes Wide Shut* (1999). (For more on Stanley Kubrick, see pages 127, 160, and 292.)

Hollywood's most famous chin goes up against one of filmdom's most memorable dueling scars. The cruel slash provides George Macready's General Mireau with a violent, unspoken history. In truth, it wasn't makeup but the result of a serious car accident suffered by the actor.

THE CAST

Colonel Dax	Kirk Douglas
Corporal Philip Paris	Ralph Meeker
General George Broulard	Adolphe Menjou
General Paul Mireau	George Macready
Lieutenant Roget/Singing Man	Wayne Morris
Major Saint-Auban	Richard Anderson
Private Pierre Arnaud	Joe Turkel
German Singer	Christiane Harlan
Proprietor of Café	Jerry Hausner
Narrator	Peter Capell
Father Dupree	Emile Meyer
Sergeant Boulanger	Bert Freed
Private Lejeune	Kem Dibbs
Private Maurice Ferol	Timothy Carey
Shell Shock Victim	Fred Bell

THE ACTORS

Paths of Glory was a great exception to **Kirk Douglas**'s boast, "I've made a career of playing sons of bitches." As Colonel Dax, an officer of rare integrity who's unable to stall the insane rush to injustice, Douglas is remarkably understated. While that signature chin is firmly clenched, his great, agonized speech directed at pompous General Broulard is a model of restraint. This from a star whose high-flying bombast led director John Frankenheimer to describe him as having "spent his whole life wanting to be Burt Lancaster." A child of impoverished Russian Jewish immigrants, Douglas never shied away from his roots and told all in his best-selling autobiography *The Ragpicker's Son* (1988). School chum Lauren Bacall got him his first screen role in *The Strange Love of Martha Ivers* (1946), but it was the boxing movie *Champion* (1949) that made him a star. He distinguished himself in *The Glass Menagerie* (1950), *Young Man with a Horn* (1950), and *Detective Story* (1951) before moving on to his most memorable decade, featuring such classics as *The Bad and the Beautiful* (1952), *Lust for Life* (1956), and *Spartacus* (1960). He continued his streak with *Town Without Pity* (1961), *Seven Days in May* (1964), and the mob saga *The Brotherhood* (1968). He made a comeback in *Once Is Not Enough* (1975) and once again in *The Fury* (1978). Following a debilitating stroke, he recuperated fully enough for several TV guest shots in the1990s. He miraculously survived a helicopter crash in 1998 and has been honored as a Kennedy Center Award recipient. And, of course, he is the proud, if often humorously competitive, father of superstar actor/producer, Michael Douglas.

Casting **Adolphe Menjou**, suave veteran actor of Hollywood's Golden Age with such credits as *Little Miss Marker* (1934) and the original *A Star Is Born* (1937), was a most pointed decision. The mustachioed Menjou was a virulent anti-Communist and one of the instigators of the Hollywood blacklist. Politically, he couldn't have been more out of step with Kubrick and Douglas. The fact that his character is unscrupulous in the extreme, a banal face of evil, may have provided their casting impetus. His performance is one of the film's great strengths.

George Macready's vainglorious General Mireau is memorable as he arrogantly strolls the trenches and greets his wounded and depressed troops with, "Good morning, soldier. Ready to kill some Germans today?" With his handsome profile, disfigured by a dueling scar, Macready looked like a former matinee idol gone to seed. He thrived in military roles in films like *The Story of Rommel, the Desert Fox* (1951), as General Kuhner in *The Great Race* (1965), and as Adm. Cordell Hull in *Tora! Tora! Tora!* (1970).

BEHIND THE SCREEN

The pretty blond German singer in the cabaret sequence, Christiane Harlan, became the second Mrs. Kubrick.

The film was shot just a few miles from the site of the Dachau concentration camp memorial.

Kubrick reneged on his promise to the studio to provide a happy ending.

THE CRITICS

"One of the greatest anti-war films ever made."—*The Motion Picture Guide*

"An unforgettable movie experience." —*Newsweek*

"As for the picture's significance, it comes to an inconclusive point." —Bosley Crowther, *New York Times*

ROLE REVERSALS

After considering Richard Burton and James Mason for the lead, Kubrick finally approached Gregory Peck, who wanted the role of Colonel Dax but was previously committed. It was then offered to Kirk Douglas, who got out of a Broadway contract to play it. By then, Peck had also freed himself up, but it was too late.

CREDITS

Producer: Bryna/Harris-Kubrick/United Artists
Director: Stanley Kubrick
Screenplay: Stanley Kubrick, Calder Willingham, Jim Thompson, based on the novel by Humphrey Cobb
Running time: 87 minutes
Budget: $935,000

THE YEAR'S ACADEMY AWARD WINNERS

Best Picture: *The Bridge on the River Kwai*
Best Director: David Lean, *The Bridge on the River Kwai*
Best Actor: Alec Guinness, *The Bridge on the River Kwai*
Best Actress: Joanne Woodward, *The Three Faces of Eve*
Best Supporting Actor: Red Buttons, *Sayonara*
Best Supporting Actress: Miyoshi Umeki, *Sayonara*

"[Kubrick] will be a fine director some day, if he falls on his face just once."
—Kirk Douglas

THE GREAT SCENE

The innocent condemned soldiers, Arnaud, Paris, and Ferol, spend a harrowing night, unable to touch their last suppers. A visit from sanctimonious Father Dupree enrages Lejeune who attacks him. Arnaud steps between them and punches Lejeune. He falls back and fractures his skull. Morning comes with the crowing of a rooster. Guards enter the cell to escort the men to their deaths. Arnaud, unconscious, must be strapped to a stretcher and carried. Paris tries to control himself but finally collapses in tears. He's reminded that the press will be on hand, and does he really want his wife and son to read of his cowardice? That forces him to straighten up, but Ferol is inconsolable. He weeps as he's pushed along to the steady, ominous drumroll. They finally reach the stakes that have been prepared for them. Arnaud's stretcher is tied to one of them and the officer-in-charge is ordered to slap his face—the generals want him awake for his death. Ferol clings to Father Dupree until his eyes are covered with a blindfold. Scores of dignitaries look on as the final judgement is passed upon the three men. The squad prepares to fire. The drumroll stops. Birds fly off their branches as the bullets shatter the still morning air.

The men died wonderfully! The economy of the firing squad scene makes it one of the most harrowing moments ever filmed. It's *Dead Man Walking* times three, and all the more agonizing because these men were innocent. Private Ferol, as played by Timothy Carey, is the most touching, because he has no shame. He doesn't care about putting up a good front. Scared of dying, he begs and pleads until the end.

THE OTHER LISTS

- American Film Institute (No)
- Roger Ebert's Top 100 (No)
- *Entertainment Weekly* (No)
- Internet Movie Database (Yes)
- Leonard Maltin (Yes)
- *Movieline* (Yes)
- National Society of Film Critics (No)
- *Premiere* Magazine (No)
- *Rolling Stone* Magazine (No)
- *Village Voice* (No)

"Anyone who has ever been privileged to direct a film also knows that, although it can be like trying to write *War and Peace* in a bumper car in an amusement park, when you finally get it right, there are not many joys in life that can equal the feeling."

–Stanley Kubrick

"There are times when I am ashamed to be a member of the human race and this is one such occasion." Kirk Douglas was one of the first A-list stars to put his activist politics on the line. He was never shy about his antiwar stance and insisted that the message of *Paths of Glory* had to be delivered, whether it scored at the box office or not. He was also one of the first stars to form his own production company, a move that provided him with the freedom to choose his projects.

72

THE MALTESE FALCON 1941

BIRDS OF A FEATHER

"I must have my little joke now and then," says the dapper, dandy thief Kaspar Gutman (Sydney Greenstreet), keeping himself amused while trying to land the richest bird in history. Those could be the words of first-time director Huston about his acerbic, tight, dark detective story in which a band of borderline psychotic—and neurotic—crooks, one femme fatale, and a hard-bitten gumshoe are kept busy betraying one another while bantering with great verbal agility. Though the seminal *noir* masterpiece lost the Oscar to Hitchcock's *Rebecca*, it was a worthy adversary. From its blistering, unforgettable dialogue ("The cheaper the crook, the gaudier the patter, eh?" says Sam Spade) to its skillful composition and camera movement, Huston knew exactly what he was doing. And what he did was explosive: He created a genre, turned Bogey into Bogey, and made film history.

Jim: The birthplace of "giving the bird." How can a movie that was never meant to be more than a low-budget "throw away" last so long? Certainly the quality of the performances, but it's the actors themselves. They just don't make people like this anymore. As fascinating as a "living museum."

Gail: The conversations are so biting, they're comic. The horrible crooks are so idiosyncratic, they're almost lovable . . . even though they're mean, mean, mean. Huston simply broke the mold.

THE PLOT

Centuries ago, a legendary statuette of a bird made of gold and encrusted with jewels went missing. Men killed to possess it. Detective Sam Spade (Humphrey Bogart) calls it "the stuff that dreams are made of." Its current pursuer, "fat man" Kaspar Gutman (Sydney Greenstreet), has followed the bird around the world. Though he and the bird are at the center of the story, they are only introduced halfway through the film. First, we meet the aggressively helpless and lovely Ms. Wonderly, or is it Miss LeBlanc, or Brigid O'Shaughnessy (Mary Astor)? She enters Sam Spade's office behind a pair of dark glasses; he sits behind a swirl of cigarette smoke. She begs him to help her. But what does she really want? To find her sister, or to snatch the "unholy grail" the bird has become? Everybody's got a trick up his or her sleeve. This labyrinthine *noir* defies summation. There's hardly a coherent story here. Instead, the film is a vehicle for blistering dialogue, knife-edged performances, and scenes that are played out with ambiguity, menace, and deceit. Hard to believe that it predated *Chinatown* by more than 30 years.

Brigid O'Shaughnessy (Mary Astor), with fox stole and veiled hat, begs for help from cool detective Sam Spade (Humphrey Bogart), admitting, "I haven't lived a good life. I've been bad, worse than you could know." Spade, in words that made Bogart "Bogey," replies, "You know, that's good, because if you actually were as innocent as you pretend to be, we'd never get anywhere."

'I couldn't be fonder of you if you were my own son. But, well, if you lose a son, it's possible to get another. There's only one Maltese Falcon." —Kasper Gutman

THE DIRECTOR

It was his directorial debut, yet **John Huston** didn't falter for even a millimeter of celluloid. Producer Henry Blanke instructed Huston to "shoot each scene as if it was the most important one in the picture; make every shot count." And he did, but his way. Taking great pleasure with the possibilities for clashes among its eccentric characters, Huston let the plot meander where it would. The film's got everything that would come to characterize Huston's work: vivid characters, greed, corruption, toughness, stylistic flair, and great shot composition. And, as always, he gave his actor father, Walter Huston, a cameo. Huston and Bogey continued on to make a number of films together, among them the director's Oscar-winning *The Treasure of the Sierra Madre* and *Key Largo* (both 1948), *The African Queen* (1951), and *Beat the Devil* (1954). Huston is also celebrated for such unforgettable films as *The Asphalt Jungle* (1950), *Moby Dick* (1956), and, later, *Under the Volcano* (1984), *Prizzi's Honor* (1985), and a brilliant adaptation of the James Joyce's novella, *The Dead* (1987). As an actor, he gave some standout performances in *The Cardinal* (1963), *Chinatown* (1974), and *Winter Kills* (1979). (For more on Huston, see page 124.)

He looked as good as he spoke in this one. The "trust no one" detective knows that Brigid O'Shaughnessy isn't always who she says she is. He has to ring doorbells to find her other identities.

THE CAST

Sam Spade	Humphrey Bogart
Brigid O'Shaughnessy/Miss Wonderly/Miss LeBlanc	Mary Astor
Iva Archer	Gladys George
Joel Cairo	Peter Lorre
Detective Lieutenant Dundy	Barton MacLane
Effie Perine	Lee Patrick
Kasper Gutman	Sydney Greenstreet
Detective Sergeant Tom Polhaus	Ward Bond
Miles Archer	Jerome Cowan
Wilmer Cook	Elisha Cook Jr.
Captain Jacobi	Walter Huston (uncredited)

THE ACTORS

Hard-boiled Sam Spade was the role **Humphrey Bogart** was born to play. He is the quintessential cynical antihero who lives by his own moral code and whose coolness seems a cover for some secret wound–most likely to his heart. Unlike any Hollywood hero before him, Bogart always stood on the outside sizing things up. In *Falcon* he sees through Mary Astor's desperate character. "You're good. . . .You're very good," he tells her, regarding her helplessness as merely a ruse. The icy private eye pulls off some great snarls and self-satisfied grins in this one. He rages like a mad dog at Gutman, throws a glass against the wall, and slams the door behind him as a slow smile spreads across his face. It's a quick change worth the price of admission. Bogart continued to play Spades of various colors in such classics as *Casablanca* (1942), *To Have and Have Not* (1944), *The Big Sleep* (1946), *Key Largo* and *The Treasure of the Sierra Madre* (both 1948), and *In a Lonely Place* (1950), and showed his more comic and romantic-lead side in *Sabrina* (1954) and *The African Queen* (1951, Academy Award-winner). (For more on Bogart, see pages 21 and 124.)

She should have taken the Oscar for her role as the fabulous liar with three aliases in *Falcon*; instead, **Mary Astor** took home the golden boy for a lesser performance in *The Great Lie*. She was "good," as Bogey said, probably the best of the bunch when it came to playing ruthless femmes fatales. And she played the part offscreen equally well. A beauty queen in her teens, Astor became one of the most desired young women in Hollywood. She made scores of movies, both comedies and dramas, including *Runaway Bride* (1930), *Red Dust* (1932), *Dodsworth* (1936), *The Prisoner of Zenda* (1937), *Midnight* (1939), and *The Palm Beach Story* (1942). As she aged, she took on "mother" roles in *Meet Me in St. Louis* (1944), *Little Women* (1949), and with a standout performance in *A Kiss Before Dying* (1956). Her final films were *Youngblood Hawke* (1964), and *Hush . . . Hush, Sweet Charlotte* (1964).

In one of the film's sublime moments, **Sydney Greenstreet**, as Kaspar Gutman, emerges from behind a vase of roses to meet Spade. It's his first appearance in the film and on any screen. After 61 years on stage, Greenstreet does a great job of portraying a madman with impeccable manners. His obsessive quest for the falcon means more than meets the eye. When he discovers that the bird in hand is a fake, he seems about to explode. Instead, he becomes oddly practical and announces his plans to move on, inviting Spade to join him in continuing his pursuit on yet another shore. It's not the object itself but the quest that he can't let go of. During the next eight years, Greenstreet made 24 films. (For more on Greenstreet, see page 21.)

Joel Cairo, the gardenia-scented little crook, provided a great character turn for **Peter Lorre**, who, prior to *Falcon*, played a psychopathic child-killer in Fritz Lang's *M* (1931). Huston made the match between Lorre and Greenstreet, clinching it when Lorre calls Greenstreet, "You, you bloated idiot!" They worked so well that they paired up again the following year in *Casablanca* and would make a total of nine films together. (For more on Lorre, see page 21.)

CREDITS

Producer: Henry Blanke/ Warner Bros.
Director: John Huston
Screenplay: John Huston, based on the novel by Dashiell Hammett
Running time: 101 minutes
Budget: $300,000

ACADEMY AWARD NOMINATIONS

Best Supporting Actor: Sydney Greenstreet
Best Picture: Hal B. Wallis
Best Writing, Screenplay: John Huston

THE YEAR'S WINNERS

Best Picture: *How Green Was My Valley*
Best Director: John Ford, *How Green Was My Valley*
Best Actor: Gary Cooper, *Sergeant York*
Best Actress: Joan Fontaine, *Suspicion*
Best Supporting Actor: Donald Crisp, *How Green Was My Valley*
Best Supporting Actress: Mary Astor, *The Great Lie*

THE OTHER LISTS

American Film Institute (Yes)
Roger Ebert's Top 100 (Yes)
Entertainment Weekly (No)
Internet Movie Database (Yes)
Leonard Maltin (Yes)
Movieline (No)
National Society of Film Critics (Yes)
Premiere Magazine (No)
Rolling Stone Magazine (No)
Village Voice (No)

The classic *noir*-blonde widow, **Gladys George** is best known for *Falcon* and as the nightclubber in *The Roaring Twenties* (1939) who delivers James Cagney's epitaph in the film's last line, "He used to be a big shot." She also appeared in *Valiant Is the Word for Carrie* (1936), for which she was nominated for an Oscar, *Madame X* (1937), *The Way of All Flesh* (1940), and *The Best Years of Our Lives* (1946).

Lee Patrick plays the secretary, who, seated on her boss's desk, leans over and lights his cigarette. She was acerbic and quick on the repartee, but also devoted. Patrick had a long career, making appearances in over 70 films, among them *Mildred Pierce* (1945) and *Vertigo* (1958).

Walter Huston made his first cameo in one of his son's films as Captain Jacobi, who delivers the bird to Bogey.

THE CRITICS

"Don't miss *The Maltese Falcon* if your taste is for mystery fare. It's the slickest exercise in cerebration that has hit the screen in many months, and it is also one of the most compelling nervous-laughter provokers yet." —Bosley Crowther, *New York Times*

"Classic detective film, but not quite the masterpiece it's supposed to be." —Ken Hanke, *Mountain Xpress*

BEHIND THE SCREEN

This was the third version of the film. Warner Bros. produced it in 1931 under the same title and in 1936 as *Satan Met a Lady*.

The Shakespeare reference that ends the film ("the stuff that dreams are made of") was suggested by Humphrey Bogart.

More than once, Spade makes derogatory references to Wilmer's presumed homosexuality (because he carries a perfumed handkerchief). In fact, he refers to Wilmer as a *gunsel*, a term that the censors assumed was a slang reference to a gunman. *Gunsel* is actually a vulgar Yiddish term for homosexual.

Two "Maltese Falcons" were used for the film. The first one is on display in the movie museum at Warner Bros. Studios, its tail feathers dented from when Bogey dropped it 60 years ago.

ROLE REVERSALS

George Raft was originally cast as Sam Spade, but he dismissed it as "not an important picture."

The role of Brigid O'Shaughnessy was originally offered to Geraldine Fitzgerald.

FIRSTS

The *Maltese Falcon* boasts some of the most important firsts in film history:

It is considered by many to be the first "film *noir*," a black-and-white mood piece in which cynical, corrupt antiheroes and -heroines are caught up in a world of moral ambiguity.

It was the first time Bogey played the cold, hard-boiled guy whose seen it all.

It was the first appearance on screen by Sydney Greenstreet.

It was screenwriter John Huston's first directing job.

It was the first pairing of Sydney Greenstreet and Peter Lorre, who went on to make nine films together, including *Casablanca* and *The Mask of Dimitrios* (1944).

"You're good ... You're real good. It's chiefly in your eyes, I think—and that throb you get in your voice when you say things like, 'Be generous, Mr. Spade,'" says the betrayed Sam Spade when he discovers that the helpless woman-in-distress was betraying him all along. The guys on the side are cops who have come to take her away.

THE GREAT SCENE

Countless scenes could be cited but this one's "cherce." Brigid O'Shaughnessy (Mary Astor) proclaims her love for Spade (Humphrey Bogart) just as she's nabbed by the cops for murdering Spade's partner. Asking him if he loves her, too, she begs him to save her. And he responds with immortally chilling words: "I hope they don't hang you, precious, by that sweet neck. The chances are you'll get off with life. That means if you're a good girl, you'll be out in 20 years. I'll be waiting for you. If they hang you, I'll always remember you."

"I couldn't be fonder of you if you were my own son. But, well, if you lose a son, it's possible to get another. There's only one Maltese Falcon," says Kasper Gutman (Sydney Greenstreet) to Spade as they cordially share a drink.

73

PATHER PANCHALI 1955

STAR OF INDIA

Satyajit Ray's masterpiece demonstrates the power of foreign films to explore truthfully an unknown corner of the world, allowing audiences to make a personal connection. Strip away the mystical, alien terrain of Indian village life circa 1910 and you're left with a universal family: young parents, their two small children, and a burdensome elder. Despite their poverty and hopeless circumstances, the dynamics are, remarkably, the same as in any other family, anywhere in the world, at any time: a mother's exhausted rage, a father's inability to protect his children from the random cruelties of life. Ray's camera lingers so long that at times you think it may be stuck. But you begin to understand that the almost meditative pace, the thorough examination of uneventful moments, are taking you somewhere you may never have been, at least on film. It's an incredible journey.

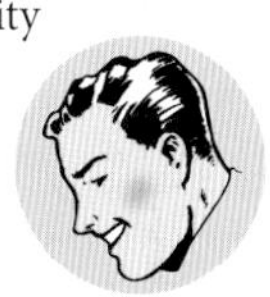

Jim: Don't wait to be in the mood for Something Important. This is very accessible, a grabber from the first minute. One of the most, no, *the* most affecting movie about being a kid I've ever seen.

Gail: Characterization, characterization, characterization. That is all you need to know, and know you will find it brilliantly achieved in Ray's unsentimental and utterly engaging portrait of childhood.

E PLOT

chronicle of the day-to-day struggles of npoverished but refined young family in n-of-the-century Indian farming village s many small surprises. Father Harihar u Banerjee) is cheerful despite his hard-ble existence but his wife Sarbojaya una Bannerjee) is worn out by the effort. s forced to eject her ancient Aunt Indur nibala Devi) from the house—there is just hungry mouth too many. Sarbojaya re-s the joyous spirit of her daughter Durga a Das Gupta) even as she coddles her g son Apu (Subir Banerjee). But Durga learns life's hard lessons when she and find Indur's corpse in the woods. There is ment of pure ecstasy as Durga dances drought-saving downpour. The result is udden illness and from that moment he tragedies pile up until the embittered y is forced to abandon their home and again in the unforgiving big city.

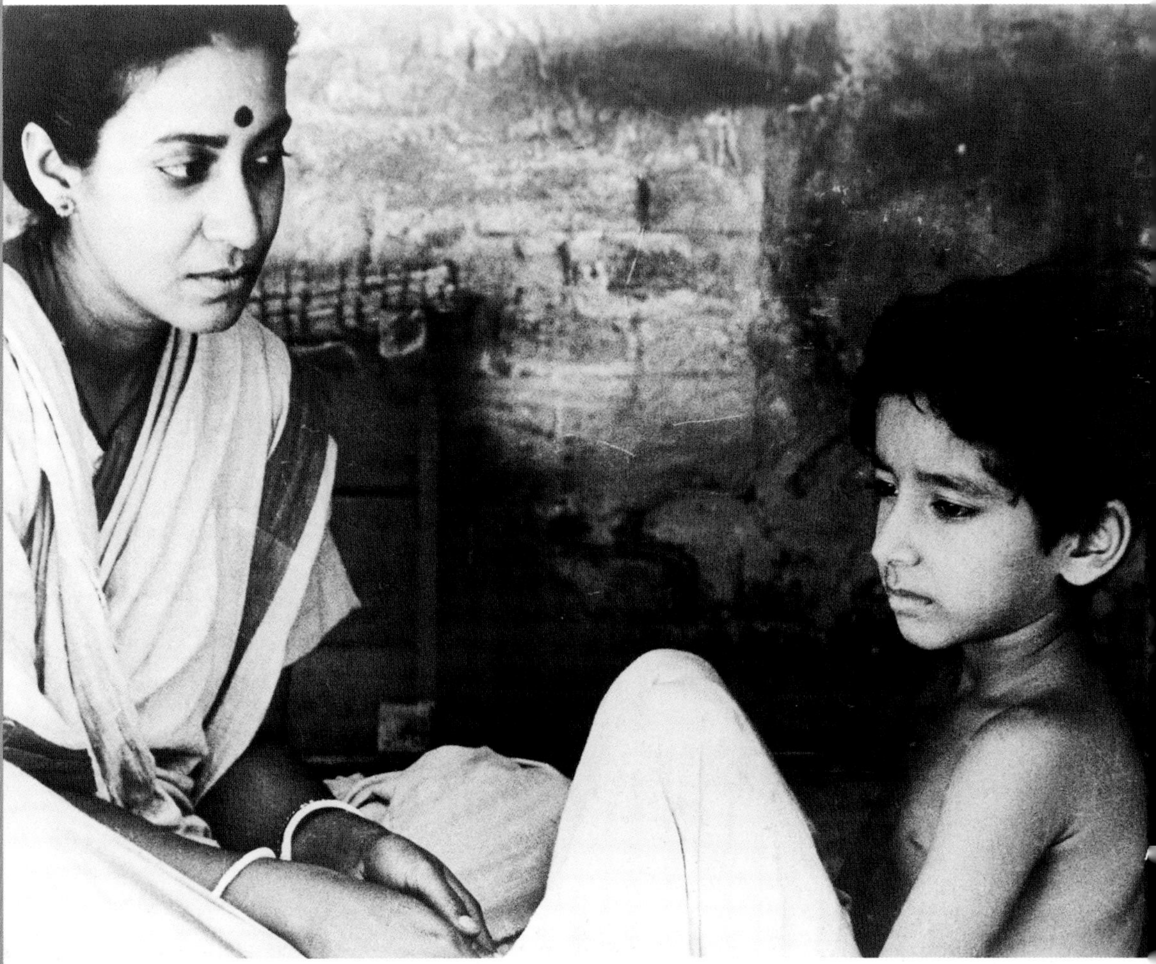

Maternal concern for her despairing child is universal. The trauma may be impossible to resolve, and Ray doesn't try to come up with an easy way out for the sake of formulaic storytelling. His camera lingers quietly to give the moment its fullest dimension.

"Whatever God does is for the best."—Harihar

THE DIRECTOR

Satyajit Ray was a young book illustrator who dreamed of making movies after seeing *The Bicycle Thief*. Unable to gain financing for the unusual film he had in mind, he pawned his wife's one good necklace to get started. He chose a small village outside Calcutta for the setting of his slowly evolving docudrama. Ray had been lucky to meet French auteur filmmaker Jean Renoir while he was in India shooting *The River* (1951), and was able to induce members of his photographic crew to assist. Another stroke of good fortune came when a few sequences of the unfinished film got into the hands of John Huston. Huston was hugely impressed and thought the film might be perfect in connection with a forthcoming exhibit of Indian art at New York City's Museum of Modern Art. With that promise, Ray managed to get the rest of his financing from the Bengal government and was able to hire Ravi Shankar to compose the indelible score. *Pather Panchali* was a sensation, the most talked about directorial debut in years. His chief young rival at the time, François Truffaut, walked out on a screening of *Pather Panchali*, claiming it was too precise, too caught up in details of the ordinary, and that he feared it would set a trend. But Ray would always be willfully out of step with prevailing cinematic fashions, content to concentrate "on the details" in dozens of films. His two most famous are the follow-ups to *Pather Panchali*, *Aparajito* (1956) and *The World of Apu* (1959) (the three films are usually referred to collectively as *The Apu Trilogy*), which cover the first 30 years of hero Apu, from village boyhood to traumatic city life to the tragedies of his early manhood. On his deathbed in 1991, Satyajit Ray received an Honorary Academy Award for his "rare mastery of the art of motion pictures and for his profound humanitarian outlook."

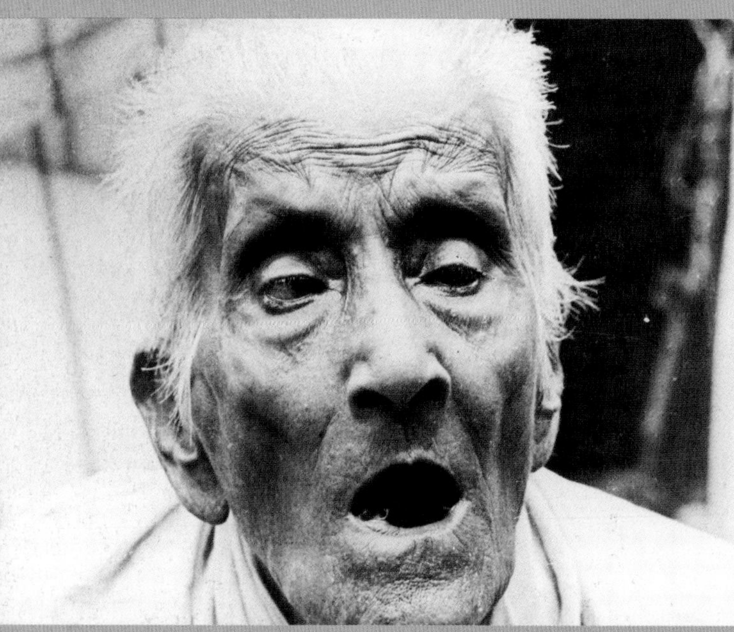

Chunibala Devi, long past her days as a famous actress, was homeless and dying until Ray rescued her, and he helped keep her alive for the duration of the production. Her performance is a raw and inspiring affirmation of the human will.

THE CAST	
Harihar Ray	Kanu Bannerjee
Sarbojaya Ray	Karuna Bannerjee
Apu	Subir Bannerjee
Durga	Uma Das Gupta
Indir Thakrun	Chunibala Devi
Little Durga	Runki Bannerjee
Seja Thakrun	Reba Devi
Nilmoni's wife	Aparna Devi

THE ACTORS

Due to cost and his desire for authenticity, Ray used primarily nonprofessional actors. A rare exception was **Chunibala Devi,** a once-famous stage actress, who played the role of the ancient aunt. Her career had come to an end as the result of illness, and by the time Ray met her, she was surviving on opium tablets. He was nervous she wouldn't make it through the shoot and took special care of her needs. Devi's performance was transcendent, and critics concurred that she gave the film its most poignant moments.

THE CRITICS

"Says and implies so much more than is ordinarily said in motion pictures that it is no wonder it towers above the thousands of films made in India, and marks the peak of the rich career of Ray." –Bosley Crowther, *New York Times*

"At the time of [*Pather*'s] release in the United States, [Ray's] achievement was occasionally misconstrued as a worthy fluke–the work of a documentary amateur from a primitive outpost of the cinematic world." –Gary Arnold, *Washington Post*

BEHIND THE SCREEN

On the very first day of shooting, Ray chose what he thought would be the easiest scene, one in which the children wander through a vast field of flowers. It went very well but he eventually lost the light and had to schedule more takes for the next day. The cast and crew returned to find all the flowers gone. In a panic, Ray interrogated a local farmer who simply smiled and explained they were filming in a grazing field. Overnight, the animals had devoured "the set."

Chunibala Devi died before the film's release.

CREDITS

Producer:
Government of West Bengal
Director: Satyajit Ray
Screenplay: Satyajit Ray, based on the novel by Bibhuti Bannerji
Running time: 115 minutes
Box Office: $500,000 (U.S.)

AWARDS

Cannes Film Festival:
Best Human Document
National Board of Review:
Best Foreign Film

THE YEAR'S ACADEMY AWARD WINNERS

Best Picture: *On the Waterfront*
Best Director: Elia Kazan, *On the Waterfront*
Best Actor: Marlon Brando, *On the Waterfront*
Best Actress: Grace Kelly, *The Country Girl*
Best Supporting Actor: Edmond O'Brien, *The Barefoot Contessa*
Best Supporting Actress: Eva Maria Saint, *On the Waterfront*

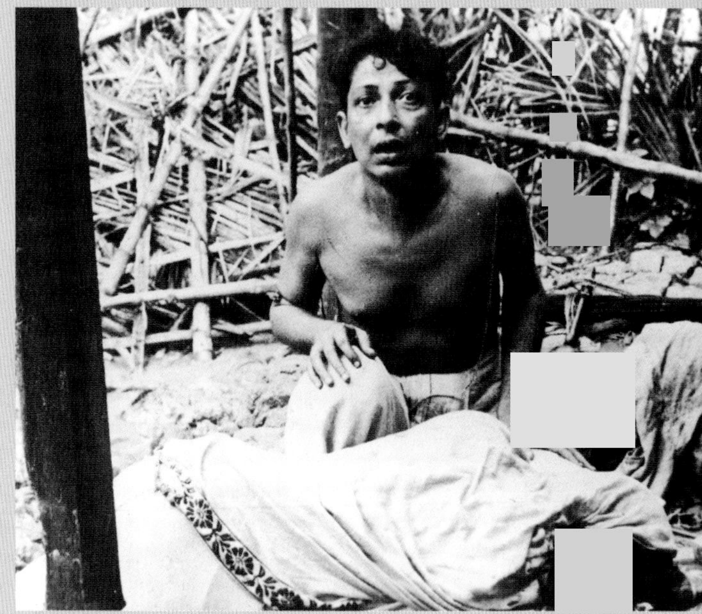

Ray's genius was in connecting us so completely with people we'd never encounter otherwise. He pulls it off without a shred of sentimentality. Remarkably, it's not depressing in the least–simply real.

"You know you worked honestly and hard, and so did everybody else. But you also know you had to make changes, compromises—on the set and in the cutting room. Is it better for them or worse? You cannot be sure. But you can be sure of one thing: you are a better man for having made it."
—Satyajit Ray

THE OTHER LISTS

- American Film Institute (No)
- Roger Ebert's Top 100 (No)
- *Entertainment Weekly* (No)
- Internet Movie Database (No)
- Leonard Maltin (No)
- *Movieline* (No)
- National Society of Film Critics (No)
- *Premiere* Magazine (No)
- *Rolling Stone* Magazine (No)
- *Village Voice* (Yes)

Apu's wide-eyed wonder makes us feel as if we're seeing the great mysteries of life for the first time. His joyous adulation of his older sister, Durga, makes every day with her an exotic adventure.

Little Apu is just happy to be in the company of his lively and imaginative sister, Durga, as they explore the wonders of the forest. They linger by a pond teeming with life before bravely foraging through a wide open field to a point beyond any they've gone before. In the distance they see a great locomotive steaming across the provincial landscape. It's the first train they've ever seen, and Apu beams with the magic of childhood's first unforgettable discoveries.

74

THE LADY EVE 1941

CRUEL TO BE KIND

The situation is simple: A beautiful, sophisticated, and wily cardsharp named Eve Sidwich (Barbara Stanwyck) pulls the wool over the eyes of the virginal, haven't-got-a-clue, "dripping with dough" ale heir, Charles Pike (Henry Fonda). Instead of falling for his money, though, she falls for his innocence against all her worldly instincts. Everything else is mind-boggling about this knowing, fast-paced, ribald, intoxicating, and painful screwball battle of the sexes, which boasts the cruelest and most competent of seductresses with a heart of melted butter. Charles is always falling at Eve's feet because she is always sticking her leg out. There's more than a touch of suppressed anger in these comic moments. After all, love is dangerous. As Eve purrs when the two finally come together, "If anybody ever deserved me you do. So richly!"

Jim: Stanwyck brings a world-weary, unspoken sexual history to her character in the way she moves, the fact that she has cigarettes for breakfast. She seems almost more eager to take on the role of mother than lover.

Gail: A femme fatale coldly humiliates a man and the end result is an exuberant, exhilarating, brain-twisting, and, yes, good-natured, comedy.

THE PLOT

On a transatlantic ocean liner, cardsharps and con artists Eve (Barbara Stanwyck) and her father, "the Colonel" (Charles Coburn), prey on shy ale millionaire ("Pike's Pale, The Ale That Won for Yale") and snake expert Charles, a.k.a. Hopsie (Henry Fonda), who has just emerged from the Amazon jungle. While he is happily ensconced in his book *Why Snakes Are Necessary*, hundreds of debutantes fall at his feet, but to no avail. It takes an Eve to snag him, which she does by dropping an apple on his head (ahem). The Amazon is nothing compared to the sexually dangerous jungle into which Eve entices Hopsie. As the plot twists snakelike around false and mistaken identities, character transformations, and cold-blooded deceptions, Eve herself loses control and falls in love with Hopsie, for better or for worse.

Try as he might to avoid Eve's feminine charms (Barbara Stanwyck), Hopsie (Henry Fonda) is lured to her bed against—or because of—all his instincts.

"I need him like an axe needs a turkey." — Lady Eve

THE DIRECTOR

After years of watching his scripts mangled by other directors, Hollywood rebel **Preston Sturges** finally threatened to leave Paramount if director Mitchell Leisen got the go-ahead to direct *The Lady Eve.* Studio chief William Le Baron assented to his wishes, and a great director was born. With *The Lady Eve* Sturges attained overnight prominence. In her biography of the director, Diane Jacobs recounts what Sturges revealed to his assistant director, Mel Epstein, about the underlying tricks of this trade: "He would write his protagonists into a box, where there seemed no hope for them. The purpose of trapping his characters was to extricate them—ingeniously." Though his star burned only briefly with a sting of brilliant and successful movies, including his Oscar-grabber for Best Screenplay, *The Great McGinty* (1940), and *Sullivan's Travels* (1941), Sturges's unique blending of barbed, sophisticated writing with outrageous slapstick remains unmatched. Hollywood threw him out the door, however, when they decided his genius made him a bit too arrogant for their liking. His downfall probably had more to do with his downright weirdness. A flamboyant cross-dresser, he may well have been wearing a smart skirt and sweater while directing prim homophobe Fonda. In the end, out of work and without savings, the great director died nearly penniless.

"Colonel" Harrington (Charles Coburn) shares some fatherly advice with his daughter as the two travel the globe in search of wealthy suckers to fall prey to their card tricks: "Don't be vulgar, Jean (a.k.a. Eve). Let us be crooked, but never common."

THE CAST

Jean Harrington/Lady Eve Sidwich	Barbara Stanwyck
Charles "Hopsie" Pike	Henry Fonda
"Colonel" Harrington	Charles Coburn
Horace Pike	Eugene Pallette
Ambrose "Muggsy" Murgatroyd	William Demarest
Sir Alfred McGlennan Keith ("Pearlie")	Eric Blore
Gerald	Melville Cooper

THE ACTORS

Often called the best actress who never won an Oscar, **Barbara Stanwyck** played everything from working-class heroines to gun molls and adulteresses. "When she was good, she was very, very good. And when she was bad, she was terrific," said Walter Matthau of Stanwyck. As Eve, arguably her greatest comic role, Stanwyck plays the female screwball lead with a difference: She's a genuinely scheming femme fatale out to "get" her man, though in the end her underhandedness is leavened by love and compassion. You can never be sure, however, when the nasties will rise again. (For more on Stanwyck, see page 79.)

Director and writer Peter Bogdanovich put **Henry Fonda**'s performance in perspective when he wrote that "*The Lady Eve* is the single time in Henry Fonda's long and valuable career that he played this sort of absentminded, innocent professor type, or did the kind of slapstick pratfall business he does repeatedly here, and with such wonderful enthusiasm that you'd think he would have made a specialty of these roles." Who knows? Had he made comedies instead of playing the decent and honest citizen, might he have won the Oscar sooner instead of as an old man in 1981's *On Golden Pond*? (For more on Fonda, see page 211.)

Playing the cantankerous but lovable character role of the Colonel, **Charles Coburn**'s dignified and hilarious performance in *Eve* is probably his best remembered, though it runs neck and neck with *The More The Merrier* (1943), for which he won the Best Supporting Actor Oscar.

Inextricable from the Sturges oeuvre, crusty old salt **William Demarest** appeared in nearly all of the director's films, including *The Great McGinty* (1940), *Sullivan's Travels* (1941), *The Palm Beach Story* (1942), *The Miracle at Morgan's Creek* (1944), and *Hail the Conquering Hero* (1944). It's difficult not to lose it remembering Demarest crashing to the ground in slapstick pratfalls that could have taught Chevy Chase a thing or two. Demarest had an active career, appearing in over 100 films, among them *Rebecca of Sunnybrook Farm* (1938), *Mr. Smith Goes to Washington* (1939), *What Price Glory* (1952), *Son of Flubber* (1963), *It's a Mad, Mad, Mad, Mad World* (1963), and *Won Ton Ton, the Dog Who Saved Hollywood* (1976). Demarest is arguably best known as Uncle Charley in the TV series *My Three Sons* (1965).

THE CRITICS

"A frivolous masterpiece. Like *Bringing Up Baby*, *Eve* is a mixture of visual and verbal slapstick, and of high artifice and pratfalls." —Pauline Kael, *The New Yorker*

"Mr. Sturges writes with a skimming but penetrating touch. He may have sacrificed a rib to the cause, but he has done the old Adam proud in his creation of the Lady Eve." —Bosley Crowther, *New York Times*

SEND IN THE CLONES

The Birds and the Bees (1956)

NOTABLE QUOTES

"I did all my directing when I wrote the screenplay. It was probably harder for a regular director. He probably had to read the script the night before shooting started." —Preston Sturges

"Put me in the last fifteen minutes of a picture and I don't care what happened before. I don't even care if I was IN the rest of the damned thing—I'll take it in those fifteen minutes." —Barbara Stanwyck

"I'm a tough old broad from Brooklyn. I intend to go on acting until I'm ninety and they won't need to paste my face with makeup." —Barbara Stanwyck

CREDITS

Producer: Paul Jones/Paramount
Director: Preston Sturges
Screenplay: Preston Sturges (based on the story "Two Bad Hats" by Monckton Hoffe)
Running Time: 97 minutes

ACADEMY AWARD NOMINATIONS

Best Writing, Original Story

THE YEAR'S WINNERS

Picture: *How Green Was My Valley*
Director: John Ford, *How Green Was My Valley*
Actor: Gary Cooper, *Sergeant York*
Actress: Joan Fontaine, *Suspicion*
Supporting Actor: Donald Crisp, *How Green Was My Valley*
Supporting Actress: Mary Astor, *The Great Lie*

THE OTHER LISTS

American Film Institute (No)
Roger Ebert's Top 100 (Yes)
Entertainment Weekly (Yes)
Internet Movie Database (No)
Leonard Maltin (Yes)
Movieline (Yes)
Premiere Magazine (No)
Rolling Stone Magazine (Yes)
Village Voice (Yes)

Jean sets her sights on Hopsie and through the lens of her compact makeup mirror voyeuristically observes a bevy of women surrounding her prey. She's literally got him in the palm of her hands as she narrates and directs what she sees to her father: "Not good enough . . . they're not good enough for him. Every Jane in the room is giving him the thermometer and he feels they're just a waste of time. He sees no one except—"

> *The Colonel: "It won't do you any good, dear, he's a bookworm, but swing 'em anyway. He'll never see it."*

Isn't it romantic? Cardsharp and gold digger Eve Sidwich (Barbara Stanwyck) literally knocks the wealthy, innocent paleontologist and ale fortune-heir Charles "Hopsie" Pike (Henry Fonda), off his feet and without a clue as to how he got there.

PRESTON STURGES'S GOLDEN RULES FOR SUCCESSFUL COMEDY

"A pretty girl is better than a plain one/ A leg is better than an arm/ A bedroom is better than a living room/ An arrival is better that a departure/ A birth is better than a death/ A chase is better than a chat/ A dog is better than a landscape/ A kitten is better than a dog/ A baby is better than a kitten/ A kiss is better than a baby/ A pratfall is better than anything."

Eve finds herself undermined by her own plan to land Hopsie for his money by falling a little bit in love with him—against her better judgment. She tries to suggest to the unworldly millionaire that she may not be as bad as she looks. "You see, Hopsie, you don't know very much about girls. The best ones aren't as good as you think they are and the bad ones aren't as bad. Not nearly as bad."

75

THE LAST PICTURE SHOW 1968

DEEP IN THE ACHING HEART OF TEXAS

It was Peter Bogdanovich's first major film and he almost got himself fired because he didn't know what a master shot was. He was young, exceptionally arrogant, but with his soul and mind utterly committed to getting the story right. The casting is just about perfect and it's no great surprise that *The Last Picture Show* launched several exceptional careers. Bogdanovich caught his actors at that precise moment when they were ready to give as much as he was. When it was first released, the film's mostly-implied sex scenes raised a few hackles. By current standards, however, there's almost an innocent charm to them. Like its infamous predecessor of small town scandals, *Peyton Place, The Last Picture Show* simply wants to remind us that even back in the repressive 1950s, people were wearing out the mattress springs. The true miracle here is Bogdanovich's ability to balance so many characters and make us care for all of them despite some nasty traits. *The Last Picture Show* is so heartfelt that one false move and it might've all turned to mush. It didn't.

Jim: You can't believe you're actually watching Cybill Shepherd steal a movie.

Gail: The desert-dry loneliness of America at the end of an era is captured beautifully by the black-and-white photography. The movie aches with lost loves and disappointed dreams.

THE PICTURE SHOW THAT INTRODUCED AMERICA TO THE FORGOTTEN 50'S.
It launched the meteoric career of its brilliant new director and its talented cast.
It won 2 Academy Awards, and nominations for 8.
If you missed it the first time, you owe it to yourself now.
If you saw it once, remember again.
ROYAL
THE LAST PICTURE SHOW
PETER BOGDANOVICH
R

[TH]E PLOT

[A]s of 1951 high school senior Sonny [Craw]ford (Timothy Bottoms) dreams of a world [beyo]nd Anarene, Texas, but he's content to hang [with] his best buddy Duane (Jeff Bridges) and [while] away his days at Sam's pool hall, the social [hub] of Anarene's good old boys. Sam (Ben [John]son) is like a father to him and when he [dies] suddenly, Sonny's life changes forever. He's [inhe]rited the pool hall but the joy of it has been [lost t]o him. He falls into a bittersweet affair with [the f]ootball coach's wife Ruth (Cloris Leachman) [but d]umps her when Anarene's dream girl Jacy [(Cyb]ill Shepherd) suddenly becomes available. [She']s tossed aside Duane who's so enraged [by] the betrayal, he comes after Sonny and [knoc]ks out his eye. Jacy weds Sonny for the thrill [but] it's quickly annulled by her rich daddy and [unfu]lfilled mom (Ellen Burstyn). Sonny recon-[ciles] with Duane on the eve of his departure for [Kore]a. They celebrate by taking in the last show [at th]e town's bankrupted theater. Day's later, [Sam]'s retarded son Billy (Joe Bottoms) is fatally [run o]ver on Main Street. Sonny is outraged by [the a]pathetic response to the tragedy and seri-[ousl]y considers leaving town. Before he does, he [mus]t make amends to long-suffering Ruth who [still p]ines for him.

Willful teen queen Jacy (Cybill Shepherd) heeds her mom's advice and takes boyfriend Duane (Jeff Bridges) for a "test drive" at a motel to see if they're sexually compatible. He fumes, she fumes, and a Texas-size heartbreak looms.

"One thing I know for sure—a person can't sneeze in this town without somebody offerin' him a handkerchief ... it's an awful small town for any kinda carryin' on ... And some people got a lotta guns." —Diner waitress, Genevieve

THE DIRECTOR

Former stage actor and film critic **Peter Bogdanovich** earned his directing stripes young with *Targets* (1967). He was turned onto Larry McMurtry's novel by Sal Mineo, who'd always thought it would be a great film. It was Orson Welles who suggested black-and-white. Bogdanovich understood at once that it would help the performances. The movie would either succeed or fail based on the acting. As a result, he refused to have lunch or socialize with anyone but the cast. The crew, feeling entirely ignored, came to detest him. When a script supervisor dared give Cybill Shepherd a line-reading, he was fired on the spot. He encouraged bonding among the cast and Ellen Burstyn admits to many nights sitting around Jeff Bridges's hotel room, singing along to his guitar and getting stoned. In a key scene in which she had to express at least eight different emotions without a word of dialogue, Bogdanovich told her, "Just eliminate everything else from your mind and think what the character thinks. The camera will read it." While discoursing with Orson Welles about Greta Garbo, Bogdanovich bemoaned the fact that she only made two great pictures. Welles studied him for a moment and said, "You only need one." And with *The Last Picture Show*, Bogdanovich had his. His following two films, *What's Up Doc*? (1972) and *Paper Moon* (1973) were sensations but he stumbled with *Daisy Miller* (1974), his unhappy transformation of the all-American corn-fed Cybill Shepherd into a 19th-century Henry James tragic heroine. He faltered yet again with *They All Laughed* (1981) but came back with *Mask* (1985). *Texasville* (1990) was an attempt to recapture the magic of *Last Picture Show* and while Bogdanovich's directorial star dimmed, he's become an accomplished author and actor with a recurring role on *The Sopranos*.

"Scarin' an unfortunate creature like Billy, just so's you could have a few laughs. I've been around that trashy behavior all my life. I'm gettin' tired of puttin' up with it." Sam is outraged by the gang of boys who've taken his retarded son, Billy, to the local $5 whore for his first "experience." Ben Johnson brought a quiet authenticity to the role of Sam the Lion, borne of his real-life cowboy years.

THE CAST

Sonny Crawford	Timothy Bottoms
Duane Moore	Jeff Bridges
Jacy Farrow	Cybill Shepherd
Sam the Lion	Ben Johnson
Ruth Popper	Cloris Leachman
Lois Farrow	Ellen Burstyn
Genevieve	Eileen Brennan
Abilene	Clu Gulager
Billy	Sam Bottoms
Charlene Duggs	Sharon Ullrick
Lester Marlow	Randy Quaid

THE ACTORS

Ben Johnson, the grizzled Western star discovered by John Ford, was resistant to the role of Sam. He turned it down three times, claiming "it had too many damn words." With an assist from Ford, Bogdanovich finally wore him down, promising he'd win an Academy Award for the performance. A youthful stint as a rodeo champion led to a long career in Westerns, many of which are genre classics, including *She Wore a Yellow Ribbon* (1949), *Shane* (1953), *Cheyenne Autumn* (1964), and *The Wild Bunch* (1969). He enjoyed a resurgence of popularity following his Best Supporting Oscar win, with *The Sugarland Express* (1974), TV-movie *True Grit* (1978) and *The Evening Star* (1996).

Jeff Bridges was chosen because he was so likeable. Bogdanovich thought that quality would bring dimension to his character, Duane, who's essentially a bastard. Bridges credits Lloyd Catlett, a local kid hired for a small role, with giving him the proper accent and sensibility. As a child of middling Hollywood royalty (his dad, Lloyd, was a ubiquitous B-movie actor), Bridges had a leg up but his dynamic work in *Last Picture Show* guaranteed him a career on his own steam. He's done especially well in roles requiring a tough guy with soul, e.g., *Thunderbolt and Lightfoot* (1974) and *Cutter's Way* (1981) and has suffered his share of disasters, most particularly the remake of *King Kong* (1976). He made a terrific villain in *Jagged Edge* (1985) and a visionary in *Tucker: The Man and His Dream* (1988). He teamed with his brother Beau for *The Fabulous Baker Boys* (1989). He played another murderous creep in *The Vanishing* (1993), Barbra Streisand's husband of convenience in *The Mirror Has Two Faces* (1996) and a coarse, fat guy in *The Big Lebowski* (1998). He appeared most recently in *Seabiscuit* (2003) and *The Door in the Floor* (2004).

Ellen Burstyn originally read for the waitress eventually played by **Eileen Brennan**. She was then asked to read for Ruth, Cloris Leachman's part. But she was fascinated by Lois, the lonely, philandering rich wife and mother of Jacy. She was so good at all of them she was told she was in the movie, no matter what, and that it was up to her who she wanted play. She was cast as yet another truly distressed mother in *The Exorcist* (1973) and finally got her chance to play a waitress in her Oscar-winning film, *Alice Doesn't Live Here Anymore* (1974). *After Same Time, Next Year* (1978) and *Resurrection* (1980), she suffered "Hollywood burnout." Her return to film wasn't particularly notable, given such fare as *Hanna's War* (1988) and *The Cemetery Club* (1992), until she roared back with her Oscar-nominated, harrowing performance in *Requiem for a Dream* (2000).

Cloris Leachman nailed the character right off with the name, Ruth Popper. "Hard to overcome a name like that." She admits to being too naive at the time to realize her husband, the coach, was homosexual. It was never played up in the movie. In her big scene, where she blows up at her teen lover, Sonny, she expected several takes. Bogdanovich was happy with her first. She was shocked and begged to do it again. He refused. It was the scene that clinched her Oscar. After being crowned "Miss Chicago" in 1946, she launched an acting career with her role in *Lassie* (1954). She made a sitcom splash with her indelible presence on *The Mary Tyler Moore Show* (1970) and her spin-off series, *Phyllis* (1975). She got some of the biggest laughs in Mel Brooks's *High Anxiety* (1977) and after cameos in dozens of TV movies, she reprised her Ruth Popper for *Texasville* (1990). She's more recently appeared in the short-lived TV show, *Ellen [DeGeneres]* (2001).

Cybill Shepherd was fatefully discovered by Bogdanovich's wife and Production Designer, Polly Platt, who saw her on the cover of *Glamour* magazine and thought she looked the part of Jacy perfectly. She had very little interest in an acting career and demanded a stipulation

CREDITS

Producer: BBS Productions/ Columbia Pictures
Director: Peter Bogdanovich
Screenplay: Peter Bogdanovich, Larry McMurtry
Running time: 118 minutes
Budget: $1.3 million

ACADEMY AWARDS

Best Supporting Actor: Ben Johnson
Best Supporting Actress: Cloris Leachman

NOMINATIONS

Best Picture
Best Director: Peter Bogdanovich
Best Adapted Screenplay: Larry McMurtry and Peter Bogdanovich
Best Supporting Actor: Jeff Bridges
Best Supporting Actress: Ellen Burstyn
Best Cinematography: Robert Surtees

THE YEAR'S OTHER WINNERS

Best Picture: *The French Connection*
Best Director: William Friedkin, *The French Connection*
Best Actor: Gene Hackman, *The French Connection*
Best Actress: Jane Fonda, *Klute*

THE GREAT SCENE

Barely awake, Sonny steps outside the pool hall and spots a commotion on the far side of Main Street. His good eye focuses on the broom lying in the dust. He runs hell-bent toward the scene where the Sheriff and local menfolk surround poor retarded young Billy. He's been struck dead by a truck. "I don't know what the hell he was doing out here in the middle of the street," one of them says without much sympathy. Sonny, with tears of rage, picks up his surrogate little brother and drags him to the sidewalk. "You sons of bitches, he was sweepin', he was sweepin'!" He lays him out lovingly, removes his own jacket and covers the dead boy's face. He then walks away in the shock of grief. A mumbled comment as he passes, "I don't know what's wrong with the kids around here. They're all crazy."

Bogdanovich avoids the pitfalls of sentimentality and nostalgia by keeping his camera at harshly realistic eye-level in every shot in the movie.

in her contract that there would be no nudity. But by the time she was to shoot her big scene at the nude swimming party, she was already Bogdanovich's lover and trusted him implicitly. She was further encouraged by the other actresses who felt it was important to her character. Shepherd followed up with one of her best roles in *The Heartbreak Kid* (1972) but, along with Bogdanovich, suffered the trials of *Daisy Miller* (1974) and her questionable musical debut in *At Long Last Love* (1975), singing and tapping with Burt Reynolds. She'll forever be remembered as Travis Bickle's love interest in *Taxi Driver* (1976) before turning to TV for another great round of success with *Moonlighting* (1985) and *Cybill* (1995). She would seem to be once again ideally cast as Martha Stewart in *Martha Stewart Inc.* (2003)

Last Picture Show provided **Timothy Bottoms** with an auspicious debut and though he continued to work he was never able to attain stardom. His second most notable role was in the *Paper Chase* (1973) before a long string of sympathetic, puppy-eyed performances in a raft of forgettable films culminating most recently in *The Prince and the Surfer* (2000).

BEHIND THE SCREEN

In the film, the last picture show to play at Anarene's Royale theater is *Red River*, starring John Wayne. Bogdanovich chose it because it took place in Texas at a time when it was full of hope and promise.

Bogdanovich's scandal-fueled personal life didn't end with his affair with Cybill Shepherd. He then courted *Playboy* centerfold Dorothy Stratten and wrote the doomed *They All Laughed* for her. Shortly afterwards, she was murdered by her estranged husband. In a strange twist, he then wed her younger sister, Louise.

Young Sam Bottoms was visiting his brother Timothy on the set when Bogdanovich spotted him, liked his natural quality, and asked him if he wanted to be in the movie. Sam had no previous experience and hadn't considered a career. The actor originally cast as mute Billy was promptly let go.

Cybill Shepherd was desperate to have Jacy's saddle shoes as a memento of the film. But Bogdanovich's wife Polly was in charge of costumes and refused the request. Commented Shepherd, "I guess she figured I had enough of a souvenir: her husband."

THE OTHER LISTS

- American Film Institute (Yes)
- Roger Ebert's Top 100 (No)
- *Entertainment Weekly* (No)
- Internet Movie Database (No)
- Leonard Maltin (No)
- *Movieline* (No)
- National Society of Film Critics (No)
- *Premiere* Magazine (No)
- *Rolling Stone* Magazine (No)
- *Village Voice* (No)

CRITICS

"The most important work by a young American director since *Citizen Kane*."—*Newsweek*

"A very decent, straightforward kind of movie, as well as one of—and I rather hesitate to use such a square phrase—human values." —VincentCanby, *New York Times*

THE SET

McMurtry's hometown, Archer City, was the inspiration for the book. It was, as a result, an ideal place to shoot. Despite the glamour of it all, the locals weren't pleased to have their dirty laundry aired for all to see.

"What am I doin' apologizin' to you? Why am I always apologizin' to you, you little bastard?" Discarded lover, Ruth (Cloris Leachman), rails out at Sonny (Timothy Bottoms) when he begs forgiveness. Finally, she takes his hand and holds on tight with the last bit of hope she has left.

76

ONE FLEW OVER THE CUCKOO'S NEST 1975

NUTS FOR CUCKOO

This novel made author Ken Kesey an overnight counterculture hero, but the film had no such aspirations. Knowing it couldn't stand up to the book's paranoid, antiwar revolutionary politics, director Forman kept the story rooted in what happens among the patients and authority figures in one particular institution. The film stands out for its portrayal of damaged souls—not unlike most—whose humanity is constantly tampered with. *Cuckoo's Nest*'s observing look at the lives lived in a hospital for the criminally insane has impressive emotional power, not from any metaphorical associations, but from the situation itself. A riot breaks out over the indiscriminate restriction of TV privileges. A young man is starved for love and life but is terrified by what might happen to him if he dares to reach out. The evil Nurse Ratched (Louise Fletcher) is a mistress of domination through humiliation until she meets her match in Randle Patrick McMurphy (Jack Nicholson), with his wild passion for freedom and self-expression.

Jim: The world finally learns that Grinning Jack can do just about anything. His mesmerizing presence may someday define film-acting history as pre- and post-Nicholson.

Gail: The performances and the struggle between spirit and suppression are what make this a classic. Jack Nicholson lets his natural acting gifts show, and what an inspiring sight they are to behold.

THE PLOT

Wiseguy Randle Patrick McMurphy commutes his short jail sentence to an endless mental hospital stay, thinking it will get him off work duty. He doesn't know what he's traded. Now, his every move will be challenged by Ward Nurse Ratched, whose job it is to maintain the status quo of the institution, even if it means depriving those in her charge of their basic human rights. McMurphy strives for control and commits a number of riotous acts of insubordination. He stages a protest against Ratched's refusal to allow the patients to watch the World Series; he hijacks a bus and takes the group sailing on a fishing boat; he arranges to escape but organizes a party beforehand that has everyone up all night drinking, and provides Billy Bibbit (Brad Dourif) the chance of his life: to sleep with a woman. In the end, though, Nicholson can't win. He undergoes electroshock treatment to the point of paralysis. Seeing this, Chief Bromden (Will Sampson), who had planned to escape with him and knows that McMurphy would rather be dead than half alive, mercifully suffocates him to death in his bed.

Crazy like a fox, Randle Patrick McMurphy (Jack Nicholson) is too smart for his own good, thinking life will be a piece of cake in a mental hospital. He gets more than he bargained for when he loses all his human rights at the heavy hands of the head nurse.

"What do you think you are, for Chrissake, crazy or somethin'? Well you're not! You're not! You're no crazier than the average asshole out walkin' around on the streets and that's it."—McMurphy

THE DIRECTOR

"I spent more time in mental institutions than the others," director **Milos Forman** said when discussing his Oscar win. Forman is one of the few foreign directors to enjoy success in Hollywood. *Cuckoo's Nest* was met with mixed reviews, as was his direction. Vincent Canby wrote, "*Cuckoo's Nest* is at its best when Mr. Forman is exercising his talents as a director of exuberant comedy that challenges preconceived notions of good taste." Though *Cuckoo's Nest* is not an out-and-out comedy, Forman avoided many of the pitfalls of a "triumph of the spirit movie," so popular for the period. There's very little sentimentality and much outright, evenhanded outrage at the kind of mindless authority running the institution. Forman was orphaned by the Holocaust and raised by relatives, and among his humorous and moving early Czech films were *Loves of a Blonde* (1965, Best Foreign Film Oscar), and a satiric social commentary on Communism, *The Firemen's Ball* (1967). His first American film was the dryly funny *Taking Off* (1971). *Cuckoo's Nest* brought him acclaim, which led to the making of *Hair* (1979), *Ragtime* (1981), *Amadeus* (1984, Best Director Oscar), *Valmont* (1989), *The People vs. Larry Flynt* (1996), and *Man on the Moon* (1999).

Billy Bibbit (Brad Dourif, right) looks to McMurphy as his liberator. Indeed, McMurphy gets the young man what he has always wanted: a night in bed with a woman. When Nurse Ratched discovers Billy in flagrante, she torments him to the point of suicide.

THE CAST

Randle Patrick McMurphy	Jack Nicholson
Nurse Mildred Ratched	Louise Fletcher
Harding	William Redfield
Col. Matterson	Michael Berryman
Ellis	Peter Brocco
Dr. John Spivey	Dean R. Brooks
Miller	Alonzo Brown
Orderly Turkle	Scatman Crothers
Warren	Mwako Cumbuka
Martini	Danny DeVito
Jim Sefelt	William Duell
Bancini	Josip Elic
Ellsworth	Dwight Marfield
Woolsey	Philip Roth
Chief Bromden	Will Sampson
Frederickson	Vincent Schiavelli
Scanlon	Delos V. Smith Jr.
Ruckley	Tim Welch
Billy Bibbit	Brad Dourif

THE ACTORS

Having spent three months as a resident of the Oregon State Asylum, along with the rest of the cast, **Jack Nicholson** told the *New York Daily News*, "Usually I don't have much trouble slipping out of a film role, but here I don't go home from a movie studio, I go home from a mental institution." The critics' response to Nicholson's performance changed the course of his career. The *New York Times*'s Vincent Canby observed, "Nicholson slips into the role of Randle with such easy grace that it's difficult to remember him in any other film." *People* magazine predicted, correctly, "*Cuckoo's Nest* should bring Nicholson his long overdue Oscar and public acceptance as the first American actor since Marlon Brando and James Dean with the elemental energy to wildcat new wells of awareness in the national unconscious." (For more on Nicholson, see page 39.)

Louise Fletcher, in her first film role as Nurse Ratched, played what would become an American type: the sexually repressed, controlling, and sadistic bureaucrat. "She was nothing short of blood-curdling as the dispassionate, ruthless, and vaguely sadistic Nurse Ratched," wrote critic Leonard Maltin. The bemused Fletcher—whose husband produced the film—couldn't help laughing as she spoke to reporters. "Suddenly, I'm having to worry about my hair," she said. "I got hot rollers for the first time in my life." Fletcher would continue to make films like *Exorcist II: The Heretic* (1977), *Strange Invaders* (1983), *Brainstorm* (1983), *Firestarter* (1984), and *Invaders from Mars* (1986). She earned an Emmy nomination for her recurring role on *Picket Fences*, but is perhaps best known to television audiences as Kai Winn from *Star Trek: Deep Space Nine*.

It was close, but no cigar at Oscar time for the intense and gentle performance of **Brad Dourif** as Billy Bibbit, the stuttering but spirited mental patient. Though he has not received the attention he deserves, his few standout performances have been characterized by subtlety and fragile intelligence in such films as *Wise Blood* (1979), *Eyes of Laura Mars* (1978), *Ragtime* (1981), *Blue Velvet* (1986), *Mississippi Burning* (1988), *Amos & Andrew* and the TV miniseries *Wild Palms* (both 1993), and his most recent outing, *Lord of the Rings: The Two Towers* (2002).

The dignified giant "deaf-mute" Chief Bromden—"as big as a goddamned tree trunk"—was played with pathos and humor by non-actor **Will Sampson**.

The diminutive and smiley Martini was one of **Danny DeVito**'s first featured roles. He has less hair now but many more starring roles to his credit, among them Louie on the television series *Taxi* (1978–83). He also appeared in *Ruthless People* (1986), which was his first directorial effort, *Throw Momma from the Train* and *Tin Men* (both 1987), *Twins* (1988), *The War of the Roses* (1989, which he directed), and *Batman Returns* and *Hoffa* (both 1992). One of the more powerful men in Hollywood, DeVito produced *Pulp Fiction* and *Reality Bites* (both 1994), and *Get Shorty* (1995), in which he also acted. Among the more recent films he's appeared in are *The Big Kahuna* (1999), *Man on the Moon* (1999), *Drowning Mona* (2000), *Heist* (2001), and *Death to Smoochy* (2002).

ROLE REVERSALS

The role of McMurphy was originally offered to James Caan. Marlon Brando and Gene Hackman were regarded as backups.

Actresses turning down the role of Nurse Ratched included Colleen Dewhurst, Jane Fonda, Jeanne Moreau, Ellen Burstyn, Faye Dunaway, Geraldine Page, Angela Lansbury, and Anne Bancroft.

Kirk Douglas bought the movie rights to the novel but couldn't get a studio to produce the film. He held onto the rights for a long time until his son Michael finally started the project. The elder Douglas had planned to star in it himself, but by the time they got around to making the film he was too old.

CREDITS

Producer: Saul Zaentz, Michael Douglas/United Artists
Director: Milos Forman
Screenplay: Bo Goldman, Lawrence Hauben
Running Time: 133 minutes
Budget: $3 million
Box Office: $112 million

ACADEMY AWARDS

Best Picture
Best Actor: Jack Nicholson
Best Actress: Louise Fletcher
Best Director: Milos Forman
Best Writing, Screenplay Adapted from Other Material: Lawrence Hauben, Bo Goldman

NOMINATIONS

Best Supporting Actor: Brad Dourif
Best Cinematography: Haskell Wexler, Bill Butler
Best Film Editing: Richard Chew, Lynzee Klingman, Sheldon Kahn
Best Music, Original Score: Jack Nitzsche

THE YEAR'S OTHER WINNERS

Best Supporting Actor: George Burns, *The Sunshine Boys*
Best Supporting Actress: Lee Grant, *Shampoo*

McMurphy calls for a vote among the usually dispirited patients about watching the World Series, which Nurse Ratched is against. He asks for a show of hands. All nine votes in the group are counted and McMurphy is feeling triumphant when Nurse Ratched decides to be the spoiler:

Nurse: "There are eighteen patients on this ward, Mr. McMurphy. And you have to have a majority to change ward policy. So you gentlemen can put your hands down now."

McMurphy: "You're tryin' to tell me that you're gonna count these, these poor son-of-a-bitches, they don't know what we're talkin' about."

Just as she announces that the meeting is closed, Chief slowly raises his hand, McMurphy is elated, but Ratched rejects the vote. Exasperated, McMurphy insists that the vote was 10 to 8, including the Chief (who barely manages to get his hand up).

Nurse: "No, Mr. McMurphy. When the meeting was adjourned, the vote was 9 to 9."

Not one to take things lying down, McMurphy finds a way to subvert her by staring and pretending to watch the game, cheering and calling an invented play-by-play. His excitement thrills the other patients who join in. As they come to believe (almost) that they are watching the game, we see their faces reflected on the dark monitor, victorious.

"Someone get me a fucking wiener before I die," says McMurphy (Jack Nicholson). He defies Nurse Ratched's refusal to allow the men to watch the World Series on television by pretending to watch the game. So convincing is his response to the blank TV screen that the men begin cheering along with him.

THE CRITICS

"Smashingly effective version of Ken Kesey's novel." —Pauline Kael, *The New Yorker*

"A comedy that can't quite support its tragic conclusion, which is too schematic to be honestly moving, but it is acted with such a sense of life that one responds to its demonstrations of humanity if not to its programmed metaphors." —Vincent Canby, *New York Times*

FILM DEBUTS

Brad Dourif, Christopher Lloyd, Will Sampson, and Dean R. Brooks (superintendent of the Oregon State Hospital in Salem, the film's main shooting location).

Ken Kesey, who wrote the original novel, said he would never watch the movie version and attempted to sue the movie's producers because the film wasn't written from Chief Bromden's perspective, as the novel was.

Jack Nicholson's girlfriend at the time, Anjelica Huston, appears in the crowd on the pier as the men return from their fishing excursion.

Jack Nicholson disappeared two months before filming started and underwent implants of hair plugs. This explains the stocking cap he wears throughout the movie.

The story was based on author Ken Kesey's experiences while working at the Veterans Administration Hospital in Palo Alto, California.

Along with *It Happened One Night* (1934) and *The Silence of the Lambs* (1991), *Cuckoo's Nest* was the third film to sweep the top five Academy Awards (Picture, Director, Actor, Actress, and Screenplay).

Actors got into character by living in the asylum for the duration of the filming, even sleeping at the facility. Nicholson couldn't handle the immersion and had to leave the building every day at lunchtime.

BEHIND THE SCREEN

Will Sampson, who plays the Chief, was discovered as a park ranger in Oregon, near the park where it was filmed.

Many of the extras wandering around the ward were actual mental patients.

The script called for McMurphy to leap on a guard and kiss him when first arriving at the hospital. During filming, director Milos Forman decided that the guard's reaction wasn't strong enough and told Nicholson to jump on the other guard instead. This surprised the actor greatly, and he can be seen punching Nicholson.

Rumor has it that Nicholson underwent electroshock therapy during the filming of the scene where his character does.

In her Academy Award-winning film debut, Louise Fletcher plays the ruthless and sadistic Nurse Ratched with chilling exactitude. As the authority figure of the institution, she sees herself as duty-bound to repress all human impulses toward self-expression, even while demanding that her patients express their feelings freely—or else.

THE OTHER LISTS

- American Film Institute (Yes)
- Roger Ebert's Top 100 (No)
- *Entertainment Weekly* (Yes)
- Internet Movie Database (Yes)
- Leonard Maltin (No)
- *Movieline* (No)
- National Society of Film Critics (No)
- *Premiere* Magazine (No)
- *Rolling Stone* Magazine (Yes)
- *Village Voice* (Yes)

77

ROSEMARY'S BABY 1968

MAMA MIA!

Roman Polanski's got a thing about old apartment buildings. In *Repulsion*, Catherine Deneuve's walls begin to pulse with blood. In *The Tenant*, renters of a particular Paris flat have a tendency to jump out the window. So when we follow Mia Farrow, at her translucent strangest, into the creepy basement laundry room of the Dakota apartment house on New York City's Central Park West, we jump almost as high as she does when a light bulb inexplicably shatters in the gloom. So much for that final rinse cycle—let's get the hell out of here! Polanski plays his hand very lightly at first, as if this were a pastel Doris Day romp. Early scenes show the attractive young newlyweds in love, redecorating, making fun of the eccentric neighbors, but slowly the honeymoon idyll turns dark. *Rosemary's Baby*, shot from the suspicious viewpoint of Rosemary herself, emerges as one of the most terrifying, paranoid thrillers ever. Even the bizarre humor—and there's plenty of it thanks to Ruth Gordon and her wacky gang of retiree Devil-worshipers—will keep you moving closer to the edge of your couch.

Jim: It's hard to get real estate out of your mind while you're watching this. Ira Levin's great 1966 joke is that an actor would sell his family to the devil in exchange for fame and fortune. Ironically, that apartment at the Dakota is probably worth more now than a three-picture deal at Paramount.

Gail: The tension in this New York nightmare reaches a pitch so high it bursts off the charts. What people wouldn't do for a job, an acting job, in New York makes me want to pack my bags and get out.

E PLOT

Woodhouse (John Cassavetes), an r who hasn't quite broken through yet, his new wife, Rosemary (Mia Farrow), n love with a rambling old Central Park apartment that unfortunately comes a dear but exasperating old couple next , Roman and Minnie Castevet (Sidney kmer and Ruth Gordon). The Castevets, ever, are not quite as harmless as they ear to be. In fact, they're Satanists plot- the birth of the Devil's first flesh-and- d son. To that end they need a mommy, who better than Rosemary? Of course, not to know. She'll be drugged for the ummation and led astray during the nancy. As a reward for sacrificing his wife, will be given every opportunity to rise to op of his profession. The only problem is Rosemary may be getting wise. Will she it them or will maternal instinct compel o come to the Devil's aid?

Rosemary (Mia Farrow): "I dreamed someone was raping me. I think it was someone inhuman." Guy (John Cassavetes): "Thanks a lot." Minnie Castevet (Ruth Gordon) has cooked up a special chocolate mousse full of sleeping powder to keep Rosemary inert for the consummation.

"He chose you, honey! From all the women in the world to be the mother of his only living son!"—Minnie Castevet

THE DIRECTOR

Rosemary's Baby was **Roman Polanski**'s first Hollywood film, and it kicked off what the 1970s golden age. "I really wanted to do a ski picture," he said, so Paramount Production Chief Robert Evans enticed him with the promise of the Robert Redford vehicle *Downhill Racer*. He got him in a hotel room and handed him Ira Levin's Manhattan Gothic horror novel. Polanski stayed up all night reading and was hooked. He agreed to direct only if he could have Dick Sylbert as his production designer. He didn't know New York well but when Polanski saw the Dakota apartment building, he knew he had his locale. He wanted to keep the ending ambiguous—"It's a horror story without the horror."—so we never see the baby, just Rosemary's reaction to it. Polanski maintains a special affection for actors, being one himself, in such pictures as *The Tenant* (1976). "I always let the actors try the scene first on their own. If I like it, I just let the camera follow them." (For more on Polanski, see page 39.)

"To 1966! The Year One!" Rosemary won't have a clue as to what the Castevets' toast really means until it's far too late. Off-screen, Mia Farrow is famously familiar with motherhood. She's had six children of her own and eight by adoption.

THE CAST

Rosemary Woodhouse	Mia Farrow
Guy Woodhouse	John Cassavetes
Minnie Castevet	Ruth Gordon
Roman Castevet	Sidney Blackmer
Edward Hutchins	Maurice Evans
Dr. Saperstein	Ralph Bellamy
Terry	Victoria Vetri
Laura-Louise	Patsy Kelly
Mr. Nicklas	Elisha Cook Jr.
Elise Dunstan	Emmaline Henry
Dr. Hill	Charles Grodin
Grace Cardiff	Hanna Landy
Dr. Shand	Phil Leeds
Diego	D'Urville Martin
Mrs. Gilmore	Hope Summers

THE ACTORS

Halfway through the production, 22-year-old **Mia Farrow** wanted to quit and return to her husband, Frank Sinatra. Paramount production chief Robert Evans showed her an hour of footage and told her she'd win the Academy Award. She proceeded with the picture, and the marriage ended in divorce. Polanski was amazed by how instinctive an actress she was: "Her choices are always so right. She has nothing of this Method business. She just concentrates, then relaxes." Mia had her own inner formula: "I know what I have to do and it doesn't start until Roman starts the camera. I don't like to talk about acting, I don't like to analyze it." Though well known for the TV series *Peyton Place* (1963-65), *Rosemary's Baby* took her career to a new level. But she muddled around in forgettable films until *The Great Gatsby* (1974), which then led to another dry spell before her resurrection as Woody Allen's star, muse, partner, and, finally, nemesis. Among her Allen films are *Zelig* (1983), *Broadway Danny Rose* (1984), *Purple Rose of Cairo* (1985), *Hannah and Her Sisters* (1986), *Alice* (1990), and *Husbands and Wives* (1992).

"I like obvious casting," Polanski said, "and **John Cassavetes** looks just like an Actor's Studio actor." At this point in his career, Cassavetes was gaining far more mileage as a pioneering indie director. Though he'd been Oscar-nominated for *The Dirty Dozen* (1967), he was soon to direct the groundbreaking *Faces* (1968), followed by *Husbands* (1970), *Minnie and Moskowitz* (1971), and *A Woman Under The Influence* (1974). Most of his films starred his wife, Gena Rowlands, and best friend, Peter Falk. Cassavetes died prematurely, never achieving the stardom of Al Pacino or Robert De Niro, though he's reminiscent of both in *Rosemary's Baby*.

"I can't tell you what an encouraging thing like this is," joked **Ruth Gordon**, 72, as she accepted her Best Supporting Actress Oscar. As Minnie Castevet, you can't take your eyes off her. It's not often you get to watch a master scenery-chewer gulp down an entire movie in one bite. She takes a line like, "Hey, we just found out a dear friend of ours is *preg-a-nant*," and transforms it into a high comic event. The screenwriting team of Gordon and her husband, Garson Kanin, churned out highly successful films like *A Double Life* (1947) and the vehicles for Katharine Hepburn and Spencer Tracy, *Adam's Rib* (1949) and *Pat and Mike* (1952). Famous as a stage actress in her youth, she came to films late in *Abe Lincoln in Illinois* (1940), and then much *much* later in *Inside Daisy Clover* (1965) and, most famously, *Harold and Maude* (1972). The autobiography of her youth, *The Actress*, was filmed in 1953 starring Jean Simmons.

SEND IN THE CLONES

The Omen (1976)
Demon Seed (1977)

ROLE REVERSALS

If Polanski had his way we would've seen Tuesday Weld as Rosemary and Robert Redford as Guy.

THE CRITICS

"If Ira Levin's story shrewdly taps into every pregnant woman's fears about the stranger growing inside her, Mia Farrow gives those fears an achingly real and human force."
—Stephen Farber, *Movieline*

"I've never received so much mail from adolescents (and post-adolescents) due to my derogatory remark about *Rosemary's Baby*. Adolescents think *Rosemary's Baby* is great because it upsets them." —Pauline Kael, *The New Yorker*

NOTABLE QUOTES

"I never know what my movies are about until I finish them."—John Cassavetes

"I like to be frightened when I see a film. Not to upset people would be an obscenity."
—Roman Polanski

"It is an error to find Ruth Gordon quaint or eccentric. She is the Queen of Hearts, Electra, and Lilith all crammed into one small frame."—David Thomson

CREDITS

Producer: William Castle Paramount
Director: Roman Polanski
Screenplay: Roman Polanski, based on the novel by Ira Levin
Running time: 136 minutes
Budget: $3.8 million
Box Office: $30 million

ACADEMY AWARDS

Best Supporting Actress: Ruth Gordon

NOMINATIONS

Best Adapted Screenplay: Roman Polanski

THE YEAR'S OTHER WINNERS

Picture: *Oliver!*
Director: Carol Reed, *Oliver!*
Actor: Cliff Robertson, *Charly*
Actresses: Katharine Hepburn, *The Lion in Winter*
Barbra Streisand, *Funny Girl*
Supporting Actor: Jack Albertson, *The Subject Was Roses*

A chance remark by a receptionist about the strange-smelling after-shave Dr. Saperstein uses makes Rosemary suddenly realize her obstetrician is part of the witch's coven. She rushes out to see her first doctor, and tells him all her suspicions about her husband and his pact. The doctor must help her and her baby! He tells her to rest, and that he'll take care of everything. As she sleeps, he makes a call. She wakes to find Guy and Saperstein ready to take her home. If she makes any more fuss they'll put her in a mental asylum. Numb with shock and betrayal, she's led out to a car driven by a smiling member of the cult.

"What have you done to him? What have you done to his eyes, you maniacs!" Polanski scored big with his American directorial debut, but after *Chinatown* (1974), he was forced to move himself Europe to avoid charges of statutory rape. His big Oscar win for *The Pianist* (2002) was seen by much of the Hollywood community as a vindication, both artistically and personally.

Rosemary's brief escape ends with betrayal. In real-life the fragile-looking Mia Farrow was able to stand her ground against domineering husband, Frank Sinatra, who commanded her to quit the picture and come home—or else.

BEHIND THE SCREEN

Tony Curtis is the voice of the blind actor on the telephone.

The ill-fated Sharon Tate appears uncredited in a party sequence.

Ira Levin wrote the suspenseful tale of another demonic Manhattan apartment building that inspired the movie *Sliver* (1993) starring Sharon Stone.

THE OTHER LISTS

- American Film Institute (No)
- Roger Ebert's Top 100 (No)
- *Entertainment Weekly* (No)
- Internet Movie Database (No)
- Leonard Maltin (No)
- *Movieline* (No)
- National Society of Film Critics (No)
- *Premiere* Magazine (No)
- *Rolling Stone* Magazine (No)
- *Village Voice* (No)

THE MUSIC

The haunting lullaby theme, sung/hummed by Mia Farrow, was a *Billboard* chartbuster for several weeks.

THE SET

The Dakota apartment house on New York's Central Park West serves as a major villain in *Rosemary's Baby*. It's perfectly designed and constructed for horror, with its complex gables, creepy ill-lit hallways, and closet walls that barely conceal doorways to the next apartment. The Dakota is additionally tainted with its notoriety as the site of John Lennon's murder. So when one of the characters early on tells us that the building was once a home to cannibal witches who partially ate then buried babies in the basement, it's not entirely implausible.

78

MIDNIGHT COWBOY 1969

ONE WHORE'S TOWN

Charles Dickens by way of *The Happy Hooker*. English director John Schlesinger brings the American class system to light, sentimentally zeroing in on the plight of those who slip between the cracks: the losers, hustlers, and street dregs who scramble for their little pieces of the action in the big, apathetic metropolis. Schlesinger and producer Jerome Hellman were initially delighted to have earned an X rating, the first and only Oscar-winning Best Picture to have done so. All these years later, the glaringly portrayed decadence seems almost charming. What hasn't grown quaint over time are two transcendent performances by Dustin Hoffman and, most particularly, Jon Voight. The tortuous path taken by his angelic but damaged manchild is as wrenching as any chapter from *Oliver Twist*.

Jim: Sometimes over the top, but a real heartbreaker. And get a load of pre-gentrified Manhattan—42nd Street actually looks dangerous.

Gail: It's a little too entertaining for a portrait of the down, degraded, and dismissed of society, but the movie manages to penetrate to the nerve endings, nevertheless. You'll never walk down 42nd Street—or board a Greyhound bus—without looking for Ratso and Joe Buck.

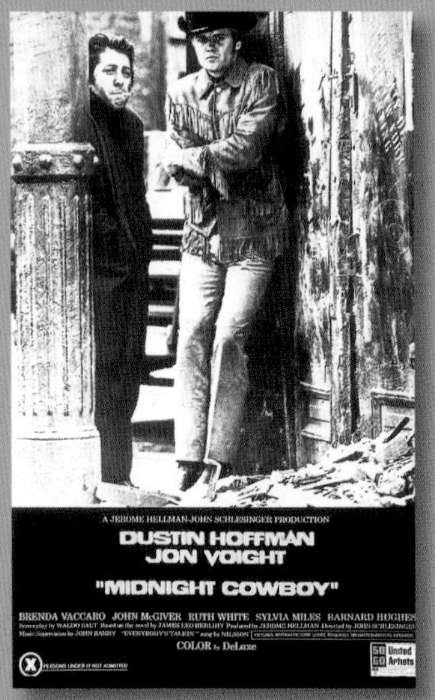

THE PLOT

Dimwit prettyboy Joe Buck (Jon Voight) quits his Texas dishwashing gig and buses to New York City to become a high-paid gigolo. He's heard that all the men are "tutti fruttis," and that the women are hungry for action. It doesn't take Joe long to realize he's been misinformed. He hardly earns a passing glimpse from any female. Drawing up his courage, he approaches sexy blonde Cass (Sylvia Miles), who turns the tables, demanding money for *her* sexual favors. He gets hoodwinked by crippled street hustler Ratso Rizzo (Dustin Hoffman). Ratso takes his money and sets him up with a Jesus freak. Joe tracks Ratso down and the little guy, feeling a touch of guilt and fearing a beating, does his best to teach Joe the rules of the game. Soon enough, Joe is working Times Square as a cut-rate stud for cigarette money. He and Ratso, probably the only real friend he's ever had, are barely surviving. Ratso's lungs are getting weaker and Joe is determined to finance a Florida getaway. He manages to score with socialite Shirley (Brenda Vaccaro), but in a follow-up with a male customer, things get violently out of hand. With his stolen stash, Joe gets himself and Ratso on the next bus bound for Miami, but a sunny future may not be in the cards.

"Uh, well, sir, I ain't a f'real cowboy. But I am one helluva stud!" Among one of Joe's (Jon Voight) paying "customers" is a young college student played by Bob Balaban, scion of one of Hollywood's pioneering dynasties, and a future regular on *Seinfeld*.

"Frankly, you're beginning to smell, and for a stud in New York, that's a handicap."—Ratso Rizzo

THE DIRECTOR

"People were looking at us as if we were embarking on the impossible. It wasn't an easy picture to make," insists **John Schlesinger**. "It wasn't even particularly enjoyable to make. Somehow one was always being confronted by something worse on the streets than one was putting in the film. There wasn't anything in the film I hadn't seen in some way, somewhere. Horrifying." As a result he didn't think the X rating was such a bad thing. "We *did* make the film for adults. It's not a film to which you'd necessarily recommend people to bring young children." Schlesinger is convinced *Midnight Cowboy* could never be made today. He ran the storyline by a studio exec recently and asked him if such a film would even be possible. The response was immediate and blunt. "I'd show you the door." Fortunately, Schlesinger already had his calling card, *Darling* (1965), and would go on to make another big winner with Dustin Hoffman, *Marathon Man* (1976). Among his best-known follow-ups are *The Falcon and the Snowman* (1985), the Yuppie thriller *Pacific Heights* (1990), and the Madonna vehicle *The Next Best Thing* (2000).

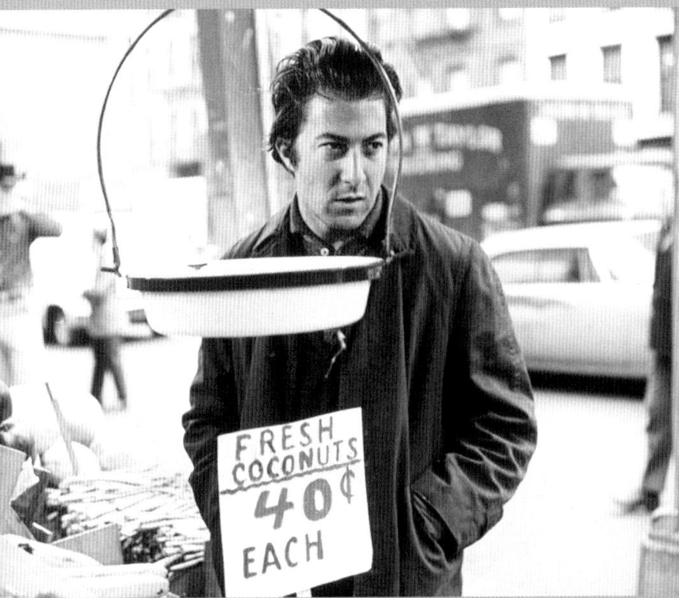

"You know, in my own place, my name ain't Ratso. I mean, it just so happens, in my own place my name is Enrico Salvatore Rizzo." It's astonishing to realize this was only Hoffman's second film. He risked his career on it, having developed a definite "clean cut" commercial image with his debut *The Graduate*, in which, at the age of 30, he played a 21-year-old.

THE CAST

Ratso Rizzo	Dustin Hoffman
Joe Buck	Jon Voight
Cass	Sylvia Miles
Mr. O'Daniel	John McGiver
Shirley	Brenda Vaccaro
Towny	Barnard Hughes
Sally Buck	Ruth White
Annie	Jennifer Salt
Woodsy Niles	Gil Rankin
Little Joe	Gary Owens
The Young Student	Bob Balaban

THE ACTORS

To eliminate any qualms that Schlesinger might have about his ability to play Ratso, **Dustin Hoffman** donned a filthy raincoat, slicked his hair back, and took the director on a tour of Manhattan's gritty pool halls and hustler dives. He blended in perfectly and got the part. A perfectionist to the last detail, Hoffman put pebbles in his shoe every day to keep Ratso's limp consistent. His extraordinary career would be full of such transformations: 100 years old in *Little Big Man* (1970), skirt and heels in *Tootsie* (1982), autistic in *Rain Man* (1988), cartoonish villain in *Dick Tracy* (1990), and Captain Hook in *Hook* (1991). (For more on Hoffman, see page 112.)

Though Warren Beatty campaigned for the role of Joe Buck, Schlesinger thought he was just too much of a box-office draw to risk playing dumb and possibly bisexual. It was the same issue that came up for Beatty in *Bonnie and Clyde*, but that screenplay was tailored to fit. Schlesinger preferred an unknown, **Jon Voight**, who auditioned by pretending to be a real midnight cowboy right off the street. Some of his improvisations wound up in the script. Known for his generosity, Voight celebrated winning the role by taking in a homeless man. A busy career followed his explosive debut in *Cowboy*, though he soon lost his innocent blond looks: *Deliverance* (1972), *Coming Home* (1978), *Table for Five* (1983) and, *Mission: Impossible* (1996). To a new generation of filmgoers, he's perhaps most famous as the father of Angelina Jolie.

BEHIND THE SCREEN

Dustin Hoffman improvised the iconic line for Ratso, "I'm walkin' here! I'm walkin' here!" when a cabbie nearly ran him over as he crossed the street in character.

With under six minutes of screen time, Sylvia Miles's performance was the briefest ever to receive a supporting actor or actress Oscar nomination.

THE MUSIC

Harry Nilsson's recording of "Everybody's Talkin'" was a filler song for the unedited version, but Schlesinger decided it worked better than anything else they tried. Bob Dylan wrote "Lay, Lady Lay" for the movie but didn't deliver it by the deadline.

THE CRITICS

"So extraordinarily good and surprising in so many ways that it's hard to give it adequate praise . . . the kind of solid work that stays superbly in one piece, a statement about our time and place that doesn't have to stand back and orate." —Archer Winsten, *New York Post*

"Schlesinger keeps pounding away at America, determined to expose how horrible the people are. The spray of venom is so obviously the director's way of showing off that we begin to discount it." —Pauline Kael, *The New Yorker*

ROLE REVERSALS

Lee Majors and Michael Sarrazin were both up for Buck. Rizzo was offered to Robert Blake, who said thanks but no thanks.

CREDITS

Producer: Jerome Hellman/UA
Director : John Schlesinger
Screenplay:
Waldo Salt, based on the novel by James Leo Herlihy
Running time: 113 minutes
Budget: $3.6 million
Box Office: $44.8 million

ACADEMY AWARDS

Best Picture
Best Director: John Schlesinger
Best Adapted Screenplay:
Waldo Salt

NOMINATIONS

Best Actor: Dustin Hoffman
Best Actor: Jon Voight
Best Supporting Actress:
Sylvia Miles
Best Editing:
Hugh A. Robertson

THE YEAR'S OTHER WINNERS

Best Actor: John Wayne, *True Grit*
Best Actress: Maggie Smith,
The Prime of Miss Jean Brodie
Best Supporting Actor: Gig Young,
They Shoot Horses, Don't They?
Best Supporting Actress:
Goldie Hawn, *Cactus Flower*

THE OTHER LISTS

American Film Institute (Yes)
Roger Ebert's Top 100 (No)
Entertainment Weekly (No)
Internet Movie Database (No)
Leonard Maltin (Yes)
Movieline (No)
National Society of Film Critics (No)
Premiere Magazine (No)
Rolling Stone Magazine (Yes)
Village Voice (No)

Joe Buck stalks the wealthy women along Park Avenue, hoping to strike fire with an opening line, "Where is the Statue of Liberty?" He is ignored until he comes upon the blonde Cass, who's coaxing her poodle to "make for Mommy." Cass gives Joe the once-over, figures him for a wiseguy, and fires back in response, "She's up in Central Park taking a leak." Nonetheless, she likes what she sees and invites him up to her place. Joe delivers with a great performance in the bedroom and isn't sure how he's to approach her about the money. He finally blurts it out as she prepares to dine with her sugar daddy. Cass throws an hysterical, teary fit: "You were gonna ask me for money? Who the hell do you think you're dealing with, some old slut on 42nd Street? In case you didn't happen to notice it, ya big Texas longhorn bull, I'm one helluva gorgeous chick!" To placate her, Joe is forced to fork over $20 for her "cab fare." He's been conned by a master.

The filly lassoes the cowboy. Joe learns the hard way that in New York City nothing comes easy.

Ratso's dream of Miami Beach, where they've got more coconut trees than anywhere, is brutally interrupted by reality. "Here I am goin' to Florida, my leg hurts, my butt hurts, my chest hurts, my face hurts, and if that ain't enough, I gotta pee all over myself."

"I'm a reluctant icon! I don't want to be put on a shelf and pointed to! I'm not the Statue of Liberty."
—Sylvia Miles

79

M*A*S*H 1970

CUT-UP IN ARMS

The anticipated smash-hit war comedy of 1970, the screen version of Joseph Heller's classic novel *Catch-22*, was an unqualified bust. Its producers were stunned. A darkly satiric indictment of American military incompetence, the movie seemed to have the right components to appeal to the public's current mood. But it was also about World War II, a war that was perhaps too safe a generational distance away in a country caught up in the quicksand of Vietnam. And let's face it: it wasn't all that funny. From out of political left field, *M*A*S*H*, Robert Altman's incendiary little film, cut deeper than mere bureaucratic corruption. It went to the heart of the problem: the absurdity of war and the irreverent lengths to which reasonable men and women will go in order to cope while serving. Altman makes no apology for the characters' cruel wit, cynicism, and flat-out denunciation of organized religion. If that's what it takes to get them through the nightmare of the front lines, then anti-Godspeed! The film's three lead characters, gifted surgeons drafted by the Army, are surrounded by horror. They survive by pretending that modern man's greatest achievement is the dry martini. When one of them turns up with an impossible-to-get jar of olives, it's a moment of unmitigated bliss, as if all their most fervent dreams for a perfect world have come true.

Jim: *M*A*S*H* may well be the birthplace of irony-as-comic-staple. Almost every line is loaded with a sly awareness that what is said is not what is meant. In this film, Elliott Gould, Donald Sutherland, and Tom Skerritt become the Marx Brothers for a new generation. Their laid-back attitude and frat house bonhomie, combined with fierce career ambition, are remarkably prescient. These boys of 1970 were way ahead of the game.

Gail: While Larry Gelbart's script delivers a devastatingly funny evisceration of "armed conflict" and its incompetent purveyors, after all those dry martinis dry up, you feel the compassion and the pain.

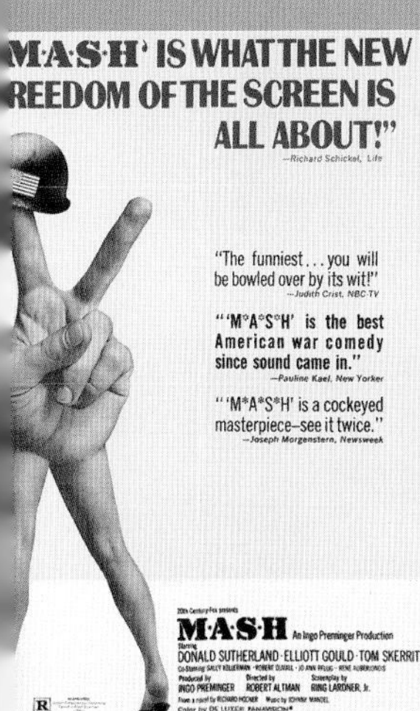

IE PLOT

ant surgeons and brothers-in-arms, ·keye" Pierce (Donald Sutherland) and e Forrest (Tom Skerritt), are drafted into ıell of the Korean Conflict and stationed Mobile Army Surgical Hospital (MASH) three miles from the front. They're forced ınk with hypocritical religious zealot ır Burns (Robert Duvall), who doesn't ıtenance their profanity, hard-drinking, wildly anarchic behavior. They manage ·ive him insane and his replacement is per John" McIntyre (Elliot Gould), who s them with his own over-the-top ribaldry. ı enough Trapper has managed to "cure" dal, latently gay dentist Captain "Painless ' Waldowski (John Schuck), and plot eyeıing revenge on imperious blonde Chief e Houlihan (Sally Kellerman). The merry ɪ of three turn the unit into a delectable of iniquity even as they perform brilliantly e operating room, a charnel house of ɪ-soaked young bodies broken on the lless wheel of war.

"I'm Dr. Jekyll, actually, and this is my friend, Mr. Hyde." Hawkeye (Donald Sutherland) and Trapper John (Elliott Gould) arrive in Japan to save the life of a Congressman's son and get laid, in either order.

THE DIRECTOR

"When I see an American flag flying, it's a joke," says **Robert Altman**, not your typical World War II veteran. But Altman, who'd served as a bomber pilot in the Pacific, has always forged a unique path across the American landscape. *M*A*S*H* was only his third film and among his most successful, though he'd gotten the job after fifteen other directors turned it down. He transformed Ring Lardner, Jr.'s script into a prototype for his own completely original form of moviemaking. It was through *M*A*S*H* that he became famous for his overlapping action and dialogue—a kind of running collage technique he has employed in many subsequent films. His camera expresses no particular point of view as it cuts and pans, allowing for hit-or-miss glimpses of the world he's created. You can't take it all in at once and Altman doesn't expect you to. He has a special gift for working with an ensemble troupe of actors, too, very often playing up secondary characters as if he's suddenly caught up in their behavior. It's a technique that can sometimes grate on the ego of a superstar but, as with Woody Allen, most of the most talented names in the business are eager to work with him. After a long apprenticeship as a TV director of dozens of episodes of *Bonanza* (1958), *Surfside Six* (1959), *U.S. Marshal* (1960), and two minor features, *M*A*S*H** marked Altman's entry into the top ranks. From there came *Brewster McCloud* (1970), *McCabe & Mrs. Miller* (1971) starring Warren Beatty and Julie Christie, *The Long Goodbye* (1973), *Thieves Like Us* (1974), his masterwork *Nashville* (1975), *3 Women* (1977), *A Wedding* (1978), the unusually moody, cartoon-inspired musical *Popeye* (1980), *Come Back to the Five and Dime, Jimmy Dean, Jimmy Dean* (1982), then, after a relative dry spell, his roaring comeback film *The Player* (1992), a searing look at the Hollywood movie game, which led to *Short Cuts* (1993), *Cookie's Fortune* (1999), the critically admired *Gosford Park* (2001), *The Company* (2003), and *Prairie Home Companion* (2006), his last film. (For more on Altman, see page 45.)

THE CAST

Capt. "Hawkeye" Pierce	Donald Sutherland
Capt. "Trapper John" McIntyre	Elliott Gould
Capt. "Duke" Forrest	Tom Skerritt
Maj. Margaret "Hot Lips" Houlihan	Sally Kellerman
Maj. Frank Burns	Robert Duvall
Lt. Col. Henry Blake	Roger Bowen
Father Mulcahy	Rene Auberjonois
Sergeant Vollmer/PA Announcer	David Arkin
Lt. Maria Schneider	Jo Ann Pflug
Cpl. "Radar" O'Reilly	Gary Burghoff
"Spearchucker" Jones	Fred Williamson
Capt. "Me Lay" Marston IV	Michael Murphy
Lieutenant Leslie	Indus Arthur
Private Seidman	Ken Prymus
Sergeant Gorman	Bobby Troup
Ho-Jon	Kim Atwood
Corporel Judson	Tim Brown
Capt. "Painless Pole" Waldowski	John Schuck
Lieutenant Storch	Dawne Damon
Capt. "Ugly John"Black	Carl Gottlieb
Pvt. Lorenzo Boone	Bud Cort

ROLE REVERSALS

Burt Reynolds passed up the chance to play "Trapper John."

THE ACTORS

Canadian-born **Donald Sutherland** was very definitely a Golden Boy of 1970s film, working with some of the world's greatest directors, including Fellini (*Casanova*), and costarring with the most glamorous women of the era, including Jane Fonda (*Klute* [1973]) and Julie Christie (*Don't Look Now* [1971]). He's never shied away from playing unappealing characters and, as a result, can often be seen in villainous roles. He's the father of Kiefer, star of TV's *24*. Sutherland got his start in *The Dirty Dozen* (1967) and thereafter became identifiable as an antiwar activist with his choice of roles in *Start the Revolution Without Me* (1970), *Johnny Got His Gun* (1971) and *Steelyard Blues* (1973). *Animal House* and *Invasion of the Body Snatchers* (both 1978) gave rise to more serious dramatic fare such as *Ordinary People* (1980), *Eye of the Needle* (1981), and *A Dry White Season* (1989). A trio of paranoid thrillers included *JFK* (1991), *Outbreak* (1995), *and A Time to Kill* (1996), and were followed by *Space Cowboys* and *Cold Mountain* (both 2003).

"Success didn't change me. I was already distorted before I became a star." Despite a few previous film appearances, **Elliot Gould** took the character of "Trapper John" and made it his own with supreme confidence. In so doing, he became an "overnight sensation," after having had a long musical comedy career off and on Broadway. That was the milieu in which he met his legendary (now ex-) wife Barbra Streisand. Like Sutherland, Gould became a poster boy of counterculture 1970s film but his career faltered badly just a decade later. Among his most memorable performances are *Bob & Carol & Ted & Alice* (1969), *Getting Straight* (1970), *The Long Goodbye* (1973), *The Silent Partner* (1978), *Capricorn One* (1978), *Bugsy* (1991), and *Ocean's Eleven* (2001).

Tom Skerritt got lucky in landing the role of Duke Forrest but his luck didn't hold. As his costars, Sutherland and Gould, both relatively new to the game, shot to major stardom, Skerritt somehow ended up with a far lesser career. It may have been a matter of timing. He was a more traditional-looking actor in an era when audiences were aligning themselves with more idiosyncratic faces. He's enjoyed a full career in TV, having won an Emmy for his long-running role on *Picket Fences*. On the big screen, he scored with *The Turning Point* (1977), *Alien* (1979), *Top Gun* (1986), *Steel Magnolias* (1989), *A River Runs Through It* (1992), *Contact* (1997), and *The Texas Rangers* (2001).

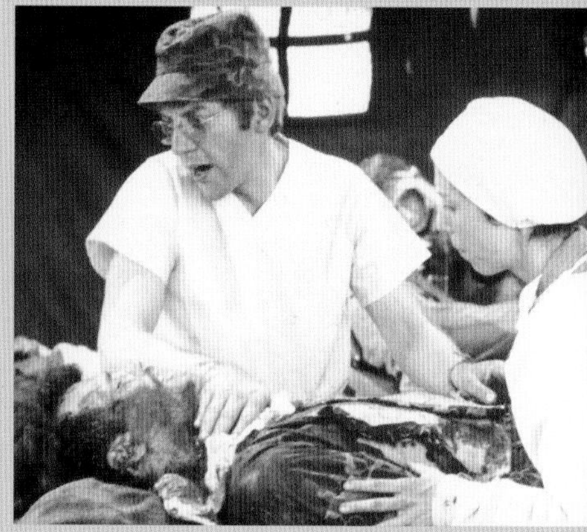

"Find me ONE nurse who's able to work in close without getting her tits in my way!" Beneath the wacked-out humor and politics, is the entrenched notion that doctors are gods. If you have the skills to save a life, you can pretty much get away with murder.

"I always wanted to be an actress. My mother told me to get a job as an elevator operator—because Dorothy Lamour was discovered that way." **Sally Kellerman** nabbed the only acting Oscar nomination for *M*A*S*H* and her distinctive looks and personality would've seemed to spell continued success. It didn't quite happen in a major way and she settled into less-than-starring roles. She's since become an acclaimed cabaret performer and can be heard as the throatily sexy voice in numerous commercials. On-screen, she was trapped in *The Big Bus* (1976), stalled in *Moving Violations* (1985), and stranded in *The Maze* (1997).

Robert Duvall is so convincing as the wildly conflicted Major Burns that you can feel him suffering as the butt of everyone's jokes. His complex and intense style of acting, combined with a forbidding countenance, has made Duvall one of the most successful anti-stars of his generation. It's hard to imagine the *Godfather* films without him, but you can't conceive of him in a larger role in them, either. He managed to rise above supporting player status by winning a Best Actor Oscar for *Tender Mercies* (1982). Among his co-stars of *M*A*S*H*, he's the only actual Korean War veteran. Duvall was unforgettable as the psychotically fearless Lieutenant Colonel Kilgore in *Apolcalpyse Now* (1979) and his ubiquitous presence in TV and films is marked by such highlights as *The Great Santini* (1979), *Lonesome Dove* (1989), *The Apostle* (1997), *A Civil Action* (1998) and as Robert E. Lee in *Gods and Generals* (2003). (For more on Duvall, see page 13 and 60.)

This was a film debut for many cast members. Among those who've since become familiar to audiences are Bud Cort (*Harold and Maude*, 1971), John Schuck (TV's *McMillan and Wife*, *Roots*), and Gary Burghoff (*M*A*S*H*, the TV series).

BEHIND THE SCREEN

Elliot Gould and Donald Sutherland tried to get director Altman fired when they felt he was ignoring their star status in order to create a more ensemble-style film. Altman exacted his revenge by never hiring Sutherland again. Gould curried favor by confessing his betrayal and worked on four other Altman productions.

There are no references to Korea in the shooting script. Altman hoped audiences would perceive the story as taking place in Vietnam. The producers found the antiwar sentiment explosive enough and added a voice-over at the beginning to tell us precisely where we are and when.

Gary Burghoff ("Radar") was the only major actor in the film to make the transition to the TV series.

Altman had done so much improvisation, he worried that screenwriter Ring Lardner, Jr. would be dejected. When he spotted him approaching the set, he called out, "Hey, somebody find the script—here comes the writer!" Lardner was, in fact, devastated that almost none of his dialogue had been used. His vindication came with an Oscar.

Studio chief Daryl Zanuck was outraged by the blood and gore of the operating scenes. He leapt out of his seat at an early screening and barked, "The public can't handle that!" His two French girlfriends, sitting on either side of him cooed, "Oh, no, that's what makes it so good!" The scenes stayed.

"That one! The sultry bitch with the fire in her eyes! Bring her to me! Take her clothes off and bring her to me!" Sally Kellerman had to be tricked into being shot nude in the shower. Her character's shocked reaction was no act. Director Altman and Gary Burghoff distracted her by dropping their own drawers.

Officious Chief Nurse, Major Margaret Houlihan, finds her only ally in teetotaling, hard-praying quack, Major Frank Burns. Together, they draft a letter to the top brass, outlining the lax morals of their M.A.S.H. unit. Thrilled by their efforts, Margaret asks if he's hungry and he dares to respond that he's ravenous—for her! They lunge at each other, ferocious in their lust. When "Radar" eyes them through the tent window, he runs for a microphone and slips it under the bed. The raucous musical *Hit Parade*, broadcast live from Tokyo, is replaced on the camp loudspeaker by the sounds of Margaret and Frank in the throes of passion. Hawkeye, Trapper, and their poker pals in the Mess Tent are riveted. When Margaret gasps, "Kiss my hot lips!" her infamous alias is born. The couple's humiliation is complete when, next morning, Hawkeye presses Frank for details of his hot night in the sack. Frank punches him out, goes completely berserk, and is taken away in a straitjacket.

CREDITS

Producer: Ingo Preminger/ 20th Century Fox
Director: Robert Altman
Screenplay: Ring Lardner, Jr., from the novel by Richard Hooker
Running time: 116 minutes
Budget: $3.5 million
Box Office: $73.2 million

ACADEMY AWARDS

Best Adapted Screenplay: Ring Lardner, Jr.

NOMINATIONS

Best Picture
Best Director: Robert Altman
Best Supporting Actress: Sally Kellerman
Best Editing: Danford B. Greene

THE YEAR'S OTHER WINNERS

Best Picture: *Patton*
Best Director: Franklin J. Schaffner, *Patton*
Best Actor: George C. Scott, *Patton*
Best Actress: Glenda Jackson, *Women in Love*
Best Supporting Actor: John Mills, *Ryan's Daughter*
Best Supporting Actress: Helen Hayes, *Airport*

THE CRITICS

"I don't know when I've had such a good time at a movie. *M*A*S*H* is the best American war comedy since sound came in." —Pauline Kael, *The New Yorker*

"At the end, the film simply runs out of steam, says good-bye to its major characters, and calls final attention to itself as a movie—surely the saddest and most overworked of cop-out devices in the comic film repertory." —Roger Greenspun, *New York Times*

THE OTHER LISTS

American Film Institute (Yes)
Roger Ebert's Top 100 (No)
Entertainment Weekly (No)
Internet Movie Database (No)
Leonard Maltin (No)
Movieline (No)
National Society of Film Critics (Yes)
Premiere Magazine (No)
Rolling Stone Magazine (No)
Village Voice (No)

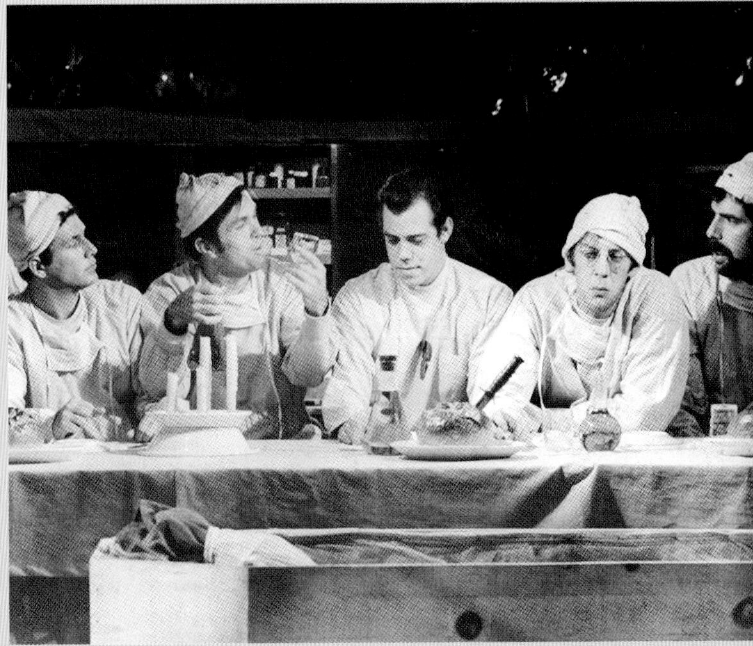

The Last Supper tableau was a sudden inspiration for Altman, who much prefers improvisation to the limitations of a tight shooting script.

80

AMERICAN GRAFFITI 1973

YOU CAN'T GO HOME AGAIN

"*Boom ba boom, ba boom, ba boom*: We're gonna rock, rock, rock 'til broad daylight . . ." And rock and roll we do, from the moment *American Graffiti* begins beating out top tunes from the early 1960s. We're transported to a time and a place on the cusp of change: JFK's presidency, the end of the security of the '50s, and the beginning of the unpredictable '60s. As in some Chekhovian play, two young men on the brink of leaving their small-town nest to fly out into the cold, unknowable world of college are torn between the universal fear of growing up and the terror of remaining a child forever. And nothing drives it home more powerfully than the music, which forms a haunting cocoon of nostalgia around their 17-year-old lives. Why does it all have to end? "Why can't we just stay here?" asks scholarship student Curt (Richard Dreyfuss), the more tormented of the two. One look at the drag-racing, James Dean-wannabe Johnny (Paul LeMat) tells you why. "You chicken fink," screams former Class President Steve (Ron Howard), his comrade on the way to college. "We're finally getting out of this turkey town and now you want to crawl back into your cell?"

Jim: Amazing to count up all the major careers that came out of this film. The cast must surely have offered up their firstborn to Lucas as a small token of gratitude. That is, except the lead, Paul LeMat, who never really went anywhere. Go figure.

Gail: The moment between the end of one era—the '50s—and the beginning of another—the '60s—is captured in one endless night of cars, girls, and music, proving that nostalgia can be dangerous to your future.

THE PLOT

It's one long night in the life of two guys at the end of childhood. Steve (Ron Howard) and Curt (Richard Dreyfuss) are each feeling the anxiety pangs of going off to college. Steve thinks its great to be getting out, but he's leaving his steady girl, head cheerleader Laurie (Cindy Williams). Curt is in absolute turmoil; he doesn't want to go. A smile from a blonde (Suzanne Somers) passing by in a white Thunderbird gives him even more reason to stay. Steve spends the night arguing and making up with Laurie. Providing a counterpoint to their story is Johnny (Paul LeMat), who has been putting off adulthood by cruisin' in his car. Tonight he's drag racing Bob Falfa (Harrison Ford), while saddled with somebody's bratty kid sister, Carol (Mackenzie Phillips). And, finally, there's Toad (Charles Martin Smith), the dorky junior and sycophant who hangs on the older guys' every word and finds love with the pretty blond waitress, Debbie (Candy Clark). Daybreak comes. One of the two guys is ready to board his flight to freedom. But which one?

Steve (Ron Howard) knows just where he's heading. He's determined to get out of this small town and make a new life for himself. After all, he was at the top of his class and is meant to go places. But will he?

THE DIRECTOR

When Universal saw the first screening and didn't like the film, executives immediately pulled out the scissors. **George Lucas** said, "It's like taking your little kid and cutting off one of her fingers. 'It's only a finger, it's not that big a deal,' they say. But to me it's just an arbitrary exercise of power. And it irritates me enormously." The cutting of *Graffiti* was all the more painful because, by all accounts, it is a semiautobiographical portrait of his own youth, with the director represented by Toad. Lucas, a child of TV culture who studied film at the University of Southern California and interned at Warner Bros., was only 28 when he made *Graffiti*, his second feature film after *THX 1138* (1971). The film's unparalleled success shot him to stardom and wealth via the *Star Wars* epics (1977, 1980, 1983, 1999, 2002, 2005). (For more on Lucas, see page 169.)

Curt (Richard Dreyfuss) is in such inner turmoil about leaving for college—which most kids in this town just don't do—that he gets himself initiated into the unlikely "bad boys" club by super-cool bad boy Joe (Bo Hopkins), and they booby-trap a cop car. Curt can't sleep and roams around town in search of answers about his life and future.

THE CAST	
Curt Henderson	Richard Dreyfuss
Steve Bolander	Ron Howard
John Milner	Paul LeMat
Terry "The Toad" Fields	Charles Martin Smith
Laurie Henderson	Cindy Williams
Debbie Dunham	Candy Clark
Carol	Mackenzie Phillips
XERB Disc Jockey	Wolfman Jack
Joe Young	Bo Hopkins
Bob Falfa	Harrison Ford

THE CRITICS

"It's a very good movie, funny, tough, unsentimental. It is full of marvelous performances. But for me its excitement comes at least partly from its indication of what may be a major new career."
—Roger Greenspun, *New York Times*

THE ACTORS

It's almost painful to watch **Richard Dreyfuss**'s Curt Henderson as he agonizes over what matters in life. Is there no place like home? If he goes away will he find his place? His heroes? It's a brilliant performance, both grave and funny. (For more on Dreyfuss, see pages 88 and 208.)

"Now you know what I want out of life. And it's just not in this town, " says former Class President Steve Bolander, played with just the right level of strait-laced certainty by **Ron Howard**. One of the most successful directors working in Hollywood today, he will always be known to audiences as the beloved little Opie on TV's classic *Andy Griffith Show*. His first adult foray into acting was in another sitcom, the nostalgic *Happy Days* (1974–80). He appeared in juvenile roles in films including *The Music Man* (1962) before finally growing up. As an acclaimed director, he would head such smart, funny, and popular films as *Splash* (1984), *Cocoon* (1985), *Parenthood* (1989), and *Backdraft* (1991). His latest films include *Apollo 13* (1995, Academy Award), *Inventing the Abbotts* (1997), *A Beautiful Mind* (2001, Academy Award), *The Da Vinci Code* (2006), and *Frost/Nixon* (2008).

Cindy Williams plays good girl and head cheerleader Laurie Henderson, the girlfriend in the oversized letterman sweater belonging to her steady, Steve. During the endless night, Steve and Laurie get into constant battles over his "seeing" other girls in college. In a more melancholic moment Laurie tells him, "You know, it doesn't make sense to leave home to look for home, to give up a life to find a new life, to say good-bye to friends you love just to find new friends." Williams is best known as Shirley in the 1970s sitcom *Laverne and Shirley*, which was a spin-off of the sitcom *Happy Days*. She and Penny Marshall (who played Laverne) had been fixed up as a writing team by Marshall's brother, Garry. Williams, along with her husband, Bill, has produced her own films, among them the *Father of The Bride* movies (1991, 1993).

Charles Martin Smith plays the nerdy, bespectacled Terry Fields, the kid they call "Toad." Sporting a '50s pink-and-black shirt and white bucks. and riding haphazardly on his Vespa, Toad admires Johnny, the cool-but-going-nowhere drag racer. Toad has, perhaps, the best luck of all in the film, as he pairs off for the night with the cute blonde waitress Debbie. Smith has appeared in a number of films as the shy guy who breaks out of his shell. He debuted in *The Culpepper Cattle Company* (1972) and went on to appear in *Pat Garrett and Billy the Kid* (1973), *Rafferty and the Gold Dust Twins* (1975), and *The Buddy Holly Story* (1978). He played one leading role, in the little-known *Never Cry Wolf* (1983). He returned to supporting roles in such films as *Starman* (1984) and *The Untouchables* (1987). Smith made his debut as a feature director with *Trick or Treat* (1986), followed by the live-action *Rocky and Bullwinkle* spin-off *Boris and Natasha: The Movie* (1989, released 1992). His most recent appearances have been in the TV film *And the Band Played On* (1993), and the feature films *Wedding Bell Blues* (1996), *Air Bud* (1997), *P. T. Barnum* (1999), and *Roughing It* (2002).

CREDITS

Producer:
Francis Ford Coppola/MGM
Director: George Lucas
Screenplay: Gloria Katz, Willard Huyck, George Lucas
Running Time: 110 minutes
Budget: $750,000
Box Office: $21.3 million (1974)
Produced on a low budget, the film now holds the record for the highest profit margin of any film.

ACADEMY AWARD NOMINATIONS

Best Picture
Best Supporting Actress: Candy Clark
Best Director: George Lucas
Best Film Editing: Verna Fields, Marcia Lucas
Best Original Screenplay: George Lucas, Gloria Katz, Willard Huyck

THE YEAR'S OTHER WINNERS

Best Picture: *The Sting*
Best Director: George Roy Hill, *The Sting*
Best Actor: Jack Lemmon, *Save the Tiger*
Best Actress: Glenda Jackson, *A Touch of Class*
Best Supporting Actor: John Houseman, *The Paper Chase*
Best Supporting Actress: Tatum O'Neal, *Paper Moon*

THE OTHER LISTS

American Film Institute (Yes)
Roger Ebert's Top 100 (No)
Entertainment Weekly (Yes)
Internet Movie Database (No)
Leonard Maltin (No)
Movieline (No)
National Society of Film Critics (No)
Premiere Magazine (No)
Rolling Stone Magazine (No)
Village Voice (No)

The daughter of John Phillips of The Mamas and the Papas fame, **MacKenzie Phillips** plays the bratty, chattering thirteen-year-old Carol, who can't believe her good luck at being thrown into Johnny's car for the night. Good-hearted Johnny wants none of it: "This better be a joke, 'cause I'm not drivin' you around." "What's the matter?" she responds. "Am I too ugly? Nobody wants me—even my mother and father hate me. Everybody hates me." Two years after *Graffiti*, Phillips landed a role on the hit sitcom *One Day At A Time* (1968). After a bout with drugs, she returned to the screen in *Rafferty and The Gold Dust Twins* (1975), *More American Graffiti* (1979), and *Double Teamed* (2002).

Debbie Dunham, the adorable, peroxide-blond bombshell waitress, played by **Candy Clark**, takes up with the not-so-adorable Toad. It's an unlikely pairing that works out sweetly for both of them. Clark got a Best Supporting Actress nomination for this touching Stella Stevens/ Shirley MacLaine-style performance. She debuted in *Fat City* (1972), and later appeared in *The Man Who Fell to Earth* (1976) and *Handle With Care* (1977). But a few years later she was doing B-movies like *Amityville 3-D* (1983), *The Blob* (1988), and, alongside rap star Vanilla Ice, *Cool as Ice* (1991). She also appeared in *Buffy the Vampire Slayer* (1992).

Harrison Ford refused to cut his locks for the role of the drag racer who eats dust. He didn't give up his handyman job for this one. That would come later. (For more on Ford, see pages 130, 169, and 289.)

Legendary DJ Wolfman Jack, the voice of a generation of young people, plays himself in this valentine to an era.

Desperate for advice, Curt finds his way to the radio station where Wolfman Jack is deejaying in the darkness. "Hey! What do you want?" asks Wolfman. Curt (thinking about the woman of his dreams he saw in the white T-bird) says: "I'm looking for this girl." Sitting at his radio console, the bearded, Hawaiian-shirted man passing himself off as the manager sucks on a Popsicle as Curt makes a plea for help: "Are you the Wolfman?" The manager replies, "The Wolfman is everywhere." Curt wants to give a note to the Wolfman—a dedication to the girl in the white T-bird to be played on the air. Speaking for the omniscient Wolfman, the manager sees Curt's pain and encourages him to move on. "I can't talk for the Wolfman," he says, "but I can tell you one thing. If the Wolfman was here, he'd say: 'Get your ass in gear!'" As Curt walks out he looks back through an open door and sees the manager speaking into the microphone in the unmistakable voice of the Wolfman, as he spins "Heart and Soul" by The Cleftones.

BEHIND THE SCREEN DISASTERS

A day before filming was due to start, a key member of the crew was arrested for growing marijuana.

Shooting on the first night began at 2 A.M. because it took so long to mount the cameras on the cars.

The city of San Rafael, where most of the outdoor footage was to be shot, revoked its permit after a bar owner complained that he was losing business due to blocked streets.

On the second night of filming, a fire in a nearby restaurant resulted in a traffic jam that killed filming for the night.

During the filming of the drag race, assistant cameraman Barney Coangelo slipped off the camera truck and was run over, suffering minor injuries.

Paul LeMat ended up in the hospital with an allergic reaction to a Waldorf salad he had one night at dinner.

LeMat threw Richard Dreyfuss into a swimming pool, which left a gash in his forehead on the day before he was due to have his closeups filmed.

Dreyfuss refused to wear the loud Bermuda shorts and shirt Lucas had chosen for his character.

During the filming of the drag race between LeMat and Ford, the latter's car axle broke. The second try broke the other axle. Finally, axles all in place, the car refused to veer off the road as planned, narrowly missing two cameramen lying on the road.

BEHIND THE SCREEN

"The Toad" pulled a toad when he lost control of his bike and really crashed into the building. Lucas kept the cameras rolling.

Note the movie marquee in the scene where the guys pull a stunt with a police car. *Dementia 13* (1963), Francis Ford Coppola's first film, is playing. Oops—the film opened in 1963, while *Graffiti* is set in 1962.

Cindy Williams proposed wearing braces so she could play the role of Carol, the part she preferred.

The obsessive-compulsive real-life owner of the '56 Thunderbird used in the film was always just a few feet away, taking every opportunity to shine up his car. Suzanne Somers didn't appreciate his constant input about how she should treat the vehicle.

NOTABLE QUOTES

George Lucas on directing: "The sound and music are 50 percent of the entertainment in a movie."

"The script is what you've dreamed up—this is what it should be. The film is what you end up with."

"I've had a very volatile relationship with Francis [Ford Coppola]. It's on both sides, like we were married and we got divorced. It's as close a relationship as I've had with anybody."

"Actually, when I was a kid I was really more aware of the star and the handprints in Graumann's Chinese more than I was aware of anything else, including the Oscar. I wanted to have a star. I wanted to be able to see, you know, old gum on my star." —Richard Dreyfuss

Breakin' up is hard to do, particularly when you've had it all and now all is about to disappear. The night before taking off for college, Class President Steve (Ron Howard) and his girlfriend, head cheerleader Laurie (Cindy Williams), dance their last dance at the high school gym. They spend the night breaking up and making up. Growing up is hard to do, too.

81

THE PRODUCERS 1968

THAT'S ENTERTAINMENT?

"Don't be stupid/ be a smarty/Come and join the Nazi party"—the lyrics to a musical number in a production called *Springtime for Hitler*. And they said it couldn't be done. Who in the universe of insane comic geniuses could have launched such an affront to decent-minded moviegoers? Who would have even thought of it but the 2,000-Year-Old-Man himself, Mel Brooks? When you're that old, who cares? But seriously, Brooks, who wrote and directed this uproarious farce about Broadway along with the most inspired pair of comedians ever, Zero Mostel and Gene Wilder, delivered us into hysterics and brought us as close to a near-death experience as you can get by laughing. The grotesque failing Broadway producer, Max Bialystock (Mostel), for whom there is no depth of degradation to which he will not descend, comes upon a scam to produce a failing musical and in the process assembles a hilarious group of people, completely lacerating all the sacred cows of the theater. He's a life force, rapacious with greed, lust (for old ladies with money), and a joyous desire to compromise any and all principals. Enter the shy, terrified accountant Leopold Bloom (Wilder)—looking like a baby chicken—whose very contact with Max has him on the ground shivering in terror. Eyes bulging out of their sockets, Max shouts at Leo, " I'm condemned by a society that demands success when all I can offer is failure! See this? I'm wearing a cardboard belt!" And he pulls off the belt and tears it to pieces. Scenes like this come like bullets out of a machine gun. Crazed desperation, shouting, screaming, running, it's a frenzied blitzkrieg into the battle of life in the theatre. That's how *The Producers* begins, and it doesn't let up for a second. This is surely one of the funniest movies ever made, and a vicious lampoon at that. Its audacity so attacks our sense of the appropriate that it's downright liberating—though some disagreed when it came out. According to a story told by Roger Ebert, a woman recognized Brooks in an elevator shortly after the movie was released and said, "I have to tell you, Mr. Brooks, that your movie is vulgar." Brooks smiled benevolently. "Lady," he said, "it rose below vulgarity."

Jim: It's been said that modern American humor can be traced back to the arrival of Jewish immigrants at the turn of the century. I think we can trace it back even more specifically—to Mel Brooks. This is the one to see if you want to die laughing.

Gail: I want to dance around the fountain at Lincoln Center sharing with Max and Leo the joy of exposing what people will do to make money on Broadway, because it makes me laugh. Yes, it makes me laugh.

[TH]E PLOT

[pani]c-stricken accountant Leopold Bloom [(Gen]e Wilder) gets more than he can handle [when] he's invited to check the books of one [Max] Bialystock (Zero Mostel), failed Broadway [prod]ucer. When Bloom discovers $2,000 miss[ing, h]e comes to a terrifying realization: "The [IRS i]sn't interested in a show that flopped." [Sudd]enly Max realizes, to his devilish joy, that [if the]y deliberately made a flop, given the tax [cons]equences, they could earn more money [than] with a hit. And the monster is out of the [cage.] With that Max goes into full throttle rais[ing m]oney from little old ladies for a piece of [the p]rofits. (What profits?) And then they find [the p]erfect success-proof musical, *Springtime [for H]itler: A Gay Romp with Adolf and Eva in [Berch]tesgarden*, featuring a chorus line of [goose-]stepping, jackbooted SS girls singing ["Sprin]gtime for Hitler." There is much ado about [how t]he Führer will be portrayed, and then the [world]'s worst director, the cross-dressing Roger [De B]ris, is hired. The camera turns on the audi[ence], who sit in stunned amazement, paralyzed [with h]orror at what is before them. A disaster, [of co]urse—but no! At intermission, after a [mom]ent of dazed silence, there is a roar of ap[plaus]e. It's a comedy hit! So bad it's . . . great!

That's not funny! Aghast at goose-stepping Nazi chorus girls singing for the Führer, the audience soon decides it's all a terrific joke and turns the show that was supposed to be a bomb into a hit—thereby foiling the producers' "fool-proof" money-making scheme.

THE DIRECTOR

Was it that he just couldn't control himself, or was it all deliberate? The incomparably manic genius **Mel Brooks** has delivered a body of work—writing, directing and acting—that challenges the greatest comics of all times. Mel Brooks started his career as a standup comic in the 1940s, heavily influenced by the Borscht Belt comedians with whom he appeared. It was there that his love affair with Sid Caesar was born, and out of it grew Brooks's participation as a writer on the groundbreaking TV comedy series, *Your Show of Shows*. Brooks' first independent film, *The Critic* (1963), put him on the map, and he went on to collaborate on the creation of TV's *Get Smart* (1965–69). That's what got him the green light to make *The Producers*. Brooks showed all the naysayers who said he was "too Jewish" when he returned with *The Twelve Chairs* (1970). The laughter and the success continued with his next feature, the cowboy-movie spoof *Blazing Saddles* (1974), and *Young Frankenstein* (also 1974), *Silent Movie* (1976), the Hitchcock parody *High Anxiety* (1977), the historical epic parody *History of the World—Part I* (1981), the remake of the 1942 classic *To Be or Not to Be* (1983, also a Nazi send-up), and the space-opera spoof *Spaceballs* (1987). During the 1980s his production company, Brooksfilm, produced some uncharacteristically serious films, including David Lynch's first commercial feature, *The Elephant Man* (1980), David Cronenberg's first Hollywood shot, *The Fly* (1986), *The Doctor and the Devils* (1985), *84 Charing Cross Road* (1987, featuring Brooks's wife, Anne Bancroft), and *Solarbabies* (1986). Brooks returned to directing with *Life Stinks* (1991) and *Robin Hood: Men in Tights* (1993). Since then, he's made several TV movies, among them *The Roman Spring of Mrs. Stone* (2002).

Estelle Winwood plays the first of a series blue-haired heiresses Max Bialystock (Zero Mostel) chases around his office—among other "amorous" games—to get seed money for his failing Broadway production.

THE CAST

Max Bialystock	Zero Mostel
Leopold Bloom	Gene Wilder
Franz Liebkind	Kenneth Mars
Hold me, Touch me	Estelle Winwood
Eva Braun	Renée Taylor
Roger De Bris	Christopher Hewett
Ulla	Lee Meredith
Carmen Giya	Andréas Voutsinas
Doc Goebbels	David Patch
Lorenzo St. DuBois (L.S.D.)	Dick Shawn
Concierge	Madelyn Cates

THE ACTORS

"That's exactly why we want to produce this play. To show the world the true Hitler, the Hitler you loved, the Hitler you knew, the Hitler with a song in his heart," says Max Bialystock to aspiring playwright Franz Liebkind, in the fine tradition of huckster for which **Zero Mostel** was well-known and highly regarded. His Bialystock will remain forever in lights—as will Mostel. Mostel was known best for his comedy—that slicked-back hair, those eyes, that head, those tiny balletic feet supporting an inflated balloon of a body, that impossible exuberance—both as a director and in performance. But he began his career as a serious actor, an intellectual, and was even blacklisted for his troubles. Early on he appeared in such dramas as *Panic in the Streets* (1950), but his career was interrupted by an appearance before the House Un-American Activities Committee and he was blacklisted. Out of work, he managed a comeback on stage in Eugene Ionesco's absurdist satire of fascism, *Rhinoceros*, for which he won a Tony Award. His second Tony came quickly with *A Funny Thing Happened on the Way to the Forum* (1966), and he received a third for his full-bodied performance as Tevye in *Fiddler on the Roof*. He continued to make films, including *The Angel Levine* (1970), *The Hot Rock* (1972), and *Journey Into Fear* (1975). In his last live-action film, *The Front* (1976), he played a victim of the blacklist, not unlike himself. His son Josh is also an actor. Mostel died in 1977.

There is only one **Gene Wilder**. There is only one actor who could have played the gentle, neurotic, stricken-unto-paralysis accountant clutching his blue baby blanket for comfort. And he pulled off a well-deserved Oscar nomination for it, too. No one is as funny at anxiety. Leopold Bloom became so synonymous with Wilder that it's difficult to remember his first appearance in a key supporting role in *Bonnie and Clyde* (1967), also as a neurotic. Wilder followed with a number of films, including *Start the Revolution Without Me* (1970). He is lovingly remembered by a whole generation as the mischievous candy maker in *Willy Wonka and the Chocolate Factory* (1971). He played a sheep-loving psychiatrist in Woody Allen's *Everything You Always Wanted to Know About Sex (But Were Afraid to Ask)* (1972), a gunslinger in *Blazing Saddles* (1974), and the title role in *Young Frankenstein* (1974, Academy Award nomination). Wilder took a stab at writing and directing, as well, with *The Adventure of Sherlock Holmes' Smarter Brother* (1975), *The World's Greatest Lover* (1977), and *The Woman in Red* (1984). He paired up with Richard Pryor in *Silver Streak* (1976), *Stir Crazy* (1980), *See No Evil, Hear No Evil* (1989), and *Another You* (1991). He also appeared in *The Frisco Kid* (1979). He met his wife, Gilda Radner, while on the set of *Hanky Panky* (1982). He also starred in *Funny About Love* (1990), as well as his own TV sitcom, *Something Wilder* (1994–95).

Dick Shawn breaks up the house in the role of "Lorenzo, baby. Lorenzo St. DuBois. But my friends call me L.S.D." The outrageous Shawn appears bedecked in flower-power glory, complete with knee-high shag boots and a Campbell's soup can necklace. Oooh baby! Shawn always seemed to be doing the boogaloo in fine camp tradition, yet his career was a bit of a game of peekaboo. His best days came in the "hippie period," in such films as *It's a Mad Mad Mad Mad World* (1963), *Way . . . Way Out* (1966), *What Did You Do in the War, Daddy?* (1966), *Love at First Bite* (1979), *The Secret Diary of Sigmund Freud*

CREDITS

Producer : Sidney Glazier/ Embassy Pictures
Director: Mel Brooks
Screenplay: Mel Brooks
Running Time: 88 minutes
Budget: $941,000

ACADEMY AWARDS

Best Writing, Story and Screenplay, Written Directly for the Screen: Mel Brooks

NOMINATIONS

Best Supporting Actor: Gene Wilder

THE YEAR'S OTHER WINNERS

Best Picture: *Oliver!*
Best Director: Carol Reed, *Oliver!*
Best Actor: Cliff Robertson, *Charly*
Best Actress: Katharine Hepburn, *A Lion in Winter*
Best Supporting Actor: Jack Albertson, *The Subject Was Roses*
Best Supporting Actress: Ruth Gordon, *Rosemary's Baby*

THE OTHER LISTS

American Film Institute (No)
Roger Ebert's Top 100 (Yes)
Entertainment Weekly (No)
Internet Movie Database (No)
Leonard Maltin (No)
Movieline (No)
Premiere Magazine (No)
Rolling Stone Magazine (No)
Village Voice (No)

(1984), *Maid to Order* (1987), and *Rented Lips* (released in 1988), with scattered TV appearances along the way. He could also be seen live, performing his bizarre one-man shows around the country in between screen appearances. Shawn died in 1987.

Christopher Hewitt's flamboyant Roger De Bris brought cross-dressing to the masses in *The Producers*. He could be seen again (though not in drag) in *The Lavender Hill Mob* (1951), on TV's *Fantasy Island* (1978), in a small-screen version of *The Elephant Man* (1982), in *Mr. Belvedere* (1985), and in the film *Ratboy* (1986).

ROLE REVERSALS

Dustin Hoffman decided he'd rather be seduced by a middle-aged woman (who just happened to be Mel Brooks's wife) in *The Graduate* than play a fun-loving Nazi, so he passed on the part of Franz Liebkind.

THE CRITICS

"This is one of the funniest movies ever made. The whole movie is pitched at that level of frenzied desperation, and one of the many joys of watching it is to see how the actors are able to control timing and nuance even while screaming." —Roger Ebert, *Chicago Sun-Times*

"Some of it is shoddy and cruel; the rest is funny in an entirely unexpected way." —Renata Adler, *New York Times*

"The star not only indulges himself gluttonously, but the director seems to be doubled up with laughter at how funny he is being through Mostel; and the film bloats into sogginess." —Stanley Kauffmann, *The New Republic*

BEHIND THE SCREEN

Early in his career, Zero Mostel was noted for his performance as the original Leopold Bloom, James Joyce's creation, in an off-Broadway production of *Ulysses in Nighttown*.

Though originally banned in Germany, the film was finally shown there in a festival featuring the works of Jewish filmmakers.

Mel Brooks almost had his own *Springtime*, but his flopped. He wrote the libretto for a Broadway musical called *All American*, which starred Ray Bolger and ran for 80 performances in 1962.

Nathan Lane as Bialystock and Matthew Broderick as Bloom appeared in a stage musical of *The Producers* adapted by Mel Brooks in 2001. It won a record-breaking 12 Tony Awards. Martin Short and Jason Alexander later starred in the Los Angeles production.

"'Gregor Samsa awoke one morning to discover that he had been transformed into a giant cockroach.' Nah, it's too good," says Max, rejecting the script for Franz Kafka's *Metamorphosis*. In another Mel Brooks film, *Spaceballs*, he makes an obscure reference to the same literary classic during the "Mega-Maid" scene.

The name "Bialystock" is taken from the Polish village that was home to Mel Brooks' ancestors. It's also the birthplace of the bagel wannabe known as the bialy.

Some say the first use of the term "creative accounting" can be traced to *The Producers*.

Mel Brooks based the character of Max on a Broadway producer he knew who used to seduce little old ladies in exchange for checks that were supposedly used to produce his plays.

It is thought that the "high five" was created by Dick Shawn in *The Producers*. Instead of putting his hand in front to "give me five," Shawn held it up in a salute and Goebbels slapped it.

THE GREAT SCENE

"I'm hysterical and I'm wet," cries Leo when he first encounters the demonically enthusiastic Max Bialystock.

"What's the matter with you?" screams Max to Bloom after he has nearly throttled the nerdy accountant in excitement over the terrified man's scheme to make a bundle on a bomb of a Broadway play. "I'm hysterical! I'm having hysterics. I'm hysterical. I can't stop when I get like this. I can't stop. I'm hysterical. Oh my god. Ah-la-la-la," cries Bloom. Bialystock then throws a bucket of water on him, thinking it will calm him down. Instead Bloom cries, "I'm wet. I'm wet. I'm hysterical and I'm wet. I'm in pain and I'm wet and I'm still hysterical! No, no, no don't hit, don't hit. It doesn't help. It only increases my sense of danger." "What can I do?" asks Max. Bloom clutches his baby blanket and whimpers, "Go away. Go away. You frighten me."

Leopold Bloom (Gene Wilder), Max, and *va-va-voom* secretary Ulla (Lee Meredith) hide from Franz Liebkind (Kenneth Mars), the gun-wielding, Nazi-uniformed, Hitler-loving author of *Springtime for Hitler*, after they hurt his feelings about his beloved Führer.

82

RASHOMON 1950

THROUGH THE EYES OF THE BEHOLDER

"I just don't understand," are the first words spoken by an 11th-century woodcutter taking shelter from a savage rainstorm under what was once a temple of faith and is now the decaying Rashomon gate. Both the language and the setting convey the ideas of this beautiful, revolutionary film which introduced director Akira Kurosawa's most frequently explored theme: that nothing can be known with absolute certainty; that everything is filtered through the pride of the observer. "Human beings are unable to be honest with themselves about themselves. They cannot talk about themselves without embellishing," said the director. Throughout its 88-minute running time, the same story, the rape of a wife and the murder of her husband as they are taking a walk through a forest, is told from four completely different points of view. This was the first time in cinema history that flashbacks were used successfully to portray the same event differently, as separate eyewitness accounts. In the end, there are three self-confessed killers, one outside viewer, and no one guilty party. So profound an impact did this new way of storytelling have that it has become part of our language; when we speak about multiple viewpoints of the same event we call it The Rashomon Effect. Above all, though, *Rashomon*'s greatest achievement is in its cinematic and dramatic artistry. The film is visually dense, evoking the heat, light, and shade of a semi-tropical forest. Twisting branches and the rays of the sun obscure our vision; every shot is composed and lighted to emphasize the impossibly of seeing clearly. Most remarkable of all are the subtly varied characterizations of each player, emphasizing the fluidity of identity. The actors are remarkable. Toshiro Mifune's bandit changes his nature depending upon the eyes through which we see him. He is by turns all twitches and jerks, full of animalistic fury, noble rage, or an insane buffoonery. Masayuki Mori, the husband, appears by turns good and noble or cowardly. Most breathtaking of all is Machiko Kyo, the wife, whose mesmerizing, seductive character varies the most from wholesome victim to treacherous manipulator, temptress, or whimpering child. And *Rashomon* is a timely film too, coming as it did just after the second World War, when the truth about world events was warped by the need to create a narrative that could be lived with in the aftermath of horrendous destruction

Jim: Kurosawa's rightful claim to fame is that he made films that were accessible to American audiences. Probably more important, they were accessible to Hollywood's power elite. Spielberg and Lucas owe him big: the two wunderkinds transformed Kurosawa's imagery into pop entertainment and made the world a far better place for escapists.

Gail: A man walking through the forest has never been revealed in so many different lights. Like the introduction of the multiple points-of-view for which this film has become a classic, *Rashomon*'s filmmaking style speaks of the varieties of experience with absolute grace.

According to one description of the crime, after resisting being raped by the bandit (the wild Toshiro Mifune), the woman (Machiko Kyo) melts into his arms.

THE PLOT

The story opens with a priest and a woodcutter, and then a commoner, who all take shelter from a torrential rain in the crumbling Rashomon Temple. The woodcutter and priest share a story. The central event is of the rape of a woman (Machiko Kyo) and the murder of a man (Masayuki Mori), possibly by a bandit, Tajomaru (Toshiro Mifune). The story is told entirely in flashback from four different point-of-view. In the first account, seen from the bandit's point-of-view, the criminal accepts culpability for the murder but refutes the charge of rape, saying that it was an act of mutual consent; that the woman had seduced him. The woman's story affirms that the bandit attacked her, but she cries that she may have inadvertently been the murderess when she fell into a faint with a dagger in her hand and stabbed her tied-up husband (the bandit had tied him up in order to take the wife). The dead man's tale is told through a medium. He claims his wife was raped, but he also insists that he killed himself out of disgrace. The only "impartial" witness, the woodcutter, weaves a story that intertwines elements of the other three, leaving the viewer wondering if he truly saw anything at all. When the film returns to the confused woodcutter at Rashomon Gate at the end, it is clear to the commoner that the woodcutter himself has told a story filled with holes.

"Look, we all want to forget something. So we tell stories." —The Woodcutter

THE DIRECTOR

Akira Kurosawa, indisputably one of the greatest international filmmakers, was the most prolific and respected of Japanese directors. *Rashomon*, with its original storytelling and acting style, catapulted the director to international acclaim. His most prominent theme, introduced in *Rashomon*, and revisited throughout his career is that we should suspect even what we think we have seen. This theme recurs in *Ikiru* (1952), in which old friends and family are made to question their assumptions about an old clerk's descent; in *The Seven Samurai*, in which the men are by turns heroes and thugs; and in *Ran*, in which an old king who has long believed in words ends up talking himself out of his own life. Kurosawa was greatly influenced by American filmmaking and, in turn, influenced American filmmakers. *The Seven Samurai* (1954) was remade by John Sturges into *The Magnificent Seven* (1960), *Yojimbo* (1961) was transformed by Sergio Leone into *A Fistful of Dollars* (1964) and by Walter Hill into *Last Man Standing* (1996). *The Hidden Fortress* (1958) was one of the inspirations behind George Lucas's *Star Wars* (1977). Kurosawa began his career in 1943 with *Sugata Sanshiro*, followed by *Drunken Angel* (1948), *The Seven Samurai* (1954), *Throne of Blood* (1957), *The Hidden Fortress* (1958), *The Bad Sleep Well* (1960), *Yojimbo* (1961), *Sanjuro* (1962), *High and Low* (1963), and *Red Beard* (1965). Among his last films was the Russian-produced *Dersu Uzala* (1975), which won the Academy Award for Best Foreign Film. American fans Francis Ford Coppola and George Lucas backed his epic *Kagemusha* (1980) and the French-financed *Ran* (1985), which earned Kurosawa his only Academy Award nomination as Best Director. Steven Spielberg presented *Akira Kurosawa's Dreams* (1990), and *Rhapsody in August* (1991), which featured American star Richard Gere. In 1989 the director was presented with an honorary Academy Award. He died in 1998. (For more on Kurosawa, see page 298.)

Machiko Kyo displays breathtaking variations on one personality: at once seductress, victim, child, and hot-tempered accomplice to murder.

THE CAST

Tajomaru	Toshiro Mifune
Masako Takehiro	Machiko Kyo
Woodcutter	Takashi Shimura
Priest	Minoru Chiaki
Commoner	Kichijiro Ueda
Medium	Fumiko Honma

THE ACTORS

Toshiro Mifune's bandit is by turns a crazed animal, scratching himself and picking off mosquitos from his body, and a brash, swaggering warrior, confident and adept with a sword. His face is a riot of expression and his voice enough to rouse you from a coma. He was one of the most famous Japanese actors ever. Kurosawa once said, "I am proud of nothing I have done other than with him." The director has much to be proud of, having made many films with the nimble actor. After starring in *Drunken Angel* (1948) he went on to play a reckless fighter in *The Seven Samurai* (1954), a stoic in *Yojimbo* (1961) and its sequel *Sanjuro* (1962), a paranoid and irrational samurai in the *Macbeth* adaptation *Throne of Blood* (1957), and a swashbuckler in *The Hidden Fortress* (1958). His one attempt at directing, *Goju Man-nin no Isan* (1963), was a failure. His American films, mainly playing a cartoonish villain, include *Grand Prix* (1966), *Hell in the Pacific* (1968), *1941* (1979), and the TV miniseries *Shogun* (1980). Less active during the past decade, Mifune recently appeared in *Shogun Mayeda* (1990). (For more on Mifune, see page 298.)

When Kurosawa cast her she was an unknown actress, but **Machiko Kyo**'s arresting, multi-faceted performance as both vixen and victim led to appearances, also both sensual and sinister, in Kenji Mizoguchi's *Ugetsu* (1953) and Teinosuke Kinugasa's *Gate of Hell* (1953), to world renown. In fact, so intense was her performance style that she came to embody sexual stereotype of the potency of the Japanese woman as a dangerous manipulator of man. Her fame led to an appearance with Marlon Brando in *The Teahouse of the August Moon* (1956). She returned to Japan to make over ninety films with a number of Japanese directors, including *Street of Shame* (1956), *Odd Obsession* (1959), *Floating Weeds* (1959), and *Sweet Sweat* (1964).

Takashi Shimura's face radiates a sympathetic and mysterious engagement with some internal presence as the woodcutter who witnessed the rape and murder. One of Japan's finest character actors, he was a member of Kurosawa's "stock company," appearing in more than twenty films for the director including *Drunken Angel* (1948), *Ikiru* (1952), *The Seven Samurai* (1954), *The Hidden Fortress* (1958), and *Kagemusha* (1980). He is often described as filling the spot of the reliable character actor for Kurosawa that Ward Bond filled for John Ford. (For more on Shimura, see page 298.)

Kurosawa saw **Minoru Chiaki** in a stage production and advised him to enter films. Chiaki became a favorite of the great director, who cast him in over a dozen of his films including *The Idiot* (1951), *Ikiru* (1952), and *The Seven Samurai* (1954).

BEHIND THE SCREEN

Rashomon was singularly responsible for bringing Japanese film to the attention of the West when it won the Grand Prize at Venice in 1951.

Leeches dropped from trees onto the cast and crew, Kurosawa recalled, and they slathered themselves with salt to repel them.

The rain in the torrential downpour in the scene at the Rashomon Gate was tinted by pouring black stain into the tank of the rain

CREDITS

Studio: RKO/Janus Films
Producer: Akira Kurosawa
Director: Akira Kurosawa
Screenplay: Shinobu Hashimoto and Akira Kurosawa
Running Time: 88 minutes

ACADEMY AWARDS

Honorary Award, Japan. Voted by the Board of Governors as the most outstanding foreign-language film released in the United States during 1951.

NOMINATIONS

Best Art Direction-Set Decoration, Black-and-White: So Matsuyama and H. Motsumoto

THE YEAR'S OTHER WINNERS

Best Picture: *An American in Paris*
Best Director: George Stevens, *A Place in the Sun*
Best Actor: Humphrey Bogart, *The African Queen*
Best Actress: Vivien Leigh, *A Streetcar Named Desire*
Best Supporting Actor: Karl Malden, *A Streetcar Named Desire*
Best Supporting Actress: Kim Hunter, *A Streetcar Named Desire*

THE OTHER LISTS

- American Film Institute (No)
- *Entertainment Weekly* (No)
- Internet Movie Database (Yes)
- Leonard Maltin (Yes)
- *Movieline* (No)
- *Premiere* Magazine
- Roger Ebert's Top 100 (Yes)
- *Rolling Stone* Magazine (No)
- *Village Voice* (Yes)

machine so it would show up against the light gray backdrop of the building.

The forest in which the film was shot was infested with leeches which dropped out of the trees onto the actors. Each morning before shooting, everyone would cover their necks, arms, and socks with salt because leeches, like slugs, avoid salt.

The music written for the film was based on Ravel's "Bolero," which had inspired Kurosawa. "The effect [of the music]," said the director, "was positively eerie."

THE VISUAL STYLE

Many special effects were used to capture the voluptuous visual style of *Rashomon*. Notably, the camera shot directly into the sun, which had been considered impossible and taboo. The visual texture of the film utilized hard sunlight casting sharp, dappled shadows on the forest floor. Because the trees were too far away from where they were filming to achieve this affect, mirrors and tree branches were placed just out of frame. At high noon, when parts of the forest were still too dark to shoot, rather than use a regular foil reflector which did not bounce enough light, Kurosawa and cinematographer Kazuo Miyagawa decided to use a full-length mirror. Light was bounced from the mirror through leaves and trees to soften it and make it look more like natural sunlight. Miyagawa later called it the most successful lighting effect he had ever used. Kurosawa places much emphasis on the scenery of the countryside, often filming the action in long-shots. Camera movement is used frequently and rhapsodically, whether following the woodcutter as he treks through the trees or circling around the woman to reveal her face when she first realizes Tajomaru's intentions are evil. Much of the staging of the scenes is rather stilted; the actors move from one carefully composed shot to the next, and fluidity of action is often sacrificed for artistic composition. Frequently during arguments, one actor turns away from the others and stares off at some imaginary distant object, a style that has come to be identified with Japanese cinema though Kurosawa may have been its only proponent.

THE CRITICS

"*Rashomon* is an artistic achievement of such distinct and exotic character that it is difficult to estimate it along conventional story films. On the surface it isn't a picture of the sort that we're accustomed to at all, being simply a careful observation of a dramatic incident from four points of view, with an eye to discovering some meaning—some rationalization—in the seeming heartlessness of man." —Bosley Crowther, *New York Times*

"The introductory and closing sequences are tedious; the woman's whimpering is almost enough to drive one to the nearest exit. Yet the film transcends these discomforts; it has its own perfection." —Pauline Kael, *The New Yorker*

THE GREAT SCENE

Masako Takehiro (Machiko Kyo) takes a rest during her walk in the woods. Great care has been taken by Kurosawa and his cinematographer to create the effect of the sharp, dappled sunlight filtering through the trees and painting and forest floor.

The opening three-and-half-minute silent sequence, in which the woodcutter journeys though the forest, is one of the most cinematic interludes in talking pictures. As the barefoot man enters new territory, it is as if he has traveled into another realm of reality. Cinematographer Kazuo Miyagawa shoots directly into the sun and we see it as a radiating orb glaring down on the little man below. The camera seems to glide through the woods, offering a kaleidoscope of black-and-white images accompanied by a dramatic and mysterious score by Fumio Hayasaka. There is constant movement, slow then fast, close-up and long-shot, cutting back and forth up to the tall treetops and then down the length of a monumentally large tree to the woodcutter below where the leaves cast upon him a web of shadows and light. As he walks through the forest we see him from varying angles and distances, the camera dancing around him, bringing the various powers of photography into play. The camera suddenly draws in to a close-up of his face, on which is registered shock as he discovers the dead body with its stiff arms still reaching out. There is a loud crash in the music and the woodcutter turns and races through the forest. As he runs, the leaves on the trees become a blur, like a leader of film run too quickly through a projector, with the desperate figure glimpsed behind it. This sequence is a marvel of mood and style, simple and yet almost a film in itself.

In this version of the rape of a woman and the murder of her Samurai husband, the wife (Machiko Kyo) begs the rapist-bandit (Toshiro Mifune) to kill her husband or be killed in order to salvage her dignity.

83

CABARET 1972

LIZA WITH AN SS

If you've ever spent enough time in a nightclub to see the grime and tack beneath the glitter, the not-as-young-as-you-thought faces behind the heavy makeup, then "Wilkommen!" to *Cabaret*'s Kit Kat Klub, in Bob Fosse's pitch-perfect period Berlin. It's the 1930s, Nazi thugs roam the streets and Liza Minnelli, as the politically oblivious chanteuse Sally Bowles, is tearing up the Kit Kat stage in cahoots with emcee Joel Grey. The only quibble is that they're so supremely talented it's hard to imagine they'd be consigned to such show biz oblivion. The Kander and Ebb score sizzles with cynicism in this Hollywood first, a realistic, very sexy musical that's actually about something and isn't afraid to delve.

Jim: Minnelli's bawdy belter is the perfect antidote to Julie Andrews' Sister Saccharina of the Alps.

Gail: Lost in a corrupt and decadent world, the habitués of the Kit Kat Club barely know there's a war coming on, let alone acknowledge the existence of the Nazis. The fact that Fosse captured all this in a musical makes *Cabaret* all the more remarkable.

E PLOT

berate to be decadent, Sally Bowles (Liza nelli), estranged child of privilege, holds as the star attraction in a sleazy but ılar Berlin show bar where she wows the dent crowd with steamy numbers like . Herr" and "Don't Tell Mama." Sexually used young British writer Brian (Michael moves into her boardinghouse where ıpports himself by tutoring English to the of wealthy young Jewish socialite Natalia isa Berenson). Sally is quick to charm vay into Brian's life and he falls under sway. Sally's hunger for everything shiny beautiful is reflected in her duet, "Money, ey, Money" with the Kit Kat Klub's weird ee (Joel Grey). Sally's affection for Brian y turns to passion and she wonders could be the solution to all her needs ybe This Time"). That bubble bursts when neets dapper German aristocrat Maximil-Helmut Griem), who uses both Sally and sexually, then abruptly casts them off. and Brian feel mutually betrayed and love turns to rage. As the Nazis rise to r, the club's emcee plays a dangerous of racial satire in "If You Could See Her gh My Eyes." Sally's self-involvement s no room for politics but she has sadder and wiser since aborting the child she will probably ever have. Brian her a wistful goodbye and returns to the y of London.

The pairing of Liza Minnelli and Joel Grey was priceless. In their triumphant duet "Money, Money, Money," all that talent comes together with truly inspired choreography by Bob Fosse.

THE DIRECTOR

Bob Fosse, whose name is synonymous with a particular blade-edge style of jazz choreography, brought raw authenticity to the Kit Kat Klub numbers. Having come up in the world of strip clubs, he knew from raunch, tinsel, bored saxophones, and cymbals. While he'd drawn from that bag of tricks as director of the original Broadway production, he was well aware that film has a unique language of its own. He flew to Germany in search of locations for *Cabaret*, insisting that it had to look right to be right. He played Marlene Dietrich records over and over to make sure his cast and crew caught the precise flavor. Though Fosse had the finished picture in his mind, he allowed his actors the chance to try it their way and he was always open to possibilities, especially if they enhanced his own concept. Conveying the narrative storyline was not his strong suit, though there are some powerful little moments in between the music. For example, there is a deft scene at the country estate of Maximilian, in which a closeup of Sally, Maximilian, and Brian drunkenly dancing together sends silent signals as to who's going to wind up in bed with whom. As a young dancer/choreographer, Fosse contributed to several Golden Age musical films including *Kiss Me Kate* (1953), *The Pajama Game* (1957), *Damn Yankees* (1958), and *How to Succeed in Business without Really Trying* (1967). His directorial follow-ups to *Cabaret* were the non-musical *Lenny* (1974), starring Dustin Hoffman as the infamous comic Lenny Bruce; the autobiographical *All That Jazz* (1979); and *Star 80* (1983). The hard-driven, chain-smoking Fosse died of a heart attack in 1987.

Boy, oh, boy! Oh, girl! A bittersweet, tense, and sexy moment as Sally (Liza Minnelli), Brian (Michael York), and rich-rich Maximilian (Helmut Griem) consider all the possibilities of the eternal triangle.

THE CAST

Sally Bowles	Liza Minnelli
Brian Roberts	Michael York
Maximilian von Heune	Helmut Griem
Master of Ceremonies	Joel Grey
Fritz Wendel	Fritz Wepper
Natalia Landauer	Marisa Berenson

THE ACTORS

The prevailing **Liza Minnelli** persona of a glamorously beleaguered superstar was born with *Cabaret*. "I was young, everything seemed so easy." She and Fosse symbiotically melded their approach to the character. "Sally is talented but doesn't care." Out of that came Liza's by now signature gestures from the movie-stopping "Mein Herr," the throwaway "bye-bye" as if bored with her own blinding light. "*Cabaret* was a time in my life, it was like the inside of a diamond. Everything was so clear." It was her golden, defining moment and she wanted full credit for it. When accepting her Academy Award, she clearly took exception to presenter Rock Hudson's suggestion that her bloodline (as Judy Garland's daughter) had a great deal to do with it. Liza had already made her debut splash in *Charlie Bubbles* (1968) and had played kookie "Pookie" in the film *The Sterile Cuckoo* (1970). Otto Preminger chose her for her first dramatic role *in Tell Me That You Love Me, Junie Moon* (1969) and after *Cabaret* came the disastrous *Lucky Lady* (1975). She fared little better in what was to be her dad Vincente Minnelli's farewell film, *A Matter of Time* (1976), and soared back in the gritty Scorsese musical *New York, New York* (1977), costarring Robert DeNiro. Since then her life has been a series of ups and downs, brief Broadway appearances, brave comebacks after bouts of substance abuse and ill health, and one of the most media-blitzed marriages of recent times to "special events" producer, David Gest.

"Either use **Joel Grey** or you're gone." That was the word Bob Fosse got from on high. Joel had done the part of the emcee on Broadway—had virtually invented it in fact—and he owned it completely. All Fosse had to do was point the camera at him and shoot. He beat out Al Pacino in *The Godfather* for the Oscar and insured his place in the history of the movie musical. He never came close again but then, how many parts are there like this one? His limited appearances on the big screen include *Man on a Swing* (1974), *The Seven-Percent-Solution* (1976), and *Kafka* (1991). On Broadway, he did a star turn in the revival of Kander and Ebb's *Chicago* as "Mr. Cellophane," hapless husband of the murderous Roxie.

Michael York was amused that the producers were looking for a "Michael York type" for the role of Brian. When he came in to audition, he blew away the clone competition. The otherwise handsome York, with his distinguishing broken nose, was already a major star in Great Britain before the rest of the world took notice in *Cabaret*. His career quickly became centered in Hollywood with *Murder on the Orient Express* (1974), *Logan's Run* (1976), Billy Wilder's final film *Fedora* (1978), and a slew of "fast forgettables"—until *Austin Powers: International Man of Mystery* (1997) and its sequel, *Austin Powers: The Spy Who Shagged Me* (1999) brought him to the attention of a new generation of filmgoers.

Marisa Berenson was an international model and debutante who made her biggest splash in *Barry Lyndon* (1975), and has been seen only occasionally outside of the social circuit since.

THE MUSIC

John Kander and Fred Ebb, the musical creators of the Broadway production, were called upon by Fosse to write a new number for the movie. He described what he wanted and they just happened to have an old, unused song in their trunk, "Maybe This Time." But in so doing, they forfeited the possibility of an Oscar nomination for Original Song.

CREDITS

Producer: Cy Feuer
Director: Bob Fosse
Screenplay: Jay Presson Allen, from the book *Berlin Stories* by Christopher Isherwood, and the play *I Am a Camera* by John Van Druten
Score: Music by John Kander, Lyrics by Fred Ebb
Running time: 124 minutes
Box Office: $42.7 million

ACADEMY AWARDS

Best Actress: Liza Minnelli
Best Supporting Actor: Joel Grey
Best Director: Bob Fosse
Best Art Direction-Set Decoration: Hoff Zehetbauer, Jurgen Kiebach, Herbert Strabel
Best Cinematography: Geoffrey Unsworth
Best Film Editing: David Bretherton
Best Musical Scoring: Ralph Burns
Best Sound: Robert Knudson and David Hildyard

NOMINATIONS

Best Picture
Best Screenplay: Jay Presson Allen

THE YEAR'S OTHER WINNERS

Best Picture: *The Godfather*
Best Actor: Marlon Brando, *The Godfather*
Best Supporting Actress: Eileen Heckart, *Butterflies Are Free*

"All the odds are in my favor," sings Sally with more than a bit of wishful thinking on her part. The object of her desire is gay and Berlin is about to be overcome by the Nazis. The lyric line is more on the money for Liza herself, who was born to Hollywood royalty and made her debut as a toddler in mom Judy Garland's In the Good Old Summertime (1949).

THE GREAT SCENE

Sally confides in Brian that she's pregnant and, in a gush of sentiment, he begs to be the surrogate father. She suddenly sees him in a new light, the possibility of a solid, true love. She sings an anthem to romantic optimism "Maybe This Time," as the scene cross-cuts to her finally consummated relationship with Brian. Maybe he's not really gay, after all. Maybe, she can finally put her trust in a man, maybe, maybe. As she sings her heart out, the jaded Kit Kat faces, particularly that of the emcee, look on in stark contrast to her buoyancy. We somehow know this is a pipe dream about to burst.

Every shade of Grey is revealed in one of the most intriguing film musical performances of all time. With all of his dialogue framed within songs, Joel Grey's emcee perfectly evokes the eeriness of an era.

THE CRITICS

"*Cabaret* is a great movie musical, made, miraculously, without compromises. The people involved must've said something like "let's do it right. If it doesn't make money, it will still make movie history." —Pauline Kael, *The New Yorker*

"Fosse makes mistakes, partly because his camera is a more potent instrument than he realizes . . ." —Roger Greenspun, *New York Times*

BEHIND THE SCREEN

In the film, the faux Third Reich anthem "Tomorrow Belongs to Me" is sung by an angelic Nazi youth to chilling effect. In reality, the song has been taken up by neo-Nazis and recorded by skinhead band, "Skrewdriver."

Cabaret holds the record of winning the most Academy Awards (a total of eight) without winning Best Picture. Another Oscar distinction: Liza Minnelli is the only Oscar-winning child of Oscar-winning parents. Mom, Judy Garland, got her special "junior" statuette for *The Wizard of Oz* (1939) and Dad, Vincente Minnelli, won his for *Gigi* (1958).

At the time of his death in 1987, Bob Fosse was attempting to put together a film version of the Kander and Ebb musical *Chicago* starring Madonna. It has since been made by Rob Marshall—featuring Renée Zellweger and Catherine Zeta-Jones, among its stars—and was the darling of the 2002 Oscar season.

THE OTHER LISTS

- American Film Institute (Yes)
- Roger Ebert's Top 100 (No)
- *Entertainment Weekly* (No)
- Internet Movie Database (No)
- Leonard Maltin (No)
- *Movieline* (Yes)
- National Society of Film Critics (No)
- *Premiere* Magazine (No)
- *Rolling Stone* Magazine (Yes)
- *Village Voice* (No)

84

RETURN OF THE KING 2003

"PRECIOUS" GEM

Here is the final triumph of questing Hobbits, sages and righteous kings and the first fantasy/adventure to win the Best Picture Oscar. And the only sequel since *Godfather II* to do so. Though author Tolkien thought his opus unfilmable, he never counted on Peter Jackson, an auteur whose admiration for the work doesn't diminish his devotion to the cinematic rules of the game. He knows how to get the heart pounding, the blood racing and have nearly four hours fly by in a magical wink. Visually startling in the massive battle scenes and almost more so when the camera pulls back in a key emotional moment to reveal the physical scale of Hobbits to humans. The imagery is all the more astonishing for seeming so completely natural.

The narration is pried from its philosophical harness, time-lines are condensed and events reconfigured. In doing so, Jackson invigorates the aura of *The Rings* without being imprisoned by it and the most diehard disciples of the books should gladly go along for the ride. The gentle tampering of the source material only manages to underscore the most powerful thematic elements: friendship, love, duty and the inevitable cycle of hope. What makes *The Return Of The King* unforgettable is its ability to give as much power to the tested alliance of Frodo and Sam as it does the earth-scorching battle scenes between The Undead and Orcs, whose precise battalions evoke the eerie images of Triumph Of The Will.

Jim: Exquisitely rendered geekfest for those with feet planted firmly on Middle Earth. Heart-grabbing cinematography and painterly set design, in tandem with gold standard performances, make this action/fantasy a near-religious experience.

Gail: Though not my usual "neck of the woods" in film, this landscape affords the operatic sweep and scope, enduring themes—less so the pyrotechnics—and most of all the great emotional pull to render it deservedly classic.

THE PLOT

The hideous Gollum leads Hobbit Frodo Baggins to Mount Doom where he's promised to destroy the Ring for the harmonic good of Middle Earth. But Frodo's devoted friend Sam overhears the creature's plan to murder him; his attempt to warn leads to mistrust. Meanwhile, Gandalf foresees via the palentir (seeing stone) his nemesis Sauron attacking Minas Tirith and rides off to confront him. But Lord Protector of Gondor, Denethor, insane with grief over the death of his favorite son, refuses to assist. The dreaded Orcs launch the attack; the only hope is Prince Aragon's induction of the Army of the Dead; their reward for victory is a glorious afterlife. Gollum tricks Frodo into the web of giant spider, Shelob. It's Sam to the rescue but he must retreat when an Orc unit comes upon the scene and kidnaps Frodo. Once again, brave Sam saves him but as they make their way to the top of Mount Doom, Gollum catches up with them and in a final struggle, bites off Frodo's finger for the Ring before falling to his death in the lava pits, taking the Ring with him. Frodo and Sam are stranded in the sudden destruction of Doom until Gandalf saves them on the wings of the Great Eagles. With the battle won, Aragon reigns over a new era of peace. Sam weds his sweetheart Rosie but Frodo has seen too much to return to a simple Shire life. He boards a ship with Gandalf to the Undying Lands.

In a heartfelt speech before battle, Aragon bids his men, "Hold your ground, hold your ground! Sons of Gondor, of Rohan, my brothers! I see in your eyes the same fear that would take the heart of me. A day may come when the courage of men fails, when we forsake our friends and break all bonds of fellowship, but it is not this day. An hour of woes and shattered shields, when the age of men comes crashing down! But it is not this day! This day we fight! By all that you hold dear on this good Earth, I bid you stand, Men of the West!"

THE DIRECTOR

"Pain is temporary—film is forever," serves as one of Peter Jackson's pet catch-phrases. New Zealand born Jackson is a cinema autodidact with no formal training who early on developed a fascination for such films as *King Kong*, which he later remade at the height of his career in 2005. He essentially put himself on the map with *Heavenly Creatures* (1994) that also launched the career of Kate Winslet. Determined to bring *The Lord Of The Rings* to the screen, he won the rights in 1997 after agreeing to a two-film production. But Jackson, as always, had his own ideas and with cooperation of the Weinstein brothers of NewLine, proceeded with the trilogy. Jackson, in his constant uniform of shorts, sneakers and a cell-phone in his back pocket, is famous for his eccentricities and offbeat sense of humor. During production he'd traverse from one set to another on a skull-decorated bike. He's a hands-on perfectionist who shoots every scene from innumerable angles. One of his trademarks is a close-up with a wide angle lens. A traditionalist in many ways, he much prefers miniatures over CGI; *Return of the King* required a veritable miniature world in varying scales. In the Hitchcockian manner, he delights in appearing in each of his films, often with an uncredited cameo. In *Return Of The King* he can be seen briefly as the blood-thirsty captain of a corsair ship who's done in by the pierce of an arrow.

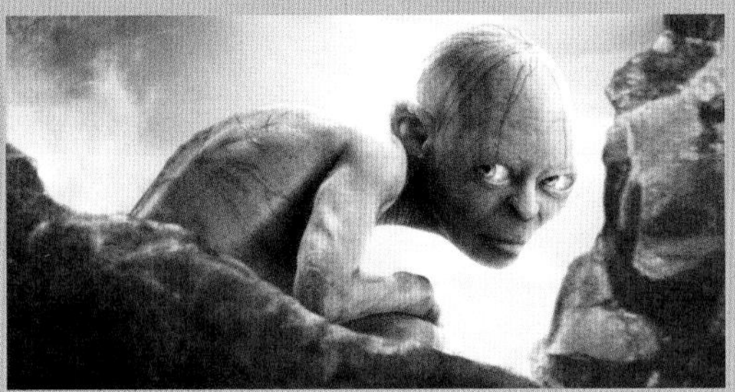

"Wake up, wake up, sleepies!" Hard to imagine nodding off during a moment of Andy Serkis's screen time as the eerily soul-tortured Gollum. The actor displayed his thorough investment in the role on his very first day on the set when he was required to film one of his very last moments in the trilogy—his finger-biting leap onto Frodo for possession of the Ring.

THE CAST	
Frodo Baggins	Elijah Wood
Samwise Gamgee	Sean Astin
Aragorn	Viggo Mortensen
Gandalf	Ian McKellen
Gollum	Andy Serkis
Meriadoc	Dominic Monaghan
Peregrin Took	Billy Boyd
Legolas	Orlando Bloom
Gimli	John Rhys-Davies
Sauron	Sala Baker
Deagol	Thomas Robins
Theoden	Bernard Hill
Eowyn	Miranda Otto
Eomer	Karl Urban
Elrond	Hugo Weaving
Arwen	Liv Tyler
Faramir	David Wenham
Denethor	John Noble
Gamling	Bruce Hopkins
Bilbo Baggins	Ian Holm
Galadriel	Cate Blanchett
Rosie Cotton	Sarah McLeod

THE ACTORS

Having worked together off and mostly on for four years (during which the entire trilogy was filmed simultaneously) the deeply engaged cast truly defines 'ensemble.' The final months were so emotionally charged that the tears shed on screen were often the result of the actors saying goodbye to one another in reality. Iowa-born former child actor Elijah Woods' Frodo, is the heart and soul of *Return Of The King*, and his saucer blue eyes capture every nuance of his character's transformations. When he first learned of the project he rightly suspected it would be his acting chance of a lifetime and relentlessly campaigned for it with a homemade video of himself as the character. His nearly constant scene companion, Sean Astin (Samwise), son of Patty Duke and stepson of the late John Astin, conversely, had never heard of the Tolkien opus before being cast. He hated having to gain forty pounds for the role and continues to view his performance as a 'big crybaby' despite critical raves. Though not originally chosen for the pivotal role of Aragon, it's hard to imagine anyone other than NYC-born Viggo Mortenson, a sensitive hunk whose career as a leading man has included *A History of Violence*, *Eastern Promises* (both 2005) and *The Road* (2009). Sir Ian McKellen breathes fiery truth into the gargantuan role of Gandalf and his performance is perfectly proportioned to the epic landscape. Though Andy Serkis (Gollum) is seen only briefly as his actual self, the eerie wit of his physical and vocal performance creates one of modern film's most iconic villains.

THE MUSIC

Canadian composer Howard Shore had long been a Hollywood fixture before his *Return of the King* assignment, for which he won Best Score and Best Song *Into The West*, lyrics by Fran Walsh and dowager of rock, Annie Lennox. Shore has since conducted his *Lord of the Rings* symphony on a world tour. As with many behind-the-scenes creators of the trilogy, he appeared in a brief cameo in *Return Of The King* in the role of a guard of Rohan. Along with such big screen entries as the scores for Martin Scorcese's *The Departed* and *The Aviator*, he also penned the theme for *Late Night With Conan O'Brien*.

ROLE REVERSAL

Viggo Mortensen was not Peter Jackson's first choice for the role of Aragorn. He replaced Stuart Townsend who was let go before the end of the first week of shooting due to "artistic differences." Hardly a euphemism for bad behavior in this case; Jackson realized he looked too young for the role.

THE CRITICS

"Here is an epic with literature's depth and opera's splendor—and one that could be achieved only in movies. What could be more terrific?" —Richard Corliss, *Time* magazine

"*Return of the King* is such a crowning achievement, such a visionary use of all the tools of special effects, such a pure spectacle, that it can be enjoyed even by those who have not seen the first two films." —Roger Ebert, *Chicago Sun-Times*

BEHIND THE SCREEN

The great battle scene was shot on an Army munitions testing site; the cast had to tread cautiously through a minefield that could not be completely cleared.

Liv Tyler refused to kiss Viggo Mortenson's double in a 'reaction shot' of their final scene together. Mortenson was rushed back to the set to save the day. He later surprised Billy Boyd with a deep kiss off-camera in the Sam/Rosie wedding sequence. Boyd's response: "I think I fell in love for a second!"

The tear-sodden farewell at Grey Haven had to be re-shot when Sean Astin forgot to put his vest back on after lunch break. The actors had to weep yet again the next day when the lab discovered the camera was out of focus.

In Orlando Bloom's very last scene, his trusty bow that had served him for 14 months broke.

CREDITS

Producer: Wingnut Films/Barrie M. Osborne/Peter Jackson/Fran Walsh/New Line
Director: Peter Jackson
Screenplay: Fran Walsh, Phillippa Boyens, Peter Jackson
Running Time: 201 minutes
Budget: $94,000,000
Box Office: $1,118,888,979

ACADEMY AWARDS

Best Picture
Best Director
Best Adapted Screenplay: Fran Walsh, Phillippa Boyens, Peter Jackson
Art Direction/Set Decoration: Grant Major, Alan Lee, Dan Hennah
Costume Design: Ngila Dickson, Richard Taylor
Sound: Christopher Boyes, Michael Semanick, Michael Hedges, Hammond Peek
Editing: Jamie Selkirk
Visual Effects: Jim Rygiel, Joe Letteri, Randall William Cook, Alex Funke
Song: ("Into The West"): Fran Walsh, Howard Shore, Annie Lennox
Score: Howard Shore
Makeup: Richard Taylor, Peter King

"Come on, Mr. Frodo. I can't carry it (the Ring) for you. . . but I can carry you!" And he does, right to the top of Mount Doom. The ultimate action/fantasy 'bromance' is played to the tearful hilt by Elijah Woods and Sean Astin. The emotionally drenching close-ups were re-shot nearly a year after the scene was filmed. .

THE GREAT SCENE

Against all odds, Aragon and his devoted men challenge 10,000 Orcs at the foot of Mount Doom as a distraction; they pray Frodo is still alive and able to destroy the Ring at its core. But Frodo is exhausted by his trials and it's up to the brave Sam to carry him on this final journey. They make it to the rim of the teeming volcano but the Ring's hypnotic evil compels Frodo to hesitate. Gollum, thought to be dead, leaps onto him in a brutal grab for the Ring and bites Frodo's finger off in order to win it. In his mad glee, he dances too close to the edge and falls into the searing river of lava below. The Ring is consumed with him and Mount Doom begins to destruct in a mighty explosion of fiery quakes. Sam pulls Frodo up from the hellish brink and together they make a desperate run for their lives as the earth opens up before them.

"There is no going back." –Frodo

"Did you die at the end?" –Jack Nicholson to Elijah Wood

THE OTHER LISTS

- American Film Institute (Yes)
- Roger Ebert's Top 100 (No)
- *Entertainment Weekly* (No)
- Internet Movie Database (Yes)
- Leonard Maltin (No)
- *Movieline* (No)
- National Society of Film Critics (No)
- *Premiere* Magazine (No)
- *Rolling Stone* Magazine (No)
- *Village Voice* (No)

Jumbo rumble! Outsized pachyderms and their precarious trunkfuls of Orcs prepare to stomp Prince Aragon's depleted battalions. Several are eventually brought down by the mighty bow of Orlando Bloom's Legolas who aims low and knocks the enemy off its lumbering feet.

85

A PLACE IN THE SUN 1951

THAT KISS!

They had faces then. And George Stevens knew how to photograph them. Forget the original Dreiser novel, with its socio-political agenda, and don't look for the traditional love-story formula of the period. This is about Montgomery Clift's obsession with Elizabeth Taylor's beauty and vice versa. From the moment he sees her walking down a long hall, the rest of the world melts away. Her first glimpse of him, after he makes a perfect hook shot in the billiard room, leaves her breathless. When the camera pulls back from their perfect facial bones, there's some nearly perfect acting going on. Clift gives one of his most spectacularly weird, early Method, sexually ambiguous performances. It threatens to lunge out of Stevens's precise cinematography and artful sort-of-*noir* lighting. Nearly every frame is frameable. As with the most imaginative directors of the period, he pulls off some neat tricks to throw off the censors. Note the weather-changing window shot indicating that George has spent the night in bed with dowdy factory-worker Alice. Costumer Edith Head certainly kept the Moral Code boys' heads spinning with the famous strapless dress she designed for Taylor, with its eye-locking bust of spring flowers. Just eighteen, Taylor holds her own in the acting department—in case you happen to notice anything else between the rack of daisies and that face.

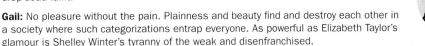

Jim: Very much of its time (they couldn't say "abortion" in 1951—they couldn't say *boo!*) but somehow timeless. If you think the kiss is the ultimate movie moment, hang in for Taylor's drop-dead faint.

Gail: No pleasure without the pain. Plainness and beauty find and destroy each other in a society where such categorizations entrap everyone. As powerful as Elizabeth Taylor's glamour is Shelley Winter's tyranny of the weak and disenfranchised.

IE PLOT

ly, ambitious young George Eastman ntgomery Clift), desperate to escape his gelical roots, takes a job at the bathing-nanufacturing company of his rich uncle es (Herbert Hayes). He hooks up with a but willing naïf on the production line, (Shelley Winters), but he soon loses his t to gorgeous deb Angela Vickers abeth Taylor), whom he meets at his e's mansion. The two become locked in ssionate mutual obsession. As George nds the social and professional ladders, eby making himself more attractive to la's family, Alice clings more desperately. s pregnant and demands he do "the right ." He goes as far as driving her to a doctor does abortions, but in her case, sensing er, the doctor refuses. She presses George arry her and he avoids the issue by running a vacation with Angela and her crowd to ickers' lakeside summerhouse. Alice sees photo in the society pages and, in a fury, s the next bus. She calls him from a phone h and demands he marry her right then, or l expose him to everyone. George is torn een duty and his heart's desire. The only ion lies at the bottom of a lake. When Alice ns while boating with him, he must some-convince a jury that it was accidental—or a final reckoning on Death Row.

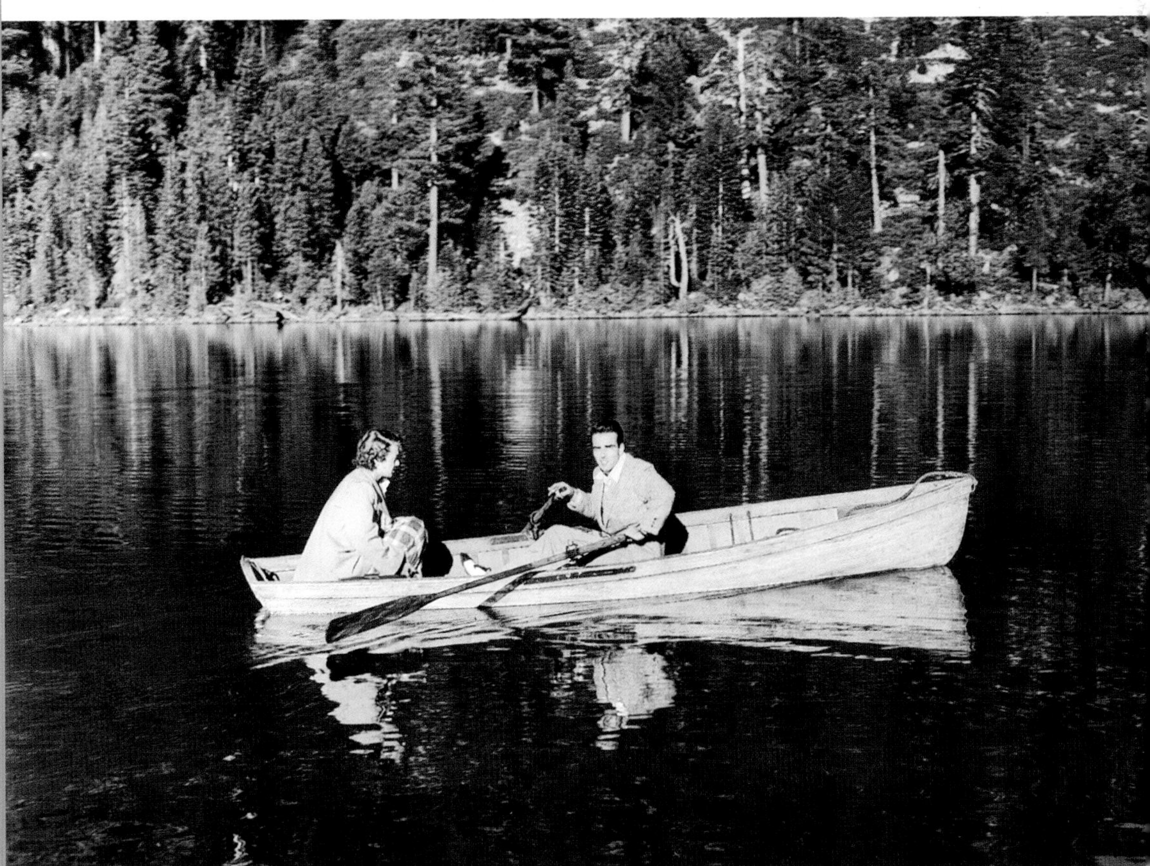

"Rest for a while, dear. We can just drift. After all, we're not going anywhere." Alice is oblivious to George's increasingly disturbed state as she rambles on about how content they'll be—poor but cozy—in their quiet, loveless marriage. He wants to kill her right now, just to shut her up, but he can't do it. A moment later, things will happen so fast he won't really remember if it was all an accident or not.

"I'm in trouble, George. Bad trouble."—Alice Tripp

THE DIRECTOR

A Place in the Sun was a hard sell to the studio until **George Stevens** laid out his plan to translate Dreiser's terse social drama into a lush romance. He dropped the theme of George Eastman's class-conscious ambition and zeroed in on his obsession with Angela Vickers. The essential storyline appealed to the director's recurring preoccupation, the outsider eager to fit in. He insisted on black-and-white, claiming that Technicolor elicited too much of an "Oh, what a beautiful morning!" feel. He wanted texture to suit his "camera as observer" style, the objective view, often clouded by shadows and featuring almost no close-ups—until the most famous one in film history: the kiss. He was also fond of the long dissolves that bled from one of George's secret lives to another. They could be especially cruel as they lingered on Angela's privileged beauty, only to fade into plain Alice's tacky boarding-house room. Stevens lent his special touch to *Swing Time* (1936), *Gunga Din* (1939), *Woman of the Year* (1942), *I Remember Mama* (1948), the Western classic *Shane* (1953), and twice again with Elizabeth Taylor in *Giant* (1956) and *The Only Game in Town* (1970).

All evidence points to the young man who wanted it all. In a precursor to his iconic courtroom role in *Perry Mason*, Raymond Burr as prosecutor Frank Marlowe accuses George of brutally trading up from Alice to Angela.

THE CAST	
George Eastman	Montgomery Clift
Angela Vickers	Elizabeth Taylor
Alice Tripp	Shelley Winters
Hannah Eastman	Anne Revere
Earl Eastman	Keefe Brasselle
Bellows	Fred Clark
Frank Marlowe	Raymond Burr
Charles Eastman	Herbert Heyes
Anthony Vickers	Shepperd Strudwick
Mrs. Vickers	Frieda Inescort
Louise Eastman	Kathryn Givney
Jansen	Walter Sande

THE ACTORS

At 29, **Montgomery Clift** was the most sought-after, intensely talented young actor in Hollywood. Mobbed by fans everywhere he went, fame didn't deter his concentration on his craft. Elizabeth Taylor was hurt that he so completely shut her out in the final days of filming; he needed to find his way inside the mind of imprisoned young Eastman. He and director Stevens were not on the same wavelength. Clift hated his "objective camera," his inflexibility with actors. "George preconceives everything through a viewfinder," he complained. The two argued bitterly over the last scenes on Death Row. Stevens wanted a clear expression of terror. Clift countered that a man about to die in the electric chair has no expression, he's emotionally paralyzed. The final moment of the film reveals the victor of the debate. Clift's debut in *Red River* (1948) launched a spectacular, if sadly brief, career in such classics as *The Heiress* (1949), *I Confess* and *From Here to Eternity* (both 1953), *Suddenly, Last Summer* with Elizabeth Taylor (1959), *The Misfits* (1961), and *Freud* (1962). (For more on Clift, see page 271.)

Until *A Place in the Sun*, **Elizabeth Taylor** was a kid, most often playing opposite dogs and horses. She later admitted they were often her most amiable costars. At 18, suddenly, in her first adult role, she displayed an acting ability that hadn't been noted among her assets. According to coproducer Ivan Moffat, she was touted as "the most beautiful woman in the world," and, as he continued, "she would be the first to agree." Taylor admitted to her free pass: "I was the pet, I got away with murder." She added that her inspiration was Monty Clift, whose acting so fascinated her that she was determined to see if she could match it. The two became instant friends, never more, and made two other pictures together, *Raintree County* (1957) and *Suddenly, Last Summer* (1959). The eight-times-wed Dame Elizabeth has made at least as much history offscreen as on. As to the latter, she made waves from the start in *National Velvet* (1944) and *Little Women* (1949), before stepping into adult roles with *Ivanhoe* (1952), *Elephant Walk* (1954), *Giant* (1956), *Cat on a Hot Tin Roof* (1958) (during whose filming her producer/husband, Mike Todd, was killed in a plane crash), *Cleopatra* (1963), *A Little Night Music* (1978), and, when not counting her millions in perfume profits, an occasional cameo like *The Flintstones* (1994) that appeals to her famously ribald sense of humor.

Shelley Winters pleaded with Stevens for the role of Alice but her image as a blonde bombshell was difficult to overcome. She solved that by dying her hair a mousy brown, skipping the makeup, and dressing like a factory worker. She'd researched her getup. Stevens strolled into the restaurant for their meeting and didn't spot her at first. He was overwhelmed by the transformation and she won the part. Once filming began, however, Shelley tried to make her character a bit more glamorous every day. She was secure enough to look like a frump for her audition, but not before her public. Stevens didn't let her get away with it, but she was back to her sexy self on Oscar night. While she missed the gold for this one, she won twice, for *The Diary of Anne Frank* (1959) and *A Patch of Blue* (1965). She turned in powerful performances in *Night of the Hunter* and *The Big Knife* (both 1955), and *Lolita* (1962), before descending into such campy, highly mannered fare as *The Poseidon Adventure* (1972) and *Fanny Hill* (1983). With her acting heyday long since over, she's probably most famous now for her "kiss and tell" Hollywood autobiographies.

BEHIND THE SCREEN

When Elizabeth Taylor stepped into the Paramount commissary for the first time there was a hushed awe; few had ever seen her lush beauty in person. Billy Wilder piped up from his table, "How the hell did she get in movies?"

CREDITS

Producer: George Stevens, Ivan Moffat/Paramount
Director: George Stevens
Screenplay: Michael Wilson, Harry Brown, from Theodore Dreiser's novel *An American Tragedy.*
Running time: 122 minutes
Budget: $2.3 million

ACADEMY AWARDS

Best Director: George Stevens
Best Screenplay: Michael Wilson, Harold Brown
Best Cinematography, Black-and-White: William C. Mellor
Best Costume Design, Black-and-White: Edith Head
Best Editing: William Hornbeck
Best Music: Franz Waxman

NOMINATIONS

Best Picture
Best Actor: Montgomery Clift
Best Actress: Shelley Winters

THE YEAR'S OTHER WINNERS

Best Picture: *An American in Paris*
Best Actor: Humphrey Bogart, *The African Queen*
Best Actress: Vivien Leigh, *A Streetcar Named Desire*
Best Supporting Actor: Karl Malden, *A Streetcar Named Desire*
Best Supporting Actress: Kim Hunter, *A Streetcar Named Desire*

Clift, unusually hirsute, had a standing monthly appointment with an electrolysist. A Paramount press agent reported, "He looks like a monkey in a bathing suit." If you'll notice the swimming scene at the lake, he's wearing a T-shirt.

Anne Revere (Clift's evangelical mother and, coincidentally, Elizabeth Taylor's mother in 1944's *National Velvet*) was blacklisted shortly after *A Place in the Sun.*

During the filming of *Raintree County*, Elizabeth Taylor was credited with saving Montgomery Clift's life after he crashed into a tree following a party at her house. She pulled the shattered teeth out of his throat to keep him from choking.

THE CRITICS

"As produced and directed by George Stevens, the movie is first rate all along the line." —John McCarten, *The New Yorker*

"Those gigantic closeups of them (Clift and Taylor) kissing was unnerving—sybaritic—like gorging on chocolate sundaes." —Andrew Sarris, *Village Voice*

NOTABLE QUOTES

"There are three things I never saw Elizabeth Taylor do—tell a lie, be unkind to anyone, and be on time."—Mike Nichols

"Montgomery Clift is the only person I know who's in worse shape than I am."—Marilyn Monroe

BELOW: "Elizabeth Taylor is a pre-feminist woman. This is the source of her continuing greatness and relevance. She wields the sexual power that feminism cannot explain and has tried to destroy. Through stars like Taylor, we sense the world-disordering impact of legendary women like Delilah, Salome, and Helen of Troy."
—Camille Paglia, *Penthouse* (1992)

THE GREAT SCENE

"I love you. I've loved you since the first moment I saw you. I guess maybe I've even loved you before I saw you." Elizabeth Taylor was just as crazy for Montgomery Clift offscreen as she was on. She trailed him like a lovesick puppy, furious that her mother wouldn't let her be alone with him. Clift was charmed but not reciprocating, though he did like to brag about her physical endowments: "My God, you should see her tits!" They remained close friends for the rest of his life, and when his career faltered, she made sure he was hired for *Suddenly, Last Summer* (1959).

George and Angela are lost in each other as they dance. He can't keep his desire a secret any longer. He admits his obsession for her and she breathlessly responds in kind. Suddenly aware of the crowded room, she panics, fearing the guests can read their thoughts, and together, they rush out onto the balcony. They kiss and the camera fairly swoons, zeroing in on what is perhaps the most famous closeup in movie history. Here they are, the two most unearthly beautiful Hollywood faces, competing for the audience's yearning. Back and forth, back and forth, Clift's face buried in her neck and Taylor, only a teenager, cooing, "Tell, Mama." The rush of lust makes us feel like bellhops walking in on a honeymoon couple. But there's no cause for embarrassment. They don't even seem to know we're there. It's as if the camera were just another star above them. And we circle again, his face, her face, his lips, her eyes, his eyes . . .

THE OTHER LISTS

- American Film Institute (Yes)
- Roger Ebert's Top 100 (No)
- *Entertainment Weekly* (No)
- Internet Movie Database (No)
- Leonard Maltin (No)
- *Movieline* (No)
- National Society of Film Critics (No)
- *Premiere* Magazine (No)
- *Rolling Stone* Magazine (No)
- *Village Voice* (No)

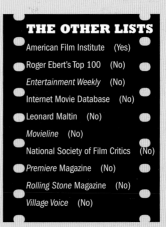

86

RED RIVER 1948

CATTLE CALL

There's a turning point in every great Hollywood career. An unusual role, a seminal moment in a film, something that tells us there's more to this personality than we thought. It happens for Monroe in *Bus Stop,* when we see the aching wistfulness beneath the comic, ditzy blonde. Brando wowed us out of our seats at his career's beginning in *A Streetcar Named Desire,* and bookended it by astonishing us anew with his transformation in *The Godfather*, just at the point when we thought he was washed up. For John Wayne, it happens in *Red River,* in a role that Gary Cooper turned down because it was too ruthless. As Tom Dunson, Wayne plays his first anti-hero. He's hard-drinking, bitter, murderous, and contemptible—and he's never been more compelling. Thoroughly committed to the performance, there's no hedging, no eleventh-hour monologue recanting his character's behavior over the course of the action. There's a bit of a Hollywood happy ending tacked on, but that's not what you'll remember about *Red River.* Wayne is so forceful he nearly blinds us to one of the great film debuts, that of Montgomery Clift as Matt. It's Wayne, the old-guard Hollywood traditionalist vs. the "Method" prettyboy from New York City. It's one of the great acting battles on film, an even draw, you keep thinking, until a moment after the final credits when you realize that it's Wayne who lingers in mind. While "Duke" is a fitting title for his place among Hollywood royalty, he emerges from *Red River* a king.

Jim: One of those very rare studio-era Westerns that exudes authenticity. You can almost smell their feet when they pull their boots off. If you've never been a fan, this is the movie in which you'll finally "get" John Wayne.

Gail: Beyond the great lyricism, the themes of frontier courage, loyalty, and leadership in *Red River*, there is the Hawksian vision of women as partners to men, no matter how rough the terrain. Joanne Dru is no exception. In fact, she overpowers the men by breaking up their stubborn enmity—with a gun.

THE PLOT

Tom Dunson (John Wayne) and his sidekick Groot (Walter Brennan) pull out of a wagon train headed for California when they see the cattle-friendly soil of Texas. Tom leaves behind his ladylove, Fen (Coleen Gray), and the very next day she and the others are slaughtered by Comanches. The sole survivor of the massacre is a boy, Matt Garth (Montgomery Clift), who stumbles into Tom's camp with his cow. He quickly proves his mettle, and, with Tom's single steer, they begin what will become the largest herd in Texas. Tom fends off Mexican land barons and gunslinging rivals to keep hold of his domain. But with the end of the Civil War, the beef market bottoms out in the South. To survive, they must drive their cattle to Missouri on the untested Chisolm Trail. It's thought to be impossible but they have no choice. Worse than the weather, Indians, and stampedes, is the pitched battle between Tom and Matt, the result of Tom's hard drinking and unnecessary cruelty to his men. Matt wrests control of the drive and Tom is sent packing with a cry of vengeance. Matt gets the herd to Kansas for a big sale, but then Tom arrives, itching for a fight to the death. That is, unless Matt's new love, Tess (Joanne Dru), can step in and save these two stubborn men from themselves.

"Why do Indians always want to be burnin' up good wagons?" Dunstan and Groot can hear the drumbeat but are too far away to help stave off a massacre of settlers. Among them is Dunson's fiancee, Fen.

"There are only two things that are better than a gun: a Swiss watch and a woman from anywhere. Ever had a good...Swiss watch?" —Cherry Valance

THE DIRECTOR

"I'm a storyteller—that's the chief function of a director. And they're moving pictures, let's make 'em move!" **Howard Hawks**, one of the most versatile directors in American film was, in his personal life, a character as large and hellbent as many of his fictional heroes. Handsome and impeccably attired, he pushed his reputation as a sportsman, gambler, and philanderer to the limit. As for women, he invented a particularly potent prototype for the screen with Katharine Hepburn in *Bringing Up Baby* (1938), and Rosalind Russell in *His Girl Friday* (1940). He was inspired by his fashionable, independent-thinking second wife, Slim Keith, when molding the screen persona of his proudest discovery, Lauren Bacall. Thorough in every aspect of filmmaking, he spent long days searching for just the right locations for *Red River* and actually screen-tested herds of cattle for their size, weight, and agility. Short of moving mountains, if a river's depth wasn't sufficient, he had dams built. Hawks was a rare breed of director who could transcend all genres from screwball comedy to crime, from war drama to the Western. He scored early after a handful of silents, with *Scarface: Shame of the Nation* (1932) and with remarkable ease, slipped into sophisticated romantic comedy with *Twentieth Century* (1934), providing John Barrymore with his best screen role. The delectable wit of *Bringing Up Baby* (1938) and *His Girl Friday* (1940) was followed by the adaptation of Hemingway's *To Have and Have Not* (1944) and the Bogart *noir The Big Sleep* (1946). His later career included *Gentlemen Prefer Blondes* (1953) and another John Wayne classic, *Rio Bravo* (1959). (For more on Hawks, see page 223.)

Matt (Montgomery Clift) loses his heart to Tess (Joanne Dru), a woman who doesn't appear to be afraid of anything, or any man. Here, she's too busy being feisty to wince. But that's gotta hurt!

THE CAST

Thomas Dunson	John Wayne
Matt Garth	Montgomery Clift
Tess Millay	Joanne Dru
Nadine Groot	Walter Brennan
Fen	Coleen Gray
Mr. Velville	Harry Carey
Cherry Valance	John Ireland
Buster McGee	Noah Beery Jr.
Dan Latimer	Harry Carey Jr.
Quo	Chief Yowlachie
Teeler Yacey	Paul Fix

THE ACTORS

John Wayne's recipe for success was, "Talk low, talk slow, and don't say too much," despite the high-volume ferocity of his best roles, including this one. It's interesting that he could contradict his own image and still not go wrong. It was always the perception of him that mattered, to the public in particular. He was considered a great war hero, but he never enlisted. He wasn't thought of as a romantic hero but he almost always got the girl. There is one story about him that has the air of myth and the authenticity of fact. While on location in Las Vegas, his hotel suite was directly above Frank Sinatra's, a man he was not overly fond of. Wayne was trying to sleep but the party down below was wildly out of control. He called the desk to complain and the noise abated for a few minutes before resuming as before. Finally he went to the door and demanded quiet. Sinatra's beefy bodyguard informed him that nobody talked to his boss that way. Wayne responded by knocking the muscleman out with a chair. The party was over (For more on Wayne, see page 73.)

Hawks discovered **Montgomery Clift** through agent Leland Hayward. Handsome and gifted, he'd just appeared on Broadway in a play with Helen Hayes. Clift initially had no interest in either Hawks or his Western. He confided in Hawks's wife, Slim, "I don't know how to ride a horse or shoot a gun or walk in funny boots." She convinced him that her husband was wonderful to work with and that his costar, Wayne, was not only a genuinely nice guy but a great and patient teacher. Clift had begun his film career with *The Search* (1948), a pseudo-documentary drama about a soldier in postwar Europe. His performance was so realistic, many viewers didn't realize he was a professional actor. After *Red River* came *The Heiress* (1949), *A Place in the Sun* (1951), *I Confess* (1953), his signature role in *From Here to Eternity* (1953), then *Raintree Country* (1957), whose filming was interrupted by his near-fatal car accident. Various addictions and ill-health resulted in fewer films, the most noteworthy being *The Young Lions* (1958), and *Judgement at Nuremberg* and *The Misfits* (both 1961), and *Freud* (1962) (For more on Clift, see page 268.)

Walter Brennan never wanted to be a star. "All I wanted from this business was to make a good living." After losing his teeth early as a stuntman, he was never out of a job as a character actor. It made him look much older than his years so that he was able to play old codgers with youthful energy. He appeared again as John Wayne's sidekick in *Rio Bravo* (1959) with Hawks at the helm. Brennan was an Oscar favorite, having won three Best Supporting statuettes for *Come and Get It* (1936), *Kentucky* (1938), *The Westerner* (1940). His wins came during the era when screen extras had the vote. As a former member of their Guild, critics suspect the loyalty he engendered may have been the basis for his rare trifecta.

John Ireland was a ubiquitous presence on TV and in nearly a hundred films, though he rarely played the lead. He had appeared alongside Wayne before *Red River*, in *My Darling Clementine* (1946), and specialized in Westerns through most of his career, including *The Return of Jesse James* (1950) and *Gunslinger* (1956). He then became a cast member on the popular early TV series *Rawhide*, costarring the young Clint Eastwood. Without spurs, he was featured in *Spartacus* (1960) and *55 Days at Peking* (1964).

THE CRITICS

"Although *Red River* is a stirring epic full of stampedes, chases, and gunfights, it's also perhaps the first Western with real complexity."
—Stephen Farber, *MovieLine*

"Several fine performances by a solidly masculine cast until they run smack into 'Hollywood' in the form of a glamorized female. The characters turn into actors and the story turns into old stuff. It ends with two tenacious cowboys kissing and making up."
—Bosley Crowther, *New York Times*

ROLE REVERSALS

Cary Grant passed on the role of Cherry Valance, thus giving a shot to relative newcomer John Ireland.

CREDITS

Producer: Howard Hawks/ Charles Feldman
Director: Howard Hawks, Arthur Rosson
Screenplay: Borden Chase
Running time: 133 minutes
Budget: $3 million
Box Office: $4.5 million

ACADEMY AWARD NOMINATIONS

Best Original Screenplay: Borden Chase
Best Editing: Christian Nyby

THE YEAR'S WINNERS

Best Picture: *Hamlet*
Best Director: John Huston, *The Treasure of the Sierra Madre*
Best Actor: Laurence Olivier, *Hamlet*
Best Actress: Jane Wyman, *Johnny Belinda*
Best Supporting Actor: Walter Huston, *The Treasure of the Sierra Madre*
Best Supporting Actress: Claire Trevor, *Key Largo*

BEHIND THE SCREEN

One cause of budget overruns was the 6,000 head of cattle rented at $10 apiece. You do the math.

Bad weather on location in Arizona required several script rewrites to include heavy rain. The conditions led to terrible colds suffered by nearly everyone in the cast.

Wayne referred to Clift as "an arrogant young son of a bitch." As for Clift, he thought Wayne's machismo was "unnecessary" and over the top. The personal animosity led to the very realistic scrapes on film.

The original ending had John Wayne's character dying, the result of a gunshot by Cherry Valance.

When Montgomery Clift saw the first rough cut of *Red River* he rightly suspected he'd become a star and it made him very anxious. He decided to "get drunk anonymously one last time." He loudly tied one on in New Orleans and managed to get himself arrested for disturbing the peace.

THE OTHER LISTS

- American Film Institute (No)
- Roger Ebert's Top 100 (Yes)
- *Entertainment Weekly* (No)
- Internet Movie Database (No)
- Leonard Maltin (No)
- *Movieline* (No)
- National Society of Film Critics (No)
- *Premiere* Magazine (No)
- *Rolling Stone* Magazine (No)
- *Village Voice* (No)

THE GREAT SCENE

It's early dawn on the prairie and all is breathlessly quiet as Dunson, on horseback, surveys the scene. Dozens of men await his command, ready to drive thousands of cattle. This is the do-or-die moment. Everything's riding on the success of this great, dangerous trek across the Chisolm Trail. Dunson seems to be summing up his entire life, the painful sacrifices of it, before he finally gives the nod to his adopted son. "Take 'em to Missouri, Matt!" And with that, there is a montage of closeups of the faces of the men, for the moment all fearless and breathless with anticipation as they shout "Yippee!" The ground trembles as the great driving herd moves forward.

Dunson: "There they are, Matt. Fourteen years of hard work. And they say we can't make the drive."

Matt: "They could be wrong."

Dunson: "They'd better be."

"I'll catch up with ya! I don't know when, but I'll catch up. Every time you turn around, expect to see me. 'Cause one time you'll turn around and I'll be there. I'll kill ya, Matt." The speech could just as well suggest the mighty old Hollywood star challenging the new kid on the lot.

87

THE CONVERSATION 1974

WIRED

"He'd *kill* us if he had the chance." Play that surveillance tape again, slowly. "He'd kill *us* if he had the chance." Is that what we hear? Are we sure? Has paranoia shaped the thoughts of eavesdropping expert, Harry Caul, to the point that the frightened comment of a possible victim could be reinterpreted as the conspiratorial challenge of a possible killer? Francis Ford Coppola hits the jackpot with *The Conversation*, as he ingeniously combines the suspense of Hitchcock with the slow character revelations of European film to mirror and comment on the discomfiting Watergate Era. *The Conversation* is one of the most studied films of the 1970s and has been painstakingly X-rayed by scholars of the medium. Critic Roger Ebert expounds on the subtext of Harry Caul's name, pointing out the significant definition of "caul" as either a spider's web or a membrane that encloses a fetus and protects it from drowning. In fact, the character was originally named Harry Call and only became Caul as the result of a memorandum typo. As they say, sometimes a cigar is quite simply a cigar. But it's to the credit of Coppola's purposeful "idea film" that so much is open to interpretation. There's even an audacious dream sequence complete with a femme fatale in the mist. Like her, nothing is entirely as it seems. Just when we assume Harry is so removed from his feelings that he's in danger of total disconnect, he reaches for his saxophone and blows a fairly decent jazz riff. Once again, thoughtful academics might argue that it's just his way of tidily filling up space; after all he's playing along to a record. But as any musician can attest, you can't help but be transported by the act of playing, whatever the quality of the performance. It might be counter-argued that Harry Caul is frightened because he's too full of feelings. One of the premier joys of the film is finding your own way through it. It's a complex treasure with Gene Hackman thoroughly astonishing in his full-force interpretation of anti-charisma.

Jim: The average consumer today could probably pick up better bugging equipment at Circuit City than Harry Caul ever dreamed about. So it's particularly amazing that, in spite of the clunky technology of 1974, the film still holds us in suspenseful thrall. Maybe it's because the best scenes have nothing to do with machinery. In one of them, Teri Garr actually matches Hackman's acting chops without even getting out of bed. Who knew? And you ain't seen nothin' til you've seen Harry's idea of apartment de-renovation in the final scene. Martha Stewart, cover your eyes!

Gail: This one is Hitchcockian in its power to draw you to the wrong side by undermining your judgment and then revealing how easily you can be had. We cheer at Caul's brilliant manipulation of technology even though we know that it will all come to a bad end.

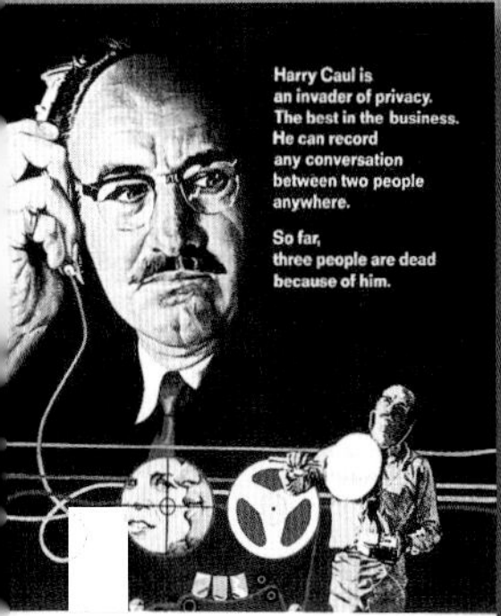

E PLOT

Caul (Gene Hackman), master of onic surveillance, has nearly eliminated elf from human interaction. He can't tolerate sharing a coffee break with his assistant, Stan (John Cazale), and he s his mistress (Teri Garr) packing when sks too many personal questions. Harry essed with his most recent job, for the or of a mega-corporation (Robert Duvall) ears his young wife, Ann (Cindy Williams), ing an affair with one the company's (Frederic Forrest). A similar assignment a ears back resulted in a triple murder and refuses to be party to such a tragedy . He withholds the evidence from the or's conniving assistant (Harrison Ford) en hires a prostitute to seduce Harry teal it. Harry comes undone and, after ting his "blood money," checks into the ing room of the hotel where he fears the ntation will be played out. Sure enough, s a terrible murder and all Harry can do en to it through the walls. But the victim urprise, and Harry realizes he's been set m the start. The conspirators are on to well aware he knows too much. To keep t bay, they've bugged his apartment and, he might, he can't find the apparatus. ecome the victim of his own technology.

In one of the most detailed, deeply resonant performances of his career, Gene Hackman plays Harry Caul, a professional eavesdropper who can't conquer his own conscience—or overcome his own suspicious nature. By the end of the story, Harry's life—and apartment—have been stripped bare.

THE DIRECTOR

The idea for *The Conversation*, about a man obsessed with and finally overpowered by technology, had been brewing within **Francis Ford Coppola** since 1966. The success of *The Godfather* (1972) finally allowed him to obtain the financing. Coppola admits to having been inspired by Antonioni's *Blow-Up*, in which a photographer thinks he may have evidence of a murder in his mundane shots of a mist-bound park. He also credits Hitchcock's *Psycho* as the inspiration for *The Conversation's* most famous scene involving a suddenly blood-flooded bathroom. Given the vital importance of sound technology in the film, Coppola wisely chose Walter Murch, an undisputed master in the field, to oversee the film's audio. Murch was left to work out the final scenes of the film when Coppola was forced to attend to his simultaneous production, *The Godfather, Part II*. Previous to his breakthrough classic, *The Godfather* (1972), there was *You're a Big Boy Now* (1966), *Finian's Rainbow* (1968), and *The Rain People* (1969), though he was better known as a screenwriter on such seminal films as *Patton* (1969). Following *Apocalypse Now* (1979), there was a sketchy period that included *One from the Heart* (1982) and *The Cotton Club* (1984) before the success of *Peggy Sue Got Married* (1986). *The Godfather, Part III* (1990) was the critically diminished distant cousin of the trilogy and was followed by *Bram Stoker's Dracula* (1992), *Jack* (1994,) and *The Rainmaker* (1996). (For more on Coppola, see pages 15 and 60.)

While handsome young Harrison Ford gives a compelling performance as a corporate bad guy, there's little to suggest that in just four years he'll burst out as the biggest box-office grossing movie star of all time.

THE CAST

Harry Caul	Gene Hackman
Stan	John Cazale
Bernie Moran	Allen Garfield
Mark	Frederic Forrest
Ann	Cindy Williams
Paul	Michael Higgins
Meredith	Elizabeth MacRae
Amy Fredericks	Teri Garr
Martin Stett	Harrison Ford
Receptionist	Mark Wheeler
The Mime	Robert Shields
Lurleen	Phoebe Alexander

THE ACTORS

Gene Hackman considers *The Conversation* his best work. His performance is almost entirely subterfuge, the embodiment of a man's estrangement from his own humanity. This is a man who can't even undress for sex. He's a cipher through most of the movie, consumed by his electronic gadgetry, and it's only when he tries to prevent a crime, a very human impulse, that he comes undone. It's been said of Hackman's acting that he's incapable of hitting a false note. His long list of outstanding credits include *Bonnie and Clyde* (1967), *The French Connection* (1971), *Young Frankenstein* (1974), *Superman* (1978), *Hoosiers* (1986), his Oscar-winning *Unforgiven* (1992), *Get Shorty* (1995), and *The Royal Tenenbaums* (2001). (For more on Hackman, see page 163.)

This was only **John Cazale**'s second film following his sensational debut in *The Godfather* (1972). His career was tragically short, ending after only six films with his death of cancer in 1978. His peers, among them Al Pacino, considered him a supreme talent who would've inevitably become a solid cinematic force. He was engaged to Meryl Streep throughout his illness. (For more on Cazale, see pages 11 and 148.)

Allen Garfield was one of the most durable character actors in 1970s film, appearing in some of the decade's most prestigious films, particularly Robert Altman's *Nashville* (1975). Garfield has always specialized in hyperactive, feisty roles and, in *The Conversation*, he combines those traits with a dangerous desperation.

The very young alumni of *American Graffiti* (1973), **Cindy Williams** and **Harrison Ford**, are unusually cast in roles that don't square with their popular images. The screwball Shirley Meany of *Laverne and Shirley* here plays a philandering young socialite; America's favorite action hero, Ford, is surprisingly effective as a duplicitous, Iago-like executive assistant. (For more on Ford, see pages 130, 169, 254, and 289.)

BEHIND THE SCREEN

The pivotal cameo role of The Director is played by an uncredited Robert Duvall.

Coppola galled Paramount execs by shooting exclusively on his own turf, San Francisco. Despite the film's success, the studio refused to finance a publicity campaign.

The score, with its famous use of only a single instrument, the piano, was composed by Coppola's brother-in-law, David Shire.

SEND IN THE CLONES

Blow Out (1981)
Enemy of the State (1998)

THE CRITICS

"Both Coppola and Hackman have done showier work than *The Conversation*, but none so chilling, real, or powerful."
– Michael Atkinson, *Movieline*

"It's a little thin . . . but it's a buggy movie that can get to you so that when it's over you really feel you're being bugged."–Pauline Kael, *The New Yorker*

"One of Coppola's very best."
–*TV Guide's Movie Guide*

CREDITS

Producer: Francis Ford Coppola/ Paramount Pictures
Director: Francis Ford Coppola
Screenplay: Francis Ford Coppola
Running time: 113 minutes
Budget: $1.6 million

ACADEMY AWARD NOMINATIONS

Best Picture
Best Original Screenplay: Francis Ford Coppola
Best Sound: Walter Murch, Art Rochester

THE YEAR'S WINNERS

Best Picture: *The Godfather, Part II*
Best Director: Francis Ford Coppola, *The Godfather, Part II*
Best Actor: Art Carney, *Harry and Tonto*
Best Actress: Ellen Burstyn, *Alice Doesn't Live Here Anymore*
Best Supporting Actor: Robert De Niro, *The Godfather, Part II*
Best Supporting Actress: Ingrid Bergman, *Murder on the Orient Express*

THE OTHER LISTS

American Film Institute (No)
Roger Ebert's Top 100 (No)
Entertainment Weekly (No)
Internet Movie Database (No)
Leonard Maltin (Yes)
Movieline (Yes)
National Society of Film Critics (No)
Premiere Magazine (No)
Rolling Stone Magazine (No)
Village Voice (No)

Harry wants to prevent the murder he fears is inevitable, but he doesn't know how to go about it. He tries to rent the very room in the hotel mentioned as a rendezvous in the tapes but it's already been taken. He checks into the one next door and drills a surveillance device into the thinly separated bathroom walls. He crouches down beside the toilet, not sure what he's hearing. Scared out of his wits, he takes refuge under the covers with the TV on. He falls asleep and when he awakens, there's a disquieting pall in the air. Not so much as a whisper coming from next door. He peeks out into the hall—no sign of activity. He jimmies the lock and enters the ill-fated room to find—nothing. Everything is immaculate, not a trace of foul play. But Harry's an old pro at the game and checks under the bathtub drain for any trace of blood. Not a speck. He stares at the toilet and finally presses the handle to see if any evidence might've been flushed. Suddenly, a blood-soaked hand towel backs up and a bright red flood spills over the bowl and gushes onto the floor. Harry backs away in horror.

Cindy Williams, in the unlikely role of femme fatale, ambles through San Francisco's Union Square with her lover (Frederic Forrest), unaware that the air is full of "bugs."

Harry sinks to a new low in hopes of "flushing" out the murderous conversation in the next room.

"I probably have genius. But no talent."
—Francis Ford Coppola

88

GRAND ILLUSION 1937

THE TIES THAT BIND

Like some military fraternal organization representing every nation, the Hallbach German POW camp is the meeting ground for genial chaos. As new prisoners are welcomed into their cosmopolitan barracks, a cacophony of languages fills the halls, and everything from tasseled caps to spiked helmets are in constant motion back and forth across the chambers. With a gentleness and humanity characteristic of the optimistic director Jean Renoir, the inanity of borders and boundaries between peoples is explored, particularly as they disintegrate at the end of World War I. *Grand Illusion* is no ordinary POW escape story, though, but a discourse on human behavior. The men, both captors and captive, treat one another with respect, and Renoir allows this to happen without denying the realities of nationalism, cultural differences, and all of the things that separate men from one another. Though he makes brotherhood look easy, he knows that it is not; he presents it as another "grand illusion," just like the illusion that war can serve some noble purpose. Here, as in *Rules of the Game*, Renoir sounds the death knell of that other grand illusion, that of an immortal aristocratic class; the old order of European civilization is about to collapse, to be replaced by the transcendence of the working man. Perhaps one of the most influential films in history, many of the *Grand Illusion*'s greatest moments have been recalled in classic films: The comic and claustrophobic escape scene recurs in *The Great Escape* (1963), and the singing of "La Marseillaise" crops up in *Casablanca* (1942). *Grand Illusion* is a beautiful film in which Renoir's camera once again sits still and lets the compositions emerge from the material. From its subtly individual characters and dialogue to the look of its prisons and the landscape outside, every aspect of the film merges artfully to tell a story of the futility of war; no one stands above it, neither victor nor victim.

Jim: Behind all his father's pretty paintings was a man in great physical pain. And like him, there's a lot beneath the affable surface of a Renoir film. There's a heart of a Communist idealist at work here. An assault on the class system in the guise of charm.

Gail: Lyrical, graceful, and poetic, *Grand Illusion* is tinged with magnificent, touching humor. Men in drag at a prison-camp musical? It's like *M*A*S*H*, but with tears.

THE PLOT

In World War I Germany two French airmen, Lieutenant Maréchal (Jean Gabin), a mechanic who works his way up to officer, and Captain de Boeldieu (Pierre Fresnay), an aristocrat, are captured by German Captain von Rauffenstein (Erich von Stroheim), whose first order is, "If they are officers, invite them for lunch." The two are transferred to a POW camp, where they become fast friends with fellow inmates, including a well-placed Jew, Rosenthal (Marcel Dalio). The three men hatch an escape plan, are discovered and transferred to another camp. The new camp's commandant is the very aristocratic Captain von Rauffenstein who had first welcomed the two men to his lunch table. He warns the men against escape attempts and reaches out to de Boeldieu, who, though an enemy, is a fellow aristocrat like himself. Maréchal and Dalio plan another escape with the selfless help of de Boeldieu, who provides the distraction. In the process, de Boeldieu is shot—reluctantly—by von Rauffenstein, who sits by the dying man's bedside like an old friend. The two other prisoners escape and are taken in by a German widow with whom Maréchal falls in love but must leave. He is still French, after all. And there's a war on.

Closing ranks. Aristocratic Captain de Boeldieu (Pierre Fresnay, left) and Lieutenant Maréchal (Jean Gabin), a mechanic who works his way up to officer, are surrounded by POWS wearing the hats of many nations as they hatch a plan to escape from their second German prison camp.

"Nature all looks alike. Frontiers are an invention of man."—Maréchal

THE DIRECTOR

The son of impressionist painter Pierre-Auguste Renoir, **Jean Renoir** fought in World War I, then quickly returned to Paris and entered the movie business. He expressed his vision of filmmaking like this: "My dream is of a craftsman's cinema in which the author can express himself as directly as the painter in his paintings or the writer in his books." A hallmark of the director's greatest films is his keen observation of and sympathy for his characters, and this can be seen in every shot; there is hardly a camera movement made for pure effect. Biographer David Thomson wrote, "Renoir's greatness lies in his repeated desire to take risks, to make new sorts of film, to be experimental." He continued, "During the 1930s there is not an adventure in natural light, camera movement, depth of focus, real location, the blending of interior and exterior that Renoir did not make." Renoir's fondness for improvisation prompted him to allow von Stroheim free range to use his extensive knowledge of the military to enlarge his part. In his long retirement, Renoir was sought out by younger filmmakers and critics. As Thomson put it, "He is the greatest of directors; he justifies cinema." (For more on Renoir, see page 157.)

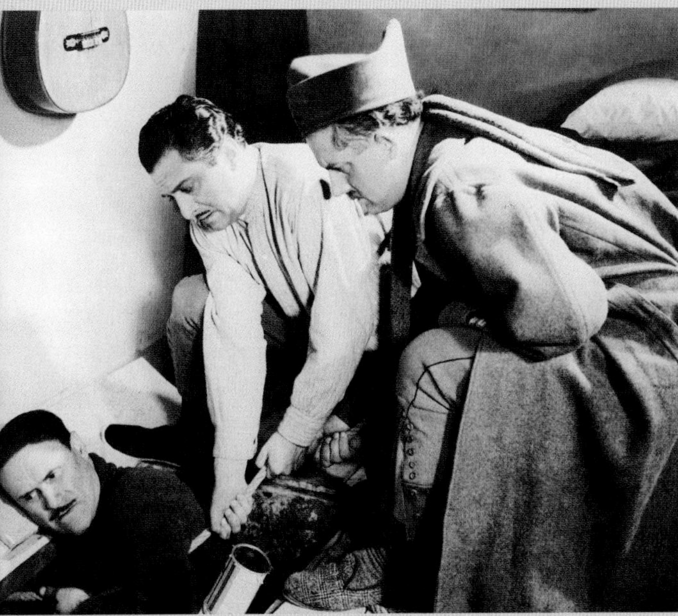

An engineer (Gaston Modot) is aided by the Jewish Lieutenant Rosenthal (Marcel Dalio) and a third soldier (unidentified) down to a tunnel through which they hope—but fail—to escape from their first German prison camp.

THE CAST

Lieutenant Maréchal	Jean Gabin
Elsa	Dita Parlo
Captain de Boeldieu	Pierre Fresnay
Captain von Rauffenstein	Erich von Stroheim
Lieutenant Demolder	Sylvain Itkine
The Engineer	Gaston Modot
Lieutenant Rosenthal	Marcel Dalio
The Showoff	Julien Carette
An Officer	Georges Péclet
Sergeant Arthur	Werner Florian
The Teacher	Jean Dasté

THE ACTORS

"The miracle of **Jean Gabin**'s performance in this good, simple-hero kind of role is that you're not aware of any performance, unlike Fresnay's and von Stroheim's where you are, and should be; they represent a way of life that is dedicated to superbly controlled outer appearances," wrote Pauline Kael in *The New Yorker*. Gabin's role as a member of the emerging proletariat in *Rules of the Game* represented the shape of things to come: The aristocrats would have to give over their places to the new nobility, the working class. As he often did, Gabin played here a hero of simple grace, nobility, and stoic strength. The French star began acting in the 1930s making such unforgettable films as *Zouzou* (1934), *The Lower Depths* (1936), *Pepe Le Moko* (1937), *French Can Can* (for Renoir in 1955), *Les Misérables* (1957), and the first of a popular series in which he played the title role, *Inspector Maigret* (1958), and *L'Année Sainte* (1976), his final film. Gabin worked briefly in Hollywood, playing Spencer Tracy-like roles in *Moontide* (1942) and *The Imposter* (1944).

In a movie performance that would enter the pantheon of iconic figures in film, **Erich von Stroheim** made an indelible impression as the World War I German commandant whose aristocratic and romantic notions of chivalry and friendship were dying as the war wound down. His stiff neck held in place by a brace gave him a haughty stature even as it reflected impairment, and we will forever see him that way, his eye squinting through a monocle. Among the greatest directors of silent films, including *Blind Husbands* (1919), and *Foolish Wives* (1922), von Stroheim's career in Hollywood is the stuff of epic tragedy. He was constantly bickering with studio management over cost overruns and his notorious penchant for decadence. His film *Greed* (1925), which is among the greatest films ever made, had been dissected by producers. His *Queen Kelly*, starring Gloria Swanson (1928), was stolen, after which he would never direct again. He remained in the industry as a character actor, however, in such films as *The Crime of Dr. Crespi* (1935), *Five Graves to Cairo* (1943), and *The Mask of Diijon* (1946). His last, most unforgettable role was as a formerly great director and devoted servant to a has-been actress played by Gloria Swanson in *Sunset Boulevard* (1950), for which he was nominated for an Oscar. (For more on von Stroheim, page 24.)

Pierre Fresnay as the senior French officer, de Boeldieu, is elegant, suave, aristocratic, and aloof, yet considerate of his fellow inmates. His *noblesse oblige* takes him so far that he is willing to sacrifice himself to help others escape. He is the quintessential heroic French officer, steeped in the chivalrous traditions of the old military academy. Sir Alec Guinness said that Fresnay was his favorite actor. Fresnay has appeared in more than 60 European films.

Marcel Dalio plays the newly wealthy Jew Rosenthal, who is only too happy to share the bounty he receives from home with his fellow POWs. It gives him pleasure, as he says, to show off his family's achievements. Ironically, Rosenthal's family members, who worked themselves up from rags to riches, become the new inhabitants of the de Boeldieu estate as the power passes from the landed aristocracy to the working rich. Maréchal, with whom Rosenthal escapes from the POW camp, finally screams at him, "You know what you are to me? A ball and chain!" Then he cuts him most cruelly: "I always hated Jews." Dalio, who was himself Jewish, also appeared in Renoir's *Rules of the Game* (1939). (For more on Dalio, see page 157.)

BEHIND THE SCREEN

Just as *Rules of the Game* was confiscated by the Germans, *Grand Illusion* was declared "cinema enemy No. 1" by Nazi propaganda

CREDITS

Producer: Raymond Blondy/ Janus Films
Director: Jean Renoir
Screenplay: Jean Renoir, Charles Spaak
Running Time: 111 minutes

YEAR'S ACADEMY AWARDS WINNERS

Best Picture: *The Life of Emile Zola*
Best Director: Leo McCarey, *The Awful Truth*
Best Actor: Spencer Tracy, *Captains Courageous*
Best Actress: Luise Rainer, *The Good Earth*
Best Supporting Actor: Joseph Schildkraut, *The Life of Emile Zola*
Best Supporting Actress: Alice Brady, *In Old Chicago*

THE OTHER LISTS

American Film Institute (No)
Entertainment Weekly (No)
Internet Movie Database (No)
Leonard Maltin (No)
Movieline (No)
Premiere Magazine (Yes)
Roger Ebert's Top 100 (Yes)
Rolling Stone Magazine (No)
Village Voice (No)

chief Joseph Goebbels, and the Germans confiscated the "camera negative" in 1940. The story of the negative's recovery is a labyrinth of seizures and retrievals worthy of its own film.

Ironically, though von Stroheim was German, he could hardly speak a word of his native tongue and had to be coached for the role.

The film was so sensitive that it was criticized for being too kind to its German characters.

When producer Raymond Blondy told Renoir he was considering von Stroheim for the role of the German commandant, the director gasped. Von Stroheim was a kind of god to him. The director was particularly taken aback when the great German director approached Renoir, gold-tipped cane in hand, and said, "Monsieur, your wish is my command."

Grand Illusion was the first foreign language film—and still one of only a handful—to be nominated for an Oscar for Best Picture.

THE CRITICS

"*La Grand Illusion* is a triumph of clarity and lucidity; every detail fits simply, easily, and intelligibly together."
—Pauline Kael, *The New Yorker*

BELOW: The differences disappear between de Boeldieu (Pierre Fresnay) and von Rauffenstein (Erich von Stroheim) as the two men share the finer things in their lives. Von Rauffenstein apologizes for having to hold his aristocratic new friend prisoner.

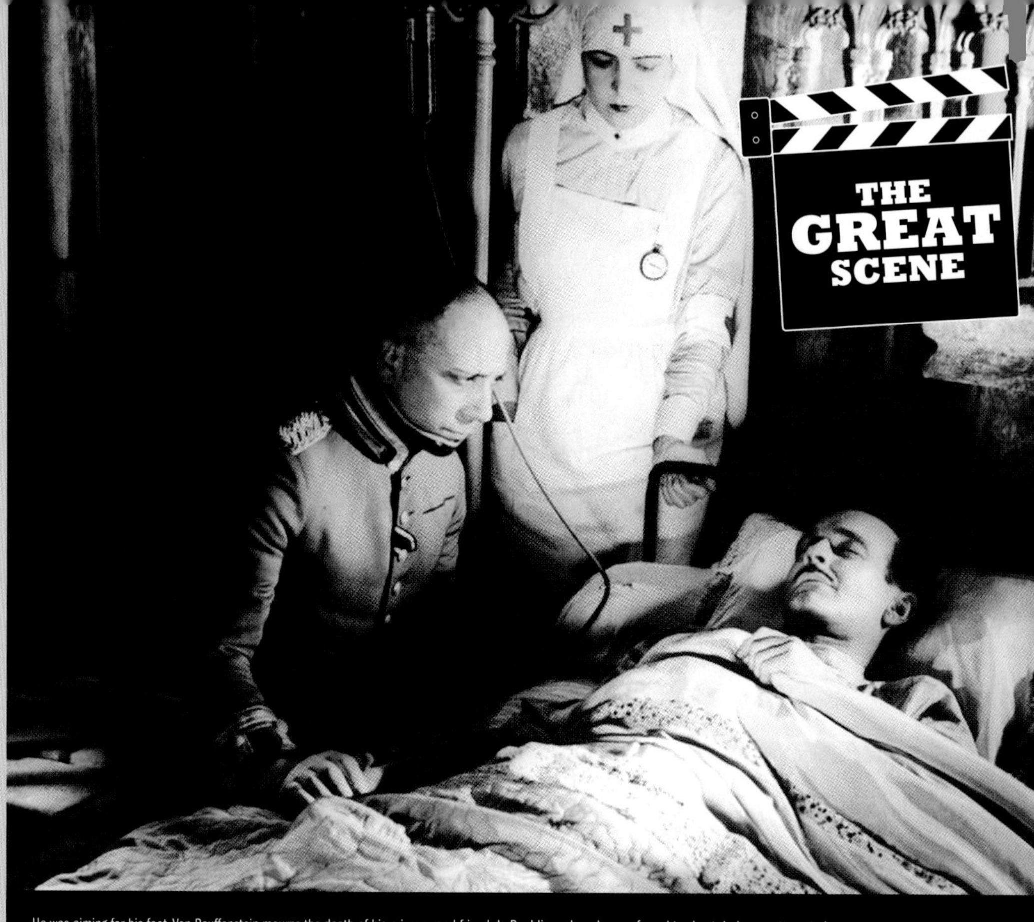

He was aiming for his foot. Von Rauffenstein mourns the death of his prisoner and friend de Boeldieu, whom he was forced to shoot during an attempted escape.

In a heart-rending scene that takes place soon after de Boeldieu and von Rauffenstein form a warm connection, de Boeldieu sacrifices his own life to provide cover for Maréchal and Rosenthal's escape. Von Rauffenstein begs de Boeldieu not to go through with the plan, telling him that if he continues to run, he will have no choice but to shoot his new friend. He does shoot him, but accidently hits him in the stomach instead of the leg, as intended. Nursing de Boeldieu at his deathbed, von Rauffenstein cannot hide his grief. De Boeldieu tries to soothe his friend, saying, "Neither you nor I can stop the march of time. For a commoner, dying in a war is a tragedy. But for you and me—it's a good way out." As de Boeldieu dies, von Rauffenstein cuts the flowers that have been growing in a pot beside the window. Earlier the two men had commented on how difficult it was to grow anything in this environment. He rests the flowers on his friend as he brushes his eyes closed with his fingers.

89

L.A. CONFIDENTIAL 1997

THE BOYS IN BLUE AND *NOIR*

FLASH!! CHRISTMAS EVE MURDERFEST IN NITE OWL CAFÉ! Slay bells ringing! You heard it here first, good people of Los Angeles, home of orange-scented breezes and the foul wind of corruption coming from City Hall! Could be that hotshot director Curtis Hanson has delivered a masterpiece of New Age *noir*. And it's no mere homage to Sam Spade or *Chinatown*, buster! It all goes down in that paper-thin slice of time between the black-and-white '40s and the Elvis '50s. The period details are subdued, you bet, but when it comes to suspense, hold onto your fedora! This is a nonstop theme park ride through Vice City! Step right up and see that new teen idol and his starlet companion caught red-handed in their marijuana-flavored love nest! And right up ahead, the whole truth about that prostitution ring full of lookalike stars! That's right, boy–o! Next time Veronica Lake comes on to you for a $25 date, better check out her autograph first. Consider yourself warned, bucko! This is a big, BIG movie full of mobsters and double whammies, with more twists and turns than the Santa Monica Freeway! All-star performances and a grand finale shootout to make your hair curl. So plant your feet in front of your own imaginary Graumann's, splash a little extra butter on that popcorn (hey, it's 1953 and it's only fifteen cents a bag) and stay tuned! This is *L.A. Confidential*, where you'll always get the real lowdown—on the Q.T.—and very HUSH HUSH!

Jim: The good news is there's too much plot, just too much movie for a single viewing. It's right up there with *Chinatown*. Not precisely next door, but in the same ultra-deluxe neighborhood.

Gail: The good guys can be bad guys and the good girls aren't much better. They're all beautiful, and wound tight, within an inch of their desperately glamorous, deadly, and exciting lives.

E PLOT

sergeant Jack Vincennes (Kevin Spacey) elebrity cop with a running cash deal rime tabloid editor Sid Hudgens (Danny o), who's always on hand with a camera s juiciest busts. Officer Bud White (Russell) is the "bone-crusher" who gets confes- for Captain Smith (James Cromwell). Lt. ley (Guy Pearce) is the most despised the division, a whistle-blower whose ity is tied to his ambition. He aches to e department but for the time being Smith's fiefdom. When a slaughter at a results in the murder of a just-retired Smith wants results fast and settles for aming of three young black men. When e abruptly released, then tracked down illed, Vincennes and White smell a rat gree to work together to sort out the in- stencies. The trail keeps leading to a call- g of star-lookalike prostitutes protected ith. One of the girls, Lynn Bracken (Kim ger), is set up to lead White astray when mes calling. Instead, she falls in love with nd gives him the boost of confidence he . Smith begins to worry when these three o close to the pile of bodies behind his grab. He sets into motion a retaliatory to stop them in their tracks.

"It's Christmas Eve in the City of Angels and while decent citizens sleep the sleep of the righteous, hopheads prowl for marijuana not knowing that a man is coming to stop them! Celebrity crime-stopper Jack Vincennes, scourge of grasshoppers and dope fiends everywhere!" Vincennes's (Kevin Spacey) lucrative association with *Hush Hush* editor Sid Hudgens has made him the most famous cop in LA.

“Oh, great. You get the girl, I get the coroner.”—Jack Vincennes

THE DIRECTOR

"Nobody really believes in a good movie except the people who are making it," admits **Curtis Hanson**. A former film critic, he began the *L.A. Confidential* project with a collection of treasured photos of the period in question. He "saw" the characters through the image of real-life stars of the early 1950s, caught the transition of Los Angeles at the time, and even had the style of furniture and architecture down cold. Producer Arnon Milchan was sold at once; Hanson was astounded that Milchan didn't even need to read a script. "I saw the movie in his eyes, that was enough for me." Hanson insists the best decision he made was to bring young screenwriter Brian Helgeland on board. Together they hacked through the jungle of James Ellroy's purposely "impossible to adapt" novel and found the bare bones of a plotline. "We wanted the characters to lead us through," Hanson reasoned. After a series of small pictures ending with *The Bedroom Window* (1987) and *Bad Influence* (1990), Hanson hit the big time with *The Hand That Rocks the Cradle* (1992) and *The River Wild* (1994). Following his success with *L.A. Confidential*, Hanson made the critically acclaimed *Wonder Boys* (2000) then Eminem's *8 Mile* (2002), and *Lucky You* (2003).

"Our justice must be swift and merciless." In keeping with Captain Smith's dictum, two of his proteges, Bud White and Ed Exley, will use it against him in one of the most vivid shootouts ever filmed. *L.A. Confidential* was a launching pad for the Hollywood careers of Australians Russell Crowe and Guy Pearce.

THE CAST	
Sgt. Jack Vincennes	Kevin Spacey
Officer Bud White	Russell Crowe
Detective Lt. Edmund Exley	Guy Pearce
Capt. Dudley Smith	James Cromwell
Lynn Bracken	Kim Basinger
Sid Hudgens	Danny DeVito
Pierce Patchett	David Strathairn
D.A. Ellis Loew	Ron Rifkin
Badge of Honor star Brett Chase	Matt McCoy
Johnny Stompanato	Paolo Seganti
Sgt. "Dick" Stensland	Graham Beckel
Susan Lefferts	Amber Smith
Leland "Buzz" Meeks	Darrell Sandeen
Matt Reynolds	Simon Baker
Mrs. Lefferts	Gwenda Deacon
Lana Turner	Brenda Bakke

THE ACTORS

"It's maybe the first real adult film I've made," **Russell Crowe** is proud to admit. "James Ellroy told me, 'In my world of tarnished people, Bud's the only one I consider a hero.' He's a racist. He's self-righteous. He's foul-mouthed. He's a son of a bitch. But he's very much a product of his time and his job.'" Hanson was sold on Crowe after seeing him in the Australian film *Romper Stomper* (1992), which displayed the full force of the primal magnetism that served him so well in *Virtuosity* (1995), and, of course, in *Gladiator* (2000), for which he won an Oscar. *A Beautiful Mind* (2001) was followed by *Cinderella Man* (2005), *3:10 to Yuma*, and *American Gangster* (both 2007).

Hanson was looking for a big star to play Jack Vincennes but one who still had some secrets left with which to surprise audiences. **Kevin Spacey** perfectly fit the bill of the wry, world-weary detective who can't remember why he became a cop, and he grabbed some of the best moments in the film. As the technical expert on a *Dragnet*-like TV show, he teaches the lead actor to walk and talk like a real cop. When a date reminds him that the actor doesn't walk and talk like him, he responds with a shrug, "Well, that's 'cause he's the television version. America isn't ready for the real me." That's hardly the case. The following year Spacey won his first Oscar for *American Beauty*. Though Spacey attracted a great deal of attention early on with such films as *Glengarry Glen Ross* (1992) and *Swimming with Sharks* (1994), it was his stunning portrayal of a mysterious criminal in *The Usual Suspects* (1995) that brought him stardom. From then on he was golden, despite the less than successful *Midnight in the Garden of Good and Evil* (1997), *Pay It Forward* (2000), *The Shipping News* (2001), and *The Life of David Gale* (2003). Spacey is famously mum about his personal life. "The less you know about me, the easier it is to convince you that I am that character on screen. It allows an audience to come into a movie theater and believe I am that person." (For more on Spacey, see page 307.)

As described by critic Peter Rainer, **Guy Pearce**'s Detective Lt. Ed Exley is "almost comically straight-arrow. But there's connivance built into his uprightness." Pearce admits his character is at first extremely unlikable. And it's to his credit that he found so many layers of Exley, enough to make audiences cheer him on in the final blowout scene. Pearce was another "Down Under" discovery, and made his first major impression on America in a dress. He was the youngest drag queen in the hilariously bizarre *The Adventures of Priscilla, Queen of the Desert* (1994). Previously, he'd been an Australian soap star and teen idol. Following *Rules of Engagement* (2000) he made his biggest splash the same year with the indie sensation *Memento*, in which he played a man afflicted with compelling memory loss. *The Time Machine* and *The Count of Monte Cristo* followed in 2002.

Playing the proverbial whore with a heart of gold and Veronica Lake tresses to match, **Kim Basinger** was Hanson's early choice, and he pursued her relentlessly for the part. She's the only constant voice of truth in the movie. Described by one critic as having the perfect look of "vanilla parfait," Basinger was the only nominated star of *L.A. Confidential* to win an Oscar. Her stunned reaction on the big night was memorable. "I just want to thank everybody I've ever met in my entire life!" Her career began as a Breck shampoo girl, Playboy model, and James Bond sex toy. She broke through in films with *9 1/2 Weeks* (1986), in which she performed unmentionable acts with ice cubes and Mickey Rourke. That was followed by *Blind Date* (1987), *Batman* (1989), *The Marrying Man* (1991), costarring her then-husband Alec Baldwin, *I Dreamed of Africa* (2000), and, for Curtis Hanson, *8 Mile* (2002), in which she plays Eminem's mother. Offscreen, she's been a walking tabloid headline, thanks to her stormy relationship with Baldwin and the purchase of the town of Braselton, Georgia, which thereafter filed for bankruptcy.

Hush Hush tabloid reporter Sid Hudgens is "the Christopher Columbus of journalism," claims **Danny DeVito**. "He has no qualms, sees all the possibilities." Diminutive, pudgy, and balding, the same might be said of DeVito. "I was sure chic Hollywood people gathered around a pool were just waiting for a five-foot-tall Italian to walk into their lives—I was wrong." But not for long. His first big break came with *One Flew over the Cuckoo's Nest* (1975), and he won millions of TV fans with his blustery character on the hit series *Taxi* (1978). On the big screen, *Terms of Endearment* (1983) and *Romancing the Stone* (1984) led to *Throw Momma from the Train* (1987), which he also directed, and *Twins* (1988), costarring with Arnold Schwarzenegger. Then came an unusually touching villainous turn as the Penguin in *Batman Returns* (1992). DeVito is a triple threat as an actor, director, and producer of such major hits as *Erin Brockovich* (2000).

Yet another Australian, **James Cromwell**, nearly manages to steal the movie from the glamorous younger men. As diabolical Capt. Dudley Smith, he exudes a falsely paternalistic air while plotting unimaginable evil. What's even more remarkable about his performance is the memory of Cromwell as farmer Arthur Hoggett in the instant classic *Babe* (1995). How could a man who skips along so joyously with an adorable pig be all bad?

BEHIND THE SCREEN

On the heels of *L.A. Confidential*, Kevin Spacey and Russell Crowe won Best Actor Oscars for *American Beauty* and *Gladiator*, respectively.

James Ellroy was insistent that Russell Crowe's character, Bud White, drink Scotch, not beer. Says Crowe, "Now I can tell what's blended and what's single malt. But I haven't actually had any since the moment we finished shooting this movie, because it's disgusting."

Producers initially balked at the idea of two unknown Australian actors in the leads of a big-budget American period piece.

THE MUSIC

Hanson chose most of the songs before writing the screenplay. All are from the early 1950s, with special emphasis on the music of jazz trumpeters Jerry Mulligan and Chet Baker. Hanson played tapes of their music on the set throughout shooting. His key directive to Kevin Spacey regarding his character was, "Think Dean Martin." In the scene at the bar in which Spacey, as Jack Vincennes, has a crisis of conscience, Dean Martin's "Smile, Smile, Smile" is playing on the jukebox.

THE SET

Filmed in Los Angeles at 45 evocative locations, the period comes fully alive without hitting you over the head with nostalgia. Many of the neighborhoods aren't glamorous but retain the look and feel of the early 1950s. One site, the Formosa Bar, is a survivor of the era. Hanson interviewed many of the actors there to imbue them with a sense of time and place.

NOTABLE QUOTES

"I'd move to Los Angeles if Australia and New Zealand were swallowed up by a huge tidal wave, if there was a bubonic plague in Europe, and if the continent of Africa disappeared from some Martian attack."—Russell Crowe

THE CRITICS

"A flawless ensemble cast and style to burn."
—Janet Maslin, *New York Times*

"Ostentatiously cynical, hyper-violent, dripping with attitude, *L.A. Confidential* holds nothing sacred." —Kenneth Turan, *Los Angeles Times*

THE OTHER LISTS

American Film Institute (No)
Roger Ebert's Top 100 (No)
Entertainment Weekly (No)
Internet Movie Database (Yes)
Leonard Maltin (No)
Movieline (No)
National Society of Film Critics (Yes)
Premiere Magazine (No)
Rolling Stone Magazine (No)
Village Voice (No)

CREDITS

Producer: Arnon Milchan/
Regency-David Wolper/
Warner Bros.
Director: Curtis Hanson
Screenplay: Brian Helgeland,
Curtis Hanson, from the novel by
James Ellroy
Running time: 138 minutes
Budget: $35 million
Box Office: $78 million

ACADEMY AWARDS

Best Supporting Actress:
Kim Basinger
Best Adapted Screenplay:
Brian Helgeland, Curtis Hanson

NOMINATIONS

Best Picture
Best Director: Curtis Hanson
Best Cinematography:
Dante Spinotti
Best Art Direction-Set Decoration:
Jeannine Claudia Oppewall,
Jay Hart
Best Editing: Peter Honess
Best Music: Jerry Goldsmith
Best Sound: Andy Nelson,
Anna Behlmer, Kirk Francis

THE YEAR'S OTHER WINNERS

Best Picture: *Titanic*
Best Director:
James Cameron, *Titanic*
Best Actor: Jack Nicholson,
As Good As It Gets
Best Actress: Helen Hunt,
As Good As It Gets
Best Supporting Actor:
Robin Williams, *Good Will Hunting*

"Don't start tryin' to do the right thing, boy-o. You haven't the practice." But Capt. Dudley Smith (James Cromwell) can't seem to get through to Jack Vincennes (Kevin Spacey) and has to make his point in a more "permanent" way.

Jack Vincennes is plagued by guilt over the murder of a young actor he'd set up for a tabloid scandal. To retrieve what's left of his integrity as a cop, he agrees to help Ed Exley explore the dark possibilities of the Nite Owl Café slaughter. He stumbles onto some potentially damaging evidence from the past and comes to the home of his mentor, Captain Smith, late one night for advice. As Smith makes them coffee, Jack lays out what he knows, unaware the information is ruinous to Smith. With his back turned to Jack, Smith asks what Exley thinks. When Jack replies, "He doesn't know yet," it's all Smith needs. He turns and fires a fatal bullet into Jack's heart. Too stunned at first to understand what's happened, Jack finally gets it and, with a hint of a smile, whispers, "Rollo Tomasi" and dies. Rollo Tomasi is the name Exley uses for any guy who thinks he can get away with murder.

"You're the first man in five years who didn't tell me I look like Veronica Lake inside of a minute." As an actress, Kim Basinger's ability to wrap men around her little finger didn't serve her well in a real LA courtroom in 1993. She lost an $8 million suit for reneging on her commitment to star in *Boxing Helena*. The decision forced her to file for bankruptcy.

90

BUTCH CASSIDY AND THE SUNDANCE KID

1969

CHARISMATIC COHORTS

It begins with the legend, "Most of what follows is true." We certainly hope so, at least with regard to the dynamic chemistry between this doomed but damnably appealing duo. Based on the real exploits of Robert LeRoy Parker (Butch) and Harry Longbaugh (Sundance), sons of starchy religious families, the film catches up with them just as the dawn of the 20th century is leaving them in the dust. Their brand of crime in the wide-open spaces is about to be done in by modern communications systems and organized legal authorities. But even as the last days of Butch and Sundance tick down, director George Roy Hill and screenwriter William Goldman provide them with the style of *Bonnie and Clyde*, the balletic shootouts of *The Wild Bunch*, and the female-as-hyphen of *Jules and Jim*. The images are indelible: Paul Newman's engaging Butch gliding around on a newfangled bicycle with Katharine Ross's Etta on the handlebars—as B. J. Thomas croons about raindrops falling on his head; a money train blowing sky high and scattering loot everywhere ("Think you got enough dynamite there, Butch?"); and Sundance's self-deprecating, eleventh-hour confessions ("I never shot nobody before"; "I don't know how to swim"). Ironic humor underscores the inevitable tragedy, and makes it all the more moving when it comes. The film ends with the frozen image of Butch and Sundance making a last stand against impossible odds. Unsubstantiated reports claim that the real-life boys survived the military onslaught in Bolivia and lived to ripe old ages under assumed identities in the Northwest. If so, their extraordinary careers lasted nearly as long and shined nearly as brightly as their Hollywood "golden boy" counterparts.

Jim: When you hear these two actors say it was the most fun they ever had making a movie, you can believe it. You want them to be your friends, too. Well, maybe not Sundance. But Butch, for sure, especially if he brings the popcorn and salad dressing.

Gail: Jumping from high cliffs to raging rapids, dancing on a bicycle, blowing train cars apart, how much more fun can two Peter Pan cowboys at the height of their seductive powers have? That they bring us along for the ride is our good luck.

THE PLOT

Butch Cassidy (Paul Newman) and his Hole-in-the-Wall gang have earned a fierce reputation as bank robbers. But the banks are getting wise and Butch, along with his mercurial sidekick, the Sundance Kid (Robert Redford), starts to focus on holding up money trains instead. The unhappy gang fails at a coup attempt and Butch leads them on several lucrative raids. Their success is derailed by the arrival of a super-posse that tracks Butch and Sundance relentlessly and corners them with no option but to dive from a precipice to save themselves. After collecting Sundance's schoolteacher ladylove, Etta (Katharine Ross), they're off to ripe-for-the-picking Bolivia after a brief stopover in New York City. Life in South America is good, especially after Etta teaches them some basic Spanish phrases like "Hands up, this is a robbery." Their luck eventually runs out but not before Etta does. She never could bear the thought of watching them die.

In fancy dress, Butch (Paul Newman), Sundance (Robert Redford), and Etta (Katharine Ross) make the best-looking threesome ever to head down Bolivia-way. A brief stopover in New York City allows for a visit to a photographer's studio. A rarity for Hollywood, the three real-life characters who inspired the movie were nearly as attractive as the stars who played them.

THE DIRECTOR

"No matter how much I screwed up, the picture should do well because the material is so good," said **George Roy Hill**, who wasn't concerned by the mix of comedy and drama, bloodbaths and belly laughs. "As long as the moment is real, it will work." Hill came late to films, having had a full career as an actor and director in theater and TV. His most successful directorial forays include *Toys in the Attic* (1963), *The World of Henry Orient* (1964), *Hawaii* (1966), *Thoroughly Modern Millie* (1967), *The Sting* (1973), *The Great Waldo Pepper* (1975), *Slap Shot* (1977), *The World According to Garp* (1982), and *The Little Drummer Girl* (1984).

Butch and Etta meet the future on a newfangled bicycle built for two stars. To the accompaniment of "Raindrops Keep Fallin' on My Head," they ride in the sunshine, Butch does a few fancy tricks and takes a comic tumble. Ross later admitted it was rather anxiety-inducing to be perched on those handlebars. She had no idea where Newman was headed.

THE CAST

Butch Cassidy	Paul Newman
Sundance Kid	Robert Redford
Etta Place	Katharine Ross
Percy Garris	Strother Martin
Bike Salesman	Henry Jones
Sheriff Bledsoe	Jeff Corey
Woodcock	George Furth
Agnes	Cloris Leachman
Harvey Logan	Ted Cassidy
Marshal	Kenneth Mars

ROLE REVERSALS

Newman agreed to play either role so long as Steve McQueen costarred. McQueen thought Newman was up to something, possibly getting his name more prominently placed on the bill, and backed out. Ironically, the same scenario would be played out in the one film they did make together, *Towering Inferno* (1974). Newman was happy with either role, fireman or architect. He wound up playing the latter. Their names were of equal size in the credits.

THE ACTORS

"I used a good deal of myself in the role. I wanted to keep it loose." Always affable on the set and full of famously bad jokes, **Paul Newman** isn't an actor to put up resistance. "I see myself as a soldier. Just tell me where to stand," he has said. He's spent a good deal of his career combating the effect of his extraordinary good looks. "To work as hard as I've worked to accomplish anything and then have some yo-yo come up and say, Take off those dark glasses and let's have a look at those blue eyes', is really discouraging." He's rarely agreed to simply romantic roles in which the camera lingers on his physicality. His most iconic performances possess a manic edge that counteracts his appearance. Among them are *Somebody Up There Likes Me* (1956), *Cat on a Hot Tin Roof* (1958), *Exodus* (1960), *The Hustler* (1961), *Sweet Bird of Youth* (1962), *Hud* (1963), *Cool Hand Luke* (1967), *The Sting* (1973), *The Towering Inferno* (1974), *Fort Apache, The Bronx* (1981), *The Verdict* (1982), *The Color of Money* (1986, Academy Award, Best Actor), *Nobody's Fool* (1994), and *Road to Perdition* (2002). He's directed his wife, Joanne Woodward, most famously in *Rachel, Rachel* (1968) and *The Glass Menagerie* (1987). Newman is almost equally well-known for the nonprofit food empire, "Newman's Own," and his charity camp for children suffering terminal illnesses, "The Hole-in-the-Wall Gang," affectionately named after Butch Cassidy's posse.

"This is the movie that changed my life," admits **Robert Redford.** "Afterwards, I couldn't live in the same way again." It's hard to imagine a time when Redford wasn't a household name and face, but until Butch Cassidy, he'd done only stage plays and a few films, most notably *Barefoot in the Park* with Jane Fonda. Though only 30 when he played Sundance, Redford possessed tremendous self-confidence. Director Hill said of him, "He's one of those hard-headed Irishmen who goes his own way." Redford has used his fame and fortune to carve the legendary Sundance Institute and Film Festival out of the Utah mountains. Some of the films that got him there are *Downhill Racer* (1969), *Jeremiah Johnson* and *The Candidate* (both 1972), *The Way We Were* and *The Sting* (both 1973), *The Great Gatsby* (1974), *Three Days of the Condor* (1975), *All the President's Men* (1976), *Brubaker* (1980), *The Natural* (1984), *Out of Africa* (1985), *The Horse Whisperer* (1998), and *Lions for Lambs* (2007). Like costar Newman, Redford has doubled as a director, winning Oscar gold his first time out with *Ordinary People* (1980) and earning critical acclaim for *A River Runs Through It* (1992) and *Quiz Show* (1994).

Director George Roy Hill thought at first that **Katharine Ross** was miscast, but her vunerability and sex appeal ultimately vindicated the choice. Ross has mixed feelings about the film. She and Hill didn't get along at all. He'd caught her trying to learn how to operate a camera on the very first day of shooting and found it offensive. He banned her from the set when she wasn't in a scene and they rarely spoke thereafter. She will forever be associated with her most famous role, Elaine Robinson in *The Graduate* (1967). (For more on Ross, see page 112.)

THE MUSIC

The Oscar-winning song, "Raindrops Keep Fallin' on My Head" by **Burt Bacharach** and **Hal David**, was offered to Bob Dylan who declined, thereby providing B. J. Thomas with the biggest hit of his career.

THE SET

Hill wanted to use the Old New York set on the Fox lot that had been built for *Hello, Dolly*, but studio chief Darryl F. Zanuck refused the request, claiming that he didn't want audiences to see it before the musical's release. Necessity is the mother of invention and Hill came up with the idea of splicing his actors into vintage sepia photos of the era.

CREDITS

Producer: John Foreman/ 20th Century Fox
Director: George Roy Hill
Screenplay: William Goldman
Running time: 110 minutes
Box Office: $97 million

ACADEMY AWARDS

Best Original Screenplay: William Goldman
Best Cinematography: Conrad L. Hall
Best Song: "Raindrops Keep Fallin' on My Head" by Burt Bacharach, Hal David
Best Original Score: Burt Bacharach

NOMINATIONS

Best Picture
Best Director: George Roy HIll
Best Sound: William E. Edmondson, David Dockendorf

THE YEAR'S OTHER WINNERS

Best Picture: *Midnight Cowboy*
Best Director: John Schlesinger, *Midnight Cowboy*
Best Actor: John Wayne, *True Grit*
Best Actress: Maggie Smith, *The Prime of Miss Jean Brodie*
Best Supporting Actor: Gig Young, *They Shoot Horses, Don't They?*
Best Supporting Actress: Goldie Hawn, *Cactus Flower*

BEHIND THE SCREEN

The real Butch's sister LuLu was still alive when the film was made, and visited the set. She had no idea what to make of it and, when she was asked to attend the premiere, she held out for cash. She and Redford remained friends until her death.

The famous dive from the cliff utilized an especially effective quick edit. Redford and Newman leapt to a wooden platform six feet below the precipice. Stuntmen finished the job in a California lake several weeks later.

This was William Goldman's first screenplay. He wrote it over the Christmas holidays in his office at Princeton, where he was a professor.

THE CRITICS

"Although *Butch Cassidy* wasn't the first movie to pair up a couple of wisecracking best friends in an action/adventure setting, this film became the model of how well that approach could work when done right."
—James Berardinelli, *Reelviews*

"All these talents are trying for something more clever than is attempted in most commercial jobs, and it's all so archly empty." —Pauline Kael, *The New Yorker*

Butch and Sundance are relentlessly pursued by a super-posse across the rugged Wyoming terrain. They try riding one horse to throw them off the scent—but that won't work with the famous Indian scout, Lord Baltimore, examining the tracks. They're finally cornered atop a rocky precipice, surrounded at every turn. They could give themselves up and face prison for life. Sundance has been there, and won't go back. They could shoot it out to the death. Or, there's the water down below.

Sundance: "I can't swim."

Butch: "Why you crazy . . . ! The fall will probably kill you."

With a gulp of panic and a scream, they dive over the edge in free-fall. They hit the water and are carried off by the rapids with Sundance clinging to Butch for all he's worth. They survive and make it back to Etta's place, where they're delighted to read newspaper reports that they've been killed.

THE OTHER LISTS

- American Film Institute (Yes)
- Roger Ebert's Top 100 (No)
- *Entertainment Weekly* (No)
- Internet Movie Database (No)
- Leonard Maltin (No)
- *Movieline* (No)
- National Society of Film Critics (No)
- *Premiere* Magazine (No)
- *Rolling Stone* Magazine (No)
- *Village Voice* (No)

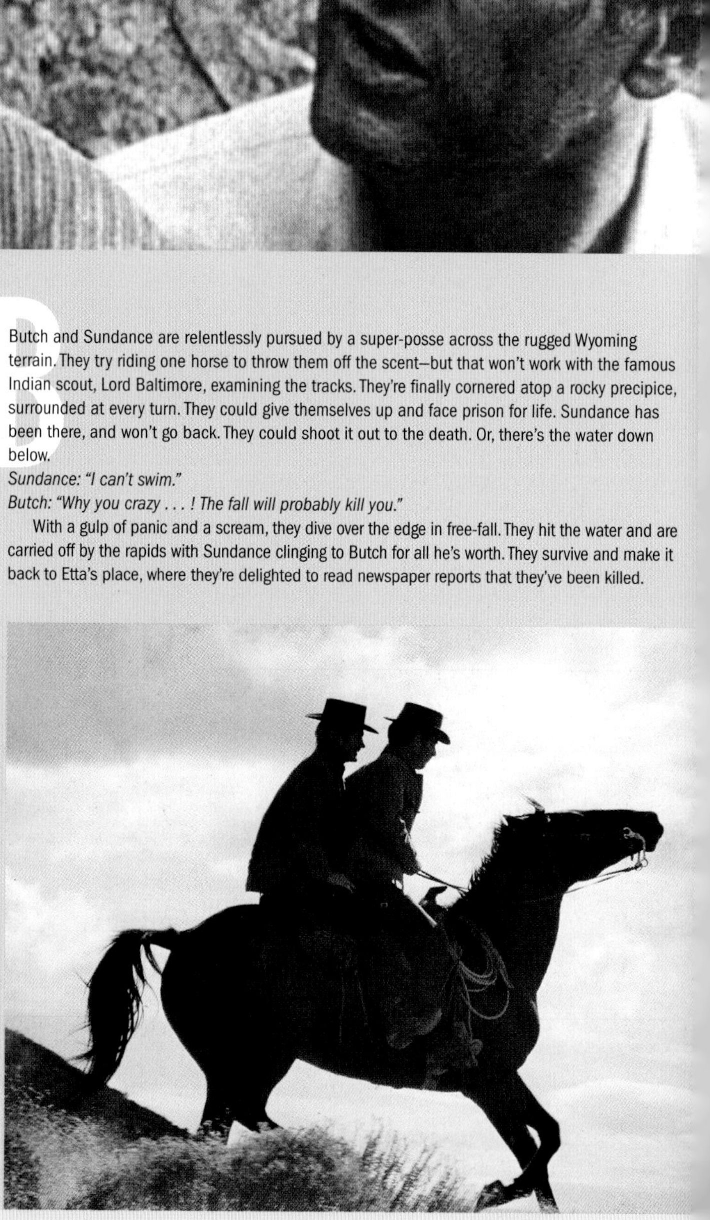

RIGHT: The image of two icons sharing a horse is all it takes to define the ultimate buddy Western. Newman, the established superstar, and Redford, the brash young newcomer, meld their combined charisma. They'll score again in 1973 with *The Sting*, but this one has the most bite.

91

IMITATION OF LIFE 1959

THE REAL THING

German Expressionism meets the all-American "weeper," and the collision is one of the luckiest accidents to emerge from the limping postwar studio system. The vividness of color and the ripe symbolism of every artfully devised set, costume, and prop put the "modern" in postmodern. Though hugely popular at the time, the movie was blasted by the critics, who closed their eyes to Sirk's style rather than promote what they pompously derided as a "woman's picture." Ironically, the film's ambitious scenario tackles pressing social issues that the "serious" films of the day skirted, in particular, the day-to-day grind of racism and the self-loathing borne of it. And *Imitation of Life* doesn't confine the color barrier to the clichéd environs of the Deep South. The film isn't shy about its melodramatic traditions and dives into the familiar pool of two women fighting for the love of one man. It's a theme that carries the weight of such genre classics as *Mildred Pierce* (1945) but serves as only one of the several layers here. The overriding premise, however, is the struggle of two single women, Lora Meredith and Sarah Jane Johnson, attempting to succeed on their own terms without the assistance—or, for that matter, the need—of a man. Downright blasphemy in 1959. Behind this thinly coded melodrama is a pre-Feminist call to arms.

Jim: Macho cinema-heads always vote for Sirk's *Written on the Wind* but this is so much more story, more fun, and it can actually make you cry. It's the quintessential '50s Technicolor melodrama. And let's face it, Dorothy Malone ain't no Lana Turner!

Gail: Only a film so operatic, so exaggerated, could feel this true.

IE PLOT

ance Coney Island encounter forever ds struggling actress Lora Meredith (Lana er), her daughter Susi (Sandra Dee), and red" Annie Johnson (Juanita Moore), s so desperate for a place to live with her daughter Sarah Jane (Susan Kohner) she agrees to work as Lora's maid for As Lora's star rises, her longtime beau, e (John Gavin), is left holding the bag, teen Susi falls hopelessly in love with Annie's got her own daughter problems the now-gorgeous Sarah Jane manages ass" for white. As Sarah Jane tries to e a life for herself, she orders her long-ring mama to keep her distance. Every Annie shows up, Sarah Jane either loses ob or her man, sometimes with violent ts. Sickly and "just plain tired of it all," e finally agrees to sever her maternal for good. Alone, her broken heart results e most spectacular, four-Kleenex-box ral ever filmed.

Lora (Lana Turner) is torn between the conflicts of love (John Gavin) and the chance to play "Raina, the juiciest role since Scarlett O'Hara!" for Italian director, Amergo Falluci. She opts for the former and, in so doing, makes herself and everyone else miserable. Lana Turner's mask-like beauty was at least partially due to the fact that, having shaved her eyebrows for an early film role, they never grew back.

THE DIRECTOR

"I would have made it for the title alone. The mirror is the imitation of life. What is interesting about a mirror is that it does not show yourself as you are, it shows you your own opposite." **Douglas Sirk** was a director who had a great deal of respect and admiration for what others thought of as lowbrow material. He was convinced that melodrama was the basis for cinema and, as such, felt he could elevate the image of ordinary lives. A Danish émigré who had a difficult time getting started in Hollywood, he found his champion at Universal in producer Ross Hunter. Together, they brought the audiences back to the movie houses in the 1950s with *All That Heaven Allows* (1955), *Written on the Wind* (1957), and *Imitation of Life*. Lana Turner, who'd been treated as an object by previous directors, described Sirk as one of the few gentlemen she ever worked with. "He wouldn't simply shout at me from his chair. He'd come over and ask to discuss the scene with me. He was the first director to make me feel I had acting talent."

Sarah Jane, all grown up and determined to make her own way in the world, plies her limited musical talents at a sleazy nightclub. Susan Kohner earned a Best Supporting Actress nomination but was never truly enamored by the idea of a film career. She'd been raised in the business and it held very little magic for her.

THE CAST	
Lora Meredith	Lana Turner
Steve Archer	John Gavin
Susi	Sandra Dee
Allen Loomis	Robert Alda
Sarah Jane	Susan Kohner
David Edwards	Dan O'Herlihy
Annie Johnson	Juanita Moore
Frankie	Troy Donahue

"[Hollywood] was all beauty and it was all talent, and if you had it they protected you." —Lana Turner

THE ACTORS

"The most important tool of my trade was a mirror. I always had a three-way, full-length mirror outside my trailer door so that I could check my appearance before I went on the set." But with *Imitation of Life*, reality intruded on **Lana Turner**'s superficial approach to her craft. While filming Annie's funeral, Turner was so overcome with emotion (images of her dead lover, Johnny Stompanato, and imprisoned daughter, Cheryl) that "I ran off the set in tears to my dressing room, verging on hysteria. My hairdresser had to slap me, but it worked. I went back to finish the scene and (Sirk) called 'cut and print.' He said I'd been brilliant, I'd given him just what he wanted." A teen sex symbol that managed to extend her career well beyond the usual Hollywood lifespan, Turner was the object of desire in every genre, from *Love Finds Andy Hardy* (1938) to the sizzling *The Postman Always Rings Twice* (1946) and *The Bad and the Beautiful* (1952). She received an Oscar nomination for *Peyton Place* (1957).

Sandra Dee, the teen dream of the 1950s, never had it so good as she did in *Imitation of Life*. A slew of dumber-than-dumb scripts and the end of her marriage to singing star Bobby Darin ended her Hollywood career. She's since penned an autobiography chronicling her personal demons and tragedies (sex abuse, drugs, eating disorders). Satirically immortalized in "Look at Me, I'm Sandra Dee" from *Grease*, the real Dee can be viewed in such fare as *A Summer Place* (1959), *Gidget* (1959), *Tammy Tell Me True* (1961), and *Tammy and the Doctor* (1963).

Talent, looks, and nepotism won the role of Sarah Jane for **Susan Kohner**. Her father Paul was Lana Turner's longtime agent. Remarkably, *Imitation of Life* was pretty much it for her. Following *All the Fine Young Cannibals* (1960) and *Freud* (1962), she retired to wed designer John Weitz, and held forth as a beloved Manhattan socialite. Her producer/screenwriter son Chris costarred in the cult hit *Chuck and Buck* (2000).

Juanita Moore profited from her Oscar nomination and maintained a nonstop career through the '70s and '80s. But like Kohner, this was her most visible highpoint. She turned up again as a maid in *Walk on the Wild Side* (1962), a nurse in *Rosie!* (1967), a slave in *Skin Game* (1971), and a Congresswoman in *Fugitive Lovers* (1975).

For **Troy Donahue**, the lyric from *A Chorus Line* says it all: "If Troy Donahue can be a movie star, than I can be a movie star." His very lucky, very brief career relied mostly on that blond mop of surfer hair. He can be seen running his fingers through it in *A Summer Place* (1959), *Parrish* (1961), *Palm Springs Weekend* (1963), and briefly in *The Godfather, Part II* (1974). His end was Hollywood Babylon tragic after having spent a homeless period sleeping on Central Park benches.

This was **John Gavin**'s first major role, and it launched him as a beefcake who could speak in *Psycho* (1960), *Spartacus* (1960), *Back Street* (1961), and *Thoroughly Modern Millie* (1967), in which he parodied his own stiffness. In the ultimate casting coup, President Ronald Reagan chose him for the role of the U.S. ambassador to Mexico. (For more on Gavin, see page 292.)

BEHIND THE SCREEN

Lana Turner wears $1,000,000 worth of jewels in the film and a $78,000 Jean Louis wardrobe—34 costume changes at an average cost of $2,294.12 each, princely sums by the budgetary standards of 1959.

Imitation of Life was Turner's return to the screen following the biggest Hollywood scandal of the 1950s, the carving-knife murder of her mobster lover Johnny Stompanato by her 14-year-old daughter Cheryl. Producer Ross Hunter made sure the script mirrored the real life mother-daughter relationship for maximum exploitation.

In the original film version (1934), Claudette Colbert, in the Lora Meredith role, plays a young widow/businesswoman who turns her long-suffering maid's pancake recipe into a multimillion-dollar industry.

Turner initially turned down the role but Hunter coaxed her back. His budget was limited so

CREDITS

Producer: Ross Hunter/Universal
Director: Douglas Sirk
Screenplay: Eleanore Griffin, from the novel by Fannie Hurst
Running time: 125 minutes
Box Office: The 4th highest grosser of 1959.

ACADEMY AWARD NOMINATIONS

Best Supporting Actress: Susan Kohner
Best Supporting Actress: Juanita Moore

THE YEAR'S WINNERS

Best Picture: *Ben-Hur*
Best Director: William Wyler, *Ben-Hur*
Best Actor: Charlton Heston, *Ben-Hur*
Best Actress: Simone Signoret, *Room at the Top*
Best Supporting Actor: Hugh Griffith, *Ben-Hur*
Best Supporting Actress: Shelley Winters, *The Diary of Anne Frank*

THE GREAT SCENE

Annie pines away for her estranged daughter, Sarah Jane, who's gone off to claim a new life for herself. Annie's health is affected and she collapses from emotional exhaustion. On her behalf, devoted Steve manages to track down Sarah Jane in Hollywood. She's passing for white in the scantily clad chorus line of the Moulin Rouge nightclub. Annie, with her last bit of strength, flies out to see her one final time. When she steps into the dressing room, Sarah Jane is horrified that she'll expose her secret to the other girls. But in a final, grand sacrifice, Annie pretends that she was Sarah Jane's childhood nanny. Sarah Jane's eyes brim with tears of gratitude and terrible guilt. Annie gives her one last beatific smile and a hug, whispering her promise to never bother her again, even if she should see her on the street.

LEFT: "Oh, Mama, Mama!" Werner Fassbinder, in an essay on *Imitation of Life*, insists it's Juanita Moore's character who's in the wrong in this searing mother-daughter battle. She keeps insisting that Sarah Jane "know her place" and does not strive for more in the white world.

she opted for half the potential profits. She wound up making more money on *Imitation of Life* than Elizabeth Taylor did on *Cleopatra* (1963).

The Hollywood myth has Lana Turner being discovered at Schwab's Drugstore in Hollywood. In fact, she was tapped for stardom at Currie's Ice Cream Parlor across the street from her high school.

Sandra Dee wed singing star Bobby Darin at the ripe old age of sixteen.

Troy Donahue's role in *The Godfather, Part II* was that of Merle Johnson Jr., his real name. His casting was the result of a long friendship with Francis Ford Coppola, who'd been a fellow cadet at a military academy.

THE CRITICS

"*Imitation of Life* is both Sirk's final film and, arguably, his masterpiece."—Stephen Handzo, *Bright Lights Film Journal*

"Good God, even strong men are crying!" —Theater owner to producer Ross Hunter

SEND IN THE CLONES

Far from Heaven (2001)

THE OTHER LISTS

- American Film Institute (No)
- Roger Ebert's Top 100 (No)
- *Entertainment Weekly* (No)
- Internet Movie Database (No)
- Leonard Maltin (No)
- *Movieline* (No)
- National Society of Film Critics (No)
- *Premiere* Magazine (No)
- *Rolling Stone* Magazine (No)
- *Village Voice* (No)

RIGHT: "Why do you have to be my mother—why, why, why?" Rebellious little Sarah Jane is caught once again trying to "pass" for white when her mama, Annie, brings her forgotten galoshes to school. Director Sirk and screenwriter Griffin made it clear that racism wasn't confined to the Deep South.

92

RAIDERS OF THE LOST ARK 1981

BOULDER DASH!

"I'm making this up as I go along," shrugs Indiana Jones as he leaps onto a gleaming white stallion to pursue a truckful of Nazis through the desert. The multi-climactic plot, like a bedtime story invented by a sugar-energized kid, suggests just that. But Hollywood's two wunderkinds, Steven Spielberg and George Lucas, are in full control of every frame. They are the masters of every wry one-liner, sight gag, and quick thrill. The movie is, of course, a rousing homage to the Saturday-afternoon serials of old. What elevates it to the level of classic escapism is Harrison Ford, in a performance as golden as the priceless ark itself. In the tradition of cartoon superheroes, Ford's Indiana has his Clark Kent side, the bespectacled college prof whose musculature is barely contained beneath a tweed jacket. He's oblivious to his swooning students, as he ponders far greater matters—he means to make history, not dates. That's why one of the best moments in the film is its quietest. After suffering the slings, arrows, asps, and blowguns of misadventure, he allows Karen Allen to kiss him on the few millimeters of skin that aren't hurting. When he gestures to his eyelid and she tenderly complies, we finally get it—this isn't a kid's movie at all. Oh, but let them watch. If nothing else, they'll learn how to outrun giant boulders and even outwit a mischievous Nazi monkey.

Jim: A venomous snake slithering its way through a discarded open-toed high heel is a terrific touch. But what isn't, in this one? Get a load of that final shot, a clever steal from the fadeout of *Citizen Kane*, of all things.

Gail: Hitler wants to get his hands on the most important of all Jewish relics, the ark containing the word of God, and Spielberg gets back at him for every step his Nazi creeps take. It's like a kid's furious fantasy of getting back at the Führer.

THE PLOT

Adolf Hitler thinks he's found the key to world domination: possession of the lost Ark of the Covenant, which once contained the Ten Commandments. It could unleash the very powers of God. The U.S. must get the jump on him and hires the only truly capable man for the job, Dr. Indiana Jones (Harrison Ford), mild-mannered archaeology professor and fearless hunter of ancient treasures. His first pit stop, a dive in Nepal run by ex-lover Marion (Karen Allen), who has a medallion required to divine the precise location of the Ark. But she's not so quick to give it up; she wants him to pay for having abandoned her long ago. She stalls and gets a visit from the Gestapo's master torturer, Toht (Ronald Lacey). Jones rescues her in the nick of time and, whether he likes it or not, the two are partners to the end in a snake and Nazi-infested adventure of biblical proportions.

Narrowly escaping certain death is all in a day's work for Dr. "Indiana" Jones. One of Harrison Ford's most appealing traits as an actor is his ability to express real fear on screen. Lucas and Spielberg give him plenty of opportunities here.

Marion: You're not the man I knew ten years ago. Indiana: It's not the years, honey, it's the mileage.

THE DIRECTOR

"If a person can tell me an idea in twenty-five words or less, it's going to make a pretty good movie. I like ideas, especially movie ideas, that you can hold in your hand." Apparently George Lucas was able to come in under the word limit and induce **Steven Spielberg** to join forces on this, their first collaboration. They would round out the franchise with two more equally successful installments: *Indiana Jones and the Temple of Doom* (1984) and *Indiana Jones and the Last Crusade* (1989). After sneaking onto studio lots as a teen to see how movies got made, Spielberg got his first shot on TV doing episodes for *The Name of the Game* (1968) and famously for *Night Gallery* (1969), in which he directed Joan Crawford as a blind woman who buys the gift of sight for one day. His first feature, *Duel* (1971), about a faceless, demonic truck driver, caused a sensation and his second, *Sugarland Express* (1974), won him critical praise. *Jaws* (1975) essentially changed the movie industry as its first summer blockbuster, and while Spielberg dismisses *Close Encounters of the Third Kind* (1977) as his youthful obsession, it revealed on screen for the first time the possibility of a peaceful galactic community. After a serious stumble with *1941* (1979), he roared back with *E.T.* (1982), took critical blows for *The Color Purple* (1985), but finally won his Oscar for *Schindler's List* (1993). Subsequent films include *Munich* and *War of the Worlds* (both 2005). (For more on Spielberg, see pages 88, 103, 136, 190, and 208.)

"Snakes. Why'd it have to be snakes?" We'll leave Jones' extreme ophidiophobia to the Freudians and just pass the popcorn.

THE CAST

Dr. Indiana Jones	Harrison Ford
Marion Ravenwood	Karen Allen
Rene Belloq	Paul Freeman
Toht	Ronald Lacey
Sallah	John Rhys-Davies
Dr. Marcus Brody	Denholm Elliott
Satipo	Alfred Molina
Colonel Dietrich	Wolf Kahler
Gobler	Anthony Higgins
Barranca/Monkey Man	Vic Tablian
Colonel Musgrove	Don Fellows
Major Eaton	William Hootkins
Bureaucrat	Bill Reimbold
Jock, Seaplane pilot	Fred Sorenson
Captain Katanga	George Harris

THE ACTORS

Spielberg describes **Harrison Ford** in *Raiders* as "a remarkable combination of Bogart in *Treasure of the Sierra Madre* and Errol Flynn." His deadpan world-weariness provides the perfect comic balance for his acrobatic heroics. Ford has a quality that makes you think he'd rather be doing something other than starring in movies. In fact, he's stated often that he was quite happy being a carpenter before his first big break. Of *Raiders*, he managed rare praise: "It was a very collaborative atmosphere, and that's the way I like to work." The highest grossing-actor in the history of American movies, Ford's beginnings were hardly auspicious, with a few uncredited walk-ons and brief TV appearances. Things began to change with a small role in *American Graffiti* (1973), a juicy, villainous part in *The Conversation* (1974), and finally the movie that changed everything for him, *Star Wars* (1977). The sci-fi classic *Blade Runner* (1982) led to the franchise gold of *Indiana Jones* and another hugely successful series as Special Agent Jack Ryan in *Patriot Games* (1992) and *Clear and Present Danger* (1994). He continued his box-office reign with *The Fugitive* (1993), *Air Force One* (1997), *K-19: The Widow-maker* (2002), *Hollywood Homicide* (2003), and *Indiana Jones III* (2008). (For more on Ford, see pages 130, 169, 254, and 289.)

Karen Allen rocketed to fame in *Animal House* (1978), which led directly to her being cast by Spielberg in *Raiders*. But a funny thing happened on the way to her enduring stardom—nothing. Following the delightful *E.T.* clone *Starman* (1984), she returned to the stage, focused on her marriage and baby, and only recently reemerged in *The Perfect Storm* (2000) and *In the Bedroom* (2001).

BEHIND THE SCREEN

While on location in Tunisia, nearly everyone got dysentery except Spielberg, who brought his own food from home, cases of Spaghetti-O's.

Despite the hundreds of live snakes in the tomb, their numbers weren't terrifying enough for Spielberg. Lengths of snake-like garden hose were tossed into the mix.

Ford and Allen were protected from the striking cobra by a glass panel.

To facilitate Ford's greatest display of set-piece heroics, being dragged beneath a truckful of Nazis, the truck's chassis was raised and the roadway was scooped out in the middle. Ford didn't think it was all that dangerous. "If it was, they would've shot a lot more of the film before I did it." Still, he got plenty of bruises for the effort.

SEND IN THE CLONES

The Mummy (1999)

Lara Croft: Tomb Raider (2001)

THE CRITICS

"One of the most deliriously funny, ingenious, and stylish American adventure movies ever made." —Vincent Canby, *New York Times*

"Children may well enjoy its simple-mindedness, untroubled by the fact that it looks so shoddy and so uninventive." —*London Observer*

ROLE REVERSALS

Indiana Jones was tailored for Tom Selleck, but he was too busy with his TV series, *Magnum PI*, to make the picture.

CREDITS

Producer: Howard G. Kazanjian, George Lucas, Frank Marshall/ Paramount
Director: Steven Spielberg
Screenplay: George Lucas, Philip Kaufman, Lawrence Kasdan
Running time: 115 minutes
Budget: $20 million
Box Office: $400 million

ACADEMY AWARDS

Best Art Direction-Set Decoration: Norman Reynolds, Leslie Dilley, Michael Ford
Best Effects, Visual Effects: Richard Edlund, Kit West, Bruce Nicholson, Joe Johnston
Best Editing: Michael Kahn
Best Sound: Bill Varney, Steve Maslow, Gregg Landaker, Roy Charman
Special Achievement Award, Sound Effects Editing: Ben Burtt, Richard L. Anderson

NOMINATIONS

Best Picture
Best Director: Steven Speilberg
Best Cinematography: Douglas Slocombe
Best Music: John Williams

THE YEAR'S OTHER WINNERS

Best Picture: *Chariots of Fire*
Best Director: Warren Beatty, *Reds*
Best Actor: Henry Fonda, *On Golden Pond*
Best Actress: Katharine Hepburn, *On Golden Pond*
Best Supporting Actor: John Gielgud, *Arthur*
Best Supporting Actress: Maureen Stapleton, *Reds*

THE GREAT SCENE

It's a manic chase through the casbah as Indiana and feisty Marion are pursued by Nazis and their minions. At every turn in the labyrinth they're confronted by masked flunkies with guns, swords, daggers, any weapon that Jones can manage to turn back on them. A knife is drawn, he pulls away in the nick of time and the jerk behind him gets it. He briefly loses Marion who hides in a giant basket until a screeching monkey gives her away. Jones trails the sound of her screams as she's carried off. This way, that way, which way? He's suddenly confronted by a devilish, red-and-black robed behemoth with a massive scimitar which he flashes back and forth in elaborate, ceremonial choreography. Is this the end? A beat. Jones pulls out his gun and simply shoots him. He's off again, finally spots the basket. He runs after it into the square and is briefly lost in a sea of nearly identical baskets. Marion's screams lead him through a maze of alleys. He finally sees her as she is being tossed into the back of a truck. In the ensuing gunfire, the truck explodes. He cries out "Marion!" His great lost love has apparently gone up in smoke. Stay tuned!

ABOVE: She went thataway! Indiana's race through the casbah in search of Marion is a cinematic catalog of sight gags and suspenseful puzzle-book chases. Hitchcock meets Charlie Chaplin.

BELOW: All trussed up with no place to go. Indiana and Marion are special guests of the evil Dr. Belloq and the Nazis, as they prepare to open the golden ark.

THE OTHER LISTS

- American Film Institute (Yes)
- Roger Ebert's Top 100 (No)
- *Entertainment Weekly* (No)
- Internet Movie Database (Yes)
- Leonard Maltin (No)
- *Movieline* (No)
- National Society of Film Critics (No)
- *Premiere* Magazine (No)
- *Rolling Stone* Magazine (No)
- *Village Voice* (No)

"The most expensive habit in the world is celluloid, not heroin, and I need a fix every few years."
–Steven Spielberg

93

SPARTACUS 1960

SUPERSTAR SLAVE

Bisexuality couched in culinary terms steams up bath time for Roman dictator Crassus, played with decadent élan by Sir Laurence Olivier. "My robe, Antoninus," he nods seductively to wary slave-boy Tony Curtis, "My taste includes both snails and oysters." And off they went, in the original release of *Spartacus*, to the cutting-room floor. The Legion of Decency wasn't having any of that, thank you very much. But iconoclastic young director Stanley Kubrick was impossible to squelch entirely. The film is nothing if not a series of revolutionary warning shots aimed at the Hollywood establishment. Star/producer Kirk Douglas flaunted his choice of screenwriter, Dalton Trumbo, chief among the "Hollywood Ten," who'd been forced to pen such classics as *Roman Holiday* under a pseudonym. Douglas made sure his real name appeared in the credits, thus effectively ending the blacklist. Trumbo attempted to use *Spartacus* as a platform for his Socialist ideals. Douglas wanted, instead, an emphasis on the Jewish struggle. A smug Kubrick simply sat out the squabble and when the smoke cleared, rewrote the script according to his own concept. The collision of such massive egos resulted in one of the most thoroughly entertaining and unusually thought-provoking costume epics ever. It's perhaps the most sturdy survivor of the genre because it transcends 1950s gloss, showboating performances, and climactic set pieces (like, say, a chariot race). The film, leading with its star's immortal chin, is a rousing tribute to the human spirit. "Maybe there's no peace in this world, for us or for anyone else, I don't know. But I do know that, as long as we live, we must remain true to ourselves."

Jim: A hugely riveting spectacle. Slaves with perfect teeth and coiffures aside, *Spartacus* is the real deal. We're talking thousands of eager extras, not computerized miniatures, fighting to the death. Kubrick's Ancient Rome provides the perfect rainy Saturday afternoon getaway.

Gail: Russell Crowe is an inanimate object in a high-tech world in *Gladiator*. The film couldn't hold the reins in a race with *Spartacus*, its cinematic grandfather, in which Kirk Douglas's Spartacus is a real, hot-blooded hero, Tony Curtis's slave-boy is unforgettable, and all of the other stars make you tingle.

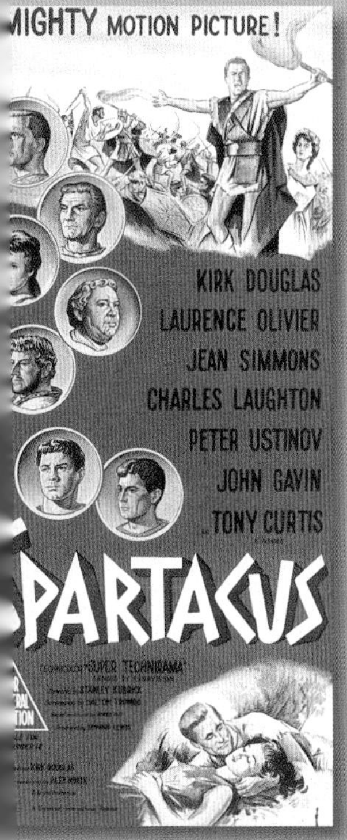

MIGHTY MOTION PICTURE!
KIRK DOUGLAS
LAURENCE OLIVIER
JEAN SIMMONS
CHARLES LAUGHTON
PETER USTINOV
JOHN GAVIN
TONY CURTIS
SPARTACUS
SUPER TECHNIRAMA

E PLOT

nine slave Spartacus (Kirk Douglas) is sold iatus (Peter Ustinov), a gladiator training-l owner. He's thrust into a world of men ed to slaughter one another for sport. In t-to-the-death display for visiting Roman a gladiator (Woody Strode) thrusts his at them rather than kill his friend. He dies s courage inspires Spartacus to revolt, zing a vast army of fugitive slaves who quick work of Rome's elite guard. With the n Empire endangered, dictator Crassus nce Olivier) uses his entire arsenal to e slaves. Spartacus's lover, Varinia (Jean ons), survives with their infant son, and n into the house of Crassus who's fallen . He orders Spartacus and his remaining be crucified along the Appian Way. escapes Rome with Batiatus. She finds cus on the cross and holds up their son, he will grow up free.

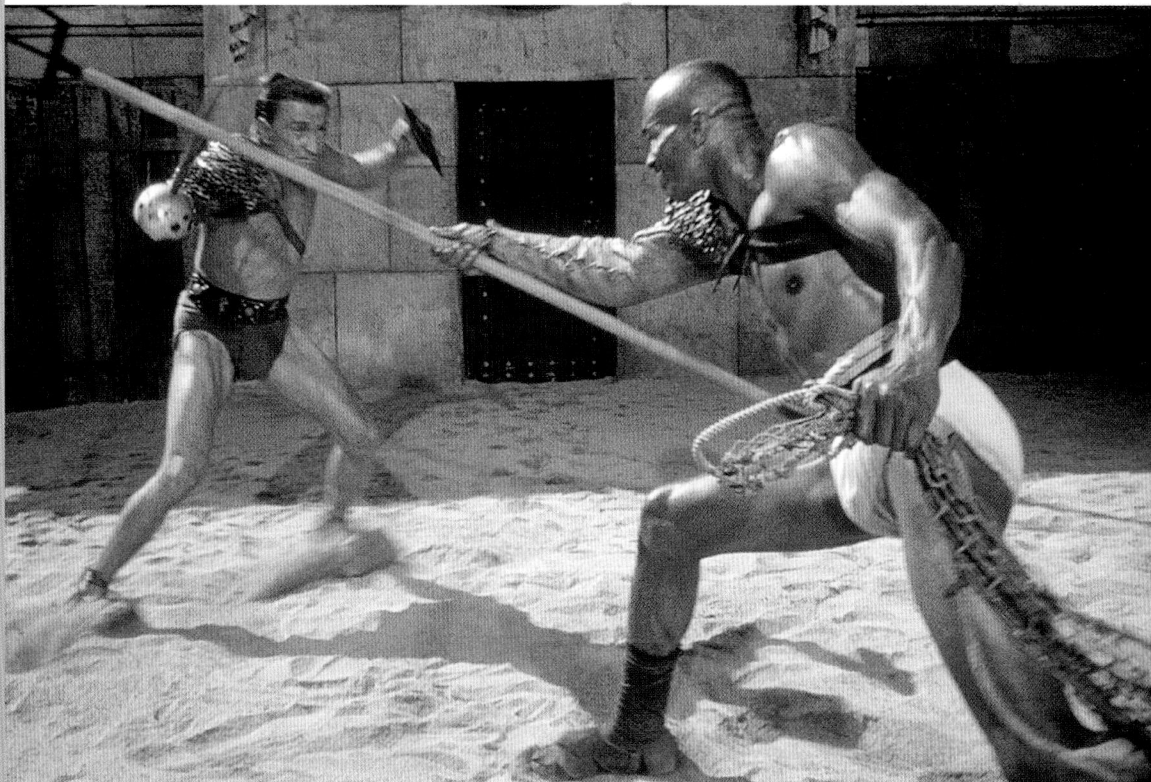

"Gladiators don't make friends. If we're ever matched in the arena together, I have to kill you." It all comes down to Draba (Woody Strode) vs. Spartacus (Kirk Douglas) for the pleasure of rich Roman visitors to the training school of Batiatus.

"Dignity shortens life more quickly than disease." —Gracchus

THE DIRECTOR

Stanley Kubrick wanted the audience for *Spartacus* to think—"a rarity in an historical film," he conceded. "I was more influenced by Eisenstein's *Alexander Nevsky* than by *Ben-Hur* or anything by Cecil B. DeMille." At 31 and with only one major feature, *Paths of Glory* (1957), under his belt, Kubrick was audacious. He launched an assault on Dalton Trumbo's script to give it a more visual conception. Kubrick's daily ego-wrestling and power plays with Kirk Douglas and cinematographer Russell Metty were as epic as the picture itself. Douglas was led to comment, "He'll be a fine director some day, if he falls flat on his face just once. It might teach him how to compromise." Oh, yeah? Kubrick remained unrepentantly isolated and independent, reveling in the meticulous production of a handful of films, each of which received a grand-scale welcome, though not always positive. His canon includes *Paths of Glory* (1957), *Lolita* (1962), *Dr. Strangelove* (1964), *2001: A Space Odyssey* (1968), *A Clockwork Orange* (1971), *Barry Lyndon* (1975), *The Shining* (1980), *Full Metal Jacket* (1987), and his final film, which was released after his death, *Eyes Wide Shut* (1999). (For more on Stanley Kubrick, see pages 127, 160, and 226.)

"The enemies of the state are known, arrests are being made, the prisons begin to fill." One of the film's great pleasures is the dextrous verbal sparring of some of the greatest English-speaking actors of the age.

THE CAST	
Spartacus	Kirk Douglas
Marcus Licinius Crassus	Laurence Olivier
Varinia	Jean Simmons
Sempronius Gracchus	Charles Laughton
Lentulus Batiatus	Peter Ustinov
Julius Caesar	John Gavin
Helena Glabrus	Nina Foch
Crixus	John Ireland
Tigranes Levantus	Herbert Lom
Claudia Marius	Joanna Barnes
Draba, Gladiator	Woody Strode
Antoninus	Tony Curtis

THE ACTORS

Midway through *Spartacus*, **Kirk Douglas** breaks into his trademark persona, all fire, fury, and intense chin-thrusting. But during the first third of the film, in which he's bought and sold, trained in the gladiator school, and falls shyly in love with a slave girl, Douglas is a particular revelation. A great deal of credit goes to Kubrick, who insisted that his dialogue in that section be almost entirely eliminated. He's an uneducated slave, after all, who's not accustomed to putting words to his thoughts and feelings. As a result, those scenes continue to resonate with rare honesty. Still, in all, it's a great, old-fashioned movie pleasure to watch Douglas stir his men to battle and shout down his oppressors with that in-your-face, Brooklyn-street-kid defiance. The boxing movie *Champion* (1949) made him a star and he distinguished himself in *The Glass Menagerie* (1950), *Young Man with a Horn* (1950), and *Detective Story* (1951) before moving on to his most memorable decade featuring such classics as *The Bad and the Beautiful* (1952) and *Lust for Life* (1956). He continued his streak with *Town without Pity* (1961), *Seven Days in May* (1964) and the mob saga *The Brotherhood* (1968). He made a comeback *in Once Is Not Enough* (1975) and once again in *The Fury* (1978). Following a debilitating stroke, he recuperated fully enough for several TV guest shots in the 1990s. He returned to the big screen with his son, Michael, in *It Runs in the Family* (2003). (For more on Douglas, see page 226.)

Sir Laurence Olivier was, for many decades, the living icon of acting, a British national treasure and one of the true greats of the stage. His film career reflected his love-hate relationship with the medium. It often showed his blatant, stagebound techniques to poor advantage (*The Entertainer,* 1960) and some of his later performances were clearly "phoned in" for the cash (*The Betsy* [1978], *The Boys from Brazil* [1978], *Inchon!* [1982]). At the same time, his *Hamlet* (1948), which he also directed, is the basis by which all film performances of Shakespeare are judged, and his Heathcliff in *Wuthering Heights* (1939) still pulses with raw passion. He was indelible in *Rebecca* (1940), and few can forget his sadistic Nazi dentist in *Marathon Man* (1976). His performance here as Crassus is considered one of his finest. He takes risks with the role and finds nearly every possible nuance of evil. Among his many romances and marriages, his most famous was undoubtedly to Vivien Leigh. Despite his amazing career and reputation, he considered acting "a masochistic form of exhibitionism, doing silly things well enough to be effective."

Jean Simmons was Ophelia in Olivier's definitive *Hamlet* (1948), which may account for their great on-screen chemistry here. Their final scene at the end of the film is loaded with fireworks and undercurrent. Conversely, in her scenes with Kirk Douglas, she can't stop laughing and it's contagious. The two of them crack up in the midst of what was, up until then, the most expensive "sandals and swords" epic ever, and it's surprisingly charming. Simmons began as a light comedienne in England but no sooner had she arrived in Hollywood than she was playing a murderess in *Angel Face* (1953). She spent most of her

CREDITS

Producer: Kirk Douglas/ Universal Pictures
Director: Stanley Kubrick
Screenplay: Dalton Trumbo, from the novel by Howard Fast
Running time: 198 minutes
Budget: $12 million
Box Office: $30 million

ACADEMY AWARDS

Best Supporting Actor: Peter Ustinov
Best Art Direction-Set Decoration, Color: Alexander Golitzen, Eric Orbom, Russell A. Gausman, Julia Heron
Best Cinematography, Color: Russell Metty
Best Costume Design, Color: Valles, Bill Thomas

NOMINATIONS

Best Editing: Robert Lawrence
Best Music, Scoring : Alex North

THE YEAR'S OTHER WINNERS

Best Picture: *The Apartment*
Best Director: Billy Wilder, *The Apartment*
Best Actor: Burt Lancaster, *Elmer Gantry*
Best Actress: Elizabeth Taylor, *Butterfield 8*
Best Supporting Actress: Shirley Jones, *Elmer Gantry*

THE OTHER LISTS

American Film Institute (Yes)
Roger Ebert's Top 100 (No)
Entertainment Weekly (No)
Internet Movie Database (No)
Leonard Maltin (No)
Movieline (No)
National Society of Film Critics (No)
Premiere Magazine (No)
Rolling Stone Magazine (No)
Village Voice (No)

"Spartacus! Spartacus!" The rise of the mighty slave king provides a thin strand of hope to those who didn't dare even to dream of it. Douglas's face and body, which seem carved from rock, suit the epic role perfectly.

Despite magnificent courage and cunning, the slave army led by Spartacus can't overcome the surprise three-flank attack of Crassus's Roman army. It's an outright slaughter and from the vast ravine of shattered bodies, only a few survivors emerge. Among them are Spartacus, his loyal Antoninus, and the remaining 6,000 of his brave, ragtag soldiers. Crassus is obsessed with wiping out the growing legend of Spartacus. He wants no trace left of him, not a song, not a poem, not a memory. To that end, he wants him to die horribly in disgrace as an example to others. Having never seen his nemesis, he must rely on his followers to denounce him. "Point out Spartacus to me and you will all be spared!" Spartacus is about to step forward, eager to sacrifice himself for the sake of the others. But before he can, his beloved cohorts, one after the other, shout "I am Spartacus! I am Spartacus! I am Spartacus!" Spartacus is overwhelmed by their profound display of loyalty. Crassus is not so well disposed. His bitter command to his men: "Crucify them all!"

early career in period costume, in *Androcles and the Lion* (1952), *The Robe* (1953), *The Egyptian* (1954), and *Desiree* (1954), before breaking into song in *Guys and Dolls* (1955). In David Lean's *Great Expectations* (1946), she played a harshly beautiful young Estella. In the 1989 TV remake, she'd come full circle to the role of Miss Havisham.

Peter Ustinov won the only acting Oscar for *Spartacus* and it's not difficult to see why he was so honored. As Batiatus, the irascible slave trader and sly survivor of treacherous Roman politics, he's got some of the best lines in the film. He addresses his gladiator recruits with "Good luck and may fortune smile on . . . *most* of you." When trapped by Crassus behind enemy lines for the duration of the war, he protests, "I'm a *civilian*! I'm more of a civilian than most civilians!" He won another Best Supporting Oscar just four years later for *Topkapi*, but his talents also included screenwriting and directing: His most famous directorial effort was *Romanoff and Juliet* (1961). He rewrote several of Trumbo's Charles Laughton scenes in *Spartacus*.

"You can't direct a **Charles Laughton** picture. All you can hope for is to referee," commented Alfred Hitchcock. The legendary star of *The Private Life of Henry VIII* (1933), *Mutiny on the Bounty* (1935), *The Hunchback of Notre Dame* (1939), and *Witness for the Prosecution* (1957) spends most of his screen time here in scenes with the handsome but less-than-likely Caesar of John Gavin. Laughton, as the womanizing Senator Gracchus, pulled more than enough acting weight for both of them. He appeared to enjoy his witty sparring with Ustinov most, and one of his best speeches emerged from a scene of theirs, most probably written by Ustinov himself: "You and I have a tendency towards corpulence. Corpulence makes a man reasonable, pleasant, and phlegmatic. Have you noticed the nastiest of tyrants are invariably thin?"

Tony Curtis began his career as a teen idol in such fare as *I Was a Shoplifter* (1950), but he quickly stepped up in class with the title role in *Houdini* (1954). He proved his acting chops in *Sweet Smell of Success* (1957) and was more than ready for his closeup in his signature film, *Some Like It Hot* (1959). (For more on Curtis, see page 48.)

THE SET

The exteriors of Crassus's home were shot at the fabled Hearst Castle in San Simeon, California.

THE MUSIC

The elaborate *Spartacus* score was composed by Oscar-winner Alex North, whose film career was launched with *A Streetcar Named Desire* (1951). His jazz score for that one was so heated, the Legion of Decency demanded the omission of a "much too carnal" solo saxophone.

SEND IN THE CLONES

Gladiator (2000)

NOTABLE QUOTES

"I act in films for free. They pay me to wait." —Sir Laurence Olivier

THE CRITICS

"A mighty tale told large." —*Life Magazine*

"In the same giant class as *Ben-Hur*." —*New York Post*

"Heroic humbug—a vast, panoramic display of synthetic Rome . . . bursting with patriotic fervor, bloody tragedy, a lot of romantic fiddle-faddle, and historical inaccuracy. Also, it is pitched about to the level of a lusty schoolboy's taste." —Bosley Crowther, *New York Times*

ROLE REVERSALS

Ingrid Bergman and Jeanne Moreau passed on the chance to play the beauteous slave, Varinia.

BEHIND THE SCREEN

In order to attract so many big names to small roles, Kirk Douglas gave each a different script that accentuated their characters.

The roar of the slave army, more than 8,500 Spanish extras, was dubbed by the cheering section of Michigan State's "Spartans."

The Legion of Decency struck out not only the Olivier/Curtis bath sequence, but the final moment of the film, in which Varinia begs Spartacus to die quickly.

Marcus Crassus teaches the new bath slave Antoninus all about oysters and snails and where to find the towels marked His and His.

94

THE MANCHURIAN CANDIDATE 1962

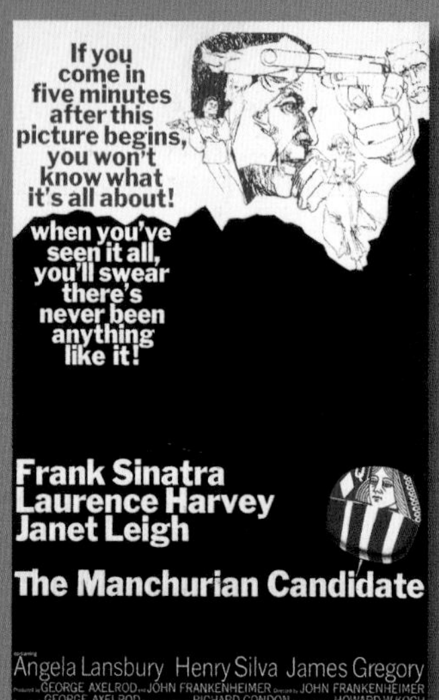

If you come in five minutes after this picture begins, you won't know what it's all about!
when you've seen it all, you'll swear there's never been anything like it!
Frank Sinatra
Laurence Harvey
Janet Leigh
The Manchurian Candidate
Angela Lansbury Henry Silva James Gregory

THE PLOT

Army Captain Raymond Shaw (Laurence Harvey) returns a hero from a Korean prisoner-of-war camp but the members of his unit can't recall exactly what he did that earned him a Purple Heart. It's only when two of them begin to have recurring nightmares about brainwashing sessions that they suspect Shaw has been transformed into a Communist mole, a sleeping assassin. One of them, Major Bennett Marco (Frank Sinatra), heads up an investigation that reveals an elaborate political conspiracy concocted by Shaw's own remarkably wicked mother (Angela Lansbury). Her aim is to get her moronic Senator husband (James Gregory) nominated to the Vice Presidency by whipping up anti-Communist fervor—in fact, she's the true Communist mole. By showing her son a particular playing card, the queen of hearts, she can set off his "killer program." Just when Raymond has found happiness with the girl of his dreams (Leslie Parrish), Mama intrudes and the slaughter begins. But she'd better take care. Thanks to Marco's tinkering, her son's program may have developed an unexpected glitch.

EERIE PREMONITION

A Soviet sleeper agent, high-powered rifle in hand, perches in a small window high above the cheering crowd. In his sights, he's got a popular presidential candidate. Cut and print! Almost precisely a year later, there's an all-too-real replay in Dallas. *The Manchurian Candidate* wasn't merely prescient. Its vehement attack on McCarthyism scared Hollywood to death at a time when the blacklist still had a stranglehold on the industry. John Frankenheimer pushed the stakes higher by casting a black actor in a non-racially defined role. And, just for the hell of it, he directed the first karate fight in an American-made film. JFK was eager to see Richard Condon's novel adapted for the screen and asked his party-time cohort, Sinatra, "Who's playing the mother?" If it had been up to Frank, one of the nastiest females in movie history would've been played by Lucille Ball. Luckily, Angela Lansbury tested meaner. Much, much meaner. The argument has been made that Lee Harvey Oswald was inspired by Laurence Harvey's indelibly creepy performance. Harvey . . . Harvey, hmm. Conspiracy theorists, start your engines.

Jim: North Korean brainwashers in the guise of the New Jersey Ladies Gardening Society—just in case you were looking for one good reason to see this.

Gail: The dearth of sophisticated political satire coming from Hollywood is made all the more apparent by the impact of this wildly penetrating thriller. A singular sensation.

"His brain has not only been washed, as they say, it's been dry-cleaned," quips Raymond Shaw's North Korean torturer. Without a thought Shaw fires point-blank at one of his own men. Laurence Harvey's angular, inexpressive face served his character particularly well.

THE DIRECTOR

A veteran of early black-and-white TV, **John Frankenheimer** was a master of deep focus, or as he put it, "the big-head-in-the-foreground shot." He believed *The Manchurian Candidate* was his most successful work and attributed it to the exceptional source material, Richard Condon's novel. Frankenheimer had to fudge or omit certain aspects due to censorship. He could only suggest, for example, the incestuous mother-son relationship with a kiss on the lips, rather than portraying the book's full-out seduction. Frankenheimer specialized in dark thrillers, preferably with political undertones. Among his best are *Seven Days in May* (1964), *Black Sunday* (1977), and *The Holcroft Covenant* (1985).

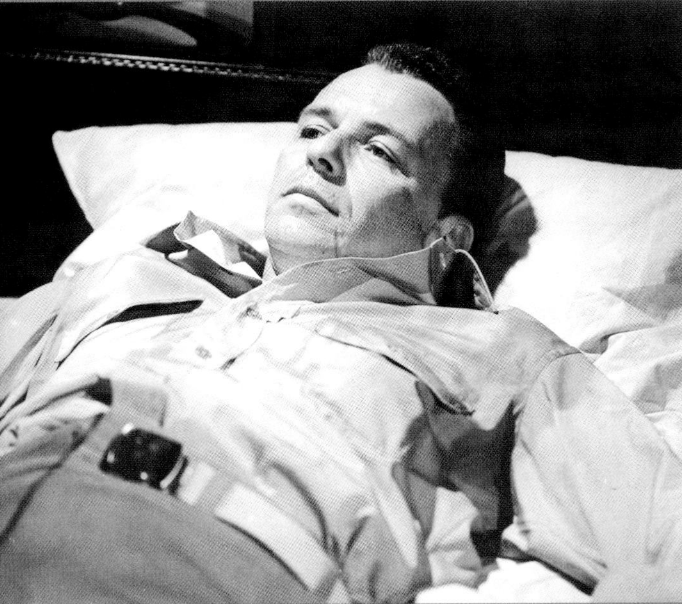

Marco has been programmed to respond, "Raymond Shaw is the kindest, bravest, warmest, most wonderful human being I've ever known in my life." The joke is that Shaw is one of the most unlikable men he's ever met. Sinatra considered this the greatest role of his career. Without his involvement, the movie would never have been made.

THE CAST

Major Bennett Marco	Frank Sinatra
Raymond Shaw	Laurence Harvey
Rosie Chaney	Janet Leigh
Mrs. Iselin	Angela Lansbury
Chunjin	Henry Silva
Senator John Iselin	James Gregory
Jocie Jordan	Leslie Parrish
Senator Thomas Jordan	John McGiver
Dr. Yen Lo	Khigh Dhiegh
Corporal Alvin Melvin	James Edwards
Colonel Milt	Douglas Henderson
Zilkov	Albert Paulsen
Secretary of Defense	Barry Kelley
Holborn Gaines	Lloyd Corrigan
Female Berezovo	Madame Spivy

THE ACTORS

Frankenheimer wasn't concerned by **Laurence Harvey**'s British accent, given the oddly un-American, Harvard-y Boston accent of JFK. With a long career as an ice-cold cad (*Darling*, *Butterfield 8*), Harvey was probably best known for his patrician bone structure. Costars of his films were apt to spout a recurring bit of dialogue: "I don't like you." It comes up in *The Manchurian Candidate* more than once. A high point of his performance here is a wonderfully wry monologue about "being unlovable." He made his first big splash in America with an Oscar nomination for *Room at the Top* (1959). Among his other major credits are *A Walk on the Wild Side* (1962), *Of Human Bondage* (1964), and *The Magic Christian* (1969).

Frank Sinatra was known in the business as "one-take Frank." But not, according to Frankenheimer, because he refused to do more. "He was always just better in the first take. He came to the role so complete, so full." In the scene in which Sinatra's character, Marco, tries to deprogram Raymond, Sinatra's closeups were out of focus. Frankenheimer was devastated. Sinatra did the scene ten more times, none as good as the first. Finally, Frankenheimer decided to keep the poor quality shots in. Critics raved. It captured Raymond's hazy point of view perfectly. Sinatra's film career was sharply defined into two parts. His early years as a pop-singing-phenomenon-turned-star included such fare as *The Kissing Bandit* and *On The Town* (both 1949). Then, the crash caused by the brief loss of his singing voice, traumatic divorces, marriages, and breakups, led to his huge Oscar-winning comeback in *From Here to Eternity* (1953). From there on, he picked and chose whatever projects interested him, and the spectrum was exceptionally wide, from the sublime *Pal Joey* (1957) and *The Detective* (1968) to such paper-thin Rat Pack quickies as *Robin and the Seven Hoods* (1964).

Janet Leigh's downright weird dialogue, especially in the train pickup scene, is taken directly from Richard Condon's novel.

"Do you speak Arabic?" she asks Sergeant Marco.

"No."

"In other words, are you married?"

Critic Roger Ebert theorized that Leigh's character, Rosie, might also be a mole. To watch the film with that in mind answers a lot of questions, particularly her rush to seduce Marco. (For more on Leigh, see page 54.)

Angela Lansbury plays Harvey's mother, even though the actress was only three years his senior. Best known for her Broadway musicals (*Mame* and *Sweeney Todd*) and the upright goo of *Murder, She Wrote*, she was clearly in top form as a bitch (though always the supporting bitch—Hollywood didn't find her pretty enough for leads). Here, as the sinister Mrs. Iselin, she plays one of the great villainesses of film with such ease and relish you begin to suspect that the sweet Mrs. Teapot in *Beauty and the Beast* (1991) must have been the real stretch for her. Her film career started at top speed with an Oscar nomination for *Gaslight* (1944) and then again for *The Picture of Dorian Gray* (1945). In between she played Elizabeth Taylor's older sister in *National Velvet* (1944). She's unforgettable in *The Long Hot Summer* (1958), *The World of Henry Orient* (1964), and *Death on the Nile* (1978).

THE CRITICS

"It may be the most sophisticated political satire ever made in Hollywood."
—Pauline Kael, *The New Yorker*

"With the air full of international tension, the film *The Manchurian Candidate* pops up with a rash supposition that could serve to scare

CREDITS

Producer: John Frankenheimer, George Axelrod/UA
Director: John Frankenheimer
Screenplay: George Axelrod
Running time: 126 minutes

ACADEMY AWARD NOMINATIONS

Best Supporting Actress: Angela Lansbury
Best Film Editing: Ferris Webster

THE YEAR'S WINNERS

Best Picture: *Lawrence of Arabia*
Best Actor: Gregory Peck, *To Kill a Mockingbird*
Best Actress: Anne Bancroft, *The Miracle Worker*
Best Supporting Actor: Ed Begley, *Sweet Bird of Youth*
Best Supporting Actress: Patty Duke, *The Miracle Worker*

THE OTHER LISTS

American Film Institute (No)
Roger Ebert's Top 100 (No)
Entertainment Weekly (Yes)
Internet Movie Database (Yes)
Leonard Maltin (No)
Movieline (Yes)
National Society of Film Critics (No)
Premiere Magazine (Yes)
Rolling Stone Magazine (Yes)
Village Voice (No)

“Raymond, why don’t you pass the time by playing a little solitaire?” The sight of the queen of diamonds will transform Raymond into his mother’s slave assassin. Director Frankenheimer was in awe of Lansbury’s work. He thought her climactic collapse was the best “fall” he’d ever seen.

some viewers half to death—that is, if they should be dupes enough to believe it, which we solemnly trust they won’t.”
—Bosley Crowther, *New York Times*

BEHIND THE SCREEN

It was suggested for years that *The Manchurian Candidate* was pulled out of circulation as a gesture of respect to the Kennedys after the assassination. Not true. It was pulled because Sinatra, a major player in the production, suspected UA of cooking the books to withhold profit-sharing.

Due to its vehemently anti-Communist subject matter, the film was not released in Eastern Bloc countries until the collapse of the Soviet Union in 1993.

In the karate scene, when Sinatra smashes the coffee table with his hand, that grimace of pain isn’t acting. He broke a finger that never completely healed.

In keeping with Sinatra’s disdain for more than one take per shot, he turned down the movie version of *Carousel* (1956) when he learned that they were going to shoot each scene twice using various lens sizes. “I was paid to make one movie, not two,” he said.

Raymond is under the sway of the queen of diamonds playing card; he can’t clear his brainwashed mind. He walks into his father-in-law’s townhouse and politely reaches into his jacket pocket while Jordan is fixing a late night snack.

Jordan: What’s that in your hand, Raymond?
Raymond: Why, it’s a pistol, sir.
Jordan: Is that a silencer?
Raymond: Yes, sir, it is.

A bullet bursts through the carton of milk Jordan is holding and into his heart. Jocelyn rushes in just as Raymond delivers a coup de grace to the head.

Jocelyn: Raymond, what have you done!

He turns the gun on her and fires, then sleepwalks over her beautiful, stunned corpse and out the door.

95

THE SEVEN SAMURAI 1954

A GENRE IS BORN

If the Roman bridge could be said to be the form on which all bridges are based, then likewise *The Seven Samurai* might to be the foundation for the heist, caper, or action-adventure movie. In these films, as in *Samurai*, a group of men is carefully hand-picked—think *The Dirty Dozen, The Magnificent Seven*, to mention only two—to carry out a mission; much time is spent assembling the team, during which we come to know and care about each individual. Kurosawa did it first, and he did it not only dramatically but with great attention to character, making the people more central to the film than the actual events. Takashi Shimura, his head shaved so that he looks like a priest, plays the wise, reliable leader who keeps his crew in line and always knows under which bush a bandit will be hiding. His gesture of rubbing his hand through the bristles of his hair becomes symbolic of his thoughtfulness. At the other end of the spectrum is the rambunctious, renegade Kikuchiyo (Toshiro Mifune), a show-off whose feral jumps and gestures betray his humble beginnings. Though Kikuchiyo's pretense at being of Samurai origin should doom him to failure to join the men, he is taken on for his abundant skills. *The Seven Samurai* is also an exquisitely composed film, made with a kind of poetry overlaying the action. Every frame of the film is assembled like a still photograph with deliberate placement of figures and landscape. Every action scene has grace and communicates the traditional values of honor, courage, honesty, and loyalty. And when people move, they move in tides, creating waves of action. Long shots show men on horseback moving against the horizon or riding down a hill in stunning choreography. Like Orson Welles and Jean Renoir, Kurosawa made great use of deep focus, in which the action that takes place in the foreground, middleground, and background carry equal and shifting weight, and enrich the story. Simply put, there's not a frame of footage in this more than three-hour film that has not been carefully constructed. Yes, this is a Japanese "Western" about good guys protecting innocent farmers in the 16th century, but it is so much more; it is one of the most striking and important films ever made.

Jim: Less than a decade after Hiroshima, this genius Japanese director exported the inspiration for our contemporary Western—*The Magnificent Seven*. Its rousing theme music by Elmer Bernstein sold ten billion packs of Marlboros, an ironic payback.

Gail: A feast for the eyes. No one knows how to utilize black-and-white motion picture film like Akira Kurosawa. Too bad his imitators turned to color when they tried—but failed—to duplicate it in the U.S.

IE PLOT

ed on a historical legend of 16th-century in, a time and place of civil war and rder, the story is set in a small village run by a band of roving bandits. In one ated village, a young man comes forward among his suffering neighbors with a . Though the Samurai are considered to bandits themselves (they are mercenary iors, more specifically), Rikichi (Yoshio hiya) suggests that the villagers hire urai to protect them against the bandits are stealing their crops. He knows the urai will protect them out of a sense of or. The next harvest is approaching and, ainly, the bandits will return to loot n. Six Samurai are chosen and soon e the city for the peasant village. Along way they encounter a seemingly crazed rambunctious warrior, Kikuchiyo hiro Mifune), who flaunts his huge d, swaggers, and tells them tales of his ries as a Samurai warrior. They know he t a real Samurai, but they take him into ranks as their seventh member. seven Samurai return to the village, arm villagers with bamboo spears, and teach how to fight. They build a fortress of es around the village, barricade the road, wait for the bandits—who appear on cue. time they are overcome by the villagers the Samurai—between whom there is an air of mistrust. A subplot tells a eo-and-Juliet story of the love affair een one of the warriors, Katsushiro, and laughter of one of the farmers.

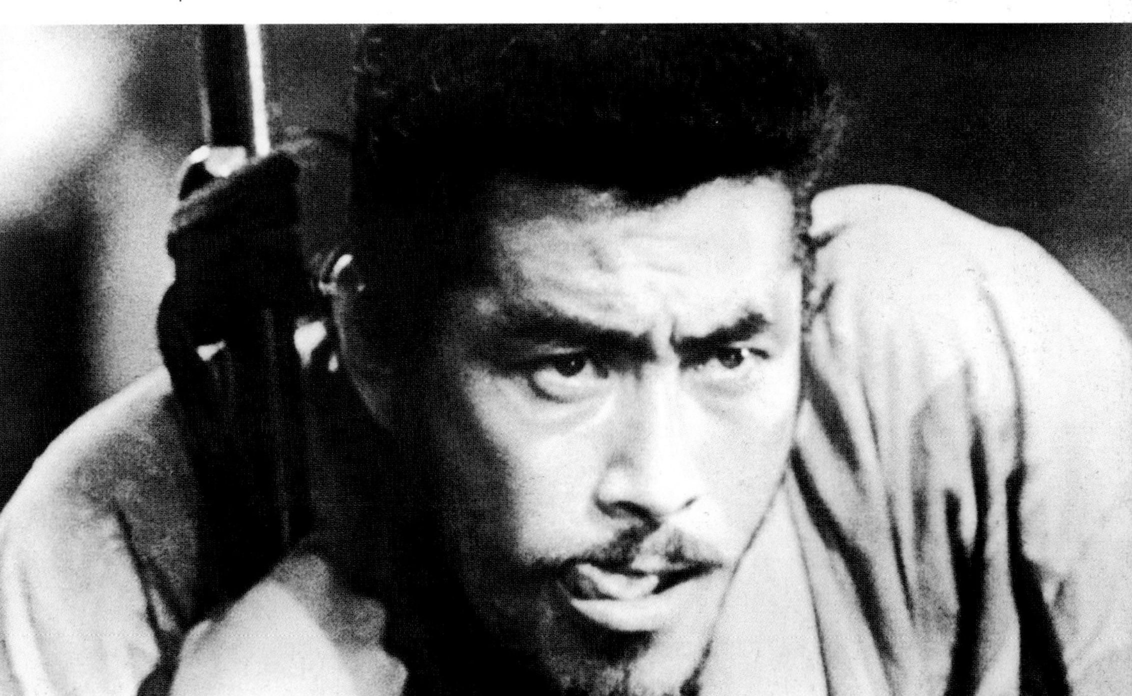

Kikuchiyo (Toshiro Mifune), the rambunctious show-off, is welcomed into the group of Samurai, though he was not born to be one, when he demonstrates his prodigious talents as a warrior.

"What do you think of farmers? You think they're saints? Hah! They're foxy beasts! They say, 'We've got no rice, we've no wheat. We've got nothing!' But they have! They have everything! Dig under the floors! Or search the barns! You'll find plenty! Beans, salt, rice, cake!"—Kambei Shimada

THE DIRECTOR

Long considered the most Western of great Japanese directors—though the performances of his actors borrowed much from traditional Japanese Kabuki—**Akira Kurosawa** had great impact on the American Western and action-adventure film. It has been said that *The Seven Samurai* represents a turning point from his earlier work in which the group, and team effort, represented the highest good. The later work emphasized the individual, as do most American films. Before becoming a filmmaker Kurosawa was trained as a painter, which explains his strong compositions and the great visual impact of his films. He gained world acclaim after his film *Rashomon* won the top prize at the Venice Film Festival, at which point Kurosawa became more popular in the West than in his native Japan. *The Seven Samurai* is considered one of the greatest works in all of film history. (For more on Kurosawa, see page 259.)

Seven Samurai are hired to protect a small farming village against the bandits (seen here on horseback) who roam the countryside looking for the spoils of the harvest.

THE CAST

Kambei Shimada	Takashi Shimura
Kikuchiyo	Toshiro Mifune
Gorobei Katayama	Yoshio Inaba
Kyuzo	Seiji Miyaguchi
Heihachi Hayashida	Minoru Chiaki
Shichiroji	Daisuke Kato
Katsushiro Okamoto	Isao Kimura
Shino	Keiko Tsushima
Rikichi's Wife	Yukiko Shimazaki
Manzo, father of Shino	Kamatari Fujiwara
Mosuke	Yoshio Kosugi
Yohei	Bokuzen Hidari
Rikichi	Yoshio Tsuchiya
Gisaku, the Old Man	Kokuten Kodo
Peasant	Jiro Kumagai

THE ACTORS

Playing the role of the Samurai who, disguised as a priest, saves a baby from a bandit, **Takashi Shimura** was one of the key actors in Kurosawa's repertory company. Shimura was actually a descendent of the warrior Samurai class, and he played many Samurai roles for the Japanese studios, appearing in six or more films per year. He was considered one of Japan's finest character actors. He is recognized outside of Japan for his role as the kindly doctor in the original *Godzilla* (*Gojira*,1954). (For more on Shimura, see page 259.)

The irrepressible **Toshiro Mifune** once again plays the role of the wild but courageous fighter, as he did in *Rashomon* (1950), with his usual athletic prowess and a voice that never falls below a yell, as if to scare off anything in hearing range. Mifune, who would become one of the most famous Japanese actors ever, was born to missionary parents working in China. In 1963, he formed his own production company, directed one film, and produced several others. In his later years, he gained wider fame in the title role of the American TV miniseries *Shogun* (1980), and appeared infrequently in cameo roles after that. George Lucas seriously considered Mifune for the role of Obi Wan Kenobi in *Star Wars* (1977) before settling on Alec Guinness. Mifune died in 1997. (For more on Mifune, see page 259.)

Isao Kimura plays the handsome and delicate young Samurai who, though he prefers lying among the daisies to fighting, neverthless wants to become a warrior. He also appeared in Kurosawa's *Stray Dog* (1949), released in the U.S. in 1963, *Ikiru* (1952), and *High and Low* (1963).

Keiki Tsushima plays Shono, the shy but amorous farm girl, and the forbidden lover of Samurai Katsushiro. She also appeared in Ozu's *Flavor of Green Tea Over Rice* (1952), released in the U.S. in 1964.

Seiji Miyaguchi, who plays the master swordsman, also appeared in Kurosawa's *Ikiru* (1952) and *The Bad Sleep Well* (1960), as well as the TV miniseries *Shogun* (1980).

KUROSAWA ON DIRECTING

"There is something that might be called cinematic beauty. It can only be expressed in a film, and it must be present in a film for that film to be a moving work. When it is very well expressed, one experiences a particularly deep emotion while watching that film. I believe it is this quality that draws people to come and see a film, and that it is the hope of attaining this quality that inspires the filmmaker to make his film in the first place. In other words, I believe that the essence of the cinema lies in cinematic beauty."

"In order to write great scripts, you must first study the great novels and dramas of the world. You must consider why they are great. Where does the emotion come from that you feel as you read them? What degree of passion did the author have to have, what level of meticulousness did he have to command, in order to portray the characters and events as he did? You must also see the great films. You must read great screenplays and study the film theories of the great directors. If your goal is to become a director, you must master screenwriting."

"During the shooting of a scene the director's eye has to catch even the minutest detail. But this does not mean glaring concentratedly at the set. While the cameras are rolling, I rarely look directly at the actors, but focus my gaze on it, but being aware of it in a natural

CREDITS

Studio: Toho Studios and Columbia Pictures
Producer: Director: Akira Kurosawa
Screenplay: Akira Kurosawa
Running Time: 207 minutes
Budget:

THE YEAR'S ACADEMY AWARD WINNERS

Picture: *On the Waterfront*
Director: Elia Kazan, *On the Waterfront*
Actor: Marlon Brando, *On the Waterfront*
Actress: Grace Kelly, *The Country Girl*
Supporting Actor: Edmond O'Brien, *The Barefoot Contessa*
Supporting Actress: Eva Maria Saint, *On the Waterfront*

THE OTHER LISTS

- American Film Institute (No)
- *Entertainment Weekly* (Yes)
- Internet Movie Database (Yes)
- Leonard Maltin (Yes)
- *Movieline* (No)
- *Premiere* Magazine (Yes)
- Roger Ebert's Top 100 (Yes)
- *Rolling Stone* Magazine (Yes)
- *The Village Voice* (Yes)

way. I believe this is what the medieval Noh playwright and theorist Zeami meant by "watching with a detached gaze."

THE CRITICS

"This three-and-a-half-hour epic of violence and action—Akira Kurosawa's masterpiece—has been widely imitated, but no one has come near it." —Pauline Kael, *The New Yorker*

"There are things about the picture to question and criticize. It is much too long for comfort or for the story it has to tell. The director is annoyingly repetitious. He shows so many shots of horse's feet tromping in the mud in the course of battle that you wonder if those horses have heads."—Bosley Crowther, *New York Times*

BEHIND THE SCREEN

Filming had to be stopped several times due to a shortage of horses for the battle sequences.

With careful filming and editing, Seiji Miyaguchi, who played the taciturn Samurai Kyuzo and who had never touched a sword before this film, was made to look like a master swordsman.

Toho Studios pulled the plug on the project several times when it ran over budget, forcing the director to go back personally and plead with the board of directors, who were convinced they were making a flop.

The character played by Toshiro Mifune has no name when he enters the story, and is given one by his companions.

A young farm girl soon loses her freshly washed hair, when her father cuts if all off so that she can pass as a boy. He fears that bandits will make off with her when they see her beauty.

Kurosawa used different theme music for each main character or group of characters.

THE GREAT SCENE

The high-spirited Kikuchiyo (Mifune), in his effort to prove himself a greater warrior than the rest, carries a longer sword than anybody, accumulates more weapons in battle, and tries to show his riding prowess when he barely knows how to mount. With all the of the Samurai and townspeople watching attentively, he struggles onto a bareback horse as if crawling up a mountain. He rides off out of control. At first, one of the other Samurai comments that Kikuchiyo seems to know what he is doing, given such a difficult horse. Soon horse and rider disappear behind a barn and emerge separately, the rider chasing after the horse brandishing his stick, screaming, "You fool! Damn you! You call yourself a horse! For shame! Hey! Wait! Please! I apologize! Forgive me!"

Thanks to the masterly eye of director Akira Kurosawa, every frame in *The Seven Samurai* appears composed like a painting or still photograph—even the tumultuous battle scenes in which the Samurai soundly thrash the bandits and save the isolated village (or what is left of it).

96

A HARD DAY'S NIGHT 1964

ALL YOU GOTTA DO IS ACT NATURALLY

A sustained chord, running, screaming, "and I've been working like a dog" . . . the thrill of the chase, Ringo's down! Fans weeping, lunging, JOHN! PAUL! WE LOVE YOU, GEORGE! To the train, quick! Out of the cars, down the back way, out into the field and fast, now, into the truly exhilarating circle of fame. There is a surprising sweetness and respectability to the boys from Liverpool, and a pure delight in the music. The gleaming young smiles, the shock of bottomless talent, the bad jokes. Money can't buy you love, you can bet on that. What it can buy you, for $500,000, is a first-time feature director, Richard Lester, with more imagination and curiosity than formal training. With his camera everywhere, up, down, in the crowd, in your face, he broke all the rules, and invented a genre. "I received a parchment that told me I was the father of MTV. I wrote back demanding a blood test." Cheeky. He was eternally young, just like the boys. Their essence was captured for all time in black-and-white and the bright pink light of undiluted joy.

Jim: They are like a pack of younger, cuter, musical Marx Brothers set loose in Swinging London. Suspicions confirmed: despite the tragedies and twists of their super-stardom, it must've been good to be a Beatle, very good.

Gail: I don't want to watch this movie, I want to be in it. Everybody is just having too much fun. Thank god Richard Lester hadn't made a movie before, because he might never have let himself—and the boys—go like this.

THE PLOT

A manic comedy of errors defines a single day in the life of England's most popular rock group. They're hounded by screaming fans in hot pursuit, uptight execs, and Paul's alleged granddad, who delights in stirring the pot. He singles out Ringo as the weak link and briefly convinces him to leave his pals and venture into the world alone. The hapless drummer winds up in police custody and John, Paul, and George rush off in a Keystone Kops rescue. They're reunited at last, the show goes on, and a new day dawns with another round of crazy possibilities.

The girls can't help it! The reaction of the teen audience in the film was almost tame compared to the first Beatles tour of America. At their concert at New York's Shea Stadium, the band could barely be heard above the mass hysteria.

Man on train: Don't take that tone with me, young man. I fought the war for your sort. Ringo: I bet you're sorry you won.

THE DIRECTOR

With a background in the quick-cut world of TV commercials and a brief directing stint on a zany *Monty Python* precursor, *The Goon Show*, **Richard Lester** came onto the project with no film training. He insists that his most noticeable asset at the time was his "exuberant amateurism." He wasn't sure how the film would finally look but he was adamant in his view that the Beatles appear natural, nothing more than themselves. To that end, he wanted to capture them in the widest range of moods and angles, thus the multi-camera approach: six rolling at all times. Trouble is, he didn't have six professional cameramen. Friends were enlisted and told to give it their best shot. In the end, theirs was the film primarily used. "A myth builds up that you knew what you were doing," he says. He broke all the rules simply because he didn't know what they were. *A Hard Day's Night* launched a busy career that never reached the height of his debut here. His followups included the Julie Christie vehicle, *Petulia* (1969), *The Three Musketeers* (1974), Audrey Hepburn's comeback film costarring Sean Connery, *Robin and Marian* (1976), *The Ritz* (1976), *Superman II* (1980), *and Superman III* (1983). "When people ask, what were the sixties like? I say, don't ask me. I was at the center of the universe."

Did anyone ever tell you, you look just like . . . ? John has a strange encounter with a woman backstage who thinks he might be somebody, then decides he couldn't possibly be. His wounded, confused expression as he walks away suggests he may be entirely in agreement with her.

THE CAST

John	John Lennon
Paul	Paul McCartney
George	George Harrison
Ringo	Ringo Starr
Paul's Grandfather	Wilfrid Brambell
Norm	Norman Rossington
Shake	John Junkin
TV Director	Victor Spinetti
Millie	Anna Quayle
Police Inspector	Deryck Guyler
Man on Train	Richard Vernon
Hotel Waiter	Edward Malin
TV Floor Manager	Robin Ray
TV Choreographer	Lionel Blair
Secretary	Alison Seebohm

THE ACTORS

The Beatles took on personae in the film, not necessarily true to who they were, that stuck for the rest of their careers.

John Lennon "The Bad Boy" "I don't mind talking to the camera—it's people that throw me. I don't want people taking things from me that aren't really me. They make you something that they want to make you, that isn't really you. We're not Beatles to each other, you know. It's a joke to us. If we're going out the door of the hotel, we say, 'Right! Beatle John! Beatle George now! Come on, let's go!' We don't put on a false front or anything. But we just know that leaving the door, we turn into Beatles because everybody looking at us sees the Beatles. We're not the Beatles at all. We're just us." The Beatle movies (including the documentary *Let It Be*) aside, Lennon made only one other significant on-screen appearance, as "Gripweed" in Richard Lester's *How I Won the War* (1967).

Paul McCartney "The Cute One" "Even the work, which was hard work, was still good fun because, you know, the film was a good laugh, mainly. I mean, even when we were sort of very tired and really knocked out, we'd do a thing, when we actually saw it on the screen it looked, sort of, quite fun. There was a sequence that I was going to do, and to this day whenever I go past the pub in Shepherd's Bush I remember going in with Ilsa Blair and filming on the second floor. She was supposed to be the object of my desire, or I was of hers. That was the idea behind this little scene-ette. I had to sort of wander around her with the camera going round and round in circles—all very sixties, all very French—and I had to repeat these very quirky lines. We had a whole day of doing that, but it didn't work because it wasn't the kind of thing we would have done in everyday life. It was all a little bit too contrived." Though considered the most telegenic member of the band, McCartney didn't pursue an acting career despite hundreds of TV appearances and even an animated guest spot on *The Simpsons* playing himself.

George Harrison "The Partyboy" "You mightn't have noticed. No, but—you know, we all go out at night. And then suddenly our day was reversed, so that we had to be up at six in the morning, but we still couldn't get the hang of going to bed at night. So we were going out at night AND getting up in the morning for the first week or so, and I just couldn't believe it. Six o'clock and somebody dragging me out of bed." Harrison can be spotted in a brief, uncredited cameo in Monty Python's *Life of Brian* (1979).

Ringo Starr "The Sad Sack" "Well, it was a hard two months. It took two months actually to make this film. But, umm, I think I found the biggest drag was when we were just sitting 'round doing nothing. The scene I got all the credit for was the walking by the canal with the camera—the lonely guy scene. That came about because I came to work, very unprofessionally, straight from a nightclub. And I was a little hung-over to say the least, you know. I was just so out of it so they said, 'Let's do anything.' So my version of it was 'Just let me walk around and film me.' And why I look so cold and dejected is because I felt like shit. So, no acting going on there." Starr had a successful, if brief, motion picture career, costarring in *Candy* (1968), *The Magic Christian* (1969), *200 Motels* (1971), *Lisztomania*—in which he played the Pope—(1975), *Sextette* (1978), and *Caveman*—in which he starred with his wife, Barbara Bach (1981).

THE MUSIC

"A Hard Day's Night"
"I Should Have Known Better"
"If I Fell"
"I'm Happy Just to Dance with You"
"And I Love Her"
"Tell Me Why"
"Can't Buy Me Love"

THE CRITICS

"The *Citizen Kane* of jukebox movies." —Andrew Sarris, *The Village Voice*

"All technology was enlisted in the service of the gag, and a kind of nuclear gagmanship exploded." —John Simon

CREDITS

Producer: Walter Shenson/UA
Director: Richard Lester
Screenplay: Alun Owen
Running time: 87 minutes
Budget: $560,000
Box Office: $11 million

ACADEMY AWARD NOMINATIONS

Best Original Screenplay: Alun Owen
Best Scoring of Music: George Martin

THE YEAR'S WINNERS

Best Picture: *My Fair Lady*
Best Director: George Cukor *My Fair Lady*
Best Actor: Rex Harrison, *My Fair Lady*
Best Actress: Julie Andrews, *Mary Poppins*
Best Supporting Actor: Peter Ustinov, *Topkapi*
Best Supporting Actress: Lila Kedrova, *Zorba the Greek*

BEHIND THE SCREEN

Never once is the word "Beatles" uttered in the film.

One of Ringo's asides inspired the film's title song, which John and Paul wrote overnight (presumably after a hard day).

Following an executive screening, it was strongly advised that the Beatles' voices should be dubbed and some of their songs shortened.

When presenting Paul McCartney with an Honorary Grammy, Meryl Streep confessed she'd been one of his screaming teenage fans at the Beatles' first American concert at New York's Shea Stadium. She blushingly admitted that she'd even held up a sign, "I love you, Paul!"

THE OTHER LISTS

- American Film Institute (No)
- Roger Ebert's Top 100 (Yes)
- *Entertainment Weekly* (No)
- Internet Movie Database (No)
- Leonard Maltin (No)
- *Movieline* (Yes)
- National Society of Film Critics (No)
- *Premiere* Magazine (No)
- *Rolling Stone* Magazine (No)
- *Village Voice* (No)

THE GREAT SCENE

It's the culmination of a long, breathless, hilarious adventure. The boys—finally—make it onto the set of a TV program in the nick of time and launch powerfully into a short concert of hits. The girls in the audience writhe in berserk ecstasy. The camera drops us right into the midst of their ear-splitting frenzy, then there's a quick cut to the control booth as images of the boys are displayed on several monitors, then back onto the live stage where John, Paul, George, and Ringo sweat, rock on, and revel in their sudden fame like lottery winners.

BELOW: Paul's mischievous Granddad (we think that's who he is but we're never quite sure) convinces Ringo to put down his book and live, live, live! Poor Ringo only manages to get lost, get knocked over by a stray inner tube, and get arrested.

It's Mrs. Harrison's bouncing boy! George admitted, along with John, Paul, and Ringo, that the scene in which they simply jumped around in an open field, was the most enjoyable to do.

97

ATLANTIC CITY 1980

TERRIFIC ODDS

The high point of his day is peeping through the blinds to watch a beautiful neighbor bathe her breasts with lemons. He's a dirty old man, forced to steal cigarettes and iron the same worn-out tie every day. You wonder how a man could fall so low. Soon enough, you begin to see that Lou Paschall, as inhabited by Burt Lancaster, was never up to begin with. He's a handsome old loser still waiting to catch the brass ring, still believing there is such a thing. When a veteran screen icon gives the performance of his career, you hope that the film in question is worthy of it. Louis Malle's *Atlantic City* is a confluence of minor miracles that include a wildly funny, offbeat script by Tony-winning playwright John Guare and perfectly cast supporting players. When a ditzy young pregnant woman prone to New Age mind-control scoffs at the idea of using seat belts ("I don't believe in gravity"), you rightly suspect you're in for a good time. Even Atlantic City itself lends a hand. The production was shot simultaneous to its grand-scale destruction/construction boom. The squalid grandeur of what was once America's most elegant ocean resort is being blasted out of existence to make way for the encroaching glitter-built casinos. In the center of all this is Burt Lancaster, years past his prime as a Hollywood stud, as Lou, a mobster wannabe who looks the part but has never quite had the heart for it. The closest he got to the big time was sharing a drunk-tank with Bugsy Siegel for ten minutes. And as Lancaster so brilliantly shows us, it takes a poetic heart to transform that ten minutes into an elaborate fabrication lasting a lifetime.

Jim: A bombastic drill-sergeant of an actor, Lancaster could hardly be accused of nuance. But this performance is a revelation of grace notes. The look on his face as he watches helplessly as his dream girl is roughed up by mobsters, well, it's like a compacted history of every man's humiliation from the beginning of time. It's one moment like that after another. The Oscar that year went to Henry Fonda. Yeah, sure, he'd never gotten one and he was sick—but come on!

Gail: There could be no grander exit for the Birdman of Alcatraz than in the achingly mortal role of Lou Paschall, a never-been has-been.

[TH]E PLOT

[Lou] Paschall (Burt Lancaster) makes his [en]ds as a numbers runner. After a lifetime [ov]er as a mob flunky, he lives in a shabby [apar]tment upstairs from bed-ridden Grace [(Kat]e Reid), widow of his late boss. She rings [a bel]l to summon him for chores and sex. He [can o]nly get excited by thinking of the girl [acro]ss the hall, Sally Matthews (Susan [Sara]ndon). She is studying to become a [dea]ler, until her scumbag husband Dave [(Rob]ert Joy), shows up with her sister, Chrissie [(Holli]s McLaren), now pregnant by him. He's [stole]n cocaine from the mob—and they are in [hot p]ursuit. Desperate to make local connec[tions], he hooks up with Lou who makes a [deliv]ery for him. Dave is killed and Lou suddenly [finds] himself with $4,000. For the first time [in hi]s life he feels like a bigshot and endears [hims]elf to Sally by taking care of Dave's funer[al ex]penses. Grateful, she sleeps with him. But [the m]ob thugs track them down and beat her [for in]formation. Lou is humiliated that he can't [com]e to her rescue, and packs his bags. She [finall]y catches up with him and demands her [share] of the cash. The mobsters corner them [but th]is time Lou shoots them down. He's [elat]ed as he and Sally drive off to a motel [on th]e outskirts to celebrate. Lou spies her [takin]g the money and lets her go. He returns [to Gr]ace who assists in one last drug deal.

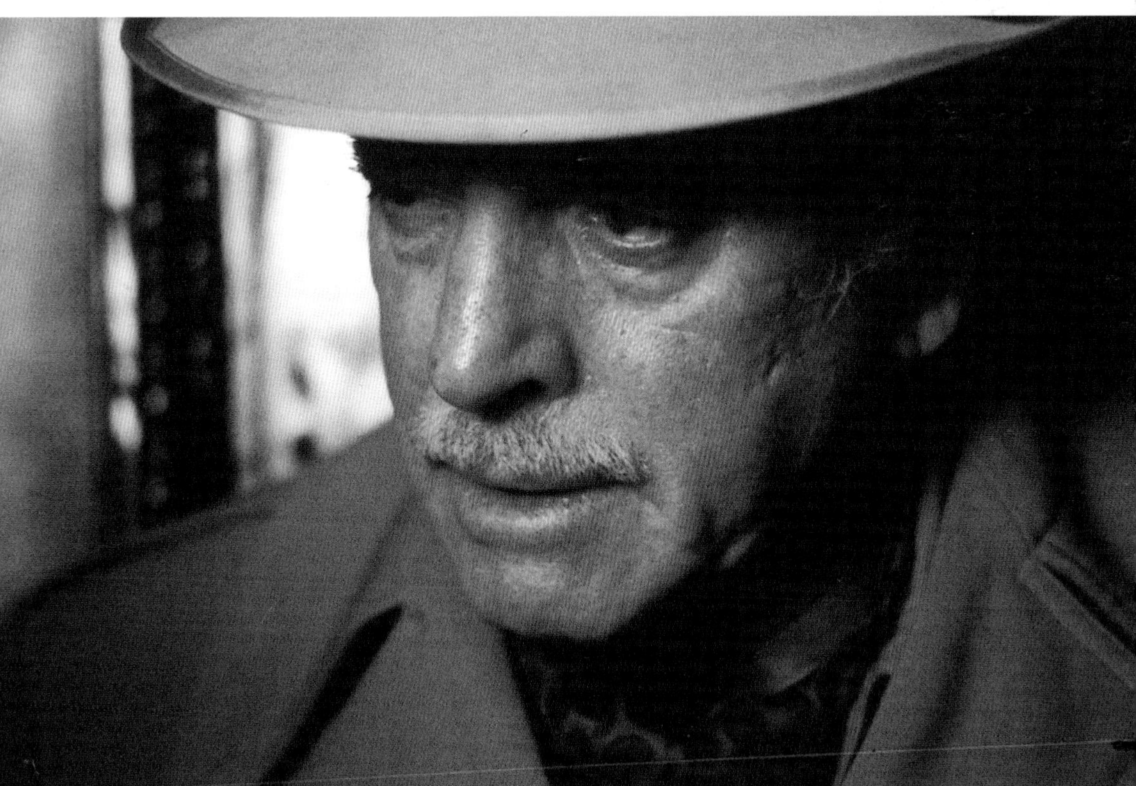

"Tits and sand—that's what we used to call sex and violence in Hollywood." Burt Lancaster was nothing if not forthright. The son of a New York City postal worker, he joined the circus and from there, went on to Broadway and the movies. His life was like a delusion his character Lou would've dreamed up.

THE DIRECTOR

Scion of one of the great family fortunes of France, **Louis Malle** got an unusual start as an underwater cameraman for Jacques Cousteau. As a fledgling auteur of New Wave cinema, his sexually explicit early features were harbingers of a career that would always be greeted with strong, not always friendly reactions. *Les Amonts* (1958) starring Jeanne Moreau, resulted in an obscenity trial in the U.S. after an Ohio theater was barred from showing it. The Supreme Court decision found in favor of the theater (and the film) with Justice Brennan's famous ruling that "to be obscene a film must be utterly without social importance." Malle once said that he "liked spectators to be disturbed." That was certainly the case with *Murmur of the Heart* (1971), an oddly charming shocker about incest. His two other most famous French films are *Lacombe, Lucien* (1974) and *Au Revoir, les Enfants* (1987), which was based on a traumatic incident from his own childhood involving a Jewish friend in hiding. He made his American debut with *Pretty Baby* (1978), featuring 12-year-old newcomer Brooke Shields as a child of a prostitute, living in a New Orleans bordello at the turn-of-the-century, happily awaiting the auctioning of her virginity to the highest bidder. Following *Atlantic City* came the offbeat but very successful *My Dinner with Andre* (1981) and *Vanya on 42nd Street* (1994). He was married to Candice Bergen at the time of his death in 1995.

When you're stuck with lemons, make lemonade. Here, Susan Sarandon delivers the most provocative scene with citrus ever filmed.

THE CAST	
Lou Paschall	Burt Lancaster
Sally Matthews	Susan Sarandon
Grace	Kate Reid
Joseph	Michel Piccoli
Chrissie	Hollis McLaren
Dave Matthews	Robert Joy
Alfie	Al Waxman
Robert Goulet	Himself

THE ACTORS

Early in his career, **Burt Lancaster** vowed, "I'm going to be the one guy who won't let Hollywood rot his soul." Whatever the outcome, Lancaster made the movies a much more lucrative place for his fellow actors and directors. He invented the percentage-sharing system whereby stars forego large salaries for a piece of the gross profits. His reputation as "difficult" didn't hurt his career a whit. He started off quite literally with a bang in *The Killers* (1946) and never looked back at his origins as a trapeze artist and occasional lingerie salesman. With each role, his image grew in stature from *From Here to Eternity* (1953) to his Oscar-winning role as the evangelist in *Elmer Gantry* (1960) and a prisoner in *Birdman of Alcatraz* (1962) to his crowning achievement here in *Atlantic City*, for which he was Oscar-nominated. Along with pioneering stars like Kirk Douglas, Lancaster very early on formed his own production company and in 1955, struck gold with his "little picture" *Marty*, which began as a tax write-off and wound up sweeping that year's Academy Awards.

"I think the only reason I remain an actor is that you can never get it quite right, " admits **Susan Sarandon**. But the facts of her career suggest otherwise. Her soap opera start on *Search for Tomorrow* (1972) led to the role of the singing bimbo in the cult phenom *The Rocky Horror Picture Show* (1975). From there, it was a major jump to the ultra-liberated baseball groupie of *Bull Durham* (1988), a film that made her a household name and led her to build a household of her own with costar Tim Robbins. Together they share a fervent political activism that's gotten her briefly arrested and earned her a reputation as the Jane Fonda of her generation. Her anti-Establishment image was forever sealed by her role as the FBI's Most Wanted housewife in *Thelma and Louise* (1991). She won an Oscar for *Dead Man Walking* (1995) but *Atlantic City* earned her a debut nomination and caused critics to take her seriously for the first time. Subsequent films include *Thelma and Louise* (1991), *Alfie* (2004), and *Enchanted* (2007).

British-born **Kate Reid** was one of the shining lights of the stage, having appeared in original productions of plays by Edward Albee and Tennessee Williams. She played Linda Loman in a TV version of Arthur Miller's *Death of a Salesman* but appeared in only a handful of films, including *This Property Is Condemned* (1966) and *Equus* (1977). Fans of the series, *Dallas* may remember her as Lil Trotter.

Robert Joy admits that his movie debut working alongside a veteran like Lancaster might have been daunting. "Burt took a mentor-like approach. His presence was genteel, he'd hold doors open and light everyone's cigarettes." Joy's death chase scene through the parking lot contraption took four months before completion. Joy recalls a great fuss made over Lancaster's classic line, "You should have seen the Atlantic Ocean in those days." The producers felt it made his character look stupid and wanted it out. Lancaster, Malle, and Guare argued vehemently and obviously won. Following *Atlantic City*, Joy appeared in *Ragtime* (1981), *Desperately Seeking Susan* (1985), *Radio Days* (1987), *Longtime Companion* (1990), *Waterworld* (1995), the mini-series *Nuremberg* (1998), and *The Shipping News* (2001).

BEHIND THE SCREEN

Louis Malle and Susan Sarandon were lovers during the making of *Atlantic City*.

Michel LeGrand wrote a score for the film that was never used.

Wallace Shawn, in a cameo as a hovering, slightly sour waiter with only a couple of inconsequential lines, would later appear as Andre Gregory's very talkative dining companion in Malle's *My Dinner with Andre* (1981).

THE SET

Shot entirely on location in Atlantic City, Malle's timing was fortunate. Many of the key scenes were played against a backdrop of major demolition and construction that fit eloquently into the storyline. The last shot of the film is particularly impressive. Burt Lancaster and Kate Reid, having found some new hope for

CREDITS

Producer: Denis Heroux/
Paramount Pictures
Director: Louis Malle
Screenplay: John Guare
Running Time: 104 minutes
Budget: $7.2 million
Box office: $13 million

ACADEMY AWARD NOMINATIONS

Best Picture
Best Director: Louis Malle
Best Actor: Burt Lancaster
Best Actress: Susan Sarandon
Best Original Screenplay:
John Guare

THE YEAR'S WINNERS

Best Picture: *Chariots of Fire*
Best Director: Warren Beatty, *Reds*
Best Actor: Henry Fonda,
On Golden Pond
Best Actress: Katharine Hepburn,
On Golden Pond
Best Supporting Actor:
John Gielgud, *Arthur*
Best Supporting Actress:
Maureen Stapleton, *Reds*

Dire circumstances compel Sally to throw in her lot with Lou. It's a roll of the dice as to whether they can outwit the mob and live long enough to enjoy the spoils.

THE GREAT SCENE

Cops track Sally down at the casino's oyster bar after finding her stolen wallet in Dave's pocket. He's lying near death in the Intensive Care Unit, having been brutally stabbed in the gut by mob soldiers in search of a stolen cache of cocaine. She's asked to come with them to the hospital at once, hoping she might get some necessary information out of him. In a state of shock, Sally is led through the reception lobby which is all tricked out for a celebration of the new Frank Sinatra Wing. Robert Goulet sings a loungy tribute to Atlantic City, written by Paul Anka, as medical staffers and patients in their gowns, swoon appropriately. Sally and her police escort barely notice, even as news photographers flash away at the absurdly cheesy proceedings. She arrives at Dave's bedside just as he breathes his last. He's covered over with a sheet and she's left to her own devices. Numb, unable to figure what to do next (this has all happened too fast), she attempts to make a collect call to his less-than-caring family back in Moosejaw, Saskatchewan. The phone booth is in the lobby and as she tries to relay the news that their son is dead, the singing Goulet serenades her through the glass. She can't even begin to make sense of any of this. Unable to cry, and far from finding it funny, all she can do is blink and wonder if maybe this sort of thing is the norm in Atlantic City. For some, perhaps it is.

their faded lives, promenade down the boardwalk with great style. Despite their ages and circumstances, they seem for the moment indestructible and forever young. Just behind them, a wrecking ball is trying its damnedest to knock down one of the grand old buildings. But the Gilded Age structure won't budge. All through the final credits we watch that ball getting no further than a lovely window frame or two. A perfect allegory for Burt and Kate. What a way to say, "We aren't letting go, either."

THE WRITER

Louis Malle credits screenwriter John Guare's gift for "exposing these grandiose lies of ours." Guare does this in his plays and films through absurdist exaggeration because, he says, "the chaotic state of the world demands it." His first important play, the darkly comic *House of Blue Leaves* (1971), caused a sensation on Broadway. He was similarly lauded for such plays as *Rich and Famous* (1974), *Bosoms and Neglect* (1977), and probably his best known work, *Six Degrees of Separation* (1991), which was later adapted for the screen. Yet Guare, with typical self-deprecation, has been known to refer to himself as "the world's oldest promising young playwright."

THE CRITICS

"This picture has just about everything. When you leave the theatre, you may feel light-headed, as if there were no problems in the world that couldn't be solved."—Pauline Kael, *The New Yorker*

"Malle's Atlantic City is a place of myth, of legends and dreams, most of them pretty tacky." —Vincent Canby, *New York Times*

THE OTHER LISTS

- American Film Institute (No)
- Roger Ebert's Top 100 (No)
- *Entertainment Weekly* (No)
- Internet Movie Database (No)
- Leonard Maltin (No)
- *Movieline* (No)
- National Society of Film Critics (Yes)
- *Premiere* Magazine (No)
- *Rolling Stone* Magazine (No)
- *Village Voice* (No)

Obsequious Lou maintains a small shred of dignity as he caters to the outlandish, petty requests of Grace (Kate Reid), the widow of Lou's former boss. She keeps him in cigarette money and, in exchange, he allows her to think she's still the greatest Betty Grable lookalike of them all.

98

AMERICAN BEAUTY 1999

NO BED OF ROSES

Deftly handled, remarkable, unexpected, there is so much beauty in this comic, pointedly cliché-ridden portrait of the turmoil that underlies the surface smoothness of the suburban American Dream that we, like one of its characters, can hardly breathe. But haven't we seen all these suburban lives of quiet desperation before? Yes, we have seen it all before, but not like this. In this film, we both abhor and care for a middle-aged father who fails at being "the man" and looks for solace and renewal in the teenage wet dream that is his daughter's best friend. We laugh at and feel the wrenching insecurity of yet another perfect mother, a Martha Stewart wannabe who plays Muzak at a silent dinner table because she wants life to seem seamless. And we are weary yet respectful of the depressed daughter who thinks she's odd and ugly and despises her parents. Like the best of directors, director Sam Mendes makes it all strange, new, and real, as if for the first time. Through him, as well as screenwriter Alan Ball, and cinematographer Conrad Hall, there are flashes of redemption in these lives. Though caricatured and very funny in how they cope with the tragic circumstances of their disconnection and lovelessness—an adulterous affair is revealed at a fast-food drive-up; a middle-aged man consults two gay men on how to look good naked; and a daughter is scolded by her mother: "You ungrateful little brat! Just look at everything you have. When I was your age, we . . . lived in a duplex! We didn't even have our own house!"—there is another layer to these lives. Kevin Spacey's is among his most unexpected performances; he is the divided self—the fool and the wise man. Annette Bening blows us away with great depths of emotional pain in what could be comic moments. The strange, intermittent unfolding of fading lives in Mendes's debut film is unique and welcome to Hollywood storytelling.

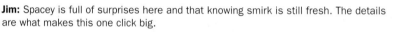

Jim: Spacey is full of surprises here and that knowing smirk is still fresh. The details are what makes this one click big.

Gail: A ballet performed by a paper bag blown about by the wind in the film-within-the-film is worthy of its own Oscar.

THE PLOT

"Look at me, jerking off in the shower . . . This will be the high point of my day, it's all downhill from here," says Lester Burnham (Kevin Spacey), beginning the jaded narration of his life within a humiliating, loveless, and dying suburban family. The thin veneer of normalcy falls away when Lester becomes obsessed with his disaffected teenage daughter Jane's (Thora Birch) blonde Lolita-like fellow cheerleader, Angela (Mena Suvari). Dreaming of seducing her, Lester finds a reason to live again; he quits his job, buys a sports car, and starts working out in order to "look good naked." Image-obsessed wife Carolyn (Annette Bening) is lost in her own self-improvement campaign, and begins a comic affair with Buddy "Real Estate King" Kane (Peter Gallagher), whose every word becomes a mantra for her. Next door, a different kind of dysfunctional family moves in: Col. Frank Fitts, U.S. Marine Corps (Chris Cooper), his catatonic wife, Barbara (Allison Janney), and their mysterious, voyeuristic teenage son Ricky (Wes Bentley) who falls in love with Jane. The center cannot hold. Believing that Lester is having an affair with his son, Col. Fitts shoots him dead. Carolyn finds his corpse. But a kind of peace settles in. The moments of redemption that have occurred almost imperceptibly throughout the film resonate in a traumatic, but, in its way, happy ending.

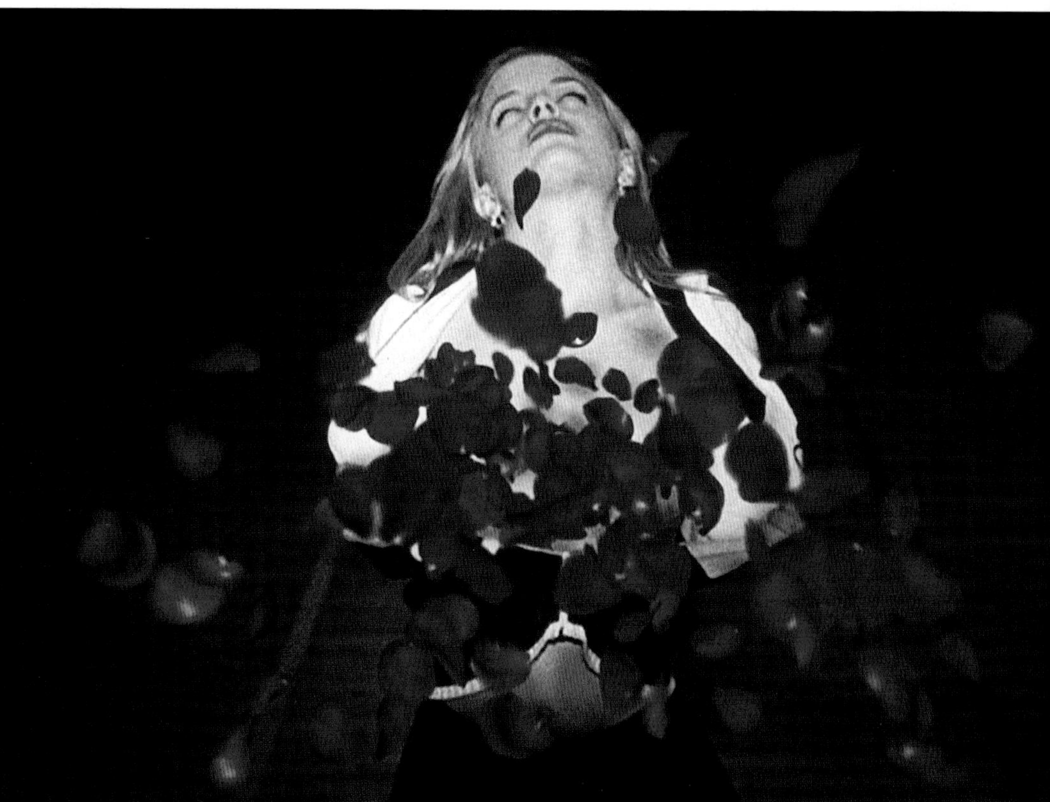

Will seducing the beautiful young nymphet (Mena Suvari) make up for all that a middle-aged father lost when he bought into the suburban American Dream?

THE DIRECTOR

Theater director **Sam Mendes**, a newcomer to film when he made *American Beauty*, not only draws delicately balanced performances from these gifted actors, but he has a visual sophistication and artistry that raise this film in a class of its own. His compositions are built around strong narrative elements, much like tableaux on the stage, and they work to make scenes visually unforgettable. With the invaluable contribution of cinematographer Conrad Hall, Mendes views the boxed-in world of suburbia from a heavenly height, implying that the lives lived within it just may be connected to something outside it after all. Screenwriter Alan Ball contributed significantly to the subtleties that are achieved against all odds in this usually predictable setting. (Ball was the scriptwriter for the also extraordinary HBO TV series, *Six Feet Under.*)

Wanting to look good naked for his dream-girl cheerleader, suburban failure Lester Burnham (Kevin Spacey) tries to resurrect his flabby body and his paralyzed life by pumping iron.

THE CAST	
Lester Burnham	Kevin Spacey
Carolyn Burnham	Annette Bening
Jane Burnham	Thora Birch
Ricky Fitts	Wes Bentley
Angela Hayes	Mena Suvari
Colonel Fitts	Chris Cooper
Buddy Kane	Peter Gallagher
Barbara Fitts	Allison Janney

ROLE REVERSALS

The role of Lester Burnham was originally offered to Tom Hanks (who later starred in Sam Mendes's follow-up project *Road to Perdition* [2002]), and to Chevy Chase.

Jeff Daniels was also considered for the role of Lester Burnham.

The role of Angela was offered to Kirsten Dunst, who turned it down.

Terry Gilliam turned down the chance to direct the film.

THE ACTORS

Kevin Spacey's delicately balanced performance—possibly the greatest of his career—is by turns creepy and moving. He can throw a dinner plate at the wall when he doesn't get what he wants, but he can also hold his married neighbor as he cries, realizing the man is gay and lonely. We know Lester is struggling, trying to recover the ideals and the optimism that once energized his life, and we cannot help but feel for him. The enigmatic and rambunctious Spacey usually turns up in roles much like his bad-boy persona. He debuted in *Heartburn* (1986), played a neurotic in the TV series *Wiseguy* (1988), revealed his gifts in *Dad* (1989), was in *Henry & June* (1990), *Glengarry Glen Ross* (1992), *Swimming with Sharks* (1994), won a supporting Oscar in *The Usual Suspects* (1995), played a corrupt cop in *L.A. Confidential* (1997), and appeared in *The Life of David Gale* (2003). Subsequent films include *Beyond the Sea* (2004) and *Superman Returns* (2006).

Carolyn, whose pruning shears match her gardening clogs, is played with over-the-top intensity by **Annette Bening**, who should have taken home the Oscar for this one. "Carolyn isn't a complicated dramatic construction, but Bening gives her a primal force . . . an actress who packs more psychological details into a single gesture than others get into whole scenes," wrote David Edelstein in *Slate*. As with every character in the film, Bening has to encompass the duality of playing a cliché and a real person at the same time. She does it, adding her own layered understanding of a woman out-of-control who sees no other recourse but to whip herself into a lather about everything including her perfectly groomed bed of deathly red roses. Bening is a highly gifted actress who deserves more attention than the wealth of it she received upon becoming the mother of Warren Beatty's baby. After her debut in *The Great Outdoors* (1988), she really excited audiences as a sexy manipulator in *The Grifters* (1990), which was followed by *Postcards from the Edge* (1990) and *Bugsy* (1991). Her winning streak was interrupted by several losers, including *Guilty by Suspicion* (1991), *Regarding Henry* (1991), and the sorry *Love Affair* in which she appeared with husband Warren (1994). She returned for a terrific comic performance in *The American President* (1995), and has most recently appeared in *Being Julia* (2003) and *Running with Scissors* (2006).

Wes Bentley's Ricky Fitts is a perfect incarnation of the haunted but self-possessed, abused teenager who transcends his awful environment by discovering "this entire life behind things, and this incredibly benevolent force, that wanted me to know there was no reason to be afraid, ever." Many young actors were clamoring for the part, but Bentley fit it to a T, delivering low-key intensity and an ability for intimacy that only he and Jane seemed to possess, which is why it makes full sense that they run away together. Bentley has appeared in *Beloved* and *Three Below Zero* (both 1998), *The White River Kid* (1999), *The Claim* (2000), *Soul Surivors* (2001), and *The Four Feathers* (2002).

Seventeen-year-old **Thora Birch** gives the most direct, authentic performance in the film as the self-hating, sad Jane who connects—finally—with her supremely confident, misfit next-door neighbor Ricky. She thinks she's ugly, especially when she's told so by her America's Sweetheart best friend, Angela. But when we

CREDITS

Dreamworks SKG
Producer:
Bruce Cohen and Dan Jinks
Director: Sam Mendes
Screenwriter: Alan Ball
Running Time: 120 minutes
Budget: $15 million

ACADEMY AWARDS

Best Actor in a Leading Role:
Kevin Spacey
Best Cinematography:
Conrad L. Hall
Best Director: Sam Mendes
Best Picture:
Bruce Cohen and Dan Jinks
Best Writing, Screenplay Written Directly for the Screen: Alan Ball

NOMINATIONS

Best Actress in a Leading Role:
Annette Bening
Best Editing: Tariq Anwar
Best Music, Original Score:
Thomas Newman

THE YEAR'S OTHER WINNERS

Best Actress: Hillary Swank, *Boys Don't Cry*
Best Supporting Actor: Michael Caine, *The Cider House Rules*
Best Supporting Actress: Angelina Jolie, *Girl, Interrupted*

THE OTHER LISTS

American Film Institute (No)
Entertainment Weekly (No)
Internet Movie Database (Yes)
Leonard Maltin (No)
Movieline (No)
National Society of Film Critics (No)
Premiere Magazine (No)
Roger Ebert's Top 100 (No)
Rolling Stone Magazine (No)
Village Voice (No)

see her looking into a mirror through the lens of Ricky's video camera, she looks every bit the breathtaking Pre-Raphaelite beauty. The eyes of the beholder show her what she cannot herself see. Starting her career at the age of four, Birch appeared in a famous Quaker Oats commercial, and by six appeared on the short-lived daycare sitcom *Day by Day* (1988). She started her film career in the children's fantasy *Purple People Eater* (1988), and went on to the TV sitcom, *Parenthood* (1990), and *Paradise* (1991). She graduated to high-profile films *Patriot Games* (1992), *Clear and Present Danger* (1994), and then into adult roles in *Now and Then* (1995), *Alaska* (1996), *The Smokers* (2000), *Dungeons & Dragons* (2000), and *Ghost World* (2001).

THE CRITICS

"Unsettling, unnerving, undefinable, *American Beauty* avoids quick and easy categorization. A quirky and disturbing take on modern American life energized by bravura performances from Kevin Spacey and Annette Bening." —Kenneth Turan, *The Los Angeles Times*

"*American Beauty* splashes vitriol on the middle class, but sinks into its own stereotypes." —Wesley Morris, *San Francisco Examiner*

NOTABLE QUOTES

"This has definitely been the highlight of my day."—Kevin Spacey, on winning the Oscar

"I read the screenplay and nearly fell out of bed. I thought I better meet [Sam Mendes] quick before someone else read it."—Kevin Spacey

"The less you know about me, the easier it is to convince you that I am that character on screen. It allows an audience to come into a movie theater and believe I am that person." —Kevin Spacey

"If you shout in the theater, people think you've gone a bit mad. But if you raise your voice on a film set, people just work a bit harder."—Sam Mendes

BEHIND THE SCREEN

"I love this story and the project, but my God, how can you like these characters?" said cinematographer Conrad Hall to director Mendes. "Well, Conrad, you have to like them. If you don't like them, we don't have a picture here," replied Mendes adding, "Against considerable odds, we do like them, and there definitely is a hell of a picture here."

Thora Birch was only 17, so filming her brief nude scene required permission from her parents, who were both on the set during the filming along with child labor representatives.

This film has been described as *Death of a Salesman* for the nineties. Early in the film, Carolyn mentions that "the Lomans" just moved out of the house next door.

The last name of Mena Suvari's character, Hayes, is probably a reference to the last name of Lolita Haze, from the Vladimir Nabokov novel *Lolita*.

And speaking of *Lolita*, if you look at the letters in Lester Burnham's name you'll find an anagram for that other famous middle-aged man who develops an infatuation with an adolescent girl: The anagram is "Humbert learns."

Executive Producer Steven Spielberg personally recommended Sam Mendes as director of this film.

Mendes personally filmed the pivotal POV shot through Ricky's camera when he zooms past the figure of Angela to "look closer" at Jane's smiling reflection in the mirror. The original script began and ended with scenes of Ricky and Jane in jail and on trial, and other events surrounding their arrest.

Seated in front of her carefully groomed dinner table, complete with background music by Montovani, Carolyn Burnham (Annette Bening) clings—with a vengeance—to her belief that the perfect setting assures the perfect life.

Carolyn straightens out her perfectly fitted suit on her way to an open house. "I am going to sell this house today," she repeats over and over again with steely determination, pep-talking herself into the winner's state of mind. She does a last-minute white-glove test and ends up on her hands and knees scrubbing floors and toilets. A few stray searchers wander in to insult her efforts. "This doesn't look like a lagoon," whines one customer while examining the swimming pool. Carolyn chirps back, "I can put up some Tiki Torches." No dice. Everyone leaves and Carolyn, grasping onto the venetian blinds, begins to break down, crying. "Shut up, you whining baby!" She masochistically upbraids herself, slapping herself on the face—the tough guy's way of gaining composure. But she keeps falling into primal, endless sobs. Finally, she stands up straight, walks away from the curtain, and out of the frame. Bening's performance is lacerating, funny, heartbreaking, and psychologically astute, and not likely to be matched for some time.

Repeating to herself over and over again, "I refuse to be a victim!" like some mantra, Carolyn breaks down behind the steering wheel of her car after her husband has caught her having an affair with Buddy, the real estate magnate.

99

PULP FICTION 1994

A WAX MUSEUM WITH A PULSE

Yes, but does it mean anything? While we're trying to figure that out, brace yourself for the exhilarating, hyper-kinetic, super-cinematic, nonstop talkathon roller-coaster ride into the "Tarantinoverse," a grungy, profane pulp/*noir* Disneyland. In Quentin Tarantino's pop-culture theme park we careen around as if we're in a cartoon computer game. Click, we're in and out of cool nightclubs (where Marilyn Monroe can be your waitress). Click, we're in a slimy boxing ring. Click, we're in a dirty pawn shop, and click, click, click, we're in a slick millionaire's pad or a carpeted, middle-class drug den where a subculture version of *The Honeymooners* could live. It's controlled madness of the most intoxicating—and, yes, lovable—kind.

Jim: Tarantino reshuffles movie clichés like a master cardsharp and invents a dictionary of new iconic images. We may never dance (or murder) the same way again.

Gail: It gets the temperature of the cool '90s right without being cold.

E PLOT

Fiction zigzags through time as various locking *noir* stories about violent, desper-haracters take turns in the foreground disorientingly switch places. All the while, es and junkies talk intensely, sometimes ically, about why a "Quarter Pounder" is d a "Royale with Cheese" in Paris, and r such stuff of everyday life. The three stories involve a mobster who is called to baby-sit his jealous boss's spacey, gy wife; a washed-up boxer who is red to take a fall but doesn't; and two s who accidentally shoot a captive in ace while driving over a bump and d the day cleaning up his blood and s. It's a good, clean, classic quest story—bracingly new context, told with an nkingly intelligent, film-savvy attitude.

Jules Winfield (Samuel L. Jackson) and Vincent Vega (John Travolta) are two of the coldest killers you'd never want meet at the other end of a gun. They are also two of the most loquacious dime-store philosophers, and, in between bloody hits, spend most of their energies arguing about such everyday fare as the difference between a Quarter Pounder in America and the Royale with Cheese in Paris.

"That's a pretty fucking good milkshake. I don't know if it's worth five dollars but it's pretty fucking good." —Vincent

THE DIRECTOR

The former video-store clerk **Quentin Tarantino** became an object of cult worship with *Pulp Fiction*, his follow-up film after the super-violent *Reservoir Dogs* (1992). Fans are still busy interpreting the film, which was cast, according to Eric Stoltz, via the laid-back director's invitation to dinner. If he enjoyed your company, you were in. It probably took a little more determination than that to drag Travolta out of has-been hell and make him a born-again movie star. Casting Samuel L. Jackson was not dumb luck either—he should have taken the Oscar.

Mia Wallace (Uma Thurman), the jealous crime boss's spacey, druggy wife, never seems to know when the fun is over. She ODs on their night out, requiring her escort, Vince, to plunge the largest hypodermic needle known to science into her chest like a stake into the heart of a vampire. Their evening is kismet composed of weird dance moves and deeply trivial conversation.

THE CAST	
Vincent Vega	John Travolta
Jules Winnfield	Samuel L. Jackson
Mia Wallace	Uma Thurman
Lance	Eric Stoltz
Jody	Rosanna Arquette
Pumpkin	Tim Roth
Honey Bunny	Amanda Plummer
Winston Wolf	Harvey Keitel
Marsellus Wallace	Ving Rhames
Captain Koons	Christopher Walken
Butch	Bruce Willis
Fabienne	Maria de Medeiros
Marvin	Phil LaMarr
Brett	Frank Whaley

THE CRITICS

"Tarantino's adrenaline rush of an American melodrama is a brash dare to Hollywood filmmakers in their current slough of timidity." —*Time Magazine*

"Jonathan Rosenbaum summed the film up quite nicely as 'a couch potato's paradise.' In the end, it's not that Tarantino has no life, it's that his life *is* the movies. Much like his characters, the director can only live by engaging cinema." —Ed Gonzalez, *Slant Magazine*

THE ACTORS

They said it couldn't be done. Could anyone reignite the flame of a burned-out Hollywood pretty boy? But this was just the ticket for **John Travolta**'s return, triumphant, showing us how good an actor he really is. What's more, his disco boogie from *Saturday Night Fever* (1977) was officially enshrined in the pop culture hall of fame by Tarantino when he put Travolta back on the dance floor in *Pulp*. Travolta has been breathing his second wind ever since with roles in *Get Shorty* (1995), *Face/Off* and *Mad City* (both 1997), *Primary Colors* and *The Thin Red Line* (both 1998), *Swordfish* (2001), and the high-heeled *Hairspray* (2007).

Tarantino wrote the role of the reflective, hell-fire and damnation-spouting Jules with the explosive **Samuel L. Jackson** in mind. When Jackson became a little too full of himself, he almost lost the part to (there are two versions) either Ving Rhames or Paul Calderon. Hearing about this, Jackson re-auditioned. Calderon appeared in a cameo as Paul, the bartender, and Rhames chomped into the meaty role of Marcellus Wallace. Jackson has been "doing the right thing" ever since that Spike Lee joint in such films as *Sea of Love* (1989), *GoodFellas* (1990), *Jungle Fever* (1991), and *Patriot Games* (1992). He appeared in major roles in such minor films as *Amos & Andrew* and *National Lampoon's Loaded Weapon 1* (both 1993). Later Jackson appeared in *Losing Isaiah* and *Die Hard With a Vengeance* (both 1995). Jackson's recent films include *Changing Lanes* and *Star Wars: Episode II—Attack of the Clones* (both 2002).

The parts of Honey Bunny and Pumpkin were written specifically for **Amanda Plummer** and **Tim Roth**. Amanda's primary passion is theater. She has appeared in many TV movies and both independent and feature films, among them, *Joe Versus the Volcano* (1990), *The Fisher King* (1991), *Whose Child Is This? The War for Baby Jessica* (both 1993), *A Simple Wish* (1997), and, more recently, *The Apartment Complex* (1999) and *Get a Clue* (2002). Tim Roth has become a regular in many indie films, among them *Reservoir Dogs* (1992), *Bodies, Rest and Motion* (1993), *Heart of Darkness* (1994), and *Little Odessa* (1995), as well as studio features including *Rob Roy* (1995) and *Everyone Says I Love You* (1996). His recent films include *Vatel* (2000) and *The Musketeer* (2001).

THE MOVIE BUFF'S MOVIE

Director Tarantino is nothing if not a devout cinephile; *Pulp Fiction* is clearly an homage to the form. Note just some of the references to earlier movies in his film:

Bande à part (Godard); *The Good, the Bad, and the Ugly*; *The Texas Chain Saw Massacre*; *The Brady Bunch*; *The Honeymooners*; *His Girl Friday*; *Halloween*; *Kiss Me Deadly*; *Body and Soul*; *The Set-Up*; *La Femme Nikita*; *Repo Man*; *Deliverance*; *Saturday Night Fever*; and *Grease*.

ROLE REVERSALS

Vincent Vega was originally to be played by Michael Madsen (who played Vega in *Reservoir Dogs*). There was also talk of Daniel Day-Lewis taking the part.

CREDITS

Producer: Lawrence Bender/ Miramax Films
Director: Quentin Tarantino
Screenplay: Quentin Tarantino
Running Time: 154 minutes
Budget: $8 million
Box Office: $212 million (worldwide)

ACADEMY AWARD

Best Original Screenplay: Quentin Tarantino and Roger Avary

NOMINATIONS

Best Picture
Best Director: Quentin Tarantino
Best Supporting Actress: Uma Thurman
Best Actor: John Travolta
Best Supporting Actor: Samuel L. Jackson
Best Editing: Sally Menke

THE YEAR'S OTHER WINNERS

Best Picture: *Forrest Gump*
Best Director: Robert Zemeckis, *Forrest Gump*
Best Actor: Tom Hanks, *Forrest Gump*
Best Actress: Jessica Lange, *Blue Sky*
Best Supporting Actor: Martin Landau, *Ed Wood*
Best Supporting Actress: Dianne Wiest, *Bullets Over Broadway*

THE OTHER LISTS

American Film Institute (Yes)
Roger Ebert's Top 100 (Yes)
Entertainment Weekly (Yes)
Internet Movie Database (Yes)
Leonard Maltin (Yes)
Movieline (No)
National Society of Film Critics (Yes)
Premiere Magazine (Yes)
Rolling Stone Magazine (Yes)
Village Voice (No)

Many maidens were up for the part of Mia: Meg Ryan, Meg Tilly, Holly Hunter, Brigitte Nielsen, Rosanna Arquette, and Alfre Woodward (which would have changed the racial balance in the Marcellus-Mia relationship).

Rumor also has it that Pam Grier (the star of Tarantino's later film, *Jackie Brown*) was originally considered for the role of Lance's wife. Tarantino decided not to cast her because he could not envision her getting pushed around the way her character does.

SEND IN THE CLONES

Year of the Dragon (1985)
True Romance (1993)
Bound by Honor (1993)
Natural Born Killers (1994)
Jackie Brown (1997)
Payback (1999)

BEHIND THE SCREEN

Jules's character was supposed to sport a huge Afro, but a crewmember bought some Geri-curled wigs instead, unaware of the difference, and there was no time to fix it.

When Vincent plunges the syringe into Mia's chest, he is actually pulling the needle out. The film was then run backwards to create the piercing effect.

The marquee on the arena where Butch boxes advertises two fights: "Coolidge vs. Wilson," and "Vossler vs. Martinez," in reference to U.S. Presidents Calvin Coolidge and Woodrow Wilson, and to Russell Vossler and Jerry Martinez, two friends of Tarantino's from his video-store days.

Mia seductively refers to Vincent as "cowboy," invoking John Travolta's starring role in *Urban Cowboy* (1980). Vincent calls Mia "cowgirl" in return; Uma Thurman starred in *Even Cowgirls Get the Blues* (1993).

Every time Vincent goes to the bathroom, something bad happens. If you look carefully you will see Vincent entering the bathroom at the beginning of the film, when Pumpkin and Honey Bunny are talking about the robbery.

Mia's overdose and her revival by an adrenaline injection into the heart was taken from a story told in *American Boy: A Profile of Steven Prince* (1978), a documentary directed by Martin Scorsese.

The word "fuck" is used 271 times.

"And now, little man, I give the watch to you," says Captain Koons (Christopher Walken) as he passes a family heirloom on to young Butch. Koons tells the young boy a meandering story of the journey taken by his grandfather's watch through several wars to finally reach safety in Butch's little hands. Let's just say, it tended to be hidden where the sun doesn't shine.

THE GREAT SCENE

Butch has a nightmare in which he relives the story of how he collected his dead father's watch. He is visited by his father's buddy in Vietnam, Captain Koons (Christopher Walken), who tells the young Butch: "The way your dad looked at it, this watch was your birthright. He'd be damned if any of the slopes were gonna get their greasy yellow hands on his boy's birthright. So he hid it in the one place he knew he could hide something: his ass. Five long years, he wore this watch up his ass. Then when he died of dysentery, he gave me the watch. I hid this uncomfortable piece of metal up my ass for two years. Then, after seven years, I was sent home to my family. And now, little man, I give the watch to you."

Strongman boxer with the soul of a poet, Butch (Bruce Willis), receives orders from crime boss Marcellus, who has a lot of money riding on this pony: "In the fifth, your ass goes down. Say it." "In the fifth, my ass goes down," replies Butch, subserviently. But when his sense of himself won't allow him to compromise, he wins the match and becomes a hunted man. He goes on the lam with Tulip, his girlfriend, in search of a better life.

100

THE SHAWSHANK REDEMPTION 19

AMAZING GRACE

It sounds like, looks like, and smells like the kind of prison movie where inmates raise birds and build hope out of libraries and comradeship while fighting off unspeakably violent fellow prisoners and even more dastardly wardens. It has all that, and though it comes close to fulfilling all the stereotypes, it rises far above them. The flood of sentimentality never overwhelms the picture, because Morgan Freeman and Tim Robbins's performances are so powerful and honest. The twenty-year friendship between them, which embodies the virtues of loyalty, patience, and the instinct for survival inside Shawshank, is the key to the redemption in the title. The deliberate pacing and the burnished cinematography together make palpable both the prisoners' numbingly bleak lives and the sense of possibility—even in Shawshank.

Jim: To borrow from Smucker's, with a title like this, you've got to be good. For my money, Stephen King is at his best when at his least creepy.

Gail: In the great tradition of *Birdman of Alcatraz* and *Cool Hand Luke*, this is a luminous character study of fortitude and friendship behind bars.

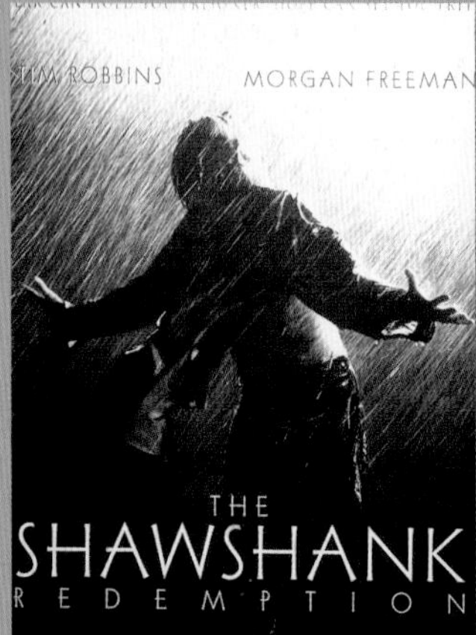

THE PLOT

Sentenced to two consecutive life terms in the brutal wards of Shawshank prison for the murders of his wife and her lover, reticent banker Andy Dufresne (Tim Robbins) insists on his innocence—even though he had intended to commit the crime. He enters the prison yard moving slowly as all eyes focus on him, sizing him up, particularly lifer Red (Morgan Freeman), who's seen so many men come and go that he places bets against this fragile-looking young man. Red, who narrates the story, witnesses Andy's subjugation—the gang rapes and the brutality—but soon learns that beneath Andy's quiet stance is an active determination to survive. The two become fast friends. As Andy develops a thriving business as a bookkeeper and tax preparer for most of the local prison officials, he observes how the power brokers amass their ill-gotten gains. He also earns the respect of inmates and staff, and inspires hope where there was none. Steady in his purpose, Andy patiently executes his escape plan and ultimately shares his most precious possession—freedom—with his loyal friend.

One has hope; the other doesn't. Innocent of the murder of his wife, Andy Dufresne (Tim Robbins) nevertheless lands in Shawshank and, from Day One, makes up his mind to get out. Red (Morgan Freeman) is doin' life, and has been through too many parole rejections to even hear the word hope. Red begins to admire Andy's survival instincts. The twenty-year friendship between the two becomes the heart of the movie.

"Let me tell you something my friend. Hope is a dangerous thing. Hope can drive a man insane."—Red

THE DIRECTOR

With many powerful friends encouraging him from the sidelines, including George Lucas and Steven Spielberg, **Frank Darabont**'s first feature film put him on the map. A writer/director, Darabont got his start writing B-horror movies including *A Nightmare On Elm Street 3: Dream Warriors* (1987) with his friend Chuck Russell and *The Blob* (1988), as well as penning several episodes of Lucas's TV series *The Young Indiana Jones Chronicles* (1992). He was the uncredited script doctor on *Saving Private Ryan* (1998) and *Minority Report* (2002). After achieving Oscar recognition and cult stature with *Shawshank*, he directed *The Green Mile* (1999), a second work by writer Stephen King. At the time of this writing, he was at work on the remake of *Fahrenheit 451*.

"I believe in two things: discipline and the Bible. Here you'll receive both. Put your trust in the Lord; your ass belongs to me. Welcome to Shawshank," says Warden Samuel Norton. A host of other killers (the prison officials, that is) oversee and over-discipline the inmates with a battery of methods including bats, solitary confinement, and the like.

THE CAST

Andy Dufresne	Tim Robbins
Ellis Boyd "Red" Redding	Morgan Freeman
Warden Samuel Norton	Bob Gunton
Heywood	William Sadle
Captain Byron Hadley	Clancy Brown
Tommy Williams	Gil Bellows
Bogs Diamond	Mark Rolston
Brooks Hatlen	James Whitmore
1946 D.A.	Jeffrey DeMunn
Skeet	Larry Brandenburg
Jigger	Neil Giuntoli
Floyd	Brian Libby
Snooze	David Proval
Ernie	Joseph Ragno
Guard Mert	Jude Ciccolella
Guard Trout	Paul McCrane
Andy Dufresne's Wife	Renee Blaine

THE ACTORS

"Yeah. The funny thing is—on the outside, I was an honest man, straight as an arrow. I had to come to prison to be a crook," says neophyte prisoner Andy Dufresne, played with intense, subtle charm by **Tim Robbins.** Director Robert Altman said of the sometimes controversial actor/director, "[Robbins] has qualities that could make him the next Orson Welles." Robbins began his film career taking minor roles in such independent films as *No Small Affair* (1984) and *The Sure Thing* (1985), and his first feature was the much-maligned *Howard the Duck* (1986). But it wasn't until he played a civil rights worker in *Five Corners* (1988) and the wild rookie pitcher in *Bull Durham* (1988) that he achieved some measure of fame. He hit pay dirt in Robert Altman's *The Player* (1992), and his directorial debut came with *Bob Roberts* (1992). He won an Oscar for his heartbreaking turn in *Mystic River* (2003).

With his powerfully resonant voice, **Morgan Freeman** as Red narrates the film like a veritable Moses. He infuses the role of murderer serving life with dignity; his eyes project hope and despair in equal measure. "These walls are funny," he intones. "First you hate them. Then you get used to them. After time passes, you get so's you depend on them." After years of working in the theater, Freeman found a wider audience on the children's PBS-TV series *Electric Company*. From the moment his face hit the big screen he was embraced by the public, garnering a Best Supporting Actor nomination for his fierce, complex pimp in *Street Smart* (1987). Once he reached stardom he played roles in *The Bonfire of the Vanities* (1990), *Glory* (1989), *Driving Miss Daisy* (1989, Academy Award nomination), and *Unforgiven* (1992). His recent best include *Gone, Baby, Gone* and *The Bucket List* (both 2007).

Bob Gunton's hellfire-and-brimstone Warden Samuel Norton likes to beat prisoners to death. His is one of several cliché roles in the film, but his performance transcends. Among Gunton's other films are *Glory* (1989), *Patriot Games* (1992), *Patch Adams* (1998), and *The Perfect Storm* (2000).

Another one of the usual suspects in the prison genre is the sadistic guard, played with conviction by **Clancy Brown**. The son of a former Congressman from Ohio, most of his work has been providing voiceovers.

The gentle, aging inmate who knows no other life than the one behind bars is played with grace here by **James Whitmore**, whose weather-beaten face resembles that of Spencer Tracy. A well-known character actor, Whitmore earned his first Oscar nomination for *Battleground* (1949), followed by roles in *The Asphalt Jungle*, *The Next Voice You Hear . . .*, and *Mrs. O'Malley and Mr. Malone* (all 1950), *Kiss Me Kate* (1953), and *Black Like Me* (1964), in which he impersonated a black man. Whitmore has also traveled the country in one-man shows, including a portrait of President Harry Truman in *Give 'Em Hell, Harry!* (The 1975 film version earned him an Oscar nomination). He starred in several TV series, including *The Law and Mr. Jones* (1960–61).

ROLE REVERSALS

Brad Pitt was slated to play the young inmate Tommy Williams.

BEHIND THE SCREEN

By order of the American Society for the Prevention of Cruelty to Animals, Brooks's crow had to be fed a maggot that had died of natural causes. The Society claimed that it was cruel to maggots to feed them live to a bird.

Did you do a double take when Morgan Freeman says, "Maybe it's 'cause I'm Irish?" I did. It was left in the script from Stephen King's original story, in which Red was an Irishman.

CREDITS

Producer: Liz Glotzer, Executive Producer, David V. Lester, Executive Producer, and Niki Marvin, Producer/Columbia Pictures and Castle Rock Entertainment
Director: Frank Darabont
Screenplay: Frank Darabont and Stephen King (based on his short story "Rita Hayworth and The Shawshank Redemption")
Budget: $25 million
Running Time: 144 minutes

ACADEMY AWARD NOMINATIONS

Best Actor: Morgan Freeman
Best Cinematography: Roger Deakins
Best Film Editing: Richard Francis-Bruce
Best Music, Best Original Score: Thomas Newman
Best Picture: Niki Marvin
Best Sound: Robert J. Litt, Elliot Tyson, Michael Herbick, Willie D. Burton
Best Writing, Screenplay Based on Material from Another Medium: Frank Darabont

THE YEAR'S WINNERS

Best Picture: *Forrest Gump*
Best Director: Robert Zemeckis, *Forrest Gump*
Best Actor: Tom Hanks, *Forrest Gump*
Best Actress: Jessica Lange, *Blue Sky*
Best Supporting Actor: Martin Landau, *Ed Wood*
Best Supporting Actress: Dianne Wiest, *Bullets Over Broadway*

For a few majestic moments Andy locks himself in a room and gets his hands on the prison loudspeaker system, through which he projects *"Che Soave Zeffiretto"* from Mozart's *Marriage of Figaro*. The effect is nothing less than soaring and Red speaks of it on the voiceover: "I have no idea to this day what those two Italian ladies were singing about. Truth is, I don't want to know. Some things are best left unsaid. I'd like to think they were singing about something so beautiful it can't be expressed in words, and makes your heart ache because of it. I tell you, those voices soared higher and farther than anybody in a gray place dares to dream. It was like some beautiful bird flapped into our drab little cage and made those walls dissolve away, and for the briefest of moments, every last man in Shawshank felt free."

"We sat and drank with the sun on our shoulders and felt like free men. Hell, we could have been tarring the roof of one of our own houses. We were the lords of all creation. As for Andy—he spent that break hunkered in the shade, a strange little smile on his face, watching us drink his beer." —Red

THE CRITICS

"*The Shawshank Redemption* is the sort of movie that sneaks up on you. Every time you're about to throw in the towel and conclude that this is all just too depressing, this fellow does something remarkable—something that convinces you that he's going to find a way to survive. When the film's conclusion starts to unfold, you suddenly realize that this is one of the more inspiring films you've seen in a long time—yet you don't feel the least bit manipulated." —Brian Webster, *Apollo Movie Guide*

"As preposterous as it as appealing, *The Shawshank Redemption* takes a straightforward, soul-stirring novella by horror maestro Stephen King and turns it into a somber, bloated prison drama designed to pump you up on inspiration." —Peter Stack, *San Francisco Chronicle*

NOTABLE QUOTES

"If you're going to succeed, you've got to be like one of those punch-drunk fighters in the old Warner Bros. boxing pictures: too stupid to fall down, you just keep slugging and stay on your feet." —Frank Darabont

"[Stephen King and I] have a joke now—because the first two films I directed were period prison movies—that my directing career will stall unless he writes another period prison story." —Frank Darabont

Andy exults in the rain as he emerges from his sewage-choked escape route to freedom. Red has come to believe in Andy, but is still amazed at the extent of the man's determination.

THE OTHER LISTS

- American Film Institute (Yes)
- Roger Ebert's Top 100 (Yes)
- *Entertainment Weekly* (No)
- Internet Movie Database (Yes)
- Leonard Maltin (No)
- *Movieline* (No)
- National Society of Film Critics (No)
- *Premiere* Magazine (No)
- *Rolling Stone* Magazine (No)
- *Village Voice* (No)

101

GROUNDHOG DAY 1993

A RODENT IS REBORN

It's a Wonderful Life meets *No Exit* in this classic romantic comedy with a spiritual allegory at its heart. Bill Murray makes it all make sense. His unlikely romantic lead is a self-important cynic, a somewhat lovable, sad emotional isolate who doesn't miss a comic beat. We hate his misanthropy. We don't want this egotistical cad to win the bright and optimistic girl, the luminous Andie MacDowell. But he does—and he makes it all surprisingly thoughtful and weighty.

Condemned to live the same day over and over . . . possibly a few too many "overs" . . . Murray grows besotted with his inexplicable power to perfect his role in the day's events as they unfold. He's like a kid in a candy store who can never get a stomachache, at one point going for the grandiose, "I'm a god. I'm not the God . . . I don't think." Ramis and Rubin milk the conundrum of how to live the same day for the rest of your life with an inspired array of diversions that keep us in stitches. But in the end, Murray can never really enjoy anything and begins to die, figuratively, from the effects of his own unending sarcasm.

Ramis and Rubin do Elisabeth Kübler-Ross proud as they structure the movie around Murray's passage through the five stages of grief, from giddy denial to desperation, depression, and finally acceptance. And they're not afraid to take this brilliantly entertaining and hilarious comedy down into the abyss (at Murray's insistence, it is said) by staging a succession of surprisingly unsettling suicide attempts. Murray's fall is visceral and, increasingly we begin to feel, "We're not in Kansas anymore." But he climbs back up. He learns. The scenes between the more mature and self-aware Murray and MacDowell sparkle like the ice sculpture he carves of her face. It never gets schmaltzy . . . well, not for long. Boy eventually gets girl by gaining himself. We can be sure, however, that the one-liners will continue happily ever after.

Jim: Murray's face is a map of deadpan irony—he never has to say a word. Every time I see this one, it's as original and hilarious as the first time. Hey . . . what's going on here?

Gail: Nietzsche confronts Bill Murray—yet he finds a light at the end of the tunnel. That's a gift.

E PLOT

3ill Murray), a surly, misanthropic TV erman, makes his miserable annual nage to Punxsutawney, Pennsylvania, ver the Groundhog Day festivities and ence "the excitement of a large squirrel cting the weather." Everything about this , except for the presence of Rita (Andie owell), his fetching and optimistic new cer. Trapped in small-town hell, Phil s up the next morning at the same time, same music and the same everything; tuck in a time warp. He savagely plays s childlike omnipotence—he robs a bank, out on pastries, wins all the women, and lose to bedding Rita under false pretens- owing that the slate will be wiped clean on as he goes to sleep at night. Too much ns into the terrifying realization that g in his life will ever change; his selfish- urns into self-destruction. He electro- himself, jumps off a building, and drives k over an embankment, but he cannot ie. He plunges into despair. Then, rising of the ashes, Phil changes. He does wherever he can, learns new skills, dis- new talents. He lives and relives the day were his last. He seizes every moment. become a better version of himself, he ita's heart and gains his freedom.

If he could report it as he saw it, world-weary TV weatherman Phil (Bill Murray) would tell the crowd of groundhog idolaters, "This is one time where television really fails to capture the true excitement of a large squirrel predicting the weather."

"You're not a god. You can take my word for it; this is twelve years of Catholic school talking." —Rita

THE DIRECTORS

Sex-drugs-and-rock-and-roll satires with heart, **Harold Ramis**'s brand of comedy grew out of the improvisational wellspring of Chicago's Second City, where he first worked with Murray. He followed the troupe to television in different incarnations. His first film, *National Lampoon's Animal House* (1978) broke all box-office records for comedies and set the mold for a legion of films featuring immature "men" passing out with beer cans smashed into their foreheads. As a writer and director Ramis has been connected with box-office winners (and a handful of clinkers), including *Meatballs* (dir., 1979), his first collaboration with Bill Murray; *Caddyshack* (dir., 1980); *Vacation* (dir., 1983); *Ghostbusters* (writer, 1984); *Analyze This* (dir.,1999); *Analyze That* (dir., 2002) ,and the low-budget, poorly received "comic film *noir*" *The Ice Harvest* (dir., 2004). In 1982, Ramis's dream project, a film adaptation of the Pulitzer Prize-winning novel *A Confederacy of Dunces*, was aborted when its star, John Belushi, died. His six-film collaboration with Murray ended with *Groundhog Day*, after some disagreement on the film's balance between the philosophical and the comic. (Murray voted for the former.)

"Boy (Bill Murray) finally gets girl (Andie MacDowell), once boy finds his higher self—without completely losing his lower self, and the laughs.

THE CAST	
Phil Connors	Bill Murray
Rita	Andie MacDowell
Larry	Chris Elliott
Ned Ryerson	Stephen Tobolowsky

"Phil goes from being a prisoner of time to become its master."
—Harold Ramis

THE ACTORS

In this, his best comic role, **Bill Murray**, the embodiment of the impudent and disaffected know-it-all, opens the closet to a working inner life. That higher and lower self would later be explored in his favorite role, the sullen loner in *Lost in Translation* (2003), for which he won a Best Actor Oscar nomination. Murray's first break came on television when he replaced Chevy Chase on NBC's *Saturday Night Live* (1977–99). He went on to star in *Meatballs* (1979), the first of six films with director Harold Ramis. His popularity soared in *Caddyshack* (1980), *Tootsie* (1982), and *Ghostbusters* (1984—in a role originally written for John Belushi). But Murray's dream project, an adaptation of *The Razor's Edge* that he cowrote (1984), was a box-office failure. With that, Murray, disappeared from films, studying philosophy and history at the French Sorbonne. He returned in the 1990s with a new muse, director Wes Anderson, appearing in *Rushmore* (1998), *The Royal Tennenbaums* (2001), *The Life Aquatic with Steve Zissou* (2004), and *Broken Flowers* (directed by Jim Jarmusch, 2005). After another break from films, he returned in a small role in Anderson's *The Darjeeling Limited* (2007). Like his characters, Murray tends toward detachment, employing neither an agent nor a manager—but he does have a wife and children.

Andie MacDowell first came to prominence for her hair. Calvin Klein commercials led to her film debut in *Greystoke: The Legend of Tarzan, Lord of the Apes* (1984). But she overcame her image as a mere model-turned-actress with critical acclaim for her role in Stephen Soderbergh's indie *sex, lies, and videotape* (1989). It led to starring roles in *Green Card* (1990), *The Object of Beauty* (1991), *Hudson Hawk* (1991), *Short Cuts* (1993), a highly acclaimed performance in *Four Weddings and a Funeral* (1994), and *Unstrung Heroes* (1995). Since then, her film appearances have been less than notable.

Oddball roles come naturally to **Chris Elliott**, who broke out as a writer and performer on *Late Night with David Letterman* in the 1990s. The son of Bob Elliott of the famous comedy team "Bob and Ray," Elliott's face is known to viewers of such television shows as the short-lived *Get a Life* (1990), *Saturday Night Live* (1994–95), *Dilbert* (1999–2000), and *Everybody Loves Raymond* (2003–5). He played an oily ladies'-man wannabe in *The Abyss* (1989), along with roles in *New York Stories* (1989), *There's Something About Mary* (1998), and *Scary Movie 2* (2001). As a writer, Elliott has several books and many scripts under his belt.

Having clocked more than two hundred roles in television, film, and theater, **Stephen Tobolowsky** does a riotous turn as Ned Ryerson, the gawky small-town insurance salesman who is a landmark in Murray's time warp. He's nothing less than ubiquitous on the small screen, having appeared in *Seinfeld* (1991), *Will and Grace* (2004), *Curb Your Enthusiasm* (2005), *Deadwood* (2005–6), *Entourage* (2007), and as a regular cast member on *Heroes* (2007). Among his film appearances are *Spaceballs* (1987), *Mississippi Burning* (1988), *Thelma and Louise* (1991), *Radioland Murders* (1994), *Memento* (2001), *Garfield* (2004), and *Loveless in Los Angeles* (2007). On Broadway, he was nominated for a Tony for his role in *Morning's at Seven* (2002).

ROLE REVERSALS

Tom Hanks was Ramis's first pick, but then the director decided he was "too nice" for the part.

Tori Amos was among the actresses considered to play Rita.

CREDITS

Producer: Trevor Albert and Harold Ramis
Director: Harold Ramis
Screenplay: Harold Ramis and Danny Rubin
Running Time: 101 minutes
Domestic Box Office Gross: $70,906,973

THE YEAR'S ACADEMY AWARD WINNERS

Best Picture: *Schindler's List*
Best Director: Steven Spielberg, *Schindler's List*
Best Adapted Screenplay: Jan Chapman, *Schindler's List*
Best Actor: Tom Hanks, *Philadelphia*
Best Actress: Holly Hunter, *The Piano*
Best Supporting Actor: Tommy Lee Jones, *The Fugitive*
Best Supporting Actress: Anna Paquin, *The Piano*

THE OTHER LISTS

American Film Institute (No)
Roger Ebert's Top 100 (Yes)
Entertainment Weekly (No)
Internet Movie Database (No)
Leonard Maltin (No)
Movieline (No)
National Society of Film Critics (No)
Premiere Magazine (No)
Rolling Stone Magazine (No)
Village Voice (No)

BEHIND THE SCENES

Murray enjoyed the small-town community spirit so much he bought five hundred Danishes and fed them to everyone who watched the film being shot.

Whenever Murray became confused about Ramis's direction, he would cut to the chase and ask, "Just tell me—good Phil or bad Phil?"

After love and wealth, getting all of the answers right on *Jeopardy* is arguably the greatest thing in life. So, why isn't Phil (Bill Murray) smiling as he reels off the answers while seated among a group of amazed and delighted septuagenarians? Because immortality has begun to take its toll. Murray's face grows blank and heavy as he begins his descent into despair.

"Well, what if there is no tomorrow?" In his attempt to answer this destabilizing existential question, Phil goes on a binge—only to find his sin of gluttony, and all his other self-destructive behaviors, expunged with the next buzz of his alarm clock.

Murray was bitten by Punxsutawney Phil (the groundhog, who played himself) twice during shooting.

Writer Rubin says he was inspired, in part, to probe the question of what it would be like to live forever when he read Anne Rice's *Interview with the Vampire*.

NOTABLE QUOTES

"At first I would get mail saying, 'Oh, you must be a Christian because the movie so beautifully expresses Christian belief.' Then rabbis started calling from all over saying there were preaching the film as their next sermon. And the Buddhists! Well, I knew they loved it because my mother-in-law has lived in a Buddhist meditation center for 30 years and my wife lived there for five years." —Harold Ramis, *New York Times*

"People can change." —Harold Ramis

THE CRITICS

"Groundhog Day is a film that finds its note and purpose so precisely that its genius might not be immediately noticeable. It unfolds so inevitably, is so enticing, so apparently effortless, that you have to stand back and slap yourself before you see how good it really is." —Roger Ebert, *Chicago Sun-Times*

"It springs straight from the heart of the great tradition of American trash surrealism, which is precisely what makes it so immediately delightfully accessible, so multilayered and rich without pretensions." —Hal Hinson, *Washington Post*

In Phil's case, man's worst enemy is—the groundhog. So tired is he of living and reliving the same day, Phil decides to end it once and for all. He hog-naps the celebrated beast at the root of his troubles in an attempt to end his (and its) interminable life. Big Phil straps little Phil in for a bumpy ride to death. With increasing speed and desperation, he drives a stolen truck over the edge of a quarry, where it blows up in an inglorious blaze. Alas, death eludes Phil. He rises again the next morning without a scratch on his body, only his spirit broken. Suddenly, this comedy is not so funny anymore...at least for the moment.

"Don't drive angry. Do not drive angry," intones Phil ironically, as he embarks on a suicidal joy ride with his nemesis.

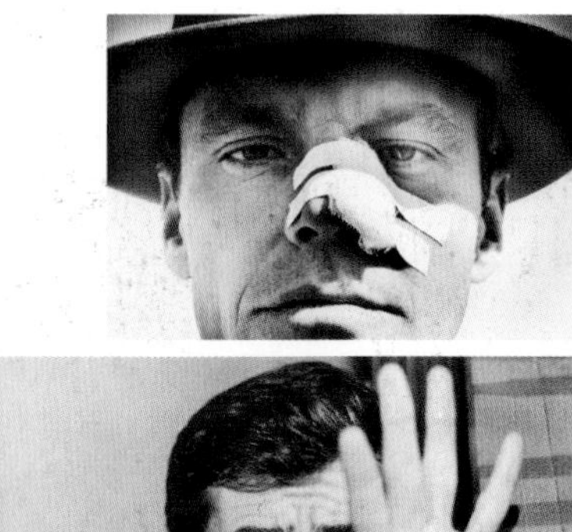

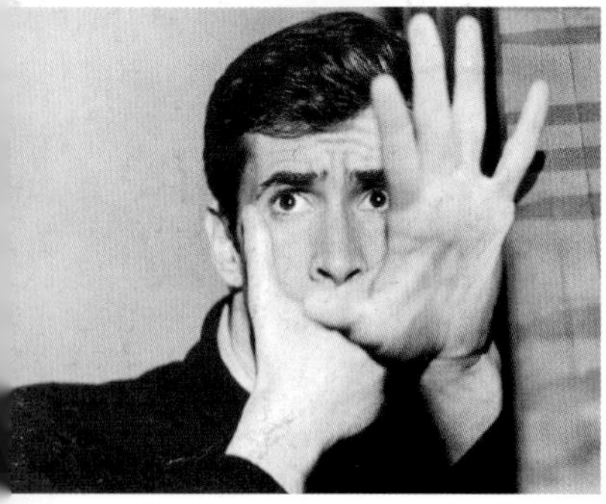

CHRONOLOGY of THE GREATEST MOVIES EVER

1930s

1931 *City Lights* (44)
1933 *King Kong* (51)
1934 *It Happened One Night* (32)
1935 *A Night at the Opera* (54)
1935 *Top Hat* (47)
1937 *Grand Illusion* (88)
1938 *Bringing Up Baby* (70)
1939 *Gone with the Wind* (18)
1939 *Rules of the Game* (48)
1939 *The Wizard of Oz* (7)

1940s

1940 *The Grapes of Wrath* (66)
1940 *Pinocchio* (61)
1941 *Citizen Kane* (2)
1941 *The Maltese Falcon* (72)
1942 *Casablanca* (3)
1943 *Shadow of a Doubt* (62)
1944 *Double Indemnity* (22)
1946 *The Best Years of Our Lives* (36)
1946 *The Bicycle Thief* (69)
1946 *It's a Wonderful Life* (34)
1948 *Red River* (86)
1949 *The Third Man* (57)

1950s

1950 *All About Eve* (13)
1950 *The Lady Eve* (74)
1950 *Rashomon* (82)
1950 *Sunset Boulevard* (4)
1951 *The African Queen* (37)
1951 *A Place in the Sun* (85)
1951 *Strangers on a Train* (31)
1951 *A Streetcar Named Desire* (29)
1952 *Singin' in the Rain* (10)
1954 *On the Waterfront* (17)
1954 *The Seven Samurai* (95)
1955 *Night of the Hunter* (56)
1955 *Pather Panchali* (73)
1956 *Invasion of the Body Snatchers* (60)
1956 *The Searchers* (20)
1957 *Funny Face* (28)
1957 *Paths of Glory* (71)
1957 *Wild Strawberries* (68)
1958 *Vertigo* (24)
1959 *The 400 Blows* (53)
1959 *Imitation of Life* (91)
1959 *North by Northwest* (6)
1959 *Some Like It Hot* (12)

1960s

1960 *Psycho* (14)
1960 *Spartacus* (93)
1961 *La Dolce Vita* (21)
1961 *Jules and Jim* (27)
1962 *Lawrence of Arabia* (5)
1962 *The Manchurian Candidate* (94)
1962 *To Kill a Mockingbird* (19)
1963 *8½* (46)
1964 *Dr. Strangelove* (38)
1964 *A Hard Day's Night* (96)
1965 *Dr. Zhivago* (58)
1967 *Bonnie and Clyde* (50)
1967 *The Graduate* (33)
1968 *2001: A Space Odyssey* (49)
1968 *The Last Picture Show* (75)
1968 *The Producers* (81)
1968 *Rosemary's Baby* (77)
1969 *Butch Cassidy and the Sundance Kid* (90)
1969 *Midnight Cowboy* (78)

1970s

1970 *The Conformist* (40)
1970 *M*A*S*H* (79)
1972 *Cabaret* (83)
1972 *The Godfather* (1)
1973 *American Graffiti* (80)
1974 *Chinatown* (9)
1974 *The Conversation* (87)
1974 *The Godfather, Part II* (1)
1975 *Jaws* (65)
1975 *Nashville* (11)
1976 *One Flew Over the Cuckoo's Nest* (76)
1976 *Taxi Driver* (15)
1977 *Annie Hall* (8)
1977 *Close Encounters of the Third Kind* (25)
1977 *Star Wars* (52)
1978 *The Deer Hunter* (45)
1979 *Apocalypse Now* (16)

1980s

1980 *Atlantic City* (97)
1980 *Raging Bull* (35)
1981 *Raiders of the Lost Ark* (92)
1982 *Blade Runner* (39)
1982 *Diner* (43)
1982 *E.T. The Extra-Terrestrial* (59)
1986 *Blue Velvet* (64)
1989 *Do the Right Thing* (67)

1990s

1990 *Goodfellas* (26)
1993 *Groundhog Day* (101)
1993 *Schindler's List* (41)
1994 *Pulp Fiction* (99)
1994 *The Shawshank Redemption* (100)
1996 *Fargo* (63)
1997 *L.A. Confidential* (89)
1998 *Saving Private Ryan* (30)
1999 *American Beauty* (98)

2000s

2003 *Return of the King* (84)
2006 *The Lives of Others* (42)
2006 *Pan's Labyrinth* (23)
2008 *Slumdog Millionaire* (55)

INDEX

A

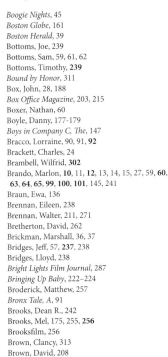

A.I., 131
Academy of Motion Picture Arts and Sciences, 52
Adams, Brooke, 193
Adler, Renata, 161, 257
African Queen, The, 21, 123–125
After Hours, 76
Agee, James, 181
Aiello, Danny, **214**
Aimée, Anouk, **75**, **76**, 150, 151, **152**
Albert, Trevor, 316
Alexander, Jason, 257
Alford, Philip, 69, 70, **71**
Alison, Joan, 21
All About Eve, 23, 50–52
All of Me, 146
Alland, William, **18**
Allen, Jay Presson, 262
Allen, Karen, 288, 289, **290**
Allen, Woody, **35**, **36**, **37**, 146, 205
Allied Artists, 193
Alpert, Herb, 184
Altman, Robert, 44, **45**, 249, **250**, 251, 313
Amato, Giuseppe, 76
Amblin Entertainment, 190
American Beauty, 306–308
American Graffiti, 252–254
American Museum of the Moving Image, 15
Amos, Tori, 316
Anastasia, Albert, 65
Anderson, James, 71
Anderson, Jeffrey M., 175
Anderson, Richard L., 289
Anderson, Wes, 315
Andersson, Bibi, 217, **217**–218
Andersson, Harriet, 172
Andrews, Dana, 120, 121, **122**
Angulo, Alex, 83
Annie Hall, 11, 35–37
Antonucci, Vittorio, **220**
Apocalypse Now, 11, 15, 59–62
Apocalypse Now Redux, 59, 61
Apollo Movie Guide, 314
Archer, Ernest, 160
Archer, Eugene, 158
Arlen, Harold, 33, 34
Armstrong, Robert, 166, **167**
Arnold, Gary, 170, 232
Arquette, Rosanna, 311
Asimov, Isaac, 160
Aspegren, Chuck, 148
Astaire, Fred, 96, 97, **98**, **153**, **154**, **155**
Astor, Mary, **228**, 229, **230**
Atkinson, Michael, 274
Atlantic City, 303–305
Atlantic Monthly, 68
Austin Chronicle, 188
Avary, Roger, 310
Avedon, Richard, 96, 98
Avenging Texans, The, 73
Avery, Brian, 111
Axelrod, George, 295

B

Bacall, Lauren, 226, 271
Bacharach, Burt, 283
Backlinie, Susan, **207**, 208
Bacon, Kevin, **141**, 142, 143
Badham, Mary, 69, 70, **71**
Badlands, 163
Baker, Chet, 281
Balaban, Bob, 246
Baldwin, Alec, 280
Ball, Alan, 306, 307
Ball, Derek, 169
Ball, Lucille, 294
Balsam, Martin, 160
Bancroft, Anne, **111**, 112, **113**, 241
Bannerjee, Karuna, **231**
Bannerjee, Subir, **231**, **233**
Bannerji, Bibhuti, 232
Baquero, Ivana, **81**, **82**
Barker, Lex, 76
Barkin, Ellen, 142, **143**
Barry, John, 169, 170
Barrymore, Drew, 190
Barrymore, Lionel, 115
Baryshnikov, Mikhail, 98
Basinger, Kim, 280, **281**
Bates, Barbara, 51
Battaglia, Aurelius, 196
Baumgarten, Marjorie, 188
Baxley, Barbara, **44**, 45
Baxter, Anne, **50**, 51, **52**
Bazin, André, 172
Beatles, The, **300**, 301, **302**
Beatty, Warren, **162**, **163**, **164**, 187, 247, 307
Beautiful Confusion, A. See *8½*.
Beggs, Richard, 60
Bel Geddes, Barbara, 84
Bellamy, Ralph, **245**
Belushi, John, 316
Benchley, Peter, 208, 209
Bender, Lawrence, 310
Benigni, Roberto, 196
Bening, Annette, 306, 307, **308**
Bennett, Joan, 193
Bennett, Joseph, 151
Bennett, Tony, 90
Bentley, Wes, 307
Benton, Robert, 163, 164
Berardinelli, James, 190, 284
Berbert, Marcel, 94
Berenson, Marisa, 262
Bergen, Candice, 113, 304
Berger, Mark, 60
Bergman, Ingmar, 172, **217**, 218
Bergman, Ingrid, 21, 22, 205, 293
Berlin, Irving, 154
Berman, Pandro S., 154
Bernstein, Elmer, 69, 297
Bertolucci, Bernardo, 132, **133**, 134
Best Years of Our Lives, The, 120–122
Bicycle Thief, The, 219–221
Birch, Thora, 307–308
Birds and the Bees, The, 235
Black, Karen, 44, 45
Black, Robert, 169
Black & White & Red All Over, 142
Blackmer, Sidney, **244**
Blade Runner, 129–131
Blake, Robert, 247
Blakley, Ronee, **44**, 45, **46**
Blandick, Clara, 32, 33
Blanke, Henry, 229
Bloch, Robert, 54
Blondy, Raymond, 277, 278
Blonigan, Colette, **143**
Blore, Eric, 154
Blow Out, 274
Blue Velvet, 199, 204–206
Boasberg, Al, 175
Body Heat, 79
Bogart, Humphrey, **20**, **21**, **22**, 123, **124**, **125**, **228**, **229**, **230**
Bogdanovich, Peter, 10, 223, 235, 237, **238**
Boileau, Pierre, 86
Bolger, Ray, **32**, 33, **34**, 257
Bolt, Robert, 188
Bondi, Beulah, 211
Bonnie and Clyde, 162–164
Boogie Nights, 45
Boston Globe, 161
Boston Herald, 39
Bottoms, Joe, 239
Bottoms, Sam, 59, 61, 62
Bottoms, Timothy, **239**
Bound by Honor, 311
Box, John, 28, 188
Box Office Magazine, 203, 215
Boxer, Nathan, 60
Boyle, Danny, 177-179
Boys in Company C, The, 147
Bracco, Lorraine, 90, 91, **92**
Brackett, Charles, 24
Brambell, Wilfrid, **302**
Brando, Marlon, **10**, 11, **12**, 13, 14, 15, 27, 59, **60**, **63**, **64**, **65**, **99**, **100**, **101**, 145, 241
Braun, Ewa, 136
Brennan, Eileen, 238
Brennan, Walter, 211, 271
Bretherton, David, 262
Brickman, Marshall, 36, 37
Bridges, Jeff, 57, **237**, 238
Bridges, Lloyd, 238
Bright Lights Film Journal, 287
Bringing Up Baby, 222–224
Broderick, Matthew, 257
Bronx Tale, A, 91
Brooks, Dean R., 242
Brooks, Mel, 175, 255, **256**
Brooksfilm, 256
Brown, Clancy, 313
Brown, David, 208

Brown, Harry, 268
Brown, Joe E., 47
Brown, Nacio Herb, 41
Bruce, Sally Jane, **182**
Bryce, Ian, 103
Bull, Peter, **128**
Bullets Over Broadway, 52
Bumstead, Henry, 70, 86
Buñuel, Luis, 37
Burghoff, Gary, 250, 251
Burnett, Murray, 21
Burns, Ralph, 262
Burr, Raymond, **268**
Burroughs, William, 130
Burstyn, Ellen, 238, 241
Burton, Richard, 226
Burtt, Ben, 169, 190, 289
Buscemi, Steve, 202, **203**
Busey, Gary, 45
Butch Cassidy and the Sundance Kid, 282–284

C

Caan, James, 10, **12**, 13, 61, 241
Caballero, Eugenio, 82
Cabaret, 261–263
Cain, James M., 78, 79
Calderon, Paul, 310
Campbell, Bruce, 203
Campbell, Charles L., 190
Canby, Vincent, 15, 37, 62, 88, 133, 149, 188, 190, 215, 239, 241, 242, 289, 305
Cantamessa, Gene S., 88, 190
Capote, Truman, 71
Capra, Frank, 108, **109**, 110, **115**, 116
Captain Marvel, 79
Cardinale, Claudia, 151
Carell, Lianella, **221**
Carette, Julien, **158**
Carey, Harry, 73
Carey, Harry, Jr., 73
Carey, Macdonald, 199
Carey, Olive, 73
Carey, Timothy, **227**
Carmichael, Hoagy, **120**
Caron, Leslie, 97
Carr, Jay, 136
Carradine, John, **210**, 211, 212
Carradine, Keith, 44, 45
Carter, John R., 208
Caruso, Fred C., 205
Casablanca, 20–22, 123
Cassavetes, John, **243**, **244**, **245**
Cassidy, Joanna, 129, **130**
Castle Rock Entertainment, 313
Catlett, Lloyd, 238
Cavalleria rusticana, 119
Cazale, John, 10, 11, **12**, 13, **15**, 16, 148, 149, 274
Chandler, Raymond, 79, 106, 125
Chapin, Billy, **182**
Chaplin, Charlie, 45, **144**, **145**, **146**
Chaplin, Geraldine, 44, 45, 145, 187
Chaplin, Oona, 145
Chapman, Michael, 58
Charade, 199
Charisse, Cyd, 41, **43**, 97
Charman, Roy, 289
Chartoff, Robert, 118
Chase, Borden, 271
Chase, Chevy, 307
Cherrill, Virginia, 144, **145**
Chew, Richard, 169
Chiaki, Minoru, 259
Chicago Sun-Times, 39, 49, 52, 55, 91, 104, 113, 116, 131, 146, 151, 166, 172, 182, 196, 203, 208, 257, 317
Chicago Tribune, 28
Chinatown, 38–40
Christian, Roger, 169
Christie, Julie, **186**, **187**
Christine, Virginia, 193
Cicognini, Alessandro, 220
Cimino, Michael, **148**, 149
Citizen Kane, 17–19, 120
City Lights, 144–146
Clark, Candy, 254
Clarke, Arthur C., 160
Clift, Montgomery, 24, **267**, **268**, **269**, 270, **271**, **272**
Close Encounters of the Third Kind, 87–89
CNN, 34
Coangelo, Barney, 254
Coates, Anne V., 28
Cobb, Humphrey, 226
Cobb, Lee J., 63, **64**, **65**
Coburn, Charles, **235**
Coen, Ethan, **202**
Coen, Joel, **202**
Cohen, Bruce, 307
Cohn, Harry, 109
Colbert, Claudette, 51, 52, **108**, **109**, **110**, 286
Coleman, Herbert, 31
Collinge, Patricia, **198**, 199
Collins, Ray, 17, 18
Collodi, Carlo, 196
Columbia Pictures, 298, 313
Comden, Betty, 41, 42
Comer, Sam, 24, 86
Coming Home, 121, 147
Comingore, Dorothy, 17, 18, 19
Condon, Richard, 294, 295
Conformist, The, 132–134
Connolly, Walter, 109
Conrad, Joseph, 60
Conversation, The, 139, 273–279
Coolidge, Calvin, 311
Cooper, Gary, 181, 270
Cooper, Merian C., 73, **166**
Coppel, Alex, 86
Coppola, Carmine, 13, 15
Coppola, Eleanor, 62
Coppola, Francis Ford, 10, 11, 13, **15**, 59, **60**, 61, 62, 139, 253, 254, 259, 273, **274**, 287
Corridan, John M., 65
Cort, Bud, 250
Cortez, Stanley, 180
Cory, Judith A., 136
Cotten, Joseph, 17, 18, **19**, **183**, **184**, **185**, **198**, 199, **200**
Cottrell, William, 196
Countess of Hong Kong, 145
Courtenay, Tom, 187–188
Coward, Noël, 28, 184
Cox, John, 28
Coyote, Peter, 190
Crane, Cheryl, 286
Crawford, Joan, 190, 289
Crime on the Waterfront, 64
Crist, Judith, 68
Crocodile, 209
Cromwell, James, 280, **281**
Cronkite, Walter, 89
Cronyn, Hume, 199
Crowe, Russell, **280**, 281
Crowther, Bosley, 19, 22, 55, 70, 76, 80, 85, 98, 101, 106, 113, 164, 172, 220, 226, 232, 235, 260, 271, 293, 295–296, 299
Cukor, George, 68
Cuny, Alain, 75
Curtis, Tony, 47, **48**, **49**, 245, 291, **293**
Curtiz, Michael, **21**, 22

D

D'entre les morts, 86
Dalio, Marcel, 157, **158**, **277**
Dalton, Phyllis, 188
Daly, Timothy, **141**, **142**
Damon, Matt, 103, 104
Dancer, Texas, Pop. 81, 142
Daniels, Jeff, 307
Darabont, Frank, **313**, 314
Darin, Bobby, 286, 287
Darling, 76
Darwell, Jane, 181, **211**, **212**
Davenport, Nigel, 160
David, Hal, 283
Davies, Jeremy, 102, 103, **104**
Davies, Marion, 19
Davis, Bette, **50**, **51**, **52**, 109, 124, 181
Davis, Ossie, **213**
Day, Doris, 113
Day, Richard, 64, 100
Day-Lewis, Daniel, 310
Day the Earth Stood Still, The, 87
De Havilland, Olivia, 66, 67
De Laurentiis, Dino, 76, 205
De Niro, Robert, 10, 11, **13**, 15, 16, **56**, **57**, **58**, 90, 91, **92**, **117**, **118**, **119**, 147, **148**, **149**, 215
De Palma, Brian, 57, 170
De Sica, Vittorio, **220**
De Vincenzo, Anthony, 65
Deacon, Richard, 193
Dead Again, 85
Dean, James, 205
Dee, Ruby, 214
Dee, Sandra, 286, 287
Deeley, Michael, 130, 148
Deer Hunter, The, 147–149
Del Toro, Guillermo, 81, **82**, 83
Demarest, William, 235
DeMille, Cecil B., 25
Demon Seed, The, 244
Dern, Bruce, 205
Dern, Laura, **205**, **206**
DeSylva, Buddy, 79
Devi, Chunibala, **232**
DeVito, Danny, 241, **242**, 280
Dewhurst, Colleen, 241
Diamond, I.A.L., 49
Dick, Philip K., 130, 131
Digirolamo, Don, 190
Dilley, Leslie, 169, 289
Dillon, Melinda, 88
DiMaggio, Joe, 113
Diner, 141–143
Dirks, Tom, 149
Disney, Walt, **196**
Disney Studios, 196
Do Androids Dream of Electric Sheep?, 130, 131
Do the Right Thing, 213–215
Dolce Vita, La, 75–77
Donahue, Troy, 15, 286, 287
Donen, Stanley, **42**, 96, **97**
Donnie Brasco, 91
Donovan, King, **193**
Doohan, James, 104
Double Indemnity, 78–80, 105
Douglas, Illeana, 91
Douglas, Kirk, **225**, **226**, **227**, 241, **291**, 292, **293**
Douglas, Michael, 226, 241, 292
Dourif, Brad, **241**, **242**
Dovima, 98
Dr. Strangelove, 126–128
Dr. Zhivago, 186–188
Dreamworks SKG, 190, 307
Dreier, Hans, 24
Dreiser, Theodore, 267
Dreyfuss, Richard, 87, **88**, **89**, 208, **209**, 252, **253**, 254
Dru, Joanne, 270, **272**
Dubost, Paulette, 157
Dullea, Keir, 160
Dumont, Margaret, 174, 175
Dunaway, Faye, 38, **39**, **40**, **162**, **163**, **164**, 241
Dunst, Kirsten, 307
Dutton, George, 86
Duvall, Robert, 10, **12**, 13, 16, 60, **62**, 69, 71, 193, 250, 274
Duvall, Shelley, 36
Dykstra, John, 169
Dylan, Bob, 163, 283

E

E.T. the Extra-Terrestrial, 189–191
Eastwood, Clint, 61, 124, 193
Ebb, Fred, 261, 262
Ebert, Roger, 39, 49, 52, 55, 91, 104, 113, 116, 129, 131, 146, 151, 160, 166, 172, 182, 196, 203, 208, 255, 257, 273, 295, 317
Ebsen, Buddy, 34
Edelstein, David, 307
Edens, Roger, 96, 97
Edlund, Richard, 169, 289
Edson, Richard, **214**
8½, 150–152
Ekberg, Anita, 75, **76**, **77**
Ekelund, Alan, 217
Elliott, Bob, 316
Elliott, Chris, 316
Elliott, Laura, 105, 106, **107**
Ellroy, James, 280, 281
Embassy Pictures, 256
Enemy of the State, 274
Englander, Otto, 196
Entertainment Weekly, 34, 140
Epstein, Julius J., 21
Epstein, Mel, 235
Epstein, Philip G., 21
Esperanto Filmoj, 82
Esposito, Giancarlo, **215**
Estudios Picasso, 82
Evans, Robert, 13, 38, 39, 244
Everyone Comes to Rick's, 21
Eyes Wide Shut, 76

F

Face in the Crowd, A, 52
Fairbanks, Douglas, 145
Falk, Peter, 244
Fan, The, 52
Fancher, Hampton, 130
Far from Heaven, 287
Farago, Alexander, 154
Farber, Manny, 185
Farber, Stephen, 244, 271
Fargo, 201–203
Farrow, Mia, **243**, **244**, **245**
Fascism, 81–83, 132–134
Fassbinder, Werner, 287
Fast, Howard, 292
FBI, 145
Feldman, Charles, 100, 271
Fellini, Federico, 37, 75, **76**, 77, 150, **151**
Ferrer, José, 27, **28**
Feuer, Cy, 262
Fields, A. Roland, 18
Fields, Verna, 208,
Fields, W. C., 34
Fiennes, Ralph, 135, **136**
Finney, Albert, 27
Finney, Jack, 193
Fiore, Carlo, 65
Fishburne, Laurence, 59, 61
Fisher, Carrie, 169, **170**
Fisher, Eddie, 169
Fitzgerald, Ella, 22
Fitzgerald, F. Scott, 66
Fitzgerald, Geraldine, 230
Flaiano, Ennio, 76, 151
Flash Gordon, 151
Fleming, Victor, **33**, 67, **68**
Flemyng, Robert, 96
Fletcher, Louise, 45, 240, **242**
Fonda, Henry, **210**, **211**, **212**, 220, **234**, **235**, **236**
Fonda, Jane, 163, 241
Fontaine, Joan, 199
Foote, Horton, 70
Ford, Harrison, **129**, 130, **131**, 169, **170**, 191, 254, **274**, **288**, **289**, **290**
Ford, John, **73**, 74, 166, **211**, 223, 238
Ford, Michael, 289
Foreman, John, 283
Forester, C. S., 124
Forman, Milos, 240, **241**, 242
Forrest, Frederic, 59, 61, **275**

Fosse, Bob, 261, **262**
Foster, Jodie, 56, **57**, 170
400 Blows, The, 171–173
Frankenheimer, John, 226, 294, **295**
Frederickson, Gray, 13
Freed, Arthur, 41
Freeman, Morgan, **312**, 313
Freleng, Fritz, 109
Fresnay, Pierre, **276**, 277, **278**
Friedhofer, Hugo, 121
Frost, Mark, 205
Funny Face, 96–98

G

Gabin, Jean, **276**, 277
Gable, Clark, 66, 67, 68, **108**, **109–110**
Gale, Eddra, 151, **152**
Galento, Tony, 65
Garfield, Allen, **46**, 274
Garfinkle, Louis, 148
Garland, Judy, **32**, 33, **34**, 65, 262, 263
Garr, Teri, 88, 273
Gausman, Russell A., 292
Gavin, John, 53, 54, **285**, 286, 293
Gazzo, Michael, 11, 13, 16
Gedeck, Martina, 138, **139**
Geffen, David, 190
Gein, Ed, 54
Gelbart, Larry, 249
George, Gladys, 230
George, Peter, 127
Gere, Richard, 259
Gershe, Leonard, 96, 97
Gershwin, George, 96, 97
Gershwin, Ira, 96, 97
Gest, David, 262
Gherardi, Piero, 76, 151
Gibson, Henry, **44**, 45
Gielgud, John, 169, 188
Gigi, 97
Gil, Ariadna, 81, 83
Gilliam, Terry, 307
Ginger and Fred, 151
Girl Who Dared, The, 154
Gish, Dorothy, 181
Gish, Lillian, 181, **182**
Gladiator, 293
Glass, Robert J., 88, 190
Glazier, Sidney, 256
Gleiberman, Owen, 34
Glotzer, Liz, 313
Go Tell the Spartans, 147
Godard, Jean-Luc, 164
Godfather I, 10–16, 62, 147
Godfather II, 10–16, 147
Goebbels, Joseph, 278
Goldman, Bo, 241
Goldman, William, 283, 284
Goldwyn, Samuel, 120, 121, 122
Golitzen, Alexander, 70, 292
Gone with the Wind, 10, 66–68, 120
Good Will Hunting, 104
GoodFellas, 90–92
Goodrich, Frances, 115
Gordon, Mark, 103
Gordon, Ruth, **244**
Gosford Park, 158
Gottlieb, Carl, 208
Gould, Elliott, **249**, 250, **251**
Graduate, The, 111–113
Graham, Angelo P., 13
Gramercy Pictures, 202
Grand Illusion, 276–278
Granger, Farley, **105**, 106, **107**
Grant, Cary, **29**, **30**, **31**, 49, 220, **222**, **223**, **224**, 271
Grapes of Wrath, The, 210–212
Grapewin, Charlie, 32, 33
Great Dictator, The, 144
Greatest Gift, The, 115
Green, Adolph, 41, 42
Greene, Graham, 184
Greenhut, Robert, 36
Greenspun, Roger, 251, 253, 263
Greenstreet, Sydney, 22, 228, 229, **230**
Gregor, Nora, **156**, **157**
Gregory, Paul, 181
Grey, Joel, **261**, 262, **263**
Griem, Helmut, **262**
Grier, Pam, 311
Griffin, Eleanore, 286, 287
Griffith, D. W., 181
Groundhog Day, 317–317
Gruault, Jean, 94
Guare, John, 303, 304, 305
Guffey, Burnett, 163
Guffy, Cary, **87**, 88
Guinness, Alec, 27, **168**, 169, 170, 188, 277, 298
Gunton, Bob, **313**
Guthmann, Edward, 15, 62
Guttenberg, Steve, 141, **142**
Guys and Dolls, 11

H

Hackett, Albert, 115
Hackman, Gene, 61, 88, 163, 241, **273**, 274, **275**
Hagen, Jean, 41, 42
Hale, Georgia, 145
Haley, Jack, **32**, 33, **34**
Haley, Jack, Jr., 33
Hall, Albert, 59, 61
Hall, Conrad L., 283, 306, 307, 308
Haller, Ernest, 67
Hamill, Mark, **168**, 169, **170**
Hamilton, Margaret, 32, **33**
Hamilton, Murray, **112**, **209**
Hammett, Dashiell, 229
Handzo, Stephen, 287
Haney, Carol, 43
Hanke, Ken, 230
Hanks, Tom, **102**, 103, **104**, 307, 316
Hannah, Daryl, 129, 130
Hanson, Curtis, 279, **280**, 281
Harburg, E.Y. "Yip", 33, 34
Hard Day's Night, A, 300–302
Harlan, Christiane, 226
Harlan, Russell, 69
Harline, Leigh, 196
Harris, Barbara, 44, **45**
Harrison, George, **300**, **301**, **302**
Hart, Moss, 43
Harvey, Laurence, **294**, 295, **296**
Hashimoto, Shinobu, 259
Hauben, Lawrence, 241
Hauer, Rutger, 129, 130
Hawks, Howard, **223**, **271**
Hayasaka, Fumio, 260
Hayden, Sterling, **126**, 209
Hays Office, 99
Hayward, Leland, 271
Head, Edith, 51, 267, 268
Hearst, William Randolph, 19
Heart of Darkness, 60
Helgeland, Brian, 280, 281
Heller, Joseph, 249
Hellman, Jerome, 246, 247
Heman, Roger, 208
Henckel von Donnersmarck, Florian, **139**, 140
Henreid, Paul, 20, 21, 22
Henry, Buck, 112, 113
Hepburn, Audrey, 96, **97**, **98**
Hepburn, Katharine, **123**, 124, **125**, **222**, 223, **224**
Herlihy, James Leo, 247
Heron, Julia, 292
Heroux, Denis, 304
Herr, Michael, 60
Herrmann, Bernard, 18, 29, 30, 55, 56, 57, 85
Hewitt, Christopher, 256
Hidden Fortress, The, 168, 259
Highsmith, Patricia, 106
Hildyard, David, 262
Hill, George Roy, 282, **283**
Hinson, Hal, 317
Hirsch, Paul, 169
Hitchcock, Alfred, 29, **30**, 31, 53, **54**, 55, 84, **85**, 86, 105, **106**, 107, 198, **199**, 200, 293
Hitchcock, Patricia, 106
Hitler, Adolf, 68
Hoberman, Jay, 30, 83
Hoffe, Monckton, 235
Hoffman, Dustin, 88, **111**, **112**, **113**, 131, 246, **247**, **248**, 257
Hokernot, Larissa, 203
Holden, William, **23**, **24**, **25**, 106
Holly, Buddy, 72, 73
Hollywood Reporter, 121
Holm, Celeste, **50**, 52
Hooker, Richard, 251
Hopkins, Bo, **253**
Hopkins, George James, 100
Hopkins, Miriam, 109
Hopper, Dennis, 60, **61**, 205, **206**
Hornbeck, William, 268
Horne, Lena, 22
Horton, Edward Everett, 154
Howard, Leslie, 66, 67
Howard, Ron, **252**, 253, **254**
Howard, Sidney, 67
Hoyt, Robert L., 208
Hudson, Rock, 57, 160, 262
Hunter, Holly, 311
Hunter, Jeffrey, 72, 73, **74**
Hunter, Kim, 99, **100**, **101**
Hunter, Ross, 286, 287
Hurst, Fannie, 286
Huston, Anjelica, 39, 242
Huston, John, 39, **124**, 125, 228, **229**, 230, 232
Huston, Walter, 229
Huyck, Willard, 253
Hymns, Richard, 103
Hynek, Allen J., 88

I

Imitation of Life, 285–287
Imperioli, Michael, 91
Independence Day, 143
Invasion of the Body Snatchers, 192–194
Invasion of the Body Snatchers (remake), 193
Ireland, John, 271
Irving Thalberg Memorial Award, 55
Isherwood, Christopher, 262
It Happened One Night, 108–110
It's a Wonderful Life, 114–116

J

Jackie Brown, 311
Jackson, Michael, 191
Jackson, Peter, 264-266
Jackson, Samuel L., 214–215, **309**, 310
Jacobs, Diane, 235
Janus Films, 157, 217, 259, 277
Jarre, Maurice, 28, 188
Jaws, 207–209
Jaws 2, 209
Jaws 3-D, 209
Jaws: the Revenge, 209
Jinks, Dan, 307
Joffe, Charles H., 36
Johnson, Ben, **238**
Johnson, Malcolm, 64
Johnson, Nunnally, 211
Johnston, Joe, 289
Jolie, Angelina, 247
Jones, Brion, 129
Jones, Carolyn, 193
Jones, Dickie, 196
Jones, Doug, **81**, **82**
Jones, James Earl, 127, 170
Jones, Paul, 235
Jones, W. D., 164
Joy, Robert, 304
Judkins, Ron, 103, 136
Jules and Jim, 93–95
Juliet of the Spirits, 151
Jurassic Park, 166

K

Kael, Pauline, 15, 19, 22, 45, 65, 74, 91, 94, 110, 116, 119, 131, 133, 157, 163, 164, 193, 206, 212, 223, 235, 242, 244, 247, 251, 260, 263, 274, 277, 278, 284, 295, 299, 305
Kafka, Franz, 257
Kahn, Michael, 103, 136, 289
Kalifornia, 163
Kaminski, Janusz, 103, 136
Kander, John, 261, 262
Kanin, Garson, 244
Karas, Anton, 184
Karns, Roscoe, 109
Kasdan, Lawrence, 289
Katz, Gloria, 253
Katzenberg, Jeffrey, 190
Kauffmann, Stanley, 28, 257
Kaufman, Boris, 64
Kaufman, George S., 43, 175
Kaufman, Philip, 193, 289
Kazan, Elia, 63, **64**, 65, **100**
Kazanjian, Howard G., 289
Keaton, Buster, 175
Keaton, Diane, 10, **11**, 12, 15, **16**, **35**, **36**, **37**
Keitel, Harvey, 56, 57
Keith, Slim, 271
Kellerman, Sally, 250, **251**
Kelly, Gene, **41**, **42**, **43**
Kelly, Grace, 65
Keneally, Thomas, 136
Kennedy, John F., 127, 294
Kennedy, Kathleen, 190
Kenyon Review, The, 151
Kern, Hal C., 67
Kesey, Ken, 240, 242
Kiebach, Jurgen, 262
Killer Fish, 209
Kilmer, Val, 206
Kimura, Isao, 298
King, Stephen, 312, 313
King, Walter Woolf, **176**
King Kong, 165–167
King Kong (remake, 1976), 166
King of New York, 144
Kingsley, Ben, 135, 136, **137**
Knudson, Robert, 88, 190, 262
Koch, Carl, 157
Koch, Howard, 21
Koch, Sebastian, 138, **139**
Kohner, Paul, 286
Kohner, Susan, **286**, **287**
Korda, Alexander, 184
Krasker, Robert, 184
Kübler-Ross, Elisabeth, 315
Kubrick, Stanley, 126, **127**, 128, 159, **160**, 161, 225, **226**, 227, 291, **292**
Kurosawa, Akira, 168, 258, **259**, 297, **298**, 298–299
Kyo, Machiko, **258**, **259**, **260**

L

L.A. Confidential, 39, 279–281
Ladd, Diane, 205
Lady Eve, The, 234–236
Lahr, Bert, **32**, 33, **34**
Lamarr, Hedy, 22
Lancaster, Burt, **303**, 304, **305**
Lanchester, Elsa, 181
Landaker, Gregg, 289
Landis, Jessie Royce, 29, 30
Lane, Nathan, 257
Lange, Dorothea, 210
Lange, Harry, 160
Langley, Noel, 33
Lansbury, Angela, 241, 294, 295, **296**
Lara Croft: Tomb Raider, 289
Lardner, Ring, Jr., 250

Last Picture Show, The, 237–239
Last Seduction, The, 79, 199
Laszlo, Aladar, 154
Laughton, Charles, 180, **181**, 182, 293
Lawrence, Martin, 215
Lawrence, T. E., 26–28
Lawrence of Arabia, 26–28
Le Baron, William, 235
Le May, Alan, 73
Leachman, Cloris, 238, **239**
Lean, David, 26, **27**, 28, **171**, **172**, **173**, 186, **187**, 188
Leave Her to Heaven, 105
Lee, Harper, 70, 71
Lee, Spike, **213**, **214**
LeGrand, Michel, 304
Lehman, Ernest, 30, 31
Leigh, Janet, **53**, 54, 55, 295
Leigh, Vivien, **66**, **67**, **68**, **99**, **100**, 101, 292
Leisen, Mitchell, 235
LeMaire, Charles, 51
LeMat, Paul, 252, 254
Lemmon, Jack, **47**, 48, **49**
Lennon, John, 245, **300**, **301**, 302
Leone, Sergio, 10
Lerner, Alan Jay, 24
LeRoy, Mervyn, 33, 110
Lester, David V., 313
Lester, Richard, 300, **301**
Levin, Ira, 244, 245
Levine, Joseph E., 112
Levinsohn, Gary, 103
Levinson, Barry, 141, **142**, 143
Life Magazine, 293
Lifeboat, 30
Liotta, Ray, **90**, 91, **92**
Lives of Others, The, 138–140
Lloyd, Christopher, 242
Lloyd, Harold, 223
Lodi-Fe, Maurizio, 133
Lolita, 145
Lollobrigida, Gina, 220
Lombard, Carole, 109
Lombardo, Guy, 184
London Observer, 289
London Tribune, 121
López, Sergi, 81, 82, **83**
Lord of the Rings, 264-266
Loren, Sophia, 145, 188, 220
Lorre, Peter, 20, **21**, 229, 230
Los Angeles Times, 83, 104, 106, 281
Louis, Joe, 65
Low Down, The, 142
Loy, Myrna, 109, 120, 121
Lucas, George, 62, 72, 168, **169**, 191, **253**, 254, 259, 288, 298, 313
Lucas, Marcia, 169
Lucasfilm, 169
Luske, Hamilton, 196
Lustig, Branko, 136
Lynch, David, 204, **205**, 206
Lynch, John Carroll, **203**
Lynn, Loretta, 45

M

*M*A*S*H*, 249–251
Mabery, Earl, 208
MacDougall, Don, 88, 169
MacDowell, Andie, 315, **316**
MacLachlan, Kyle, **204**, **205**
MacMurray, Fred, **78**, **79**, **80**
Macready, George, **226**
Macy, William H., **202**, 203
Madonna, 263
Madsen, Michael, 310
Maggiorani, Lamberto, **219**, 220, **221**
Magic Christian, The, 128
Magnificent Seven, The, 297
Magnolia, 45
Mainwaring, Donald, 193
Majors, Lee, 247
Making of the African Queen..., 124
Mako: The Jaws of Death, 209
Malden, Karl, 63, 64, 65, 99, **100**, 101
Malle, Louis, 303, **304**, 305
Maltese Falcon, The, 21, 22, 228–230
Maltin, Leonard, 241
Man Who Knew Too Much, The, 85
Manchurian Candidate, The, 294–296
Mandell, Daniel, 121
Manhattan, 146
Mankiewicz, Herman J., 18
Mankiewicz, Joseph L., 50, **51**, 52
Mann, Hank, **146**
March, Fredric, **120**, 121
Marcos, Ferdinand, 62
Mars, Kenneth, **257**
Marsh, Terence, 188
Marshall, Frank, 289
Marshall, Garry, 253
Marshall, Penny, 253
Marshall, Rob, 263
Marshman, D. M., 24
Martí, David, 82
Martin, Mardik, 118
Martin, Niki, 313
Martin, Steve, 146
Martinez, Jerry, 311
Marvin, Lee, 209
Marx, Chico, **174**, 175, **176**
Marx, Groucho, **174**, **175**, **176**
Marx, Harpo, **174**, 175, **176**
Marx, Minnie, 175
Marx Brothers, 174
Mascagni, Pietro, 119
Masina, Giuletta, 151
Maslin, Janet, 142, 281
Maslow, Steve, 289
Mason, James, **29**, 30, 124, 226
Masters, Anthony, 160
Mastroianni, Marcello, **75**, **76**, 77, **150**, **151**, 152
Mathison, Melissa, 190, 191
Matthau, Walter, 235
Mauriello, Tami, 65
Maurier, Claire, **172**
Mayer, Louis B., 24, 34, 205
Mayhews, Peter, 170
Mayo, Virginia, 120
McBride, Joseph, 172
McCarten, John, 269
McCarthy, Kevin, **192**, **193**, **194**
McCartney, Paul, **300**, 301, 302
McCune, Grant, 169
McDaniel, Hattie, 67
McDonald, Edward, 91
McDonell, Gordon, 199
McDormand, Frances, **201**, 202, **203**
McGuinness, James Kevin, 175
McKelvy, Frank R., 86
McLuhan, Masrhall, 37
McMurtry, Larry, 238
McQueen, Steve, 88, 209, 283
Mean Streets, 57
Medved, Michael, 206
Meehan, John, 24
Meeker, Ralph, **225**
Meet the Stewarts, 33
Mellor, William C., 268
Mendes, Sam, 306, **307**, **308**
Menjou, Adolphe, 226
Meredith, Lee, **257**
Merrill, Gary, **50**, **51**, **52**
Methot, Mayo, 22
Metty, Russell, 292
Meyer, Emile, **227**
MGM, 175, 253
Midnight Cowboy, 111, 246–248
Mifune, Toshiro, **258**, 259, **260**, **297**, 299
Mighty Joe Young, 166
Milchan, Arnon, 280, 281
Miles, Sylvia, 247, **248**
Miles, Vera, 54, **74**
Milford, Gene, 64
Milius, John, 60, 62, 72, 169
Millan, Scott, 136
Miller, Arthur, 65
Miller, Laura, 185
Mills, John, 124
Milo, Sandra, 150, **151**, **152**
Mineo, Sal, 238
Minkler, Bob, 169
Minnelli, Liza, 33, 91, **261**, **262**, **263**
Minnelli, Vincente, 262, 263
Minority Report, 131
Miramax Films, 172, 310
Mission Impossible II, 30
Mitchell, Margaret, 10, 66
Mitchell, Thomas, 66, 115
Mitchum, Robert, **180**, **181**, **182**, 215
Miyagawa, Kazuo, 260
Miyaguchi, Seiji, 298, 299
Modot, Gaston, **277**
Moffat, Ivan, 268
Molen, Gerald R., 136
Mollo, John, 169
Monroe, Marilyn, **47**, **48**, **49**, **50**, 51, 269
Montgomery, Robert, 109
Moore, Juanita, 286, **287**
Moorehead, Agnes, 18
Moravia, Alberto, 133
Moreau, Jeanne, **93**, **94**, **95**, 241, 293
Morgan, Frank, 32, 33
Mori, Masayuki, 258
Moriarty, Cathy, **118**
Morley, Robert, 123
Mostel, Josh, 256
Mostel, Zero, 255, **256**, **257**
Motion Picture Guide, The, 226
Mountain Xpress, 230
Moussy, Marcel, 172
Movieline, 244, 271, 274
Moyer, Ray, 24
Muhe, Ulrich, **138**, 139, **140**
Mulligan, Jerry, 281
Mulligan, Robert, **70**, 71
Mummy, The, 289
Mungle, Matthew W., 136
Muráti, Lili, 188
Murch, Walter, 60, 62, 274
Murder on the Orient Express, 21
Muren, Dennis, 190
Murray, Bill, **315**, **316**, **317**
My Son John, 106
Myers, Harry, **146**
Mystic Pizza, 142

N

Nabokov, Vladimir, 145
Narcejac, Thomas, 86
Nashville, 44–46
Nashville Blue, 45
Nashville Red, 45
Nation, The, 185
National Society of Film Critics, 136, 142
Natural Born Killers, 163, 311
Navarro, Guillermo, 82
Neeson, Liam, **135**, 136
Nelson, Andy, 103, 136
Nelson, Earle Leonard, 199
Nelson, George R., 13
New Republic, The, 28, 257
New York, 72
New York Daily News, 45
New York Observer, 85
New York Post, 247, 293
New York Press, 80
New York Times, 15, 19, 22, 24, 28, 30, 37, 49, 55, 62, 65, 68, 70, 76, 80, 83, 85, 88, 98, 101, 106, 113, 133, 142, 149, 166, 161, 172, 190, 212, 215, 220, 223, 226, 232, 235, 239, 242, 251, 253, 257, 263, 271, 281, 289, 293, 295–296, 299, 305
New Yorker, The, 15, 19, 22, 45, 65, 74, 91, 94, 110, 116, 119, 131, 133, 157–158, 206, 212, 223, 235, 242, 244, 247, 251, 260, 263, 269, 274, 277, 278, 284, 295, 299, 305
Newcom, James E., 67
Newman, David, 163, 164
Newman, Paul, 76, 209, **282**, **283**, **284**
Newsweek, 226, 239
Nicholls, Allan, 45
Nichols, Dudley, 223
Nichols, Mike, **112**, 169, 269
Nicholson, Bruce, 289
Nicholson, Jack, **38**, 39, **40**, 61, 226, **240**, **241**, **242**
Nielsen, Brigitte, 311
Night at the Opera, A, 174–176
Night of the Hunter, 180–182
Nights of Cabriria, 151
Niland brothers, 104
Nilsson, Harry, 247
Nimoy, Leonard, 193
Niven, David, 124
Normand, Mabel, 24
North, Alex, 101, 160, 293
North by Northwest, 29–31, 87
Nourse, Alan, 130
Novak, Kim, 84, **85**, **86**
Noyes, Betty, 43
Nugent, Frank S., 68, 73, 212, 223

O

O'Brien, Willis, 166
O'Connor, Donald, **42**, **43**
O'Donnell, Cathy, 120, **121**
O'Neill, Eugene, 145
O'Toole, Peter, **26**, **27**, **28**
Obsession, 85
Odets, Clifford, 116
Of Human Bondage, 109
Oklahoma, 52
Olivier, Laurence, 169, 188, 291, **293**
Olmos, Edward James, 129, 130
Olson, Nancy, 23, 24
Omen, The, 244
OMM, 82
On the Waterfront, 63–65
100 Best Movies, International Movie Database, 149
Once in a Lifetime, 43
One Flew Over the Cuckoo's Nest, 45, 240–242
Orbison, Roy, 206
Orborn, Eric, 292
Orr, Mary, 51
Orry-Kelly, 47, 49
Osservatore Romano, L', 76
Owen, Alun, 301

P

Pacino, Al, **10**, **11**, 12, **14**, **15**, 16, 61, 274
Page, Geraldine, 241
Paglia, Camille, 269
Pakula, Alan J., 70
Pan's Labyrinth, 81–83
Pather Panchali, 231–233
Paramount Pictures, 235, 268, 274, 289, 304
Parker, Bonnie, 164
Parker, Dorothy, 116
Parsons, Estelle, 163
Pasternak, Boris, 186, 188
Paths of Glory, 225–227
Patrick, Lee, 230
Payback, 311
Pearce, Guy, **280**
Peck, Gregory, **69**, **70**, **71**, 226
Peckinpah, Sam, 193
Pederson, Steve, 136
Peel, Dave, 45
Penn, Arthur, **163**
Penner, Erdman, 196
Penthouse, 269
People, 241
Peoples, David, 130
Pereira, Hal, 86

Perez, Rosie, 214, 215
Perkins, Anthony, **53**, **54**, **55**
Pesci, Joe, 90, **91**, **92**, 118, **119**
Peters, Brock, 69, **70**, 71
Peverall, John, 148
Philby, Kim, 184
Phillips, John, 254
Phillips, Julia, 58, 88, 89
Phillips, Mackenzie, 254
Phillips, Michael, 58, 88
Pianist, The, 136
Pickens, Slim, 126, **127**
Pickford, Mary, 145
Pileggi, Nicholas, 91
Pinelli, Tullio, 76, 151
Pinocchio, 195–197
Piranha, 209
Pitt, Brad, 313
Place in the Sun, A, 267–269
Platt, Polly, 238, 239
Plummer, Amanda, 310
Polanski, Roman, **39**, 136, 243, **244**
Pollack, Sydney, 139
Pollard, Michael J., 163
Poltergeist, 191
Ponti, Carlo, 188
Postman Always Rings Twice, The, 79
Powell, Dick, 79
Powell, William, 199
Preminger, Ingo, 251
Presnell, Harve, 102
Previews, 206
Producers, The, 175, 255–257
Pryor, Thomas, 24
Psycho, 30, 53–55
Pulp Fiction, 309–311
Puzo, Mario, 10, 13

Q

Quinn, Anthony, 27, 28

R

Radner, Gilda, 256
Raft, George, 22, 47, 79, 230
Raging Bull, 11, 117–119
Raiders of the Lost Ark, 288–290
Rain, Douglas, 160
Rain Man, 111
Raindrops Keep Fallin' on My Head, 283
Rainer, Peter, 142, 280
Raines, Cristina, 45
Rains, Claude, 20, 21
Rambaldi, Carlo, 190
Ramis, Harold, 315, **316**, 317
Rashomon, 258–260
Ravel, Maurice, 260
Ray, Satyajit, 231, **232**, 233
Reagan, Nancy, 191
Reagan, Ronald, 22, 113, 191, 286
Rear Window, 30, 65, 85
Rebecca, 30
Red River, 270–272
Redeker, Quinn K., 148
Redford, Robert, 113, 208, 244, **282**, **284**
Reed, Carol, **184**
Reed, Donna, **114**, **115**, **116**
Reed, Rex, 45
ReelViews, 190, 284
Reid, Kate, 304, **305**
Reiser, Paul, 142
Remembrance, 142
Rémy, Julien, **173**
Rennahan, Ray, 67
Renoir, Claude, 157
Renoir, Jean, **156**, **157**, 232, 276, **277**
Renoir, Pierre-Auguste, 277
Reservoir Dogs, 91
Resnais, Alain, 158
Return of the King, 264–266
Revere, Anne, 269
Revuelta, Pilar, 82
Reynolds, Burt, 250
Reynolds, Debbie, 41, 42, 169
Reynolds, Norman, 169, 289
Rhames, Ving, 310
Rhodes, Erik, 154, **155**
Ribé, Montse, 82
Richardson, Ralph, 188
Richter, W. D., 193
Ringwald, Molly, 206
Riskin, Robert, 109
Ritter, Thelma, 50
Rizzoli, Angelo, 151
RKO, 166, 223, 259
Robbins, Tim, 304, **312**, 313, **314**
Roberts, Tony, 36
Robinson, Edward G., 78, 79, **80**
Robson, May, **224**
Roche, Henri-Pierre, 94
Rochester, Art, 274
Rodat, Robert, 103
Roeg, Nicholas, 187
Rogers, Ginger, **153**, 154, **155**
Rolling Stone, 52, 74, 137
Roman, Ruth, 105, 106
Rondi, Brunello, 76, 151
Roos, Fred, 13
Rope, 85
Rosemary's Baby, 243–245
Ross, Katharine, 111, 112, **113**, **282**, **283**
Rossellini, Isabella, 91, **204**, 205
Rossellini, Roberto, 21, 205
Rosson, Arthur, 271
Rota, Nino, 13, 76
Roth, Tim, 310
Rourke, Mickey, **141**, **142**, **143**
Rowlands, Gena, 244
Rubin, Danny, 315, 316
Ruddy, Alfred S., 13
Rules of the Game, 156–158
Russell, Chuck, 313
Russell, Harold, **120**, **121**, 122
Ryan, Meg, 311
Rydstrom, Gary, 103
Ryerson, Florence, 33
Ryskind, Morrie, 175

S

Saba, Joseph, 196
Saint, Eva Marie, **29**, **30**, **63**, 64, 65
Salon.com, 185
Salt, Waldo, 247
Sammon, Paul D., 205
Sampson, Will, 241, 242
San Francisco Chronicle, 15, 62, 170, 314
San Francisco Examiner, 175
Sanda, Dominique, 132, 133, **134**
Sanders, George, **50**, 51, **52**
Sandrelli, Stefania, 132, 133
Sandrich, Mark, **154**
Santa Claus Conquers the Martians, 128
Sarandon, Susan, **304**, **305**, 313
Sarrazin, Michael, 247
Sarris, Andrew, 85, 125, 194, 220, 269, 301
Savage, John, 147, **148**, 149
Saving Private Ryan, 102–104
Sayles, John, 191
Scenes from the Class Struggle in Beverly Hills, 158
Scheider, Roy, 208, **209**
Schindler's List, 135–137
Schlesinger, John, 246, **247**
Schoedsack, Ernest, **166**
Schoonmaker, Thelma, 118, 119
Schrader, Paul, 58, 72, 89, 118
Schuck, John, 250
Schulberg, Budd, 64
Scorsese, Charlie, 118
Scorsese, Martin, 19, 56, **57**, 58, 72, **91**, **118**, 136, 205, 311
Scotch and Milk, 142
Scott, A. O., 83
Scott, Allan, 154
Scott, George C., 127, **128**
Scott, Hazel, 22
Scott, Ridley, **130**
Searchers, The, 72–74
Sears, Ted, 196
Seitz, Matthew, 80
Selleck, Tom, 289
Sellers, Peter, **126**, 127, **128**
Selznick, David O., 22, 66, 67, 68, 110, 166, 184, 220
Selznick, Myron, 68
Sententia Entertainment Telecino, 82
Serre, Henri, **93**, 94, **95**
Seven Samurai, The, 297–299
7th Voyage of Sinbad, 166
Shadow of a Doubt, 198–200
Shankar, Ravi, 232
Sharif, Omar, 26, **27**, **186**, **187**, **188**
Sharpsteen, Ben, 196
Shaw, Robert, 208, **209**
Shawn, Dick, 256–257
Shawn, Wallace, 304
Shawshank Redemption, The, 312–314
Sheen, Martin, **59**, 60, 61, 62
Shenson, Walter, 301
Shepherd, Cybill, 56, 57, **58**, **237**, 238–239
Sheppard, Anna B., 136
Sheridan, Ann, 22
Sherwood, Robert E., 121
Shimura, Takashi, 259, 297, 298
Shire, David, 274
Shire, Talia, 10, **12**, 13, 15, 16
Shooting Party, The, 158
Short, Martin, 257
Shwarzbaum, Lisa, 140
Siegel, Don, 192, **193**
Silver Streak, 30
Simmons, Jean, 244, 292–293
Simon, Abe, 65
Simon, John, 37, 301
Simon, Paul, 36, 112, 169
Simon and Garfunkel, 111, 112
Simoni, Dario, 28, 188
Sinatra, Frank, 65, 244, 271, **294**, **295**, 296
Singin' in the Rain, 41–43
Sirk, Douglas, 285, **286**, 287
Siskel, Gene, 129
Sizemore, Tom, 103
Sjöstrom, Victor, **216**, **217**
Skerritt, Tom, 249, 250,
Slate, 307
Sleeper, 146
Sleeping with the Enemy, 199
Sloane, Everett, 18
Slumdog Millionaire, 177-179
Smiles of a Summer Night, 158
Smith, Charles Martin, 253
Smith, Christina, 136
Smith, Dick, 57
Smith, Howard K., 89
Smith, Kenneth, 190
Smith, Ludlon, 223
Smith, Paul J., 196
Smith, Webb, 196
Snyder, Ruth, 79
Some Like It Hot, 47–49
Sommaren med Monika, 172
Son of Kong, The, 166
Sondergaard, Gale, 34
Sopranos, The, 91
Sorvino, Paul, 90
Southern, Terry, 127
Spaak, Charles, 277
Spacek, Sissy, 170
Spacey, Kevin, **279**, 280, 281, 306, **307**, 308
Spartacus, 291–293
Spiegel, Sam, 27, 29, 64, 65, 124, 187
Spielberg, Steven, 27, 87, **88**, 89, 102, **103**, 104, 135, **136**, 137, 169, 189, **190**, 207, **208**, 259, 288, **289**, 290, 308, 313
Spikings, Barry, 148
Stack, Peter, 170, 314
Stagecoach, 19
Staiola, Enzo, **219**, 220
Stanwyck, Barbara, **78**, **79**, **80**, **234**, **235**, **236**
Star Trek, 104
Star Wars, 55, 62, 89, 168–170
Star Wars: Episode I–The Phantom Menace, 170
Star Wars: Episode II–Attack of the Clones, 170
Star Wars: Episode III–Revenge of the Sith, 170
Star Wars: Episode V–The Empire Strikes Back, 170
Star Wars: Episode VI–The Return of the Jedi, 170
Starr, Ringo, **300**, 301, **302**
Starski, Allan, 136
Stears, John, 169
Stefano, Joseph, 54
Steiger, Rod, 63, 64, 187
Steinbeck, John, 210
Steiner, Max, 22, 66, 166
Stern, Daniel, **141**, **142**
Stevens, Georges, 267, **268**
Stewart, James, **84**, **85**, **86**, **114**, **115**, **116**, 184, 211
Stockwell, Dean, 206
Stoll, John, 28
Stoltz, Eric, 310
Stompanato, Johnny, 286
Stone, Sharon, 245
Storaro, Vittorio, 60, 132
Stormare, Peter, 202, 203
Stothart, Herbert, 33
Strabel, Herbert, 262
Strada, La, 151
Strange Days, 131
Strangers on a Train, 105–107
Strasberg, Lee, 11, 13, 16
Stratton, Dorothy, 239
Stratton, Louise, 239
Strauss, Richard, 160
Streep, Meryl, 148, **149**, 169, 274, 302
Streetcar Named Desire, A, 11, 99–101
Streisand, Barbra, 45, 196, 250
Strode, Woody, **291**
Sturges, Preston, **235**, 236
Sullivan, Margaret, 109
Summers, Gary, 103
Summertime, 124
Sunset Boulevard, 23–25, 52
Sutherland, Donald, 193, **249**, **250**, **251**
Sutherland, Kiefer, 250
Suvari, Mena, **306**, 308
Swanson, Gloria, **23**, **24**, **25**
Swerling, Jo, 115
Sylbert, Dick, 244

T

Tarantino, Quentin, 309, **310**
Tatara, Paul, 34
Tate, Sharon, 245
Taubin, Amy, 119
Tavoularis, Dean, 13
Taxi Driver, 11, 56–58
Taylor, Elizabeth, 267, **269**
Taylor, Robert Lewis,
Taylor, Sam, 86, 154
Taylor, William Desmond, 24
Tequila Gang, 82
Temple, Shirley, 34
Tentacles, 209
Thalberg, Irving, 175
Third Man, The, 18, 183–185
Thomas, B. J., 283
Thomas, Bill, 292
Thomas, Henry, **189**, **190**, 191
Thomas, Jameson, 108, 109
Thomas, Kevin, 106
Thompson, Jim, 225, 226
Thompson, Kay, **96**, 97, 98
Thomson, David, 244, 277
Thorpe, Richard, 33

Thulin, Ingrid, **218**
Thurman, Uma, **310**, 311
Tilly, Meg, 311
Time Out, 98, 101
Tintorera ... Bloody Waters, 209
To Kill a Mockingbird, 69–71
Tobolowsky, Stephen, 316
Todd, Mike, 268
Toho Studios, 298, 299
Toland, Gregg, 120
Tomlin, Lily, 45, **46**, 146
Tootsie, 48, 111
Top Hat, 153–155
Total Recall, 131
Toto, 32
Toutain, Roland, **157**
Towne, Robert, 38, 39, 40
Tracy, Spencer, 223
Trainspotting, 91
Travers, Henry, 114, **116**
Travers, Peter, 52, 74, 137
Travolta, John, **309**, 310, 311
Trintignant, Jean-Louis, **132**, **133**, **134**
Trouble with Harry, The, 85
True Romance, 311
Truffaut, François, 88, 93, **94**, 95, 164, 171, **172**, 232
Trumbo, Dalton, 116, 291, 292
Tsushima, Kaiki, 298
Turan, Kenneth, 83, 104, 281
Turkel, Joe, 129
Turman, Lawrence, 112
Turner, Lana, **285**, 286
Turturro, John, 118, **214**
TV Guide, 196
TV Guide's Movie Guide, 125, 154, 274
Two Jakes, The, 39
2001: A Space Odyssey, 159–161
20th Century Fox, 169, 251, 283

U

UFO Experience, The, 88
United Artists, 145, 181, 226, 241, 247, 301
Universal Pictures, 190, 199, 208, 214, 286, 292
University of Aberdeen, 128
Unsworth, Geoffrey, 262
Ustinov, Peter, 292, 293

V

Valles, 292
Valli, Alida, **184**
Van Doren Stern, Philip, 115
Van Druten, John, 262
Vangelis, 130
Variety, 166, 175, 194
Varney, Bill, 289
Verdon, Gwen, 43
Verdú, Maribel, 81, 82
Verniere, James, 39
Vertigo, 84–86
Victor/Victoria, 48
Vidor, King, 33
Viertel, Peter, 124
Vietnam War, 59–62, 147–149
Village of the Damned, 194
Village Voice, 30, 83, 119, 125, 194, 208, 220, 269, 301
Viva Zapata, 11
Vogue, 15, 96
Voight, Jon, **246**, **248**
Von Stroheim, Erich, 23, 24, **25**, 277, **278**
Vossler, Russell, 311
Vreeland, Diana, 96

W

Walken, Christopher, **147**, 148, **149**, **311**
Walker, Robert, **105**, **106**, **107**
Wallace, Edgar, 166
Wallis, Hal B., 21, 22, 229
Walshe, Pat, **33**
Wanger, Walter, 193
Warner, Frank, 88
Warner, Jack, 22, 110, 164
Warner Bros., 163, 229, 281
Warrick, Ruth, 17, 18, **19**
Washburn, Deric, 148
Washington, Ned, 196
Washington Post, 170, 232, 317
Waxman, Franz, 24, 268
Wayne, John, **72**, 73, 74, 182, 270, 271, **272**
Weaver, Sigourney, 36
Webb, Charles, 112
Webster, Brian, 314
Weegee, 127
Weiler, A.H., 30, 49, 65
Weintraub, Jerry, 142
Weitz, Chris, 286
Weitz, John, 286
Weld, Tuesday, 244
Welles, Gwen, 44
Welles, Orson, **17**, **18**, **19**, **183**, 184, **185**, 238
Werner, Oskar, **93**, **94**, **95**
West, Kit, 289
West, Mae, 24
West, Ray, 169
Wheeler, Lyle, 67
When You Wish Upon a Star, 196
White Hunter, Black Heart, 124
Whitmore, James, 313
Whitney, C.V., 73
Whitney, Eli, 73
Who Framed Roger Rabbit, 39
Wild Strawberries, 216–218
Wilde, Hagar, 223
Wilder, Billy, 23, **24**, 25, 47, **48**, 49, 74, 78, **79**, 80, 136, 268
Wilder, Gene, 255, **257**
Wilder, Thornton, 198, 199
Williams, Cindy, 253, **254**, 274, **275**
Williams, John, 55, 136, 169, 170, 190, 191, 208
Williams, Robin, 104
Williams, Tennessee, 89, 100, 101
Williamson, Kim, 203
Willingham, Calder, 112, 226
Willis, Bruce, **311**
Willis, Gordon, 10
Wilmington, Michael, 28
Wilson, Dooley, **20**, 21, 22
Wilson, Michael, 28, 268
Wilson, Woodrow, 311
Winkler, Irwin, 91
Winsten, Archer, 247
Winters, Shelley, **181**, **267**
Winwood, Estelle, **256**
Wisdom of Eve, 51
Wiseguy, 91
Wizard of Oz, 32–34
Wolfman Jack, **254**
Wolper, David, 281
Wood, Lana, 74
Wood, Natalie, 73, **74**
Wood, Sam, **175**
Woodward, Alfre, 311
Woodward, Joanne, 283
Woolf, Edgar Allan, 33
World War I, 123–125
World War II, 76, 102–104, 115, 120–122, 135–137
Wray, Fay, **165**, 166, **167**
Wright, Frank Lloyd, 52
Wright, Teresa, 120, 121, **122**, 199, **200**
Wyler, William, 120, **121**, 122
Wynn, Keenan, 45
Wynter, Dana, **192**, **193**, **194**

Y

Year of the Dragon, 311
York, Michael, **262**
Young, Freddie, 28, 188
Young, Sean, 129, 130, **131**
Youngman, Henny, 92

Z

Zaentz, Saul, 241
Zaillian, Steven, 136
Zanuck, Darryl F., 51, 211, 212, 251, 283
Zanuck, Richard D., 208
Zavattini, Cesare, 220
Zehetbauer, Hoff, 262
Zellweger, Renée, 263
Zeta-Jones, Catherine, 263
Zinner, Peter, 148
Zsigmond, Vilmos, 88, 89

David Ferguson

GAIL KINN has conceived and edited a wide range of film books, among them, *Screwball: The Great Romantic Comedies, Hollywood at Home: The Photographs of Sid Avery, The Zanucks of Hollywood, The Scorsese Picture* by David Ehrenstein, *The James Dean Scene,* and *Those Lips, Those Eyes.* She lives in New York City.

JIM PIAZZA is a screenwriter and playwright whose personal essays and writings about the media have appeared in *The Village Voice* and *Out Magazine*. He has also been a script analyst for Columbia, Fox, and Paramount Pictures. He lives in New York City.

Gail Kinn and Jim Piazza are the co-authors of *The Academy Awards: The Complete Unofficial History*.